♻ NatWest

BUSINESS HANDBOOKS

If you are running your own business then you probably do not have time for the general, theoretical and often impenetrable subject areas covered by many business and management books. What works for the major corporation may not work for you. What you do need is to-the-point guidance on how to implement sound business skills in a growing enterprise.

The NatWest Business Handbooks deliver this practical advice in an easy-to-follow format.

Written by authors with many years' experience and who are still actively involved in the day-to-day running of successful businesses, these handbooks provide all the guidance you need to tackle the everyday issues that you and your business face. They will enable you to adopt a step-by-step approach to isolating and resolving problems and help you meet the entrepreneurial and organisational challenges of a growing business.

♺ **NatWest**

BUSINESS HANDBOOKS

BOOK-KEEPING AND ACCOUNTING

Keeping track of the growing business

Fourth Edition

GEOFFREY WHITEHEAD

FINANCIAL TIMES MANAGEMENT
128 Long Acre, London WC2E 9AN
Tel: +44 (0)171 447 2000
Fax: +44 (0)171 240 5771
Website: www.ftmanagement.com

A Division of Financial Times Professional Limited

First published in Great Britain 1989
Fourth edition 1998

© Financial Times Professional Limited 1998

ISBN 0 273 63564 6

British Library Cataloguing in Publication Data
A CIP catalogue record for this book can be obtained from the British Library.

10 9 8 7 6 5 4 3 2 1

Typeset by Northern Phototypesetting Co. Ltd, Bolton
Printed and bound in Great Britain by Bell & Bain Ltd, Glasgow

The Publishers' policy is to use paper manufactured from sustainable forests.

About the Author

Geoffrey Whitehead has been a teacher and lecturer in accounting for over 40 years, and was formerly Head of the Professional Studies Division at Thurrock Technical College, lecturing in both financial and management accounting. He has acted as small business accounts adviser to Croner Publications Ltd, the publishers of *Reference Book for Self-employed and Smaller Business*. He also acts as consultant to the Simplex Advice Bureau, solving book-keeping problems for many small businesses. As a self-employed author who has sold over three million books, he has had practical experience of running a small business.

Contents

Preface

This book has been prepared as a practical accounting guide to all those entering business for the first time. It is based on my experiences in over 40 years' lecturing and consultancy work at a grass roots level. It starts at 'dawn on day 1', and explains how to open very simple account books, using one of the systems readily available at any stationer's shop.

It then goes on to look at all the other systems available, giving a detailed account of several of them. This section includes a full explanation of double entry, and also a section on computerised accounting. A full list of all the manual and computerised systems on the market is given in Chapter 13. How to do bank reconciliation statements is covered in this section also, and VAT records are explained fully.

The book then proceeds to explain the final accounts of manufacturers, sole traders, partnerships and limited companies. It concludes with chapters about control of the business in its various profit-making activities, analysis of the results using the commoner accounting ratios, and ends with some practical advice on dealing with the Inland Revenue. You no longer have to submit accounts to the Inland Revenue – just declare your profits in the self-assessment tax return sent to you each April – but all your records must be archived for six years for possible inspection. The self-assessment system is explained in Chapter 20. Finally, there is a chapter on the accounts of clubs and charities.

In writing this book I have been greatly helped by all the firms whose systems are described, and by numerous other people. Their assistance is acknowledged on p. xv. While their help and encouragement have been invaluable, I must take responsibility for all the statements made, which have been made in good faith. In using names for exercises and so on no intentional reference has been made to any particular firm or company, and I must apologise if I have inadvertently mentioned an actual company.

Geoffrey Whitehead

Acknowledgements

The assistance of the following persons and organisations is gratefully acknowledged. Some kindly permitted the use of artwork to illustrate their systems, and their permission to reproduce this copyright material is much appreciated.

The Accounting Centre
Acorn Books
Alternative Investment Market (AIM)
Arena Software Ltd
Ataglance Publications
Burgan Publications
Casdec Ltd (YBS System)
The Charity Commission
CRC Ltd
Evan Jackson CBS Ltd
Evrite Ltd
Freeway Sofware Ltd
Kalamazoo Security Print PLC
Micro-Retailer Systems Ltd
National Westminster Bank PLC
Observe Business Computing Ltd
Safeguard Systems Ltd
Sage Group PLC
Simplex Accounting Systems Ltd
Tollit and Harvey Ltd
Twinlock Acco-UK Ltd
George Vyner Ltd (Simplex Manual Systems)

Solving the book-keeping problem

WHY DO I NEED TO KEEP BOOK-KEEPING RECORDS AT ALL?

The Finance Act 1994 requires sole traders and partnerships to keep book-keeping records, and if you set up as a limited company there is a positive requirement in section 221 of the Companies Act 1985. It begins 'Every company shall cause accounting records to be kept in accordance with this section' and it goes on to require that the accounts shall be sufficient to show and explain the company's transactions, financial position and so on. So, if you set up as a company, you must keep accounts. If you trade as a sole trader or a partnership, you must keep all your records for six years under the Finance Act 1994. The requirement is that you keep all the records necessary to substantiate the statements made in your tax returns – now called SA tax returns (self-assessment tax returns). The Inland Revenue's literature specifies documents, chequebook stubs, bank reconciliation statements, accounts and so on, and a fine of up to £3000 can be imposed for failure to keep proper records.

You need to keep proper books of account for the following reasons.

- You need to keep track of all aspects of your business activities, and the simplest way to do this for the financial aspects of the business is to keep a set of books of account.
- If your turnover (in other words, the takings of the business) exceeded £50,000 in the past 12 months, or if the likely turnover in the next 30 days will bring the past 11 months' total over the £50,000 threshold figure, you must register for VAT. Many traders whose sales are not as high as £50,000 per annum register voluntarily for VAT (because this means you can reclaim the input tax you pay on everything you buy and on your overhead expenses). In that case, you must keep VAT records from the moment you start business – which we will call 'dawn on day 1' – a vital moment in the life of every business. These VAT records must, by law, be kept for six years, so they must be put into apple-pie order each year and then archived in the bottom drawer of a convenient filing cabinet so that you have them available if Customs and Excise require them.

    In the first few weeks after you are registered for VAT you will receive a visit from the VAT inspector. The purpose of the visit is to ensure that you are using an adequate system and are clear about the VAT procedures.
- The profits declared in your self-assessment tax returns become the basis for your assessment for taxation, and are derived from the records you have kept during the year. Apart from companies with a

turnover greater than £90,000, it is not necessary for these accounts to be drawn up by a professional accountant, and this book will explain how to draw up your own accounts with very little trouble. Of course, many people do have their accounts drawn up by an accountant and therefore have the peace of mind that comes from having professional support in their financial affairs. One consultant told the author of this book, 'A sole trader would be as well advised to draw up his own accounts as he would be to draw his own teeth.' Actually, that is going a bit too far – at least half a million sole traders and partnerships draw up their own accounts and declare them to the Inland Revenue every year, without any real trouble. On the other hand, we all need the help of accountants at times – for example, when the business grows or perhaps when preparing a submission in connection with a loan request to a finance company or institutional investor – so there is much to be said for establishing a link with a reputable accountancy firm.

For these three main reasons, you need to keep book-keeping records.

WHAT SORTS OF RECORDS DO I NEED?

Since the Middle Ages, the system of book-keeping has traditionally been the double entry system. Every time people discuss book-keeping, they refer to this system, which is fully described later in this book (see Chapter 6). Indeed, most of the words commonly used in accountancy relate to the double entry system. For example, the ledger is the main book of account, and is full of pages called 'accounts'. An account is a leaf in the ledger (that is, two pages), though these days it may just be some pattern of magnetic records in the memory store of a computer. For example, if you have an account with one of the High Street banks, it simply means that they have allocated you a page in their ledger, and they tell you the page number so it can be referred to at any time. The number is embossed on the bottom of every cheque in magnetic ink, as shown in Figure 1.1. The bank's computer can read this magnetic ink and it is used to speed up cheque clearing, and debit the amount of the cheque in the customer's account.

Today, a full double entry system is not essential for most businesses, although those who have studied double entry book-keeping will always have a great advantage in understanding their accounts. You can learn double entry book-keeping at an evening class or you can use one of the many self-study textbooks on the market – a good one is *Frank*

Wood's Book-Keeping and Accounts by Frank Wood (3rd edition, Pitman, 1992). However, it takes a year to learn the subject really well.

> *Whatever duties the state imposes on you – like collecting VAT for the government or keeping proper pay records if you employ anyone – you have to carry them out.*

For the person starting up in business, this full knowledge of double entry is not necessary, as explained in the next section. What records, then, do you need? To some extent, it depends on the type of business you are running, but, to begin with, you could make a list as follows:

- VAT records;
- 'dawn on day 1' records;
- cash records (to keep track of receipts and payments) and enable you, eventually to work out the profit or loss you have made in the year;
- pay records (if you employ anyone);
- a full double entry system if you prefer to keep full records, without taking any short-cuts;
- specialised records (which are chiefly short-cuts on a full double entry system – these are described later);
- you might keep computerised records, which involves some small capital cost at the start, though you can buy everything you need for about £1500.
- then, you need to be able to prepare your final accounts at the end of the year, for declaration to the Inland Revenue – these are called the trading account (in which is found the gross profit), the profit and loss account (in which is found the net profit) and the balance sheet (which gives a snapshot picture of the state of your business after closing the doors on the last day of the financial year) – and preparing these is really very simple (you will find lots of practice exercises to help you in this book);
- finally, and it is really a part of the balance sheet work, you need to understand the effect of the year's trading on the owner of the business, whether you are trading as a sole trader, as partners in a partnership or as a limited company with shareholders.

That may sound quite a lot, but actually it isn't too bad. In any case, the first lesson you must learn in business is that whatever duties the state imposes on you – like collecting VAT for the government or keeping proper pay records if you employ anyone – you have to carry them out, even if they are a bit of a problem. It is no good throwing up your hands in horror as if it was all too much for you. Parliament has imposed certain duties on you, and you must carry them out or get someone to do them for you. None of this is very difficult, as this book will show you.

Fig. 1.1 CHEQUE SHOWING THE CUSTOMER'S ACCOUNT NUMBER IN THE BANK'S LEDGER

SOLVING THE BOOK-KEEPING PROBLEM FOR DIFFERENT TYPES OF BUSINESS

■ Systems for the very small business

People who are setting up in business don't want general answers to their questions – they want a specific answer that will solve their problems, whatever they are. In the accounting department, so far as the very small business is concerned, the answer to the question 'What system of book-keeping shall I use for my ordinary financial accounts?' is simple: it is 'Use the Simplex system.'

■ *The Simplex system*

You can see the weekly page of this system illustrated in Figure 1.2. The advantages of the Simplex system are as follows.

- It is an inexpensive (about £10) one-book system that lasts a whole year.
- Each week's accounts are separate. The system provides 53 weekly pages – one for each week in the year and one extra, because every few years you get an extra week ($52 \times 7 = 364$, but there are 365 days in a year and 366 in a leap year).
- There is a line on the page for each item of expense so you can see exactly where to put everything. When they first see a Simplex page, some people say 'It looks very complicated' – but having a place for everything isn't complicated at all. If you are paying travelling

Example No. 1 – Bank in Credit

Week No ....1.... Commencing ....2ND JANUARY 19..

Receipts / Paid to Bank

Day/Date	Daily Gross Takings Cash Col 1	Cheques, Credit Cards and EFTPOS Col 2	Other Receipts Col 3	Particulars of Other Receipts	Lottery etc. Takings Col 4	Cash Col 5	Cheques Col 6	Credit Cards & EFTPOS Col 7	Total Col 8
Sun 2/1	196 27		40000 00	MORTGAGE GRANTED	37 00				
Mon 3/1	232 44	45 75	10000 00	LOAN ARRANGED	141 00	88755 00			88755 00
Tues 4/1	256 26		88805 00	CAPITAL CONTRIBUTED	84 00				
Wed 5/1	112 27	12 64			67 00	882 00	45 75		927 75
Thur 6/1	289 85	60 79			151 00				
Fri 7/1	364 24	26 34			162 00	418 00	78 43		491 43
Sat 8/1	322 72	136 45			337 00				
Sub totals	1824 05	290 97	88805 00 Total		Totals 979 00	90055 00	119 18		90174 18

Gross Weekly Takings (Cols 1+2) **2105 02** EFTPOS = Electronic Funds Transfer at the Point of Sale

Payments for Business Stock

Date or Chq No	To whom paid	Cash Col 9	Cheque Col 10
1 JAN	A. SUPPLIER		5045 00
3/1	J. CONLAN & SONS	48 50	
659	J. BREWER & CO LTD		36 50
660	A.J. GOOD LTD		136 85
5/1	J. BROWN & CO LTD	33 80	
7/1	F. LIVESEY & CO LTD	26 70	
661	A. NEWCOMBE		86 25
662	M. LOMAX		230 00
	Totals	109 00	5534 60
		109 00	
	Total payments (to Summary)	5643 60	

Payments other than for Stock

Nature of payment	Cash Col 11	Cheque Col 12
Employee Costs (i) Wages	65 75	
(ii) Inland Revenue PAYE & NI		127 96
Premises Costs (i) Rent and Rates	35 00	
(ii) Light, Heat and Insurance		63 50
(iii) Cleaning	5 00	
Repairs		15 78
Gen.Admin. (i) Telephone		
£2·38, £9·45 (ii) Postage £1·70, 24·p	13 77	
£27·46, £23·20 (iii) Stationery, etc.		50 66
Motor Expenses (i) Fuel	16 12	
(ii) Servicing and Repairs		86 50
Travel and Subsistence	7 32	
Advertising and Entertainment		
Legal and Professional		
Interest Payable		
Other Financial Charges		
Other Expenses	1 05	
Lottery prizes paid		
Scratch card prizes paid		
MOTOR VEHICLES		9450 00
Customs & Excise (VAT)		
Drawings of Proprietor/Partner 1	85 00	
Drawings of Partner 2		
Drawings of Partner 3		
Capital Items (i)		64500 00
(ii)		8260 00
Totals	229 01	82554 40

Weekly Bank Report

	Opening Balance b/fwd from last week	–	–
Add	Total paid to bank during week (Col 8)	90174	18
	Start-up Allowance/Other Direct Credits	–	–
	Total	90174	18
	Cash drawn for office use	–	–
	Stock (Col 10) Cheques only	5534	60
Deduct	Other Payments (Col 12)	82554	40
	Standing Orders	–	–
	Direct Debits	–	–
	Bank and Interest Charges	–	–
	Total	86089	00
	Closing Balance carried forward	4085	18

Weekly Cash Report

	Cash in hand (as counted) b/fwd from last week	–	–
	Gross Weekly Takings (Col 1 + Col 2)	2105	02
Add	Other Receipts (Col 3)	88805	00
	Lottery etc. Takings (Col 4)	979	00
	Cash drawn from bank for office use	–	–
	Total	91889	02
	Stock payments (cash) (Col 9)	109	00
Deduct	Other payments (cash) (Col 11)	229	01
	Amount paid to bank (Col 8)	90174	18
	Total deductions	90512	19
	Cash balance as per weekly page	1376	83
	Cash in hand (as counted) carr. fwd	1376	83
	Difference on Books (if any) (+ or –)	–	–

Fig. 1.2 THE SIMPLEX WEEKLY PAGE

expenses, you put the money spent on the 'travelling expenses' line – easy. If you don't pay any travelling expenses that particular week the line is left blank. So it is an easy system, not a complicated one. Complicated systems give you a set of ruled paper with no headings at all and you just don't know where to put anything unless you understand the whole of double entry book-keeping.

■ The only figures you have to carry forward from one week to the next are your bank balance (according to your weekly page) and your cash in hand at the end of the week. You count that up and carry it forward to the next week.

■ You don't have a lot of accounts to keep – there are no accounts – only summaries where you gradually build up the profits and losses of the business.

■ At the end of the year, all these summary figures are ready to carry into the trading account and profit and loss account to find the profits of the business.

■ Finally, you draw up a balance sheet and are ready to declare your profits on the self-assessment tax return (SA tax return) sent to you each April. This new self-assessment system of taxation is described in some detail in Chapter 20. Briefly, instead of sending your accounts to the Inland Revenue for assessment each year, you simply declare them on the SA tax return and the assessment for tax is based on the profits you declare.

■ You can buy the Simplex D account book from any reputable stationer, or by post from George Vyner Ltd, PO Box 1, Holmfirth, Huddersfield HD7 2RP. Phone them on 01484 685221 to ask the current price and send a cheque with your order.

■ They do sell a book called *Simplified Book-keeping for Small Businesses*, which is by the present author, but, of course, it deals only with their systems. It explains every detail of the system, although much of it is explained later in this book anyway. They also offer a free advice service to all Simplex users, and any problem you pose will be answered in great detail at no cost to you, other than for your phone call.

■ The Simplex VAT system

I did say the Simplex system was a one-book system, but if you are registered for VAT, you do need a Simplex VAT book as well. A good set of VAT records is simple enough, but there are various VAT systems and nearly all VAT users have three sets of records to keep, which are the following.

- **Input tax** based on the invoices you receive from your suppliers, and kept by what is known as the 'normal method' – the method used by people who have invoices to cover every purchase/or sale.
- **Output tax** based either on the invoices you issue to your customers or on one of the five retailers' schemes. A 'retailer' in VAT terms is not just a shopkeeper, but anyone who supplies goods or services for payment without making out an invoice for every supply. If you issue invoices, these output records are kept by the normal method.
- If you don't issue invoices, you have to use a VAT retail scheme, and your output tax is calculated on a 'reconciliation of daily takings' set of figures.

All these records are kept in the Simplex VAT book – very easily – and, once again, you have the backing of the Simplex advisory service if you run into any difficulties.

Simplex computerised accounts

If the owner of a small business wishes to avoid tedious manual book-keeping, it is possible to use a computerised version of the Simplex system. In it, the rulings of the Simplex D book appear on the computer screen and entries can be made on the screen directly by means of the keyboard. The system is user-friendly, in that it has been designed with safeguards to prevent a trader making wrong entries. For example, suppose the trader is entering the 'daily takings', which today come to £428.37. When the entry has been keyed in the computer asks a friendly question, for example:

> You are asking me to record £428.37 as your daily takings. Is this correct? Y/N

Y means 'Yes' and N means 'No'. A touch on the Y key will bring another question:

> Are you sure?   Y/N

Another touch on the Y key will instantaneously:

- record the figure for daily takings in the records;
- add it to the previous total to give a total figure for the month to date;
- carry it to the summary of takings for use in working out the profits at the end of the year;
- make the necessary VAT entries, including calculating the amount of VAT in £428.37, and so on.

A touch on the N key will delete the entry that is not correct and the screen will read something like this:

Ready to enter your correct daily takings figure.

Simplex's computerised accounts are described fully later in this book (see Chapter 12).

■ Systems for the slightly larger business

■ Simultaneous records systems

An embryonic business will operate perfectly happily using the Simplex system or the computerised version. However, a business that has been growing for a year or two, and is becoming too large for these basic systems, should move on to one of the more advanced systems that give the benefits of full double entry, but do so by means of short-cuts that reduce some of the more laborious work of double entry. Such systems are often called 'three-in one' systems, or simultaneous records systems, because three sets of records are prepared at one time, using carbon or NCR paper (paper where no carbon is required) In the latter case, the paper itself is covered with tiny droplets of colourless ink, which becomes visible only when pressed with a ballpoint pen, which bursts the tiny globules. These systems marketed by firms such as Kalamazoo Security Print PLC and Safeguard Systems Ltd – are described in detail later in this book.

A good example of a three-in-one system is one for pay that prepares a payroll, an employee's individual pay record and a payslip for the week, all in one operation. The payslip gives you an account of the pay earned and the deductions made, to go in the pay packet. The employee's record card builds up to give the total pay and tax deducted and so on for the whole year, while the payroll has every employee's pay on it for the week (or the month) and thus gives a clear record of pay given to staff and deductions made, for the week (or month) concerned.

■ A full double entry system

Any business can, of course, use a full double entry system, but to keep it properly, you do have to understand double entry book-keeping. The system is explained in detail in Chapter 6, but you cannot really say you have mastered the system without doing a great many exercises in keeping the various books. The books required include:

- **five day books, or journals** – the purchases day book, purchases returns book, sales day book, sales returns book and journal proper (which deals with all the rather tricky things that happen, such as bad debts, depreciation, dishonoured cheques and so on).

■ **The ledger** – is the main book of account. It may be split up into a debtors ledger, a creditors ledger, a general ledger and a private ledger.

■ **Finally, you need a four-column cash book and petty cash book** – (the first was formerly called the three-column cash book, but in the United Kingdom you need an extra column for VAT).

With these books (and you could have several more), you can keep a full accounting record for every type of firm and company.

■ Systems for medium-sized enterprises

As the firm increases in size (by this time, often, it will become a private limited company), it will usually move over to a fully computerised system of accounts. Even so, it is surprising how long quite large firms can keep going with smaller systems they have become familiar with. For example, I recently found two companies with over £1 million turnover where they were still using the Simplex system – the easiest system of all – which is described in Chapters 1–5 of this book. When remonstrated with about not moving on to some more sophisticated system, they both maintained that they were happiest with a foolproof system they understood well.

All medium-sized enterprises need a system based on double entry book-keeping, but computerised to reduce the routine book-keeping activities. Chapter 13 of this book gives a chart showing all the manual and computerised systems available. Proprietors of growing enterprises would do well to contact the providers of a system that is appropriate to their needs. I could have mentioned Micro-Retailer and Sage accounting as two of the most popular (see pages 177 and 192).

Apart from reducing the routine book-keeping activities, the great advantage of a fully computerised system is the management information that it generates. All the ratios and control figures featured in this book in Chapter 17 can be generated on request, by most of the computerised systems on the market, and give sound control of all aspects of the business.

■ Systems for large companies

Generally speaking, it is true to say that the books of even the largest company can be kept with the double entry system and the books listed in the section above. In fact, practically every large company has a

computerised accounting system. However, this is not a book about large companies and so I will not try to describe

Documents have important legal consequences.

these systems in detail here. Most small traders will become very familiar with computerised records from their banking activities, and their
purchasing from wholesalers and large suppliers of every kind.

THE IMPORTANCE OF DOCUMENTS IN BUSINESS

It is impossible to over-stress the importance of documents in business.
Whatever the nature of the activity, there is almost always a document
to trigger it and another to bring it to an end. Documents have important legal consequences – not just documents like the deeds to property,
wills, summonses, and so on, but ordinary documents like invoices,
credit notes, receipts, petty cash vouchers, statements, cheques and the
like. They may be presented as evidence in court; VAT inspectors and
the Inland Revenue authorities expect to see documents to bear out the
statements made in sets of figures presented to them, and severe penalties can be imposed for falsifying records. It follows that you should
always take great care of documents, even the tiny till receipts for small
items purchased and the VAT slips you demand from the garage for
petrol purchased. All these documents supplied by outsiders (people
not in your own business) have to be kept as financial records and,
under the rules laid down in the Finance Act 1994, must be retained for
six years.

■ Petty cash vouchers

For some purchases it is impossible to obtain proof of purchase from an
outside organization. For example, railways issue a ticket that is collected at the other end of the journey. In such cases it is advisable to
make out an internal petty cash voucher, signed by yourself to prove
that money was disbursed. Of course this might seem a bit pointless if
you are writing a certificate for your own expenses, but it is certainly
essential for expenses incurred by an employee. In general the principle is: 'Have a piece of paper to cover every item of expenditure.' The
general name for these chits is 'petty cash vouchers' and internal
vouchers for your own use can be purchased in pads of about 50 copies
at any stationery shop. Such a voucher is illustrated in Figure 1.3.

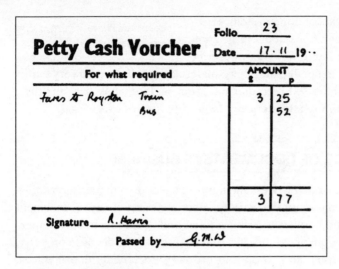

Petty Cash Voucher

Follo_____23_____

Date_____17 · 11__19 · ·

For what required		AMOUNT
		£	p
tares to Royston Train	3	25
Bus		52
	3	**77**

Signature_____R. Harris_____

Passed by_____G. M. W_____

Fig. 1.3 **AN INTERNAL PETTY CASH VOUCHER**

■ Invoices

The most important document is the invoice, which is often made out in sets. The smallest set consists of two copies: the top copy for the customer who is purchasing the goods (or services) you supply; the second for your own book-keeping records. It will probably finish up in your VAT file, but if you are not registered for VAT put it in a lever-arch file. Lever-arch files are the very best files for small businesses and will keep your records in apple-pie order. They are very cheap – from about £1.75 to £3.75 according to quality. They can be purchased from any stationery shop, or by mail order over the telephone from such firms as Neat Ideas, Freepost, Sandall Stones Road, Kirk Sandall, Doncaster DN3 1BR (telephone 01302 890999).

A typical simple set of invoices is shown in Figure 1.4. It is an appropriate set for a small trader who supplies goods by mail order and wishes to collect the cash for the order as soon as possible. Of course, often such sales are made on cash with order (CWO) terms, but in these days of telephone ordering it is sometimes inconvenient to demand that the customer write out an order and enclose a cheque. If you agree to supply goods ordered by telephone it is convenient to have a 'statement copy' to send out with the order. The customer therefore receives two copies, the 'sales invoice' copy and the 'statement' copy. Some firms call the 'statement' copy a 'remittance advice' copy. The third copy is retained in the office and becomes the VAT record, or the sales day book record if a full double entry system is being used.

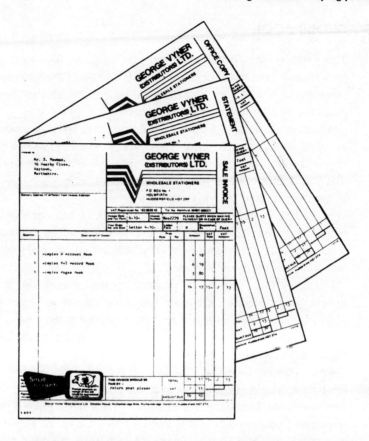

Fig. 1.4 A SIMPLE THREE-COPY INVOICE SET (*courtesy of George Vyner Ltd.*)

■ 'Dawn on day 1' and documents

More will be said about particular documents in later chapters, but it is worth mentioning here that documents begin to arrive from the very earliest moments of your business' existence. It is vital not to lose these records, so take care of them, even though you have so much on your mind. You can buy a very inexpensive file known as a concertina, or expanding, file from any stationers. These have 16–20 pockets, labelled alphabetically. They provide a place to put every document received until you have time to deal with it. With all the invoices under I and the petty cash vouchers under P you are well placed from 'dawn on day 1'. Of course, an empty cardboard box is quite satisfactory, until someone uses it for some other purpose and disposes of your bits and pieces in the process. The Criterion Expanding File is a good one, or if you want to spend a little more you could get a Denton or a Tuff-Nette expanding wallet.

ABOUT THIS BOOK

This book is intended to give you practical, down-to-earth advice on how to start your book-keeping records and keep them going until you come to the end of your first financial year. You will then declare your profits on the SA tax return, and archive your account book, documents and so on for six years in case they are required. This book does not suggest that you do not need an accountant, but it does argue that the vast majority of your routine records should be kept by you, or someone in the family who is prepared to do the work. The finishing touches can then be done by an accountant if you wish, at very little inconvenience to the accountant and very little cost to you.

The first requirement of any business person is to keep honest records. ... Never re-write your records.

Naturally there are many systems on the market and it has been impossible to mention them all, but those mentioned have been well tried over a number of years and have proved satisfactory. Whatever system you use, you may find it necessary to adapt it to suit your own business, but without destroying the accounting principles on which the system is based. Don't be afraid to ask for help from the advice bureau run by the system you adopt or to telephone the suppliers if, for any reason, your computer system won't work. They will soon tell you what is wrong and how to correct it. Remember that the office side of the business is still the relatively easy side, given a little attention, especially in the first year. Later it will become a routine activity.

One final point is this: the first requirement of any business person is to keep honest records. Don't worry if you make a mistake, cross the figure out, initial the alteration and put the correct figure in. Never re-write your records, whether for the sake of neatness or because you have made a lot of alterations. The Inland Revenue expects a few mistakes in placing figures in the books. A neat record is a false record, generally speaking, especially in the first year. All account books are coded and if the Inland Revenue finds that your January accounts are written in a book that didn't roll off the presses until July, it will not like it. Keep a proper record from 'dawn on day 1', have all your pieces of paper neatly filed to support your written records and pay what tax you are charged. Only those making profits have to pay taxes, and the amount you will be charged will be fair and reasonable. Put something away every week for taxes and put away your VAT money every week, in a deposit account. Then, when the time comes to pay it, you can look cheerful and pay up.

CHECKLIST

- Make up your mind early about whether or not you want to register voluntarily for VAT. If you do, you can reclaim your input tax right from the start, but of course you must charge your customers output tax – that is, add $17\frac{1}{2}$ per cent (at present) to their bills.

- If you don't register for VAT at once, you must keep an eye on your takings. A total of £50,000 a year is £12,500 per quarter or roughly £1000 a week. If your takings are approaching anywhere near £1000 a week, register for VAT at once. Of course, if you wish, you may register voluntarily even when your turnover is well below £1000 a week.

- The main method of book-keeping is the double entry system, handed down to us by our ancestors from the Middle Ages. You can keep a full set of books by double entry yourself if you wish to (see Chapter 6).

- Better, for the very small business, is a simple system like Simplex. This has been computerised as the Simplex computer system.

- Other useful systems for slightly larger businesses are the three-in-one systems of simultaneous records, such as the Kalamazoo and Safeguard systems.

- Documents are vital parts of any record-keeping system. Never throw documents away. Have a concertina file (an expanding file) to put documents in as they arrive. After recording them, file them in a permanent file – preferably a lever-arch file. Have a piece of paper for every outlay. If necessary, make out an internal petty cash voucher.

- Under the Finance Act 1994, all documents of every sort must be kept for six years. You should archive your year's documents in one of the special 'archive boxes' sold at any stationers, putting into the box such documents as cease to be useful or current as the year progresses. For example chequebook stubs must be preserved. At the end of the financial year, your account books, lever-arch file of documents and so on should be placed in the box to give a complete record. The two chief parties interested are HM Customs (for your VAT records) and the Inland Revenue. The attitude of the Inland Revenue is that you should preserve all documents that substantiate the statements about your business profits made in your declaration of profits in your SA tax return, which is sent to you in April each year.

- *Never re-write your records!* The Inland Revenue does not demand neat accounts; it does demand honest records. If you make a slip by entering something in the wrong place, cross out the wrong figure, initial the correction and write in the correct figure.

- For medium-sized enterprises, it is desirable to move on to a computerised system of accounting as it not only reduces the amount of routine book-keeping work but also provides detailed management control figures that relate to every aspect of the business.

'Dawn on day 1'

THE SIGNIFICANCE OF 'DAWN ON DAY 1'

The first moment of the first day of your new business is a very important moment. It signals the start of your new business and when a new 'business entity' is born. It may be a sole trader enterprise, a partnership or a limited company, but it comes into existence at dawn on day one. It is separate from you in many ways, and in the case of a limited company is totally separate from you – with a separate legal personality. A company can own assets, borrow money, employ people, buy and sell goods, supply services and demand payment for them and so on. A company is a totally separate legal person, and you are just a director of the company. Do not be misled by that title. We often see company directors referred to as if that status conferred rank, honour and position on them, but it doesn't. Anyone can become a company director by buying a company off the shelf for about £100. No particular merit or attribute is required, no skill or qualification is implied. Company directors are just as fallible as other mortals; perhaps more so.

> *The first moment of the first day of your new business is a very important moment. It signals the start of your new business and when a new 'business entity' is born.*

Sole traders and partnerships are not separate legal personalities from their owners and, consequently, sole traders and partners are responsible for their businesses directly and personally to the full extent of their worldly wealth. They do not have the limited liability that the company director has, which means that the latter is liable to lose only the actual capital put into the business – often as little as £100. More of this later.

The most important aspects of 'dawn on day 1' are the following.

- As that is the start of the business, it is a moment that should be recorded carefully so the accounting activities begin in a proper manner and everyone who needs to look at our books can see what the starting position was. The chief people who might want to look at your books at some time in the future are:
  - the accountants, if you decide to use the services of an accountant;
  - HM Customs, if you register for VAT;
  - the Inland Revenue, should it query the accounts you have submitted;
  - your lawyers, should you die and they need to sort out your will or your financial position if we died intestate (without leaving a will);
  - your partners or other persons interested in the business, such as

the representatives of shareholders or debenture holders or the receiver if the company goes into liquidation.

The records that such people would want to look at start with the opening entry', which is the official accounting term for the entries made at 'dawn on day 1'. You will see how to make these entries later in the chapter.

- The other aspect of 'dawn on day 1' is that the pieces of paper (documents) that trigger every sort of business activity begin to arrive from that time and you should be ready for them and have somewhere safe to put them. A full explanation of start-up requirements is given later in this chapter.

THE 'OPENING ENTRIES' OF THE BUSINESS

Every new trader starts with a certain accumulation of goods and money that enables them to commence trading. This may consist of physical assets – such as premises, machinery, tools, motor vehicles and stock – but may also include money, cash at the bank or in a building society, say.

A certain amount of confusion exists about the terms to be used for these assets, because the word 'capital' has several different meanings. For example, a person seeking to start up in the clothing trade may say, 'I must see the bank about some capital – I shall need about £30,000.' The use of the word capital to mean 'money capital' is very common, but, actually, money capital is only a part of the true capital of a business, as you will see.

To digress for a moment, consider the Start-up Allowance Scheme, run by the government to assist new small enterprises. It is a condition of joining the Scheme that the budding entrepreneur (one who shows enterprise) should have capital of £1000, or if two people are going into partnership the sum required is £2000. It is easy enough to find such capital, for almost any bank will lend you the money at the drop of a hat, provided you make a reasonable case for borrowing it. Joining the Scheme is reason enough in most cases. What is the purpose behind the requirement? Probably it is the feeling of those officials who run the Scheme that it is some sort of guarantee that the new business will have a minimum amount of liquid funds (that is, funds in cash form) for the first few weeks of its life. There is no requirement to leave the money in the business beyond that time, and a great many people do not. The first question they ask is, 'Is it all right if I repay the bank (or repay Aunt Lucy who loaned me the money) because I don't need it for the business really?' This problem is considered later once you have been shown how to open the books of a business.

To open the books of a business, you take a piece of paper and write down on it all the assets you have contributed to the business, and any liabilities the business is taking over. A list of assets and liabilities is called a 'balance sheet'. That name is appropriate because the total value of the assets and the total value of the liabilities are always exactly the same, and therefore if put into the scales of a balance the balance would settle horizontally, as shown in Figure 2.1.

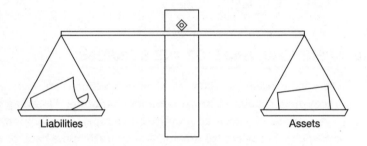

Liabilities   Assets

Fig. 2.1 ASSETS AND LIABILITIES ALWAYS BALANCE

Let us draw up a list of the assets and liabilities of Tom Smith, who is starting off in business under the Start-up Allowance Scheme as the proprietor of a snack bar operating from a layby on a busy main road. His wife Mary is a partner, and, at 'dawn on day 1', 1 July 199X, they had:

- a caravan, newly purchased for £2850;
- various items of crockery, kitchenware, gas cylinders and so on worth £340.56;
- a car to tow the van, which is worth £2250, but only two-thirds of this is to be regarded as business, the other third is for domestic use, which means the business value of the car is £1500;
- stocks of various types of food, confectionery and so on worth £168.30.

They had borrowed £2000 from the Helpful Bank PLC, as required by the Start-up Allowance Scheme, and this money, together with £225.40, which is all that is left of their own savings after purchasing the items listed above, is in a current account at Helpful Bank PLC. They also have £25 cash in hand, which is regarded as a till float for use on the first day. The list of assets and liabilities is as follows:

Assets	£	Liabilities	£
Caravan	2850.00	Bank loan	2000.00
Crockery, etc.	340.56		
Car (²/₃)	1500.00		
Stock	168.30		
Cash at bank	2225.40		
Cash in hand	25.00		
	£7109.26		

It is clear that the assets and liabilities do not balance; the assets total £7109.26 while the liabilities (owed to the bank) are only £2000. The reason for the imbalance is that I have left out one of the liabilities: what the business owes to the owners of the business, Tom and Mary. This is called the 'capital they have contributed to the business' and it totals £5109.26.

> *Capital is what the business owes to the owner of the business.*

The true meaning of 'capital' is not money alone. Money capital is only a part of the true capital, which is the total value of the assets contributed by the proprietor or proprietors. Tom and Mary have assets of £7109.26, of which the bank contributed £2000 and they provided all the rest: £5109.26. Putting in this capital, Tom and Mary's balance sheet is as shown in Table 2.1.

Table 2.1 TOM AND MARY SMITH'S BALANCE SHEET

Tom and Mary Smith Balance Sheet as at Dawn on 1 July 199X			
Assets	£	Liabilities	£
Caravan	2850.00	Bank loan	2000.00
Crockery, etc.	340.56	Capital	5109.26
Car (²/₃)	1500.00		
Stock	168.30		
Cash at bank	2225.40		
Cash in hand	25.00		
	£7109.26		£7109.26

It is worth learning the following definition of capital by heart:

> Capital is what the business owes to the owner of the business. It is the difference between the total value of the assets and the total external liabilities, owed to, for example, banks, building societies and other creditors.

This capital will be repaid to the proprietor when the business ceases to trade, at close of business on the last day. Close of business on the last day may be said to be the opposite of 'dawn on day 1'. What starts at dawn on day 1 does not end until close of business on the last day, which may be many years after, and is often the day the proprietor dies and their solicitor takes steps to carry out the last will and testament of the deceased.

You now know what the starting position of this business is. In a full double entry system you would start the books by doing what is called an 'opening journal entry'. This is explained in Chapter 6. For a simple system of books, such as the Simplex system, you record the opening balance sheet at the beginning of the book on the special blank balance sheet provided. When completed, it is as shown in Figure 2.2. Study this, and the notes to it, now.

OPENING THE BOOKS AT 'DAWN ON DAY 1'

Recording the 'dawn on day 1' position does not actually open the books. You now know what the assets and liabilities were at dawn on day 1, but you still have to enter them all in the books, whatever system you decide to use. With the Simplex system, you enter all these items on the first weekly page, which is of course week 1 of your business. As shown in Figure 1.2, the weekly page has separate sections for 'receipts', 'paid to bank', 'payments for business stock' and 'payments other than for stock'. For convenience, the entries from your opening balance sheet have been shown in their separate sections in Figures 2.3, 2.4, 2.5 and 2.6. What you are pretending is that all these assets and liabilities were taken on at the first moment of day 1, even if in real life some of them were bought or arranged in the weeks before the business actually opened. If you look down the list of activities necessary to get the week 1 page started and then look at the figures, you will follow the ideas.

- **The 'receipts' section** I shall pretend that the £2000 kindly loaned by Helpful Bank PLC, and the £5109.26 put into the business by Tom and Mary Smith are both contributed in cash on day 1. Of course, they weren't; the arrangements had really been made in the run-up period before day 1 (see Figure 2.3).
- **The 'payment for business stock' section** I shall pretend that stock to the value of £168.30 is purchased at this time with some of the money received (see Figure 2.4).
- **The 'payment other than for stock' section** Three of the items you started business with are capital items – in other words, fixed assets. You need a small digression here to explain the terms 'capital items' and 'capital expenditure'.

BALANCE SHEET AT START OF BUSINESS/YEAR

As at 1st July 19..

Liabilities

	£	p	£	p
CAPITAL ACCOUNT (Tom and Mary) SMITH				
Balance at 1st July 19..	—	—	5,109	26
Add Net Profit during year	—	—		
Extra Capital Contributed	—	—		
Total	—	—		
Less Drawings & Income Tax	—	—	—	
Total			5,109	26
LONG TERM LIABILITIES				
Mortgage				
Loan HELPFUL BANK PLC	2,000	00	2,000	00
CURRENT LIABILITIES				
Sundry Creditors	—	—		
Accrued Charges	—	—		
Bank Overdraft	—	—	—	
Total			7,109	26

Assets

	At Cost		Less Depreciation		£	p
FIXED ASSETS						
Goodwill					—	—
Premises			—	—	—	—
Fixtures & Fittings	340	56	—	—	340	56
Motor Vehicles	4,350	00	—	—	4,350	00
Total					4,690	56
CURRENT ASSETS						
Stock in Trade			168	30		
Sundry Debtors			—			
Cash at Bank			2,225	40		
Cash in Hand			25	00		
Payments in Advance			—		2,418	70
Total					7,109	26

Fig. 2.2 THE OPENING BALANCE SHEET OF A NEW BUSINESS

(See notes on page 24)

Notes to balance sheet in Figure 2.2

- A balance sheet is just a list of balances on the accounts of a business, listed as either assets or liabilities. It may be written down with the assets on the left and the liabilities on the right or vice versa. In the United Kingdom, it is traditional for the assets to be on the right-hand side, as shown in Figure 2.2.
- The assets are divided into 'fixed assets' and 'current assets'. Fixed assets are those that are used in the business over many years, and are sold only when they have depreciated to such an extent that they have come to the end of their useful life. Current assets are those that have been purchased to sell again. This means that the stock in trade is sold and so turns into cash or it may turn into debtors and so becomes cash when they eventually pay.
- The liabilities may be current liabilities, which are those due for payment very shortly. For example, if you buy goods on credit to sell again, you usually pay for them within one month. The suppliers you owe the money to are called 'trade creditors' or, more simply, creditors. The dividing line between current liabilities and long-term liabilities is one year. A long-term liability is usually one where you have made a contractual arrangement to repay over a period of several years. For example, bank loans may be spread over one to five years, and mortgages are usually repayable over even longer periods – up to 25 years.
- The other liability, as explained in the text, is the capital owed back to the proprietor. In Figure 2.2, which is only the starting position at dawn on day 1, there is simply the figure for the total assets supplied by the proprietors, Tom and Mary Smith, but, as the illustration shows, this would change at the end of every year. Suppose that, in the first year, they made £20 000 profit, and each drew out £6000 as drawings. 'Drawings' is the term used when a proprietor of a business draws out money to live on during the year. A proprietor cannot draw 'pay'. Instead, what they do draw is 'drawings in expectation of profit earned'. So, if Tom and Mary drew a total of £12 000 and the profits proved to be £20 000, there would be £8000 left in the business. This £8000 would be added to the capital to give them £13 109.26 by the end of the year. That is how a business grows in value – by ploughing back the profits.
- There is one final point that I will not go into in detail here because it is explained in Chapter 15. As this is a partnership business, you should really show how much each partner has contributed as capital, instead of showing a single figure of £5109.26. The partners could have contributed equally (that is, £2554.63 each) or unequally – say £1000 by Mary and £4109.26 by Tom. For the moment, to save a long explanation of partnership accounts, I will leave it as a joint figure.

■ Capital expenditure and revenue expenditure

It is very important to understand the two terms 'capital expenditure' and 'revenue expenditure'.

Capital expenditure' is expenditure on fixed assets, which last a long time and are used in the business during their lifetime. They are not bought to sell again – you sell them only at the end of their working life when you may trade them in for a new item, or sell them for scrap. They are bought to use in the business and make it possible to carry out your activities. Thus Tom and Mary have a car to tow the caravan, the caravan itself is fitted out as a mobile canteen and has various items of crockery, frying pans and so on. These are all capital items.

'Revenue expenditure' is expenditure on things that do not last a long time. For example, you buy business stock and sell it the next day or in the next few days – it is part of your turnover. You buy petrol, postage stamps, stationery and so on. These are revenue expenses, incurred in the process of earning 'revenue' – that is, takings. If you like, you can remember these revenue expenses as items you will account for at the end of the year when you have dealings with the Inland Revenue, who will expect to see that your profit and loss account shows the revenue you earned (your takings) and the revenue expenditure you incurred (your expenses) and the difference between them – your profit (on which the Inland Revenue will levy a rate of tax).

Returning to those capital items – the car, caravan and crockery – they are recorded on the capital items lines of the weekly page. There are only two lines for capital items, but if there are three, you use one of the spare lines provided, as shown in Figure 2.5.

Week No....1........ Commencing...1ST JULY 19..

Day/Date	Daily Gross Takings		Other Receipts Col 3		Particulars of Other Receipts	Lottery etc. Takings Col 4
	Cash Col 1	Cheques, Credit Cards and EFTPOS Col 2				
Sun 1 JULY			5109	26	CAPITAL T. & M. SMITH.	
Mon 2 "			2000	00	LOAN FROM HELPFUL BANK PLC.	
Tues 3 "						
Wed 4 "						
Thur 5 "						
Fri 6 "						
Sat 7 "						
Sub totals					Total Totals	

Gross Weekly Takings (Cols 1+2)   EFTPOS = Electronic Funds Transfer at the Point of Sale

Fig. 2.3 RECEIVING THE CAPITAL AND SO ON ONTO THE BOOKS

■ **The 'paid to bank' section** You now have to pretend that you are paying into the bank the £2225.40 (which, in fact, is in the bank already). You enter this in the 'paid to bank' section, as shown in Figure 2.6.

Payments for Business Stock					
Date or Chq No	To whom paid	Amount paid			
		Cash Col 9		Cheque Col 10	
I JULY	A. SUPPLIER.	168	30		
Totals					
Total payments (to Summary)					

Fig. 2.4 PRETENDING TO PURCHASE THE STOCK ON DAY 1

■ Do you understand the 'cash' situation now?

On Tom and Mary's Balance Sheet, it says that the proprietors provided £5109.26 and the bank provided a loan of £2000, making £7109.26. I have entered this as if it came in, in cash, at 'dawn on day 1'. I have then pretended that Tom and Mary paid out for the following:

	£
Three capital items	340.56
	1500.00
	2850.00
Business stock	168.30
Cash banked	2225.40
Total	£7084.26

As they contributed £7109.26 and have 'spent' £7084.26, the balance left unspent is £25.

	£
	7109.26
	− 7084.26
	£25.00

Payments other than for Stock				
Nature of payment	Amount paid			
	Cash Col 11		Cheque Col 12	
Employee Costs (i) Wages				
(ii) Inland Revenue PAYE & NI				
Premises Costs (i) Rent and Rates				
(ii) Light, Heat and Insurance				
(iii) Cleaning				
Repairs				
Gen.Admin. (i) Telephone				
(ii) Postage				
(iii) Stationery, etc.				
Motor Expenses (i) Fuel				
(ii) Servicing and Repairs, etc.				
Travel and Subsistence				
Advertising and Entertainment				
Legal and Professional				
Interest Payable				
Other Financial Charges				
Other Expenses				
Lottery prizes paid				
Scratch card prizes paid				
CAPITAL ITEM (CROCKERY).	340	56		
Customs & Excise (VAT)				
Drawings of Proprietor/Partner 1				
Drawings of Partner 2				
Drawings of Partner 3				
Capital Items (i) CARAVAN	2850	00		
(ii) CAR (⅔ RDS VALUE).	1500	00		
Totals				

Fig. 2.5 BRINGING THE ASSETS ONTO THE BOOKS AS CAPITAL

Paid to Bank			
Cash Col 5	Cheques Col 6	Credit Cards & EFTPOS Col 7	Total Col 8
2225 40			2225 40

Fig. 2.6 PAYING THE FUNDS (APART FROM THE TILL FLOAT) INTO THE BANK

This £25 is left in their till as a till float. I don't need to enter it anywhere. The books are open and they are ready for the first week of their business, up and running.

HOW TO REPAY AUNT LUCY!

Of course, a person who has just started up in business is usually short of capital, and doesn't want to repay any loan borrowed until the business has really started to pay off. However, this business of providing capital to satisfy the Start-up Allowance Scheme's requirement does mean that many small traders who start in business are forced to borrow a capital sum that they don't really need. How do they repay it if they don't really want the money, and would rather not be in debt? The answer is very simple. You write Aunt Lucy a cheque for £2000, and enter it in the 'payments other than for stock' section, on one of the spare lines:

Repaid Aunt Lucy   2000.00

The £2000 is entered in the 'By cheque' column because you have paid by cheque. Aunt Lucy has her money back again, and you have only £225.40 in the bank. There is nothing difficult about paying any debt – just write out the cheque and post it to your creditor, and enter the payment on the appropriate line in 'payments for business stock' or 'payments other than for stock', whichever is the correct section for the payment you are making.

READY TO GO AT 'DAWN ON DAY 1'

This chapter has explained how important a moment 'dawn on day 1' is. It remains to say that you should be ready to be 'businesslike' on the day your business begins. Whatever it is, you can't just concentrate on the technicalities; you have to get the business side organised as well. Of course the budding pizza restaurateur is worried about producing good pizzas, and is busy ordering flour, salt and toppings and all the rest of the paraphernalia of a pizza parlour. What they must not do is forget to register for VAT; £50 000 per annum is only £965 a week, and a pizza parlour will take a lot more than that, so VAT registration will be compulsory. Other traders may only be going to register voluntarily, but don't delay if you are planning to register so you can claim back your input tax straight away. To be businesslike and ready to go you should do the following.

■ Decide on your accounting system. I recommend that you consider the Simplex system first, because it is cheap, easy, comprehensive and has a sound advisory service to help you if you get into any book-keeping difficulty. Buy a Simplex D book, and a Simplex VAT book well before day 1. If you want a computerised system, try the Simplex computer system. If you understand double entry book-keeping and need a full double entry system, decide what system to use after reading this book – and actually buy the system and be ready to do your opening entries in it.

■ Decide whether or not you are going to register for VAT and, if you are, register well in advance before day 1 arrives. Buy a Simplex VAT book and go into the whole subject of VAT (see Chapters 11–12) so you know which scheme you are going to use. If you are not going to use a VAT retail scheme you have to issue an invoice to every customer, so visit your local print shop and have a good invoice designed and printed before day 1. Make sure your full details are on all documents – including postcode and telephone numbers. You will lose orders if people can't find your postcode and telephone number; it is very frustrating to want to place an order and not be able to locate the supplier, even when you are looking at their printed document.

■ Buy a basic set of office requirements – an expanding file for documents, a filing cabinet helps (however old), a two-hole punch, a stapler, a pair of scissors, a decent telephone system that meets your needs, a couple of lever-arch files, a calendar, a memo pad for telephone messages, some paper-clips and so on. All these things are very cheap, they last for years and will soon be 'all shiny from long years of handling' – as much a part of you as an arm or a leg. Obtain bills for all of them – remember, you want a piece of paper for everything you buy (and sell – though the sales might be on a till roll).

With this sort of set-up you are poised to start in business. Like the British soldier, who is said to have a field marshal's baton in his knapsack if he just knows where to find it, you are ready to become a tycoon. Whether you become one or not, enterprise activity is never dull, and there are nearly always new avenues to explore as you become more knowledgeable and more experienced. Life begins at 'dawn on day 1'.

'DAWN ON DAY 1' AND MEDIUM-SIZED ENTERPRISES

By the time you have become a medium-sized enterprise, day 1 of the business and its 'opening balance sheet' have retreated into the distance far behind you. However, this is not entirely true because every financial year has its own 'day 1', and if you do end your financial year on the anniversary of the day you started up, then you shall be reminded every year of the original day 1 when it all began.

If you do not trade to the anniversary of the start-up, but to the end of the calendar year (31 December) or the end of the tax year (5 April) each year, then you must either have a short year or a long year. Thus, if you start business on 1 October and decide to trade to the end of the tax year, your first year will be a short year – 1 October to 5 April. With companies, the end of the year is always 31 March, so, once again, a short year or a long year might apply. A year would be 'long' if you started on 1 February, for example. There would be little point in doing a set of final accounts on 5 April, only 5 weeks after start-up, so you would work to the next year and your accounts would cover the longer period of 1 year and 5 weeks.

The main point is this. At the end of the year, you do a set of 'final accounts'. These consist of a trading account, a profit and loss account and a balance sheet. The first two of these work out the profit for the year. A balance sheet lists the assets and liabilities at the end of the year, on day 365. The balance sheet then rolls over into the new year, and becomes the opening balance sheet on day 1 of the new year. So, every year has its day 1, with its opening balance sheet. If you want to see how a business has grown, look at its balance sheets year by year. You will gradually see the proprietor becoming wealthier as a larger and larger collection of worldly goods surrounds them. Of course, if the business does not make profits, the collection becomes smaller and smaller, and eventually the proprietor disappears to the bankruptcy court. Every added penny made by a prosperous 'medium-sized enterprise' can be traced back to its origin in one of the balance sheets of years gone by.

What is the significance of the annual calculations of profits and the preparation of a balance sheet at the end of the financial year? It is quite simple. It gives a moment in time, each year, when the state can take its share of the wealth created by the citizens, particularly the entrepreneurs. In a civilised society, with its Head of State, there are many things the citizens cannot do for themselves. The state exercises its fiscal power to tax citizens according to procedure laid down officially, so that it has funds to do such things as educate the young, care for the sick, maintain law and order and so on. Fiscal power is the power to tax ('fisces' meant the Roman Emperor's purse). The Inland Revenue used to assess each citizen for tax. Today, we are considered intelligent and knowledgeable enough for it to have introduced 'self-assessment'. We are charged with the duty of working out what we should pay and sending the money in before the due date. How the Roman Emperor would smile if he knew how things are done today!

EXERCISE ON OPENING ENTRIES

To practise drawing up opening entries, you might like to try the following exercise. You will find it a lot easier to draw up your own opening entry if you have tried this first.

A. Starter commences business on 1 February 199X, bringing in the following assets:

- tools and equipment £1240;
- an electronic till £380;
- supplies for resale already purchased £1585.50;
- a motor vehicle (to be shared 50 per cent business, 50 per cent domestic) and valued at £3850;
- cash in hand £48.50;
- cash at bank £1732.85.

A. Starter has an outstanding bank loan of £2500 from Helpful Bank PLC. Draw up the owner's opening balance sheet.

Answer
Capital £4411.85, totals of balance sheet £6911.85.

CHECKLIST

- 'Dawn on day 1' is the moment when your new business comes into existence.

- Get ready for it, ahead of time.
  - Register in advance for VAT if you intend to register voluntarily or feel sure your takings will exceed £961 per week, on average, so that registration will be compulsory for you.
  - Get your accounts system ready – either a Simplex book for small businesses or a full double entry system or a computerised system.
  - Buy an expanding file to hold all documents as they arrive or are generated in-house.
  - Establishing a basic office set-up, so you are not driven frantic for the sake of a paper-clip or a petty cash voucher.
  - Buy an archive box (they are usually sold in flat packs of three or five at any stationer's). Make one of them up and start to accumulate all documents, chequebook stubs, bank statements and so on as they arrive during the year. In this way, you will comply with the requirements of the Finance Act 1994 to keep all the records that substantiate the statements you make in your SA tax return.

- Draw up your opening balance sheet at 'dawn on day 1', using a piece of scrap paper. When you have written down all the assets you are bringing into the business and placed a fair value on them and all the liabilities the business is taking over, work out your capital.

- Record this balance sheet on the opening balance sheet in the front of your Simplex D book, or do an opening entry if you are using a full double entry system.

- Carry these opening figures into week 1 of your book-keeping records so that all the assets and liabilities are properly recorded on the books.

- Although I have talked about drawing up a balance sheet at 'dawn on day 1' of the business, in fact every year has its day 1, and the balance sheet drawn up on day 365 of the first year becomes the day 1 figures for year 2. If a business prospers, the balance sheets year by year show increasing assets and increasing liabilities. Let us hope that the increasing liabilities are not external liabilities owed to banks and other organizations, but simply extra sums due to the proprietor as their investment in the business grows.

Recording takings (sales)

THE NATURE OF TAKINGS

Every business must have 'takings' in some form or another. If a business is to survive, it must have cash flows into it, and we often hear business advisers talking about the importance of 'cash flow'. The trouble, is of course, that cash can flow out as well as in, and if too much flows out and too little flows in you finish up in the bankruptcy court.

Takings may be defined as sums of money received as a result of business activity. The easiest forms of takings to understand are the takings of a shop dealing only in cash – in other words, payment is demanded as the goods are supplied and the property (right of ownership) in the goods passes to the buyer as they give the money payment (the price) to the seller. These terms – 'buyer', 'seller', 'property' and 'price' – all come from the Sale of Goods Act 1979 (as amended), where Parliament has laid down a whole host of rules about the sale of goods that makes very interesting reading. Even in such a simple matter as cash sales the payment may be made in cash, by cheque, credit card, EFTPOS cards, such as NatWest's 'Switch' card, and tokens and vouchers from some of the minor trading houses that help poor people buy household goods, for which they pay a local tally man who calls weekly.

Shop takings of this sort occur every business day and also lead to a considerable amount of banking. It is unwise to keep excessive amounts of cash on the premises and cheques and vouchers must be paid in before they can be turned into cash at the bank. Always pay in every day if you can, and if you do have amounts overnight, cash them up at closing time and take them home with you, including the separate till float, which you keep for change next day. It is better to have a small safe at home for these overnight moneys than to leave them in a safe in a small shop premises. Leave the till open and empty; this saves the burglars breaking it open, only to find it empty. The loss of your till can be as big a nuisance as the burglary itself.

Other traders do not handle cash every day, but are paid only when they finish a job. If your business is of that kind, record each amount you receive on the day you receive it. You should supply an invoice for the job done, and if you do not give invoices for some reason, at least give the person concerned a receipt. You can buy pads of receipts from any good stationers, usually with counterfoils so that the customer is given the original and you retain the counterfoil. Giving a receipt is a way of proving your good faith in financial matters, for not only has your customer proof of payment but you have proof of the amount of your takings, which is very useful in your dealings with the VAT authorities and the Inland Revenue. The person who takes payments in cash and does not record them may think they are getting away with it, but untraced income shows up sooner or later and is subject to serious penalties when discovered. Many a householder has complained that the burglars stole a tin containing savings from their wardrobe only to find that the next letter received is from the Inland Revenue, asking how the press reports can be true in view of recent tax returns and enclosing a supplementary assessment form with an immediate deadline for payment. The Inland Revenue watches for such press reports as unbanked savings are usually a sign of undeclared income.

RECORDING TAKINGS AND OTHER RECEIPTS

All firms record their cash takings in some sort of 'cash book'. In the Simplex system being used here, the weekly page has a special section for recording receipts. In Figure 3.1, you can see this 'receipts' section, showing how a shopkeeper taking cash on a regular daily basis will record it. These daily takings records are important because they form the basis of the VAT records for use in determining the VAT payable under the VAT retail schemes. The takings figures are entered gross (inclusive of VAT), either in the cash column (Col. 1) or in the cheques column if payment is made by cheque, credit card or EFTPOS card. Study the notes to Figure 3.1.

Week No...1...   Commencing...2 JANUARY 19..

Day/Date	Daily Gross Takings		Other Receipts Col 3		Particulars of Other Receipts	Lottery etc. Takings Col 4	
	Cash Col 1		Cheques, Credit Cards and EFTPOS Col 2				
Sun 2 JAN	186	27		40000	00	MORTGAGE GRANTED.	37	00
Mon 3 "	232	44	45	75	10000	00	LOAN ARRANGED.	141	00
Tues 4 "	256	26		38805	00	CAPITAL CONTRIBUTED.	84	00
Wed 5 "	112	27	12	64		67	00
Thur 6 "	289	85	60	79		151	00
Fri 7 "	364	24	26	34		162	00
Sat 8 "	382	72	135	45		337	00
Sub totals	1824	05	280	97	88805	00 Total Totals	979	00

Gross Weekly Takings (Cols 1+2)   2105 02

EFTPOS = Electronic Funds Transfer at the Point of Sale

Fig. 3.1 RECORDING 'DAILY TAKINGS' AND 'OTHER RECEIPTS'

Notes to Figure 3.1
● The daily entries are simple enough. Towards the end of the day – say 30 minutes before closing time – the till is emptied, and any till float in use – say £25 – is returned to the till in small coins and so on for change. The rest – which is the day's takings – is put into suitable bags for banking purposes, notes are put together with rubber

bands, and cheques and credit card vouchers are prepared for paying in. Any further takings that day are left in the till with the float and will count as tomorrow's takings.

- The paying-in book for the next day can be prepared at this time if preferred.
- The entries are now made on the appropriate lines and in the appropriate columns as shown in Figure 3.1. If the trader is registered for VAT, the total takings will be entered in the Simplex VAT book in the 'daily takings' section (see Chapter 11). The figures are entered gross – that is, inclusive of VAT.
- At the end of the week, the total takings for the week – cash, cheques and credit cards – will be taken to the 'weekly summary of takings' (see Figure 3.3 on page 38).
- Any receipts which are not ordinary takings are entered in the 'other receipts' column and a short explanation of them is written in the 'particulars' column. These are then carried to summaries at the back of the book. The mortgage and the loan will be carried to the loan summary at the back of the book. The capital contributed is carried to the 'summary' of other receipts section.
- The lottery takings are rather special. As this money belongs to the National Lottery authorities and not to the trader, it is not part of the trader's takings. It is carried to a special Summary of National Lottery Transactions section and is extracted from the trader's bank account by direct debit every Wednesday morning.

Figure 3.2 shows the much more sparse entries for a trader who is paid only when a job is completed. Thus plumbers, electricians, decorators and so on may spend several days on a job and, consequently, have only one or two entries a week. Authors are paid only once or twice a year and so have very few entries in the 'receipts' section of the book.

Week No ...17...... Commencing ...13 AUGUST 19..

	Receipts						
Day/Date	Daily Gross Takings		Other Receipts Col 3		Particulars of Other Receipts	Lottery etc. Takings Col 4	
	Cash Col 1	Cheques, Credit Cards and EFTPOS Col 2					
Sun 13 AUG							
Mon 14 "							
Tues 15 "		246 50					
Wed 16 "							
Thur 17 "							
Fri 18 "		788 90					
Sat 19 "							
Sub totals	–	–	1035 40	–	–	Total	Totals	–	–

Gross Weekly Takings (Cols 1+2) | 1035 40 | EFTPOS = Electronic Funds Transfer at the Point of Sale

Fig. 3.2 RECORDING RECEIPTS FOR A TRADER WHO DOES NOT RECEIVE CASH EVERY DAY

CARRYING THE WEEKLY TAKINGS TO THE 'SUMMARY OF TAKINGS' SECTION

The whole purpose of keeping accounts is to discover the profits made by the business, both for management purposes (to decide whether or not it is worth while being self-employed at all) and for taxation purposes (to supply figures for the Inland Revenue). One of the vital figures is the 'sales' figure for the trading year. This is often called the 'turnover' of the business. Under the Simplex system, you find it by transferring the weekly takings figure, both cash and cheques, into a 'weekly summary of takings' section that builds up into four quarterly totals, and eventually into an annual total. This is illustrated in Figure 3.3. Note that in the Simplex system, these figures are all gross of VAT, in that the takings figures include the VAT – it is actually removed later when preparing the final accounts of the business. Study Figure 3.3 now and the notes to it.

PAYING MONEY AND VOUCHERS INTO THE BANK

Every day, or every few days, you have to pay your funds into the bank. We make out the usual paying-in slips as illustrated in Figure 3.4. Note the warning on the paying-in slip that, as it is not unknown for cheques to be lost in the course of clearing, it is wise to keep a note of the names and addresses of those who are paying you by cheque. Where a cheque is valued at less than £50, it is advisable to ask for a cheque card and record the number of the card on the back of the cheque. This causes the bank to honour the cheque, for it has virtually validated the payment made. Cheques over £50 are not covered, and

> *It is wise to keep a note of the names and addresses of those who are paying you by cheque.*

if you accept them, you run the usual risk of taking a cheque – that it may be dishonoured. This is of course a criminal offence, which may lead to the person passing the cheque being punished, but that will not get you the money owed.

A rather similar paying-in slip is provided by credit card companies for paying in vouchers signed by customers and imprinted with their card details. It is not necessary to reproduce one of these here as you will be instructed in its completion when you become an authorised retailer for any particular card. (If you wish to become an authorised retailer your local NatWest branch will be happy to put you in touch with the Access authorities.) The total amount of the vouchers

Weekly Summary of Gross Takings

Week No.	Cash		Cheques and Credit Cards		EFTPOS		TOTAL		Week No.	Cash		Cheques & Credit Cards		EFTPOS		TOTAL	
1	1725	62	–	–	–	–	1725	62	14	987	76	213	16	185	56	1386	48
2	958	64	235	29	132	80	1326	73	15	1586	24	496	50	156	98	2238	72
3									16								

Week No.	Cash		Cheques and Credit Cards		EFTPOS		TOTAL		Week No.	Cash		Cheques & Credit Cards		EFTPOS		TOTAL	
12	525	80	179	64	188	27	893	71	25	946	32	128	70	246	50	1321	52
13	626	50	211	74	156	12	994	36	26	1464	28	358	27	167	21	1989	76
Total 1st Qtr.	20294	45	2658	27	4333	58	27286	30	Total 2nd Qtr.	23265	70	2275	65	2500	29	28041	64

Week No.	Cash		Cheques and Credit Cards		EFTPOS		TOTAL		Week No.	Cash		Cheques & Credit Cards		EFTPOS		TOTAL	
27	2466	37	451	38	255	20	3172	95	40	985	25	417	27	326	95	1729	47
28	2133	28	346	62	528	60	3008	50	41	1384	74	329	56	471	12	2185	42
36									49								
37	958	60	174	20	159	90	1292	70	50								
38	1215	56	136	20	269	90	1621	66	51								
39	1786	56	–	–	–	–	1786	56	52	1725	60	311	18	237	77	2274	55
	–	–	–	–	–	–	–	–	53	–	–	–	–	–	–	–	–
Total 3rd Qtr.	24916	56	5816	76	3644	10	34377	42	Total 4th Qtr.	24926	17	4361	88	3586	70	32874	75

SUMMARY	Cash		Cheques & Credit Cards		EFTPOS		TOTAL	
1st Qtr.	20294	45	2658	27	4333	58	27286	30
2nd Qtr.	23265	70	2275	65	2500	29	28041	64
3rd Qtr.	24916	56	5816	76	3644	10	34377	42
4th Qtr.	24926	17	4361	88	3586	70	32874	75
TOTAL	93402	88	15112	56	14064	67	122580	11

TOTAL SUMMARY FOR YEAR		
Gross Takings for Year	122580	11
Plus Debtors at end of Year	475	27
Sub-total	123055	38
Less Debtors at start of Year	952	60
Gross Takings for Year	122102	78

Fig. 3.3 BUILDING UP THE 'TOTAL SALES' FIGURE (ABBREVIATED)

Notes to Figure 3.3

- Each week, the total takings figure for cash, cheques, credit card vouchers and EFTPOS is taken to the 'weekly summary of daily gross takings'. Some traders prefer to carry the detailed figures for cash, cheques, credit cards and EFTPOS and space is provided for this. Others simply carry the total only.
- Every quarter the figures are totalled and carried to the 'final summary' as shown.
- Depending on the way they are treated, it may be necessary to do an adjustment for debtors at the start and the end of the year. This is explained more fully later on. As can be seen in the 'total summary' for the year, the debtors who owed money on the last day of the year are added in, but the debtors who owed money on the first day of the year (because, although they paid us in the current year, the takings had already been counted in last year's figures) and to include them again would be double-counting.
- This gives the total sales for the year – in other words, the turnover of the business.
- Note that in the Simplex system, a trader who is registered for VAT records the figures gross of VAT (that is, including the VAT collected from customers). The VAT will be removed, for VAT-registered traders, when the final accounts are done, but this need not bother us at this stage.

submitted is recorded on a paying-in slip for your bank as if it were a single cheque, and this amount will be credited to your bank current account.

As far as the Simplex D Account Book is concerned, each weekly page has a section headed 'Paid to Bank' on which the sums paid in can be recorded. In Fig. 3.5 we see a typical entry by a trader who pays in on Wednesday and Friday only.

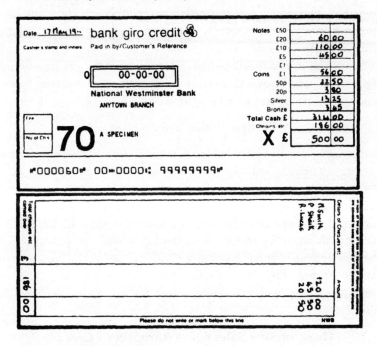

Fig. 3.1 A PAYING-IN SLIP
(courtesy of National Westminster Bank PLC)

Day/Date	Paid to Bank							
	Cash Col 5		Cheques Col 6		Credit Cards & EFTPOS Col 7		Total Col 8	
Sun 14 MAY								
Mon 15 "								
Tues 16 "								
Wed 17 "	314	00	186	50	217	50	718	00
Thur 18 "								
Fri 19 "	726	00	332	80	195	26	1254	06
Sat 20 "								
Totals	1040	00	519	30	412	76	1972	06

Fig. 3.5 THE 'PAID TO BANK' SECTION

USE OF THE 'SUMMARY OF TAKINGS' FIGURE IN DETERMINING PROFITS

The figures for takings collected together in the weekly summary of takings add up at the end of the year to a total takings figure, which is the 'sales' figure of the business. It is, in fact, swollen by having the VAT output tax included in it, but this need not concern us at the moment. The sales figure is a most important figure, and is often called the 'turnover' of the business. This term 'turnover' is discussed more fully in Chapter 18.

The chief use of this figure is in working out the profits of the business. Everyone knows that profit is the difference between cost price and selling price, and may be written down as:

Profit = Selling price – Cost price

In business, this can be extended to make a slightly different formula as we are not dealing with the profit on a single item, but with a vast number of goods or services supplied in the trading period under consideration. Profit is still very much concerned with cost prices and selling prices, but also many 'overhead expenses' have to be taken into account as well. For this reason I shall deal with the profits of a business in two parts. First 'gross profit', which means 'fat' profit or 'overall' profit, found by taking the cost price from the selling price. This is set out in the form of an account, called a 'trading account', but the formula is:

Gross profit = Sales figure (turnover) – Cost of sales

Second, 'net profit', which means 'clean' profit, which is worked out by taking away the overhead expenses from the gross profit. The formula is:

Net profit = Gross profit – Overheads

You will find out how to do this later in the book, but here all that one needs to say is that the records you have kept so far (see Figure 3.3) have found one of these vital figures for you. The sales of your business are the total takings, which come to £122,102.78. This figure will be used in the trading account when the gross profit is found at the end of the year (see Chapter 4).

KEEPING A RECORD OF DEBTORS

Debtors present many problems. For many small businesses, there is no need to become involved with debtors, and so you will see notices saying 'Please do not ask for credit as a refusal may offend'. These days if people cannot pay cash for something, or pay by cheque backed by a banker's cheque card (for items costing £50 or less), they can usually use a credit or debit card instead. In this way the retailer, provided they have kept within the operating rules laid down by the card company concerned, has no fear of a bad debt. The organisation that knows how to arrange credit, is a registered credit broker and has vetted the customer for creditworthiness, has all the problems; you as the retailer have none. The first rule, then, about debtors is:

'Don't offer credit unless you have to.'

Where you do supply goods or services without immediate payment the following problems arise:

- you must record the debt in some simple way;
- you have to exercise credit control, not only over that transaction but over all future transactions;
- you must make up your mind how to do the book-keeping entries because, of course, although you have sold the goods, no 'takings' have been received.

A word or two about each of these problems is necessary.

■ Recording the debt

With a full double entry system, every debtor is allocated a separate account, with the sum owing appearing on the debit side of the account. The debit side is the left-hand side, and such an account looks like this:

T. Smith, 1275 Camside, Cambridge CB4 1PQ

199X	£	
23 May Goods	118.54	

Simple systems of book-keeping do not have such accounts and, instead, work on the 'butcher's book method'. Victorian butchers, to help customers in temporary difficulties, used to keep a book near the till in which they recorded any unpaid bills. When the customer paid up, the date of payment was recorded in the customer's presence, and the debt struck through with a ruled line. A simple example is shown in Figure 3.6.

19..		Date paid	£	P
May 17	Mrs. J. Brown, 21 River Walk		3	27
~~17~~	~~Mr. T. Appleyard, 4 Deansbury~~	21 May	~~7~~	~~32~~
19	R. Grimes, 19 Caffice Way		7	48
21	T. Lark, 27 Totterdown Passage		24	25
24	K. Ahura, 19 High St.		19	36
		£	61	68

Fig. 3.6 A SIMPLE RECORD OF DEBTORS

■ Exercising credit control

For straightforward debtors kept under personal control by the proprietor of a business, there is little difficulty. You simply decide on a policy and stick to it, except on rare occasions when you exercise discretion within a policy. Thus, the policy for some debtors might be 'no further credit until an outstanding earlier item has been settled'. With another customer, it might be for all the previous month's transactions to be settled by the seventh of the following month. On special pleading – for example, where there is a postal strike and allowances are held up – you might use your discretion and still supply goods even though the seventh has passed.

Some small businesses (and medium-sized businesses too) are held to ransom by larger firms that won't place orders unless they can have three months' credit. This is a big problem and is dealt with in detail later, in Chapter 17. An excellent booklet available from your local Enterprise Agency is called *Prompt Payment Please*. Telephone your local branch on Freefone Enterprise to obtain a copy. Included in it are stickers that the small firm can place on its invoices. They are brightly coloured and read 'Prompt payment please – help small businesses'.

■ The book-keeping entries

Apart from recording your customer's debt in the 'butcher's book' you have purchased for that purpose, how will you deal with the problem of the book-keeping records?

There are two ways to treat these sales, which we will call the 'Sale of Goods Act' method and the 'sales deferred' method. In strict law, the former is the correct method, but it is less convenient than the 'sales deferred' method, which is therefore often used.

■ The 'Sale of Goods Act' method

The Sale of Goods Act says that when a contract for the sale of goods is made, the property in the goods passes at the time the parties intend it to pass, irrespective of when payment is made. Thus, if a customer takes goods from you and promises to pay later, the sale of the goods has taken place and they are now the customer's goods, and as far as you are concerned they are sales (and should be included in your daily takings even though you haven't received the money for them, but only a debtor's promise to pay). Therefore, strictly speaking, you should add these sales in with your daily takings at the end of the day.

It then becomes a problem what to do with the money when the customer comes in and pays; you can't put it into the till because that would swell the daily takings for the day, when in fact this sale has already been included in daily takings much earlier. The money must be kept separate. As a result the 'Sale of Goods Act' method, while legally correct, is a little awkward in everyday practice.

■ The 'sales deferred' method

With the 'sales deferred' method, you record the debt in the 'butcher's book' but don't regard the sale as having been made until you actually receive the money. When the customer comes in and pays the debt, you cross out the debt in the book and put the money in the till, where it becomes takings on the payment date, not takings on the earlier date when the sale was actually made. In strict legal terms, you regard the stock sold as not sold at all, but only out on location with the customer, until the day of payment arrives. Of course, that is really a silly idea because the customer's family may have eaten the stock, say, so you can hardly pretend that it is still available and could be reclaimed. There does come a time though when you do have to recognise that these debts do represent actual sales, and that is on the last day of the year. At this date, when we do the final summary of daily takings, you record the outstanding debts in the butcher's book as sales, on the summary. You can see this figure for trade debtors, £475.27, if you look back to Figure 3.3 for a moment.

SECURITY AND DAILY TAKINGS

Takings are always vulnerable – from burglaries, highway robberies, embezzlement and petty theft. Some of the more obvious security measures are to:

- use proper tills with in-built security devices so that cash is properly handled, till receipts are given and sharp practices are avoided;
- collect high-value notes from tills at regular (or irregular) intervals;
- insist that staff call witnesses when giving change for large notes, or when giving change to young children;
- pay in regularly – if necessary, more than once a day – and avoid taking the same route to the bank each time;
- watch out for shoplifting, credit-card frauds and passing-out (staff giving excess change to friends and accomplices);
- remove overnight money and till floats and either use the night-safe service at your local bank or a secure safe at home to protect it;
- never discuss the level of your takings with anyone, especially in places like public houses;
- leave tills empty and open at night;
- do see your local crime prevention officer if you feel uncertain about the adequacy of your security measures.

EXERCISE ON RECORDING RECEIPTS

In Figure 3.7, there is a blank 'receipts' section of a Simplex page. You may photocopy a few copies of it and use them to do the exercise that follows, to give you practice in recording receipts.

Peter Morgan uses the Simplex D account book. It is Week 21 and the week commences on Sunday 22 May. Sales each day are as follows:

- Monday £197.20 cash; cheques £148.56; credit cards £84.72; EFTPOS £136.40; lottery £56
- Tuesday £285.50 cash; cheques £132.78; credit cards £90.60; EFTPOS £138.49; lottery £38
- Wednesday £248.90 cash; cheques £29.50; credit cards £127.35; EFTPOS £197.20; lottery £126
- Thursday £886.50 cash; cheques £584.44; credit cards £195.62; EFTPOS £163.45; lottery £84
- Friday £879.25 cash; cheques £628.74; credit cards £421.70; EFTPOS £97.65; lottery £258
- Saturday £662 cash; cheques £316.40; credit cards £238.65; EFTPOS £378.64; lottery £295

Week No .... Commencing ....

Receipts

Day/Date	Daily Gross Takings		Other Receipts Col 3	Particulars of Other Receipts	Lottery etc. Takings Col 4
	Cash Col 1	Cheques, Credit Cards and EFTPOS Col 2			
Sun					
Mon					
Tues					
Wed					
Thur					
Fri					
Sat					
Sub totals				Total	Totals

Gross Weekly Takings (Cols 1+2)

EFTPOS = Electronic Funds Transfer at the Point of Sale

Fig. 3.7 A BLANK SIMPLEX 'RECEIPTS' SECTION OF THE WEEKLY PAGE
(courtesy of George Vyner Ltd)

You may photocopy this page for training purposes only, and do the exercises on these copies. Do not do any entries on this blank page or you will spoil it for copying purposes.

On Wednesday, Peter is notified that he has won £928.50 on the football pools and decides to put £600 in as extra capital. Make all these entries and total the various columns.

Answer

Peter Morgan: cash takings £3159.35; column 2 takings £4110.89; other receipts total £600.00; lottery takings £857.00.

CHECKLIST

- 'Takings' is another word for 'sales'. The takings of a business are the sole source of funds to run the business, apart from the original capital provided by the proprietor. From the sales money, you must be able to afford to purchase all the goods and materials you need, and to pay all the overheads.

- Takings should be recorded every day, and surplus funds not required in the business should be banked as soon as possible. This includes cash, cheques, credit card vouchers and EFTPOS taking. EFTPOS takings are 'electronic funds transferred at the point of sale' by debit cards and credit cards of various sorts. A daily total is made available by the issuers of each card.

- Ensure that you take adequate security measures with takings. Think through all the possibilities and if necessary seek advice from your local crime prevention officer.

- The daily takings form the basis of your VAT figures if you are using one of the VAT retail schemes. Remember, in VAT, the word 'retailer' means anyone who provides taxable supplies of goods or services without issuing an invoice to the customer.

- The daily takings figures accumulate into weekly, quarterly and annual totals for sales. It is the annual total which is used to work out the profit at the end of the financial year.

Recording purchases (payments for business stock)

THE MEANING OF 'PURCHASES' IN BUSINESS

In business, the word 'purchases' has a special meaning; items purchased for resale or items purchased to be embodied in a product or in a finished piece of work. The test as to whether an item is a 'purchase' or not is whether an invoice will eventually be raised to charge a customer for the goods supplied or the work done. Equally, if a future supply will be made only against a cash payment by a customer, the goods purchased for resale or the goods embodied in the work done are 'purchases'.

It follows that many things you may buy are not 'purchases'. For example, if you buy tools, machinery, motor vehicles, furniture and other assets of the business, these are not 'purchases' because they are bought for use in the business, not for resale. Similarly, if you buy stationery, advertising brochures, pencils and ballpoint pens for use in the office these are not 'purchases'.

By contrast, for a grocery business, cheese, bacon, butter, sugar, coffee and similar products are 'purchases' that are bought to sell again. To a landscape gardener, paving stones, gravel, trees and shrubs and so on are 'purchases', for when embodied in the landscaped grounds that are the subject of their contract, they will become the customer's property, embodied in the price for the job.

To take another example, suppose a garage buys 12 cars, 2 of which are to be used by the managing director and the sales director, while the other 10 are for resale. Clearly the first two are assets of the business, and the last ten are 'purchases' for resale. You may like to refer back to an earlier section in which the distinction was made between capital expenditure (expenditure on assets) and revenue expenditure (expenditure on items that will be part of your revenue accounts in the current financial year and used in the calculation of your profits). The first two cars are capital expenditure; the other ten cars are revenue expenditure – in this case, 'purchases of the business'.

PURCHASES OF BUSINESS STOCK

Whether goods are purchased for resale (without any alteration) or to be embodied in a finished product as a result of some manufacturing or craft process, they are purchases and form part of the stocks of the business. They can be paid for in three ways:

- in cash, on delivery;
- by cheque, on delivery;

- at a later date – in other words, you are given a credit period (time in which to pay).

Where credit is given, in many organizations the period is not very long – for example, perishables like meat are usually required to be paid for within three days. Other companies may give you 7, 15 or 30 days to pay, from the invoice date. If you are dealt with by your suppliers on 'open account' terms, it usually means that you will be sent a 'statement' once a month showing all the purchases made

Most firms use a system of 'cyclical billing', in which 4 per cent of their accounts are sent out every day.

in the month (and any returns for which credit notes have been given). You are then required to pay the balance on the statement within a given period, usually 30 days. To avoid having to send out thousands of accounts at the end of the month, most firms use a system of 'cyclical billing', in which 4 per cent of their accounts are sent out every day. This means that you may get an account on the 16th of every month, which will be payable within 30 days of that date.

In the Simplex system, which has been followed closely in these first few chapters, you record these payments in the following ways:

- **cash payments** are recorded in the 'cash' column, as shown in Figure 4.1, on the day they are made;
- **payments by cheque** are recorded similarly, but in the 'by cheque' column;
- **credit deliveries** are not entered until they are actually paid for, when the entries are made on that date (clearly it is important to keep the invoice safely until the due date).

A useful tip here is to have an expanding file labelled 1–31. You can buy one from stationers Neat Ideas by telephone on 01302 890999. It will be labelled A–Z, but you can change these to numbers. When an invoice or a monthly statement arrives, you work out the date it must be paid by and put it in the file accordingly. If the company offers a discount if it is paid within a certain time, put it in at the date that will earn you the discount. On that date, write the cheque, enter it into your records and post it off.

Now look at Figure 4.1 to see how the 'purchases' entries are made, and Figure 4.2 to see an expanding file for storing invoices until the date of payment.

Payments for Business Stock					
Date or Chq No	To whom paid	Amount paid			
		Cash Col 9		Cheque Col 10	
1 FEB	BANBURY & CO.	37	56		
3 FEB	F. GILES.	3	50		
4 FEB	R. HAY SEED.	27	55		
326541	NEAT IDEAS.			8	73
326543	R.T. MORGAN.			214	27
6 FEB	BANBURY & CO.	49	84		
Totals		118	45	223	00
				118	45
Total payments (to Summary)				341	45

Fig. 4.1 RECORDING PURCHASES (PAYMENTS FOR BUSINESS STOCK)

Notes

- The date is the date of payment or, if paid by cheque, the cheque number may be inserted instead (it helps with bank reconciliations later).
- Cash payments and cheque payments are differentiated in columns 9 and 10.
- The total of payments for the week will be carried to the 'summary of payments for business stock' section at the back of the Simplex book.

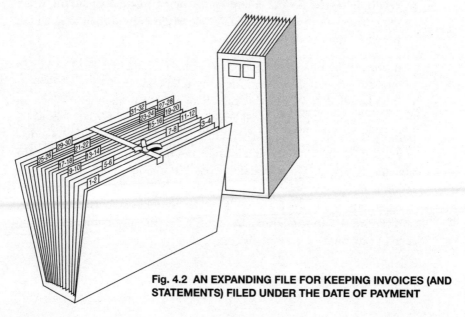

Fig. 4.2 AN EXPANDING FILE FOR KEEPING INVOICES (AND STATEMENTS) FILED UNDER THE DATE OF PAYMENT

INVOICES, DELIVERY NOTES AND ADVICE NOTES

An invoice from a supplier for goods for resale is usually spoken of as a purchase invoice. It will usually be part of a multicopy set, as shown in Figure 1.4, though many invoice sets consist of more than the three copies shown in that illustration. The copies you are likely to see are the following.

■ The delivery note

The delivery note will usually be presented by the delivery driver, who will ask you to sign it. What the driver wants is a 'clean' signature, preferably just your signature, but they may ask you to print your name in one box and sign in the next. From the appearance of the package, you may be prepared to do this, but if it is unsatisfactory at all, such as showing signs of damage, or if it is a mixture of goods, some of which may have been pilfered, do not give a 'clean' signature. For example, you could write 'Signed, contents unchecked' or something like that. In these circumstances, the driver may have been told to request an immediate check, and to wait while this is done. Even when the package seems quite sound, some cautious people sign 'Received in apparent good order and condition', which is just a little less than a 'clean' signature.

The delivery note is retained by the driver and you will not see it again.

■ The advice note

The advice note will usually either be enclosed with the goods in their crate or parcel, or tied on or otherwise affixed to the goods in a special envelope. The idea is that you should check the contents against the advice note, and report any discrepancy (usually there is a time limit of three days to give notice of any partial loss or shortage). The advice note can then either be discarded or clipped to the top copy of the invoice, which is usually sent by post, though it may be delivered by the driver of a delivery vehicle.

■ The top copy of the invoice

This copy may be labelled 'customer's copy' and is the purchase invoice for your purposes. It will often go into the VAT records in the first place and then be used to record payment for the purchases, on the day of payment, as recorded in Figure 4.1. If you are being supplied as a trusted customer on 'open account' terms, you will not pay on the invoice but on the monthly statement, as explained above. Keep your top copy of the invoice, with the advice copy clipped to it if you received one, as part of your VAT records. If this means you cannot keep it in a concertina file until payment, put a piece of scrap paper giving the details in your concertina file so that you do not fail to pay it on the due date.

A SUMMARY OF PURCHASES

At the end of the week, the total of the payments for business stock is carried to the 'summary of payments for business stock' at the back of the Simplex D account book, and these figures total into quarterly totals and then an annual total in the special box provided.

Once again, as it is possible that you will have a few invoices from suppliers that you have not yet paid, it may be necessary to do what is called an 'adjustment' to the figures. You add on to the four quarterly totals any invoices as yet unpaid, because they are really purchases of the year that is just ending. However, at the beginning of the year there may have been outstanding invoices from the previous year, which were paid after the end of that year and are consequently included in your first quarter figures. If you now deduct these, you arrive at your correct payments for business stock in the current year. This total of purchases comes, in Figure 4.3, to £30,594.36. Notice that this is a great deal less than the figure for total sales for the year (see Figure 3.3), so it is clear that you are leading up to a profitable result at the end of the financial year.

Weekly Summary of Payments for Business Stock

Week No.	Amount		Week No.	Amount		Week No.	Amount		Week No.	Amount		Summary and Reconciliation for Year		
1	223	43	14	325	72	27	525	36	40	538	11			
2	416	56	15	426	36	28	472	25	41	861	49			
3	219	72	16	375	49	29	684	46	42	772	90			
4	375	61	17	209	56	30	396	72	43	249	82			
5	296	17	18	623	72	31	838	38	44	951	63			
6	341	45	19	443	21	32	925	29	45	973	71			
7	423	14	20	329	49	33	701	71	46	884	43	Summary and Reconciliation for Year		
8	815	29	21	217	36	34	1272	49	47	717	29	1st Qtr.	5229	04
9	316	31	22	361	72	35	1138	72	48	1108	34	2nd Qtr.	4922	44
10	275	42	23	552	63	36	1047	68	49	1342	71	3rd Qtr.	10062	12
11	385	58	24	449	48	37	929	86	50	1051	60	4th Qtr.	10335	62
12	426	66	25	336	59	38	456	71	51	377	32	Purchases Creditors at end of Year	237	25
13	714	70	26	271	11	39	672	49	52	511	27	SUB-TOTAL	30786	47
									53			Less Purchases Creditors at start of Year	192	11
Total 1st Qtr.	5229	04	Total 2nd Qtr.	4922	44	Total 3rd Qtr.	10062	12	Total 4th Qtr.	10335	62	TOTAL	30594	36

Fig. 4.3 THE SUMMARY OF PAYMENTS FOR BUSINESS STOCK (PURCHASES)

USE OF PURCHASES IN FINDING THE PROFITS OF THE BUSINESS

In Chapter 2 use of the sales figure in determining the profits of the business was referred to in the general formula:

Gross Profit = Sales figure (turnover) – Purchases figure

Now that you have seen how the total purchases figure for the year is found we can see how to work out the gross profit because you have both the figures required for the formula given above – the sales figure and the purchases figure. According to the formula, the gross profit would be found, using the figures in Figures 3.3 and 4.3, as follows:

Gross profit = Sales – Purchases
= £122 102.78 – £30 594.36
= £91 508.42

However, this isn't really the correct answer for the gross profit of the business because the formula used is just a little too simple. The reason is that it does not take account of unsold stock. You will very rarely manage to sell out all the stock by the last day of the year and that unsold stock is included in the 'purchases' made in the year. As it hasn't been sold, you really need to deduct it from the 'purchases' figure for the year. Of course, you may also have had some opening stock, at the start of the year, that will almost certainly have been sold during the year and, thus, needs to be added in with your 'purchases' figure. Let us, therefore look at 'stock' closely for a moment.

■ Stock and stocktaking

What is stock? Well, obviously it is the result of purchasing goods for resale – what the Simplex system calls 'payments for business stock'. However, although everything you buy goes into stock (and if you had a burglary you would certainly be asked by the police to make a list of all the stock stolen), you don't usually talk about 'stock' in that general sense. The word 'stock' usually refers to the 'closing stock' figure, which is the amount of stock left on the shelves at the last moment of the last day of the financial year. This 'closing stock' is carried over to next year and, of course, becomes the 'opening stock' of the new year, at exactly the same figure. To value the closing stock, you have to carry out a stocktake, and as this is rather a lot of hard work and takes a few hours you may have a 'stocktaking sale' just before the end of the financial year to get rid of as much stock as possible. Having done that, you must then count the stock still on the shelves, and value it. There is a special rule for stock valuation, laid down by the professional bodies of accountants. The rule is that *Stock is valued at cost price, or net realisable value, whichever is the lower.*

> Stock is valued at cost price, or net realisable value, whichever is lower.

This is a very important rule. Most of your stock will be valued at cost price. Suppose a menswear shop has a suit priced at £50 to the customers, but it cost the shop £23.50 from the wholesaler. It will be valued at the cost price of £23.50 when you do the stocktaking. However, suppose that the suit has been used as a display model and is rather shop-soiled because customers have been feeling the quality of the material. You might decide you'll be lucky to sell it for £30, and to do that you'll have to send it to another branch in an area where people are looking for bargains. It will cost £3 to send it to the other branch, so the 'net realizable value' is only £27. However, this is still more than the cost price, so the stocktaking value is still £23.50. 'Cost price or net realizable value, whichever is the lower.' Suppose the damage is such that, honestly, you could get rid of the suit only by offering it at £15 at the other branch. The result would be that the 'net realizable value' is only £12, because of the £3 expenses involved. On the stocktaking lists, this suit would be valued at only £12, because the net realizable value is less than the cost price.

The rule is an example of another rule in accountancy – the 'prudence' rule. The prudence rule says that *any business person behaves prudently, never take a profit until you've actually made the profit and always take a loss as soon as it is clear you have suffered a loss*. In the case just mentioned, you don't value stock at the selling price of £50 or even the reduced selling price of £27, because if you did that we would be pretending to yourself that you'd made a profit, when you hadn't actually sold the article. On the other hand, if the net realizable value is less than the cost price, you value the item at this lower figure because you've made a loss on this garment (the most you can hope to recover is £12, so you've lost £11.50 on the garment). Always take a loss the moment you realise you've suffered one.

So, to carry out the stocktake:

- count the items on the shelves;
- appraise the items to decide the cost price and the net realizable value (what you can hope to sell it for);
- value it at cost price or net realizable value, whichever is the lower;
- if necessary, multiply the value decided on by the number of items (so, 26 tins of baked beans at a cost price of 24p = £6.24);
- add up all the figures for all the items to reach a grand total for the 'closing stock' figure. Let me pretend this figure comes to £3894.68.

With this closing stock figure, you are ready to calculate the gross profit of the business.

CALCULATING THE GROSS PROFIT IN A TRADING ACCOUNT

The profits of a business are worked out in two stages – the gross profit and then the net profit. The first is worked out in a trading account, which, as its name implies, tells us the profit that has been made on trading, but before deducting the overhead expenses to find the net profit (or clean profit). As you will see in Figure 4.4, the process is very simple. On the 'sales' side, you simply have the total figure for sales for the year. In the Simplex book, there is a line for 'value of goods taken for own consumption', but we can ignore this for the present. On the 'purchases' side you have slightly more complicated figures. You need to know the cost of the sales. What did the things you sold for £122 102.78 actually cost you? The answer is that at the start of the year – at 'dawn on day 1', you had an opening stock of £168.30. You then purchased a great deal of stock to add to this opening stock, making £30 594.36 of stock that went on to your shelves during the year. At the end of the year, when you did the stocktake, you had unsold stock to the value of £3894.68. If you take the closing stock from the total stock available, you find you have sold stock to a total of £26,867.98. You sold this stock for £122,102.78, so you made an excellent gross profit of £95,234.80. Note that some firms like to show last year's figures for comparison purposes, and companies are required by law to do so. As this is a new business, you cannot show these figures anyway, but the Simplex book has a place for them to be shown in future years if you wish to do so. Study the layout of the trading account in Figure 4.4 carefully.

EXERCISE IN RECORDING PAYMENTS FOR BUSINESS STOCK

In Figure 4.5, you have an illustration of the Simplex 'payments for business stock' section. Photocopy it for your personal use and then do the following exercise to make sure you understand how purchases are recorded.

R. Mansfield records on his Simplex page under the heading 'payments for business stock' the following items during the week:

July 7   Paid Media Supplies Ltd by cheque £25.74 (cheque no. 725311) and R. Jones in cash £5.40

July 8   Paid Computer Software PLC by cheque £885.50 and Prepared Data Ltd £46.50 by cheque (cheque nos 725312 and 725313 respectively)

July 9   Paid R. Masters by cheque £27.25 (cheque no. 725316) and the Mason Paper Co. Ltd in cash £25.85

July 13   Paid R. Jones in cash £17.25

Enter these items and total the 'cash' and 'cheque' columns.

EXERCISE ON CALCULATING THE GROSS PROFIT

Using the same layout as is shown in Figure 4.4, draw up the trading account for the following business.

R. Mortenson for the year ended 31 December 199X:

- sales £135 856.20
- purchases £27 386.75
- stock at 1 January £3727.60
- stock at 31 December £9512.60

Answer to recording payments exercise
Books of R. Mansfield: cash payments £48.50; payments by cheque £984.99. Total for summary £1033.49.

Answer to gross profit exercise
Books of R. Mortenson: gross profit £114 254.45.

Trading Account for year ending 31 ST. DECEMBER 19...

Previous year		This year			Previous year		This year	
	Opening stock at 1 · 1 · 19...	168	30			Sales or Work completed	122.102	78
	Purchases of Business Stock during year	30594	36			Value of goods taken for own consumption	—	—
	Total	30762	66			Total turnover	122.102	78
	Less Closing Stock at	3894	68					
	Cost of Sales Total	26867	98					
	Gross Profit (Carried to Profit & Loss Account	95234	80					
	TOTAL	122.102	78			TOTAL	122.102	78

Fig. 4.4 FINDING THE GROSS PROFIT ON TRADING

Payments for Business Stock			
Date or Chq No	To whom paid	Amount paid	
		Cash Col 9	Cheque Col 10
	Totals		
	Total payments (to Summary)		

Fig. 4.5 A BLANK 'PAYMENTS FOR BUSINESS STOCK' SECTION

(Courtesy of George Vyner Ltd)

CHECKLIST

- 'Purchases' has a special meaning in business. Not everything we buy is 'purchases'. Purchases are things we buy to sell again (business stock) or things we buy to make up into a finished product, in some sort of manufacturing process, assembly work or service (such as landscape gardening).

- Purchases of consumables (stationery, postage stamps and so on) are not purchases, neither are purchases of assets for use in the business.

- When you purchase business stock, it may be for cash or a cheque (which is as good as cash) or you may purchase on credit, and promise to pay later. You pay your creditors when they send a statement, and the terms of payment will be written on it (for example 'cash, 30 days').

- The individual payments are collected together in summaries, or possibly in a purchases account, to give the monthly, quarterly and, eventually annual total.

- The total purchases figure is used in a trading account to work out the gross profit of the business, using the formula:

  Gross profit = Sales – Cost of sales

- Cost of sales is found by adjusting the 'purchases' figure for opening and closing stocks, using the formula:

  Cost of sales = (Opening stock + Purchases) – Closing stock

Recording payments other than for stock

PAYMENTS OTHER THAN FOR STOCK

You will recall that in Chapter 4, I said that one of the chief types of expenditure incurred in a business is expenditure on purchases – that is, expenditure on goods for resale or on raw materials, components and so on to be worked into a finished product for which a customer will eventually be invoiced. You now have to look at all the other types of expenditure incurred in a business. Payments other than for stock consist of several types:

- payments for consumable items, such as paper, stationery, cleaning materials and so on;
- payments for overhead expenses, such as rent and rates, light and heat, travelling expenses, repairs, renewals and so on;
- payments for staff pay, and National Insurance contributions (NIC) associated with employing staff;
- payments for capital items, such as the purchase of premises, motor vehicles, furniture and fittings, plant and machinery, computers and so on; even goodwill – a rather strange asset that we have to purchase when we buy some kinds of business – is a capital item. It consists of the good opinion of customers in the area around the business, and is called an intangible asset because there is nothing we can really touch when we buy goodwill;

> *'Consumables' are items that are used up in the course of business activity.*

- repayments of loans and mortgages;
- payments of 'drawings' to the proprietor or partners of the business.

All these types of payment need a few words of explanation.

WHAT ARE CONSUMABLES?

'Consumables' are items that are used up in the course of business activity and, while the business gets some benefit from them, it is a very temporary benefit. For example, if you buy postage stamps, stick them on letters and post the letters, you have 'consumed' the postage stamps in the course of business. Similarly, the letterhead you wrote on and the envelopes you used are consumable items. These types of expenses are revenue expenditure, a term explained earlier. They are deductible business expenses when working out the profits as they were incurred for business purposes to advance the activities of the business. These weekly expenses must be carried to some sort of summary and added up over the year, so that at the end of the year the total expenditure on postage, stationery and so on can be deducted from the takings to determine the profitability of the business. In the Simplex system, this summary is called the 'summary of payments for expenses'. Remember that the dividing line between revenue expenditure and capital expenditure is one year, and you can always decide whether or not an item is revenue expenditure by asking ourselves the question, 'Do I expect this item I have just purchased to still be benefiting the business one year from now?' For a postage stamp the answer would be 'No', but for a pair of scales to weigh the letters the answer would be 'Yes'.

WHAT ARE OVERHEAD EXPENSES?

Consumable items are often considered part of 'overheads', but for the moment I shall use this term to refer to the very large body of expenses concerned with keeping a roof over our heads and a place to work in, such as rent, rates, light and heat, telephone expenses, repairs and renewals and so on. These are similar to consumable expenses, and will be collected together in the summary of expenses before being deducted from the profits at the end of the year as legitimate business expenses.

HOW DO I TREAT WAGES, AND NATIONAL INSURANCE CONTRIBUTIONS?

Pay and any other expenses connected with the employment of staff are an expense of the business. The reason for mentioning them separately is to point out that certain legal obligations are imposed on employers that make them unpaid collectors of taxes for the government. For example, you must operate a PAYE (pay as you earn) system to deduct tax from the employees' pay, and send it monthly to the Inland Revenue. You must also deduct National Insurance contributions (NIC) from the employees' pay, as well as paying a large contribution as an employer, for every person you employ. Full details of these payments are given in Chapter 10. These various deductions result in a considerable amount of money being in your possession that does not belong to you, but to the government. As a result, the government imposes two further burdens on you. It requires you to pay sickness benefit (Statutory Sick Pay) to staff entitled to receive it because of absence from work and also maternity benefit (Statutory Maternity Pay) to female employees taking maternity leave. You pay this money out of the funds you have collected, so it is not your money, but it does save the government a great deal of work if these payments are made through people's pay. Of course, you then need to send in only the net amount (taxes collected minus disbursements) to the Inland Revenue each month. It used to be the case that the whole amount paid to employees for Statutory Sick Pay (SSP) and Statutory Maternity Pay (SMP) could be deducted from the money due to the Inland Revenue. In 1994, the government became more penny-pinching and the employer was forced to carry some of these costs.

As far as book-keeping is concerned, the important point about all these payments, whether they are in the pay slip or sent to the tax office, is that they are all part of the expense of employing staff and, therefore, a deductible revenue expense so far as you are concerned The total payments (pay, National Insurance contributions for both employer and employee and the tax deducted from the pay) are shown in a profit and loss account at the end of the year as a deduction from the gross profit – as part of the calculations to discover the net profit.

WHAT ARE CAPITAL ITEMS?

'Capital items' have already been described as items that last longer than a year and, therefore, permanently benefit the business by giving lasting service to it. Land and buildings are generally recognised as lasting for such a long time that they may be regarded as permanent assets. Plant and machinery may last 20 or 30 years, motor vehicles about 5 to 8 years, furniture about 15 years and so on. The important point about these is that they are capital, not revenue, expenditure and cannot be written off the profits at the end of the year. However, where they do decline in value by 'fair wear and tear', you are allowed to charge a certain amount of their value against the profits each year. This is called 'depreciation', and there are many ways of

> *'Capital items' permanently benefit the business by giving lasting service to it.*

working out the correct value. However, as a small business proprietor you need not worry about this, because whatever system you use, the Inland Revenue will disregard it, for the following reason. Suppose Mr Smith, a decorator, has had a good year and made £20 000 profit. He purchased a new car for £8000 this year and, to save tax, decides to depreciate it by 100 per cent – which will reduce the value of the car to nothing on his books, and reduce his profits to £12 000. Clearly this would not be correct, because the car is really worth about £6000 and only £2000 is depreciation. Mr Smith would therefore be cheating the Inland Revenue of some tax and giving a false picture on his balance sheet at the end of the year (it appearing that he had no car, whereas in fact he has an almost new one).

To get over this problem, Parliament has enacted the rate of depreciation you may take. The £8000 Mr Smith has deducted from his profits will be added back and the Inland Revenue inspector gives him what he is entitled to. The rate has for some years been 25 per cent, on the 'reducing balance method' (this is explained below). The figure does sometimes change in the Budget, depending on governmental policy, and in June 1997, the rate for the first year of a machine's life was raised to 50 per cent. This has the effect of encouraging traders to switch over to new assets. Ignoring this one-off change and staying with 25 per cent, think of Mr Smith's car.

	£
Value when new	8000
Depreciation 25%	2000
Balance left	£6000

This £6000 is recorded by the Inland Revenue in Mr Smith's 'pool'. This is a pool of assets carried over from one year to the next. So the next year the figures would be:

	£
Amount in pool	6000
Depreciation 25%	1500
Balance left	£4500

The next year, the figures would be as shown below, because what is deducted as depreciation is 25 per cent of the reducing balance. Thus:

	£
Amount in pool	4500
Depreciation 25%	1125
Balance left	£3375

Of course, it would not be just Mr Smith's car, but all his other assets (but not land and buildings) that are in the pool, and the depreciation (Parliament calls it a 'capital allowance') would be a composite figure. The limit of depreciation on a car is £2000, so if you buy a Rolls-Royce for £40 000 you will receive only £2000 depreciation. If you want a fancy car, by all means have one, but you can't expect the tax authorities to pay a large contribution towards it.

REPAYMENT OF LOANS AND MORTGAGES

When you borrow money, you have to repay it, usually in monthly instalments. These are often paid by standing order or direct debit, but these terms are explained later. When you pay an amount due on a loan, the payment must be recorded, and the amount paid must be deducted from the loan as you then do not owe as much as before. Of course, from time to time the bank or building society will notify you of interest added to the loan because your repayments are partly interest and partly repayments of the sum borrowed, but this need not worry us for the moment, it is explained later. You will see that recording repayments is a very simple matter.

WHAT ARE DRAWINGS?

The last type of payment you need to take note of is 'drawings'. The sole proprietor of a business is not allowed to receive any pay, neither is a partner of a partnership business. What they are entitled to is the profits of the business, but as these are computed only at the end of the financial year, the proprietor(s) are in difficulty. They have to meet their household expenses and pay for food and clothing like everyone else. Therefore, to get round the difficulty, they are allowed to take 'drawings'. The full term for drawings is 'drawings in expectation of profits made'. You hope that your activities are making a profit, and, on the assumption that you are, you draw out some of your money and use it for domestic purposes. How much you draw depends on your family needs, and whether or not you have funds. Suppose you draw £60 a week, but are, in fact, making £200 a week profit. You would lead a fairly frugal life, but your business would be building up useful bank balances and, at the end of the year, you would have plenty of money to pay your taxes. You could then draw out the rest of your profits if you wished, or leave them in the business to keep it in good heart.

By contrast, suppose you draw £300 per week when you were actually making only £200 profit (although you don't actually know this). It would not be long before you would notice that you were running short of cash, and found yourself asking the bank for an overdraft or a loan. The first question a prudent banker would ask is, 'How much are you taking out each week as drawings?' When you reveal the figure the bank manager would say, 'Well, look here, you're not making that amount of profit.' Even if you had plenty of funds at the start of your business, at the end of the first year, you would have the following figures:

	£	
Capital at start (say)		25 000
Add profits	10 400	
Less drawings	– 15 600	
		– 5 200
		£19 800

Because of excessive drawings, the funds you originally contributed have declined. You are said to be 'living on your capital', and if this continues for a few more years, you'll soon be in the bankruptcy court. As the Americans say, 'You're living too high on the hog' and must cut back your standard of living until it is more in line with the profits you are earning.

RECORDING ALL TYPES OF EXPENDITURE OTHER THAN FOR STOCK

Recording all these different types of payments varies with the system of book-keeping you are using. In these early chapters, you have been using the Simplex system and, as you can see in Figure 5.1, this system is really a simple cash book in which you can record payments either in cash or by cheque. The notes to Figure 5.1 explain useful points about the records. Study them now.

Payments other than for Stock				
Nature of payment	Amount paid			
	Cash Col 11		Cheque Col 12	
Employee Costs (i) Wages	68	00		
(ii) Inland Revenue PAYE & NI				
Premises Costs (i) Rent and Rates			236	50
(ii) Light, Heat and Insurance				
89p. £1·35 (iii) Cleaning £29·76	32	00		
Repairs				
Gen.Admin. (i) Telephone				
£1·16. £1·90 (ii) Postage £3·72. 54p.	7	32		
(iii) Stationery, etc.				
Motor Expenses (i) Fuel			9	12
(ii) Servicing and Repairs, etc.				
Travel and Subsistence				
Advertising and Entertainment				
Legal and Professional				
Interest Payable				
Other Financial Charges				
Other Expenses				
Lottery prizes paid				
Scratch card prizes paid				
LOAN REPAYMENT.			50	00
Customs & Excise (VAT)				
Drawings of Proprietor/Partner 1	60	00		
Drawings of Partner 2				
Drawings of Partner 3				
Capital Items (i) COMPUTER.			246	50
(ii) POST SCALES.	8	75		
Totals	176	07	542	12

Fig. 5.1 RECORDING PAYMENTS OTHER THAN FOR STOCK

Notes to Figure 5.1

- As when making purchases of stock (see Chapter 4), you record the payments only when you actually make them. For example, you have certainly used the telephone this week, but as you pay the telephone bill once a quarter, there is no entry for payment this particular week on the 'telephone' line. You did pay the rates this week, by cheque, and £236.50 appears in the 'by cheque' column.

- With some items – postage for instance – you may need to use the spare space to record several items as the week proceeds, putting the total in the column only at the end of the week. It is helpful to remind yourself what some money was spent on – for example, the 'capital items' lines remind you that you purchased a computer and a weighing machine for postal items. Where there are more than two capital items purchased in a week, you put the extra item on one of the spare lines provided.
- Notice that as you employ someone, you must have deducted tax and National Insurance contributions, but there is no entry on the 'Inland Revenue' line. This money is paid over monthly, and you don't happen to have paid it this week. The records would be kept in a simple wages book (see Chapter 10).
- The proprietor has drawn £60 in cash this week. This money must have been taken from the till or the cash box, but it makes no difference whether cash is taken in this way or a cheque is drawn to take money from the bank (except that the £60 would be entered in the 'by cheque' column).
- Note that the 'loan repayment' has been entered in the bottom part of the spare lines, rather than on the next line below 'sundries'. This is because the top group of entries are all revenue expenses, which can be carried to summaries and eventually appear in the profit and loss account as losses for the year. The items at the bottom are all to do with rather more unusual things, which go into special summaries and are dealt with rather differently from revenue expenses.

CARRYING THE WEEKLY FIGURES TO SUMMARIES TO COLLECT THE ANNUAL FIGURES

The payments incurred every week have to be carried to summaries where the annual totals can be collected together and, of course, every type of payment must have its appropriate summary. This requires the reader to look carefully at the illustrations in Figures 5.2, 5.3, 5.4 and 5.5 and read the related notes so that the system is followed fully.

Summary of Payments for Expenses

Week No.	Wages	IR PAYE & NI	Rent & Rates	LL, H, & Ins	Cleaning	Repairs	Telephone	Postage	Stationery	Motor Fuel	Motor Servicing etc.	Travel & Subsistence	Advertising & Entertainment
1	68 00		520 00		32 00			12 36		16 94			
2	68 00				32 00			4 56		9 12			
3	68 00		236 50		32 00			7 32		13 16			
4	68 00				34 50			6 15		16 12			
5	68 00			136 25	32 00	36 25		5 24				13 24	
6	68 00	137 00		42 60	32 00		324 00	2 34		14 10			
7	68 00				32 00			13 75		15 12			
8	66 00				32 00			12 94		11 27	–		300 15
9	150 00	145 00			42 50			104 25	36 38	36 19			
10	150 00				32 00			7 13		14 12			
11	150 00				32 00			8 01		15 08			
12	150 00				32 00			4 94		12 59			
13	150 00	130 00			36 00			200 28	36 38	13 25			
1st Qtr	1311 00	412 00	756 55	178 95	437 00	36 25	324 00			174 72	–	13 24	300 15
14	150 00				32 00			11 34		17 46			
15	150 00		520 00		32 00			5 17		12 37			
16	150 00				32 00			3 20		11 96			23 68
17	150 00				34 50			8 51		8 51			
18	150 00	60 00			32 00			10 05		12 59			
19	150 00				32 00			4 95		13 25			

Summary of Payments for Expenses (continued)

Week No.	Wages	IR PAYE & NI	Rent & Rates	LL, H, & Ins	Cleaning	Repairs	Telephone	Postage	Stationery	Motor Fuel	Motor Servicing etc.	Travel & Subsistence	Advertising & Entertainment
35	85 55				35 00			8 40		12 90			
36	85 55				35 00			6 95		16 75			
37	85 55				35 00			4 32		10 50			
38	85 55				36 00			8 51		15 76			
39					35 00			12 54		21 83			
3rd Qtr	1606 85	416 00	754 00	165 20	477 56		375 00	338 00		250 57	–	31 17	
40	173 40				35 00			4 42		23 74			
41	173 40				35 00			14 86		12 44			
42	173 40	85 60	520 00		35 00			7 71		14 62			
43	173 40				35 00			19 39	18	25 57			
44	173 40				48 50		28 94	7 71		26 38		86 71	
45	173 40	77 30		108 78	35 00			13 58		10 26			
46	173 40			62 80	39 50		416 00	12 88		12 43			
47	173 40				35 00			2 29		27 51			
48	173 40				36 00			3 84		15 17			163 60
49	173 40				36 00			8 14		19 36			
50	168 00				43 25			104 12		18 20	131 26		
51	168 00	81 60			35 00			14 61		11			
52	168 00				35 00			17 16					
53													
4th Qtr	2238 50	244 50	520 00	171 59	481 25	28 94	416 00	230 60	18 15	217 17	131 26	86 71	163 60
Annual Total	7222 35	1829 32	2553 00	539 04	1877 75	192 51	1538 00	930 66	101 75	795 83	299 90	177 08	522 50

Fig. 5.2. SUMMARY OF PAYMENTS FOR EXPENSES

Notes to Figure 5.2 above

This is arranged in four quarters of 13 weeks, and totals to annual figures on each category of expense. The entries in Figure 5.1 are actually line 3 of the summary, but the figures for a whole year have been entered to show how the total expenses for the year are arrived at. These become important, as explained later in this chapter, when you come to work out the profits of the business.

The headings on this summary are those permitted by the Inland Revenue for declaration of expenses in the tax return under the self-assessment system.

Notes to Figure 5.2 continued

Notice that all the items in the top section of Figure 5.1 appear in the 'summary of payments for expenses' secction, but the items in the bottom part of Figure 5.1 do not. They are either capital items, drawings or the repayment of a loan, and are entered in other summaries.

Summary of Loan/Mortgage Repayments

Loan from: HELPFUL BANK PLC.

Mortgage from: MANOR BUILDING SOCIETY.

DATE		MORTGAGE		LOAN	
1 JAN.	BALANCE B/FWD (IF ANY)	49950	00	–	–
	TOTAL AMOUNT BORROWED			2000	00
	INTEREST CHARGED	4095	50	250	00
	INSURANCE PREMIUM CHARGED	1240	00	95	60
	BANK ARRANGEMENT CHARGES			25	00
	TOTAL FOR YEAR				
	LESS REPAYMENTS (SEE BELOW)				
	BALANCE C/FWD TO NEW YEAR				

DATE	REPAYMENTS	MORTGAGE		LOAN	
31 JAN	DIRECT DEBITS	825	60	197	55
	ETC... ETC... ETC...				
	TOTAL REPAYMENTS IN YEAR				

Fig. 5.3 SUMMARY OF LOANS AND REPAYMENTS

Notes to Figure 5.3

1. Enter the amount of the mortgage or loan in the top section.
2. Enter any interest charge at the start of the contract or notified to you during the course of the year. This may be a deductible business expense and should be carried to the summary of payments for expenses section in the 'Interest payable' column.
3. You may also be charged an insurance premium. If so, enter the amount in the top section. This may also be a deductible business expense and should be treated in the same way as interest charges.
4. If the bank has charged you for making the arrangements and these charges have been added to the loan, record them on the line provided. These too will be a deductible business expense and should be carried to the 'expenses summary' as in (2) above.
5. Enter any initial payments and all repayments, as they are made, in the lower section.
6. The balance outstanding at any given time is the difference between the top figure and the total repayments in the lower section.

Capital Expenditure Incurred During the Year

Date	Nature and Full Details of Expense	Invoice Value		Net Value of Asset		VAT	
1 JAN.	SECOND HAND VAN (H997 XYT).	460	00	391	49	68	51
18 JAN.	LETTER SCALES.	8	75	7	45	I	30
18 JAN.	COMPUTER.	246	50	209	79	36	71
	TOTALS						

Fig. 5.4 SUMMARY OF CAPITAL EXPENSES

Notes to Figure 5.4

Here you record any capital items purchased in the course of any week. Note that the two items in Figure 5.1 have been recorded, and show the element of VAT in their purchase prices (which will, in fact, be reclaimed as VAT input tax). The figures at the end of the year would be totalled and the value of the assets purchased would be added to the assets shown in the balance sheet. As these are capital expenses, they cannot, of course, be treated as expenses deductible in the profit and loss account at the end of the year.

PAYMENTS BY DIRECT DEBIT AND STANDING ORDER AND BANK CHARGES

Besides payments in cash and by cheque, you do pay sums of money for all sorts of purposes by standing order and direct debit. These types of payment are dealt with more fully later when bank reconciliation statements are discussed in Chapter 8. For the present though, let us just say that if we authorise the bank to make a series of regular payments for us (for example, mortgage payments or hire purchase instalments), it is called a 'standing order'. However, in some cases we may agree that instead of paying our creditor, the creditor may demand payment instead. This is helpful where the sum to be demanded is variable (as, for example, with rates or electricity bills, which differ each year). Many breweries deliver variable quantities of goods to tied houses and, after delivery, ask the publican's bank for the amount required. This type of arrangement is called a 'direct debit' because the customer's account is debited with the sum payable. As we don't always know what amount the

Summary of Drawings of the Proprietor or Partners

Week No.	Proprietor or Partner 1		Partner 2		Partner 3		Week No.	Proprietor or Partner 1		Partner 2		Partner 3	
1	150	00					27	150	00				
2	150	00					28	150	00	750	00		
3	150	00					29	150	00				
4	150	00	750	00			30	150	00				
5	150	00					31	150	00				
6	150	00					32	160	00	750	00		
7	150	00					33	150	00				
8	150	00	750	00			34	150	00				
9	150	00					35	150	00				
10	150	00					36	150	00	750	00		
11	150	00					37	150	00				
12	160	00	750	00			38	150	00				
13	150	00					39	150	00				
1st Qtr.	1950	00	2250	00			3rd Qtr.	1950	00	2250	00		
14	150	00					40	150	00	750	00		
15	150	00					41	150	00				
16	150	00	750	00			42	150	00				
17	150	00					43	150	00				
18	150	00					44	150	00	750	00		
19	150	00					45	150	00				
20	150	00	750	00			46	150	00				
21	150	00					47	150	00				
22	150	00					48	160	00	750	00		
23	150	00					49	150	00				
24	150	00	750	00			50	150	00				
25	150	00					51	150	00				
26	150	00					52	150	00	750	00		
TAX.	2174	00	2856	00			53	2174	00	2856	00		
2nd Qtr.	4124	00	5106	00			4th Qtr.	4124	00	5856	00		

Yearly Summary — Proprietor or Partner 1

1st Qtr.	1950	00
2nd Qtr.	4124	00
3rd Qtr.	1950	00
4th Qtr.	4124	00
Total	12148	00

Yearly Summary — Partner 2

1st Qtr.	2250	00
2nd Qtr.	5106	00
3rd Qtr.	2250	00
4th Qtr.	5856	00
Total	15462	00

Yearly Summary — Partner 3

1st Qtr.		
2nd Qtr.		
3rd Qtr.		
4th Qtr.		
Total		

Fig. 5.5 SUMMARY OF DRAWINGS FOR SELF

Notes to Figure 5.5

In this illustration, just to show how partnership drawings are recorded, the summary has been completed as if there were two partners, and it can be seen that they have different patterns of drawings. One draws £150 a week, while the other draws £750 a month. Notice also that if they pay their tax out of the business bank account, it is treated as extra drawings. What happens with drawings is that, at the end of the year, you divide the profits between the partners, and they are then entitled only to whatever amount is due to them less amounts already drawn. Remember, drawings are really 'drawings in expectation of profits made'. Of course, if a partner has already drawn more than they are entitled to, it would present a problem. This is explained later in the book.

bank is paying these creditors, we cannot make them in the week they actually occur. We have to wait until we receive a bank statement (usually requested on a monthly basis). When the bank sends the statement, we go through it and find any direct debits, standing orders, bank charges and so on and record them as if they all happened in the week the statement arrives. The result is that we carry out a simple bank reconciliation process that reconciles our cash book with the bank's ledger account in our name. (See Chapter 8 for a full explanation of this process.)

FINDING THE NET PROFIT OF THE BUSINESS: THE PROFIT AND LOSS ACCOUNT

You have already learned how to prepare a trading account and find the gross profit on trading. You are now able to go further and work out the net profit of your business, for you have now discovered the total value of all the expenses (overheads) of the business. When these figures are brought into a profit and loss account, you have the situation shown in Figure 5.6.

Notice one point before you study Figure 5.6. You may have registered for VAT, either because your turnover exceeds £50,000 per year and you are compelled to register or because you have registered voluntarily so that you can reclaim your input tax, on the things you buy, out of the output tax you collect from your customers. In either of these cases, you will be making a VAT return every quarter (or every month if you sell zero-rated goods). Simplex's profit and loss account has some extra lines on it about VAT. You should only write anything on these lines if you are VAT registered. If you are not, ignore these lines and leave them blank.

In studying Figure 5.6, note the following points.

- On the right-hand side of the page, you have all the profits of the business. These include the gross profit brought down from the trading account, and any other profits, such as the miscellaneous receipts from the summary of other receipts, Customs and Excise VAT repayments (for VAT-registered traders who sell mostly zero-rated goods) and a Start-up Allowance for new businesses receiving this help from the government.
- On the left-hand side, you have all the overhead expenses of the business, including two lines for VAT payments and VAT on capital items.

- When you take the total of the left-hand side (expenses) from the total of the right-hand side (profits earned), you find the net profit of the business. This belongs to the proprietor. Of course, if the expenses were more than profits earned, we should have a net loss instead of a net profit.

The notes below explain one or two further points about Figure 5.6.

Profit and Loss Account for year ending..3l.s⊤ DECEMBER 19...

Previous year			This year		Previous year			This year	
	Employee costs		9051	67		Gross Profit (brought down from Trading Account)		95234	80
	Premises costs		4969	79					
	Repairs		192	61		Miscellaneous Receipts		150	00
	General Administration Expenses		2570	31					
	Motor Expenses		1095	63		Customs & Excise VAT Repayments		–	–
	Travel and Subsistence		171	08					
	Advertising and Entertainment		522	50		Start-up Allowance (if any)		2080	00
	Legal and Professional		–	–					
	Bad Debts		–	–			TOTAL	97464	80
	Interest Payable		115	99					
	Other Financial Charges		–	–					
	Depreciation and Loss/Profit on Sale		535	00					
	Other Expenses		–	–					
	Customs & Excise VAT Payments		14428	32					
	VAT on Capital Items		106	52					
		Total	33759	32					
	Net Profit During Year		63705	48		Net loss (if no profit made)			
		TOTAL	97464	80			TOTAL	97464	80

Fig. 5.6 CALCULATING THE NET PROFIT IN A PROFIT AND LOSS ACCOUNT

Notes to Figure 5.6
- The miscellaneous receipts, and the Start-up Allowance have been included just to show that other figures contribute to profit apart from the gross profit coming in from the trading account.
- On the left-hand side, the losses of the business are those coming from the summary of expenses (see Figure 5.2), but some depreciation figures have been inserted as well. When the total expenses are deducted from the total receipts, you find the net profit of the business, which you will declare to the Inland Revenue in your tax return in April, under the self-assessment system.
- You should now try the exercise that follows.

EXERCISE ON CALCULATING THE NET PROFIT

In the exercise, you are required to draw up a profit and loss account in the style shown in Figure 5.6, using the figures supplied.

Books of Tom Price:

- gross profit £37 217;
- miscellaneous receipts £350;
- Start-up Allowance £2080;
- employee costs £7856.50;
- premises costs £3517.65;
- repairs £328.50;
- general administration expenses £720.70;
- motor expenses £756.50;
- travel and subsistence £280.00;
- advertising and entertainment £238.80;
- legal and professional £128.60;
- bad debts £28.46;
- interest payable £120.00;
- other financial charges £98.95;
- depreciation and loss (profit) on sale £1630.00;
- other expenses (including VAT paid) £1746.50.

Answer
Books of Tom Price: net profit £22 195.84

MEDIUM-SIZED ENTERPRISES AND ROUTINE BOOK-KEEPING

Routine book-keeping is a major feature of all business enterprises. The activities described in Chapters 3–5 of this book have been very simple examples of records that are fundamental to all enterprises. Receipts, payments for raw materials and goods for resale and overhead expenses are the foundations on which profitability and business success are built. As the business grows, the volume of transactions increases and the figures are bigger. An invoice for 50 million barrels of crude oil is just the same as a garage's voucher for a can of motor oil. The difference lies in the size of the order and the way you record this.

Medium-size enterprises move on to more advanced systems, often starting with those that simplify a section of the work and deal with it by a small group of reliable book-keepers. This may be a payroll system (see Chapter 10) or a sales ledger or purchases ledger section (see Chapter 9). A cashier may take charge of all receipts and payments and a budgeting department may develop future plans. All such systems are based on a clear understanding of what is known as 'double entry book-keeping', which is the subject matter of our next chapter.

The one different feature of these activities in the medium-size enterprise is that the question of security raises its ugly head. In a small enterprise, the sole trader or the partners know what is going on and can correct abuses or remedy wrong decisions very quickly. However, when you subdivide the work so it is done by groups of people, you lose the direct, hands-on control of these procedures. It is necessary to build in safeguards to ensure that abuse of any system is quickly detected. For example, it is usual to separate the buying activities from the delivery section. Buyers who are authorised to purchase items on the company's behalf will not receive them when they arrive. Instead, they will go to a goods inward section and staff there will record the arrival of, and pass the goods on to, the department that indented for them originally.

You may insure key staff (for example, cashiers) with a fidelity bond (a guarantee of faithful behaviour). If the cashier steals funds, the company will be reimbursed by the insurance company after the cashier has been convicted of the offence. You cannot say, 'Well, we'll forgive you this time, and meanwhile we'll ask the insurer for the money.' Reimbursement depends on successful prosecution.

In larger organizations, an internal audit department looks at every department from time to time by random selection. This means that you do not give prior notice of an audit, but each audit is selected in a random and unexpected way. Unsatisfactory results may indicate embezzlement, or theft of product or, perhaps, weak procedures that call for improvements, retraining of staff and so on.

CHECKLIST

- The chief types of payments, apart from purchases of goods for resale, are payments for consumables, overhead expenses, wages, capital items, repayment of loans and mortgages and payments to the proprietor.

- Of these expenses, payments for consumables, overheads, and wages are revenue expenses, deductible in the profit and loss account at the end of the year as legitimate business expenses.

- Capital items and repayments of loans and mortgages are not business expenses in the sense that term is used by the Inland Revenue, but capital expenditures, which are not deductible from the profits at the end of the year.

- The weekly expenses of all types have to be collected together in some sort of summary to give annual totals that can then be used in preparing the final accounts. The revenue expenditures are losses of the business and go in the profit and loss account.

- The capital expenditures finish up on the balance sheet at the end of the year, but do not affect the profits of the business, except for depreciation charges for fair wear and tear.

- Medium-sized enterprises may not use simple systems for the basic book-keeping activities of recording receipts, payments for business stock and overhead expenses. Instead, they will develop specialist cost centres and departments to handle these matters, but they still lie at the centre of business activity, and profitability and prosperity depend on them.

- In developing such specialist groupings, the problem of security arises as hands-on control of the activity is no longer possible. Management must develop control procedures to ensure supervision of all such areas is achieved.

Using a full double entry system

THE NATURE OF THE FULL DOUBLE ENTRY SYSTEM

The double entry system is the basis of all book-keeping systems, whether they are manual (handwritten) systems or computerised systems. To be able to 'think in double entries' is a great advantage because it can answer every problem that ever presents itself in accountancy. You can learn the double entry system at any evening school or technical college in the United Kingdom, and it takes only one year, one evening a week, to master the whole subject. Alternatively, you can use one of the simple introductions, such as my own *Book-keeping Made Simple* (Butterworth-Heinemann, 1997).

Those who already have this knowledge, or are prepared to acquire it before going into business, will find it a very great help in running any system of accounts and, if you keep a full double entry system, you will certainly know exactly where you are. On the other hand, it is time-consuming and that is why this whole book is largely about short-cuts to double entry. These are best understood if you have some general knowledge of the double entry system. The whole layout is illustrated in Figure 6.1. The numbers 1–5 by the headings that follow guide you through the system, and you should look at the part numbered 1 and study the illustration, then read the notes that begin with section 1. Having followed that section, proceed to part 2 of the illustration and so on.

LAYOUT OF THE DOUBLE ENTRY SYSTEM

1 Every transaction has a business document related to it

A 'transaction' is a business arrangement of any sort whatsoever. The most common transactions, which you will already be familiar with because of the content of Chapters 1–5, are listed below. At the end of each is the document related to it, as illustrated in Figure 6.1.

> *A 'transaction' is a business arrangement of any sort whatsoever.*

- **Purchases** of goods for resale or to be worked into a finished product for resale. (The document is the **invoice**; the top copy of the **invoice** from the supplier who sold you the goods.)
- **Sales** (the document is the **second copy of your invoice** – the top copy having gone to the customer).
- **Purchases returns** (the document is the **credit note**, the top copy of the supplier's credit note that is sent to you when the supplier receives back the returned goods).

- **Sales returns** (this time it is the **second copy of your credit note**, the top copy having gone to the customer who returned the goods to you).
- **Purchases of consumables** (there will usually be an **invoice** or **bill** for the supply of these items. It will be the top copy of the supplier's invoice. If there is no invoice for a small item, the till receipt or some other **petty cash voucher** – perhaps an internal petty cash voucher made out and signed by the proprietor – will be used.)
- **Purchase of capital items** (there will always be an invoice from the supplier of the capital item, and it will be the top copy). With some items, there may be a **deed** (premises) or a formal **hire purchase document**.
- **Payments in cash and by cheque**. Here the **receipt** you obtain (the top copy) or give (the duplicate copy) or the **cheque** (inwards or outwards) will be the valid document. If you use a petty cash book (see Chapter 9) these receipts will become **petty cash vouchers**.

2 These documents are entered in books of original entry

Originally, in the Middle Ages, there were only two books – a book of original entry called the journal, or day book, and the main book of account, called the ledger. Later, it was found that having only two books was inconvenient, as only two book-keepers could work on the books at any one time. It was therefore found to be helpful if the journal was divided into five parts.

- the purchases day book;
- the sales day book;
- the purchases returns book;
- the sales returns book;
- the journal proper (note that the first four are all to do with the things you buy and sell – activities that you repeat many times every day – while the journal proper was kept for rarer items, such as the purchase of capital items, bad debts and depreciation, and so on).

The other two books of original entry are the cash book and the petty cash book, which, as their names suggest, refer to incoming cash and cheques and outgoing cash and cheques.

The chief idea of books of original entry is to make a permanent record of documents that can easily be lost. Keeping books of original entry in this way does give a great deal of work for very little benefit, and it is chiefly in this field that short-cut systems are widely used today. Computers do all such things with effortless ease, and this explains why computerised systems are so popular.

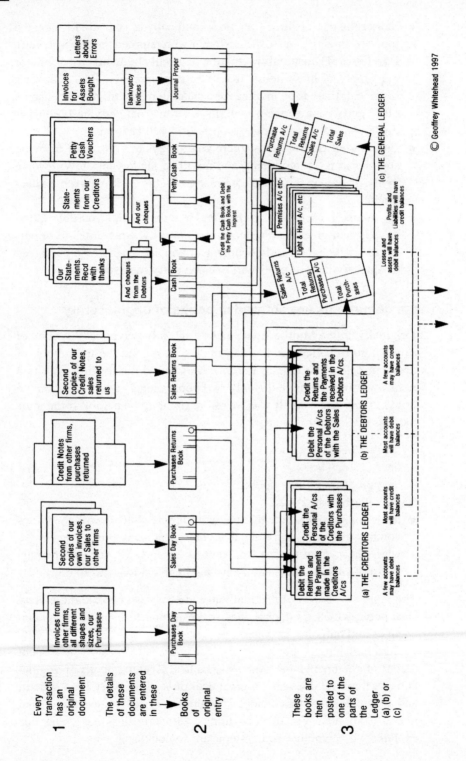

© Geoffrey Whitehead 1997

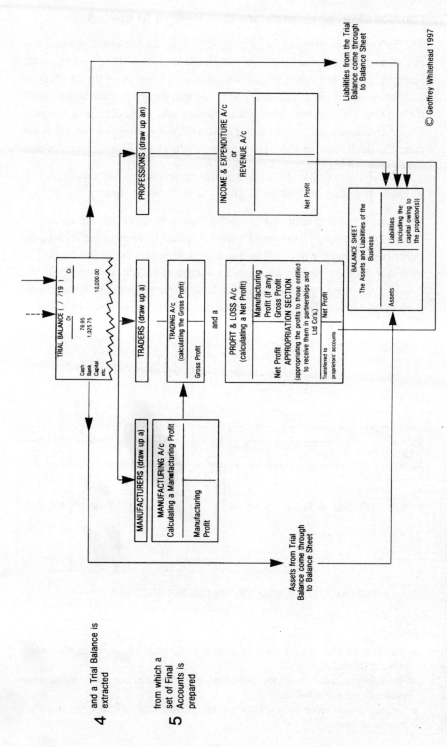

4 and a Trial Balance is extracted

5 from which a set of Final Accounts is prepared

Fig. 6.1 HOW THE DOUBLE ENTRY SYSTEM WORKS

3 The books of original entry are then posted to the ledger

The ledger is the main book of account in the double entry system. An account is a page in the ledger or, rather, a leaf in the ledger, because both sides of a page are devoted to each account. If you open up an account with someone, it simply means you give them a page in your ledger, with their name and address, telephone number and such details at the top. Every transaction with them then goes on the page, either on the left-hand side (the debit side) or the right-hand side (the credit side). The rules are:

- debit the account that receives goods or services or money;
- credit the account that gives goods or services or money.

This rule is usually shortened to debit the receiver, credit the giver.

So, if you supply Catherine Timms with envelopes worth £28.50, you debit her account with £28.50 because she is receiving value. She is now our debtor (she has an unpaid balance of £28.50 on her account). Later, if she sends you a cheque for £28.50, you can credit her account – credit the giver. This leaves her account clear; there is no outstanding balance owing on her account.

Dr.							Cr.
Debit Side				Credit Side			
Date	Details	Folio	Amount	Date	Details	Folio	Amount

Fig. 6.2 THE LAYOUT OF A TRADITIONAL LEDGER ACCOUNT

Notes
- The page is divided down the middle.
- The left-hand side is called the debit side, or debtor side, and often has the abbreviation Dr. printed at the top.
- The right-hand side is called the credit side, or creditor side, and often has the abbreviation Cr. printed at the top.
- Columns are drawn on each side for the date, details, folio numbers and the amount received or given.

Note that because there are so many accounts (one firm in the United Kingdom has over 8 million debtors alone), the ledger is split into sections. There is a 'creditors' ledger' (with all your suppliers' accounts in it), a 'debtors' ledger' (with all our debtors' accounts in it) and a 'general ledger', with the rest of your accounts. More of this later.

It will not detract from your understanding of Figure 6.1 if you consider for a moment the layout of a traditional ledger account, such as would be found in all the sections of the ledger illustrated in Figure 6.1. You can see this layout in Figure 6.2, and it is described in the notes below it.

FURNITURE ACCOUNT								L.1
Dr.								Cr.
19–			£					
Aug. 17	A. Trader	L2	100.00					

				A. TRADER				L.2
Dr.								Cr.
				19–			£	
				Aug. 17	Furniture	L.1	100.00	

Fig. 6.3 A DOUBLE ENTRY

Notes
- The two accounts affected are the furniture account and A. Trader's account.
- Each account (page in the ledger) has a reference number written in the top right-hand corner. It is called a 'folio number' (Latin: *folium* = leaf).
- When the entries are made, it is usual to record the folio number of the other account in the folio column. This tells anyone looking at an account where to find the other half of the double entry.
- Note that the furniture account received value and so it is debited, but A. Trader gave value so his account is credited. Remember the rule – debit the account that receives value, credit the account that gives value.
- Later, when A. Trader is paid by cheque, A. Trader's account will be debited and the bank account (which is giving the money) will be credited.

It is when you make entries in the ledger accounts that the term 'double entry' comes into use, for every accounting transaction requires two entries, not one. Imagine a transaction in which you purchase a piece of furniture worth £100 from A. Trader, on credit, payable in one month's time. A. Trader gives you a piece of furniture worth £100. Can you think in double entries? Which account will receive a piece of furniture worth £100? Obviously it must be the furniture account. Debit furniture account with £100.

Which account is giving you £100-worth of value? Clearly it is A. Trader's. Credit A. Trader's account with £100. A. Trader is now one of your creditors, and you owe him £100 for furniture received.

Later, of course, you would pay A. Trader £100, probably by cheque. Who will receive the £100 cheque? Clearly it is A. Trader, so you debit A. Trader's account, and that wipes out the debt and leaves his account clear. The bank account has given the cheque. Credit the giver, so credit the bank account, which loses £100 of the money in the bank. The first of these double entries is shown in Figure 6.3.

4 A trial balance is extracted

Under the double entry system, entries are being made in accounts all the time, some on the debit side and some on the credit side. The busiest accounts are probably the cash account and the bank account, which are separated out into a special book – the 'cash book', kept by a bookkeeper who is fairly high in the accounting team, and called the 'cashier'. Other busy accounts are the purchases account and the sales account. Like dealings in cash and by cheque, purchases and sales take place all day, every day, in many businesses.

As a result of all these efforts, it is helpful to check up on all your entries at least once a month, and this is done by taking out a 'trial balance'. As the name implies, you try the books to see if they balance, because if they do you must have made all your double entries correctly.

To draw up a trial balance, you balance off each account in the ledger, including the cash account and bank account in the cash book. The final balance on any particular account will be on either the debit side or the credit side. If you make a list of these balances and total them, you should find that the two sides come to the same figure.

In Figure 6.1, there is only a very brief indication of what the trial balance looks like, so it is helpful now to look at one more closely. Before you do so, look at the three accounts shown in Figure 6.4 to see how the balancing-off procedure is done. For simplicity, the accounts have been shown without the full rulings.

Mrs M. Jones A/c, 2173 Camside, Cambridge CB4 1PQ   *L32*

199X	£		
27 January	137.56		

Commission Received A/c   *L 199*

		199X	£
		4 January Motor car sale	25.00
		11 January Motor car sale	38.94
		23 January Finance contract	72.65

Land & Buildings A/c   *L252*

199X	£	199X	£
1 January Balance b/d	147 256.55	19 January Sale of Pett St.	38 250.00
14 January Garages	8 285.60	31 January Balance c/d	122 157.15
29 January Shopfront	4 865.00		
	£160 407.15		£160 407.15
199X	£		
1 February Balance b/d	122 157.15		

Fig. 6.4 BALANCING OFF ACCOUNTS BEFORE TAKING OUT A TRIAL BALANCE

Notes
- The first account has only one entry on the debit side. Clearly this is a debit balance and you can see at once what the figure is. There is no need to tidy up this account at all – just record it on your list of balances as a debit balance of £137.56.
- With the Commission Received Account, there are several entries, all on the same side, the credit side. You might think, with a name like 'Commission Received Account' these would be debit entries, because of the rule that you debit the account that receives goods or services or money. In fact, this money has been received but it will be debited in the Cash Account (or the Bank Account if you received the money as a cheque). This account is the other half of the double entry – the one that says: 'Who gave this money to the business?' The answer is that it has been given by the 'Commission Received Account'– though that may be a number of individuals who pay us for the service rendered to them. For example, garages often allow people wishing to sell a car to exhibit it on the forecourt and take 10 per cent of the sale price as commission. This is a profit of the business and goes on the credit side of the account.

  Do you need to tidy up this account? Yes – but you need not balance it off. All you do is add it up in pencil and enter the figure in your trial balance – a credit balance of £136.59.
- The third account is the Land and Buildings Account and it has items on both sides of the account. What do you do here? The answer is that you balance off the account. One side is clearly larger than the other. There is £160 407.15 on the debit side, and only £38 250.00 on the credit side. Taking the smaller side from the larger, you have a difference of £122 157.15. This is the balance on the account; the value of the buildings owned when you balance the books on the last day of the month. Note that you add this balance to the credit side, making both sides equal at £160,407.15, but immediately bring the balance down on to the left-hand side, where it shows clearly in a single figure the balance on the account.

PERSONAL ACCOUNTS, NOMINAL ACCOUNTS AND REAL ACCOUNTS

There is one further point to make about these accounts. They show the three types of account you have in every business.

Mrs M. Jones' account is obviously a 'personal account' – that is, an account with one of the persons you deal with in business. Personal accounts are always either debtors (people who owe you money) or creditors (people to whom you owe money). There is one rather special personal account, and that is the 'capital account' – the account of the proprietor. As you owe the proprietor everything put into the business, it is almost always a creditor account, with a credit balance.

The land and buildings account is a 'real account' – that is, an account that tells you about some real asset the business owns. Thus land and buildings, motor vehicles, plant and machinery, furniture and fittings and cash are all real things, things you can actually touch and handle. This business has land and buildings worth £122,157.15. Assets are always debit balances, and so appear on the debit side of the trial balance.

The commission received account is not a real account. It is a record of money received, but the real money is in the cash box or in the bank. It is said to be a 'nominal account', because the money is there 'in name only'. All nominal accounts are either profits or losses, and you keep a record of them only until the end of the year so you can work out the profits of the business.

Figure 6.5 shows a trial balance. This one has been taken out at the end of the year, although trial balances are always done monthly. Written alongside each item are notes showing whether the item is an asset, liability, profit or loss. Some items are called 'trading account items' because they appear in the trading account. Don't forget that to prepare a trading account you also need the closing stock figure, which is given separately at the end. One special item is the 'drawings' of the proprietor – which is explained more fully later. This trial balance is worked into a full set of final accounts in the next section.

T. Sanderson
Trial Balance as at 31 December 199X

Ledger Accounts	Notes	Dr. £	Cr. £	Notes
Premises Account	Asset	86 000.00		
Capital Account			130 675.70	Liability
Debtors:				
R. Green Account	Asset	394.00		
P. Colne Account	Asset	426.60		
Creditors:				
M. Shah Account			872.50	Liability
P. Driver Account			729.30	Liability
Plant and Machinery Account	Asset	38 240.50		
Office Furniture Account	Asset	7 246.38		
Cash Account	Asset	294.72		
Bank Account	Asset	13 825.60		
Bad Debts Account	Loss	238.60		
Advertising Account	Loss	3 294.60		
Commission Paid Account	Loss	25.60		
Discount Allowed Account	Loss	128.54		
Discount Received Account			236.35	Profit
Business Rates Account	Loss	894.56		
Carriage Out Account	Loss	328.70		
Salaries Account	Loss	27 925.50		
Motor Expenses Account	Loss	1 727.36		
Rent Received Account			1 850.00	Profit
Stock at 1 January 199X	Trading Account item	9 275.50		
Purchases Account	Trading Account item	29 312.65		
Sales Account			98 325.50	Trading Account item
Purchases Returns Account			2 275.56	Trading Account item

Fig. 6.5 A TYPICAL TRIAL BALANCE
(continues overleaf)

Fig. 6.5 (continued)

Sales Returns Account	Trading account item	2 425.50
Drawings	Special item	12 960.00
		£234 964.91 £234 964.91

At 31 December, stocktaking revealed that the 'closing stock' figure was £13 925.60.

Note

In abbreviated form, these notes can be condensed into the following groups:

Trial Balance	Dr.	Cr.
	• Assets	• Liabilities
	• Losses	• Profits
	• Three trading items	• Two trading items
	• Drawings	

Special note: Figure 6.6 opposite is a set of 'final accounts' drawn up from the trial balance given above. It is introduced on page 92 but is put in here to display it all on one page.

T. Sanderson
Trading Account for Year Ending 31 December 199X

	£		£
Opening stock	9 275.50	Sales	98 325.50
Purchases	29 312.65	*Less returns*	2 425.50
Less returns	2 275.56	Net turnover	95 900.00
	27 037.09		
Total stock available	36 312.59		
Less closing stock	13 925.60		
Cost of sales	22 386.99		
Gross profit	73 513.01		
	£95 900.00		£95 900.00

Profit and Loss Account for Year Ending 31 December 199X

	£		£
Bad debts	238.60	Gross profit	73 513.01
Advertising	3 294.60	Discount received	236.35
Commission paid	25.60	Rent received	1 850.00
Discount allowed	128.54		75 599.36
Business rates	894.56		
Carriage outwards	328.70		
Salaries	27 925.50		
Motor expenses	1 727.36		
Total losses	34 563.46		
Net profit	41 035.90		
	£75 599.36		£75 599.36

Balance Sheet as at 31 December 199X

	£		£
Capital (at start)	130 675.70	Fixed assets	
Add net profit 41 035.90		Premises	86 000.00
Less drawings 12 960.00		Plant and machinery	38 240.50
	28 075.90	Office furniture	7 246.38
	158 751.60		131 486.88
Long-term liabilities	–	*Current assets*	
		Closing stock 13 925.60	
Current liabilities		Debtors 820.60	
Creditors	1 601.80	Bank 13 825.60	
		Cash 294.72	
			28 866.52
	£160 353.40		£160 353.40

Fig. 6.6 SOLE TRADER T. SANDERSON'S FINAL ACCOUNTS

5 From which you prepare a set of 'final accounts'

The final stage in double entry book-keeping is to prepare a set of final accounts to discover:

- the net profit of the business;
- the financial situation of the business at the start of the new financial year.

This is done by producing a balance sheet. As you have now learned how to produce a trading account and a profit and loss account, it is relatively simple to use the trial balance given in Figure 6.5 to produce a set of final accounts, which show the profitability of the business and its exact financial position at the date of the trial balance.

Notes to final accounts shown in Figure 6.6
- The only difference in the Trading Account from the one shown in Figure 4.4 is that there are some purchases returns and sales returns that have to be deducted from the purchases and sales figures to give a true 'net' figure for purchases and sales.
- The Balance Sheet is shown in traditional United Kingdom style, with the assets on the right-hand side. This is illogical, and is the result of a mistake in an Act of Parliament in 1858, but this need not bother us here. Balance sheets are done the correct way in the rest of Europe and the United Kingdom should start to do this soon. Being simply a sheet of paper – the balance sheet – having the figures in the traditional style does not affect the double entry, though it is a bit confusing to newcomers. See Figure 6.1 (pages 82–3) for a balance sheet in correct European style, with assets on the left and liabilities on the right.

PRACTICAL REQUIREMENTS FOR KEEPING A FULL SET OF DOUBLE ENTRY BOOKS

We now come to the crucial question regarding keeping a full set of double entry books: what books do you need, and where do you get them? The answer is that you need:

- a journal proper;
- four day books:
  - a purchases day book
  - a sales day book
  - a purchases returns day book
  - a sales returns day book;
- a four-column cash book – this used to be a three-column cash book, but now that VAT is a constant feature of our lives, you need an extra column for the VAT;

- a petty cash book – for small cash outgoings;
- a loose-leaf ledger – divided into sections for debtors and creditors, and a 'general ledger' section.

This is an awful lot of books compared with, say, a Simplex D account book or one of the other systems shown later in this book. If you want to keep a full set of books, and already know how to do double entry book-keeping, by all means do, but it is better to use the Simplex system or one of the simple adaptations of double entry book-keeping described in the chapters which follow.

ADAPTATIONS OF THE DOUBLE ENTRY SYSTEM

In general, adaptations of the double entry system deal with sections of the system, rather than the entire system. There are, for example, clever systems for keeping the day books (such as the sales day book and the purchases day book) by means of simultaneous records or what are called three-in-one systems. The name comes from the use of carbon paper or, perhaps, NCR paper to prepare three records at once. The term NCR stands for 'no carbon required' – the paper itself is covered with globules of transparent ink, which when pressed by a ballpoint pen, turn to a visible ink as they react with the air.

Another three-in-one system deals with wages, and enables a payroll sheet, individual pay records for each employee and weekly or monthly payslips for insertion into pay packets to be prepared in one operation. This system is described later in the chapter on wages.

Another system, the YBS system, which is described in detail in the next chapter, is an adaptation of the double entry system that keeps certain parts of the records very clearly – for example, purchases and sales records, cash and bank records. It includes a final accounts section which enables you to prepare your trading account, profit and loss account and balance sheet. It is also ideal for larger firms that are definitely intending to use the services of an accountant for the finer points of their book-keeping activities.

Finally, any computerised system will offer great economies of operation once the initial familiarization with it has been undertaken. Because the computer program can decide what to do with any particular item of information, it can perform all the double entry activities in the twinkling of an eye, at speeds of millions of processes per second. Thus, if you imagine the double entries for the purchase of an item of business stock, once the operator feeds in the code for the supplier concerned and the amount of the invoice with the VAT included, the computer will do both the VAT records and the financial records in a hundredth of a second, updating the supplier's account, the VAT input tax, the stock records and anything else covered by the program. The chapters on computerization later in this book explain some systems on offer and give you names and addresses to contact.

CONCLUSIONS ABOUT THE DOUBLE ENTRY SYSTEM

What can be said in conclusion about the double entry system?

- It is the only perfect book-keeping system that will answer every difficulty that arises.
- There is everything to be said for getting to know the full double entry system and being able to think along double entry lines.
- At the same time, it is too cumbersome to be used by a person who is a 'one-man (or one-woman) band'. It really needs a specialist book-keeper and is thus most suitable for the slightly larger business that has reached the stage where it can afford one. Smaller firms should use one of the simple systems – either Simplex or one of the more advanced systems described in the next few chapters.
- Even the firm that does have a specialist book-keeper should consider the use of simultaneous record systems for purchases, sales, wages and so on.
- In the last analysis, the true answer to accounting problems is a computerised system. The computer works on a perfect double entry system built into the programs provided by the systems analyst. The computer operator is not aware of what the computer is doing, and only needs to ensure that the data keyed in is correct.

EXERCISE ON DRAWING UP A SET OF FINAL ACCOUNTS

Here is P. Morris's Trial Balance as at 31 December 199X. Draw up his Trading Account, Profit and Loss Account and Balance Sheet as at that date.

	Dr. £	Cr. £
Capital		83 500.00
Cash	285.50	
Cash at bank	17 350.00	
Stock at 1 January 199X	21 334.50	
Sales returns and sales	4 998.50	219 275.60
Purchases and purchases returns	85 497.25	600.75
Debtors and creditors	21 950.00	2 226.10
Discount allowed and received	501.60	3 238.20
Repairs	14 500.00	
Stationery	2 102.50	
Light and heat	4 376.50	
Business rates	13 503.50	
Motor vehicle expenses	2 102.60	
Salaries	27 539.90	
Drawings	15 000.00	
Office expenses	6 500.00	
Freehold premises	55 000.00	
Motor vehicles	8 500.00	
Fixtures and fittings	10 560.05	
Interest received		2 761.75
	£311 602.40	£311 602.40

The stock at the end of the year was valued at £18 500.

Answer
Books of P. Morris: gross profit £126 546.10; net profit £61 419.45
Balance Sheet totals:

- fixed assets £74 060.05
- current assets £58 085.50
- capital at close £129 919.45
- current liabilities £2226.10
- final totals £132 145.55

MEDIUM-SIZED ENTERPRISES AND THE DOUBLE ENTRY SYSTEM

As a business grows, more and more pressures are exerted on management from the accounting point of view. The original management may have no real knowledge of accounting, because they brought other skills, such as technical skills, marketing skills or IT to the firm. It suddenly becomes necessary to find someone who can handle at least some accounting work and keep routine activities under control. The most affordable person is a part-qualified accountant – not necessarily a chartered accountant because their expertise is in the professional field, auditing and so on. A better choice is a part-qualified member of the Chartered Association of Certified and Corporate Accountants (ACCA). Such a person will have a good grasp of double entry and will be able to deal with the vast majority of accounting events that occur.

An 'accounting event' is anything that is not absolutely routine. For example, such everyday occurrences as a bad debt or an insurance claim after a break-in or a motor vehicle that becomes a write-off as a result of vandalism, call for clear thinking about double entries. When management starts to ask, 'Well, what do we do about this event?', the young accountant will say, 'Give me ten minutes and I'll tell you'.

There are all sorts of such day-to-day problems, and they are recorded in a special book called the journal. Journal means 'day book' and, at one time, every transaction that took place was recorded in the journal. Later, the routine transactions were separated off into special 'day books' – the purchases day book, the purchases returns book, the sales day book and the sales returns book. This leaves the journal proper, kept by the accountant, for all the unusual, non-recurring events. The accountant shows the steps needed to do a perfect double entry to deal with whatever matter arises.

Remember that a part-qualified accountant will need to complete their qualification by part-time study and, while doing so, will also be familiarizing themselves with the firm's own particular needs. It is usual to offer a 'package' of support for such an employee – help with the purchase of textbooks, exam fees, perhaps day release and revision time before important examinations. In return, it is often prudent to require that the employee, as a matter of good faith, serve a reasonable period (say two years) with the firm after qualifying. Such a clause is valid in law if its terms are reasonable. A clause that is too onerous would be struck out by the Court and would have no validity.

CHECKLIST

- Double entry book-keeping is the basis of all sound accounting and it is a great help to be able to think along double entry lines.

- The chief books of account are the journal and the ledger, but these days the journal is split up into a number of day books, and the ledger is also split into several parts, notably a debtors' ledger, a creditors' ledger and a general ledger. The cash book and the petty cash book are also specialised parts of the ledger.

- If you want to learn double entry book-keeping, you can do so at an evening class or study a simple introduction to the subject, such as my own *Book-keeping Made Simple*.

- Most new entrants to self-employment don't need to learn double entry or keep a full set of books, but instead use a simple system like the ones described in this book.

- As your firm grows large enough to employ a specialist book-keeper, you may find it helpful to move on to a full double entry system, but, even then, you will probably find that using some of the short-cuts to double entry, such as three-in-one simultaneous records systems, is advantageous.

- Finally, the use of a computerised system, such as those described later in this book, is the ultimate solution to the book-keeping problem and enables all sorts of statistical control figures about your business to be calculated instantaneously.

- A medium-sized enterprise will need to give the accountancy function proper status within the organisation. At first, a young, part-qualified accountant may be adequate for the work involved, but later a fully qualified accountant, with a seat on the Board, will be essential.

YBS: (your book-keeping system) – nearly a double entry system

1
2
3
4
5
6
7
8
9
10
11
12
13
14
15
16
17
18
19
20
21

THE NATURE OF THE YBS SYSTEM

The YBS system is a simple system of book-keeping for small businesses that is, in part, double entry as some records are cross-referenced, where appropriate, between two sections of the coloured pages system. It is a fully comprehensive system with sections for:

- bank records (white);
- cash records (blue);
- sales records (pink);
- purchases records (yellow);
- payroll records (green);
- VAT computations records (orange);
- profit and loss and balance sheet (grey).

The profit and loss and balance sheet sections satisfy the self-assessment statutory requirements, which demand that all businesses keep business records. The Finance Act 1994 imposes swingeing penalties for failure to do so. The system can be supplied in a 'de luxe' loose leaf system, but the most popular, and economic, style is a one-year wire-bound version. Both the above systems come with a

As long as monthly figures are recorded and totalled each month, a quarterly VAT return can be completed by almost anyone, using the monthly figures as recorded on a monthly analysis sheet.

comprehensive training book with fully worked examples. In addition, they both have simple instructions and a worked example at the front of each section.

The sections are designed to be completed and totalled at the end of every month. This provides valuable management financial figures and is convenient for VAT returns and so on. Routine entries should be made on a daily basis as transactions are completed.

At one time, many small business proprietors left book-keeping to accountants and book-keeping services. With the advent of self-assessment, there is now a statutory requirement for firms to keep financial records and simple systems like this are ideal for small businesses.

The system is arranged so as to have a number of analysis columns for the main headings under which expenses and/or payments can be recorded, with a miscellaneous column for the others. A simple coding system, which is fully explained, allows for those who wish to do their own profit and loss account and balance sheet. Although many still leave this to an accountant or book-keeper, the statutory need to keep records makes it preferable to work these accounts out yourself.

■ VAT returns

One of the impressive features of the system is the fact that, as long as monthly figures are recorded and totalled each month, a quarterly VAT return can be completed by almost anyone, using the monthly figures as recorded on a monthly analysis sheet. This is done by simply transferring the monthly figures into prepared boxes that match the boxes on the VAT return.

ELEMENTS OF THE YBS SYSTEM

The elements of the YBS system are:

- 24 monthly pages of bank account records, showing receipts and payments – these are on white paper, and the 32 lines on each page should be enough for most businesses;
- 24 monthly pages of cash records, on blue paper – these are very similar to bank account records, and allow for the VAT element to be recorded (where applicable). The pages allow for the recording of all cash transactions and give a running balance;
- 24 monthly pages of sales records – this is virtually a sales day book, with analysis columns to bring out the sales activity in any particular area and to record the VAT output tax, payable eventually to Customs and Excise (any credit notes received have to be entered in red ink or in brackets to show a deduction on the sales record: they are deducted at the end of the month from the total sales figure – the goods being returned to stock);
- 24 monthly pages of purchases records – this is virtually a purchases day book, with analysis columns to divide the purchases into various departments, and to extract the recoverable VAT input tax (again, purchases returns must be entered in red or by using brackets);
- 24 pages of payroll records – these are not strictly arranged on a monthly basis as some people might be paying staff weekly, so the records simply take up as much space as they require, and Statutory Sick Pay (SSP) and Statutory Maternity Pay (SMP) are catered for in the records (the one thing not directly recorded is the employer's need to pay over such sums as have been deducted from staff pay for the Inland Revenue (tax and National Insurance contributions – less any reclaimed SSP and SMP), so the book-keeper must remember to pay these amounts on the due date, using the Inland Revenue forms provided for this purpose);

- 24 quarterly VAT record sheets provide records of input tax and output tax drawn from the purchases, sales, cash and bank records, but they are a little difficult to follow for a trader using one of the VAT retail schemes.

The blank page provided each quarter for the VAT retail scheme calculation enables traders to make their scheme calculation, but the daily takings figures have to be catered for by means of a separate daily analysis sheet. If the total sales are entered daily, scheme calculation can be used to derive the correct figures for output tax.

The YBS pages are too large to reproduce in a book of this size, but I shall point out the features of some of the pages as this may prove helpful. The system is also referred to in Chapter 13, which gives the names and addresses of all the suppliers of simple book-keeping systems.

THE YBS BANK RECORD

Taking the bank record first, as illustrated in Figure 7.1, the notes on page 104 explain the main points.

YBS

BUSINESS NAME: Egg. SAMPLE & Co.

BANK RECORD

PERIOD from 01.04.92 to 30.04.92 Page No.

DATE	DESCRIPTION	CHEQUE No.	RECEIPTS Total	Sales	Cash	Misc.	Details	PAYMENTS Total	Cash	Purchases	Payroll	Drawings	Misc.	Details	Accountant use only	BALANCE
	Brought forward															
April 5	Cash Banked		600 00		600 00											600 00
" 6	D. Egg		700 00			700 00	Capital									1300 00
" 6	Echo Papers	14231						70 50		70 50						1229 50
" 8	Carter & Co.		102 23	102 23												1331 73
" 10	S. Sample		700 00			700 00	Capital									2031 73
" 21	Blank Limited	14232						470 00		470 00						1561 73
" 21	Cash	14233						50 00	50 00							1511 73
" 21	Playfair Ltd.	14234						327 50		352 50			(25 00)	Due		1184 23
" 29	Wages	14235						1579 52			1579 52					(395 29)
" 29	White Ltd.		1075 00	1175 00		(100 00)	Discount									679 71
" 30	D. Egg	5701						400 00				400 00				279 71
" 30	S. Sample	5701						250 00				250 00				29 71
" 30	Red Bros' Council							120 00		120 00						(90 29)
" 30	Chicks & Sold Ltd.		470 00	470 00												379 71
Carried forward or Month April			3647 23	1747 23	600 00	1300 00		3267 52	50 00	1013 00	1579 52	650 00	(25 00)			379 71

Accountant use only

© Caslac Ltd 1971 · 1990 Form 1971-2366 X Checked Analysed

Fig. 7.1 THE YBS BANK RECORD
(See notes on p106)

Notes to Figure 7.1

- The description column appears only on one side of the page and, as it may refer to either a receipt or a payment, the eye has to run right across the page to the far side where the running balance may be seen. This balance will, of course, increase when a receipt is recorded and decrease when a payment is recorded.
- Where cheques are paid away, the cheque number is recorded. This helps later with bank reconciliations (see Chapter 8).
- The two sides of an account have a limited amount of analysis work, but the provision of a 'details' column permits individual items that might need special attention when doing the final accounts to be pinpointed when required.
- The running balance gives an immediate check on the financial position relative to the bank.
- Cross-totalling keeps an effective check on the entries made in the analysis columns, and one total subtracted from the other should give the running balance in the end column.

THE YBS SALES RECORD

These pages are illustrated in Figure 7.2.

The sales record illustrates how quickly VAT builds up. Remember that the seller of goods charges VAT at the standard rate on most of the things sold, so that at the 17½ per cent rate on VAT, almost a fifth of the money received from the customer belongs to the VAT authorities. A small trader taking £2000 a week therefore has several hundred pounds of VAT funds, and in 13 weeks (most VAT is accounted for quarterly), it comes to about £5000. It is important to put away VAT regularly in a special deposit account to ensure funds are available to meet this obligation if your business is the type where output tax collected always exceeds deductible input tax.

APPRAISAL OF THE YBS SYSTEM

The main YBS system is in loose-leaf form and is capable of infinite expansion, so it is of use to businesses however large they become. More recently, a 'one-year system', with a limit of 20 pages, has been added to the range for the smaller businesses. If you are considering using YBS, you should be careful to buy the system that is most suitable to the size of your business. For example, the bank account record shown in Figure 7.1 has 323 lines, which must cover both receipts and payments. A person paying in takings every day would perhaps find it better to buy the larger loose-leaf system so that extra pages could be inserted if necessary. For smaller businesses 32 lines per month may well be adequate.

YBS

BUSINESS NAME: Egg. SAMPLE & Co.

SALES RECORD

PERIOD from 01.04.92 to 30.04.92   Page No. 1

INVOICE No.	DATE	CUSTOMER	GROSS	VAT	Does	Windows	Junction	Windows	Misc.	Details	RECEIVED DATE
		Brought forward									
–	April 1	Daily Takings	117 50	17 50	80 00			20 00			Cash
–	" 8	Daily Takings	285 00	85 00		200 00					Cash
001	" 8	Easton & Co.	108 23	15 23		87 00					April 8
002	" 8	A. Brooks	84 81	3 61	50 00			20 60			Cash
003	"	Daily Takings	282 00	48 00	50 00	65 00	40 00	85 00			Cash
003	" 10	G. Soap Ltd	441 90	65 90		376 00					April 29
004	" 10	White Ltd	705 00	105 00	600 00						April 29
005	" 12	White Ltd	470 00	70 00	200 00	150 00		50 00			April 29
006	" 15	Daily Takings	176 25	26 25	70 00	20 00	60 00				Cash
	" 15	G. James	28 50	3 50					80 00	Soap	
–	" 25	Daily Takings	817 58	82 58	100 00	110 00	250 00	15 00			Cash
007	" 30	Stickton & Slott Ltd	470 00	70 00		110 00	230 00	60 00			April 30
008	" 30	Knobs & Knockers Ltd	1251 58	186 58	800 00	265 00					
009	" 30	KS Dyke	564 00	84 00	200 00	240 00	40 00				
		Carried forward / Month April	5090 25	756 55	2100 00	1313 00	590 00	366 60	80 00		

OUR INVOICE ANALYSIS (Net)

Accountant use only

© Gestetner Ltd 1981–1990 Form 6H1–4/90X   Checked □ Analysed □

Fig. 7.2 THE YBS SALES RECORD
(See notes on p106)

Notes to Figure 7.2

● The activity under various headings for the particular business is found in the analysis columns.

● If applicable, VAT is recorded against every entry, at the standard rate. Some traders (using VAT retail schemes) might need to modify this procedure (if selling goods at more than one rate, for example).

● Some items are not ordinary sales – such as the sales of scrap or machinery surplus to requirements. These are separated out into a 'miscellaneous' column.

● When customers are invoiced for goods and pay later, the date of payment is recorded in the 'received' column. The blank spaces in this column indicate a debtor and these should be scanned to keep a check on late payers and to stop further orders until earlier invoices have been paid. Summation of unpaid items in these blank spaces does conveniently give 'aged debtor' control.

Full details of the system, sample sheets, an instruction book and a price list are available from the suppliers, Casdec Ltd, 22 Harraton Terrace, Birtley, Chester-le-Street, County Durham DH3 2QG (telephone 0191 410 5556).

One of the main strengths claimed for YBS is its facility to provide financial management control data.

CHECKLIST

■ The YBS system is a suitable book-keeping system for small and growing firms.

■ It is particularly suitable for a new enterprise, facing the problem of keeping day-to-day records for the first time.

■ The system has a profit and loss and balance sheet facility for those wishing to produce such figures monthly.

■ As both a one-year system and a long-lasting permanent system, using loose-leaf pages, are available, it is sensible to check whether or not the one-year system is adequate for your needs before embarking on it.

■ One of the main strengths claimed for YBS is its facility to provide financial management control data. This is assisted by the supply of monthly analysis sheets for recording current data for comparison with figures from the previous year. To assist this control facility, a number of optional extras are available. These include:
 – bank reconciliation
 – aged debtor control

- aged creditor control
- cash flow and profitability control
- payslips
- purchases ledger system
- sales ledger system.

Bank statements and bank reconciliation statements

The nature of a bank statement

Why it is necessary to reconcile the two sets of
   records

The procedure on receiving a bank statement

Checklist

THE NATURE OF A BANK STATEMENT

Every trader who runs a current account with a bank should ask for a bank statement once a month. As banks have millions of accounts, they spread the workload of sending out statements by using a cyclical billing method. Andrew Specimen's statement shown in Figure 8.1 is dated 12 June 19XX, and he will receive a statement on the 12th of each month. The computer prints hundreds of thousands of statements every day, which are posted to customers – a considerable volume of work in itself. The statement shows every transaction between the bank and the customer since the last statement (12 May 19XX). All the debit entries on the account are called 'withdrawals', and mean that the account holder has received back some of the money previously deposited, though it may not have been drawn in cash but paid to various people at his request. All the credit entries are called 'deposits', which means that the account holder has paid money into the account, so that the bank is a creditor for the amount deposited. In Figure 8.1 there is only one such entry, £51.60, which is a dividend transferred to the credit of Andrew Specimen's account by a bank giro transfer.

Study the statement in Figure 8.1 closely now, and the notes to it.

Notes to Figure 8.1
- Study the 'key', which shows the computer codes used to indicate what type of receipt or payment is involved. Thus DD is 'direct debit' and DV is 'dividend'.
- Note that there is only one deposit in the month, a dividend from Guardian Royal Exchange. Andrew did not pay in any cash or cheques in the month. Rather surprisingly perhaps in view of his small balance in hand (he finished up with an overdraft) he transferred £35 into a deposit account.
- Where a cheque was made out and passed through the clearing system, the cheque number is printed, but no other details except the amount paid to the payee named on the cheque.
- There are two direct debits (where authorized parties asked the bank to debit Andrew's account directly and pay them the sums due to them).
- Andrew drew £25 from the automated teller machine (ATM) at King's Cross.
- Note that withdrawals reduce the running balance and deposits increase it.
- There is a standing order, paid monthly probably, to Swandene Council.
- Note that the account is overdrawn on 12 June 19XX by £2.95. The bank would conceivably have been able to return that last cheque for £10 to the bank that presented it, there being insufficient funds in the account to honour it, but as Andrew appears to have some money in a deposit account it did honour it (the bank has a right of set-off against the money in the deposit account should Andrew in fact be in financial difficulties).

♻ NatWest

Confidential

200 PENTONVILLE ROAD
LONDON
N1 9HL

ACCOUNT CURRENT
ANDREW SPECIMEN ESQ

SHEET NUMBER 7

19XX	TELEPHONE 1234-6583	STATEMENT DATE 12 JUN 19XX		ACCOUNT NO. 99999999

DATE	DETAILS	WITHDRAWALS	DEPOSITS	BALANCE (£)
26MAY	BALANCE FROM SHEET NO. 6			93.40
27MAY	037079	3.40		90.00
2JUN	EAGLE STAR INS DD	4.55		85.45
3JUN	GUARDIAN RYL EX DV		51.60	137.05
	037080	10.00		127.05
4JUN	SWANDENE COUNCIL SO	30.00		97.05
	AA DD	21.00		76.05
5JUN	DEPOSIT A/C TR	35.00		41.05
8JUN	KINGS CROSS AC	25.00		16.05
	037081	9.00		7.05
10JUN	037082	10.00		2.95 ‰
12JUN	BALANCE TO SHEET NO. 8	National Westminster Bank Plc		2.95 ‰

Key	SO = Standing order	TR = Transfer	CP = Card purchase	Auto withdrawals	AC = Automated cash	Interest – see over
	EC = eurocheques	CC = Cash &/or cheques	PY = Payroll		DD = Direct debit	
	DV = Dividend		OD = Overdrawn			

Please advise change of address, telephone number or occupation on this form:

To the Manager, NatWest   **STAFF TRAINING**

My/Our account number is   **99999999**   Please note my new address/occupation will be from (Date) _____

Address _____ Post code _____
Telephone   New
number   occupation   Signature

60-77-12

MR A SPECIMEN
46 GRANVILLE GARDENS
SWANDENE
YORKSHIRE
SD4 9AG

☒

Fig. 8.1 ANDREW SPECIMEN'S BANK STATEMENT FOR 12 JUNE 19XX

Having studied the statement, consider the bank account of Andrew Specimen in his own account books. He is self-employed as a freelance artist and graphic designer. The account is as shown in Figure 8.2.

Cash Book (Bank Account only)

19XX	£	19XX	£
13 May Balance b/d	93.40	14 May T. Smith (037079)	3.40
12 June R. Lomax	185.75	17 May R. Lyon (037080)	10.00
		25 May M. Lark (037081)	9.00
		26 May P. Jones (037082)	10.00
		7 June P. Patel (037083)	17.50
		8 June Cash (King's Cross)	25.00
		10 June R. Shah (037084)	12.50
		12 June Balance c/d	191.75
	£279.15		£279.15
19XX	£		
13 June Balance b/d	191.75		

Fig. 8.2 THE CASH BOOK (BANK COLUMN ONLY) IN ANDREW SPECIMEN'S BOOKS

Notes

- You will notice that, according to his cash book, Andrew Specimen has £191.75 in the bank, whereas the bank says he is overdrawn by £2.95.
- Clearly this difference needs some explanation, and to do this, it is necessary to scrutinize both records carefully, as explained under the heading Why it is necessary to reconcile the two sets of records.

WHY IT IS NECESSARY TO RECONCILE THE TWO SETS OF RECORDS

When two organisations keep records about the same thing, it is always possible that one will be better informed than the other and, consequently, that the records will differ. For example, if a bank is authorized to pay standing orders at certain times in the month, and is also permitted by direct debit mandates to allow insurance companies, district councils and clubs and associations (such as the AA or RAC) to ask for money from time to time, it may well be better informed about these matters than the account holder. The first the account holder may know about a direct debit is when they receive the bank statement. So, Andrew Specimen may not know about the direct debits for Eagle Star Insurance and the AA. He does know that there is a standing order for the Swandene Council, but he doesn't know whether or not the bank has paid it until he receives the statement and sees it has been. Similarly, he doesn't know about the dividend of £51.60 received on 3 June, and he seems to have forgotten to enter the transfer of £35.00 to his deposit account, although he must have been to the bank to make the transfer.

Similarly, the bank is not aware of some of the things Andrew has done in the month. The cheques sent to P. Patel and R. Shah are still in the clearing system, and the bank has not recorded the deposit of £185.75 made by Andrew on 12 June – it hasn't had time to key in the entries to its branch computer network or transmit them to the bank's computer centre. This will happen overnight.

It is therefore necessary to reconcile the two sets of records because:

- the bank does not know everything the customer has done;
- the customer cannot be certain about what the bank has done until the statement arrives;
- there are time lags in the cheque presentation and clearing system, which mean that differences occur between the two sets of records;
- either side could make a mistake – there are sometimes stories in the press of a computer error leading to millions of pounds being credited to an ordinary householder's account, and there have been civil and criminal cases about such events.

What is the procedure for reconciling the two sets of records?

THE PROCEDURE ON RECEIVING A BANK STATEMENT

When you receive a bank statement, you must, for your own peace of mind, immediately undertake a bank reconciliation procedure to ensure that you, and the bank, have the same ideas about your account. The procedure is as follows.

- Go through the two sets of records and tick the items that appear on both – on the bank statement and in your own books.
- Examine the items that are unticked on the bank statement. These will all be things that the bank has done of which the customer may

be unaware. They must now be entered in the customer's bank records, either in the bank account or, if a special system is being used, in whatever cash book records are provided.

■ This will leave some items that the account holder has entered in the cash book records of which the bank is not yet aware. These are the items that must be taken into account by drawing up a 'bank reconciliation statement'. They are time-lag items, which will be covered as soon as the bank gets to hear about them.

Let's do this now for Andrew Specimen's records– Figures 8.1 and 8.2.

1 Ticking the items that appear on both sets of records

The bank statement where this has been done is shown in Figure 8.3. There are five items on the bank statement that have not been ticked – two direct debits, a dividend, a standing order and an error on Andrew's part because he seems to have forgotten to enter on his own records the transfer he made into his deposit account.

Andrew's cash book is shown in Figure 8.4, ticks again showing the items that appear in both sets of records.

₰ NatWest

Confidential

280 PENTONVILLE ROAD
LONDON
N1 9HL

ACCOUNT **CURRENT**
ANDREW SPECIMEN ESQ

SHEET NUMBER **7**

	TELEPHONE				ACCOUNT NO.
19XX	1234-6583		STATEMENT DATE **12 JUN 19XX**		**99999999**
DATE	DETAILS	WITHDRAWALS	DEPOSITS	BALANCE (£)

DATE	DETAILS		WITHDRAWALS	DEPOSITS	BALANCE (£)
26MAY	BALANCE FROM SHEET NO. **6**				93.40 ✓
27MAY		037079	3.40 ✓		90.00
2JUN	EAGLE STAR INS	DD	4.55		85.45
3JUN	GUARDIAN RYL EX	DV		51.60	137.05
		037080	10.00 ✓		127.05
4JUN	SWANDENE COUNCIL	SO	30.00		97.05
	AA	DD	21.00		76.05
5JUN	DEPOSIT A/C	TR	35.00		41.05
8JUN	KINGS CROSS	AC	25.00 ✓		16.05
		037081	9.00 ✓		7.05
10JUN		037082	10.00 ✓		2.95 ✓

Fig. 8.3 TICKING THE ITEMS ALREADY KNOWN TO BOTH PARTIES ON THE BANK STATEMENT

Notes

● These items would also be ticked in Andrew's books.
● Note that Andrew did not seem to know about the items for £4.55, £51.60, £30 and £21. He has also forgotten to enter the transfer for £35 in his own records.
● The first thing to do is to update Andrew's cash book to take account of these entries (see Figure 8.5).

Cash Book (Bank Account only)

19XX	£	19XX	£
13 May Balance b/d ✔	93.40	14 May T. Smith (037079)	3.40✔
12 June R. Lomax	185.75	17 May R. Lyon (037080)	10.00✔
		25 May M. Lark (037081)	9.00✔
		26 May P. Jones (037082)	10.00✔
		7 June P. Patel (037083)	17.50
		8 June Cash (King's Cross)	25.00✔
		10 June R. Shah (037084)	12.50
		12 June Balance c/d	191.75
	£279.15		£279.15
19XX	£		
13 June Balance b/d	191.75		

Fig. 8.4 TICKING THE ITEMS ALREADY KNOWN TO BOTH PARTIES IN ANDREW'S CASH BOOK

Notes

- You can see from this record that the bank does not know about the cheques sent to P. Patel and R. Shah. These have not reached the bank it via the clearing house mechanism or BACS (the Bankers' Automated Clearing Service).
- The bank also does not know about the deposit of £185.75 made on 12 June. This has been paid into Andrew's branch, but has not yet been keyed into the bank's computer system.
- Andrew's records must now be updated by adding the missing items revealed on the bank statement. This is done in Figure 8.5.

2 Updating the entries in the records of the business to take account of those things the bank has done, which Andrew has not done

To do this, start with the balance on Andrew's books of £191.75 and make the necessary entries. These are shown in Figure 8.5. First, note the following points.

- Items that appear as deposits (credits) on the bank statement appear on the left-hand side of Andrew's books as debits. This is because the two records are kept from different points of view. The bank regards the £51.60 deposited as a liability – it credits Andrew's account because Andrew is a creditor and the bank owes him the £51.60.
- Items that appear as withdrawals (debits) on the bank statement appear as credits in Andrew's bank account. So far as the bank is concerned Andrew is receiving back the use of his money, but so far

Cash Book (Bank Account only)

19XX	£	19XX	£
13 June Balance b/d	191.75	13 June Eagle Star Insurance	4.55
13 June Dividend received	51.60	13 June Swandene Council	30.00
		13 June AA (motor expenses)	21.00
		13 June Deposit A/c	35.00
		13 June Balance c/d	152.80
	£243.35		£243.35
19XX	£		
13 June Balance b/d	152.80		

Fig. 8.5 ANDREW SPECIMEN'S REVISED CASH BOOK

Notes
- The revised balance is £152.80. This does not agree with the balance of £2.95 (overdrawn) on the bank statement, but it is a little closer than before.
- The final agreement can be achieved only when the time-lag items sort themselves out. To test if this is so, a bank reconciliation statement is prepared, in which the two balances are reconciled. The word 'reconcile' means 'get them to agree'.

as Andrew is concerned he is giving the money in his bank account to the AA, the Eagle Star Insurance Co., and so on. Now study Figure 8.5 carefully.

■ Although the bank made these entries on various dates, Andrew cannot go back and make all these entries on those dates. It would make an awful mess of his accounting records if he tried to add these things at different places. Instead, Andrew makes the entries on the day he became aware of them, which is 13 June, the date the statement reached him.

3 Drawing up the Bank Reconciliation Statement

Having entered all the things the bank has done into Andrew Specimen's books, now the two records are as close to agreement as it is possible to make them, but they still don't agree. This is due to the time-lag items, where certain cheques and other information are still in the course of transmission to the bank. It is possible to check these by preparing a bank reconciliation statement. This starts with the new balance in Andrew Specimen's cash book and tries to explain why it is different from the bank's balance as given in the bank statement. Look at the bank reconciliation statement opposite, and read the notes below it.

Bank Reconciliation Statement as at 13 June 19XX

	£
Balance as per revised bank account (in Andrew Specimen's cash book)	152.80

Add:

Cheques drawn but not yet presented (because the bank thinks he still has this money)

P. Patel	17.50	
R. Shah	12.50	
		30.00
		182.80

Deduct:

Cheque paid in but not yet cleared (because the bank does not yet know he has this money)	185.75
Balance as per bank statement	£2.95o/d

Notes

- The two figures can be reconciled.
- Starting with the cash book balance, each of the time-lag items is considered. As the aim is arrive at the figure on the bank statement, ask the question, 'What does the bank think about this particular item?'
- In the case of the two cheques for Patel and Shah, the bank thinks he still has the money, so these are added back.
- In the case of the cheque Andrew paid in on 12 June, the bank does not know this money has been paid in – it hasn't been put through the computer yet. This must then be deducted to find what the bank thinks his balance is.
- The result is that the bank thinks he is overdrawn by £2.95. This is the balance on the bank statement. As the same figure has been arrived at it can be concluded that Andrew's and the bank's books are correct, and when the time-lag items sort themselves out, both books will read the same.

■ *What actually happens to bank reconciliation statements?*

The answer is that they are filed away in a file marked 'bank reconciliation statements' and kept as proof that you have checked on your bank account and on the bank's work and found both to be satisfactory. Write or type a fair copy and file it away.

■ *What to do if you cannot reconcile the two sets of records*

The most likely reason for this is that you have not made the calculations properly or have made a slip in your own records. Check them carefully. Find out what the difference is, and see if you can remember an item for that amount.

It is much less likely that the bank has made an error, but if you do discover one, draw it to the bank's attention at once. In the United Kingdom, dishonest bank staff are, fortunately, very rare – but there are a few cases every year. By drawing attention to a disparity on your statement you may reveal to the bank that it has a problem.

> *Never use money put into your account in error*

Never use money put into your account in error. It has been held in the courts that a person who does so deliberately is a thief as a simple bank reconciliation procedure should have told them that the money had been credited to the account in error. You want bankers to deal honestly with you, and so you must be equally honest in your dealings with them.

EXERCISE ON DRAWING UP A BANK RECONCILIATION STATEMENT

....

M. Lever's bank statement reads as follows for the month of March 199X:

Date	Details	Dr.	Cr.	Balance
		£	£	£
1/3/199X	Balance C/fwd			427.40
3/3/199X	Cheque (019260)	31.30		396.10
5/3/199X	Sundries		460.00	856.10
12/3/199X	Cheque (019263)	489.50		366.60
14/3/199X	Sundries		600.00	966.60
14/3/199X	Cheque (019262)	28.86		937.74
15/3/199X	Sundries		750.00	1687.74
19/3/199X	Sundries		650.00	2337.74
26/3/199X	Cheque (019264)	846.24		1491.50
31/3/199X	Charges	22.50		1469.00
31/3/199X	Bank of England (transfer)		83.80	1552.80

On 31 March, his cash book (bank columns only) read:

M. Lever's Cash Book (bank columns only)

199X		£	199X	£
1 March Balance	b/d	427.40	3 March R. Lamb (019260)	31.30
5 March Cash	c	460.00	7 March M. Peters (019261)	24.90
14 March Cash	c	600.00	8 March B. Green (019262)	28.86
15 March Cash	c	750.00	10 March K. Ahmed (019263)	489.50
19 March Cash	c	650.00	21 March R. Onobanjo (019264)	846.24
30 March Cash	c	550.00	31 March Wages	340.62
			31 March Balance c/d	£1675.98
		£3437.40		£3437.40

199X		£
1 April Balance	b/d	1675.98

You are asked to update M. Lever's cash book by entering any items not already entered and then to draw up a bank reconciliation statement to reconcile the revised cash book figure with the bank statement balance of £1552.80.

Answer

Revised cash book balance £1737.28. The two accounts can then be reconciled.

CHECKLIST

- It is most unlikely that your own cash book (bank) records will agree with your bank statement because:
  - the bank does things, like paying standing orders and direct debits and collecting bank giro credit transfers, without telling you until some time later when you receive a statement;
  - you write out cheques and don't tell the bank;
  - there are time-lags in the clearing process;
  - both sides can make mistakes.

- When you receive a bank statement, compare it with your own records and tick all items that appear on both records.

- Now update your cash book by putting into the bank entries any items listed on the statement that do not appear in your own records, as if they happened on the day you received the statement.

- When your records are up to date, there may still be entries on your books that are not in the bank's records. You can't go to the bank and update its records, you will have to wait for the time-lags to clear the bank's records in due course. What you can do is draw up a bank reconciliation statement. If it tallies, write out a neat copy and file it away.

- If it doesn't tally, search all your records for an error and, if necessary, approach the bank about the difficulty.

- It is an offence to use money put into your account in error.

Simultaneous records (two-in-one and three-in-one systems)

What is a simultaneous records system?

How a simultaneous records system fits into double
  entry book-keeping

The Safeguard sales ledger system

Simultaneous records and medium-sized enterprises

Checklist

WHAT IS A SIMULTANEOUS RECORDS SYSTEM?

Any simultaneous records system depends on the preparation of several records at once, by writing on a top record that is immediately reproduced, either by creating a carbon copy or an NCR copy (NCR stands for no carbon required) on to other records below. As the pressure exerted by an ordinary ballpoint pen (other pens are not so good for this type of system) is only enough to make two decent copies, it means that a system involving three documents is best. Hence the name 'three-in-one systems', which is often used to describe these systems. In some systems, only two records need to be processed simultaneously. Another name is 'one-write' systems.

There are a number of famous names in this field. Two of the leaders are Safeguard Business Systems and Kalamazoo. In this chapter, Safeguard Business Systems is featured, but a similar system from Kalamazoo is featured in Chapter 10, dealing with wages.

To return to the aspects of book-keeping that lend themselves to this treatment, the following sections describe some of them. (Note that in all the Safeguard systems, the word 'journal' has its normal meaning in book-keeping of 'day book' or 'daily record'. The journal is in sheet form and will be archived in stiff cardboard binders.

■ Sales

With a sales system, you need to record all the invoices made out to customers, including the VAT output tax. The customers, of course, become debtors for the amounts owed. You also need to record any credit notes issued for returns, and any payments received. The Safeguard sales system is illustrated in this chapter and so need not be discussed any further here. The various components are the following.

- Debtor's statement
  on top of
  debtor's ledger card
  on top of
  sales journal and output VAT record;

  or:

- debtor's statement
  on top of
  debtor's ledger card
  on top of
  sales returns book;

- debtor's statement
  on top of
  debtor's ledger card
  on top of
  cash received journal.

- As a subsystem, you can have a paying-in slip that will allow you to give a list of cheques and cash amounts paid in.
- An aged accounts journal can be prepared as the new statements are headed up ready for the next monthly period. This can be used for credit control.

■ Purchases

With a purchases system, you need to record the invoices received from suppliers, the VAT on them (input tax), any credit notes received against returns or allowances subsequently made and your payments to the supplier when made. As the payment needs to be covered by a document (the remittance advice note), this is prepared at the same time.

- Remittance advice note
  on top of
  creditor's ledger card
  on top of
  purchases journal and input VAT record;

- remittance advice note
  on top of
  creditor's ledger card
  on top of
  purchases returns book;

- cheque
  on top of
  remittance advice note
  on top of
  creditor's ledger card
  on top of
  payments cash book.

■ Wages

With a wages system, you need to record the pay of each individual as part of a total payroll, but also as an individual tax record that can be discussed with the employee without the other people's pay being seen. You also need a payslip to go in the wage packet or to be given to the individual if all payments are made to the employees' bank accounts by bank giro credit transfers.

A further subsystem is required at the end of the year to notify the employee, the Contributions Agency and the Inland Revenue of the total amounts earned, deductions and so on in the year. The official forms are the P14, P35 and P60.

- Payslip
  on top of
  individual tax record
  on top of
  payroll record;

- P14 (end of year return)
  on top of
  P60 (certificate of pay, tax and NIC)
  on top of
  P35 (end of year payroll summary).

■ Petty cash

With the petty cash system, you can keep control of all petty cash items because an entry can be made by means of special carbon-backed petty cash vouchers, supplied in sets to give a pack of 'shingled' vouchers. The term 'shingled' means that each voucher overlaps the one below it, the vital details being written on the top edge of the voucher, which is carbon-backed, and this reproduces itself on the petty cash journal below it. Thus, the document (a petty cash voucher) must be made out for every expense entered and, apart from the actual details written on the edge, there is ample space to describe the expenditure incurred and to clip on any bill, or receipt. The person being reimbursed for the expenditure then signs the slip and draws the money.

- Petty cash voucher
  on top of
  petty cash journal

HOW A SIMULTANEOUS RECORDS SYSTEM FITS INTO
DOUBLE ENTRY BOOK-KEEPING

Be clear in your mind that when you decide to cover a particular area of your book-keeping by a simultaneous records system, what you are doing is removing that area from ordinary double entry book-keeping and adopting a short-cut that will both save you work and prevent possible errors by making several entries at the same time. It involves a certain amount of preparation as you move over to the new system. You need to purchase the posting boards, posting trays, forms and binders required to start up, but, once installed, it will function for as long as you are in business. It is therefore well worth while to start the system, learn how to use it and liaise closely with the distributor in the teething-problem period.

In a book of this size, I can feature only one of the systems, but there are several that may be helpful to you. The address of Safeguard Business Systems (Europe) Ltd is Duchy Road, Crewe, Cheshire CW1 6ND (telephone 01270 500921).

THE SAFEGUARD SALES LEDGER SYSTEM

The system consists of six documents, three of which are used in the main system and the others in subsidiary parts. The three main documents are:

- the monthly statement
  placed on top of
- the debtor's ledger card (a loose-leaf card that is virtually a page in the debtor's ledger, and thus forms the debtor's account)
  placed on top of
- the sales journal page, which is also the VAT output tax register.

■ Starting up the system

Before you can start up the system, you must head up a ledger card for each customer whose account is active and from whom you expect to receive orders month by month. The details required are:

Name.......................................Contact..
Address.....................................Telephone No...
....Balance forward £ ....

You now need to head up a monthly statement, simply with the name and address of the customer. These two documents – the statement and the ledger card – are kept together in the indexed posting tray, in alphabetical order. Having done this with all the active ledger accounts, you have a posting tray with numerous ledger cards, each with its statement ready to record any events that may occur in the coming month.

You now need to take the posting board, with its spring clip. Open the clip and insert a sales journal sheet in it. Lower the spring clip and your day book record is now ready for the first entry you wish to make.

■ Posting sales invoices

- Total the batch of invoices to be posted. Using an add-listing calculator, draw up a list of the invoices' gross values, VAT and 'net of VAT' values and total them.
- Select the statement and ledger card to be posted and align the first blank line on the statement with the first blank line on the ledger – use the 'previous balance' column to make the alignment easier. Hold them together and place them under the spring clip – align the first blank line of the statement directly opposite the number on the clip that denotes the first blank line on the journal. The first blank lines on all three records are now aligned together.
- First, enter the 'previous balance' and 'account name'. Then enter on the statement (using firm pressure) the 'date' (day and month is sufficient), 'invoice number' and, in the two debit columns, enter the 'amount of goods/services' and the 'VAT' to be charged. The account has now been debited with the value of the invoice and the statement has been updated to show the invoice that has been entered.
- Add the total invoice amount (goods/services and VAT) to the previous balance to obtain the new balance – enter this total in the balance column on the statement.
- On the right-hand side of the journal are some analysis columns that can collect details of the activity for any particular product or area. Analyse the charge for goods/services into these columns as required.
- Return the statement and ledger to the posting tray. Repeat this procedure for each invoice.
- If an item is exempt from VAT or zero-rated, the word 'exempt' or 'zero' should be written in the VAT column to prove the VAT has not just been overlooked.

■ Posting credit notes

These may be posted at any time of the month, but if you wish, they can be held until month-end and posted in one straight run.

In the reference column, enter 'CN' and the number – the amount of the credit should be apportioned between goods/services and VAT in the ratio in which it was originally charged and these amounts entered in the appropriate 'credit' columns on the ledger card. If analysis columns are being used on the right of the journal, the amount of the credit should be entered in brackets in the appropriate column. Entering in brackets implies that the activity in that class of goods must be reduced by the amount of the figure in brackets.

Note

The total of the VAT credit column must be deducted from the VAT debit column. This will ensure you remit only the VAT you are liable to pay.

■ Proving the journal

It is best to check the work done at the end of each set of postings, and at the foot of each journal page (which means after 30 entries have been made). The columns should be totalled and the totals should equal the totals obtained on the adding-listing obtained before the posting run began. This proves the entries have been correctly made. There is a check section at the bottom of the page to record the totals arrived at, and to confirm that all entries have been made correctly.

■ Conclusion

This is perhaps sufficient to show how helpful the Safeguard systems are. Similar entries will be made to record cash or cheques received and, when the end of the month arrives, the statements are ready to be sent out, informing the customer of all the changes in the account during the month – purchases made, returns and payments received and the balance outstanding. This avoids telephone calls to query how the figures were arrived at – and excuses for the debtor to delay payment. The full facts are disclosed and the customer is invited to pay the balance due.

The system is illustrated in Figure 9.1 and the full range of Safeguard systems is shown in Figure 9.2.

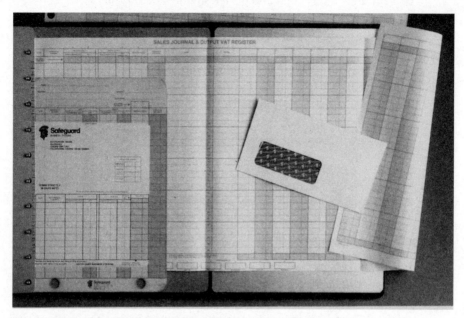

Fig. 9.1 **THE SAFEGUARD SALES LEDGER THREE-IN-ONE SYSTEM**

SELECT-A-SYSTEM CHART

Safeguard
BUSINESS SYSTEMS
Centurion House,
Gateway, Crewe,
Cheshire, CW1 1XJ

DID YOU KNOW

that most businesses can use two or even three Safeguard Systems. Locate the business classification below then read across for the Safetuard systems applicable

	Cheque-writing	Sales Ledger	Purchase Ledger	Wages/Salaries	Travel Agency Accounting	Insurance Brokers Accounting	Job Costing	Tab Ledger	Account Balance Verification	Solicitors Accounting	Time-Cost System	Cash Receipting	Goods Received	Petty cash
Accountants	•	•	•	•					•			•		•
Associations	•	•	•	•									•	•
Auctioneers & Estate Agents	•		•	•									•	•
Builders, Contractors & Allied Trades	•	•	•	•		•							•	•
Computer Service Bureaux	•	•	•	•										•
Employment & Secretarial Agencies	•	•	•	•										•
Farmers & Nurserymen	•	•	•	•										•
Franchises	•	•	•	•										•
Garages & Motor Car Dealers	•	•	•	•									•	•
Hotels & Motels	•	•	•	•			•							•
Insurance Brokers	•	•	•	•	•							•		•
Manufacturers	•	•	•	•			•						•	•
Property Management	•	•	•	•						•		•		•
Religious & Educational	•	•	•	•			•					•		•
Restaurants & Entertainment	•	•	•	•				•						•
Retailers	•		•	•								•	•	•
Service Industries	•	•	•	•			•					•	•	•
Solicitors	•	•	•	•						•	•	•		•
Travel Agents	•	•	•	•	•							•		•
Wholesalers	•	•	•	•								•	•	•

In today's economy, the efficiency in office accounting routines is more important than ever. Safeguard's One-Write systems – the WORK-SAVERS – are designed to replace antiquated methods with modern, accurate, labour-saving routines. Safeguard's systems provide maximum accounting control and ensure up-to-the minute financial information for the business managers of today and provides a perfect audit trail for your accountant.

Fig. 9.2 A USEFUL RANGE OF SIMULTANEOUS RECORDS SYSTEMS

SIMULTANEOUS RECORDS AND MEDIUM-SIZED ENTERPRISES

It will be clear from what has been said already that the drive to use simultaneous records systems comes from the need in a growing company for management to delegate some aspects of the accounts to reliable personnel. Each system – for example, the purchases ledger or the sales ledger – is a collection of transactions that can easily be separated off and handed to an individual, who assumes responsibility for the success of that particular set of records. The system is usually self-balancing, in that the total figures each month are fitted into the general accounting system and so the employee can be seen to have done a good job. Any difficulties that arise can be sorted out and explained to the book-keeper concerned, who soon acquires confidence.

The chart in Figure 9.2 lists the wide variety of activities that can be dealt with in this way.

CHECKLIST

- A simultaneous records system is one where two or three sets of records are prepared with a single writing.

- To do this, carbon paper or NCR paper is required, and a ballpoint pen is the most efficient writing instrument as it enables firm pressure to be exerted while entries are being made.

- These systems are sometimes called 'three-in-one' or 'one-write' systems.

- If you decide to adopt such a system, what you are really doing is removing one area of accounting (say, the debtors' ledger or the creditors' ledger) from your ordinary double entry system and using a simplified, more easily controlled system. These systems are therefore most suitable for firms that have grown enough to employ a specialist book-keeper or book-keepers. They are not so appropriate for 'embryo' firms just starting up.

- Famous names in this area are Safeguard Systems Ltd and Kalamazoo Security Print PLC. Both offer a range of systems (for example, Kalamazoo's wages system is illustrated in Chapter 10).

- These systems are most appropriate where a business has grown to the point where management cannot exercise personal control over all the record-keeping activities and so needs to delegate the more routine matters to reliable members of staff.

Simultaneous records: wages systems

EMPLOYING STAFF

If every new business employed one more person, it would make a considerable dent in the unemployment figures, and those who believe in encouraging enterprise believe that, eventually, all small businesses grow enough to take

> *Once you decide to employ someone, you come immediately under the general umbrella of a whole field of law called 'employment law'.*

on one or two people, even if in the first few years they are often only part-timers. This is an accountancy book – not a book describing how to start up a new business – but it is helpful to give the subject of employing staff a general airing, if only for this reason.

Once you decide to employ someone, you come immediately under the general umbrella of a whole field of law called 'employment law'. You are at once 'an employer' and, as such, have a number of general duties to perform, such as providing a safe system of work, keeping adequate wages records and deducting tax and National Insurance contributions and paying them over to the Inland Revenue on a monthly basis. You also have to assume certain 'social security' duties – for example, to pay your employees' Statutory Sick Pay (SSP) and Statutory Maternity Pay (SMP) if they qualify for these benefits. You don't pay it out of your own pocket, hopefully, because the idea is that as you have certain government moneys in your possession (the tax and National Insurance contributions you have deducted from your employees' pay), you can use this money to pay SSP and SMP, and send in only the balance.

The Inland Revenue publishes a leaflet called *Thinking of Taking Someone On?* (IR53), and it tells you a great many things you need to know about the PAYE (pay as you earn) system of income tax, the tables you need from the Inland Revenue (Tables A and B) and so on. A telephone call to your local Inland Revenue number will procure the leaflet and other explanatory material, for example about SSP and SMP. The leaflet lists five things you must do:

- tell the tax office when an employee starts to work for you;
- work out the tax and NIC due each pay day;
- pay this over to the Accounts Office each month (the Accounts Office is part of the Inland Revenue and collects or receives your payments);
- tell the tax office when an employee leaves.

- tell the tax office at the end of each tax year how much each employee has earned and how much tax and NIC you have deducted (the tax year runs from 6 April one year to 5 April the next, and your PAYE instructions include an income tax calendar showing how the tax year is divided into tax weeks and months).

Although this all sounds fairly daunting, it soon becomes routine, and even the SSP and SMP duties are fairly easy to follow, especially if you are using one of the simple schemes outlined in this chapter.

THE SIMPLEST WAGES SYSTEM

Although the Simplex wages book is not featured in this chapter, it is mentioned here because it is a very simple system for a firm that employs only a very small number of people. It has space for 26 employees. Those who have decided to use the Simplex D account book or elect to use the Simplex VAT book – see Chapter 11 – may feel that the Simplex wages book is adequate for their records. It is obtainable from George Vyner Ltd, PO Box 1, Holmfirth, Huddersfield HD7 2RP. Phone them on 01484 685221 to ask the current price, and send payment with your order.

SIMULTANEOUS RECORDS SYSTEMS

As explained in Chapter 9, a simultaneous records system is one where a number of records are prepared simultaneously, one on top of the other. There are two parts of the wages system that can be prepared by simultaneous methods.

- Payslip
- on top of
- individual pay record
- on top of
- payroll record.

- P14 (end-of-year return)
- on top of
- P60 (certificate of pay, tax and NIC)
- on top of
- P35 (end-of-year payroll summary).

Only the first of these sets of records is described in this chapter. If you decide to adopt a simultaneous records system, your supplier will show you the forms and procedure for the end-of-year summary.

The two chief names in this field today, as pointed out in Chapter 9, are Safeguard Systems and Kalamazoo. The illustrations in Figures 10.1 and 10.2 are provided by Kalamazoo, and full details are available from Kalamazoo Security Print PLC, Northfield, Birmingham B31 2RW (telephone 0121-411 2345).

THE KALAMAZOO WAGES SYSTEM

About three million people in the United Kingdom alone are paid each week or month via the Kalamazoo system. The essential feature of the system is that it provides an individual pay record for each employee distinct from everyone else's records and not part of a general payroll. This makes it possible to take out the individual's record from the locked file in which they are kept, for personal discussions with the employee about pay, deductions, discrepancies and so on without the employee seeing anyone else's pay details. The wages record shows either 10 or 15 weeks' records, and a year's records are kept in the file so that any difficulty can be cleared up for the financial year under discussion. Transfer binders are available for archiving past records.

Besides the individual pay record, the system provides a payroll sheet showing the total payroll in any given week/month, and a payslip for the pay envelope. If an employee is paid in cash, the money will be provided in the same envelope, but if payment is direct into a bank account by bank giro credit, the employee receives the payslip only, as a record of the payment transferred.

The system is best described by looking at the illustrations in Figure 10.1, which shows the Kalamazoo copywriter – a solid plastic writing surface with a set of studs on which documents can be laid, with the perforations on the documents engaging the studs firmly and retained by a spring-loaded cover. First, a layer of 10 (or 15) blank pay advice notes is positioned on the copywriter. A payroll sheet is then placed over them and, as they are coated with NCR (no carbon required) material, anything written on one will appear on the other. As each employee's pay is dealt with, the individual pay record for that employee is positioned over the top of the other two documents and positioned so that the current weekly column covers the next available column on the payroll sheet, and therefore, the next available payroll slip on the set of pay advice notes. Figure 10.1 shows the way in which these documents are used. A pay advice note is shown in Figure 10.2.

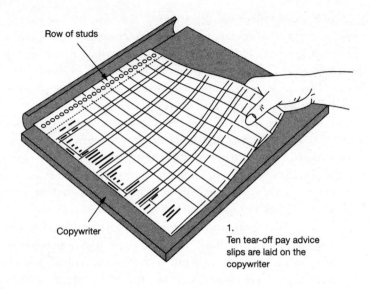

Row of studs

Copywriter

1.
Ten tear-off pay advice slips are laid on the copywriter

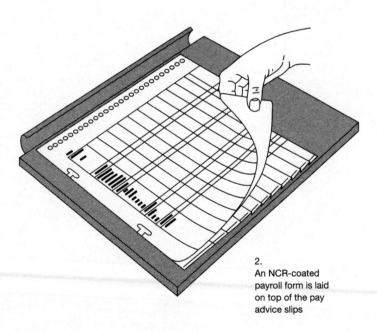

2.
An NCR-coated payroll form is laid on top of the pay advice slips

Fig. 10.1 THE KALAMAZOO WAGES SYSTEM
(Reproduced by courtesy of Kalamazoo Security Print PLC)

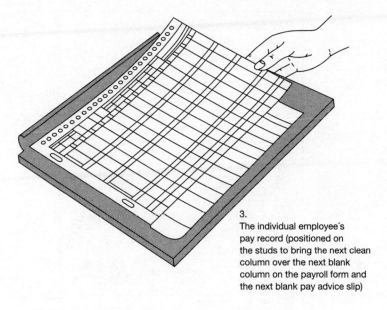

3.
The individual employee's pay record (positioned on the studs to bring the next clean column over the next blank column on the payroll form and the next blank pay advice slip)

4.
The torn-off pay advice slips folded once to go into the pay packets. If paid in cash, the money is inserted in the same envelope

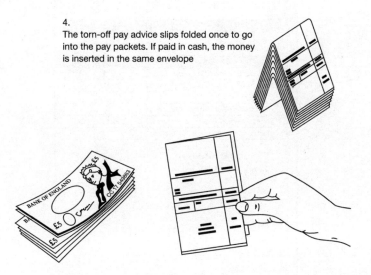

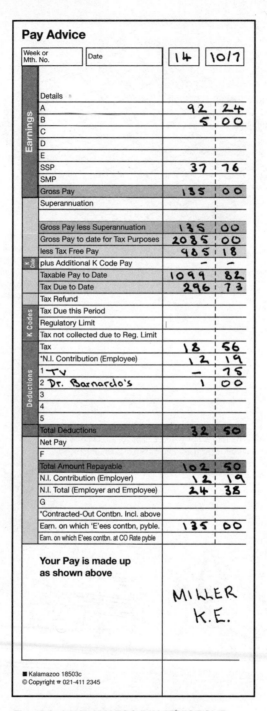

Pay Advice

Week or Mth. No.	Date	14	10/7

	Details		
Earnings	A	92	24
	B	5	00
	C		
	D		
	E		
	SSP	37	76
	SMP		
	Gross Pay	135	00
	Superannuation		
	Gross Pay less Superannuation	135	00
	Gross Pay to date for Tax Purposes	2085	00
	less Tax Free Pay	985	18
K Code	plus Additional K Code Pay	—	—
	Taxable Pay to Date	1099	82
	Tax Due to Date	296	73
	Tax Refund		
K Codes	Tax Due this Period		
	Regulatory Limit		
	Tax not collected due to Reg. Limit		
	Tax	18	56
	*N.I. Contribution (Employee)	12	19
Deductions	1 TV	—	75
	2 Dr. Barnardo's	1	00
	3		
	4		
	5		
	Total Deductions	32	50
	Net Pay		
	F		
	Total Amount Repayable	102	50
	N.I. Contribution (Employer)	12	19
	N.I. Total (Employer and Employee)	24	38
	G		
	*Contracted-Out Contbn. Incl. above		
	Earn. on which 'E'ees contbn. pyble.	135	00
	Earn. on which E'ees contbn. at CO Rate pyble		

**Your Pay is made up
as shown above**

MILLER
K.E.

■ Kalamazoo 18503c
© Copyright ☎ 021-411 2345

Fig. 10.2 A KALAMAZOO PAY ADVICE SLIP
(Reproduced by courtesy of Kalamazoo Security Print PLC)

Notes to Figure 10.2

- The week or month number is shown and the date it commences.
- There are seven lines for types of earnings, such as basic pay, overtime, commission and so on. One of these is for SSP and another for SMP. The total of these gives the gross pay.
- Superannuation is then deducted, because it is not taxable. In this case, the employee is not part of any superannuation scheme.
- The gross pay for tax purposes is then used to find the tax payable, using the tax tables provided by the Inland Revenue (Tables A and B). K codes are used to tax employees who receive non-cash rewards (such as use of a car, cheap petrol and so on). The Inland Revenue PAYE pack includes full details should you offer employees 'perks' of this kind.
- The deductions are then listed, which gives the net pay.
- There is then one line for any addition to net pay – such as refunds of tax overpaid or expenses incurred. This gives the total amount payable.
- The employer also needs to know the total cost of National Insurance – in this case the employer had to pay £12.19, making £24.38 in all.

STATUTORY SICK PAY (SSP) AND STATUTORY MATERNITY PAY (SMP)

SSP and SMP are methods of paying through the ordinary pay system what are, in effect, two types of social security payment. This is administratively convenient for the government, but rather inconvenient for the employer as it places an obligation on employers to keep records of both schemes (to ensure that the sums reclaimed from the Inland Revenue by deduction from PAYE tax and NIC contributions are correct).

> *SSP and SMP are methods of paying through the ordinary pay system what are, in effect, two types of social security payment.*

The arrangements for SSP are that employees who are sick reach a 'PIW situation' on the fourth day of absence. A PIW is a 'period of incapacity for work'. Employees provide self-certificates of absence and an absence record must be kept by the employer, which may be subject to periodic checks by DSS officers. The detailed arrangements are too involved for a book of this nature, but, briefly, the absence record will reveal the days of sickness and consequently the PIWs and from this, the number of days' SSP payable. The rate will be worked out as a daily rate based on the average earnings, and the amount due will then be added to the employees' pay.

The maximum liability for SSP is 40 days a year – those absent for more than 40 days will be paid their sick pay directly by the DSS.

A useful record system for SSP is provided by Formecon Services Ltd, Gateway, Crewe CW1 1YN (telephone 01270 500800), which includes a full explanation of the system.

The arrangements for SMP are also fairly complicated. An employee who is pregnant is entitled to receive SMP for a total of 18 weeks, either before and after the EWC (expected week of confinement). Even if she ceases work earlier, she cannot receive it until the 11th week before the EWC, and if she works after that date she cannot receive it until she does stop work. Details of the rates payable, the method of reclaiming money paid and so on are available in the scheme literature.

A useful record system, with all the necessary forms for control of SMP procedures, is also produced by Formecon Services Ltd.

It used to be the case that the whole of the money paid to employees as SSP and SMP was recoverable by employers from the money already in their possession belonging to the Exchequer (the income tax and National Insurance contributions deducted from employees' pay each week or month). This position changed in the early 1990s. The government, increasingly pressed for money to meet high social security costs during a recession, required employers to pay this money themselves (but owners of small firms were only required to pay a contribution towards the total burden).

PAYING STAFF BY BANK GIRO

Making up pay packets can be a tedious and time-consuming activity, subject to risks as money is collected in bulk from the bank and distributed from pay office windows. More and more people today receive nothing in their pay envelopes but an advice note similar to that illustrated in Figure 10.2. The money is simply credited to their bank accounts and no actual cash is handled. This is the 'bank giro credit system' and it is strongly recommended as the best way to pay staff if you have a number of employees.

The payroll is done in the usual way, using the Kalamazoo system, but instead of going to the bank to draw the payroll in cash and notes, to put in the pay packets, the cashier takes to the bank a slip for each of the employees. Each slip states the amount due to that employee, which the bank then transfers through the clearing system to the employee's account. The cashier authorizes the bank to debit the firm's account with the total payroll. The firm has thus paid its staff in a very safe and economical way. No security guards are needed and there is no tedious counting of notes or handling of coins. Also, the funds are available in the employee's account to be used at once through the ordinary banking system, and the employee also has the benefit of greater security. If you want to use this system, approach your local bank manager.

EXERCISE ON THE KALAMAZOO WAGES SYSTEM

You are asked to complete pay advice slips for the four employees shown below whose pay details are as follows.

	R. Brown	P. Green	T. Jones	F. Brand
Week	1	7	9	16
Date	12/4/199X	24/5/199X	7/6/199X	26/7/199X
Earnings A	136.30	106.25	174.62	138.62
Earnings B	4.50	14.20	15.55	24.74
Gross pay	?	?	?	?
Superannuation	8.60	5.80	9.20	8.80
Gross pay for tax purposes	?	?	?	?
Gross pay to date for tax purposes (NB it is week 1)	?	750.25	1712.20	2360.50
Free pay	48.64	191.03	676.62	642.88
Taxable pay to date	?	?	?	?
Tax due to date	20.75	139.75	258.75	429.25
Tax paid up to last week	–	124.60	272.65	401.75
Tax	?	?	? (careful)	?
NI contribution	7.80	9.50	10.20	11.15
Charity	0.50	0.50	–	1.00
Total deductions	?	?	?	?
Net pay	?	?	?	?
Refunds (if any)	?	?	?	?
Total amount payable	?	?	?	?
NI contribution from employer	7.80	9.50	10.20	11.15
NI total	?	?	?	?

Answers

	R. Brown	P. Green	T. Jones	F. Brand
Total amount payable	103.15	89.50	184.67	114.91
NIC total	15.60	19.00	20.40	22.30

Note: To complete a full set of Kalamazoo pay records, you must have the correct stationery and invent imaginary names, code numbers and so on. Schools and colleges wishing to purchase such stationery should approach the Education Department of Kalamazoo Ltd, Mill Lane, Northfield, Birmingham B31 2RW. For the purpose of the exercise above, it is suggested that pay advice notes similar to Figure 10.2 should be ruled up.

CHECKLIST

- Employing staff places onerous responsibilities on the employer. There is no gradual path into the employer–employee situation – whoever decides to take on an employee must immediately carry the full administrative burden of record-keeping.

- The Inland Revenue will supply you with an explanatory booklet called *Thinking of Taking Someone On?*, which explains all about the PAYE (pay as you earn) system.

- Simultaneous records systems enable you to prepare at one writing:
  - a pay record for each individual you employ;
  - a payroll;
  - a pay slip for the employee's pay packet.

- When the end of the year arrives, a further three-in-one system is available for the various end-of-year records that have to be supplied, both to employees and the Inland Revenue authorities.

- SSP (Statutory Sick Pay) and SMP (Statutory Maternity Pay) both impose on employers further duties and obligations that affect the pay staff receive.

- As mentioned at the end of the previous chapter, these simultaneous records are most appropriate for the medium-sized enterprise where management wishes to delegate some of the routine record-keeping to reliable employees.

Value added tax

THE NATURE OF VALUE ADDED TAX

Value added tax was first introduced in 1973. It gets its name because it is charged as a percentage of the value added to a product by each and every producer who handles it. For example, a trader who sells an item for £100 must add to it tax called 'output tax'. At the time of writing, the tax is 17½ per cent, so that the sale price, including tax, is £100 + £17½ = £117.50 However, the trader probably did not actually add value to the article of £100, because they purchased the item or, perhaps, the raw material for the item, at a lesser price. Suppose it was purchased for £40 + VAT = £47. Therefore, the trader actually added value to the item of only £60 (it was purchased for £40 and sold for £100). To correct the tax payable, the trader is allowed to deduct the £7 paid to the supplier (the trader's 'input tax') from the £17.50 collected from the customer (the output tax).

Output tax – Input tax = Tax due to HM Customs and Excise
£17.50 – £7 = £10.50

The effect of this is that, although the trader collects the tax and pays it to Customs and Excise, they are not paying the tax at all. It is the customer who pays all the tax, £17½, of which £10.50 is given to the VAT authorities by the trader, and the other £7 is given to the supplier. The supplier then has to account for this £7 to the VAT authorities, unless, of course, some part of it was paid to another supplier further back in the chain of production.

You must account for VAT accurately and by law keep your records for six years.

This is a rather awkward way of collecting tax, and some people do say it is a very cumbersome business. The fact remains that traders must become used to the idea that VAT money is not theirs, that it is quite separate from their money and belongs to Customs and Excise. Not surprisingly, the VAT authorities are very aggrieved if VAT is not paid promptly or if the accounting records are inadequate. You must account for VAT accurately and must by law keep your records for six years and make them available for the VAT inspector when required.

REGISTRATION FOR VAT

The arrangements for VAT registration are important. It is compulsory to register if your turnover has exceeded £50 000 in the past 12 months or if you feel that the likely turnover in the next 30 days will bring the cumulative total of the last 11 months over the £50 000 threshold figure for the 12-month period. A total of £50 000 per annum is only £961 a week, and many traders will exceed this level of trading and be caught by the registration procedure. The danger is that you may find you have become liable for tax that you have not in fact collected. It is therefore safer to register for VAT voluntarily before it becomes compulsory and thus enter the VAT system. It also means that the trader can claim back input tax added to all the things purchased for the business – both stock for resale and capital items. An unregistered trader cannot reclaim input tax, but is treated like a consumer – in other words the VAT falls on the trader. The only way the trader can recover the VAT paid is by raising the profit margins on goods sold, which puts them in a less competitive position than other traders.

To register, you complete form VAT 1, obtainable from your local VAT office (see your telephone directory). Once you have registered for VAT, you must do the following.

- Record your inputs, the figures being taken from the invoices received from your suppliers.
- Record your outputs, as shown on your invoices to your customers. Of course the top copy of the invoice will have been sent to the customer, but the second copy becomes your VAT record, and must be kept for six years. Some traders do not make out invoices but sell for cash over the counter. All VATable goods must be marked up by 17½ per cent for VAT, and the figures for calculating output tax are obtained from the 'daily takings' record under one of the VAT special retail schemes. These are explained later.
- Complete your VAT return every three months (or every month if you are a trader dealing in zero-rated items). The VAT return is a statistical control form that enables you to calculate the VAT due, and the tax authorities to apply certain checks to ensure that your figures are roughly correct. More detailed inspection of cases where error is indicated will be made by the Inspection Department.
- Keep and maintain accurate records for these purposes.
- If the tax exceeds £1, pay it at the same time as the VAT return is sent in. Payment may be by cheque, bank giro, National Giro or BACS.
- If you trade with customers in other countries that are members of the European Union, you must observe some special rules about VAT. It used to be the case that sales to 'foreigners' were free of VAT, to help the export drive. Today the countries in the European Union have agreed not to call one another 'foreigners' — we are all part of one big 'Union'. Consequently, sales to nationals in these countries

are not 'exports', and purchases from them are not 'imports'. The special rules for trading with EU nationals are explained later in this chapter.

The reason the zero-rated trader completes forms monthly rather than quarterly is that they will usually be entitled to a refund of tax. As the trader does not collect output tax but does buy many items (for example, capital equipment) that are taxed, the trader's input tax usually exceeds output tax. The trader is therefore out of pocket and is allowed to claim the refund each month, instead of waiting for three months for a quarterly refund.

There is a leaflet available from your local VAT office (see under 'Customs and Excise' in your telephone directory) entitled *Should I be registered for VAT?* If you are thinking of registering for VAT, call them and ask for a copy. Their slogan is, 'If you have a problem, don't guess at the answer; *ask for advice.*' It saves a lot of trouble to start on the right track straight away.

METHODS OF ACCOUNTING FOR VAT

There are two methods of accounting for VAT – the 'normal' method and the 'VAT retail' method. Where a trader conducts business using invoices – in other words, where all customers are invoiced for the goods supplied (output invoices on which tax has been added to the sale price) – the invoices are called 'tax invoices' and form the basis of the VAT records. As all traders buy their supplies from manufacturers or wholesalers, they receive invoices from suppliers (input invoices on which VAT has been added to the purchase price). Therefore, both input and output records can be made from the invoices and this is called the 'normal' method of VAT.

Some traders do not make out invoices, but sell for cash over the counter or cash on delivery. Such people can still use the normal method for their input records, but are unable to record invoices for outputs because none is issued They have to find their output tax figure from the 'daily takings' figure when they cash up at the end of the day. Because of the wide variety of business activities, there were originally about 15 retail schemes, but the pattern of schemes proved too cumbersome and, in 1997–8, the number of schemes was reduced to three – called by names that indicate the principles on which they are based. These are the:

- 'point-of-sale scheme'
- 'apportionment schemes' – two types
- 'direct calculation schemes' – again, two types.

However, the very largest firms – with annual turnover in excess of £10 million – may not use these schemes, but must agree a 'bespoke scheme' – one tailored to meet the particular requirements of their business. This gives HM Customs and Exise a close relationship with such large firms, and it appraises their VAT arrangements on an individual basis.

VAT BY THE 'NORMAL' METHOD

The normal method for accounting for VAT is to use tax invoices. Input tax is calculated from the purchase invoices received from suppliers and output tax is calculated from the sales invoices sent to customers. Of course, you may receive credit notes from suppliers if you return goods to them, and you may also send credit notes to customers if they return goods to us. These returns would affect the liability for VAT, reducing the input tax you can claim or the output tax you must pay. They must therefore be taken into account when calculating VAT by the normal method.

The chief point about any VAT record is that it must be clear, easy to follow, systematic and easily archived for six years. Whatever bookkeeping records you keep, you must have a VAT system that meets these requirements. In my own experience, the simplest record is the Simplex VAT book, which consists of:

- a bound book, with 4 quarterly records – these can each be divided into 3 parts if you are a zero-rated trader and need 12 monthly records;
- adequate space for input invoices (purchases) and output invoices (sales);
- adequate space for returns, input credit notes (from suppliers) and output credit notes (sent to customers);
- adequate pages for recording 'daily takings' if you use a VAT retail scheme;
- each quarterly section has three VAT returns, each with room for a scheme calculation (which must be kept and be available for inspection by the VAT authorities);
- each quarterly section has a special page for recording goods acquired from suppliers in other member states of the European

Union – the trader receiving such goods needs to pay 'VAT on acquisition' at the UK rate and, consequently, these are called 'acquisition pages', and they enable you to keep a clear record of such purchases.

The advantage of a bound book for VAT records is that it is obvious to the VAT inspectors that you have a system that cannot be rewritten or otherwise tampered with (but, of course, a slip can be crossed out and corrected; the alteration being initialled).

Besides a VAT book, it is best to have a lever-arch file for storing the documents. The lever-arch file should be divided into two sections – inputs and outputs – and each invoice recorded is filed in the correct order (with the most recent invoice on top). The number allocated to it as it was entered in the VAT book is written prominently on the invoice, and if the item is small (for example, VAT vouchers issued by garages), two or three of them, each with its reference number, can be clipped to an A4 page.

At the end of the year, you thus have a VAT book with a file of input and output invoices, relating to the VAT records for that year and manifestly in apple-pie order.

Details of the normal method are as shown in Figures 11.1 and 11.2. To make the illustration clear, I have imagined a multi-rate VAT system, although, at times there are only two rates of tax. For example, for many years, there were only two rates – a standard rate and a zero rate. Today (1998), there are three rates – standard rate (17½ per cent), lower rate (5 per cent on fuel) and zero rate. For the purposes of the example, I have also imagined a higher rate of 30 per cent.

■ The input records

In Figure 11.1, there is an imaginary invoice from a supplier Smith & Jones with four items on the invoice – £50.00 for a standard-rated item on which VAT at 17½ per cent has been charged (£8.75); £40.00 at the 5 per cent rate (VAT = £2.00); £100.00 at the 30 per cent rate (VAT = £30.00) and £5.00 at the zero rate (VAT = £0.0). The total VAT is therefore £40.75 on this particular invoice. When this is repeated many times in the month with various suppliers' invoices, you get the total VAT payable for inputs of £4732.25.

However, you may also have to return some goods to suppliers, who will send a credit note for them. These are recorded in the input returns section and, at the end of the VAT period, which is either monthly or quarterly, these returns will be deducted from the VAT input tax recoverable, because you are no longer entitled to reclaim the input tax on the returned items. Spend some time studying Figure 11.1 now.

■ The output records

The output records are drawn up from the second copies of the invoices you sent to customers (the top copy is sent to the customer and the second copy is retained for your sales records). The books are kept in the same way as shown in Figure 11.2. Any goods returned by your customers give rise to credit notes that are sent to the customers, and the second copies become your record of sales returns. These have to be deducted from the total output records for the VAT period, as you are not liable for the output tax on these goods now they have been returned to you. Spend a little while studying Figure 11.2 now.

■ The VAT account

The quarterly results obtained from calculating VAT output tax and input tax by the normal method enable you to draw up a VAT account similar to that shown in Figure 11.3. Note that, for most traders, the output tax will always exceed the input tax because you always charge more for the goods you sell than you pay for them. Therefore, 17½ per cent of the sale prices (the output tax) must be more than 17½ per cent of the purchase prices (the input tax). Traders selling zero-rated items will collect no output tax and, although many of the inputs will also be zero-rated, some will not – for example, plant and machinery, office supplies and so on. Therefore, there will be input tax to reclaim from the VAT authorities.

Each quarter (or month for zero-rated traders) you receive a VAT return from Customs and Excise. All you have to do is copy the figures from the VAT account on to the VAT return and send it in with the money (in Figure 11.3, the amount is £3409.78). This is a very considerable sum for most small traders, and it is important to put away the VAT collected. Some books will tell you that having VAT money accumulating in this way helps the small business with its working capital, but it is no help to use this money in your business if you do not have it available on the due date to pay to Customs and Excise. The wisest course is to put it in a deposit account at the bank, so that you do make a little interest on it. Remember, it belongs to Customs and Excise, not you! You are only an unpaid tax collector.

INPUT ACCOUNT – PURCHASES OF GOODS, SERVICES AND CAPITAL ITEMS				Cost of Goods (excluding VAT)			Zero rated Goods	Input Services	Deductible VAT Input Tax	Exempt and non deductible (inc. VAT)
Invoice Date	Number	From whom purchased	Invoice Total	Standard Rate	Positive Rate 'A'	Positive Rate 'B'				
APL. 3	1	SMITH & JONES.	235 75	50 00	40 00	100 00	5 00		40 75	

"ETC... ETC... ETC..."

If this page is your last for the current VAT period, do not use the 'Totals carried forward' line but complete your records below:

	Invoice Total	Standard Rate	Positive Rate 'A'	Positive Rate 'B'	Zero rated Goods	Input Services	Deductible VAT Input Tax	Exempt and non deductible
Totals for accounting period	33784 25	13450 00	4017 50	5268 00	3407 50	2724 00	4732 25	185 00
Less totals from 'Input returns (Credits) account'	479 48	108 00	44 70	221 00	17 00	-	88 78	-
Net totals for accounting period	33304 77	13342 00	3972 80	5047 00	3390 50	2724 00	4643 47	185 00

Carry this total to the VAT Account ⟶

Fig. 11.1 THE SIMPLEX VAT INPUT RECORDS

OUTPUT ACCOUNT – INVOICED SALES, SERVICES, WRITTEN HP & CREDIT SALE TRANSACTIONS

Invoice Date	Invoice Number	To whom sold	Gross Invoice Total	Standard Rate	Positive Rate 'A'	Positive Rate 'B'	Liable at Zero Rate	Exempt	VAT Output Tax	Export and European Union Sales
				Value of Sale –excluding VAT						
Apl. 1	1	R.T. BROWN	297 00	80 00	60 00	100 00	10 00		47 00	

"ETC... ETC... ETC..."

If this page is your last for the current VAT period, do not use the 'Totals carried forward' line but complete your records below:

	Gross Invoice Total	Standard Rate	Positive Rate 'A'	Positive Rate 'B'	Liable at Zero Rate	Exempt	VAT Output Tax	Export and European Union Sales
Totals for accounting period	59093 07	26146 00	821 41	9765 00	4012 90		8161 96	2795 80
Less totals from 'Output returns (Credits) account'	757 31	325 00	48 00	160 00	11 40		108 71	104 20
Net totals for accounting period	58335 76	25821 00	773 41	9605 00	4001 50		8053 25	2691 60

Carry this total to the VAT Account →

Fig. 11.2 THE SIMPLEX VAT OUTPUT RECORDS

THE VAT RETAIL SCHEMES

In VAT law, the word 'retailer' has a special meaning. It means anyone who takes payment from customers without making out an invoice or a simplified VAT voucher, such as a petrol voucher issued by a garage. For such people, the money received is deemed to include VAT at an appropriate rate if the trader is VAT-registered. The VAT will have been added to the prices charged. As there are no invoices, the 'normal' method of VAT cannot be used, and the trader must use one of the five 'VAT retail schemes'. These are described in Notice No. 727. A word about each is desirable.

■ The point-of-sale scheme

To use this scheme, you must be able to separate your takings at the point of sale into their separate VAT categories. If all your sales are at standard rate or all your takings are at lower rate (fuel, say), then there is no problem and you *must* use this scheme. If you sell at more than one rate, a mix of standard rate, lower rate or zero rate, then you can only use this system if you can distinguish the sales at the point of sale. This usually means you have a sophisticated till that can collect together all the standard-rated sales, lower-rated sales and zero-rated sales. If you don't have that sort of till, but you can use separate tills for each class of goods, that is acceptable (but it is not very easy if a customer has a mixed basket of goods).

Once you know your daily gross takings, all you do is apply the VAT fraction for each VAT rate to the total for that rate. This is explained below under the heading VAT fractions. Full details of the point-of-sale scheme are given in Notice No. 727/3.

■ The apportionment schemes

There are two 'apportionment schemes', but Scheme 1 can only be used by traders with a tax exclusive turnover of less than £1 million. The name of the scheme comes from the following set of circumstances.

- The trader cannot distinguish sales easily at the point of sale and ends each trading period with a total of daily gross takings, but no real idea how much is standard-, lower- or zero-rated.
- As what you sell is what you buy, you can tell what proportion of your purchases is at standard rate, lower rate and so on. After all, you have the invoices, so it is no problem.

- Therefore, you can assume that your takings will be in the same proportions. If 60 per cent of your purchases are standard-rated, then 60 per cent of your takings will be standard-rated. If you apply the VAT fraction for standard-rated tax (at present 7/47) to 60 per cent of your takings, you will find your VAT output tax for standard-rated goods. The same applies to lower-rated goods.
- An alternative way of calculating the proportions is to work, not from the purchase prices but from the expected selling prices (ESPs). To find your ESPs, add the profit margin you hope to make on each class of goods to the purchase price and use the resulting figures to decide what proportion of your sales are at standard rate, lower rate and zero rate.

Full details of the apportionment schemes are given in Notice No. 727(4).

■ The 'direct calculation' schemes

There are two of these schemes, which work by calculating the expected selling prices of a trader's 'minority goods' (the ones they sell least of). When this total has been found, it can be subtracted from the total daily gross takings to find the figure for standard-rated takings, and the VAT output tax can be calculated from this figure.

For details of this scheme, see Notice No. 727(5).

■ Bespoke schemes

Finally, for the very largest retailers – those with sales in excess of £10 million – it is necessary for them to agree a bespoke scheme with the VAT authorities. A bespoke scheme is a 'made to measure' scheme that fits the retailer's business exactly. The relationship between such businesses and HM Customs is very close, and the contributions they make to VAT funds are enormous. A bespoke scheme ensures that all aspects of the business's very diverse activities are brought under control, and their correct contribution to government funds is assessed.

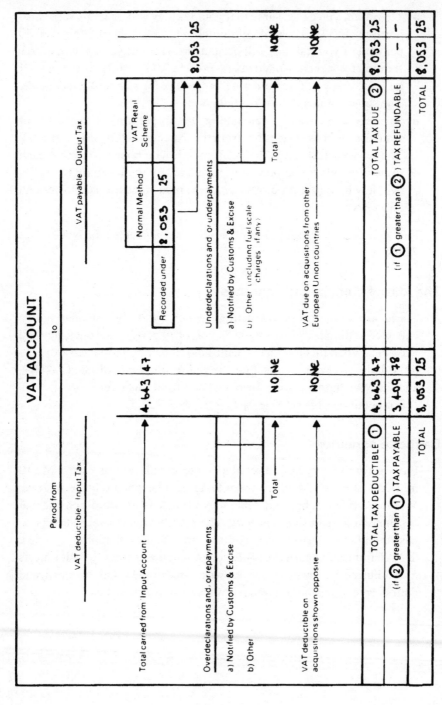

Fig. 11.3 A VAT ACCOUNT AT THE END OF A VAT PERIOD

RECONCILIATION OF DAILY TAKINGS — ONE MONTH

SUM TOTAL OF DAILY GROSS TAKINGS

Day	Date	Week No
Sun	APL 1	1
Mon	APR 2	1
Tues		
Thurs		
Fri		
Sat		

Daily Takings (1)	Tax not press al goods applied to personal use (2)	Amounts charged on goods supplied against credit cards (3)	Face value of trading checks coupons vouchers accepted (4)	Total Daily takings (add cols 2 3 and 4) (5)	Cash refunds for damaged or returned goods or redeemed 'raid stamps (6)	Output Taxable Services (except Schemes A and F) (7)	Takings against written HP or credit sale agreements (8)	Cash/Cheque payments to trading stamp companies for trading stamps (9)	Sub total (add cols 6 7 8 and 9) (10)	Daily Gross Takings for calculation of outputs (subtract col 10 from col 5) (11)
236.75	8.25	–	–	245.00	–	–	25.00	–	25.00	220.00
344.76	6.40	–	–	351.16	–	–	47.50	–	47.50	303.66
				"ETC…ETC…ETC…"						
		–	–	–	–	–	–	–	–	
		–	–	–	–	–	–	–	–	
		–	–	–	–	–	–	–	1377.50	15063.15
16284.40	156.25	–	–	16440.65	–	27.50	1350.00	–	1377.50	15063.15

Use this Figure in Schemes A C D D1 E E1 H and J

ZERORATED OR LOWEST RATED TAKINGS

Day	Week No 1 Date	Amount	Week No 2 Date	Amount	Week No 3 Date	Amount	Week No 4 Date	Amount	Week No 5 Date	Amount	Total
Sunday	APL 1	205.20	APL 8	210.50	APL 15	206.20	APL 22	251.30	APL 29	189.20	1062.40
Monday	APL 2	186.30	APL 9	175.30	APL 16	158.70	APL 23	262.50	APL 30	174.25	957.05
Tuesday											
Friday	APL 7	74.50	APL 14	98.72	APL 21	229.42	APL 28	285.60	–	–	618.24
Saturday										363.45	5336.46
Total		1145.15		1145.17		1333.04		1344.65	Total	363.45	5336.46

"ETC…ETC…ETC…"

Deduct 5336.46

9726.69

Use this Figure in Schemes B, B1, B2 and F

Where calculations are made on a quarterly basis, add together the three monthly figures

Fig. 11.4 FINDING THE TOTAL TAKINGS FOR A MONTH (OR QUARTER)

VAT FRACTIONS

One cause for concern when making VAT calculations is the nature of VAT fractions. In the VAT retail schemes, the calculations are based on selling price figures and the fraction of the selling price that is VAT is often a source of puzzlement. For example, the present standard rate of 17½ per cent makes for a VAT fraction of $\frac{7}{47}$ – a rather difficult fraction. You add 17½ per cent to the intended selling price to increase it for output tax, but this becomes $\frac{7}{47}$, not $\frac{17½}{100}$ of the final selling price. The explanation is quite simple.

Let us call the intended selling price 100. When you add 17½ per cent to this, you have 117½ per cent as the final price. Now the VAT element in this final price is:

$$\frac{17½}{117½} \quad \text{not} \quad \frac{17½}{100}$$

17½ of the 117½ parts represents output tax. When this awkward fraction is sorted out, you we have:

$$\frac{17½}{117½} = \frac{35}{2} \div \frac{235}{2} = \frac{35}{2} \times \frac{2}{235}$$

If you cancel the 2s, and the other numbers by 5 you have:

$$\frac{35}{2} \times \frac{2}{235}$$

$$= \frac{7}{1} \times \frac{1}{47}$$

$$= \frac{7}{47}$$

This is the VAT fraction, which you need to apply to any calculation where you are trying to work out what part of your daily takings is VAT output tax and must be paid over to HM Customs.

EXAMPLE

A. Smith has total sales, including VAT, of £8756.50 in July. How much of this is VAT output tax?

Output tax = $\frac{7}{47}$ × 8756.50

            = £1304.16 (using a calculator)

Check: If you take £1304.16 from £8756.50, you arrive at a true selling price (without tax) of £7452.34. If you find 17½ per cent of this, you will have the VAT figure to be added on. Here, 17½ per cent = £1304.16, which is the answer found with the calculation above – the VAT is £1304.16.

Every VAT rate has its own VAT fraction. Suppose the Chancellor were to announce a higher rate of VAT for luxury items, at 25 per cent. You would have to add 25 per cent to the intended selling price for output tax.

- *Question:* What is the VAT fraction when 25 per cent is added to the intended selling price to reach the final selling price?
- *Answer:* the VAT is $^{25}\!/_{125}$ of the final price.

$$^{25}\!/_{125} = \frac{1}{5} \text{ (cancelling by 25)}$$

The VAT fraction for a tax rate of 25 per cent is therefore ⅕.

EXAMPLE

A. Smith's higher-rate sales total £16 274.60 in the month. What is the VAT element in this? The answer is one-fifth.

⅕ × £16 274.60
= £3254.92

Check: Take £3254.92 from £16 274.60 to find the intended selling price – £16 274.60 – £3254.92 = £13 019.68. Taking 25 per cent, or ¼, of £13 019.68 = £3254.92, which is the figure found for VAT above. The VAT fraction of ⅕ of the final selling price is therefore correct.

VAT AND TRADE WITH EUROPEAN UNION COUNTRIES

Since the European Single Market came into existence in 1993, changes have been made to the VAT rules about trading with suppliers and customers in other member states. The important points are:

- selling to someone in another EU country is no longer called 'exporting' (because we are technically all one big country as far as the market is concerned) – instead, it is called 'supplying';
- similarly, when you buy from someone in another EU country, you are not 'importing' – such purchases are now called 'acquisitions'.

The invoices for such transactions are still exempt from VAT – that is, they do not have VAT added. So, the invoices you make out for supplies to an EU customer have no UK VAT charged and the invoices you receive about acquisitions from, say, Holland, do not have Dutch VAT charged.

It is simplest to consider the various effects of these rules on purchases and sales separately.

■ Purchases from a registered EU trader in another member state

- Your EU supplier will need to know your VAT number with the country prefix, which is GB. So, a typical number notified to an EU supplier would be GB 214 7320 94.
- The invoice will arrive at the cost price, free of VAT, but you will be liable for 'tax on acquisitions' at the appropriate GB rate. You must work this out based on the Sterling value of the invoice. If this is quoted in sterling, there is no problem, but if it is quoted in a foreign currency you should convert it to sterling at the rate of exchange on the day of acquisition. To enable you to record the tax due easily, the publishers of the Simplex system have inserted a special page at the end of the input section, called the acquisition section.
- You do not need to pay any money over to the VAT authorities at the time of recording it, but the amount due has to be declared on the VAT return, on the 'VAT due on acquisitions' line. However, as these supplies are usually inputs, you will be able to recover the money again as 'inputs recoverable on acquisitions' on the VAT return. The two amounts therefore usually cancel one another out (but there are one or two special cases where it cannot be reclaimed and it will therefore increase the VAT payable in the quarter). The entry of this type of invoice is shown in Figure 11.5.

■ Sales to a registered EU trader in another member state

- Your invoice to the EU customer is made out at the normal selling price, exempt of VAT, and they are liable for 'tax on acquisitions' at the local rate in their country. Your invoice must bear the customer's VAT registration number with the country prefix. However, there is a difficulty here. If the customer does not pay VAT on acquisitions as they should do, you could be liable for the VAT at the UK rate when the customer's non-payment becomes clear – possibly months later. One of the ways they might escape payment is by giving a false VAT number. If you have any doubt about the correctness of the number, your local VAT office has ways to check it.

ACQUISITIONS SECTION INVOICED SUPPLIES FROM EU TRADERS (ZERO RATED) TREATED AS ACQUISITIONS

Invoice Date	Invoice Number	Name of EU Supplier	VAT No with Country prefix	Supplier's Invoice Total	Value of goods taxable on acquisition Standard Rate	Positive Rate 'A'	Positive Rate 'B'	Liable at Zero Rate	Tax payable on acquisitions	Services (if any)
7·11·19..	1	G. HOLST	DE 214 732094	1,568 40	1,568 40				274 47	
8 11 19.	2	T. GAUTIER	FR 496 123456	2,564 40		2,564 40			205 15	
Total for accounting period (carried to foot of page)				17,254 60	12,380 94	4,823 66			2,556 55	

RETURNS SECTION CREDIT NOTES FOR GOODS RETURNED TO EU SUPPLIERS (CARRY DOWN TOTALS TO FOOT OF PAGE)

11·11·19..	1	T. GAUTIER	FR 496 123456	462 80	462 80				37 02	
Totals carried down				1,924 45	721 56	1,202 89			222 50	

Acquisitions figures for VAT Account

Totals for accounting period (see above)				17,254 60	12,380 94	4,823 66			2,556 55	
Less totals from Returns Section (above)				1,924 45	721 56	1,202 89			222 50	
Net totals for accounting period				15,330 15	11,659 38	3,620 77			2,334 05	

Carry this total to the VAT Account as tax on acquisitions

Fig. 11.5 ENTERING VAT ON ACQUISITIONS

- Enter the invoice in the output account in the usual way.
- If the goods do not leave the UK for any reason, you will become liable for the VAT on them at the UK rate. It is therefore important to keep any carrier's document or electronic evidence of the supply of goods as proof that the goods left the UK. Special care is necessary if an EU customer collects goods from your premises. You have to have some 'proof of removal', such as a document proving dispatch by sea, air, road haulage, or rail. As it is unlikely that this will be immediately available it is advisable to take a deposit at the UK rate of tax, which is refundable when you receive the 'proof of removal' document.

■ Sales to an EU customer who is not registered for VAT

With the Single Market, it is taken for granted that anyone can sell goods direct to the consumer in any country of the European Union, but it does pose some problems as far as VAT is concerned. The rules are as follows.

- If goods are to be installed or assembled at a customer's premises, the premises become the 'place of supply', and the UK supplier has to register for VAT in the customer's country, and collect VAT at the local rate. This means that the UK supplier makes out the invoice at the selling price (free of UK VAT), but adds on VAT at the customer's local rate, and pays it over – not to the Customs in the UK, but to the VAT authorities in the destination country. Clearly, a firm supplying such goods to every country in the EU would have to register for VAT in every country. If this becomes too burdensome, it is possible to make arrangements with a 'tax representative' in each country who will take care of the documentation of VAT on your behalf.
- If the product being supplied is a new means of transport (NMT), the purchaser has to account for VAT at the local rate in the destination country. There is a special form for this – VAT 411. The invoice is made out at the selling price, free of UK VAT, and the form VAT 411 alerts the VAT authorities in the destination country that a new vehicle has been supplied, and they will call for the payment from the customer, at the local VAT rate.
- 'Distance selling'. The authorities felt that it would be impossible to collect 'VAT on acquisitions' from ordinary citizens who have purchased a mass of small items from suppliers (by mail order, for example). They would have no knowledge of the VAT system in their own countries. Therefore, the sensible thing is for the supplier

to add VAT to the price of the goods and the customer pays the VAT inclusive price. However, as VAT rates are not the same in all countries and the UK VAT added to the invoice will be paid over by the trader to the UK Customs – and therefore to the UK Treasury – it means that consumers in other member states are paying taxes to the UK government, not their own government. In order to reduce the unfairness of such an arrangement, there is a 'distance selling threshold'. It varies a little from country to country, but is about the £11 500 level at present. If a trader's total sales reach this threshold, they must register with the customers' member state and levy tax on the goods at the local rate, paying the money collected over to the VAT authorities in the destination country. Once again, if this becomes too arduous, it is possible to make an arrangement with a tax representative who will deal with the local VAT on your behalf.

- If goods are subject to UK excise duty, the EU customer must declare them to their own authorities, before the goods are dispatched and guarantee, that the duty will be paid. On receipt of the guarantee the goods may be invoiced at zero rate, and sent with an Administrative Accompanying Document (AAD). This is returnable as proof of payment of the excise duty, and the VAT is paid by the customer as 'tax on acquisitions' at the local rate.

■ Country codes for VAT in the EU

Austria	AT	Italy	IT
Belgium	BE	Luxembourg	LU
Denmark	DK	Netherlands	NL
Finland	FI	Portugal	PT
France	FR	Spain	ES
Germany	DE	Sweden	SE
Greece	EL	United Kingdom	GB
Ireland	IE		

THE VAT RETURN

Each month (for zero-rated traders) or each quarter (for other traders) the VAT computer sends out an official form – the 'VAT return' – to every registered trader. It must be completed to show the essential abbreviated details of your VAT trading. Some imaginary figures have been inserted below, and are explained in the notes below the calculation.

The VAT Return

1. VAT due in this period and other outputs	5 725.60
2. VAT due in the period from other EU member states	776.50
3. Total value due (the sum of boxes 1 and 2)	6 502.10
4. VAT reclaimed in this period on purchases and other inputs (including acquisitions from the EU)	1 451.56
5. Net VAT to be paid to Customs or reclaimed by you (difference between boxes 3 and 4)	5 050.54
6. Total value of sales and all other outputs, excluding any VAT (include your box 8 figure)	32 717.00
7. Total value of purchases and all other inputs, excluding any VAT (include your box 9 figure)	3 857.00
8. Total value of all supplies of goods and related services, excluding any VAT, to other EU member states	00.00
9. Total value of all acquisitions of goods and related services, excluding any VAT, from other EU Member States	4 437.00

Notes

Box 1

Show the VAT due on all goods and services you supplied in this period.

Box 2

Show the VAT due (but not yet paid) on all goods and related services you acquired in this period from other EU member states.

Box 3

Show the total amount of VAT due – that is, the sum of boxes 1 and 2. This is your total output tax.

Box 4

Show the amount of VAT deductible on any business purchases, including acquisitions of goods and related services from other EU member states. This is your input tax.

Box 5

If this amount is under £1.00 you need not send any payment, nor will any payment be made to you, but you must still fill in this form and send it to the VAT Central Unit.

Boxes 6 and 7

In box 6, show the value, excluding VAT, of your total outputs (supplies of goods and services). Include zero-rated, exempt outputs and EU supplies from box 8.

In box 7, show the value, excluding VAT, of all your inputs (purchases of goods and services). Include zero-rated, exempt imports and EU acquisitions from box 9.

Boxes 8 and 9

Use these boxes if you have supplied goods to, or acquired goods from, another EU member state. Include related services, such as transport costs where these form part of the invoice or contract price. The figures should exclude VAT. The other EU member states, at present, are: Austria, Belgium, Denmark, Finland, France, Germany, Greece, Ireland, Italy, Luxembourg, Netherlands, Portugal, Spain and Sweden.

EU SALES LISTS AND INTRASTAT

If your EU sales reach 15 000 ECU (about £11 000), HM Customs will require you to submit an EU sales list (Form VAT 101). This shows the customers dealt with, their VAT registrations and country codes and the total value of supplies to each customer.

Trade figures are important for many government purposes. The Single Market has reduced the controls over EU trade, but the statistics are still needed. This is done in two ways:

- The VAT return has two extra lines requiring traders to give details of sales to, and purchases from, EU traders.
- Larger firms with 'dispatches' or 'arrivals' valued at over £135 000 per year, must submit statistics called 'INTRASTAT' on special forms, or by electronic data interchange (EDI).

VAT INSPECTIONS

Certainly in your first year, and from time to time later on, you will receive a visit from a VAT inspector. Newspapers often feature horror stories about people in difficulties with the VAT office, and such incidents are also featured in television documentaries. The vast majority of Customs' investigations relate to sophisticated frauds that need not concern us here. So far as the normal trader is concerned the inspector wants to see that the records are kept in an honest and systematic way and are being preserved for the requisite period of six years. If a manifest error is found – such as VAT being reclaimed on expenses that were not business expenses but domestic expenses – the investigation would lead to an assessment of the tax thus wrongfully reclaimed and, possibly, to some financial penalty. The legal rule is that 'ignorance of the law excuses no one' – we are all deemed to know all the details of VAT law, even though, in fact, none of us does. However, any penalty imposed would be fairly nominal in the case of a genuine error. It would be quite different if deliberate misdeclarations had been made, and a persistent misdeclaration penalty can be imposed.

To avoid trouble with Customs and Excise, the following rules should be observed.

- Get to know the VAT system thoroughly as it affects you. Familiarise yourself with your own scheme and the calculation it entails.

  Put away your VAT output tax regularly in a separate savings or deposit account in your own name.

- Whichever system of VAT records you adopt, keep them systematically, and preserve each year's records as a separate collection, filed away in a filing cabinet or archived in a special cardboard box. You can buy quite reasonable boxes for about £2 in most stationers or from postal sources such as Neat Ideas, Freepost, Sandall Stones Road, Kirk Sandall, Doncaster, South Yorkshire DN3 1QU.
- Put away your VAT output tax regularly in a separate savings or deposit account in your own name. This will earn you interest, but, most importantly, it will be available for Customs and Excise when it becomes payable. Remember, it is not your money, except to the extent that you can reclaim from it the input tax you have paid. The vast majority of it is tax you have collected for the VAT authorities, and they will expect it to be available. You must pay it before the due date, which is the last day of the month after your VAT period ends.

CHECKLIST

- **Value added tax is a tax added to every supply you make of either goods or services, except that certain supplies are exempt and some are zero-rated.**

- **The tax is added to the invoice price of the goods or services, and is called 'output tax'. At present, there are three rates – standard rate (17½ per cent), a lower rate on fuel (5 per cent) and zero rate. Other rates may be introduced at any time, but a multi-rate system that is too complicated is not desirable.**

- **Traders must register for VAT if sales exceeded £50,000 in the past 12 months or if you believe that the next 30 days' sales will bring the year's sales over the threshold figure of £50 000. These limits rise each year in line with inflation, and the latest figures can be obtained from the VAT office. Many traders register voluntarily so that they can reclaim input tax.**

- The tax payable is the output tax collected, less the input tax suffered on purchases for the business, whether these purchases are goods for resale, consumable items or capital items for use in the business.

- If tax invoices are used as the basis for keeping VAT records, the system of record-keeping is called the 'normal' VAT method. All traders keep their input tax records by the normal method, but if they do not issue tax invoices for every supply, they are unable to use this method for output tax and must use one of the VAT retail schemes.

- Choosing which scheme is the most appropriate for their business is the task of the proprietor or proprietors. All the schemes depend on keeping accurate records of daily takings, and the scheme calculation is then based on these records. For the very largest retailers – with sales in excess of £10 million per annum – an agreed bespoke scheme will be devised.

- Since the introduction of the Single Market in the European Union, there are special rules about 'supplies' and 'acquisitions' from other member states, and 'distancing selling' to citizens of other member states by mail order. Traders who deal with such customers must familiarise themselves with these VAT rules.

- The simplest VAT book on the market is the Simplex VAT book, obtainable from most stationers or by post from the address given on page 7.

Computerised accounting

THE NATURE OF COMPUTERS

Computers can be programmed to do a great number of routine business activities at very fast speeds. Most of them operate at speeds in excess of ten million processes per second, so that complicated activities (such as calculating the percentage of VAT in today's daily takings) appear to be done in the twinkling of an eye. A computer system is made up of 'hardware' and 'software'. Hardware consists of pieces of technical equipment, such as the computer itself (central processing unit, or, CPU), a keyboard for gaining access to the computer and for keying in instructions to it, a mouse or trackball, a visual display unit (VDU), which is like a television screen, and a printer. Their uses are described below.

■ The computer

The computer is the 'thinking' end of the system, though it does not really think. It consists of a number of parts, the chief of which is the 'central processor'. This is able to accept a program of instructions and further data that it will process according to the program – hence the term 'data processing'. As the computer works so fast, it can be instructed to do numerous things one after the other. For example, if the 'daily takings' figure was keyed in at the end of the day, it would not only be recorded on the sales account records, but the VAT output tax would be calculated and recorded as a credit in the VAT account because the VAT officer is now a creditor for this amount. The total sales would be added to the sales figure for the year, and would eventually be used to find the gross profit in the trading account. A particular figure needs to be entered only once and then all the activities and uses it can be put to are carried out automatically and instantaneously.

■ The keyboard

This allows you to communicate with the computer and input new data. This data can be processed immediately or stored within the computer or on a disk to be worked on later.

■ The visual display unit (VDU)

The VDU is an instantaneous output device that will display on its screen any particular set of information as it is presently stored in the computer. It will then display any item keyed in and, after a number of user-friendly hesitations, will pass the new data into the computer for processing. For example, suppose you have a debtor, D. Smith, who has just sent a cheque to settle the balance owing on her account on 31 January. You first choose 'debtors' ledger from the menu and then 'D. Smith' from the new menu. The account will be displayed, showing a balance on 31 January of £226.50, and one further invoice for goods sold to her on 4 February. You can then instruct the computer to deduct £226.50, cheque received. The computer program might then display the following user-friendly question:

> You are asking me to deduct £226.50 from D. Smith's account.
> Is this correct? Y/N

A touch on the Y key, meaning 'Yes', brings a further question:

> Are you sure? Y/N

A further touch on the Y key and the computer will perform the following:

- deduct the £226.50 from D. Smith's outstanding balance;
- add £226.50 to the bank account balance because a cheque has been received;
- issue a 'transaction number' that will appear on the screen: 'The transaction number for this entry is 213'.

The computer records every transaction on an 'audit trail' so that the auditors can see every entry made in the accounts. It may do several other things with the number if the program includes some sort of statistical analysis (for example an 'age of debtors' analysis).

If the operator making this entry is looking at a remittance advice note and the cheque, they will record the transaction number 213 on the remittance advice note to show that it has been entered in the accounts, and the cheque can now be paid into the bank.

■ The printer

The VDU gives an instantaneous picture of the item requested, but once it is cleared from the screen, there is no record of what was displayed. If you need a printed copy (called a 'hard copy') you can instruct the printer to print out what you require. For example, if you wish to send D. Smith a statement of her account because she telephones to say that no statement has been received this month, you can call up the account, print off a hard copy and put it in the post to her at once. The computer will also, if a suitable program is installed, produce a trial balance of the accounts, a list of unpaid creditors or a list of overdue debtors or draw up a trading account and profit and loss account whenever you want one.

■ Software

A piece of software is a program of instructions written to enable the computer to perform a particular task. For example, you could have a payroll program, a debtors' ledger program, a paid to bank program or a cash sales program. Having programs written specifically for you can be an expensive business, but fortunately there are a good many suitable programs (packages) on the market that can be purchased 'off the shelf'. Very few people need to have software written for them these days, certainly in the accountancy field, but if you want to use your computer for some technological purpose (such as detecting dangerous waste in the effluent from your factory) you are sure to be able to find someone who will write appropriate software for you (at a price). Your local Enterprise Agency will advise you and help you to find a specialist programmer with the expertise you require.

THE ADVANTAGES OF COMPUTERISED ACCOUNTING

There are several advantages of computerised accounting.

■ Every accounting procedure can be computerised, and most businesses will find that suitable software of proven quality, with all the problems sorted out years ago, is readily available at reasonable prices.

■ Any figure needs to be entered only once, and the computer will then undertake every process required with that item of data, automatically. Thus, an invoice from a supplier will be credited to the supplier's account and debited to the purchases account – which is the basic double entry process. If the trader is registered for VAT, the VAT on the purchase will be extracted and debited to Customs and Excise as it is deductible input tax, and Customs will have to refund it to you (unless you are able to deduct it from the output tax you have collected).

Every accounting procedure can be computerised.

■ The basic activity in computerised accounting is simple keyboard work, which anyone can learn in a single morning. The dealer who sells you the hardware and software will induct you into the simple procedures necessary and for the first few days will answer any calls you make if you come up against some difficulty. A well-written and proven piece of software will give you very little trouble and within a few weeks you will be perfectly happy operating the system.

- The actual accounting records for a small business can be completed in about half an hour a day. Therefore, the proprietor who establishes a simple system – for example, putting all items due to be entered in a file or a tray as they arrive and then dealing with them at a convenient moment – keeps on top of the accounts and does not fall hopelessly behind with the records.

- The computer does the work, with plenty of user-friendly guidance as you need it to make the entries, and the results are always correct (no mistakes in addition, subtraction, multiplication and so on), as long as you have entered the data accurately, of course.

- Since computerised accounting programs are always devised by knowledgeable and qualified accountants, you can rely absolutely on the correctness of the accounting work done with each piece of data you input into the system. Many systems will go right through to final accounts, and will ask you for any figures you need to input as they are required. For example, in preparing the final accounts the message might appear, 'Please insert the figure for closing stock now.' If you have just carried out your stocktaking, the figure will be available and the computer will accept it and carry on with the preparation of the trading account, profit and loss account and balance sheet.

To discuss computerised procedures, it is essential to choose a particular system. As there was some discussion of Simplex book-keeping earlier in the book, it is convenient to discuss Simplex Accounts™ Software here – the computerised version of the manual Simplex system. This is followed by a discussion of the more sophisticated 'retailer' systems devised by Micro-Retailer Systems Ltd. Finally, in Chapter 13, there is a section giving details of all the main computerised systems available to small businesses, with the addresses and telephone numbers of their suppliers. If you decide to approach a particular firm, a phone call will bring you their literature, price lists and so on. Note that the prices given in Chapter 13 were those prevailing at the time of publication (1998).

SIMPLEX COMPUTERISED ACCOUNTING

Simplex Accounts™ Software is a registered trademark owned by George Vyner Ltd, the company that originally devised the manual Simplex system. It is marketed exclusively by their Simplex Accounts Office, PO Box 1, Holmfirth, Huddersfield HD7 2RP (telephone (sales line) 0800 7836204 (support line) 01625 421999).

Simplex Accounts™ is a unique, computerised cash accounting system that enables you to keep complete records of all your business transactions as required by law and to control your business and optimise its activities. The system is easy to understand and operate and you do not need any specialist knowledge of computers or even to understand double entry book-keeping.

When you use the program, you key in information about sales, purchases, overhead expenses and so on and it is processed in such a way as to make a complete record. It will prepare VAT returns and draw up a profit and loss account at any time. It is a tried and tested system with thousands of business users.

The whole procedure of keeping your accounts can be divided into three parts:

- setting up your business books;
- keeping your business books;
- monitoring your business.

Briefly, the first requires inputting everything it is necessary to know about the business for the system to commence to keep records for you. For example, the business name is important and its address, telephone number, fax number, possibly, and Internet address. It must know whether or not you are registered for VAT and, if so, your VAT number, the VAT start date, rates of VAT applicable and so on.

Setting up the books (in computer terms it is called 'configuring the system') can take quite a lot of time because there are many necessary details to enter. You will want the system to keep track of the various classes of goods sold (for example, groceries, cigarettes, wines, dried goods and so on) so you will need to designate codes to them so that the system can collect purchases together under the various headings. Similarly, you will want it to sort out your sales under various headings so that you can see the activity of various product lines, and you will also want the various overhead expenses incurred to be classified. These days, to tie in with the tax system the expenses are grouped under 13 main headings, but a wider analysis is possible for everyday use, and for management reports, with the figures being grouped later for the profit and loss account.

The following is a brief introduction to the Simplex computerised system.

■ Setting up your business books

'Housekeeping' is a general term for the basic activities the system will perform. Figure 12.1 shows the first screen you will see, calling for details of your business name, address, telephone number, fax number and Internet address.

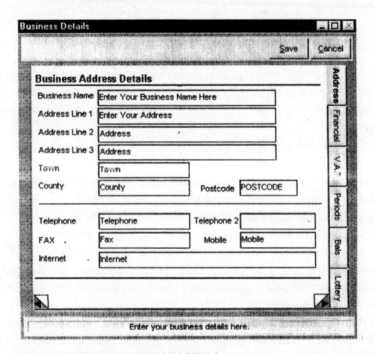

Fig. 12.1 ENTERING BUSINESS DETAILS

A second screen calls for your financial details, including the start date of your financial year, whether you want to keep your records weekly, or monthly and so on.

A further screen calls for your VAT details – whether or not you are registered for VAT, whether or not you are trading as a 'retailer' (see Chapter 11), when your VAT trading periods commence and so on.

You then move on to enter your requirements about how you wish your accounts to be analysed. For example, sales may be grouped under various headings to show the activity in various products or areas. Receipts may be daily sales, other receipts (such as capital contributed or loans arranged) and lottery receipts. Lottery receipts are not receipts of your business – you only receive them in your role as agent for the lottery's organiser – and they do not form part of the turnover of your business. Payments may be payments for business stock or payments other than for stock (the overhead expenses of the business).

Other screens are available to record supplier details, banking details, preferences (for example, whether or not you want to have current cash and bank balances showing on the screen and other accounting preferences).

Finally, there are sections for security purposes.

■ Keeping your business books

Once the housekeeping arrangements have been entered, the computer will accept whatever entries you wish to make. You simply click on the type of entry you wish to make and the system will then deal with the entry.

You have seen that there are receipts entries of three kinds – sales receipts, other receipts and lottery receipts. For entries in these three categories, a screen display will enable you to enter the appropriate figures, and these will be analysed and totalled at once according to the details you have entered.

Similarly, bills received from outside the business for goods supplied or for overheads of various sorts can be added to your list of bills payable, their due date will be calculated, VAT input tax worked out and, if discounts are available for prompt payment, these can be taken into account as well.

With all entries made, the computer generates a transaction number so that every transaction can be traced and a complete audit trail is available. This transaction number is written on each document that is processed before it is archived in an appropriate way.

■ *Preparing a VAT return*

Figures for VAT output tax and VAT input tax will have been extracted from the sales and purchases entries as they have been made throughout the quarter (or month for traders in zero-rated goods). At the end of each VAT period, you will be invited to make any amendments that are necessary – for example, there may need to be adjustments to allow for private use. You can then print out a VAT return that you can use to complete the official VAT return sent to you by HM Customs. This must be sent in, with the money due, by the agreed due date.

■ Monitoring your business

■ *The final accounts of your business*

At the end of your financial year, the takings of your business will have been accumulated from the various receipts entered during the year. The system will set against this the total takings figure, the total payments for stocks sold (the cost of sales) and also the overheads, listed in the categories required by the Inland Revenue for the self-assessment system. It will produce a profit and loss account, showing the net profit for the year. After producing the profit and loss account, the computer system automatically asks the user, 'Would you like to prepare a self-assessment tax return?' The report can be printed out and used in the preparation of your self-assessment tax return, which is required by the Inland Revenue.

■ *The balance sheet*

The present version of Simplex Accounts™ does not produce a closing balance sheet, but all the figures required for assets and liabilities are available within the system and for those actually requiring a balance sheet, one can be prepared manually within a few minutes.

MORE SOPHISTICATED ACCOUNTING FOR RETAILERS

More sophisticated systems to exploit all the potential of the computer in the small- to medium-size business fields are available. You can perhaps consider the full range of systems by looking at all the different features available from a typical system – the award-winning Retailer 90 system, available from Micro-Retailer Systems Ltd. Their address is Kings House, Royal Court, Macclesfield SK11 7AE (telephone 01625 615000). Its systems cater for all sizes of retail outlets – for example, up to 50 branches, with hundreds of suppliers and every type of point-of-sale payment by thousands of customers.

Some of the main features are as follows.

■ Sales and banking

- Full analysis by department of cash and credit sales using an unlimited number of headings for each branch.
- Banking analysis between cash, cheque, credit cards, debit cards, and paying-in branches.
- Multiple bank accounts with on-screen display.

- Handles all VAT retail schemes.
- Summary reports available as required.
- Operates weekly or monthly
- Optional links to customer credit accounts and point-of-sale systems.

■ Purchases

- Retailer 90 has powerful facilities for recording and analysing details of payments made by cash or cheque (a cash book) and bills to be paid at a later date (purchases ledger with an unlimited number of accounts).
- Entry and full analysis by departments for goods for resale and for overheads and expenses for each branch.
- Multiple VAT rate facility.
- Handles cash and credit purchases, credit notes and returns.
- Invoice approval facilities.
- Calculates and monitors selling prices, gross margin and mark-up for retail stock control and VAT retail schemes.
- Provides for settlement discounts and payments on account.
- Allows for payment by cheque, clearing house, due date and/or supplier.
- Remittance advice note production.
- Reports on the status of all customers' accounts, with their telephone numbers and full details on screen if a customer queries their account.
- Entry of bank charges, interest and standing orders.
- Journal facility for transfers between headings or recording goods transferred between branches.
- Summary of expenditures by department or category for the period and the financial year.
- Audit trail by invoice, supplier or cost heading to screen or printer for either range or year to date.
- An optional link to financial stock control is available.

■ Trading and profit and loss accounts

- Retailer 90 stores information so that a profit and loss account is available at the press of a key. It can be prepared *monthly* with period and year-to-date figures in a format you set up for yourself. Individual reports are produced for head office and each branch, with a company consolidation. You can view your profit progress every month if you so wish.

■ VAT reporting

Retailer 90 is unique in the way it caters for the needs of all businesses having to prepare VAT returns. In particular, it covers all the retail schemes, the point-of-sale scheme, the two apportionment schemes and the two direct calculation schemes.

It is also a suitable basis for the very largest firms to agree a bespoke retail scheme with HM Customs.

■ Reports to management

Retailer 90 produces many reports, most of them on request so that you don't end up with lots of paper. Most historical data is available for the whole of the financial year, on a year-to-date basis.

A number of specialist modules are also available, including a financial stock control module, a retail sales ledger system and a till reconciliation module for those who have to cash up multiple tills in a large shop. Installation and training are provided and a telephone hotline supports customers who are experiencing any difficulties.

SERVICES OF THE ACCOUNTING CENTRE LTD

One disadvantage of computerised accounting for new businesses is that a dedicated system (one designed to fit a particular trader's exact requirements) is difficult to introduce, expensive to set up and is almost sure to have teething problems. This is precisely what the new small business does not want.

If you can use the existing expertise of an established computer centre that has afforded the most expensive and versatile programs, has well-proven systems and is a well-developed organisation, with a consultancy facility to give advice or warn of dangers looming ahead, you will enjoy the best of all possible worlds. Such a service is provided by the Accounting Centre Ltd, Elscot House, Arcadia Avenue, Finchley Central, London N3 2JE (telephone 0181-349 3191).

What the Accounting Centre does is place the facilities of an advanced and sophisticated computer system at the service of the small business. After a relatively brief analysis of your requirements, such of the various services available as are needed are linked together to give you a dedicated system that meets all your requirements. The basic services are:

■ sales ledger services, including credit control, monthly statements, sales analysis and customer history;

- bought ledger services, including analysis of purchases, remittance advice notes, cash flow control and supplier history;
- payroll services, including PAYE and NIC administration, payslips, and end-of-year returns;
- monthly management accounts, including cash and cheque movements, profitability, cash flow management, future planning and end-of-year final accounts (these aspects are the most important in business today);
- local consultancy services – a 'hand-holding' service, provided by local accountants where necessary, to give tailor-made advice and general supervision of book-keeping and VAT accounts, and assist in the interpretation of the monthly management accounts supplied by the computer system.

Once you have provided basic details of sales, purchases and cash received and paid, the Accounting Centre turns it not only into financial records but management accounting records, to give you a total picture of your business' performance. Profits, cash flow, debtors and creditors, bank balances, overheads and so on are all at your fingertips within a few days, and updated monthly. The added financial management and credit control eliminates a large part of the risks and uncertainties so common to businesses that have no computerised analysis of results on a regular basis.

There is a small initial charge for the evaluation and the adaptation of the computer programs necessary to give a tailor-made service, followed by a monthly payment that is a deductible expense for tax purposes. No specialist staff need be employed, no capital equipment needs to be purchased (and there is no need for expensive bank loans to purchase it). Lengthy consultations with accountants are not required because the system is organised month by month and records are always in apple-pie order. Any consultancy services that you require will be discussions of a financial situation that the computer system has made crystal clear, and prompt, inexpensive advice will therefore be forthcoming.

In particular, there are no onerous long-term contracts, tied to expensive monthly payments. The well-established system depends for its success on mutual advantages – client satisfaction and enduring relationships between the Accounting Centre, the small business client and the local consultant (if required).

CHECKLIST

- Computer programs are now available for a very wide range of business uses, and accounting aspects are particularly well catered for by the software houses.

- A PC, consisting of a CPU, VDU, keyboard, printer and so on, plus packages for particular specialist functions are readily available.

- Some simple manual systems have been computerised. For example, Simplex's accounts software throws the ordinary manual Simplex system on to the screen, with identical rulings, so that those familiar with the manual system, can convert to the computerised system very easily.

- The chief advantage of computerisation is that once a piece of data has been fed into the computer, the programs will do with it everything that should be done – for example, a sale to a debtor will be debited to the debtor's account, credited to the sales account, the VAT will be extracted and worked into the VAT records and so on.

- Computerising final accounts means that a set of final accounts can be prepared by pressing a single key – every day if necessary.

- A complete audit trail is made available so that every transaction can be traced, and its validity established to the satisfaction of the owners, the accountants and the Inland Revenue.

- For medium-sized enterprises, the following advantages of a computerised system can be realised by using programs such as the Retailer 90 system from Micro-Retailer Systems Ltd. The system suits businesses of all sizes and has adequate facilities to cater for an unlimited number of debtors, creditors, tills, and bank accounts. It also caters for all the VAT retail schemes.

A complete set of manual and computerised accounting systems

MANUAL SYSTEMS OF ACCOUNTS

Most businesses start in a very small way and do not justify either very detailed records or the purchase of expensive computer hardware or software. There are various manual systems on the market, most of them quite inexpensive. Some have been described fairly extensively in this book, but the full list of manual systems is described in the first section of this chapter (see pages 185–8).

COMPUTERISED ACCOUNTS

As explained in Chapter 12, computerisation of accounts brings great advantages to any firm, and some of the fully developed systems for large-scale retailers, with their point-of-sale terminals are miracles of ingenuity. The tables of computerised packages show all the systems appropriate for small businesses and give details of the suppliers and the range of services offered (see pages 189–92).

THE NATURE OF THE TABULATIONS

The tabulations are given in alphabetical order in two parts – manual systems and computerised systems. Not all systems cover all aspects, so it is best to study the indications – a cross in any box indicates that the system concerned can handle the aspect named in the 'coverage' category at the top of the page.

In choosing a system for use in your business, it is advisable to scan the information given very closely and approach the publishers or suppliers of the systems that seem most appropriate for your class of business.

INVITATION TO OTHER SUPPLIERS

It is just possible that systems do exist that are not included in the charts, although in recent years I have made every attempt to contact all those offering such systems. It is also possible that new manual or electronic systems are being developed. If any publishers wish to have a system included in the next edition of this book, I shall be delighted to hear from them. There is no charge for this mention – it is hoped that all readers will benefit from the fuller description of systems available.

Simple Accounting Systems   Page 1

Name of System	Coverage (X indicates Yes)							VAT	Final Accounts	Handbook available	Free advice service	Advice service with nominal charge	Other features	Cost (Prices subject to revision)	Available from RS = Reputable stationers P = Publisher (see end col.)	Address of Publisher or Supplier
	Bank	Cash	Sales	Purchases	Receipts	Payments	Payroll									
Acorn Small Business Day Book	X	X	X	X	X	X							Wkly Cash and bank reconciliations. Payment of expenses from private funds	£3.50 inc. VAT	P & RS	Acorn Books 19 Broadmead Killay, Swansea West Glamorgan SA2 7EE Tel: 01792 202181
Ataglance VAT Account Book for Retailers	X	X	X	X	X	X		X			X			£8.00	P	Ataglance Publications 4 Granary Close CODFORD Warminster BA12 0PR Tel: 01985 850191
Small Trader Book	X	X	X	X	X	X					X			£4.00	P	
Sub-contractors Account Book	X	X	X	X	X	X					X			£2.55 Plus VAT	P	
Burgan Publications Cashflow Manager	X	X	X	X	X	X		X			X		Simple instructions in each section includes Bank Rec. Monthly summary etc.	£24.00 inc. VAT	Publisher/ Supplier	Burgan Publications (UK) Ltd, Rochester House 275 Baddow Road Chelmsford, Essex CM2 7QA Tel: 01245 492220 Fax: 01245 491120
Collins Self Employed Account Book (for the building industry)	X	X	X	X	X	X		X	X				Sub-contractors covered	£22.65	RS	
Collins Complete Traders Account Book	X	X			X	X		X						£22.65	RS	
Collins Essential Account Book	X	X	X	X		X								£9.15	RS	
Collins Essential VAT Book				X				X						£13.30	RS	

Fig. 13.1 SIMPLE MANUAL ACCOUNTING SYSTEMS (continued overleaf)

Simple Accounting Systems   Page 2

Name of System	Coverage (X indicates Yes)											Other features	Cost (Prices subject to revision)	Available from RS = Reputable stationers P = Publisher (see end col.)	Address of Publisher or Supplier
	Bank	Cash	Sales	Purchases	Receipts	Payments	Payroll	VAT	Final Accounts	Handbook available	Free advice service / Advice service with nominal charge				
Evrite Traders Weekly Account Book (VAT edn. Ref. 500S/D)	X	X	X	X	X	X		X			X		£17.94	P & RS	Evrite Group Ltd. Evrite House Haden Road Cradley Heath West Midlands B64 6ES Tel: 01384 566042
Evrite 707 D Multi-Rate VAT Book	X	X	X	X	X	X		X			X		£17.45	P	
Evrite 500 Non-VAT Account Book	X	X	X	X	X	X					X		£15.72	RS	Evrite 500 has an IR SA guide
Evrite 701 Weekly Analysis Book	X	X	X	X	X	X	X	X			X		£23.37		
Guildhall Account Box	X	X	X	X	X	X	X	X					£17.95 inc. VAT	RS	Tollit & Harvey King's Lynn Tel: 01553 696666
Kalamazoo Small Business Pack	X	X	X	X	X	X		X	X	X	X	Cashflow forecast Age analysis Stock valuation Budget	£205.15	P	Kalamazoo Security Print Mill Lane Northfield Birmingham B31 2RW Tel: 0121 411 3333
Kalamazoo Wages							X						£164.10		
Safeguard 'One-write' Systems	X	X	X	X	X	X	X	X	X	X	X	Local installation service	£100+	P	Safeguard Systems Europe Ltd Duchy Road, Crewe Cheshire CW1 6ND

Fig. 13.1 (continued)

Simple Accounting Systems   Page 3

Name of System	Bank	Cash	Sales	Purchases	Receipts	Payments	Payroll	VAT	Final Accounts	Handbook available	Free advice service	Advice service with nominal charge	Other features	Cost (Prices subject to revision)	Available from RS = Reputable stationers P = Publisher (see end col.)	Address of Publisher or Supplier
					Coverage (X indicates Yes)											
Simplex Account Books D Self-assessment style	X	X	X	X	X	X		X	X	X	X			£10.30	RS or P	George Vyner Ltd. PO Box 1 Holmfirth Huddersfield HD7 2RP Tel: 01484 685221 (Handbook is called *Simplified Book-keeping for Small Businesses* £7.99)
VAT Book	X	X	X	X	X	X		X	X	X	X			£12.13	RS or P	
Wages Book		X					X			X				£7.32	RS or P	
Licensees and Caterers Account Book														£14.73	RS or P	
Farm Account Book (Simplex Everall)	X	X	X	X	X	X		X	X	X	X		Livestock record	£12.97	RS or P	
Club Accounts Book	X													£5.78	P	For recording business and private mileage. All prices include VAT
Mileage Record Book														£3.50	RS or P	
Twinlock Paymaster 87 Wages and Salaries System									X					£190.00	RS	Twinlock Acco-UK Ltd. Gatehouse Road Aylesbury Bucks HP19 3DT Tel: 01296 397444
Twinlock Triform 73 Book-keeping System	X	X	X	X	X	X		X		X				£312.50	RS	
Twinlock Variform Loose-leaf Account & Analysis Books	X	X	X	X	X	X		X		X			Refills and replacement stationery widely available from stationers	Depends on application	RS Money back guarantee	
Twinlock Complete Accounts Book for Small Businesses	X	X	X	X	X	X		X	X	X				£17.95	RS	Prices shown are net of VAT
Twinlock Crown Loose-leaf Accounting Books	X	X	X	X		X		X						Depends on application	RS	

Fig. 13.1 (continued)

Simple Accounting Systems   Page 4

Name of System	Coverage (X indicates Yes)									Handbook available	Free advice service	Advice service with nominal charge	Other features	Cost (Prices subject to revision)	Available from RS = Reputable stationers P = Publisher (see end col.)	Address of Publisher or Supplier
	Bank	Cash	Sales	Purchases	Receipts	Payments	Payroll	VAT	Final Accounts							
Twinlock Self-Assessment Made Easy Record Set Organiser Complete Filing System													Ideal system to record, store and organise tax records to help complete tax return	£7.50 £12.99 £19.99 ex. VAT	RS	As shown on page 3 opposite
Your Book-keeping System (YBS)* (a) with VAT (b) Non-VAT	X X	X X	X X	X X	X X	X X	X X	X X	X X	X X	X X		Financial control sheet and new training book included (48 pages)	£17.99 £7.99	RS & P	Casdec Ltd. 22 Harraton Terrace Birtley Chester-le-Street Co. Durham DH3 2QG Tel: 0191 410 5556 Fax: 0191 410 0229
* Adopted by Lloyds Bank An electronic version is in preparation																

Note: Every attempt has been made to give a comprehensive coverage of the systems available. Publishers wishing to change the record shown, or to have their system included, are invited to submit details for evaluation and inclusion.

Fig. 13.1   (continued)

There are countless organisations offering specialised packages for all sorts of business purposes, and the state of the computer industry is such that it is very difficult to keep track of developments. The organisations shown below offer different services which may be of interest. We shall be glad to add other systems to this display if firms offering particular packages will kindly give us full details.

Computerised Small Business Systems   Page 5

Name of System	Is hardware supplied?	What software packages are available?	Costs	Back-up provided	Other details
The Accounting Centre Ltd. Elscot House, Arcadia Avenue Finchley Central London N3 2JE Tel: 0500 130813 (sales enquiries only) Fax: 0181 346 2038	No	We operate as a service provider. Payroll bureau – processing and administration. Monthly management accounts (input manually or by disc). Sales. Bought ledgers and book-keeping services.	Contact company giving details of service required. Payroll from £23 per month. Management accounts from £25 per week.	Qualified staff. Free helpline	Manuals available. Established 25 years. UK's number one monthly management accounting company, specialising in SME sector.
Arena Accounts Arena Software Ltd. 3 Rayleigh Close Cambridge CB2 2AZ Tel: 01223 464194 Fax: 01223 460920	It can be	Accounting package available in modules: Nominal ledger, Purchase ledger, Sales ledger, Cash book, Budgets, Full VAT analysis, Logon/password system, Job costing, Report generator. Nominal, Sales and Purchase ledgers in small/medium/full sizes. ODBC database.	£270 – £2500 depending on modules and sizes purchased.	Full telephone/fax or modem service plus training and seminars	Detailed manual available. One days training usually included. Optional link to a job costing system.
PC Cashflow Manager Burgan Publications (UK) Ltd. Rochester House 275 Baddow Road Chelmsford Essex CM2 7QA	No	Entry level small firm accounting package. Export facility plus reporting on general ledger, transactions, statement of receipts and payments and monthly summary. Includes cheque and cash payments, receipts, bank rec. and cash rec. and reports.	£99.00 (inc. VAT) for complete package	Full back-up available via freephone telephone support for six months.	Windows-based, for people with little or no computer experience. Detailed manual included and demo-disk available.

Fig. 13.2 COMPUTERISED SMALL AND MEDIUM BUSINESS SYSTEMS

Computerised Small Business Systems   Page 6

Name of System	Is hardware supplied?	What software packages are available?	Costs	Back-up provided	Other details
Small and medium Business Accounting Systems by: C.R.C. 22 Roxwell Trading Park Argall Avenue London E10 7QE Tel: 0181 556 5331	Yes – various	Payroll, SSP & SMP, Invoicing, Sales Ledger, Bought Ledger, Nominal Ledger, Stock Control, Word processing, Database, Spreadsheets etc.	£350 – £5000 for complete systems, according to specifications.	Comprehensive maintenance by own service organisation plus full software support.	Total Support Provided. Large workshop.
FREEWAY SOFTWARE Freeway Software Ltd. The Standish Centre Cross Street, Standish Lancashire WN6 0HQ Tel: 01257 472006 (Sales) 01257 472010 (Support) Fax: 01257 426671	No	Freeway Ledger-Master Freeway Paye Master Freeway Cashbook Freeway Paye-Master for Windows	Disks plus manual £60 per product.	Yes – at a small charge of £60 plus VAT per annum approx.	1990 Best Accounting Software award.
KALAMAZOO Kalamazoo Computer Group Mill Lane, Northfield Birmingham B31 2RW Tel: 0121 411 2345	Yes	Esprit Accounting & Distribution, Legend, Tetra CS/3 accounting packages. A range of specialist packages for various trades and professions. Computerised payroll.	From £490 per module £199	Telephone advice service. Software support. Training. Installation. Hardware maintenance.	
Micro Retailer Systems Ltd Kings House, Royal Court Macclesfield Cheshire SK11 7AE Tel: 01625 615000 Fax: 01625 612546	Yes, a wide selection of computers and point-of-sale devices	A wide range of retail software; Accounts, Management information, Stock Control, Customer Accounts, Customer Profiles and Loyalty Schemes.	According to system supplied – modules priced appropriately	Telephone hotline, training, telesales of consumables, till rolls, tapes and disks.	Developed by retailers for retailers.

Fig. 13.2   (continued)

Computerised Small Business Systems   Page 7

Name of System	Is hardware supplied?	What software packages are available?	Costs	Back-up provided	Other details
SIMPLEX ACCOUNTING SYSTEMS. George Vyner Ltd. PO Box 1 Holmfirth Huddersfield HD7 2RP	No, but advice given	A full, easy-to-use account service with emphasis or systems for retailers and services by tradesman. Sales, purchases, receipts, payments, cash and bank activities, debtors, creditors, VAT (all schemes) Final Accounts and Self-assessment.	£199 plus VAT	Sales line 0800 783 6204 Help line 0800 783 6205 Free for 30 days. Software Support £75 per year (£50 if paid on first joining)	User manual provided. Demo disks available before purchase of software.
OB-SERVE – RETAILER Observe Business Computing Ltd. Crossways House Enderby Road Blaby, Leics. LE8 4DD Tel: 0116 277 3747 Fax: 0116 277 7447	No	Retail accounting package incorporating cash book with sales and purchase ledgers, all VAT schemes, detailed analysis of sales and expenditure with full audit trails, year end summaries and profit and loss reports.	£400.00 plus VAT	Full back-up available for installation and training. Telephone support line.	Detailed manual and tutorial available.
PEACHTREE PBAS ACCOUNTING SYSTEM Evan-Jackson CBS Ltd. 44-46 Monks Road Lincoln LN2 5HY Tel: 01522 542399	Can be supplied to users' specifications if required	Fully-integrated accounting system for small to medium sized companies. Sales Ledger, Sales Invoices/Credit Note Production, Purchase Ledger, Nominal Ledger, Stock (Inventory) Management, Payroll.	Software only – Payroll. £159. Ledgers £129 each or Turnkey system including PC, printer and all software. Prices depend on specification.	Telephone software support. Service. Training. Hardware maintenance.	Full details available upon request. Operational demonstration disk available.

Fig. 13.2 (continued)

Computerised Small Business Systems   Page 8

Name of System	Is hardware supplied?	What software packages are available?	Costs	Back-up provided	Other details
SAGE LINE 50 The Sage Group plc, Benton Park Road Newcastle-upon-Tyne NE7 7LZ Tel: 0191 255 3000 Fax: 0191 255 0308	Available from 1800 dealers throughout UK, most of whom can also supply hardware.	Accountant Accountant Plus Financial Controller (For Windows and DOS)	Accountant £350 Accountant Plus £500 Fin. Controller £700 Fin. Controller Network £1450	Free Hotline support for first 3 months then available for annual fee, also training and seminars.	Comprehensive manuals supplied. DOS or Windows. Single user and Multi-user.
SAGE LINE 100 The Sage Group plc, Benton Park Road Newcastle-upon-Tyne NE7 7LZ Tel: 0191 255 3000 Fax: 0191 255 0308	Available from 500 dealers throughout UK, most of whom can also supply hardware.	Sales Ledger, Purchase Ledger, Nominal Ledger, Cash Book, Sales Order Processing, Purchase Order Processing, Stock Control, Invoicing, Payroll, Job Costing, Bill of Materials, Fixed Assets.	Price on application to dealers.	Dealers provide full support.	Over 150 vertical market applications to link in with modules. Dealers can develop bespoke programs.
SAGE INSTANT ACCOUNTING The Sage Group plc, Benton Park Road Newcastle-upon-Tyne NE7 7LZ Tel: 0191 255 3000 Fax: 0191 255 0308	Available direct from Sage through High Street computer re-sellers, most of whom can also supply hardware.	Sage Instant Accounting (For Windows)	£299.00 inc. VAT	Free Help line for 30 days.	It is an entry level small business accounts package. Data compatibility with Sterling products. Windows. Single user.

Fig. 13.2 (continued)

The final accounts of a business

INTRODUCTION

In Chapter 6, you learned how to do a set of final accounts for a sole trader business, and found that it consists of a trading account, a profit and loss account and a balance sheet. The starting point for a set of final accounts is the trial balance of the ledger taken out after the close of business on the last day of the financial year. If you are not using a double entry system, you do not have a trial balance and so have to draw up your final accounts from the various summaries provided by the system you are using. This is quite easy with a system like Simplex's, because all the details you need are provided in the summaries and you are guided through the preparation of the final accounts very clearly. It is not quite as easy with some of the abbreviated systems described earlier and so it may be necessary to turn your records over to an accountant and allow them to prepare your final accounts for you.

The advantage is that you find out a lot more about your business if you prepare these accounts yourself.

The aim of this chapter – and, indeed, the next two chapters – is to encourage you to attempt to prepare your own set of final accounts, rather than passing them over to an accountant. The advantage is that you find out a lot more about your business if you prepare these accounts yourself, and you will do them more quickly than an accountant, who usually has a large backlog of work, especially at the end of the calendar year (in December) and the tax year (in April). These are the times of year when most people finish their accounting years. If you finish your accounting year on the anniversary of starting your business, you may finish at any time of the year, and this is of course quite acceptable to the Inland Revenue.

Later in this chapter, I will be looking fairly closely at one further element in preparing final accounts – the manufacturing account, which is necessary for manufacturing businesses and precedes the trading account, the profit and loss account and the balance sheet. You will then have a full sequence, as follows:

- the manufacturing account, which gives you a manufacturing profit, if you wish to work this out separately;
- the trading account, which gives you the gross profit of the business;
- the profit and loss account, which gives you the net profit of the business;
- the balance sheet, which is a snapshot of the current state of affairs of the business at a given moment in time, which is the last second

of the last day of the financial year – the next day you start again, at 'dawn on day one' of a new year.

Before beginning with the manufacturing account, you must first mention one or two special points about adjustments.

ADJUSTMENTS

■ What are adjustments?

At the end of the year, there are several situations you need to know about, which come under the general heading of 'adjustments'. The idea of adjustments is that the figures arrived at in a firm's book-keeping for receipts and expenditure should be adjusted to take account of generally accepted accounting principles, so that the final accounts produced give a 'true and fair view' of the profits and losses of the business for that financial year. These basic accounting principles are as follows:

■ the accounts should bring in every penny of income that has been earned in the accounting period under consideration,
■ set against this income, there should be ranged every penny of expense incurred in earning the income.

When these expenses have been deducted from the receipts earned in the period, you reveal the true profit of the business for the period. Having found the true profit, you then arrive at the true tax payable for the period.

At one time, the Inland Revenue permitted professional firms – such as accountants, financial advisers and similar bodies – to keep their books on a different basis, but this privilege was withdrawn in 1997, to take effect from 1998. This more favourable 'receipts and payments basis' has therefore been discontinued.

If you understand double entry book-keeping, you will understand adjustments. If you employ an accountant, they will, of course, understand adjustments, and you will then have your books done on an 'accruals basis', which means that all necessary adjustments will have been done. The word 'accruals' means 'things that have become due'. Adjustments simply adjust the final accounts to include anything that had become due and must count as a profit (or a loss) for this year. They also exclude anything that has not become due, but ought properly to be deferred and treated as a profit of next year or a loss of next year. That is all adjustments do, but as there are rather a lot of them, and they sometimes call for very clear thinking about principles of accounting, they can be worrying to the beginner.

Take one very simple example to illustrate the point. Suppose you have a sub-tenant who pays you £500 a quarter for rent. This is a little bit of profit for your business. Suppose it is due on 31 March, 30 June, 30 September and 31 December. In the year 199X the Rent Received Account looks like that shown in Figure 14.1.

	Rent Received A/c		L.21
	199X		£
	31 March	A. Tenant	500.00
	30 June	A. Tenant	500.00
	30 September	A. Tenant	500.00

Fig. 14.1 AN INCOMPLETE RENT ACCOUNT

The tenant, who lives in Glasgow, has gone home for Hogmanay and you have not received the money on 31 December. If you were keeping your books on a receipts and payments basis' the rent received for the year would be £1500. However, everyone can see that this does not give a true and fair view of the profits of the business, because the Rent Received Account should read £2000 for the year. Therefore, the accountant would transfer £2000 to the Profit and Loss Account as a profit for the year. The accounts would then look like those shown in Figure 14.2.

Rent Received A/c					L.21
199X	£	199X			£
31 Dec. Transfer to		31 March	A. Tenant		500.00
P & L A/c	2000.00	30 June	A. Tenant		500.00
		30 Sept.	A. Tenant		500.00
		31 Dec.	Balance c/d		500.00
	£2000.00				£2000.00
199X	£				
1 Jan. Balance b/d	500.00				

Profit and Loss A/c for Year Ending 31 December 199X		L.97
	199X	£
	Gross profit	27 295.60
	Rent received	2 000.00

Fig. 14.2 CLOSING OFF THE RENT ACCOUNT AT THE END OF THE FINANCIAL YEAR

Notes
- As A. Tenant has not paid the last £500, it appears as a debit balance on the Rent Received Account.
- Remember that any debit balance on an account is either a loss or an asset (see Figure 6.5). As the Rent Received Account is a profit account, it cannot be a loss – it must be an asset. We have a debtor, A. Tenant, who owes us £500. As soon as the tenant gets back after Hogmanay, he will give us the money, and we shall pay it into the bank. It will then be an asset, cash at the bank, and the £500 balance on the Rent Received Account will disappear as you credit the account with the £500 received.

It is impossible at this stage to go into all the possible types of adjustments. Anyone who is really interested should obtain a copy of my book *Book-keeping Made Simple*.

■ Adjustments and the balance sheet

Whenever you do an adjustment, you finish up with a balance on an account that, had there been no adjustment, would have been clear. Thus, in Figure 14.1, if the tenant had been up to date with the rent and paid the full £2000 for the year, the £2000 would have been transferred to the Profit and Loss Account, and the Rent Received Account would have been clear. Instead, it finished up with a balance on the Rent Received Account of £500, a debt from the debtor, A. Tenant.

Now, every balance at the end of the year, on any account, must appear on the balance sheet, which is, as its name implies, a list of the outstanding balances that are being carried forward to the next year. As the balance left on any account must either be an asset (something the business owns) or a liability (something the business owes) the balances that result from adjustments appear on the Balance Sheet either as assets or liabilities. In the case of the debtor, A. Tenant, the £500 rent due is an asset – you own this debt – and the figure of £500 will appear on the assets side of the Balance Sheet as 'Rent due from sub-tenant, £500'.

Salaries A/c

199X	£	199X	£
Jan.-Dec. Sundry entries totalling	9777.50	31 Dec. Transfer to Profit & Loss A/c	9900.00
31 Dec. Balance c/d	122.50		
	£9900.00		£9900.00
		199X	£
		1 Jan. Balance b/d	122.50

Fig. 14.3 PAY ACCRUED DUE AT THE END OF THE YEAR

Taking a different example, supposing the salaries for the year total £9777.50, but you owe one employee £122.50 because he is in hospital and his pay has not yet been taken to him. The adjusted salaries figure is therefore £9900.00. The Pay Account looks as shown in Figure 14.3.

This credit balance is a liability (you owe the man his salary) and this will therefore appear on the Balance Sheet as a liability, 'Salaries due £122.50'.

The general names for these outstanding balances are 'accrued charges' for the liabilities and 'payments in advance' for the assets.

■ Depreciation – a special type of adjustment

One adjustment that affects small businesses in a special way is depreciation. Depreciation is a reduction in the value of a capital asset as a result of fair wear and tear. The principle of depreciation is that as all assets wear out as the years pass, they should diminish in value on the balance sheet over time, and each year the fair amount of loss in value should be written off on the profit and loss account as a loss for the year. As the amount to be treated as depreciation is, to some extent, left to the discretion of the trader concerned, there is a danger that, from the tax point of view, a trader could take advantage of the tax system. For example, suppose as a trader I am making good profits, I could decide to write off more than a fair amount of depreciation. This would reduce my profits and, consequently, reduce the tax payable.

To avoid such problems, Parliament has decreed that whatever the depreciation decided on by the business person, the amount shall be treated as a disallowable expense and, instead, a statutory 'capital allowance' shall apply to all small- and medium-sized firms. This allowance is at present 50 per cent of the original cost in year 1 on capital assets purchased after 2 July 1998 and 25 per cent of the diminishing balance in subsequent years. Thus, whatever the depreciation deducted in a profit and loss account, it will be added back to the profits and the capital allowance will be taken instead. Under the new self-assessment tax system, you declare the depreciation in your tax return, but it is later disregarded and the official allowance is deducted instead.

MANUFACTURING ACCOUNTS

If you run a small manufacturing business, you must really prepare a manufacturing account as part of your final accounts. The point here is that you cannot begin trading until some goods have been made, with which to trade. This means that the value of the goods manufactured has to be worked out and transferred into the trading account ('cost of goods manufactured' instead of 'purchases') and then these goods can be sold and a profit

> *If you run a small manufacturing business, you must really prepare a manufacturing account as part of your final accounts.*

arrived at. The procedure is fairly simple, but a few terms used in relation to them need to be explained first.

- **Prime costs** Prime costs are the first costs incurred in manufacturing, and are usually taken to include the costs actually embodied in the manufacturing of the products. They therefore include raw materials, any special components bought in, the direct pay of workers employed in the production process and any other costs directly attributable to production, such as the power for machines. These costs are collected together in a section of the manufacturing account called the prime cost section (see Figure 14.4), and are then carried down into a further section called the cost of manufactured goods section.

- **Overheads** Besides the prime costs of any manufactured goods, there are a great many overhead expenses that have to be added to the prime costs to get the total costs of the manufactured goods. As all these expenses have to be recovered from the customer, you must build them into the 'cost of manufactured goods' before you work out a selling price. Typical overheads are supervision salaries, factory rent, lighting, repairs and depreciation.

- **Work-in-progress** At the end of the year, you know that any trader will have stocks of goods unsold on the shelves, and these stocks must be taken into account when working out the trading account (see Chapter 4). In the same way, any manufacturer will have partly finished goods going through the manufacturing process and, what is worse, they will be at all sorts of stages. Some will be still practically raw materials, having only just entered the production phase, and some will be almost complete. If you are going to take these stocks of work-in-progress into account we have to value them at some fair figure and this will usually mean you value them all as if they were half-finished (that is you take an average value). You can therefore say that work-in-progress is an adjustment made in the cost of manufactured goods section of the manufacturing account to take account of goods going through the manufacturing process that are as yet incomplete.

To avoid having too many figures to look at when preparing a manufacturing account, I shall take you through only part of a trial balance, which shows only the manufacturing and trading items. This will enable us to prepare a manufacturing account and a trading account, but I will not go on to produce a profit and loss account or a balance sheet, as these will be explained later.

Notice that there will now be three types of stock:

- stocks of raw materials;
- stocks of work-in-progress;
- stocks of finished goods.

As with the trading account, there will be opening stocks at the start of the period and closing stocks at the end of the period. Study the figures given in Example 1 and the Manufacturing and Trading Accounts given in Figures 14.4 and 14.5.

EXAMPLE 1

R. Marshall is a manufacturer. Let's see how to prepare his Manufacturing Account and Trading Account for year ending 31 December, 199X.

	£
Stocks at 1 January, 199X	
Raw materials	27 824
Work-in-progress (valued at factory cost)	3 259
Finished goods	36 297
Purchases of raw materials	46 358
Sales	338 566
Returns in	1 566
Factory:	
Wages (prime cost)	24 268
Power (prime cost)	1 896
Factory:	
Salaries (overhead)	23 258
Rent (overhead)	5 960

Lighting (overhead)	1 265
Repairs (overhead)	1 792
Depreciation (overhead)	1 160

Warehouse: (Trading Account)	
Wages	29 254
Business rates	3 756

Stocks at 31 December 19X9	
Raw materials	19 964
Work-in-progress (valued at factory cost)	4 416
Finished goods	27 348

Method

The Manufacturing Account is prepared first, as shown in Figure 14.4 with its two sections: the Prime Cost Section and the Cost of Manufactured Goods Section. Then the Trading Account is prepared in the usual way as in Figure 14.5. Notice that the Prime Cost Section simply collects together all the prime costs, and these are then carried down into the next section – the Cost of Manufactured Goods Section. In this section the overheads are added to the prime costs, the adjustment is done for the work-in-progress and the final cost of the manufactured goods is carried to the Trading Account. You are advised to work carefully through the example to see how the gross profit is finally arrived at.

Manufacturing Account
for Year Ending 31 December 199X
Prime Cost Section

		£		£
Raw materials:			Prime costs (carried to	
Stock at start		27 824	Cost of Manufactured	
Purchases	46 358		Goods Section)	80 382
Less returns	–			
		46 358		
Total available		74 182		
Less closing stock		19 964		
Cost of raw materials used		54 218		
Wages		24 268		
Power		1 896		
		£80 382		£80 382

Cost of Manufactured Goods Section

	£		£
Prime costs	80 382	Cost of manufactured goods (transferred to Trading	
Overheads:		Account)	112 660
Salaries	23 258		
Rent	5 960		
Lighting	1 265		
Repairs	1 792		
Depreciation	1 160		
	33 435		
	113 817		
Work-in-progress:			
Stock at start	3 259		
Less Closing stock	−4 416		
	−1 157		
	£112 660		£112 660

Fig. 14.4 R. MARSHALL'S MANUFACTURING ACCOUNT

Notes

- The work-in-progress needs a word of explanation. At the start of the year, there was £3259 of work-in-progress in the workshop, and in Week 1 of the new year, this went through into production. At the end of the year, the work-in-progress closing stock was greater: £4416. Therefore, more was held back (and carried over to next year) than was handed on to this year from last year. The result is, in effect, that you must deduct the difference (£1157) from the cost of manufactured goods as some of the raw materials and so on used in the year were not manufactured this year, but left behind for next year's output.
- The final result is a Cost of Manufactured Goods figure of £112 660. These finished goods were handed on to the Trading Account to be sold in the year. Now see the Trading Account in Figure 14.5.

Trading Account
for Year ending 31 December 199X

	£		£
Opening stock of		Sales	338 566
finished goods	36 297	*Less* returns in	1 566
Cost of manufactured		Net turnover	337 000
goods	112 660		
	148 957		
Less closing			
stock	27 348		
Cost of stock sold	121 609		
Warehouse wages	29 254		
Business rates	3 756		
Cost of sales	154 619		
Gross profit	182 381		
	£337 000		£337 000

Profit and Loss Account
for Year Ending 31 December 199X

	£
Gross profit	182 381

Fig. 14.5 THE TRADING ACCOUNT OF A MANUFACTURER

Notes
- This is exactly the same as any ordinary trading account, except that instead of purchasing goods for re-sale, we manufacture them. Therefore the item 'purchases' does not appear and is replaced by 'Cost of manufactured goods', which comes in from the Manufacturing Account.
- One or two additional items have been included. For example warehouse staff's wages and business rates have been added to the costs incurred (for operating the warehouse). The final result is that the cost of sales is deducted from the sales figure (the net turnover) to give the gross profit.

BRINGING OUT A MANUFACTURING PROFIT

Some traders like to bring out a manufacturing profit, because they want to know whether it is worth while having a factory at all. Would you do better if you bought-in everything you wished to sell, and did not have the worry of manufacturing?

To understand what is necessary to bring out a manufacturing profit, look back to Figure 14.4, where, on the right-hand side, £112 660 is given as the cost of manufactured goods. Suppose you can get a good idea of what these manufactured items would cost if you could purchase them. Suppose it was £140 000. This means that the manufacturing profit is £140 000 − £112 660 = £27 340. By simply putting the market value of the goods on the right-hand side, instead of the 'cost of manufactured goods', you can bring out the manufacturing profit, as shown in Figure 14.6. This means that you will charge the trading account with the market value of the goods manufactured, not their cost. This will reduce the gross profit by £27 340, and you will have the same profit in the profit and loss account, but in two parts − a manufacturing profit and a gross profit on trading. You can thus see that your factory is a valuable unit, contributing a useful sum to your total profitability. The final profit figure of £182 381 is the same as before, but you can now see that it is made up of two parts:

- the results of the manufacturing effort;
- the results of the trading activities.

You might like to work out what these profits would have been if the market value of the manufactured goods had been:

- £230 000
- £98 000.

From the results you could then give an answer to the question, 'What should we do about our factory?'

Cost of Manufactured Goods Section

	£		£
Prime Costs	80 382	Market value of manufactured goods (transferred to	
Overheads:		Trading Account)	140 000
Salaries	23 258		
Rent	5 960		
Lighting	1 265		
Repairs	1 792		
Depreciation	1 160 33 435		
	113 817		
Work-in-progress:			
Stock at start	3 259		
Less Closing stock	–4 416		
	–1 157		
Cost of manufactured goods	112 660		
Manufacturing profit	27 340		
	£140 000		£140 000

Trading Account
for Year Ending 31 December 199X

	£		£
Opening stock of		Sales	338 566
finished goods	36 297	*Less* Returns in	1 566
Market value of		Net turnover	337 000
manufactured goods	140 000		
	176 297		
Less Closing stock	27 348		
Cost of stock sold	148 949		
Warehouse pay	29 254		
Business rates	3 756		
Cost of sales	181 959		
Gross profit	155 041		
	£337 000		£337 000

Profit and Loss Account
for Year Ending 31 December, 199X

	£
Manufacturing profit	27 340
Gross profit	155 041
	£182 381

Fig. 14.6 A MANUFACTURING ACCOUNT TO BRING OUT THE PROFIT ON MANUFACTURING

EXERCISE ON PREPARING A MANUFACTURING ACCOUNT

K. Hoyle is a manufacturer. From the information below, prepare his Manufacturing Account and Trading Account, and open his Profit and Loss Account for the year ended 31 December, 199X.

	£
Sales	375 281
Stocks at 1 January, 199X	
Raw materials	29 464
Work-in-progress (valued at factory cost)	7 295
Finished goods	47 327
Purchases of raw materials	103 528
Stocks at 31 December, 199X:	
Raw materials	17 247
Work-in-progress (valued at factory cost)	9 756
Finished goods	86 924
Factory:	
Wages	58 874
Wages due at 31 December, 199X	625
Factory and machinery maintenance	6 725
Depreciation on plant and machinery	9 800
Factory power (prime cost)	5 254
Factory salaries	17 295
Factory expenses:	
Rent and business rates	8 240
Lighting and heating	1 959

Answer

Books of K. Hoyle: prime cost, £180 498; cost of manufactured goods, £222 056; gross profit £192 822.

EXAMPLE 2

M. Thomas has capital at the start of the year of £6785.00 and makes a profit in the year of £16 968.50. Of this he has already drawn out £650 a month for 12 months and has also taken home goods for personal use valued at £238.50. Show his Capital Account, the closing balance on his Profit and Loss Account and his Drawings Account after the preparation of his Final Accounts at the end of the year, 31 December 199X.

Profit and Loss A/c (final profit only) 31 December, 199X   L.194

199X	£	199X	£
31 Dec. Transfer to		31 Dec. Balance (net	
Capital A/c	16 968.50	profit) b/d	16 968.50

Drawings A/c (M. Thomas)   L.15

199X	£	199X	£
Jan.-Dec. Sundry entries		31 Dec. Transfer to	
to a total of	7 800.00	capital A/c	8 038.50
Jan.-Dec. Goods	238.50		
	£8 038.50		£8 038.50

Capital A/c (M. Thomas)   L.1

199X	£	199X	£
31 Dec. Drawings	8 038.50	1 Jan. Balance b/d	6 785.00
31 Dec. Balance c/d	15 715.00	31 Dec. Net profit	
		transferred	16 968.50
	£23 753.50		£23 753.50
		199X	£
		1 Jan. Balance b/d	15 715.00

Notes
- First the profits are transferred to the Capital Account. The business now owes M. Thomas not only his original capital but also the profits earned.
- Then the drawings are transferred in, on the debit side because Thomas has already received them (debit the receiver). As a result, you can see that the total funds now invested in the business by the proprietor are £15 715.00.

END-OF-YEAR ACCOUNTS FOR A SOLE TRADER

Under the self-assessment system of taxation introduced in 1997, you no longer send in your accounts to the Inland Revenue. You simply declare your profits in the self-assessment tax return. Some useful points about this are given in Chapter 20. Here you are simply practising the preparation of final accounts for a sole trader and, in order not to neglect those who are involved in manufacturing, the first exercise shows a trial balance of a manufacturing business. Do not be dismayed by the look of this exercise. It is simple enough because it shows the trial balance of the business at the end of the year. The rules for preparing a set of final accounts are as follows.

- The starting point is the trial balance of the books at close of business on the last day of the financial year. If you are using a specialist system like the Simplex system, it will be the figures in the summaries collected together at the end of the year.
- You then prepare a manufacturing account if your business is engaged in manufacturing. If not, you start with the trading account.
- You then prepare the trading account, but some businesses do not trade, they are fee-earning, and in that case you will not have a trading account. The trading account gives you the gross profit (see Chapter 4).
- You then prepare a profit and loss account starting with the gross profit. If you are a non-trading business, all the fees earned will be recorded in the profit and loss account. Either way, the result is the net profit of the business (see Chapter 5).
- Finally, the net profit is carried into the capital account and any drawings are also carried to the capital account where they reduce the profits available (because they have already been drawn). To clarify this procedure, a simple example is given below. You should then try the two exercises at the end of the chapter.

EXERCISES ON THE FINAL ACCOUNTS OF A SOLE TRADER

1. Frank Dearden is in business as a manufacturer. On the last day of the financial year, 31 December, 199X, his trial balance is as follows:

	£	£
Stocks at 1 January		
Raw materials	9 560	
Work-in-progress	1 280	
Finished goods	13 925	
Purchases of raw materials	28 565	
Sales of finished goods		184 726
Factory wages (prime cost)	34 768	
Power (prime cost)	1 295	
Factory overheads	48 954	
Office expenses	27 246	

	£	£
Rent, insurance, etc.	5 980	
Commission received		18 256
Furniture and fittings	14 250	
Motor vehicles	16 750	
Debtors	3 248	
Creditors		4 921
Cash at bank	11 855	
Cash in hand	247	
Capital at start of year		16 250
Drawings	9 830	
Loan from bank		3 600
	£227 753	£227 753

Closing stocks at 31 December were found to be: raw materials £11 750; work-in-progress £3 960; finished goods £19 890. Prepare a full set of Frank Dearden's Final Accounts.

2.   Mark Farmer is a professional person who does not manufacture or trade and who therefore starts his Final Accounts with what would be his Profit and Loss Account, but by choice he calls it his Revenue Account as it contains details of his income and expenses for the year. The traditional name for incomes and expenditures is revenues. Here is his Trial Balance. Draw up his Revenue Account and Balance Sheet, taking account of the two adjustments shown below his Trial Balance. Remember that any adjustment not only adjusts the figures in the Revenue Account but also appears as a balance on his Balance Sheet, either as a liability (accrued expenses) or as an asset (payments in advance).

	Dr.	Cr.
	£	£
Capital (at 1 January, 19XX)		90 000
Drawings	24 000	
Premises	117 120	
Furniture, etc.	7 000	
Motor vehicles	48 000	
Fees received		134 625
Commission received		37 965
Rent from subtenant		2 350
Light and heat	1 865	
Cleaning	3 250	

	Dr. £	Cr. £
Loans made to clients (current asset)	72 500	
Other debtors	4 850	
Creditors		1 264
Office expenses	3 266	
Office salaries	40 840	
Mortgage on premises		71 000
Advertising materials	3 750	
Computers, etc.	2 318	
Cash in hand	240	
Cash at bank	8 205	
	£337 204	£337 204

Adjustments (at 31 December, 19XX)

- An electricity bill for £240 is due and unpaid.
- Advertising materials (brochures) to the value of £650 are in stock and will be used up next year.

Answers
1. Books of Frank Dearden: prime costs, £62 438; cost of manufactured goods, £108 712; gross profit, £81 979; net profit, £67 009; capital at close of year, £73 429; Balance Sheet totals £81 950.
2. Books of Mark Farmer: net profit, £122 379; capital at close of year, £188 379; Balance Sheet totals £260 883.

CHECKLIST

- The last act of the book-keeper at the end of the financial year is to work out the final accounts of the business, and credit any profit to the proprietor's capital account.

- Today all traders are required to prepare their accounts on an 'accruals' basis, taking account of any adjustments that are necessary, so that it is possible to arrive at a true and fair view of the profitability of the business. The aim is to include every penny of income earned in the trading period, and set against this income every penny of expense incurred in earning the income. You adjust the income and the expenses to leave out of the accounts anything that belongs to the next year, and anything that belonged to the previous year.

- If a business is a manufacturing one, the first stage of the final accounts is a manufacturing account. This usually finds the cost of manufactured goods, but, if preferred, it can also be used to find a manufacturing profit.

- The 'cost of manufactured goods' is made up of two parts – the prime costs and the overheads.

- All manufacturers and all traders need a trading account in which the gross profit is discovered.

- The gross profit is then carried into the profit and loss account, where the net profit is found. Professional people, who do not trade, start their final accounts with the profit and loss account, which they often call the 'revenue account'.

- The final part of a set of final accounts is the balance sheet, which is a snapshot of the affairs of the business at a given moment in time – the last second of the last hour of the last day of the financial year.

- In former times, a copy of a firm's final accounts was submitted to the Inland Revenue, which, in due course, sent the trader(s) an assessment for tax that had to be paid in two parts, by 1 January and 1 July. In April 1997, a changeover to a self-assessment tax system was implemented. This is explained more fully in Chapter 20 of this book. The money due as tax under the self-assessment system is now payable by 31 January and 31 July each year, with automatic penalties for failure to pay by the due date, and interest on the overdue balance beginning to be charged from 1 February and 1 August respectively.

Keeping the books of a partnership

What is a partnership?

Partnership deed

What are the differences between sole trader and
   partnership accounts?

Appropriation account

Other partnership accounts

Checklist

WHAT IS A PARTNERSHIP?

A partnership is legally defined as a relationship between persons carrying on a business together with a view to earning profits. It is a very ancient form of business arrangement and the legal rules surrounding it grew up over centuries until they were finally set down in the Partnership Act of 1890. Partnerships come into existence at will – that is because the partners wish to work together – and may be dissolved at will. This means that one partner can give notice to the other partner, and to anybody else likely to be affected (such as suppliers and customers) that they no longer wish to be associated with the other. An oral arrangement (one made by word of mouth) is sufficient to form a partnership, but to prove that it came into existence you need a witness.

> *A partnership is legally defined as a relationship between persons carrying on a business together with a view to earning profits.*

PARTNERSHIP DEED

A written agreement is better, both because it is easier to establish that a partnership does exist, but also because in setting down in writing what is agreed between the partners, a number of future difficulties may be aired and resolved. For example, it may be agreed that A, who is a good salesperson, shall handle that side of the business, while B, who is good at accounts, and putting up most of the money, shall sign cheques. Best of all, if a solicitor is asked to draw up a formal partnership deed, the relationship will be more carefully investigated to cover many points that should be agreed between those who set up in business together. For example:

- the partners' shares of profits, and losses;
- the amounts of capital to be contributed;
- the areas of responsibility in the work to be done;
- whether or not any partner is to have a salary or interest on the capital subscribed;
- what level of drawings should be allowed.

'Drawings' are sums of money taken out in expectation of profits made. A partner has to live in the course of the year while the business is established and is making its profits, and, as the final profit figure is not arrived at until the end of the year, some money must be released beforehand. If, in fact, the business is not making profits, the sums withdrawn will be deducted from the capital subscribed, and the partners are said to be 'living on their capital'.

There are many more points. Solicitors will tell you that it is not unknown for partners who agreed to work together one week to be at daggers drawn within a month or two, so the fullest airing beforehand of the likely problem areas forewarns the partners that a bit of give and take is essential if a partnership is to prosper.

WHAT ARE THE DIFFERENCES BETWEEN SOLE TRADER AND PARTNERSHIP ACCOUNTS?

For the vast majority of simple transactions, there is no difference between the accounts of a sole trader and partnership accounts. Manufacturing, buying and selling, the payment of overheads and the employment of staff are exactly the same. The differences lie in the arrangements for capital, drawings and the sharing of profits. Here the important points are as follows. First, I shall explain the various accounts. Then an example shows in detail what the accounts look like.

■ Capital accounts

Instead of a single capital account, each partner has a capital account on which is recorded the amount of capital they have contributed. It is usual to keep this figure on the capital account unchanged, except at very rare intervals when some fundamental rearrangement of the partnership's affairs takes place (as, for example, when a new partner is admitted). Partnership capital accounts are therefore said to be 'fixed'.

With a sole trader, it is usual to transfer the profits made to the capital account at the end of the year and so the capital account of a sole trader is liable to fluctuate. This is not allowed to happen in the case of partnerships. As with all capital accounts, the balances on the accounts will be credit balances because they record what the business owes back to the owners of the business. The owners are 'creditors' of the business who have given the capital contributed to the business (credit the giver).

■ Current accounts

If the capital accounts are fixed, it is necessary to have an account to which the profits earned by the partnership can be transferred, in the appropriate shares as laid down in the partnership agreement. Each partner, therefore, has a second account called a current account that does fluctuate from year to year and receives the partner's share of the profits earned.

The balance on a current account will usually be a credit balance, because the business owes the profits to the partner, but it is possible to have an overdrawn current account, with a debit balance. For example, if a partner draws out more in the year than the business earns in profits, the debit entries on the current account will be greater than the profits earned on the credit side and a debit balance will result. This is not transferred to the capital account except if the partnership is being wound up, when the partner's balance will be cleared to the capital account and they will be unable to withdraw the full amount originally subscribed.

■ Drawings accounts

Each partner also has a drawings account in which the sums of money drawn out can be collected together over the year and a clear record of all sums drawn made available.

Cash may be drawn on a regular basis. A partner is not allowed to have 'wages' in the normal sense of that word as a partner is only entitled to a share of the profits as a reward for their efforts. The cash drawn, as explained earlier, is 'in expectation of profits made'.

Other forms of 'drawings' are sums paid by the partnership for the benefit of a partner; for example, tax moneys due, pension contributions to private pension schemes, goods taken for own consumption and other items taken for personal use (for example, a partner might buy a redundant computer for home use).

These various accounts are set out later in this chapter, but first I must mention one further account that is used to bring all these partnership accounts into order and share out the profits in whatever way has been agreed. It is called the appropriation account.

APPROPRIATION ACCOUNT

The term 'appropriation account' is used both in partnerships and companies to designate an account that is used to divide up the profits made and 'appropriate', or allocate, them to the particular uses the partners or the directors of a company decide is the best. In the case of a partnership, the most common usages are as follows.

- It is quite common to reduce the value on the books of any intangible asset, of which goodwill is the chief example. Goodwill is a sum of money paid to the previous owner of a business for the good opinion they have established in the minds of people in the locality – which it is believed will bring in profits to the business in years to come. One judge said, 'Goodwill is a payment for the probability that an old customer will return to the old place for further supplies at some time in the future'. If you pay out £1000 for a piece of machinery, you get an asset, a machine, in exchange for the money. When you pay out £1000 for goodwill, you get an asset, 'goodwill', for your money, but it is a pretty intangible asset as it consists of a good opinion in the minds of the people in the locality. It is usual to write off this intangible asset out of profits in the first few years – say at 25 per cent a year.
- It is sometimes agreed that a junior partner shall be paid a salary to ensure that a certain basic income is available to them. As partners cannot really receive a salary as such, the sum agreed is regarded as a first charge against the profits and is appropriated to the partner concerned as the first claim on the profits, after arrangements for goodwill have been completed.
- It is sometimes agreed that partners shall receive interest on capital. Usually this is done where one party has contributed much more capital than the others. This interest on capital is treated as a prior charge on the profits before the residue of the profit is shared.
- Finally, the residue of the profit is shared between the partners in whatever manner is agreed.

The workings of the appropriation account is best illustrated by an example.

EXAMPLE

Paul and Jean are in partnership, sharing profits ⅔ to Paul and ⅓ to Jean. The partnership agreement makes the following provisions.

- Paul to contribute capital of £20 000 and Jean £5000;
- interest on capital to be allowed at 8 per cent, to both partners;
- Jean, the younger partner, is to have a basic salary of £5000 as a first claim on the profits – she is a fashion designer, whose designs the business is to market;
- they are to pay £2500 for goodwill to the vendor of the business they are taking over – this intangible asset will be written off in equal instalments over the first five years of the business.

In the first year, the profits are £39 285. Drawings in the year were: Paul £19 500 and Jean £12 600.

Paul and Jean's Appropriation Account is shown below, with some explanatory notes. The other accounts are shown under the heading Other partnership accounts.

Appropriation Account
for year ending 31 December 199X

199X		£	199X	£
Goodwill		500.00	Profits (from P&L A/c)	39 285.00
Salary (Jean)		5 000.00		
Interest on capital				
Paul	£1 600.00			
Jean	£ 400.00			
		2 000.00		
Share of residue of profit				
Paul	£21 190.00			
Jean	£10 595.00			
		31 785.00		
		£39 285.00		£39 285.00

Notes
- The net profit comes in from their Profit and Loss Account as a credit entry (it is what the business owes to the partners for the year's profitable activities).
- The goodwill instalment is then written off – bringing the Goodwill Account down to a balance of £2000 only. This is a capital transaction, not revenue expenditure, so it cannot be claimed as a reduction from the profits in their Profit and Loss Account. It is an appropriation of profit.
- Jean is then given her salary. It is taken to her Current Account, on the credit side.
- Each of the partners is then given the interest on capital. Again this is taken to their Current Accounts.
- Finally, the residue of the profit is shared in the agreed ratio, and taken to Paul and Jean's Current Accounts. This leaves the Appropriation Account clear – all the profits have been given away or used for the purpose the partners intended.
- For the rest of the accounts, see the next section.

OTHER PARTNERSHIP ACCOUNTS

In partnership accounts, each partner has three accounts – a capital account, drawings account and current account. If you now look at these accounts, continuing the example given above, you find that the accounts of Paul and Jean are as shown below. Each set has some notes attached.

Capital A/c Paul

199X	£
1 Jan. Capital contributed	20 000.00

Capital A/c Jean

199X	£
1 Jan. Capital contributed	5 000.00

Notes

● The accounts are opened on the day the business starts, in order to record the original capital contributions.

● As these are fixed Capital Accounts, no further entries will be made, except if some fundamental rearrangement of the partnership takes place (perhaps on the admission of a new partner). The accounts therefore remain as shown year after year, and appear on the partnership's Balance Sheet, as shown later in this section.

Drawings A/c Jean

199X	£	199X	£
31 Jan. Bank	1 000.00	31 Dec. Transfer to	
		Current A/c	12 600.00
28 Feb. Bank	1 000.00		
etc., etc., each			
month			
14 Dec. Computer A/c	600.00		
31 Dec. Bank	1 000.00		
	£12 600.00		£12 600.00

Notes

● Only one Drawings Account has been shown – the other would be similar.

● The younger partner, Jean, draws £1000 a month for living expenses and also took over a computer that was surplus to requirements, making the total drawn £12 000. These are all debit entries because the partner has received the cash and so on.

● This total for drawings is carried to Jean's Current Account, leaving the Drawings Account clear to start a new year.

● The Drawings Account is just a collection account where the various amounts drawn can be collected together, ready to be written off the partner's Current Account at the end of the year.

Current A/c Paul

199X	£	199X	£
31 Dec. Drawings	19 500.00	31 Dec. Interest on capital	1 600.00
31 Dec. Balance	3 290.00	31 Dec. Share of residue	21 190.00
	£22 790.00		£22 790.00
		199X	£
		1 Jan. Balance b/d	3 290.00

Current A/c Jean

199X	£	199X	£
31 Dec. Drawings	12 600.00	31 Dec. Salary	5 000.00
31 Dec. Balance	3 395.00	31 Dec. Interest on capital	400.00
		31 Dec. Share of residue	10 595.00
	£15 995.00		£15 995.00
		199X	£
		1 Jan. Balance b/d	3 395.00

Notes
- It is the current account in partnerships that fluctuates with the earning of profits and their withdrawal by the partners.
- All the items due to the partners appear on the credit side, because the money is owed to the partner by the business.
- Against these profits earned, the drawings are debit entries because the partner has received the money (or goods for personal use). The balance is still owing to the partners and will be carried over to the next financial year.
- Imagine that Jean had drawn the same as Paul, £19 500.00. This would have meant she had overdrawn on her Current Account, and instead of a credit balance there would have been a debit balance: she would have been a debtor of the business for the excess amount drawn.

Goodwill A/c

199X	£	199X	£
1 Jan. Goodwill acquired	2500.00	31 Dec. Appropriation A/c	500.00
		31 Dec. Balance c/d	2000.00
	£2500.00		£2500.00
199X	£		
1 Jan. Balance b/d	2000.00		

Notes
- The asset 'goodwill' is an intangible asset – there is not much to show for it really.
- If you decide to write it off, you must do so out of profits – it is not deductible as a revenue expense in the profit and loss account.
- The result here is that the asset, goodwill, is reduced in value to £2000.
- Accountants talk about the 'paradox of goodwill'. When you take over a business with goodwill, you have on your books an asset at a high valuation. The truth is that, at that time, the public bears you no goodwill at all, for they do not even know that you exist! The goodwill they bear is to the previous owner. As the years pass you write off the intangible asset by a series of appropriations of profit. The goodwill gradually reduces until it is written off completely. At the same time, the local people have now learned about you; people realise your goods or services are reliable and they now bear you some goodwill. This is the 'paradox' of goodwill; it is valued at a high figure on the books when it is worthless, and at nothing on the books when it is quite valuable.

■ Special note about the balance sheets of partnerships

The following special features of a partnership balance sheet should be noted.

- As there are two fixed (unvarying) capital accounts, these appear on the liabilities side, simply added together.
- The partners' current accounts would normally have credit balances (meaning that the business owes the partners some undrawn profits at the end of the year). These would appear on the liabilities side and, once again, they would be added together to show the total owed to the partners. However, it is possible for one, or both, of the partners to be overdrawn on their current accounts – that is, they have drawn out more money as drawings than they earned as their shares of the profits. In that case, the balance will be a debit balance, and must be carried over to the assets side. It is probably best to treat this as an unusual asset, neither 'fixed' nor 'current', and it would therefore appear below the 'fixed assets' and above the 'current assets'.

Today, because the Start-up Allowance Scheme is available to both husbands and wives if both are genuinely unemployed and seeking to become self-employed, there are a great many people setting up 'husband and wife' partnerships. There is a specimen set of partnership accounts available free of charge from George Vyner Ltd, Holmfirth, Huddersfield HD7 2RP. The balance sheet of this specimen set is shown here as Figure 15.1.

If you are in business as a partnership or if you are thinking of setting up in business with a partner, try the following exercises. The first is an exercise to get you used to appropriation accounts. The second is a full set of final accounts.

EXERCISES ON PARTNERSHIP ACCOUNTS

1. Brighton and Hove go into partnership on 1 January, 199X with capitals of £25 000 and £5000, respectively. Their partnership agreement makes the following provisions:

- that Hove will have a salary of £4000 per annum as a first call on the partnership's profits;
- that both partners will receive interest at 8 per cent on capital;
- that any profit after these prior claims have been paid will be shared in the ratio ³⁄₅: ²⁄₅ with Brighton taking the larger share.

Net profit for the first year was £48 250. It was agreed on the last day of the year that the goodwill of £9000 paid to the previous owner of their business,

Balance Sheet of a Partnership

Liabilities

Previous year		Capital Account	This year	
25000	00	(i) MR. B.	25000	00
2000	00	(ii) MRS. A.	2000	00
27000	00	(iii)	27000	00
		Current Account		
2600	00	(i) MR. B	10120	00
(800	00)	(ii) MRS. A.	2510	00
1800	00	(iii)	12630	00
		Long Term Liabilities		
28000	00	Mortgage	25000	00
–		Loan	–	
			25000	00
		Current Liabilities		
2808	46	Sundry Creditors	4736	02
860	54	Accrued Charges	54	98
3669	00		4791	00
60469	00	TOTAL	69421	00

Assets

Previous year		Fixed Assets	At Cost	Less Depreciation to date	This year	
3000	00	Goodwill	4000	2000	2000	00
37000	00	Premises	37000	–	37000	00
2600	00	Fittings	3200	1200	2000	00
3450	00	Plant and Machinery	4600	2300	2300	00
3000	00	Motor Vehicles	3800	1600	2200	00
49050	00			Total	45500	00
		Current Assets				
8750	00	Stock	13296	00		
864	00	Debtors	594	00		
1756	00	Cash at Bank	9994	50		
49	00	Cash in Hand	37	50		
–		Payments in Advance	–			
11419	00				23921	00
60469	00	TOTAL			69421	00

Fig. 15.1 THE BALANCE SHEET OF A PARTNERSHIP

and standing at that figure on the Goodwill Account, should be written off the profits to the extent of 50 per cent, before any other appropriations of profit were made. Draw up the Appropriation Account on that date.

2. Kadar and Sharif conduct a trading business in partnership on the following terms:

- interest is to be allowed on the partners' Capital Accounts at 8 per cent per annum;
- Sharif is to be credited with a partnership salary of £6000 per annum;
- the balance of profit in any year is to be shared by the partners in the ratio ¾ to Kadar, ¼ to Sharif.

After preparing their Trading and Profit and Loss Accounts for the year ended 31 March, 199X, but before making any provision for interest on capital or for partnership salary, the following balances remained on the books.

	Dr. £	Cr. £
Capital Accounts:		
Kadar (as on 1 April previous year)		22 000
Sharif (as on 1 April previous year)		3 000
Current Accounts:		
Kadar (as on 1 April previous year)		2 500
Sharif (as on 1 April previous year)	2 000	
Drawings Account:		
Kadar	13 700	
Sharif	11 000	
Profit and Loss Account – net profit for year		28 652
Stock at end of year	4 250	
Goodwill Account	2 000	
Plant and machinery	14 000	
Office equipment	3 600	
Fixtures and fittings	4 000	
Hire purchase loans		2 950
Trade debtors and creditors	2 942	1 823

Continues overleaf

	Dr.	Cr.
	£	£
Loan from Helpful Bank PLC		3 000
Rent owing		200
Insurance unexpired at 31 March (current asset)	258	
Cash at bank, Current Account	6 375	
	£64 125	£64 125

It is agreed by the partners to reduce the book value of goodwill by writing off £500 at 31 March, 199X (to be charged to the appropriation section of the Profit and Loss Account).

You are asked to prepare the appropriation section of the firm's Profit and Loss Account and the partners' Current Accounts for the year ended 31 March, 199X, together with their Balance Sheet on that date.

Answers
1. Books of Brighton and Hove. Shares of residue: Brighton, £22 410; Hove, £14 940.
2. Books of Kadar and Sharif. Shares of residue: Kadar, £15 114; Sharif, £5038. Current Account balances: Kadar, £5674 credit; Sharif, £1722 debit. Balance Sheet totals £38 647.

CHECKLIST

- Partnership is a relationship that exists between people carrying on a business together with a view to earning profits.

- It is desirable to enter into a written agreement about the terms of the partnership and if this is drawn up by a solicitor as a formal agreement, it is called a partnership deed.

- As far as accounting goes, the ordinary business transactions are the same as for a sole trader. The differences arise in preparing the final accounts of the partnership.

- Each partner has a capital account to which the capital they subscribe is credited at the start of the business. This account is fixed at the original figure, except if some fundamental rearrangement of the partnership takes place (for example, the admission of a new partner).

- Each partner also has a current account, which can vary as profits are credited to it and drawings are debited to it. Each partner also has a drawings account where the drawings for the year are collected together before being written off the current account at the end of the year.

- To allocate the profits at the end of the year in the manner agreed between the partners, the net profit is transferred to an appropriation account (sometimes called the appropriation section of the profit and loss account) where it is appropriated to the partners in the agreed way.

- The balance sheet of a partnership is similar to the balance sheet of a sole trader, except that there will be two capital accounts added together, showing the original capitals contributed, and there will be two current accounts, usually shown as liabilities (the business owes the partners any profits not as yet drawn). If a partner should be overdrawn on their current account, the debit balance will appear on the assets side of the balance sheet as an asset that is neither fixed nor current.

The final accounts
of a company

1
2
3
4
5
6
7
8
9
10
11
12
13
14
15
16
17
18
19
20
21

THE NATURE OF A COMPANY

In this book, I have been covering accounting for small- and medium-sized enterprises, and it is a fact that thousands of companies are very small and most start life as '£2 companies', which means they have capital of only £2. A company is an organisation with a separate legal status from the people who form it. Two or more people may form a company by subscribing their names to a 'memorandum of association' (which records the fact that they wish to join together in a company for some lawful purpose). When this and other formalities associated with the registration procedure have been complied with, the company will be 'incorporated' ('given a body') and will then become a legal 'person' able to do all the things an ordinary person can do, except the very personal ones. It can own property, employ staff, buy plant, machinery and motor vehicles, have a bank account and become a debtor and a creditor. It cannot fall in love, marry, have children or die, for these are personal acts.

Some companies are so large, have such prestigious premises and own such enormous amounts of property that there is a popular belief that all companies are rich, powerful, stable, reliable and so on. It is also believed that company directors are always honest, upright and respectable. Many of them are of course, but you cannot rely on it. For example, if Mr A., a penniless, ill-educated, lazy individual, sets up as Builders' Suppliers (Wilmot) Ltd, with a total capital of £2, he may call himself a company director, but will it turn him into a prosperous, skilful, energetic, go-getter overnight? Manifestly it will not! Always be wary of companies, and expect the worst from them. More of this later.

REASONS FOR CHOOSING THE COMPANY FORMAT

The sole reason for the development of the company format is that those who become members of the company, and own it by having shares in it, have limited liability. They can lose their money and be responsible for the debts of the business only to the extent of the money they have invested in it. If it is a £2 company, this means that there is only £2 that can be recovered by any creditor of the company. Therefore, those who supply companies must be very wary of providing them with large orders until they have a proven track record of payment. If you do supply them and payment is not forthcoming, you cannot sue the person who received the goods or the directors personally for the price of those goods. Your action lies against the company, and even if the company is insolvent but the directors display every appearance of prosperity, you cannot sue them for your money.

An interesting sidelight on limited companies is that, by law, the name of the company must end in 'limited' or the Welsh equivalent, unless it is a public limited company shares in which may be quoted on the Stock Exchange. Such a company's name must end in the wording 'Public Limited Company' usually abbreviated to PLC, or the Welsh equivalent. These words – Ltd, or PLC – are meant by Parliament to act as a warning that the companies concerned have limited liability and should not be supplied with goods on credit unless the supplier is prepared to take the risk or has confidence in the company's viability and ability to pay on the due date. Remember this every time you receive an order from a limited liability company and ask yourself whether or not you are absolutely confident that the company will honour its debts in due course.

If you decide to set up as a company yourself, you will probably do so in order to have limited liability so that your home, personal belongings and so on cannot be taken to pay off the debts of the business. You will not expect then to receive large deliveries from suppliers on credit straight away, for they will naturally be unwilling to supply. You should therefore be prepared to pay cash for supplies until such time as the company has established a track record for prompt payment. Of course, you could give a personal guarantee, but that would lose you the privilege of limited liability, which is the reason for taking up company status in the first place.

One great advantage of company status is that a company cannot die. The company has a separate status from the founder members, and from the directors and shareholders. If they die, the company still continues, and there is no need for it to go out of existence. The only way a company can cease to exist is for it to go through a process called 'liquidation'. You can go into 'voluntary liquidation', which is when the members decide to discontinue the company, or 'compulsory liquidation', where the Court orders the company to be wound up.

'Liquidation' in accountancy means that all the assets are converted into a liquid asset – cash. The cash is then paid in a correct order of priority to those entitled to claim it. The list starts with those with a right to repayment prior to other creditors – usually the Inland Revenue, other official bodies and the secured creditors (who have a debenture or a mortgage on the property). Then the unsecured creditors may claim and, finally, the shareholders may get their money back, together with any profits ploughed into the business over the years.

SETTING UP AS A LIMITED COMPANY

It is simple enough to promote a company, but the simplest way of all is to buy one 'off the shelf' from a local company registration agent. They cost about £130. You will find local firms listed under 'company registration agents' in the *Yellow Pages*. If in difficulty, contacting Richard Keene or Michael Clifford, 72 New Bond Street, London, W1Y 9DD (telephone 0800 289773) will bring you all the help you need. Alternatively, your accountant (and if you set up in business as a company it is advisable to have one) will make the arrangements for you, for a reasonable fee. Once a company is set up, it is possible to change the name, ownership, names of the directors and the company secretary by a simple procedure. Most registration agents keep a variety of companies 'on the shelf' and if you want one to manufacture or engage in retail trade, they will have one or two for you to choose from.

■ The 'objects' clause

The Registrar of Companies only approves companies to operate in a particular field, as laid down in the objects clause. Thus, if you wish to operate road haulage vehicles and you started to trade on the sugar market, you would be outside your objects clause, and outside the law (*ultra vires*). If you buy a company off the shelf and its objects clause is not quite appropriate to your business, you must register a change in the company's objects before you start engaging in any of these other activities.

ROUTINE ACCOUNTING FOR COMPANIES

Routine accounting for companies is exactly the same as for sole traders and partnerships. You must still record your purchases and sales, receipts and payments, overheads and assets, and prepare a set of final accounts in the usual way. However, there is an element of public interest in the affairs of any company because of the privilege of limited liability that Parliament has conferred on this type of business unit and, as a result, all important companies are subject to some element of control. In general, the situation is as follows:

- very small companies (those with a turnover of less than £90 000 per annum) may do their own accounts without the need to have an accountant or to have their books audited by an auditor;
- small companies (defined in the Companies Acts 1985–9 as companies that have a turnover of less than £2.8 million, balance sheet

totals of less than £1.4 million and less than 51 employees) need not subject themselves to a rigorous external audit, but may meet the law's requirements by asking an accountant to draw up a more limited 'compilation report' (this certifies that the accounts have been kept in a satisfactory manner, but that the full rigour of an audit has not been conducted);

■ for larger companies, the Acts require that the Board appoints auditors who are members of one of the bodies of accountants recognised as professionally qualified (a full audit will take place each year and an 'auditor's report' will form part of the final accounts, and will, in the case of public limited companies, appear in the published accounts available to the general public).

One final point that establishes firm control of even the smallest company is that a change in the law has made those who go into liquidation as a result of bad management and lack of decision liable for losses incurred in this way. For example, if a company is trading at a loss and getting into a deteriorating condition, the directors must be alert to the situation and go into liquidation. They must not simply drift. For example, to go on placing orders with suppliers when manifestly it will not be possible to pay for these goods or services is irresponsible. In these circumstances, the privilege of limited liability can now be lost and the directors made personally liable for the losses, just like a sole trader or a partnership.

THE FINAL ACCOUNTS OF LIMITED COMPANIES

The chief difference between the accounts of sole traders and partnerships and those of limited companies is that, being a separate legal entity from the members of the company, the profits earned belong in the first place to the company. How much of the profits earned is actually distributed to the shareholders depends on the recommendation of the directors at the annual general meeting. They will normally recommend a reasonable dividend, but any undistributed profit will remain as a balance on the accounts and is called a 'revenue reserve'. Revenue reserves belong to the ordinary shareholders, who can expect to receive them at some future time, but the reserves are often used to expand the business. In that case, the only way the shareholders may eventually receive them is in the form of bonus shares, when the company passes a resolution to recognise that the revenue reserves have been turned into fixed capital (by being spent on extra premises, machinery and so on).

231

It then decides to issue shares to recognise that these profits have now been turned into capital assets.

It is possible for a business to have another kind of reserve called a 'capital reserve', arising from profits that were not earned in the normal way as laid down in the objects clause, but in some other way. For example, if a company's premises were valued on the books at the purchase price of £25 000 (many years ago), it might be deemed desirable to raise the book value to the present value, say £100 000. Increasing the assets by £75 000 means you must increase the liabilities side of the balance sheet by £75 000 and this would be a capital profit (not a revenue profit). The figure would be entered on the credit side of an account – 'Appreciation of Premises A/c' – to show the extent by which the premises had risen in value and contributed to the capital value of the business. Capital reserves may not be distributed to the shareholders as a dividend, but they may be capitalised and distributed as bonus shares to existing shareholders.

As with partnerships, the net profit of a company is transferred to an Appropriation Account (or an appropriation section of the profit and loss account). The profits are then distributed or used in the ways recommended by the directors and approved by the shareholders at the annual general meeting. You can follow what happens most easily by looking at a simple example.

EXAMPLE

Triumvirate Ltd made profits in the year 199X of £183 267. At 1 January 199X the balance on the Appropriation Account of undistributed profit from the previous year was £27 301. The directors recommended as follows:

- that a reserve of £60 000 be set aside for Corporation Tax;
- that £25 000 be put in its Plant Replacement Reserve and £25 000 in its Computer Renewals Reserve;
- that a dividend of 20 per cent be paid on the preference shares of £50 000, and a dividend of 32 per cent on the ordinary shares of £100 000;
- £40 000 will be placed in its General Reserve Account and any balance left, in its Appropriation Account.

The Appropriation Account of Triumvirate Ltd would look as shown in Figure 16.1. One of the reserve accounts is shown as well (see Figure 16.2), so that you can see how these accounts would look after these transfers have been made. A few imaginary figures have been inserted to make the account realistic.

Appropriation Account: Triumvirate Ltd

199X	£	199X	£
31 Dec. Corporation Tax			
Reserve	60 000	1 Jan. Balance	27 301
Plant Replacement		31 Dec. Net Profit	183 267
Reserve	25 000		210 568
Computer Renewals			
Reserve	25 000		
General Reserve	40 000		
Preference Share			
Dividend	10 000		
Ordinary Share			
Dividend	32 000		
	192 000		
Balance c/d	18 568		
	£210 568		£210 568
		199X	£
		1 Jan. Balance b/d	18 568

Fig. 16.1 THE APPROPRIATION ACCOUNT OF TRIUMVIRATE LTD, A LIMITED COMPANY

Corporation Tax Reserve A/c

199X	£	199X	£
3 Jan. Inland Revenue	48 421	1 Jan. Balance b/d	67 500
31 Dec. Balance c/d	79 079	31 Dec. Appropriation A/c	60 000
	£127 500		£127 500
		199X	£
		1 Jan. Balance b/d	79 079

Fig. 16.2 A TYPICAL NOMINAL ACCOUNT TO HOLD RESERVES OF PROFITS

Notes

- Accounts like this receive sums from the appropriation account on the liabilities side. The reason for this is that all the balances on these accounts really belong to the ordinary shareholders (because they are profits that have not been distributed). The shareholders cannot have them because the directors have decided that they shall be used for other purposes – in this case, to pay the Corporation Tax.
- Eventually, as these accounts are used for the purpose intended, they will be debited as the profits in reserve are paid away to the Inland Revenue or the preference shareholders or to buy new plant, computers and so on.

THE BALANCE SHEET OF LIMITED COMPANIES

The balance sheet of limited companies is similar in many ways to other balance sheets in that it has the assets set against the liabilities and the two sides should balance. However, limited companies are controlled by the Companies Act 1985, which sets out (in Schedule 4) two alternative presentations of the balance sheet that companies are to use. One of these presentations is in continuous style, which means it is a balance sheet in vertical style. The other is in horizontal style, with the assets first (that is, on the left-hand side) and the liabilities second on the right). You therefore have the balance sheet in the correct European style in the way shown in Figure 18.3(b) (see page 270). This is the same style as the trial balance, with assets on the left and liabilities on the right.

> *Limited companies are controlled by the Companies Act 1985.*

This is not the place to go into too detailed an account of all the special features of limited company accounts because most small businesses are only private limited companies, and they rarely have more than £1000 capital. However, the chief features of a company Balance Sheet are listed and explained below, and then illustrated in Figure 16.3.

■ The assets side of the balance sheet

▦ The divisions of fixed assets

Fixed assets are divided into three classes – intangible assets, tangible assets and investments.

- **Intangible assets** are assets that cannot be touched – there is nothing real about them. 'Goodwill' has been mentioned already as being an intangible asset. Other intangible assets are trademarks, patents, licences and so on.
- **Tangible assets** are the real assets every one is familiar with – buildings, cars and so on.
- **Investments** are divided into two classes, one of which is regarded as a fixed asset. These are investments in subsidiary companies (companies where you have 51 per cent of the voting shares) and related companies (where you have a substantial, but not a controlling, interest). All such shares could be sold off, but if you did sell them, you would lose control of the subsidiary or your influence with the related company, and so it is better to regard them as fixed assets. They used to be called 'trade investments' as they were in companies in the same trade as the investing company.

Balance Sheet of Triumvirate Ltd, as at 31 December 199X

Assets		£	Liabilities			£
Fixed assets						
Intangibles	– Patent rights	12 000	*Preference shareholders'*			
Tangibles	– Land and buildings	140 000	*interest in the co.*		*Authorised*	*Issued*
	Plant and machinery	44 500	Preference shares of £1 fully paid		50 000	50 000
	Fixtures and fittings	19 742				
		204 242	*Ordinary shareholders' interest*		*Authorised*	
			in the co.		*& issued*	
Current assets			Ordinary shares of £1 fully paid		100 000	
Stock	49 460					
Debtors	5 984		Plant replacement			
Investments	132 186		Reserve	17 000		
Cash at bank	27 250		+ additions	25 000	42 000	
Cash in hand	240					
		215 120	Computer Renewal Reserve (new)		25 000	
			General Reserve	32 000		
			+ additions	40 000	72 000	
			Balance on Appropriation A/c		18 568	
			Ordinary shareholders' interest			257 568
			Corporation Tax Reserve			79 079
			Current liabilities			
			Creditors		2 715	
			Preference dividend due		10 000	
			Ordinary dividend due		32 000	44 715
		£431 362				£431 362

Fig. 16.3 THE BALANCE SHEET OF TRIUMVIRATE LTD

■ *Current assets*

These are the usual current assets, stocks, debtors and so on, but you must add 'investments'. This is the second class of investments, which are not kept for the purposes of control, but as a way of holding spare cash so that it earns interest. If you have profits put away in plant replacement reserves or a general reserve account, it is unwise to leave the money represented by these profits loose in the cash system. If, instead, you invest the surplus funds, either on the money market or in stocks and shares, they will earn some income for the future. Your banker will be happy to arrange this for you. For example, you might put it on the money market for 28 days and then the bank will come back to you and say 'Well – do you want to keep it on the money market, or do you want it back in your current account to buy new machinery?' It is a flexible arrangement that is useful both to you and the bank.

■ The liabilities side of the balance sheet

■ *The shareholders' interest in the company*

The only unusual feature of the liabilities side of the balance sheet is that the capital contributed by the ordinary shareholders originally, and all profits ploughed back into the business since it started, belong to the ordinary shareholders. If there are any preference shareholders, they do not own any of the profits ploughed back, unless they own participating preference shares. You should now study Figure 16.3.

EXERCISE ON COMPANY FINAL ACCOUNTS

A limited company has an authorised capital of 200 000 ordinary shares of £1, of which 100 000 are issued, and 50 000 9 per cent preference shares of £1, of which 30 000 are issued. On 31 March, 199X, it was found that the net profit was £93 420 for the year. There was also a balance on the Appropriation Account of £4450 from 1 April the previous year. The directors resolved to:

- put £25 000 into a new General Reserve and £18 500 to a new Plant Replacement Reserve;
- reserve £25 000 for Corporation Tax;
- pay the 9 per cent preference dividend;
- recommend a 20 per cent dividend on the ordinary shares.

Show the Appropriation Account and the Balance Sheet. In addition to the current liabilities resulting from the Appropriation Account, there were £2300 of debts to creditors outstanding. Fixed assets totalled £178 000 and current assets £52 170.

CHECKLIST

- A company is an incorporation – that is, a legal entity that has been given its personality by force of law. The usual way to form a company is to register it under the Companies Acts 1985 and 1989.

- In practice, you can buy companies 'off the shelf' from company registration agents or ask them to register a specific company for you.

- Limited companies must have names that end in the word 'Limited' or 'Public Limited Company', or the Welsh equivalent. This is a warning to suppliers that the directors of the company have limited liability.

- Do not think that all companies are rich and powerful – many of them are only £100 companies – which means creditors can only expect to recover £100 between them in the event of liquidation (apart from what can be realised by selling the company's assets).

- If you set up as a company, do not expect to be given credit (unless you give a personal guarantee) until you have established a track record as a good payer.

- Companies with a turnover of less than £90 000 per annum may do their own books without using the services of an accountant. Small companies – as defined in the Companies Acts 1985–9 – must use an accountant to inspect their books and draw up a 'compilation report'. This certifies that the accounts appear to have been properly kept, but have not been subjected to a full audit. The very largest companies must appoint auditors for the year ahead at their annual general meeting and an auditor's report must form part of their final accounts.

- The final accounts must conform to Schedule 4 of the Companies Act 1985. It is worth buying a copy of the Act and the 1989 Act as you will often need to refer to them. Phone HMSO for a copy on 0171-873 9090. You can pay for them by credit card and they will be sent to you by post.

Aspects of controlling small- and medium-sized enterprises

THE IMPORTANCE OF CONTROL

Control is the process of supervising every aspect of a business so that it is able to continue and grow. A business has to make enough profit to give a reasonable standard of living to the proprietor/s, but, in the early years, survival may be more important than enjoyment of current income, and the budding entrepreneur is more concerned with ploughing profits back into the business than in enjoying high living.

When you think of control, you usually think of financial control, and businesses most often fail because they run out of cash. Cash is spent at every level. For example, you can overspend by buying too many capital items or raw materials, too much stock or paying too many people too much. Financial aspects enter into all areas of business activity and are of the greatest importance in a book that is concerned with accounting, but other aspects of control may be touched on – such as, production, marketing, personnel and research, which are all areas that must be controlled and developed if any economic activity is to be successful.

Control may be exercised at any time, particularly in the small business, where the eagle eye of the proprietor can detect waste and bad practices as they occur, and economies as they become possible. At the same time, control operates best in a formal way, with a structure that gives each aspect of the business a known, established procedure that is reviewed regularly. For example, pay increases should not be granted at the whim of the proprietor or at the urgent request of an employee, but should be given as the result of a review procedure, either six-monthly or annually. The formal review designates a time when the pattern of pay will be considered. It delays impetuous demands for rises, is seen to be fair and reward steady work rather than petulant behaviour, and measures the levels of pay against the overall prosperity of the firm or company.

Even the smallest firm or company should have regular meetings, with a proper agenda, and particular aspects of the work that are due for review featuring in the agenda in rotation. Thus, the order book may be a feature of every agenda, but 'health and safety at work' may come up for annual review only. In this way, proper plans can be drawn up to cover the item to be featured, reports of weaknesses revealed in recent months can be presented and considered, and a blueprint laid down for the year ahead. Without the formality of regular meetings, it is impossible to get all staff to know the true situation of the firm or company, problems are dealt with on an *ad hoc* basis, perhaps at the whim of the proprietor, and labour turnover may be higher than it otherwise would be as individuals become dissatisfied with sudden changes of procedure made in a haphazard way.

THE ORDER POSITION

The order position is a vital component in the conduct of the business because it influences the rate of production, the stocks you feel you need to hold, the purchases you need to make, the cash flow position and staffing levels. You not only need to know what the current figures are but, preferably, comparable figures for a year ago as orders fit into a pattern of activity that tends to repeat over the years. This is especially true in businesses like the fashion or toy trades, but some sort of pattern will be apparent in most.

Where a firm has only one product, the important figures are the new orders (the current month's figures), the cumulative position since the start of the year, and the average per month since the start of the year. Where a firm has several products, it will be necessary to analyse the figures within the product range as the overall figures might give a distorted view. For example, if 50 per cent of the orders were for one particular line, it would be necessary to produce more of that line than the others. This is carried out more easily with a computerised system if there are numerous products. This analysis might be made in terms of units rather than cash. Figure 17.1 shows a typical order summary, in value terms, for a particular month.

■ The fulfilment of orders

The ability to fulfil orders should be reviewed whenever order book figures are looked at. Ideally, orders should be fulfilled at once as this pleases customers, allows invoices to be despatched and cash flows inwards to increase. Where a manufacturing or fabricating procedure is to take place, immediate fulfilment is impossible, but you should give estimated delivery dates and these should be checked up on by some sort of progress-chasing procedure. If the order book is growing and a backlog is developing, you may need a review of procedures. Is the factory too small? Are there bottlenecks in production or in the supplies of components from subcontractors? Do you need new machinery, more staff, more skilled labour in some areas? More seriously, do you need to increase the scale of your business, with all that means in terms of extension of premises, purchase of plant and machinery, capital finance, and so on?

	Current Year			Previous Year		
	This Month £	Total to date £	Average per month £	This month £	Total to date £	Average per month £
1. Balance C/Fwd at 1/5 199X	23 500			14 800		
2. Orders Received	15 000	72 000	14 400	11 500	62 000	12 400
3. Orders Fulfilled	19 500			13 000		
4. Orders Cancelled	500			1 000		
5. Orders C/Fwd at 31/5.199X $(1+2-3-4)$	18 500			12 300		

Fig. 17.1 ORDER SUMMARY (IN VALUE TERMS) 31 MAY, 199X

Notes
- In the current month, new orders were just above average for the year so far, which is satisfactory.
- Compared with the same figures last year, orders are up by 30 per cent on the month $(3,500 \times \frac{100}{11\,500})$ and 16 per cent on the first five months of the year $(\frac{10\,000}{62\,000} \times 100)$.
- Fewer orders have been cancelled than in the same month last year, which is encouraging.
- The ability to fulfil orders has improved by 50 per cent.

CONTROLLING CASH FLOW

The most common cause of business failure is the problem of cash flow. It is no good having a full order book if the people placing the orders do not pay. Clear terms of payment when allowing customers to place orders are essential. Strict credit control procedures must be applied and prompt action taken where payment is not forthcoming. Where customers are paying in a proper manner but cash flow problems still arise, there can be a number of reasons for the difficulty. All these must be looked at so that you understand the problems.

> *The most common cause of business failure is the problem of cash flow.*

Why is cash flow such a problem? The answer is because you must yourself pay your way, and if you don't, you can expect someone to whom you owe money to take steps to recover it, and put you out of business. If you are to avoid this and you face cash flow problems, you must borrow working capital from the bank. As interest rates are high, this creams off a lot of your profit, which goes into the bank's or finance company's pocket instead of your own.

To study your cash flow position, start with a cash flow forecast, which estimates what receipts and payments will be in the months ahead.

It is usual to have a rolling forecast over a period of three or six months. As the months pass, you roll the forecast forward, filling in the figures for the months ahead as they become easier to forecast. For each month, you have a 'budget' column and an 'actual' column. You fill in the 'actual' column at the end of every month, and then compare the two figures. Any difference between the two is called a 'variance', which can be positive or negative. First, consider the cash flow budget given in Figure 17.2 and the notes below it.

	January		February		March	
	Budget (£)	Actual (£)	Budget (£)	Actual (£)	Budget (£)	Actual (£)
1. Cash at start (cash & bank)	2 340		12 100		–5 793	
Receipts						
2. Sales in cash	10 000		12 000		15 000	
3. Debts collected (1 mth old)	4 500		5 600		4 250	
4. ,, ,, (2 mths old)	2 750		2 250		2 800	
5. ,, ,, (3 mths old)	1 650		2 750		2 250	
6. Other receipts	250		550		850	
7. Extra capital contributed	–				2 000	
8. Loans arranged	–				5 000	
9. Total receipts (2 to 8 inclusive)	19 150		23 150		32 150	
10. Total cash available (1 + 9)	21 490		35 250		26 357	
Payments						
11. Business stock	5 390		18 560		6 620	
12. Overheads & consumables	850		2 428		1 250	
13. Wages	2 425		2 955		3 500	
14. Capital items	125		16 500		–	
15. Payments out (11 to 14 inclusive)	8 790		40 443		11 370	
16. Drawings	600		600		600	
17. Total payments (15 + 16)	9 390		41 043		11 970	
18. Final cash balance (c/fwd) (10–17) or (17–10)	+12 100		–5 793		+14 387	

Fig. 17.2 A CASH FLOW FORECAST

Notes to Figure 17.2

- The budgeted receipts for the month include the estimated sales, and the estimated receipts from debtors. It is believed, in this example, that 50 per cent of the debtors will pay within 1 month and 25 per cent each will pay in 2 and 3 months respectively. Thus, in January, you have £4500 coming in from last month's debtors, and £2250 coming in during February and March respectively.
- The total receipts are added to the estimated cash balance at the start of the month to give the total cash available.
- The external payments are made up of those to suppliers for stock, consumables and capital items, and those to employees for wages. The drawings of the proprietor have to be added to this figure to give the total payments for the month.
- When total payments are deducted from the total cash available, you have the final cash balance envisaged at the end of the month.
- The actual figures can only be inserted at the end of the month, and when you do insert them, you shall be able to see what the variance is between the estimate and the actual figures. This is discussed in Figure 17.3 (see page 246).
- As the February budget shows, the cash flow forecast can reveal that a shortage of cash will develop in the months ahead. There are all sorts of reasons for this being so. For example, a dealer in fireworks lays in huge stocks in August and September for sale in October and November. They may be short of cash in August and September, but in funds again by November. In this case, re-stocking in February and the purchase of capital equipment is the cause of the shortage. Forewarned, arrangements are made to cover the deficit by means of a loan from the bank and the contribution of further capital from the proprietor's savings (say, £5000 loan and £2000 extra capital contributed).
- Where possible, 'cash flow smoothing' should be tried. This is explained in the main text.

	Budget (£)	Actual (£)	Variance (£)	Reason
1. Cash at start	2 340	4 250	+1 910	Good Xmas cash sales
Receipts				
2. Sales in cash	10 000	7 400	−2 600	Competition from Y Ltd
3. Debts collected	4 500	3 800	− 700	Economy depressed
4. ,, ,,	2 750	2 400	− 350	− no bad debts
5. ,, ,,	1 650	990	− 660	envisaged
6. Other receipts	250	850	+ 600	Sale of spare van
7. Extra capital	−	−	−	
8. Loans arranged	−	−	−	
9. Total receipts	19 150	15 440	−3 710	
10. Total cash available	21 490	19 690	−1 800	
Payments				
11. Business stock	5 390	4 250	−1 140	Reduced orders in view of (2) above
12. Overheads etc.	850	1 150	300	Water rate increase
13. Wages & salaries	2 425	2 025	− 400	Part-time staff dismissed
14. Capital items	125	−	− 125	Postponed this expenditure
15. Payments out	8 790	7 425	−1 365	
16. Drawings	600	750	+ 150	Promised wife to increase this
17. Total payments	9 390	8 175	−1 215	
18. Final cash balance	+21 100	+11 515	− 585	

Fig. 17.3 CASH FLOW VARIANCES – JANUARY

Notes to Figure 17.3
- Some variances are positive and some are negative.
- On Line 1, cash at the start of January had a favourable variance, and this is found to be due to good Christmas cash sales.
- As far as receipts are concerned *(Lines 2–9)* a negative variance is an unfavourable variance as receipts are less than was hoped. Looking at each line it can be said that:
  - **Line 2** the poor sales were due to fierce competition from a new trader, Y Ltd.
  - **Lines 3, 4 and 5** the debts collected were less than hoped, and this is believed to be due to the depressed state of the economy. However, none of the debts is believed to be bad, so it is hoped all the debtors will pay in due course.
  - **Line 6** this favourable variance arose as a result of a decision to sell one of the motor vehicles as an economy measure.
  - **Line 9** the final total on the variances on receipts is a negative variance of £3710.00 and this wipes out the favourable cash variance at the start leaving us with a negative variance of −£1800.
- A negative variance on payments is a favourable variance because you did not have to pay away as much as you expected. Taking each of these negative variances in turn, management might justly claim:
  - **Line 11** the fall in payments for business stock resulted from quick reactions by them to the drop in the sales (Line 2). They reduced purchases to cut costs.
  - **Line 13** reduction in staff pay was achieved by dismissing part-time staff not required in the slack January period.

Notes to Figure 17.3 continued
   - **Line 14** the budgeted capital expenditure of £125 was postponed to save money.

The only increase in outgoings over budget was due to a rise in water rates, which could not be avoided (Line 12).

The increase in drawings was the result of a long-term promise to the proprietor's wife (Line 16).

The final result is a reduction of the unfavourable variances on the receipts side (Line 10) to £585.00, achieved by economies on the payment side (Line 17). The final cash balance was £11 515.00.

■ Analysing cash flow variances

Suppose the budgeted and actual cash flows in January are as shown in Figure 17.3. By placing a sheet of paper alongside them, you can make a note of the variances and suggest reasons for them in each case (see opposite.)

'Cash flow smoothing' is a procedure whereby you move cash payments that can be moved to a position in the payments year when you are flush with cash and can pay most easily. Payments such as insurance premiums, car tax, loan repayments and so on can be rearranged to be made at a time when you know you will have funds. The purchase of capital items can be postponed to the most appropriate time for you (rather than when the supplier would like you to purchase the item).

CONTROLLING STOCK

There are three aspects of stock which need controlling:

- the general stock position;
- stock losses of various sorts;
- stocktaking for accounting purposes.

■ The general stock position

Close control of stock positions is required as you never want to be out of stock if you can avoid it, yet, at the same time, to be overstocked means that capital is tied up in unsold stock, which is not selling and therefore not yielding any profit. It is only when stock turns over that a profit is made, so slow-moving stock ('shelf-warmers') are a great disadvantage. Such slow-moving stock is a sign of bad buying and may necessitate you having a word with the buyers.

The kinds of things that need to be considered in relation to stock are as follows.

- What is the achievable monthly sales or utilisation figure for each type of stock, and how does it vary from month to month? Many items are seasonal, selling at particular times of the year. Orders must be placed to allow stocks to be high at peak selling periods and low (or non-existent) at other times.
- Can suppliers be relied on to deliver on time or should you keep higher stocks to allow for possible short deliveries?
- If you are manufacturing components yourself, you may need to manufacture batches of components to meet anticipated production targets. Sometimes idle time on machines can be filled by producing small batches of parts you know will be required at a later date.
- You can rarely achieve 100 per cent consumer satisfaction, because to do so requires you to keep stocks of even very slow-moving items. With such items, it is better to order them as requested and to add some margin to the price to cover the expense of any 'small order' procedure that is required.
- Except in the very smallest businesses where personal supervision of stocks is possible, a stock control procedure should be implemented to keep control of each type of stock, with a bin card or similar document being completed as stocks arrive or are issued. Such procedures do cost money and take a lot of time, so the cost of the procedures have to be weighed against the losses that will occur if less strict controls are instituted. A typical bin card is illustrated in Figure 17.4.

BIN CARD

Description Socket (white) Maximum stock 100
Bin number 28 Minimum stock 30
Code number PS17 Re-order level 40
Unit of issue 5 Re-order quantity 60

Received			Issued			Balance
Date	Ref.	Quantity	Date	Ref.	Quantity	Quantity
1 Jan 19..						65
			8 Jan	Req 217	30	35
19 Jan 19..	Order 126	60				95
			24 Jan	Req 297	40	55

Fig. 17.4 EXAMPLE OF A BIN CARD

■ Stock losses of various sorts

Stock losses arise from a variety of causes and measures must be instituted to correct them. Some of these causes are known as 'merchandise' qualities, which are 'inherent vices of the goods.' Strawberries rot, bananas go bad, crockery breaks, materials fade, powders blow away, insects attack many products and so on. You must train staff to understand the merchandise they are handling and help them reduce losses that are the result of 'inherent vices' in the goods themselves. Don't order perishables in large quantities, don't put clumsy people in charge of fragile goods, firmly discourage horse-play and so on.

Other stock losses occur because of staff malpractice. Theft is not uncommon, 'passing out' (the giving of goods to friends without them paying) is common, turning a blind eye to shoplifting by friends and relatives is rather similar. The same sorts of practices occur with money (giving excess change is not uncommon). To reduce such losses, it is essential to train staff so that they know the detection of any such practices is highly likely and the consequences will be unpleasant. Emphasise the serious nature of having a police record, even for tiny offences, the impossibility of getting a character reference, the chances of dismissal. Even in these days when unfair dismissal is a serious matter for employers, summary dismissal for theft is generally regarded as not being unfair, and a succession of offences, with formal warnings, is certainly a justifiable cause for dismissal.

Certain events throw up situations where such malpractices may be discovered, for example stocktaking. If stocktaking is carried out randomly without warning, with a particular type of merchandise being carefully checked and costed, any discrepancies will be discovered. If staff are unwilling to take holidays or days off, or work late regularly, or arrive early on a regular basis, the circumstances should be investigated. Of course, everything may be all right, but the investigation will warn others that any departure from standard procedures is, to some extent, suspicious. Customer complaints are another source of information that may lead to investigation. It is best to open all mail yourself if that is possible. If you read every letter, you will know what is going on. Complaints about non-delivery, short delivery, damaged goods and so on should always be investigated.

■ Stocktaking for accounting purposes

Technically speaking, you only need to do stocktaking for final accounts purposes once a year, but it is preferable to do a full stocktake more frequently. Every three months you have to complete a VAT return, a situation that calls for a quick review of sales, purchases and daily takings. This is a suitable time to do stocktaking and you can then take out a set of interim final accounts, just to see how the profits of the business are coming along.

When stocktaking, you have to count all the items in stock at a given time, as explained on page 54. By going through the stocktaking procedure, serious stock losses may become apparent and show up as a drop in gross profit percentage (see page 263) when the interim final accounts are worked out. Making a fuss about stock losses tightens up procedures and warns anyone engaging in malpractices that the proceeds are not worth the risk.

CREDIT CONTROL

Credit is the supply of goods or services without immediate payment. When you supply goods or services, the time of payment is a matter between the parties, who must make it clear to one another what terms they are trading on. Thus, a person who is only prepared to supply for cash should make this clear in any pre-contract negotiations. In a shop, you may see notices that read, 'Please do not ask for credit as a refusal may offend'. For shop trading these days, the problem of granting credit hardly arises as the use of credit cards has separated the credit problem from the selling problem, and the card companies have assumed the risks of extending credit. Become a credit card trader – an easy and almost cost-free arrangement – and enjoy the benefits.

If you trade on cash terms, it means that payment must be made at the same time as the goods or services are supplied. If the customer is to be allowed to pay by cheque, a cheque guarantee card should be insisted on. Recording the card number on the back of the cheque is sufficient to guarantee payment, provided the value does not exceed the card limit (usually £50, but some cards have a £100 value). The card must be current (not expired). If the payment is to be made by credit card, obviously no cheque is required; the credit card voucher is made out by the supplier and signed by the customer. There is a 'floor' value above which the supplier must phone for authorisation, but sums of any amount may be paid in this way, provided the payment is authorised. One South-coast marina phoned to say a customer was trying to buy an £80 000 yacht with his credit card. The purchase was authorised without any hesitation.

Supplies that are not made against cash payments are said to be 'on credit'. If you are to allow customers credit, you should only do so if you know them to be creditworthy. This usually means that only after they have become a regular customer, placing orders regularly and after you have taken up references from them, should you agree to deal with them on 'open account'. 'Open account' means that you deal with them in the way that is usual in the trade. This often means that they pay monthly in arrears. Thus, they are sent a statement once a month showing what they owe to the date of the statement, and they must then pay the statement within 30 days. These terms can be varied – for example, payment within 7 or 15 days is quite common.

Shorter credit terms may be agreed. For example, payment within seven days of invoice date means that they have to pay each invoice as they receive it. This is less convenient for the customer as it may mean making several payments in a month, but it is advantageous for the supplier because cash flow improves.

The following are the general principles of credit control.

■ Do not supply goods on credit to new customers except in very special circumstances – for instance, if they have been known to you personally for a very long time or if you have a clear statement from a bank that they are of excellent reputation. The sort of cautious banking reference 'Believed to be good for normal business transactions' is not enough to justify credit.

■ Be more careful about giving credit to companies than to sole traders or partnerships. Company directors have limited liability, which means that the business is a separate entity in law from the directors and so they cannot be held personally liable for debts. If you contract with a company, you cannot enforce the contract against a director unless you have asked them for a personal guarantee. Where a company asks to be supplied on credit, do not agree until you have had time to sort out their creditworthiness to your satisfaction. You can ask for a banker's reference and for trade references – firms that have supplied them in the past. Check with such people personally, both by telephone and by writing to find out their opinions about the potential customer. You may be advised to do a company search. The idea here is that, as directors of a company have limited liability (limited to the amount of capital they have invested in the business), all the creditors can look to is the capital of the company. This may be as little as a few pounds, and is often less than £1000. By asking a specialist firm to do a company search for you, you will at least find out what that capital is. It is a good idea to draw up a set of 'terms of payment', which states the terms on which you expect to be paid.

Send a copy of such conditions to your customer when you start to allow a credit period and insist on acknowledgement of the conditions before supplying the first order. If you are a member of a trade association of some sort, it will usually let you use its set of 'trading conditions' for a nominal charge.

Many large firms insist on negotiating more favourable credit terms than are usual in the trade, and often insist on larger discounts. You have to weigh up the advisability of dealing with such firms against the cash flow difficulties they create. You need to be sure that you can survive the first period before payment becomes due. Problems can often be avoided by planning ahead.

- If you do decide to allow a customer time to pay, set a credit limit on them by marking it on their account. Do not let this credit limit be exceeded. It is a common practice by unreliable traders to place one or two small orders and pay promptly, but then put in a very large order for which there is no real intention to pay. A single big bad debt can cripple a small firm. Never let any order go out if the previous statement has not been paid. If the payment date has not yet arrived and the new order brings the total due above the agreed credit limit, don't fulfil the order. Phone and ask for payment first.

- It is always advisable to send statements out promptly. Firms never pay until they get a statement and so the earlier they get it, the sooner you should have your money. Check that there are no petty errors in the statement since these are often used as an excuse to delay payment.

- Do not be bashful about asking for payment the moment an account is overdue. The person who demands payment and makes a fuss is more likely to be paid than a person who does not ask. A telephone call, or a personal visit if the customer is local, is more likely to produce a result than a mere letter, but if this does not produce an immediate result, send a letter stating a deadline for payment. If you arrange with your solicitor to refer all debts to them as soon as the deadline you set in your request for payment is exceeded, a formal letter requesting payment will be sent at once. Failure to respond to such a letter can be followed by legal action to recover and is therefore a threat to the slow payer. Payment will usually be forthcoming. A poor payer who has a number of debts to pay will usually pay the person who is bothering them rather than the person who is not yet complaining. A useful booklet entitled *Prompt Payment Please* is available from official organisations such as Enterprise Agencies.

CREDIT CONTROL OVER PURCHASES

Although credit control is usually thought of as an activity that exercises control over customers and ensures that bad debts are avoided, it is just as bad to fail to exercise control over payments for purchases. A business cannot be laid low by its debtors; it is the unpaid creditors who can force the business into bankruptcy. You should pay your bills promptly for the following reasons.

■ Because, on the principle of 'Do as you would be done by', you should be as careful about your supplier's welfare as about your own. If you wish to be paid promptly for your own goods or services, in accordance with the agreed contractual terms, you should be equally prepared to honour our own debts according to contract.
■ Because prompt payment is the best way of building a sound supplier–customer relationship. The supplier who knows you pay promptly is unlikely, even at times of shortage, to divert our goods to another customer and will honour urgent requests for supplies promptly.
■ A good name is an invaluable asset and can only be established slowly over a period of years. It can quickly be lost by a single late payment, and totally destroyed by a succession of them.

It is the common practice of new suppliers to ask other suppliers for an opinion of your reliability should you be seeking supplies from them, and an unhesitating confirmation that you pay promptly is the best recommendation.

A satisfactory procedure on payments for supplies is as follows:

■ Always open the mail yourself as then you will know exactly what has been purchased in your name and be able to detect any fraudulent behaviour at the earliest possible moment.
■ If you have to pay on the invoice, work out the due date and file the invoice, or a reminder to pay it, on a date just prior to the due date so that you are sure it is paid in time, yet you have taken advantage of whatever credit period is available.
■ Always sign all cheques yourself. If you are paying on a statement rather than a single invoice, check that all goods charged for have in fact arrived and that any returns have been credited.
■ If your organisation is growing, establish a proper control procedure to check that all goods ordered are received, in good order, not paid for before the credit period is approaching its end, and that cheques are signed only by authorised officials. It is wise to put a limit on the

cheque values that may be signed by people other than yourself and to notify the bank that your personal signature is required on cheques above this limit.

■ If cash flow is good, it may be desirable to take cash discounts given for paying more promptly and not using the full credit period.

■ If cash is short and some payments have to be delayed, it is well to review all payments and pay those where the moral obligation to pay is strong or where the natural objection of the supplier can be least easily borne.

■ All payments to suppliers are reduced if proper control of stocks prevents the placing of unnecessary orders. This means having maximum stock and reorder levels and designating someone as the sole 'purchasing officer' to prevent haphazard small orders being placed by individuals unaware of the cash flow position.

■ One final point about scrutinising invoices as they arrive is that the prices shown are the latest prices and these may have important implications for pricing goods for re-sale, costing jobs and estimating or quoting prices to customers. The small business is often much too slow in raising its prices. It is most unwise to get left behind in an inflationary spiral – you need to price ahead of inflation or your profit margins will be eaten into. Alert staff to the need to reprice and keep yourself familiar with the price elements built into your costing activities so that you are quick to spot a raw material that is becoming more expensive.

STAFF PERFORMANCE

No single element of control is as important as the control of staff. You need staff to perform various aspects of your work and, for this reason, you must

No single element of control is as important as the control of staff.

check that they have the skills you require or at least the potential to acquire these skills. Once employed, staff are difficult to get rid of, and poor staff are even harder to get rid of because they have little incentive to go elsewhere.

Besides the skills you require them to have, you also hope to have a reasonably agreeable working environment. People who cannot get on with others or work willingly without endless supervision soon become a bore. Impress on new arrivals before they are appointed that you are looking for cooperative, helpful people, self-starters who don't need to be driven all day but believe in a fair day's work for a fair day's pay.

Build such sentiments into letters of appointment so that if, at some future time, the employee behaves unreasonably, that in itself (after several warnings) will justify their dismissal.

This does not imply that you can be anything less than scrupulous in your own behaviour. Good control of staff requires leadership, example, fair treatment and consultation, rather than niggling rectitude.

Just as production, marketing and distribution require a clear organisational structure to secure control, the area of employee relations needs a definite structure if it is to ensure proper control of the workforce. The embryo firm is under the personal supervision of the proprietor and, as such, the structure is clear and control is exercised directly. As the business grows, it becomes necessary to establish a framework of clear responsibilities of key staff over certain areas of the work. Job descriptions that define the tasks to be done by any person appointed (but also call for adaptability and willing cooperation across boundaries where the situation requires it) are part of this framework. Clear statements of employee conduct on punctuality, self-certification of sickness, racial discrimination, sexual discrimination and so on are also desirable. Arbitrary management should be ruled out as unfair, authority should be clearly specified, discretion within a policy conceded and appeal to a higher level laid down as a natural right. The principles of natural justice, which are that everyone has a right to be heard and that no one shall be judge in a dispute in which they are one of the parties, must be applied.

The question may be asked, 'What has all this to do with accounting?' The answer is, 'A very great deal'. Employer–employee confrontations have enormous impact on the financial stability of firms. The inability of management to manage is a frequent cause of failure, but, equally, arbitrary management brings costs in higher labour turnover, stoppages, awards for unfair dismissal, fines for breach of regulations, loss of licences and so on. Anything that raises costs, causes delays on delivery dates or disaffection in the surrounding locality is of interest to accountants.

CONTROL OVER PROFITABILITY

This subject is best dealt with by looking at the various accounting ratios that can be calculated once the final accounts or the interim final accounts are worked out. These are dealt with fully in Chapter 18.

BREAKEVEN ANALYSIS

A business only reaches breakeven point when its sales to customers bring in enough income to cover all the costs that have been incurred. Suppose the prime costs of an article are £15 (these, remember, are the costs of the raw materials and labour actually embodied in the finished product). Suppose also that you can sell it for £35. You thus have a contribution to profits from each article sold of £20. However, that contribution is not enough to lead you into profit until it has covered all the 'overhead' costs of the business, both the manufacturing overhead (see Chapter 14 for the manufacturing account) and the selling, distribution and general overheads for the rest of the business. The prime costs are the variable costs (because they vary with output), but the overheads are called fixed costs because they do not vary with output. For example, if you make 200 articles, you will need 200 lots of raw materials, and if you make 2000 articles, 2000 lots. By contrast, whatever output you produce, you only need one factory (although eventually you could need another one). Overhead costs are, to a very considerable extent, fixed costs.

To reach breakeven, you must cover both variable costs and fixed costs. Where will this point occur? You can see it if you draw a breakeven chart like the one shown in Figure 17.5. In this graph the fixed costs are £40 000 and variable costs are £15 per unit. The selling price is £35 per unit, giving a contribution towards fixed costs (and eventually to profits) of £20 per unit. You can see that, at £20 profit per unit, you will need to make and sell 2000 units if you are to cover the £40 000 of fixed costs (2000 x £20 = £40 000). Therefore, the breakeven point is going to be at an output of 2000 units. Study the chart shown in Figure 17.5.

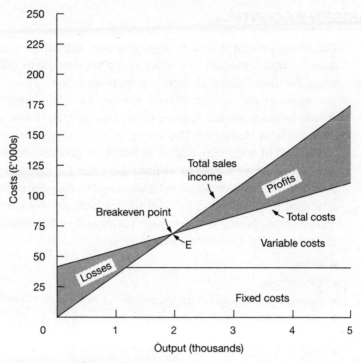

Fig. 17.5 A BREAKEVEN CHART

Notes

- The fixed costs are £40 000, as indicated by the horizontal line on the graph.
- On top of these fixed costs you have variable costs of £15 per unit, which, at an output of 5000 units, makes a total of £75 000. On top of the £40 000 fixed costs, that is £115 000 in all.
- By selling the articles at £35, 1000 units brings in £35 000 and 5000 units brings in £175 000.
- You can see that the breakeven point is at an output of 2000 units (E on the diagram), which is where the sales proceeds cover both the fixed and the variable costs and you start to make profits.
- From that time on, each unit sold brings in a contribution to profits of £20.
- You might like to answer the following questions.
  - What loss will be made if only 1500 can be sold?
  - What profit will be made if output and sales reach 4500 units?
- You could now draw a similar diagram if the selling price that could be achieved was £40, not £35.

BUDGETARY CONTROL

Budgetary control is a very large, involved subject. It is mainly practised in large firms and so it is not really appropriate to discuss it fully here. The basic ideas, though, are outlined below. Those particularly interested in the subject should see my book (in conjunction with Arthur Upson) entitled *Success in Management Accounting: An introduction* (John Murray, 1992).

The idea of budgetary control is that the accountant draws up (or has others draw up) budgets for departments that are detailed forecasts of the costs, outputs and so on to be achieved in the year ahead. You usually need a budget officer to call for the budgets, vet them and agree them as being in line with company policy and setting attainable targets of performance. Common budgets are for:

- sales
- production
- manufacturing (direct materials, direct pay, factory overheads)
- administration, selling and distribution costs
- purchases
- cash
- plant utilisation
- capital expenditure
- research and development.

The budget in each of these cases sets a standard against which all sorts of controls can be established. For example, a movement of raw material prices could be easily detected. Can you find a cheaper supplier? Can you use an alternative material? Can you rebut the price rise in any way? Can you push it on to the customer by raising your own prices? You will see at once that budgetary control sparks off a train of ideas from each variance that becomes apparent between budgeted and actual costs.

Budgetary control may be defined as a technique for relating the responsibilities of an executive to the requirements of policy via a system of budgets. It enables comparisons to be drawn between budgeted and actual costs and performances to correct any adverse variances, or, if they are insusceptible to correction, to revise the budget and feed the revision through to final prices so that budgeted profits are still achieved.

As mentioned, setting up a full system of budgetary control is an advanced technique, inappropriate to this book, but an awareness of the basic principles is still vital to the proprietors of small- and medium-sized businesses.

CHECKLIST

- Every aspect of a business requires control. With sole traders, the control is direct and easily exercised. As your business grows, you must establish an organisation that has control over all aspects, both in routine matters and emergency situations.

- Control over the order book is often a first requirement. You must attract a steady flow of customers and ensure that you can fulfil all the orders you accept.

- Cash flow control is an essential element of management. A cash budget should be drawn up and shortages anticipated and financed. Cash flow smoothing should be practised wherever possible.

- A 'variance' is a difference between a budgeted and an actual figure. If you analyse the variances that arise, you may be able to control costs or at least act quickly to pass them on in the form of increased prices to customers (and, thus prevent your profit margins being eroded).

- Stock should be controlled by a system that specifies maximum stocks, reorder points, reorder quantities and so on. Be aware of the dangers of stock losses by pilfering, inherent vices of the goods and bad buying, which cause stocks to be sold off at cut prices to prevent deterioration.

- Control over purchases is important. Open mail yourself so that you see the invoices and know what has been ordered in your name. Pay bills just before the due date to take full advantage of any credit period, unless you decide to take the settlement discount offered for paying earlier. Be solicitous of your suppliers' needs to be paid and, thus, establish a good name in the trade for prompt payment.

- Exercise good control over staff, so as to obtain a fair day's work for a fair day's pay, and avoid disruption due to petty disputes, claims of unfair dismissal and so on.

- A breakeven chart is useful for predicting when a new product will prove profitable.

- As the business grows, implement a system of budgetary control to keep costs and performance under constant review.

Accounting ratios

The nature of accounting ratios

Analysis of the trading account

Analysis of a profit and loss account

Some comments on balance sheets

Interpreting a balance sheet

Checklist

1
2
3
4
5
6
7
8
9
10
11
12
13
14
15
16
17
18
19
20
21

THE NATURE OF ACCOUNTING RATIOS

A ratio is a quantitative relationship between two figures that clearly brings out how many times one goes into another. For example, if your average stock of a particular item is £1000 at cost and you sell £26 000 of it per

> *The use of accounting ratios is to tell management what is happening to the business and bring out the relative not the actual changes.*

annum (at cost of sales price), then it is clear that your average stock turns over 26 times in a year. A rate of turnover of 26 is very good for many items (but it would not do for newspapers because it would mean that, on average, each paper sold was 2 weeks' old).

This type of figure is helpful to know, but you can only interpret it in the light of your knowledge of a particular business. For the self-employed person, the business you are interested in is your own business, and these simple ratios can tell you a lot about it. They are even more important when you have collected them over several years and can compare this year's performance with last year's. A further point is that if you take out a set of final accounts more frequently than once a year (say quarterly), you can compare results of not only this quarter with last quarter, but, more importantly, this quarter with the same quarter last year and that gives you a very good idea of how you are getting along.

The use of accounting ratios, then, is to tell management what is happening to the business and bring out the relative not the actual changes. Suppose an advertising campaign increases sales by 500 items, this might seem a satisfactory increase. If the previous sales were 40 000 and the increase brings them to 40 500 you can see that the relative increase, expressed as a percentage, is:

$$\frac{500}{40\ 000} \times 100\% = 1.25\%$$

The increase in sales does not seem much when you can see it relative to the original sales. Relative figures are usually more informative than actual figures.

Accounting ratios are found by an analysis of the final accounts. They include the following.

- Analysis of the trading account reveals:
  - the gross profit percentage;
  - the rate of stock turnover.
- Analysis of the profit and loss account reveals:

- the net profit percentage;
- the expense ratios (for all expenses).
- Analysis of the balance sheet reveals:
  - the working capital ratio or current ratio;
  - the liquid capital ratio or acid test ratio;
  - the return on capital employed (ROCE);
  - the return on capital invested (ROCI).
- Analysis of the balance sheet of a company reveals:
  - the ordinary shareholders' interest in the company;
  - the value per share.

ANALYSIS OF THE TRADING ACCOUNT

Figure 18.1 shows the trading account of Tasty Sweets, an imaginary sole trader business.

Trading Account for Year Ending 31 December 199X

199X		£	199X	£
Opening stock		5 250	Sales	139 500
Purchases	42 160		*Less* returns	1 500
Less returns	410		Net turnover	138 000
Net Purchases		41 750		
Total stock available		47 000		
Less closing stock		4 500		
Cost of stock sold		42 500		
Gross profit		95 500		
		£138 000		£138 000

Fig. 18.1 TASTY SWEETS' TRADING ACCOUNT FOR APPRAISAL

From Tasty Sweets' Trading Account, you can work out the ratios listed above.

■ The gross profit percentage

The formula is:

$$\text{Gross profit percentage} = \frac{\text{Gross profit}}{\text{Turnover}} \times 100$$

Substituting the figures from Tasty Sweets' Trading Account, we have:

$$\text{Gross profit percentage} = \frac{\pounds95\ 500}{\pounds138\ 000} \times 100$$

$$= \frac{9550}{138}\ \%$$

$$= \underline{\underline{69.2\%}}$$

■ Comments on this percentage

- The gross profit percentage should always be quite a high figure because you have to cover a great many overhead expenses with this gross profit. One of the commonest causes of failure in business is not taking a big enough gross profit percentage. You simply cannot keep going on a gross profit of 20 per cent – you need at least 50 per cent, and 200 per cent or 300 per cent is not uncommon. If your circumstances are so competitive that you cannot charge a high enough margin, leave the industry and seek a more lucrative outlet for your talents.

- The important point about gross profit percentage is that it should be the same from year to year (that is, it should be a constant), unless you yourself are doing something to make it change (like introducing more efficient methods of working). Always compare this year's ratio with last year's. Suppose last year you were making 75 per cent gross profit percentage. What can have happened to cause the decrease? It can only be something within the Trading Account. What could it be?

  - It could be the manager/manageress stealing the sales money.
  - It could be some member of staff stealing the sales money. Who, on the staff, is looking like a million dollars these days? It could be your million dollars they're looking like!
  - It could be that stocks are down because of theft by the staff or theft by customers or 'passing out' (giving of stock to friends and relations).
  - It could be increased purchase prices that have not been passed on as increased selling prices to customers.
  - It could be stock losses due to poor buying (perishables thrown away or slow-moving stock sold at marked-down prices). It could be skylarking in the crockery department. Anything that means a lower stock means a lower gross profit, and hence a lower gross profit percentage.

■ The rate of stock turnover

The rate of stock turnover can be found using either of the following two formulae.

$$\text{Rate of stock turn} = \frac{\textbf{Cost of stock sold}}{\textbf{Average stock at cost price}}$$

$$\text{Rate of stock turn} = \frac{\textbf{Net turnover}}{\textbf{Average stock at selling price}}$$

The point is that the two figures used must be in the same form – either both at cost price or both at selling price.

Using the cost price figures from Figure 18.1 we have:

$$\text{Rate of stock turn} = \frac{£42\ 500}{\text{Average stock}}$$

$$\text{Average stock} = \frac{(\text{Opening stock} + \text{closing stock})}{2}$$

$$= \frac{£5250 + £4500}{2}$$

$$= \frac{£9750}{2}$$

$$= £4875$$

$$\therefore \text{Rate of stock turn} = \frac{£42\ 500}{£4875}$$

$$= 8.7 \text{ times a year}$$

Whether 8.7 times in a year is a reasonable rate of turnover or not depends on the type of goods being sold. It gives a better picture if the figure is turned into another related figure – namely the amount of time the average stock is on hand before it is sold. You can do this by dividing the rate into the number of days, weeks or months in the year. Thus:

$$\frac{12}{8.7} = 1.4 \text{ months an average item is in stock}$$

$$\frac{52}{8.7} = 6.0 \text{ weeks an average item is in stock}$$

$$\frac{365}{8.7} = 42.0 \text{ days an average item is in stock.}$$

Whether the sweets dealt in by this trader would be in a satisfactory condition after about 6 weeks in stock is a matter for management to ponder.

ANALYSIS OF A PROFIT AND LOSS ACCOUNT

Figure 18.2 shows Tasty Sweets' Profit and Loss Account at the end of the same year.

Profit and Loss Account for Year Ending 31 December 199X

199X	£	199X	£
Mortgage interest	5 250	Gross profit	95 500
Light and heat	2 350	Rent received	2 500
Telephone expenses	1 460	Discount received	350
Salaries	27 640		98 350
Insurance paid	420		
Interest paid	350		
Community charges (rates)	4 875		
Motor vehicle expenses	2 536		
Packaging and selling			
expenses	4 419		
	49 300		
Net profit	49 050		
	£98 350		£98 350

Fig. 18.2 TASTY SWEETS' PROFIT AND LOSS ACCOUNT FOR APPRAISAL

From its Profit and Loss Account and the turnover figure in the Trading Account, you can work out the ratios listed at the start of this chapter.

■ The net profit percentage

The formula is:

$$\text{Net profit percentage} = \frac{\text{Net profit}}{\text{Turnover}} \times 100$$

$$= \frac{£49\ 050}{£138\ 000} \times 100$$

$$= \frac{4905}{138}$$

$$= \underline{35.5\%}$$

■ *Comments on this percentage*

- The net profit percentage can vary enormously between firms according to the type of industry concerned and the competitive state of the industry. You want the return you earn from risking your capital in business to be higher than the 8–10 per cent you could earn from a safe investment in a building society or a gilt-edged security. The 35.5 per cent figure is well above this level.

- What was the net profit percentage last year? If you know that it was 38.5 per cent, you could ask yourself why it has fallen this year. Provided the gross profit percentage had remained more or less the same, the fall in net profit percentage must be due to something within the Profit and Loss Account. Has a particular expense item risen considerably in the current year? You can find out by taking out expense ratios (see below). Has some source of profit you enjoyed last year (other than gross profit) fallen considerably, or even ceased to be earned for some reason? You can look at these situations. For example, if the rent received figure has fallen because you had to use rooms formerly let to cater for your own expansion, there is nothing you can do to recover the sums lost. If you have failed to pursue possible profits, you should take steps to recover them in the coming year.

■ The expense ratios

Expense ratios are those where you relate particular expenses to turnover to arrive at a percentage. Thus the salaries ratio is found by the formula:

$$\text{Salaries ratio} = \frac{\text{Salaries paid}}{\text{Turnover}} \times 100$$

$$= \frac{£27\,640}{£138\,000} \times 100$$

$$= \frac{2764}{138}$$

$$= \underline{\underline{20.0\%}}$$

Thus, 20 per cent of your turnover was used up in salaries, but suppose last year the figure was 16.5 per cent. Clearly there is a problem here. Some people collect employees, because it makes them feel powerful if they have a little empire of 'hangers on'. If extra staff have been appointed with little real effect on the expansion of the business (an increase in turnover), you should want to know why this is so.

If every expense ratio is calculated and compared with the same ratio in previous years, you will be able to pinpoint areas where action is necessary. If you cannot avoid the increases in overheads, you must pass the increases on to your customers by raising prices.

To familiarise yourself with these ratios, you should now try the exercises below. The answers are given at the end of the exercises.

EXERCISES ON EVALUATING A TRADING ACCOUNT AND PROFIT AND LOSS ACCOUNT

1. A. Trader had in stock on 1 July 600 articles costing £2.00 each. During the month, he bought 1800 more of these articles at £2.40 each and sold 2020 at £4.00 each, of which 20 of the most recent items were returned. He sells stock on a first in, first out basis. Draw up a statement showing the gross profit earned, and express the gross profit as a percentage of the turnover.

2. On preparing the Trading Account of R. Lyons, a retailer, for the financial year ended 31 March 199X, it was found that the ratio of gross profit to sales was 15 per cent, whereas for the previous financial year the corresponding ratio had been 25 per cent. State, with your reasons, whether or not the following may have contributed to causing the decline:

- the stock at 31 March 199X was undervalued;
- the cost of a new delivery van had been included in the purchases for the year ended 31 March 199X and charged to the Trading Account;
- the sales for the year ended 31 March 199X showed a decline compared with the previous year.
- in both years, R. Lyons and his family had been supplied with goods from the shop, but the value of these goods had not been recorded in the books of the business;
- on the last day of the financial year, an employee was successfully convicted of dishonesty with regard to the theft of takings from the tills.

3. A trader carries an average stock of £8000 (valued at cost price) and turns this over five times a year. If he marks up his stock by 25 per cent on cost price, what is his gross profit for the year?

4. A trader carries average stock valued at cost price of £6250 and turns this over 14 times a year. If his mark-up is 20 per cent on cost and his overheads came to £6200, what is the net profit for the year?

Answers
1. Gross profit = £3440; gross profit percentage = 43 per cent.
2. Yes – undervalued closing stock increases the cost of sales and reduces the profit and, hence, the gross profit percentage.
   - Yes – including a motor vehicle in purchases increases the cost of sales as in (a) above.
   - No – decline in sales should not affect the ratio, which is a constant.

- Possibly. These goods reduce the stock and, consequently, affect the gross profit percentage as in (a) above. However, as it happened last year, too, it would only affect the gross profit percentage if the quantity of goods taken was greater this year than last year.
- Yes – theft of sales money reduces the sales figure and, consequently, the gross profit.

3. £10 000 gross profit.
4. £11 300 net profit.

SOME COMMENTS ON BALANCE SHEETS

Before looking at the analysis of balance sheets, there are one or two points that may confuse you whenever balance sheets are studied. The idea of a balance in everyday life is that two sides of a situation should be weighed against one another and considered to see whether or not they are of equal weight. You can see this idea if you think of the statue of Justice on the Old Bailey in London, where Justice holds up the scales to see whether or not the 'good' or the 'evil' in a case is greater. A balance – both in the scientific laboratory and in justice – must be horizontal.

The balance sheet was invented in 1536 by Simon Stevin of Bruges, and he called it a 'statement of affairs'. This is a very good name, for it describes exactly what a balance sheet is – a statement of the affairs of a business at a given moment, the last second of the last day of the accounting period. Unfortunately, as a balance sheet is derived from a trial balance, where the assets are on the left-hand side and the liabilities are on the right-hand side, it is a great pity that Stevin got in a muddle when he drew up his statement of affairs, and crossed the balance sheet over to put the liabilities on the left and the assets on the right. This became the traditional British balance sheet, as shown in Chapter 6. Other nations quickly changed the balance sheet round the correct way, so that most European nations and the United States do their balance sheets the correct way round.

However, the most confusing thing for traders today is that the United Kingdom's accountancy bodies have started to do balance sheets in vertical style, with the assets above the liabilities or, perhaps, the liabilities above the assets. This makes a mockery of the name balance sheet, let alone justice. It is as sensible to have a balance sheet in vertical style as it would be for justice to have the good side of a case on top of the evil side or vice versa. If, therefore, your balance sheet from your accountant is in vertical style, remember that, really, it should be horizontal, and you are trying to weigh the assets against the liabilities to ensure that they are equal.

To explain the points made in this section, Tasty Sweets' balance sheet is presented in all three forms (see Figure 18.3(a–c)).

Balance Sheet as at 31 December 199X

199X		£	199X		£
Capital			*Fixed assets*		
At start		43 332	Premises		68 000
Add net profit	49 050		Plant and machinery		28 500
Less drawings	18 750		Motor vehicles		13 820
		30 300	Furniture, etc.		9 250
		73 632			119 570
Long-term liabilities			*Current assets*		
Mortgage	50 000		Stock	6 500	
Bank loan	5 000		Debtors	1 850	
		55 000	Cash at bank	5 214	
			Cash in hand	738	
Current liabilities					
Creditors		5 240			14 302
		£133 872			£133 872

Fig. 18.3(a) TASTY SWEETS' BALANCE SHEET FOR APPRAISAL IN TRADITIONAL UK STYLE

Balance Sheet as at 31 December 199X

199X		£	199X		£
Fixed Assets			*Capital*		
Premises		68 000	At start		43 332
Plant and machinery		28 500	Add net profit	49 050	
Motor vehicles		13 820	*Less* drawings	18 750	
Furniture, etc.		9 250			30 300
		119 570			73 632
Current assets			*Long-term liabilities*		
Stock	6 500		Mortgage	50 000	
Debtors	1 850		Bank loan	5 000	
Cash at bank	5 214				55 000
Cash in hand	738				
			Current liabilities		
		14 302	Creditors		5 240
		£133 872			£133 872

Fig. 18.3(b) TASTY SWEETS' BALANCE SHEET FOR APPRAISAL IN CORRECT 'EUROPEAN' STYLE

Balance Sheet as at 31 December 199X

	At cost £	Less depreciation £	Value £
Fixed assets			
Premises	68 000	–	68 000
Plant and machinery	35 000	6 500	28 500
Motor vehicles	18 000	4 180	13 820
Furniture and fittings	12 000	2 750	9 250
	£133 000	£13 430	119 570
Current assets			
Stock		6 500	
Debtors		1 850	
Cash at bank		5 214	
Cash in hand		738	
			14 302
			£133 872
Financed by:			
Capital at start			43 332
add net profit		40 050	
less drawings		18 750	
			30 300
			73 632
Long-term liabilities			
Mortgage		50 000	
Bank loan		5 000	
			55 000
Current liabilities			
Creditors			5 240
			£133 872

Fig. 18.3(c) TASTY SWETS' BALANCE SHEET FOR APPRAISAL IN VERTICAL STYLE

Note on Figure 18.3(c)

You can see the advantage of the vertical-style balance sheet – it is much easier to set out across a typewritten page. For example, the details of the depreciation to date have been set out in full. However, this can be done just as easily with the European style if the balance sheet is set out across a double page. The term 'Balance Sheet' is then much more appropriate, for the two sides do 'balance'. A balance is essentially a horizontal affair, and the vertical style is therefore not really appropriate.

INTERPRETING A BALANCE SHEET

Remember that as a balance sheet is taken out at the very end of the financial year, it is essentially a historical statement – this is how things were at the end of the accounting period. When you come to analyse it, it is too late to correct anything – all you can do is learn lessons for the future.

■ The working capital ratio or current ratio

Before considering the working capital ratio, you must learn the vocabulary of balance sheets. You know that fixed assets are those that last a long time (more than a year) and current assets are those that are not held for long-term use, but are only temporary (they last less than one year). For example, you hope you will sell all your stock in the first few weeks of the new year, and you hope your debtors will pay you within one month (or any other agreed credit period).

You often call the fixed assets 'fixed capital' because the capital you have spent on them is tied up in long-term assets and is no longer liquid money capital.

The current assets are often called 'working capital' because they are used to keep the business working, pay staff, buy more raw materials or goods for resale and so on. Shortage of working capital is one of the chief problems of businesses, for these reasons. It is the working capital (particularly the cash in hand and the cash at the bank) that you use to pay off your current liabilities (your creditors). If you have insufficient working capital to pay your creditors, one who cannot be paid may start legal proceedings against you and you may finish up in the bankruptcy courts.

Buying too many fixed assets and leaving yourselves too few current assets is called overtrading.

The best definition of working capital is:

Working capital = Current assets – Current liabilities

In the case of Figure 18.3, it is:

Working capital =   £14 302 – £5240
=   £9062

The more useful management figure is:

$$\text{Working Capital Ratio} = \frac{\text{Current assets}}{\text{Current liabilities}}$$

$$= \frac{\pounds14\ 302}{\pounds5240}$$

$$= \underline{\underline{2.7\ \text{times}}}$$

In other words, you could, if you realised all your current assets, pay your creditors 2.7 times over. Thus, you are perfectly safe, and no creditor could possibly put you out of business because you have plenty of funds to pay everyone.

The usual guiding rule is that the working capital ratio should be at least 2.0 – that is, you can pay all your debts twice over.

■ The liquid capital ratio or acid test ratio

Although the working capital ratio referred to above is a good guide to the state of our business as far as capital goes, there is an even more vital ratio – such a strict ratio that it is called the acid test ratio.

This states that when you test for your current viability, you should not include the stock in your current assets, because stock can be notoriously hard to sell, and if you want to realise it (that is, turn it into cash), you often have to reduce it in price. Liquid capital is therefore defined as (current assets – stock) – current liabilities. The acid test ratio formula is:

$$\textbf{Acid test ratio} \ = \ \frac{\textbf{Current assets – stock}}{\textbf{Current liabilities}}$$

In the case of Figure 18.3, it is:

$$\text{Acid test ratio} \ = \ \frac{\pounds14\ 302 - \pounds6500}{\pounds5240}$$

$$= \frac{\pounds7802}{\pounds5240}$$

$$= \underline{\underline{1.5\ \text{times}}}$$

This is a satisfactory liquid capital ratio. Accountants hold that with our liquid assets, you should be able to pay all your creditors – that is, the liquid capital ratio should be at least 1.0. However, just suppose the figures had had rather more stock in them. Say:

$$
\begin{array}{lr}
 & £ \\
\text{Stock} & 9\ 500 \\
\text{Debtors} & 2\ 850 \\
\text{Cash at Bank} & 1\ 214 \\
\text{Cash in Hand} & \underline{738} \\
 & \underline{\underline{14\ 302}}
\end{array}
$$

You would then have had:

$$
\text{Working capital ratio} \ = \ \frac{14\ 302}{5240} = 2.7 \text{ times}
$$

$$
\text{Liquid capital ratio} \ = \ \frac{4802}{5240} = 0.92 \text{ times}
$$

Clearly, you have not enough liquid capital to pay all your debts, and there is some chance that you could be in financial difficulties.

■ The return on capital employed (ROCE)

When you discover the return on capital employed, you are, to some extent, comparing your business as an investment with other investment opportunities open to you. Various measures are used (not everyone has the same ideas about what should be included in the term 'capital employed'). For example, if you look at any balance sheet, it is a simple fact that whatever assets you have on the assets side have been obtained with the capital listed on the other side. So, in Figure 18.3, the total assets are worth £133 872. How have these been obtained? The answer is that the proprietor originally provided £43 332 and has also ploughed in profits earned worth £30 300, making the total of the proprietor's contribution £73 632. Then, you also used capital from a building society or bank mortgage, and a bank loan to a total of £55 000, and you managed to persuade creditors to lend you £5240. All these various bits of capital financed the purchase of the assets.

It is usual to leave out the creditors (because, to some extent anyway, they are balanced by the debtors on the other side who are using your capital to finance their business activities). It is also usual to average out the profits ploughed back and say, 'Well, really, we've only had the use of that capital for half the year on average'. A similar averaging process would be necessary if you borrowed the long-term liabilities at some time during the year. However, you will pretend both the bank loan and the mortgage have been used for the whole year.

The capital employed is therefore worked out as follows:

Capital employed = £43 332 + £15 150 + £55 000
= £113 482

The return on capital employed is the profit you made in the year expressed as a percentage of that capital. Here, the profit is £49 050. However, as you are counting the loan and the mortgage as part of the capital employed, you must include the interest paid on these amounts as part of the profit, which was £575 and £5250 respectively. This makes the full profit £49 050 + £575 + £5250 = £54 875. Therefore, you have:

$$\text{Return on capital employed} = \frac{£54\,875}{£113\,482} \times 100$$

$$= \underline{\underline{48.4\%}}$$

This appears to be a very satisfactory return – comparing it, for example, with the same capital invested in gilt-edged securities where you might get about 9 per cent. It seems it is well worth while being in business!

■ The return on capital invested (ROCI)

A more subtle ratio – which applies more particularly to the proprietor – is to work out the return on capital invested. This term refers to the capital invested by the proprietor at the start of the year. As with all sophisticated ratios, you have to think carefully about the figures you are using and, perhaps, adapt them if necessary. The profit earned was £49 050 on original capital of £43 332 invested at the start of the year. However, to find out whether or not it has really been worth while being in business, you have to see what extra benefit the proprietor is gaining. When you take up the opportunity of being self-employed, you give up any chance of doing other things and these lost opportunities mean you have lost money. Thus, if we cannot now take a job, we have lost the opportunity to earn money. You have also lost the opportunity of putting £43 332 in a safe bank account earning a high rate of interest. These losses are called the opportunity costs of being self-employed – the lost opportunities.

What were the opportunity costs in Figure 18.3? They are not known, but imagine that the proprietor of Tasty Sweets could have earned £8500 a year as the manager of a sweet shop, and could have invested their savings in a high-interest account earning 9.5 per cent.

The opportunity cost is therefore £8500 + £4117 (the interest calculated at 9.5 per cent on £43 332 if it had been invested instead of being used in the business). This means the extra profit actually earned by being in business is:

$$£49\,050 - £12\,617 = £36\,433$$

Therefore, the return on capital invested (ROCI) in this case is:

$$\text{ROCI} = \frac{\text{Net profit} - \text{Opportunity cost}}{\text{Capital at start}} \times 100$$

$$= \frac{£36\,433}{£43\,332} \times 100$$

$$= 84\%$$

Clearly, it is well worth being in business.

You should now try the following exercises to familiarise yourself with these control ratios.

EXERCISES ON THE INTERPRETATION OF A BALANCE SHEET

1. M. Brown's current assets total £27 300 and his current liabilities total £8500. Find the working capital ratio and comment on its adequacy.

2. R. Bird's current assets are as follows:

	£
Stock	15 500
Debtors	3 400
Cash at bank	5 800
Cash in hand	200

Her only liability is to a single creditor – £8600. Work out (correct to two decimal places) R. Bird's working capital ratio and her acid test ratio. Say whether or not each of these is adequate.

3. Here is M. Ross' Balance Sheet. Answer the questions which follow (with calculations if needed).

Balance Sheet as at 31 December 199X

199X		£	199X		£
Capital			Fixed assets		
At start		56 000	Goodwill		2 000
Add Additions during					
year		2 000	Premises		36 000
		58 000	Plant and machinery		24 000
			Motor vehicles		4 000
Add net profit	16 600				66 000
Less drawings	7 200				
		9 400			
		67 400			
Long-term Liabilities			Current Assets		
Mortgage		10 000	Stock	9 192	
			Debtors	2 548	
Current Liabilities			Cash at Bank	2 762	
Creditors	3 228		Cash in Hand	144	
Accrued			Payments in		
Charges	104		Advance	176	
		3 422			14 822
		£80 822			£80 822

- What is the capital owned by the proprietor at the end of the year?
- What is the capital employed in the business? You should assume that prof-
  its were earned at an average rate throughout the year and that current lia-
  bilities are not part of the capital employed. The additions to capital were
  invested on 1 January.
- What is the working capital?
- Calculate the working capital ratio (correct to two decimal places).
- What is the liquid capital?
- Calculate the acid test ratio (correct to two decimal places).
- Work out the return on capital invested (correct to one decimal place), assuming that Ross could earn £9000 a year in an alternative position with none of
  the responsibilities of a small businessowner and could invest his capital at a
  rate of 10 per cent if he had no business to use it in. Comment on the results.

Answers

1. Working capital = £18 800; working capital ratio = 3.2. This is more than adequate.
2. Working capital = £16 300; working capital ratio = 2.90; acid test ratio = 1.09. Both
   are adequate.
3. £67 400; £72 700; £11 400; 4.33; £2208; 1.65; 3.1 per cent. The extra profit hardly
   seems worth the effort and risk.
   Perhaps there are non-monetary satisfactions.

CHECKLIST

- The trading account enables you to work out a gross profit percentage, using the formula:

$$\text{Gross profit percentage} = \frac{\text{Gross profit}}{\text{Turnover}} \times 100$$

- You can also work out a rate of stock turnover using the formula:

$$\text{Rate of stock turn} = \frac{\text{Cost of stock sold}}{\text{Average stock at cost price}}$$

- The profit and loss account enables you to work out a net profit percentage using the formula:

$$\text{Net profit percentage} = \frac{\text{Net profit}}{\text{Turnover}} \times 100$$

- You can also work out expense ratios for each expense item, using the formula:

$$\text{Expense ratio} = \frac{\text{Expense item}}{\text{Turnover}} \times 100$$

- Working capital is found by the formula: current assets *less* current liabilities.

- The working capital ratio is found by dividing the current liabilities into the current assets. It tells you how many times you can pay your current liabilities with your available current assets.

- The liquid capital ratio is the same sort of calculation, but the stock is left out of the current assets. It is the acid test ratio of whether or not you can meet your obligations.

- The return on capital employed compares your business, as an investment, with other investment opportunities open to you.

- The return on capital invested tells you whether or not it is worth while being in business.

Finding funds to start, or expand, your business

THE NEED FOR MONEY CAPITAL

As far as a balance sheet is concerned, the word 'capital' means 'what the business owes back to the owner of the business'. The initial capital may consist partly of money and partly of other assets that the proprietor has contributed to the business, such as a motor vehicle, tools and equipment, premises, perhaps, and a stock of goods for resale. As the years go by, if the business is profitable, and if the proprietor does not draw out all the profits for personal consumption, the assets will grow as surplus profit is ploughed back into the business. As the assets increase, so will the proprietor's capital. Often called the 'net worth' of the business to the owner of the business, this capital gradually increases as the assets accumulate.

However, suppose you want to expand faster and cannot wait for the slow ploughing back of profits into the business. Suppose you strike a cash flow problem and get into an illiquid situation where you are forced to make creditors wait for their money. You must ask for a loan from someone outside the business, such as a bank or a finance house or a specialist type of investor called a 'venture capitalist'. These sources can provide the funds you need, but, of course, for a price. The usual price is 'interest', charged at a fair rate according to the degree of risk being run. Part of the price you may need to pay is to give the lender some degree of control over your business – perhaps a seat on the Board of your company or a right to see the books of the business.

SOURCES OF FUNDS

■ Self-financing

If a business is self-financing, it is experiencing the ideal situation. It means that the expansion of the firm can be achieved by ploughing back the profits year by year, while at the same time giving the proprietor a reasonable standard of living. To be able to do this, a firm must be generating really good profits, which it can do perhaps because it has a popular, unique product and a monopoly conferred by an unexpired patent right or some official status. For example, Parliament sometimes confers a statutory monopoly on a developer for a limited period – say 25 years. Thus, a bridge-builder who spans a river may be given 25 years to get their money back from bridge tolls before the bridge becomes part of the public road network.

Without such a monopoly situation, the expansion of a firm by means of self-financing alone will be a slower process, subject to the competitive situation in the industry concerned.

■ *Fixed assets and current assets*

Whenever you need finance for your business, it is because you need more assets of one sort or another. You know that any balance sheet divides assets into fixed assets and current assets. Fixed assets are assets that are used in the business over many years, such as premises, plant and machinery, fixtures and fittings and motor vehicles. Current assets are assets that you hope will only feature on your balance sheets for less than a year. The boundary line between fixed assets and current assets is set at one year. Examples of current assets are debtors, stock, cash at bank and cash in hand.

The most likely finance required for fixed assets is money for the original purchase of the asset concerned – a motor vehicle or a machine, say. You can finance the purchase of such assets by hire purchase via a finance company, a loan from a bank or other financial institution, contributing further capital from private funds and so on.

The most likely finance needed for current assets is working capital. Working capital is capital that is required to run the business on a day-to-day basis, to bridge the gaps between receipts and expenses when business is seasonal or fluctuating. For example, a firm may buy in stock for resale at festival times, such as Christmas or Easter. The purchase of this stock is easy if you have plenty of cash in the bank, but if you haven't, you must borrow some working capital. Later you can repay the funds borrowed with the proceeds of the busy, festival trading. Such funds may be obtained by means of an overdraft, loan from a bank or other institution, short-term credit, such as by using a credit card and so on.

One point to note about working capital is that a shortage can easily develop if you are too relaxed or open-hearted in business. For example, if you buy too much stock, much of which sells only slowly, you will need to pay for it before you have managed to sell it. Stock control is an important part of a trading or manufacturing business. Similarly, if the figure for debtors increases, your receipts will be lower than you expected and your working capital will not be replenished as you hoped. A sound credit control policy is essential to reduce the 'debtors' figures.

■ Banks

Banks are in business to earn a living by lending money to those who need it and who have excellent prospects of repaying the sums borrowed with interest. Most banks can offer a huge range of services to meet the needs of all types of businesses, and various financial arrangements are possible with your chosen bank. The banks also want a continuing arrangement if possible, that will bring in business in the years ahead. Chopping and changing banks is often recommended by the popular press, in pursuit of the cheapest rate of interest, but cheapness in borrowing is like cheapness in other fields, it often indicates lack of quality.

The best time to discuss a package of banking services with your bank is not when you have an emergency, but when all is well with your business. A discussion that features such points as your occasional need, perhaps, for working capital, your need to invest working surpluses in short- and medium-term deposits, for seasonal overdraft facilities on reasonable terms and loans for specific assets or particular projects, expansion and so on, is going to open up many pathways through the finance network.

For the small firm making its first approach to a bank, a helpful way to start is to set down on a sheet of paper the basic details of the firm, its name, address, chief activities, turnover (or hoped-for turnover) and balance sheet at the present moment. You should then set down the types of services you require, and it promotes confidence in you by the bank if you regard them as the natural supplier of these services as far as you are concerned. For example, if you envisage insurance as being one service you require, putting the business the bank's way will naturally increase their interest in you. A list of such services would include the following, for even the smallest firm.

- **Current account services** including chequebooks, debit cards, credit cards, standing orders, direct debits, overdraft facilities, when required, and a monthly bank statement.
- **Deposit account** for short-term storage of surplus funds, particularly VAT money, taxes payable under the self-assessment rules and corporation tax of a company. Some fair rate of interest needs to be agreed and the bank will have several alternatives to suggest.
- **Insurance** particularly that which is compulsory under the Employers' Liability Acts, but also contents insurance, motor vehicle insurance and even life assurance.
- **Credit card merchant facilities** may be required by traders. The process of accreditation takes a few weeks and this is one area where

you may need to approach all the main banks so that you can offer a full range of choice to customers.

A discussion of these basic points will bring out many useful ideas and will get a small firm off to a good start. The question of bank charges should be discussed and kept under review. If you are a poor risk, the rate will be high (say 5 or 6 per cent above base rate), but if your business activity shows that, in fact, you are no longer a poor risk, a request for a more reasonable rate (say 3 or 4 per cent above base rate) will be listened to.

■ Overdraft arrangements

One way to obtain finance from a bank is by means of an overdraft. The bank agrees to allow the customer to write cheques to meet their everyday commitments even though there is no money left in the trader's account. They have 'overdrawn' and the deposit is a negative figure. Interest is charged on the outstanding balance and is a business expense of the borrower. Generally speaking, there is a limit on the overdraft (say £1000) and any attempt to exceed the sanctioned amount incurs punitive rate of interest.

An overdraft is really the provision of working capital by a bank at the most opportune moment (whenever you run out of money). Sanctioning an overdraft is therefore a very helpful act, and the bank may charge a few pounds for obliging you in this way. If your cash flow forecast shows that you will run out of funds in the month ahead, a quick telephone call may be all that is necessary to arrange an overdraft.

One disadvantage of overdrafts is that they can be withdrawn at any time, which means you must repay the amount owed at once. This can obviously be a problem, but a bank will usually make it possible for you to do this by allowing you to change the overdraft into a formal loan. This means the drawing up of a simple loan agreement, the amount of the loan being put into the current account where it cancels the overdraft. As with many loans, the bank may demand security, such as the deeds of your house, until the loan is repaid.

■ Small-scale loans from banks and similar institutions

Many firms build up relationships with banks, finance houses and similar institutions so that they can borrow money for general purposes (working capital) or expansion purposes. Such loans are the subject of loan applications, which call for a clear statement of the purposes the money is to be put to and the proposed method of repayment. This is discussed in detail later in this chapter, but the result is, if favourable, a decision to sanction the loan on agreed terms. The amount of the loan will be made available in the current account of the borrower. At the same time, a second account – the loan account – is opened for the borrower, and debited not only with the amount of the loan but also with the interest and charges. The firm is now a debtor in the books of the lender for this total amount, which will be gradually repaid according to the terms of the loan. As the loan is repaid, the amounts will be credited to the loan account and will gradually extinguish the loan. Typical entries in such an account are shown in Figure 19.1.

A. Borrower (Current Account)

Date	Details	Debit (£)	Credit (£)	Balance (£)
25 July	Loan sanctioned	–	5000.00	5000.00

The customer's current account transactions will continue using the funds made available. In due course, repayments will begin.

Date	Details	Debit (£)	Credit (£)	Balance (£)
25 October	Direct debit	350.00		
25 January	Direct debit	350.00		

Quarterly repayments of £350.00 will be extracted from the current account by direct debit.

A. Borrower (Loan Account)

Date	Details	Debit (£)	Credit (£)	Balance (£)
25 July	Loan sanctioned	7000.00	–	7000.00 Dr
25 October	Direct debit	–	350.00	6650.00 Dr
25 Jan	Direct debit	–	350.00	6300.00 Dr

The regular repayments will extinguish the loan in 5 years.

Fig. 19.1 A. BORROWER'S CURRENT AND LOAN ACCOUNTS

Besides these two accounts, the bank's ledger will have an account showing the profits it hopes to earn during the course of the loan. This account will complete the double entry (see Figure 19.2).

Interest and Charges Receivable Account

Date	Details	Debit (£)	Credit (£)	Balance (£)
25 July	Loan to A. Borrower	–	2000.00	2000.00

Fig. 19.2 THE ENTRY IN THE BANK'S LEDGER FOR A. BORROWERS' LOAN

At the end of the financial year, a fair proportion of these profits will be carried to the bank's profit and loss account as profit earned in the year.

■ Medium-sized enterprises and financing

For the medium-sized enterprise, there is a wider range of sources for funding expansions and they divide into internal funding and external funding.

■ Internal funding

Retained profits

Hopefully, internal funding will come from a healthy and profitable range of activities that yield enough funds to not only satisfy the shareholders, by permitting the payment of reasonable dividends, but also to leave a surplus for expansion of the business.

Retained profits, ultimately, do belong to the shareholders, but it is for the Board to manage the company and if it chooses to expand the business, the profits used in this way cannot be distributed as dividends. However, eventually profits become 'bonus shares' given away to the existing shareholders.

The issuing of bonus shares to existing shareholders is recognition that the profits that were retained by the company have now been turned into fixed assets, and are no longer available in cash form. Consequently, they cannot be distributed as dividends. The shareholders must take that part of their profits in shares (which, of course, they are free to sell if they prefer to have money). An increase in retained profits is the best way to fund expansion internally.

Depreciation as a source of funds

It is not widely realised that the depreciation of assets makes funds available for investment. When you enter an amount of depreciation on the profit and loss account (see Figure 5.6), it reduces the profit available to the owners of the business, but it does not actually remove the money itself, which is left lying around loose in the general funds of the firm or company. Ideally, the profits kept within the business in this way and denied to the owners or shareholders, should be invested so that funds are accumulated with which to purchase a new asset when the present asset is fully depreciated (and therefore fully worn out).

Such an investment may be merely put on deposit with a bank, earning interest that should be added to the deposit to allow for price increases when the machine, motor vehicle or whatever is replaced. Alternatively, the money could be used to buy a small portfolio of investments that will earn dividends year by year. All such dividends should be reinvested until the time to replace the assets arrives. At that time, the investments will be sold for the best price possible and the funds used to purchase a new asset. Funds of this sort are called 'sinking funds'.

Although depreciation is another source of funds, it is rarely available for expansion of the firm as it is related to the need to replace a particular asset, when the time comes. However, in some circumstance – where, for example, a new production line is being added and the deteriorating machine will not be part of the new set-up – the sinking fund for the replacement machine can be realised and used to meet the general capital costs of the new layout.

Leasing and 'sale and leaseback' arrangements

A great deal of funds in every business are tied up in fixed assets, which are essential to the running of the business and cannot therefore be disposed of to raise money for expansion. If you can find a way of replacing these permanent assets and turning them into funds that are available for expansion purposes while at the same time retaining their use by leasing them back from the new owner, you will have the best of both worlds. This is the 'sale and leaseback' method.

The assets sold disappear from the books of the business and from the balance sheet, but they are replaced by a series of lease payments as you purchase the right to go on using them for the foreseeable future. These lease payments are an expense of the business and, therefore, a charge against the profits, so there may be a tax advantage as well.

■ External funding

Funds may be obtained from outside the business in a variety of ways, and they may call for a more formal approach than the simple loans referred to earlier. Before discussing this, a word or two about venture capital.

'Venture capital' is capital made available by institutional investors as part of a 'balanced portfolio' of investments.

■ Venture capital

'Venture capital' is capital made available by institutional investors as part of a 'balanced portfolio' of investments. An institutional investor is someone who manages funds for other people, keeping control of them to achieve a good return for the depositor while, at the same time, running as little risk as possible.

The idea is that a balance is found between safety (safe investments do not yield a large return) and more risky investments (where an investment is risky it is usual to charge more interest and, thus, get a bigger return). If a fundholder decides to make a small part of investable funds available as 'venture capital', they will be prepared to lend it to a small business, even though there is some risk. Further, certain government schemes – to encourage funding for risky enterprises – allow investors to claim such venture capital as a deductible expense. Suppose a very wealthy person has plenty of funds to lend, but hesitates to lend to a business that needs urgent finance. Suppose the borrower needs £10 000. As the rich person is paying tax on their profits at the top rate (40 per cent), the chance to treat the loans as a deductible expense means that they will save £4000 tax. The borrower receives £10 000 from the venture capitalist, but the true cost to the lender is really only £6000 because the other £4000 will be recouped because tax will not be collected. Thus, the investor gets an investment of £10 000 at a cost of only £6000. This is a great incentive for the venture capitalist.

Venture capitalists are obviously interested in large-scale loans. Clear documentation on the venture, whatever it is, must be prepared, risks must be assessed and so this is only worth while if the sum involved is quite large. Venture capitalists can 'specialise', some being mainly in property development, some in shipping or speculative aviation projects, some in films or theatrical occasions and so on.

APPLYING FOR A LOAN

In the UK, there is no shortage of capital for investment purposes, and money can be found for every type of expansion or new project. The shortage is in viable projects that clearly demonstrate

When it comes to larger amounts, the banks will require a more detailed and thoughtful proposal from the borrower.

a potential for success. Penniless investors with what they believe to be marketable ideas find they cannot offer real prospects of success and so are starved of funds, while, at the same time, millions of pounds pour into the Stock Exchange for established businesses.

Small loans are readily available at most banks and a borrower with a good record of financial probity can usually obtain the limited funds they require by completing a simple form, often over the telephone. When it comes to larger amounts, the banks will require a more detailed and thoughtful proposal from the borrower. The bank needs to know the exact nature of the project, the past background of the borrower, the present situation in which it is to be launched, the timetable and what progress is envisaged at each stage, the security that can be offered against possible failure and what method of repayment is envisaged.

The borrower must put forward a business plan that covers the following main points:

- the nature of the business to be established or the expansion proposed;
- the status of the borrower, or borrowers, their skills, talents, experience in the field under consideration and commitment they are making to the project;
- the borrower's analysis of the market situation, likely demand for the product or service proposed, competition envisaged and marketing plan;
- the financial requirements, preferably broken down into detailed costings;
- the yield envisaged, the breakeven point and extent of the profit when the proposal finally comes on stream;
- the proposed method of repayment and what security is available for the loan should the project fail.

If the proposal is deemed sound, the bank or finance company will make the necessary arrangements to provide the finances. For the larger projects, the company will put together a package of support from venture capitalists and other institutions and, as a sign of its confidence in the project, take a reasonable share of the burden itself. All this cannot be the work of a few moments – negotiations may take months or even years as further detailed forecasts are called for.

In greater detail, the information required may be as follows.

■ Nature of the business

- Give the exact nature of the business, goods to be manufactured or handled or services to be offered.
- State where you propose to operate from, the adequacy of the premises for the proposed activity or expansion and type of organisation (sole trader, partnership or private limited company).
- If the proposal is an expansion, give exact details of the expansion required, successes to date and whether or not there is any new product or untried service. What proportion of the expansion will be of untried good or services? Is planning permission required and has it been granted?

■ Personnel

- The lender will expect full details of the proprietor, partners or chief members of a company. These details should include age, education, professional qualifications and their relevance to the proposed activity, experience in this industry and general track record.
- A clear account of other staff should be given, with the names of any key staff not already mentioned. If family members are working in the business, this should be made clear.
- If there are other people who are not employees – such as subcontractors – their relationship with the firm should be explained and their degree of commitment outlined (it is preferable to show these people what you are writing about them and to get their approval of it as banks and venture capitalists always check on such statements and it will do your image no good if it is clear they do not even know you are claiming to have a clear understanding with them). State in your proposal that the persons named have approved your reference to them and give their telephone numbers.
- Many loans call for personal guarantees from the proposer, partners and Board members. Ask for permission to reveal their names and addresses, and their bankers, so that references can be taken up.

■ The detailed proposal

- Here you should expand on the outline of the nature of your business, discussed above. If it is a new venture, give full details of the project, likely costs involved, any planning permission required, an estimate of the market, competition to be faced, general timetable and estimated breakeven point. If it is an expansion, give the fullest details of the situation to date, accounts for the last five years (or since start-up if the business has not yet been operating for five years). Give details of the staff, present organisation, accounting system, analysis of financial situation, turnover, profitability and extent of personal drawings.
- Give a clear account of the timetable of events – any deadlines that must be met, plans for meeting contingencies – such as the loss of a major customer, departure of key personnel, shortage of raw materials – and so on.

■ Assessment of the market

- You should present a detailed appraisal of the market for the good or service you aim to supply. What are the likely numbers of interested customers, and the amounts each can be expected to demand. Is it a 'niche' market or a widespread general demand. What percentage of the available spending power do you hope to attract.

- If supportive figures can be provided from trade associations, official publications, market research and other such sources, give them in reasonable detail.
- If you have firm orders or firm promises from particular customers, provide documentary evidence of this.
- Give your analysis of the competitive situation in the proposed field of activity. Give any reasons you have for believing you can resist this competition on grounds of quality, price, patent exclusivity or whatever.
- If the market is international, give details of your knowledge of export trade or the key personnel who will handle this aspect. Are there any VAT problems in EU states or licence requirements in those you hope to deal with?

■ The financial requirements

You must now present the figures for your capital requirement. Give detailed costings for all aspects of the project – raw materials, power, manufacturing costs, warehousing costs, transport and distribution, marketing, advertising and so on.

Often, a major weakness of such applications is a failure to think the thing through to a logical conclusion. Your costings must include all aspects of the activity. It is easy to forget such items as insurance, transport, packaging, warehousing and so on, but these must feature in your plans.

By setting against these costs the funds you have at present and the amounts you hope to earn week by week as the product or service comes on stream, you can draw up a cash flow forecast that shows you the funds you will have and the expenses to be incurred for each month. The difference between the two will be your borrowing requirement for the month.

■ The yield envisaged from the project or expansion

In the long run, the crucial figures from this business plan are the profit figures you hope to achieve. It is these profits that have to pay the interest on the money borrowed and repay the capital itself. Unless the prospects of profitability are good, you will never convince anyone that it is worth while providing the funds you require. You must do a breakeven chart (see Figure 17.5, page 257), which shows how long it will take before income will exceed expenditure.

The terms of the loan have to be such that it is possible to finance the loan (pay the interest on it) in the first year or two before profits actually start to be made. It must be possible to pay the interest out of the money borrowed because it is just one more cost of the project. In this way, the lender will receive a reward for lending the money from the start and, eventually, the total cost will be repaid out of the profits.

■ The proposed method of repayment

The borrower should propose a clear method of repayment that, to some extent, is convenient to the borrower rather than the lender. For example, some businesses have seasonal demand and make most of their profits in a few months of the year and so it may be possible to arrange an irregular pattern of repayment, with the majority of repayments being made in the high season when funds become available.

When the loan is granted, don't let anyone go on a spending spree.

If the business is not seasonal, offer a regular payment, monthly or quarterly, of a figure you feel sure will be achievable. The vital thing is not to default on any repayment because this at once casts doubt on your management of the business. If payments can be made by standing order or direct debit, this is preferable, but you then have to manage your cash flow to ensure funds are always available to meet the repayments as they fall due.

Anticipate problems that may arise and build a review clause into the contract that entitles you to call for a change in the arrangements made if circumstances external to the business make the contract unachievable. For example, a serious rise in interest rates could adversely affect the viability of the project. Closure of a particular market – for example as a result of war or civil unrest – may have a similar impact.

Finally, when the loan is granted, don't let anyone go on a spending spree. If money is there people will spend it, but make sure every bit of the money is tightly controlled so that it is used for the agreed purpose for which the loan was sanctioned. In due course, the use of every penny of the money has to be justified, by you. You must establish and maintain your own integrity in the eyes of the lenders.

You will see that major loan negotiations of this sort tie the borrower down to a clear relationship with the lender, or a group of lenders, and failure to honour the obligations may have very serious consequences. It is always well to ask 'Are the binding commitments equally good on the lender's sides? Is there any clause in the agreement where they unequivocally express their willingness to see the venture through to a successful conclusion?' This is rarely so, and the frequent occasions when one hears the phrase, 'The bank pulled the rug from under my feet', while only anecdotal evidence, does appear to show that it is not an uncommon occurrence.

Thus, if you can find new shareholders prepared to buy into the business with new equity capital, it may be preferable. 'Equity' means 'taking an equal part' with other shares – an equal share of the profits and an equal share of the risks. Indeed, equity shares are often called 'risk' shares. For a company at the right level, with a good deal of success already behind it, this may be the better route to expansion. This is the method offered by the Alternative Investment Market (AIM).

THE ALTERNATIVE INVESTMENT MARKET (AIM)

The Alternative Investment Market is the London Stock Exchange's public market for small, young and growing companies. It enables such businesses to raise capital and see their shares more widely traded. Joining the AIM has been made as simple as possible, given the need to comply with the Public Offers of Securities (POS) Regulations (1995).

When joining the AIM, the applicant companies must nominate an adviser from a register of nominated advisers who will shepherd them through the introduction process. The adviser will ensure that the directors and other key personnel understand the market's rules and the serious implications of such matters as the disclosure of insider knowledge, which might affect the proper functioning of the market. The adviser will certify to the Stock Exchange at the time your company is admitted to the market that you have complied with the relevant rules.

Besides a nominated adviser, the applicant must also appoint a nominated broker. However, it is possible to use the same firm for both functions. The broker's work will be to bring buyers and sellers of your shares together in the course of normal operations on the market. Buyers and sellers therefore know that at least one firm is always ready to do its best to match transactions in your shares.

The admission procedure includes:

■ The drawing up of a prospectus giving:
  – a full description of the company, its main activities and its capital;
  – a financial history of the company and its performance in recent years;

  – details of the management structure, administration and supervision;

■ a formal application for admission to the market signed by the directors;

■ a declaration by the nominated adviser that the rules have been complied with;

■ a statement from the nominated broker confirming its appointment.

Full details of all these matters are given in the official *Guide for Companies*, published by, and available free of charge from, the Alternative Investment Market, The London Stock Exchange, London EC2N 1HP.

The advantage of membership is that shares issued by the company can be marketed to interested investors in a variety of ways. The adviser will be familiar with these methods and also be able to offer advice on the price to ask for a share. The funds made available are at the service of the company.

CHECKLIST

■ **All firms and companies need money capital to start up and, once launched, need to generate or obtain extra capital from time to time, particularly if expansion is envisaged. A firm that is only generating small profits, most of which are being used by the proprietor(s) to finance a limited standard of living, cannot usually grow, except very slowly.**

■ **An expanding firm may need funds for fixed assets or for current assets. Fixed assets are premises, plant and machinery, fixtures and fittings, and motor vehicles. Current assets are stock, debtors and liquid funds, cash at bank or cash in hand. Finance for fixed assets is called 'fixed capital'; finance for current assets is called 'working capital'.**

■ **Extra capital may be found internally (within the company) or externally (from outsiders).**

■ **The chief sources of internal funding are retained profits, funds held back from the proprietors for depreciation purposes (to finance replacement assets eventually) and the disposal of fixed assets on a 'sale and leaseback' arrangement.**

■ **The chief sources of small-scale external funding are banks and finance houses. A good relationship with a bank is essential for all** firms and they should be able to provide a range of services. The best time to agree a package of services is when all is going well with the firm or company. Do not postpone creating a relationship until a crisis has arisen.

■ Small-scale loans are readily available at any time, with a minimum of formality. Larger loans call for a detailed loan application, giving full details of the proposed expansion, personnel involved, financial requirements and so on.

■ Venture capital is capital made available by experienced investors who are prepared to lend to more risky proposals than usual, under terms that permit them to have some hands-on knowledge of the project in hand. Some venture capitalists can obtain a tax advantage as an incentive to participation in new ventures that are not entirely straightforward.

■ Equity capital is capital made available by taking shares in a company. For medium-sized enterprises, the Alternative Investment Market (AIM) is an official market of the London Stock Exchange where equity capital can be obtained, provided the rules on entry to the market have been followed.

The Inland Revenue: self-assessment and your business

THE NATURE OF THE INLAND REVENUE

At one time, the money needed to run the government of the United Kingdom was relatively small and could be obtained from taxes imposed on luxury goods entering the country, such as furs, jewellery, wine and tobacco. Later, as government activities increased, it became necessary to impose taxes on wealth-creating activities at home – an 'inland revenue' as well as customs duties on imports. Today, government activities are so extensive that about 38 per cent of the entire national income has to be taken in taxes to finance defence, health, education, law and order, and so on. In one recent year it was £263 793 million.

It is the Board of the Inland Revenue that is charged with the duty of collecting these enormous sums, according to well-defined rules laid down in a number of Acts of Parliament. These Acts are varied from time to time, but especially by decisions announced on the day of the budget in the spring and enacted into law later in the Parliamentary year in the Finance Act.

The Inland Revenue has a tax office in every district, staffed by a number of 'inspectors' of taxes, and there is a rather smaller number of officials called 'collectors' who act like the cashiers to take the payments as they come in, issue receipts and pay the money into bank accounts. The funds eventually reach the Bank of England and are used to pay for all government activities.

The local inspector of taxes is the person you will deal with regarding your tax affairs and now that self-assessment has been adopted, a new relationship with the Inland Revenue is developing. You no longer submit your accounts to the inspector and wait for their comments, and assessment of how much you must pay. Instead, you declare your profits in the tax return sent to you by the inspector in April, completing at the same time those supplementary pages essential to the inspector's understanding of your tax situation. This new system requires a fairly detailed explanation, which is given below.

SELF-ASSESSMENT

The new self-assessment system of taxation began in April 1997, when the new self-assessment tax returns were issued for the first time. The term 'self-assessment' is a bit misleading as those taxpayers who don't want to work out the actual tax bill themselves can ask the Inland Revenue to do it for them. However, in that case, they must send in the completed return by 30 September. From April to the end of September is plenty of time to fill in the tax return and you are strongly advised to complete a return in any year as soon as you have collected all the records you need to deal with it. The Inland Revenue will then send you an assessment showing how much you must pay, and the first part must then be paid by the following 31 January. A fine (£100 at present) will be added to all unpaid bills on 1 February, automatically, and interest on the unpaid money begins to accrue from that date too.

In the first year of self-assessment, about half the 9 million people who were sent a tax return sent them in by 30 September. Unless your tax affairs are very complicated for example, you have many different sources of income), it is unlikely that you will need to seek professional advice from an accountant, but, of course, you are free to do so if you wish. The Inland Revenue has provided plenty of telephone lines and tax advice centres to help those who are having difficulties.

The first thing to say about the self-assessment system is that, for the first time, all the income of a taxpayer is to be collected in a single tax return. If the only income you have is the profits you make from your business, then your tax affairs will be very simple. You declare what these profits are in the tax return and that is that. However, nearly everyone has more than one income. Some business people have part-time jobs, so they have income from employment as well as income from their business. Some also have rent from property, some have pensions from former employments and some have alimony from divorced spouses. Almost everyone has some savings and receives small incomes in the form of interest. All these incomes are mentioned together in one tax return, and an assessment of tax due has to be calculated and paid on this total income.

■ How the self-assessment system works

At the start of the tax year in April, you will receive from the Inland Revenue a tax form called the tax return. This is a 'user-friendly' tax form, because it takes you through the whole self-assessment procedure step by step. Accompanying the form is a tax return guide that offers extra information.

Page 1 of the tax return simply tells you about the new arrangements. Page 2 tells you about the many supplementary pages that must be completed by those who have certain types of income. By going carefully through the information on page 2, you can discover which of these pages apply to you. For example, question 1 asks:

1. Were you an employee, office holder, director or agency worker? Yes/No

If we reply 'Yes', you must fill in the 'employment' pages.

Question 2 is about the earnings of directors of privatised (former nationalised) industries and need not concern us.

Question 3 asks:

3. Were you self-employed (but not a partner)? Yes/No.

If you answer 'Yes', you must fill out the 'self-employed' pages. And so the questions continue.

There are nine sources of income that have their own supplementary pages and several more sources are dealt with in the tax return itself. The nine sets of supplementary pages concern employment, share schemes, self-employment, partnerships, land and property, foreign earnings, trust incomes, capital gains and non-residence.

The other sources of income dealt with in the tax return include interest on savings, dividends from investments, pensions, maintenance payments and alimony. A final category is 'other income'.

Whatever the Inland Revenue may say, the sheet volume of these pages is daunting, but, remember, the majority of people have only one or two types of income to account for.

Having introduced the topic of self-assessment, I will now turn to other aspects of dealings with the Inland Revenue before considering the self-employment pages in more detail.

NOTIFYING THE AUTHORITIES ABOUT YOUR NEW BUSINESS

There are three bodies that are interested when you start a new business. They are the Inland Revenue, the Contributions Agency and HM Customs. They have joined forces to bring out a booklet entitled *Starting Your Own Business*, which has lots of helpful advice for those about to become self-employed. Included in the booklet is a form that must be completed and sent to the Contributions Agency, which will copy it and sent it to the other two bodies, so that all are fully informed. It is called Form CWF 1.

There are three bodies that are interested when you start a new business.

The Contributions Agency is interested because self-employed people have to pay weekly contributions called Class 2 contributions, of about £6.15. These are usually paid by direct debit, monthly, from your bank account, but they can be paid quarterly. You will receive a bill for this every quarter. If you have a job as well as being self-employed, you will be paying contributions as an employee as well. To prevent hardship, those with low earnings can apply for exemption from this liability.

Self-employed people who are making good profits are also required to pay Class 4 contributions, at levels set by the Chancellor in the budget. At present, the rate is 6 per cent on all profits between £7010 and £24 180. So, a person with profits of more than £24 180 will pay Class 4 contributions of £1030.20. These are payable with your income tax, to the Inland Revenue.

HM Customs is interested in case you are likely to need to register for VAT. This subject was referred to in Chapter 11. You will recall that you may register voluntarily if you wish, but it becomes compulsory if your turnover rises to £50 000 a year (roughly £1000 a week). If your takings are approaching that level, register at once or you will be subject to penalties.

The Inland Revenue is interested because it will need to include you in the tax system, sending you a 'tax return' in April each year so that you can assess how much tax you must pay. It will also want to know if you intend to employ anyone in your business. If you do, it will send you an employer's pack, which explains the responsibilities all employers have to collect tax from their employees under the PAYE system of taxation.

THE ACCOUNTING DATE

The basic principle behind the taxation of profits is that the net profit of the business is the income of the proprietor or is shared between the proprietors if there are two (or more) partners. It is therefore important to ensure that profits are worked out in an easy way that is uniform for all businesses, so that the assessments eventually arrived at are fair between one business and another. To ensure that this is so, there are several rules. The first is that the accounts are prepared for a set 12-month period. It is up to you to decide what accounting date to pick, but if you are registered for VAT, it is very awkward if you pick a date that is not the end of a month because VAT records work on month-end dates and your financial accounts and VAT accounts will not be synchronised. The alternative dates are:

- the anniversary of the day you start business – this seems a logical date to pick, but if you start business on a date that is not the first day of the month, you will have the difficulty referred to above;
- the anniversary of the end of the month you started business in – this

means that your first year may be a week or so longer than a real year;

- the end of the calendar year (31 December) – this means that unless you start business on 1 January, your first 'year' will be short (for example, if you start on 1 February, your first year will be 11 months long);
- the end of the month nearest to the end of the tax year – this is 5 April, so many people work out their accounts to 31 March each year;
- the actual end of the tax year, 5 April – this is an awkward date to pick because it means your VAT records are not synchronised with your financial records, as explained above;
- for companies, the tax year ends on 31 March.

One further point is that if you have a VAT date that varies from your financial records, even though it is a month-end date, it can be slightly awkward. Thus, a trader who is VAT-registered on a quarterly basis might have to submit VAT records on the last day of February, May, August and November. This is awkward if the accounting date chosen for the financial records is, for example, 31 December. It is quite possible to manage with such a difference in dates, but it is a bit irritating to close off your financial records and have your VAT records still open. A letter to the VAT authorities to ask them to allow you to change your dates to fit in with your financial records will sort this out, and they will let you have a long '4-month' quarter in order that you can get your records synchronised. Once that long quarter is over you will be sending in VAT records at the end of March, June, September and December.

To be truthful, it doesn't much matter to the Inland Revenue which date you pick. As far as the tax inspector is concerned, you can calculate your assessment for any accounting period and for any accounting date, by following the rules laid down. You need to know the following.

- **Accounting period** This is the period for which you are providing details of your business income and business expenses. It will usually be a 12-month period, but, at the start of business, it may be less than a year or more than a year.
- **Accounting date** This is the date when your accounting period ends.

For example, a person who starts in business on 1 January and keeps accounts to 31 December has an accounting period of a year, and an accounting date of 31 December.

- **Basis period** This is the basis used to identify the profits that are taxable in any particular year. You must provide details of the income and expenditure for each accounting period that relate wholly or partly to your basis period. The rules are a little difficult for the first year of self-assessment because the Inland Revenue has changed over from a 'preceding year' (PY) basis to a 'current year' (CY) basis. Business people have traditionally paid tax on the preceding year's profits, but from now on the tax is to be based on the profits of the current year. A full explanation is given in *Help Sheet 1R222* (for businesses starting up after 6 April 1994) or *1R2 30* (for those already in business before 6 April 1994 and still in business on 6 April 1997). Simply phone the orderline number given on your tax return if you want one of these (Tel: 0645 000 404).

SHARED EXPENSES – PART BUSINESS, PART DOMESTIC

In many small businesses, there are certain expenses that are shared. For example, if you run your business from home, charges for telephone, electricity, gas and so on are partly used for business and partly for domestic purposes.

The rule here is that you must decide some fair share of the expense for business purposes and only put that part down as a business expense. The usual proportion is a simple fraction for each expense heading. Thus a car might be shared half and half, but the telephone might be two-thirds business and one third domestic. If you occupy one room in a five-roomed house, you will be allowed one fifth of the expenses for lighting, heating and so on, but if you are able to argue that the garage is your archive for out-of-date documents, the inspector may concede one quarter. Note, however, that if you claim these allowances as business expenses, you are liable to capital gains tax on any capital gain made on the part of the premises designated for business if you move. This can be a considerable sum and, for that reason, some people do not always charge such expenses to the business.

In deciding these simple fractions for shared expenses, you have two courses of action open to you.

- You can make the decisions yourself and not bother with the tax inspector's opinion until you declare your profits at the end of the year. The fraction has to be a fair one for both parties so if you carefully consider all aspects of each case, you will probably arrive at a correct figure. An important point to note is that you cannot claim any part of your mortgage payments as a business expense. This is because the interest paid is already taken into account in another way when you fill out your tax return, and to give it to you as a business expense would be to give you an allowance twice. The other part, the repayment of capital, is not allowed as a business expense because it is capital expenditure, not revenue expenditure.

If you do decide to make your own decisions, it is important to set them out in your tax return. There is a box for 'additional information' at the end of the return. Any disagreement with the fractions used will then be discussed.

■ Alternatively, you can ask for a meeting with the inspector to get a firm decision right from the start. This is perhaps the better way, but sometimes there is so much to do at the start of a new business that it is difficult to find time. The Inland Revenue is busy too, and while staff will always find time to interview you if you wish it, they are also content to let it go. If everyone is reasonable about what is a fair proportion of such expenses, there will be no difficulty at all. The only other thing to be said about meeting the inspector is that their manner will soon convince you that your tax affairs are an important part of being self-employed.

While you hope dealings with the Inland Revenue will always be amicable, it is your duty to keep honest records and put away your tax money throughout the year so that you have the money ready to pay, when you need to pay it. The Inland Revenue knows the exact position of every firm in the country. It can soon see if your records are suspect in any way because your results will then be manifestly different from what they expect to find, and they will call you in for a discussion if they are at all unhappy. The majority of bankruptcy cases start with non-payment of tax. Sometimes the kindest thing the inspector can do is to declare you insolvent. That is the one occasion when all the people who owe you money will have to pay up. If they don't do so when the official receiver is handling your affairs, they may themselves be made insolvent.

One point many people find strange is that if someone uses an accountant to produce their accounts, based on the figures that they have provided, the responsibility for the figures is still theirs. If a dispute arises with the Inland Revenue and they are called for an interview, the questions will be addressed to them and they must answer them even if their accountant is present.

THE DISTINCTION BETWEEN CAPITAL AND REVENUE EXPENDITURE

This has been referred to earlier, but it is important to remember all the time when making book-keeping entries. If an expense only brings in a short-term benefit, lasting less than one year, it is a revenue expense. As long as it was incurred wholly and exclusively for the purposes of the business, it is a deductible expense of the business. This means it may appear either on the manufacturing account, trading account or profit and loss account as a deduction from income. If it is a shared expense, you should write the fraction on the document (for example, two-thirds and one-third), then adjust the amount of expense down to the correct figure. This reduced figure is the one to be used in both your VAT records and your financial records.

Capital items are not deductible expenses, and even depreciation, however you calculate it, will be added back if you deduct it from your profits. The inspector will then give you the capital allowance to which you are entitled instead. This was explained in Chapter 14.

DECLARING YOUR BUSINESS PROFITS IN YOUR SELF-ASSESSMENT TAX RETURN

You saw earlier (pages 193 to 211) how to prepare a set of final accounts at the end of the financial year. For most people, this means a trading account, profit and loss account and balance sheet. Anyone running a small factory will have a manufacturing account as well, and those who do not trade will have only a revenue account (a profit and loss account by another name).

Of course, you may ask an accountant to draw up your final accounts for you, but this will cost you a reasonable fee, according to how much work is involved and the state of the records you present to them. There is much to be said for doing your own accounts, but another method is to do your own set of final accounts and ask your accountant to put them in apple-pie order, ready for you to declare them to the Inland Revenue in your self-assessment tax return.

The actual declaration is made in a format known as 'vertical style'. That is, the trading account and profit and loss account are not reproduced in horizontal form – with debit and credit sides that balance – but in a continuous style that states the trading income (sales turnover) first and the trading expenses below – deducting from the income to produce the gross profit. This gross profit is then increased by any non-trading profits and the various overhead expenses are then deducted to arrive at the net profit. The only real advantage of this form of presentation is that it lends itself easily to computerisation.

COMPLETING THE SELF-EMPLOYMENT PAGES

These make a four-page document. The first page (page SE1) simply asks for details of your business and then has a short section for very small businesses.

The point about very small businesses (those with a *turnover* less than £15 000) is that the proprietors may not have to pay tax at all because you just can't make much profit on a turnover as small as £15 000. Therefore, all the Inland Revenue asks for are three-line accounts:

Takings – Expenses = Profits

This small section might be completed as shown in the example below.

Income and expenditure – turnover below £15 000

Turnover, goods taken for personal use and other business receipts	£14 256.89
Expenses allowable for tax	£7 642.54
Taking the expenses from the receipts, we have: Net profit (put figures in brackets if a loss)	£6 614.35

You will find the figures you need in your final accounts and you only need to give the total figures. The detailed expenses, for example, need not be given.

Those firms that have a turnover of less than £15 000 need not complete the detailed account of their receipts and payments, which is described next, and which makes up the next section of the Self-employment pages.

■ Declaring your profits if your turnover exceeds £15 000 per annum

Firms with a turnover of more than £15 000 must complete a full declaration of income and expenditure in the format laid down on page 2 of the self-employment pages. The same layout appears on page 3 of the partnership tax return. If you look back to the Final Accounts of T. Sanderson, on page 91 and note the presentation of the same figures in the illustration (Figure 20.1), this is the style of presentation required by the Inland Revenue in the self-employment and partnership pages. There is only one further point to note.

Because it needs to be able to follow the profit declarations of millions of self-employed taxpayers, the Inland Revenue has laid down the headings to be used when expenses and profits are declared, and the order in which these headings are to be arranged. This means that firms will either adopt the new headings as a basis for the collection of costs and expenses in their everyday activities or, if they stick to their traditional expense headings, at least devise some way of drawing together items that must be declared together. For example, the Inland Revenue's first heading is 'employee costs'. These would include pay, National Insurance contributions (by both employer and employees), Statutory Sick Pay, Statutory Maternity Pay, reimbursement of expenses and so on. No doubt many firms would need to keep track of these individual costs, but by the time they come to declare their profits, they have to be merged into a single heading 'employee costs'. Turning the trading and profit and loss account on page 91 of this book into a profit declaration appropriate to the self-assessment system, the result is as shown in Figure 20.1.

	£	£
Sales/business income (turnover)		95 900.00
Cost of sales	22 386.99	
Construction industry subcontractor costs	–	
Other direct costs	–	
Total trading costs		22 386.99
Gross profit/(loss)		73 513.01
Other income/profits		2 086.35
		75 599.36
Employee costs	27 925.50	
Premises costs	894.56	
Repairs	–	
General administrative expenses	–	
Motor expenses	1 727.36	
Travel and subsistence	–	
Advertising, promotion and entertainment	3 320.20	
Legal and professional costs	–	
Bad debts	238.60	
Interest	–	
Other finance charges	457.24	
Depreciation and loss/(profit) on sale	–	
Other expenses	–	
Total expenses		34 563.46
		£41 035.90

Fig. 20.1 DECLARING YOUR PROFITS FOR SELF-ASSESSMENT

Notes
- This is not quite a full presentation because the actual entries include arrangements for deducting certain 'disallowable expenses'. For example, although 'depreciation' is listed as shown, it is, in fact, later recovered as a disallowable expense and is replaced by a 'capital allowance'.
- You will see that the limited number of expense headings is a little awkward as all expenses must be squeezed into one or other of the headings given. In the above example, 'advertising' and 'commission paid' had to be put together (they are both marketing expenses).

The remaining self-employment pages are adjustments of your net profit or loss to take account of a variety of minor points. There are help sheets available on some of these points, and the Inland Revenue advice lines and its tax advice centres will be able to answer your queries.

The final result of your self-employment calculations will give you the total of your earnings from your business activities.

If you are a partner in a partnership business, one of the partners will have been completing the partnership pages and the final result will give you the total profit of your partnership business. This has to be shared among the partners in the agreed way (see pages 6 and 7 of the partnership tax return) and copies must be given to each partner so they can complete their tax return each year.

Take a photocopy of your tax return and any supplementary pages you complete before sending them in to the tax office.

When the other schedules that you are affected by have also been completed, the total for the column provided in the tax calculation guide will show your total income from all sources. It is this income on which tax will be assessed by the inspector if you send your tax return in before 30 September. If you prefer to do so (or cannot complete your tax return by 30 September), you will have to do your own assessment and send both the return and the assessment calculation to the tax inspector and the money to the tax collector before 31 January. An automatic fine is imposed on non-payers on 1 February.

You are strongly urged to take a photocopy of your tax return and any supplementary pages you complete before sending them in to the tax office. These should be archived with your other accounting records for the year.

CHECKLIST

- The Inland Revenue is a government department charged with the duty of collecting income tax, corporation tax and so on. It has no interest in killing enterprise, but it does have to collect the government's share of the proceeds of enterprise.

- All those setting up in business should obtain a copy of publication CWL 1 *Starting Your Own Business*, and should complete and submit Form CWF 1 from the back of the booklet.

- An accounting date should be selected and used year after year as the date to which accounts will be completed. It is no longer necessary to submit your accounts to the Inland Revenue. Instead, you declare your profits in the self-assessment tax return form each year, and archive your records in case any query arises. Records must be kept for six years.

- In drawing up these accounts it is essential to remember that the only deductions from income allowed are revenue expenses incurred wholly and exclusively for the purpose of the business.

- Any shared expenses – part-business, part-domestic – should be divided on the basis of simple fractions like half and half, or two-thirds and one-third. These fractions may be agreed with the inspector first if preferred. If this is not done, a full explanation of the fractions chosen should be given in the boxes provided on the tax return and its supplementary pages. These are headed 'additional information'.

- Under self-assessment, payment dates have been moved to 31 January and 31 July for all taxpayers affected by the self-assessment regulations. For companies, corporation tax is payable on 1 January in a single amount.

- Large companies must have their books audited by professional accountants and it would normally be best to allow the accountants to draw up the final accounts for submission to the Inland Revenue. Smaller companies do not now need a full audit, but a less detailed procedure that leads to a 'compilation report'. Companies with a turnover below £90 000 per annum may prepare their own accounts, but are, of course, free to use the services of an accountant if they wish.

Accounts for clubs and charities

Clubs and charities as non-profit-making bodies

The accounts of a club

The receipts of a club

The payments of a club

The monthly cash and bank reports

The annual general meeting

Income and expenditure accounts and balance sheets
for clubs and charities

More advanced final accounts for clubs and societies

Accounts for charities

The new regulations for charities

CLUBS AND CHARITIES AS NON-PROFIT-MAKING BODIES

Business people often act as treasurers for local clubs and societies of every sort, so it is not inappropriate to introduce as the final chapter of this book a special chapter about club accounts. The general feature of club accounts and accounts for charities is that such bodies are 'non-profit-making', though many of them do, in fact, make profits. The point is that the organisation comes into existence for other reasons – notably, to provide some centre of activity and organise functions

> *The general feature of club accounts and accounts for charities is that such bodies are 'non-profit-making', though many of them do, in fact, make profits.*

that are of interest to the members. Thus, a local bowls club will have its greens, club house, refreshment-making equipment and so on and will run competitions and organise meetings of interest to the members. In the course of these activities, it will receive a good deal of income and make a great many payments on its members' behalf. At the end of the year, it may have made a profit on some activities, but these were not deliberately aimed at. They therefore, are not regarded as profits but as 'surpluses' – excess amounts contributed by the members, surplus to the expenditure of the club. Similarly, if, at the end of the year, 'payments' exceed 'receipts', this will not be called a 'loss', but a 'deficiency'.

The person in charge of the accounts is called the 'treasurer' and they will naturally be anxious to avoid a deficit on the year's accounts. Treasurers may not be keen to amass a large surplus, preferring that members enjoy their simple pleasures as economically as possible, but it may be club policy to build up adequate reserves to provide for the replacement or improvement of assets from time to time.

THE ACCOUNTS OF A CLUB

The accounts of a club therefore consist of a record of 'receipts' and 'payments'. One of the receipts, for example, is 'subscriptions from members' and another would be 'refreshment income'. Payments would be made for 'Equipment' (a capital expense) and 'refreshment expenses' (a revenue expense). Clearly there would be many such receipts and payments.

When keeping this type of record, you need an analysis cash book. There is such a book on the market, at a very inexpensive price – the Simplex club accounts book. The illustrations in this chapter are taken from it, by kind permission of the publishers, George Vyner Ltd, from which company it may be obtained. The address is George Vyner Ltd., P.O. Box 1, Holmfirth, Huddersfield HD7 2RP.

Bank managers, accountants and others who read this chapter might like to advise the treasurers of clubs whose accounts they appraise of the existence of the Simplex club accounts book. It includes one year's accounts and the summaries at the end lead straight into the 'final accounts' – receipts and payments account of the club, to be presented to the members at the annual general meeting.

> *The treasurer must be a person of integrity whose conduct of the club's financial affairs is above reproach.*

The Simplex club accounts book has space for all the receipts and payments of the club, on a monthly basis. The amounts received and paid are analysed off under various headings so that similar items can be collected together and monthly totals are built up under these various headings. These records occupy 36 of the 48 pages, and are explained below, and illustrated in Figures 21.1 and 21.2.

Each month, the various totals for receipts and payments are taken to summaries on the 'summary of receipts and payments' page at the back of the book, while a monthly bank report and monthly cash report are also prepared (see Figures 21.3, 21.4 and 21.5 for these summaries). The cash report each month should of course agree with the cash in hand, while a bank reconciliation statement (see Chapter 8) should be drawn up from time to time, and agreed with the monthly bank statement.

Finally, the totals of the 'Summaries' for the whole year are used to prepare a receipts and payments account of the club, which is presented to the members of the society at the annual general meeting (AGM).

Let us now look at these sections of the book in detail.

THE RECEIPTS OF A CLUB

Figure 21.1 shows the 'receipts' side of the club's account book.

Amounts received are entered in the 'cash' or 'cheque' column (columns 10 and 11) and analysed under appropriate headings (Columns 1–9). Some columns have printed headings, while others are left blank to enable the treasurer to write in suitable classes of receipts. The receipts are totalled monthly and may be cross-totalled to check for accuracy. Columns 1–9 should make, when cross-totalled, the same total as columns 10 and 11. The totals are then carried to the summary at the back of the book (see Figure 21.4).

THE PAYMENTS OF A CLUB

Figure 21.2 shows the 'payments' page of the club accounts book.

Again, the payments are entered either in the cash or bank columns and analysed under appropriate headings of expenditure. Once again, these are totalled at the end of the month and cross-totalled to check for accuracy before being carried to the summary of payments at the back of the book (see Figure 21.5). It cannot be emphasised too strongly that, for most clubs and societies an accurate record of receipts and payments is all that is required from the treasurer of the club. The treasurer is frequently untrained in accountancy and their only aim is to play a useful part in the affairs of the club, and ensure that funds meet the club's expenses and are paid out to meet its commitments. As will be seen later (Figure 21.6), the way the treasurer accounts to the members is by producing an audited copy of the receipts and payments (called a receipts and payments account) at the annual general meeting of the club. By using a Simplex club accounts book, these figures – recorded and summarised at the end of each month – may be drawn together easily in a receipts and payments account when the AGM comes around.

The treasurer must be a person of integrity whose conduct of the club's financial affairs is above reproach. This is especially crucial when such services are provided as the collection of funds for a 'Christmas club' or for an annual 'club holiday', which involve the handling of considerable sums of money. It is usual to ensure that two people sign cheques for such accounts, and that special security arrangements are made when funds are withdrawn from the bank for an annual share-out.

The keeping of the monthly cash and bank records is part of the general process of checking on the financial affairs of the club. It is therefore the aim of a good treasurer to have a book of account that will bear inspection at any time, and can show that the affairs of the club are in perfect order. This includes such facts as up-to-date records, available cash in hand in a separate cash box (not muddled in with the treasurer's own money) and a bank account in good order that can be reconciled with the club's book of accounts at any given time.

Generally, two members are appointed as 'auditors', who will act for the club by inspecting the records from time to time and conducting a formal audit prior to the AGM to vouch for the accuracy of the treasurer's records.

Receipts for the month *(in cash and by cheque)*

Month of JANUARY ___ Year 199X

Date	Details	P.C.V.	1 Subs. £ p	2 Donations £ p	3 Ref. Sales £ p	4 Raffles £ p	5 Theatre Visits £ p	6 £ p	7 £ p	8 Misc. £ p	9 Cash drawn from bank £ p	10 In Cash £ p	11 By Cheque £ p
Jan 4	Subs 5 members		10 00									10 00	
5	Gift – Mrs Clark			5 25									5 25
11	Refreshments				3 25							3 25	
12	Subs Jones & Family		6 00										6 00
18	Refreshments				3 55							3 55	
19	Theatre Visit						8 50						8 50
25	Refreshments				2 80							2 80	
26	Subs Brown & Smith		4 00									4 00	
30	Refreshments				2 95							2 95	
30	Raffle & Refreshments				4 20	2 45						6 65	
31	Cash from Bank										10 00	10 00	
	Totals *(cross-tot to check)*		20 00	5 25	16 75	2 45	8 50				10 00	43 20	19 75

Analysis Columns – You may head the spare columns to suit your own club or school

Amount Received

If entries have been analysed correctly total of columns 1–9 will equal total of columns 10 and 11.

At the end of the month carry the 1–8 column totals to the 'Summary' pages at the end of the book. Use the totals of columns 10 and 11 in the cash and bank reports opposite.

Fig 21.1 THE RECEIPTS OF THE CLUB

Payments for the month *(in cash and by cheque)* | Month of JANUARY | Year 199X

Date	Details	P.C.V.	1 Equipment £ p	2 Refreshments £ p	3 Stationery £ p	4 Theatre Visits £ p	5 Raffle Prizes £ p	6 £ p	7 £ p	8 Misc. £ p	9 Cheques for cash £ p	10 In Cash £ p	11 By Cheque £ p
Jan 9	Table Tennis Table		24 50										24 50
10	Refreshments			1 40								1 40	
17	Refreshments			1 55								1 55	
19	Duplicating Paper				1 85							1 85	
20	Theatre Visits					9 25							9 25
25	Refreshments			1 42								1 42	
29	Refreshments			2 05								2 05	
30	Raffle Prizes						1 85					1 85	
30	Dart Board Lighting		15 00									15 00	
31	Cash from Bank										10 00		10 00
	Totals *(cross-tot to check)*		39 50	6 42	1 85	9 25	1 85				10 00	25 12	43 75

Analysis Columns – You may head the spare columns to suit your own club or school

Amount Paid

Fig 21.2 THE PAYMENTS OF THE CLUB

Paid to Bank

Date	Cash		Cheques	
January 6	10	00	5	25
" 13			6	00
" 20			8	50
Total	10	00	19	75

Monthly Bank Report

		£	p
Opening balance from last month		86	45
Add total paid to bank in month		29	75
Total		116	20
		£	p
Less	Total Payments (ch)	43	75
	Bank st. orders (if any)	–	–
	Bank charges (if any)	–	–
	Total	43	75
Balance at bank at end of month		72	45
Was a Bank Reconciliation done		Yes/No	

Monthly Cash Report

		£	p
Add	Cash in hand on 1st day	2	45
	total paid to bank in month	43	20
	Total	116	20
		£	p
Less	Total cash payments	25	12
	Cash paid to bank	10	53
	Total	35	12
Cash balance carried forward which should agree with		10	53
Cash Balance (as counted) on last day		10	53

Fig 21.3 THE MONTHLY CASH AND BANK REPORTS

© George Vyner Ltd

315

SUMMARY OF MONTHLY RECEIPTS

Month	1 Subscriptions £ p	2 Donations £ p	3 Refreshment Sales £ p	4 £ p	5 £ p	6 £ p	7 £ p	8 £ p
January								
February								
March								
April								
May								
June								
July								
August								
September								
October								
November								
December								
Total								

Fig 21.4 THE ANNUAL SUMMARY OF RECEIPTS

SUMMARY OF MONTHLY PAYMENTS

Month	1 Equipment		2 Refreshment Purchases		3		4		5		6		7		8	
	£	p	£	p	£	p	£	p	£	p	£	p	£	p	£	p
January																
February																
March																
April																
May																
June																
July																
August																
September																
October																
November																
December																
Total																

Fig 21.5 THE ANNUAL SUMMARY OF PAYMENTS

THE MONTHLY CASH AND BANK REPORTS

As shown in Figure 21.3, these monthly summaries present no difficulty to the treasurer and give them a monthly check on the accuracy of the book-keeping. As mentioned earlier, the cash report should agree with the total of cash in hand, while the bank report must be periodically checked by comparing with a bank statement and preparing a bank reconciliation statement.

THE ANNUAL GENERAL MEETING

At the AGM, the treasurer must account to the members for the conduct of the club's financial affairs. They do this by presenting them with a receipts and payments account, which shows the members what the balance was at the start of the year, the receipts and payments made during the year and concludes with the final balance at the end of the year. The balance of cash in hand should be available at the meeting for checking, if required, and a bank reconciliation statement should have been prepared as at the last day of the financial year.

If the club has appointed auditors from among the members, they should be asked to check the records for the year and sign the statements submitted to the members. If reprographic equipment is available, sufficient copies should be produced to meet the needs of the members in attendance. Figure 21.6 shows a typical receipts and payments account prepared in a Simplex club accounts book (see pages 320–1).

EXERCISES ON CLUB RECEIPTS AND PAYMENTS ACCOUNTS

1. The following sums of money were received and paid by the Treasurer of the University Cricket Club during the season April–September 199X. On 1 April, the club had a cash balance of £55.00 brought forward from the previous season. Moneys received were subscriptions £125.00, donations £100.00, refreshment sales £178.00, sales of ties and blazer badges £165.50, grant from University Student Body £50.00.

Moneys spent were postage £14.65, refreshment expenses £125.00, gift to groundsman £50.00, new equipment £386.50, Secretary's honorarium £25.00.

Draw up the receipts and payments account for the year, for submission to the AGM on 30 September, 199X. Bring out clearly the cash balance on 30 September.

2. The following particulars are supplied to you by the Treasurer of the Leyside Tennis Society, who asks you to draw up a receipts and payments account. Bear in mind the point he makes in the note below the figures:

Cash balance	1 March	£13.50
	31 October	£7.84
Bank balances	1 March	£48.24
	31 October	£138.24

Receipts during the season were subscriptions £150.00, sales of spectators' tickets £129.50, entrance charges to functions £112.85, competition fees £48.50, refreshment sales £95.80, donations during season £135.99.

Payments during the season were refreshment expenses £125.50, nets and waterproof sheeting £186.50, groundsman's charges £136.65, postage £18.50, stationery £14.85, heat and light £21.50, secretary's expenses £84.80. *Note:* A debt is owing for equipment of £42.00, which is to be included in the above costs as it will be paid at once by cheque, the bank balance being reduced accordingly.

Answers
1. Balance £72.35, totals £673.50.
2. Balances – cash £7.84, bank £96.24, totals £734.38

RECEIPTS and PAYMENTS A/c
Annual General Meeting
Year Ending 31 March 19**

Receipts	£	p
Opening Balances at Start of Year:		
Cash in Hand	3	54
Cash at Bank	86	45
Col. 1 Subscriptions	142	50
Col. 2 Donations	5	50
Col. 3 Refreshment Sales	286	45
Col. 4 Trip to France	735	60
Col. 5 Xmas Parties	48	24
Col. 6 –		
Col. 7 –		
Col. 8 Miscellaneous	1	84
	£1310	12

Payments	£	p
Col. 1 Equipment	62	50
Col. 2 Refreshment Purchases	250	00
Col. 3 Trip to France	719	25
Col. 4 Xmas Parties	56	50
Col. 5 Funeral Expenses	5	25
Col. 6 O.A.P. Charity Donation	10	00
Col. 7 –		
Col. 8 Miscellaneous	3	64
Closing Balances at End of Year:		
Cash in Hand	4	62
Cash at Bank	198	36
	£1310	12

Auditors' names . . . .

and Signatures: . . . .

Treasurer's Name . . . .

and Signature: . . . .

Fig. 21.6 ACCOUNTING TO THE MEMBERSHIP AT THE AGM

Notes to Figure 21. 6

- The account is a list of receipts, set against a list of payments and showing, as a result, the balance of cash in hand and at the bank at the end of the club's financial year.
- The 'receipts' figures and the 'payments' figures have come from the two summaries drawn up as the months went by (see Figures 21.4 and 21.5).
- The account starts with the opening balances at the beginning of the year, and finishes with the closing balances at the end of the year.
- The balance of cash in hand at the end of the year (£4.62) would be available for checking at the AGM.
- Similarly, the balance on the bank account could be checked by any member wishing to do so by looking at the bank statements (particularly the last one provided) and referring also to any bank reconciliation statement provided.
- The treasurer might refer in the report to the small profit made on refreshments – it not being thought necessary to charge more for these – any outstanding debts of the club not brought out in a receipts and payments account, any assets of the club – for example, vehicles, camping equipment and so on – and where they are kept (as a receipts and payments account does not tell us anything about assets, except 'cash in hand' and 'cash at bank'); whether or not the club has any debtors (usually members who have not paid their subscriptions'.

INCOME AND EXPENDITURE ACCOUNTS AND BALANCE SHEETS FOR CLUBS AND CHARITIES

While the receipts and payments account described earlier is satisfactory for small organisations such as the local tennis club, it has certain defects. For example, it does not show:

- whether or not a surplus or a deficiency has resulted from the year's activities (it only shows the 'cash in hand' and 'cash at bank' positions);
- any debts owed by the club to creditors, nor any sums payable to the club (for example, members who are enjoying the facilities without paying their club membership fee);
- any assets owned (and usually clubs have quite a lot of assets of one sort or another) and nor does it show any liabilities (for example, there may be a mortgage on premises or loans repayable to members).

To bring out these points and present them clearly to any interested parties, most large clubs draw up a more advanced accounting statement called an income and expenditure account, and it is followed by a balance sheet that reveals the full state of the club's affairs on the last day of the financial year. From this type of statement, the sorts of records required by, for example, the charity commissioners can easily be provided, while for other clubs the members can see the full position. Remember, some clubs are enormous organisations (for example, the AA, with millions of pounds in subscriptions and hundreds of employees covering the entire country).

The records needed to prepare an income and expenditure account and a balance sheet are as follows:

- an opening balance sheet, either drawn up on the first day the club started its activities or the one drawn up at the end of the previous year, which becomes the starting point for the present accounting period;
- a receipts and payment account prepared from the detailed figures of receipts and payments, however these were kept (they might, for example, be in a Simplex club accounts book like the one described earlier in this chapter or they might be in a full set of double entry book-keeping accounts).

From these records, you can then go on to draw up an income and expenditure account, which may be described as the profit and loss account of a club. Like every profit and loss account, it has all the income for the financial year on the right-hand side, and all the expenditure (equivalent to the losses of a business) on the left-hand side. The difference between the two sides is, of course, the 'net profit' for the year, but as it is a club, it is not called a profit, but a 'surplus of income over expenditure'. Of course, it could be a loss for the year, but it is not called a loss, it is called a 'deficiency'.

Sometimes a club that supplies refreshments or has a bar or restaurant, will prepare a bar trading account or refreshments trading account. In that case, the profit on the bar or the refreshments is called a profit, and appears as one of the items of income on the right-hand side of the income and expenditure account.

Having arrived at the surplus or deficiency for the year, you then ask the question, 'What happens to the surplus?' or 'What do we do with the deficiency?' The answers are as follows:

- as there is no proprietor, the profits cannot go to the proprietor and the losses cannot be suffered by the proprietor;
- the surplus belongs to the members generally, and the losses must be borne by the members generally;
- this is done by adding any surplus to a fund called the accumulated fund (sometimes called the capital fund) or taking any deficiency away from the accumulated fund (or capital fund);
- if this means you have more in 'the funds' than you really need, you

can use it up either by reducing the membership fee in the years ahead or increasing the services available (cheaper refreshments and so on);

■ sometimes clubs put money away in special funds – for example a rebuilding fund.

The best way to see all this in practice is to do an exercise for a club of this sort. As can be seen from the above, you start with an opening balance sheet and a receipts and payments account.

EXAMPLE

The Happy Valley Young Farmers' Club has the following assets and liabilities at 1 January 199X:

■ assets: club house £18 500;
  games equipment £8250;
  bar stocks £7825;
  club house equipment £886;
  subscriptions due £60 (12 members at £5 each);
  cash in hand £124;
  deposit account at bank £4650.

■ Liabilities: loan from A. Member £8000 (interest free);
  creditors £426 (for bar supplies).

The receipts and payment account at the end of the year is shown below.

Receipts and Payments A/C for year ending 31 December 199X

Receipts	£	Payments	£
1 Jan. Cash in hand	124	Bar purchases	7 500
Subscriptions	3 560	Rates	1 378
Donations	284	Heat and light	298
Dance takings	1 266	Purchase of new club	
Refreshments takings	1 842	equipment	344
Bar takings	14 858	Postage and printing	89
		Dance expenses	553
		Refreshment expenses	469
		Club house repairs	272
		Transfer to deposit account	7 000
		Bar pay	3 100
		Cash in hand c/d	931
	£21 934		£21 934
Balance b/d	931		

From these figures and the following information, prepare a trading account for the bar, an income and expenditure account and a balance sheet as at 31 December 199X.

- The bar stocks at the end of the year were worth £6125.
- At the end of the year, subscriptions were due from 11 members at £5 each and 3 members had paid in advance for next year.
- At the end of the year, £196 was owing for bar supplies and a printing bill for £45 was due and unpaid.
- All the subscriptions for last year were eventually paid, and it is expected this year's outstanding subscriptions will be paid in due course.
- The member who made the loan last year did not ask for any repayment in the year.

To solve this problem, there are several points you must first sort out.

- **The accumulated fund at the start of the year.** At the start of any year, just as with an ordinary business, you can draw up a balance sheet for the club, and the accumulated fund will be in the same position as the capital of a business. If you list the assets and liabilities of the club at the start of the year, you find:

Liabilities	£	Assets	£
Loan	8000	Club house	18 500
Creditors	426	Games equipment	8 250
	£8426	Bar stocks	7 825
		Club house	
		equipment	886
		Subs due (debtors)	60
		Deposit Account at	
		bank	4 650
		Cash in hand	124
			£40 295

It is clear that the missing item is the accumulated fund – the capital of the club. It is £40 295 – £8426 = £31 869. Putting in the accumulated fund on the liabilities side will make the two sides balance.

- **Adjustments.** You can have adjustments in club accounts just as you do in an ordinary business. Once again, the rule is to make sure every penny of this year's income is included in the accounts for this year, and every penny of this year's expenses is borne by this year's accounts. So, for example, on subscriptions, you have the following points to consider:

- subscriptions received in the year, £3560;
- this would include £60 from last year's subscriptions;
- £55 is due from this year's late payers;
- £15 has been received in advance for next year.

To find the subscriptions actually received for this year, you must deduct the £60 for last year and the £15 for next year, and count in the £55 due from the late payers who have not yet paid:

$$\text{Subscriptions} = £3560 - £75 + £55 = £3540$$

Note that at the end of the year, the subscriptions due will be an asset (the members are debtors for £55), but the subscriptions in advance will be a liability. (You owe the members a year's entertainment. They are creditors for £15.)

■ **The creditors for bar stocks at the beginning of the year.** These present a problem. If payments for bar purchases in the year were £7500, this must include the money owed for last year, £426. The amount owing at the end of the year is for this year's stocks and must be counted in So the purchases in the year are £7500 − £426 + £196 = £7270.

The final accounts will now be prepared as follows:

■ everything in the opening balance sheet must appear somewhere in the final accounts – this includes the accumulated fund at the start;
■ everything in the receipts and payments account must appear somewhere in the final accounts;
■ all the adjustments given in the extra information must appear twice in the final accounts, once in the final accounts and once in the balance sheet as they are carried over to next year.

The final accounts of the club are as shown below.

Bar Trading Account for Year Ending 31 December 199X

	£	£		£
Opening stocks		7 825	Bar takings	14 858
Purchases	7 500			
Less last year's	426			
	7 074			
Add this year's due	196			
		7 270		
		15 095		

(continues overleaf)

	£		£
Less Closing stock	6 125	c/fwd	14 858
	8 970		
Bar pay	3 100		
	12 070		
Profit on bar	2 788		
	£14 858		£14 858

Income and Expenditure Account for Year Ending 31 December 199X

		£			£
Rates		1 378	Subscriptions		3 560
Heat and light		298	Less subs due at start		60
Postage and printing	89				3 500
Add sum due	45		Add subs due		55
		134			3 555
Dance expenses		553	Less subs in advance		15
Refreshment expenses		469			3 540
Repairs to club house		272	Donations		284
		3 104	Dance takings		1 266
Surplus for year		6 616	Refreshment takings		1 842
(to Accumulated Fund)			Profit on bar		2 788
		£9 720			£9 720

Balance Sheet as at 31 December 199X

Accumulated Fund		£	*Fixed Assets*		£
At start		31 869	Club house		18 500
Add surplus for year		6 616	Games		
		38 485	equipment		8 250
			Club house		
			equipment	886	
			Add new items	344	
Long-term Liability					1 230
Loan from A. Member		8 000			27 980
			Current Assets		
			Bar stocks	6 125	
Current liabilities			Deposit		
Bar supplies	196		account	4 650	
Printing bill due	45		Add new		
Subs in advance	15		deposit	7 000	
		256		11 650	
			Cash in hand	931	
			Subscriptions		
			due	55	
					18 761
		£46 741			£46 741

MORE ADVANCED FINAL ACCOUNTS FOR CLUBS AND SOCIETIES

EXERCISES

1. From the information below, produce an income and expenditure account and a balance sheet for the Amateur Photographer's Club for the year ending 31 December 199X.

On 1 January 199X equipment was valued at £1630, there was a Bank balance of £120 and the Cash balance was £288. Subscriptions due amounted to £25 for the previous year and subscriptions paid in advance for the current year were £50. During the year, there were the following receipts and payments.

Receipts and Payment Account for Year Ending 31 December 199X

	£		£
Bank balance	120	Rent and rates	385
Cash in hand	288	Insurance	64
Subscriptions	1825	Wages of part-time staff	360
Refreshments sales	288	Postage and printing	68
Competition fees	160	Refreshment expenses	194
Collections	48	Prizes	85
Donations	425	Repairs	162
		New equipment	625
		Bank balance	630
		Cash in hand	581
	£3154		£3154
Bank balance	630		
Cash in hand	581		

Additional information is as follows. On 31 December, the rates due were £42, wages due £46, subscriptions due £40. The insurance payment includes £23 for next year and subscriptions in advance for the year ahead were £75. Old equipment is to be depreciated by 20 per cent.

2. The Leyside Cycling Club has assets and liabilities as follows at the start of its financial year, 1 April 199X.

■ **Assets** club premises £35 000, practice machines £3485, furniture and fittings £1765, subscriptions due £65, stock of spare parts £864, bank balance £426, cash in hand £63.

■ **Liabilities** subscriptions in advance £126, telephone expenses due £48, mortgage on premises £18 000.

The treasurer prepares two receipts and payments accounts:

Receipts and Payments in Cash for Year Ending 31 March 199X

	£		£
Cash in hand at start	63	Payments for spare parts	156
Subscriptions	2950	Prizes	200
Competition fees	760	Refreshment expenses	125
Refreshment sales	827	Premises expenses	384
Sales of spare parts	825	Repairs	185
		Payment to bank	4000

Receipts and Payments by Cheque for Year Ending 31 March 199X

	£		£
Balance at start	426	Rates	486
Rent from subtenant	2080	Purchases of spare parts	2255
Subscriptions	240	Telephone expenses	199
Cash banked	4000	Mortgage interest	1592
Sales of spare parts	1624	Mortgage repayments	1564

At the end of the year, subscriptions of £126 were due and £185 had been received in advance for the next year. Stocks of spare parts were valued at £956. Show the calculation of the accumulated fund at the start of the year, a receipts and payment account (cash) and a receipts and payment account (bank), a trading account for spare parts, an income and expenditure account for the year and a balance sheet as at 31 March 199X. Note that mortgage repayments decrease the mortgage. They are not a revenue expense, but a capital movement.

Answers
1. Accumulated Fund at start, £2013; Surplus for year £1027, totals £3203.
2. Accumulated Fund at start £23 494, cash balance £375, bank balance £2274, profit on spares £130, surplus £3866; balance sheet total £43 981.

ACCOUNTS FOR CHARITIES

With the passing of the Charities Act 1993, the accounts of charities have come under stricter control. Although the accounts of charities are essentially club accounts, in that they are the accounts of non-profit-making organisations, there are some special points to be made about the general conduct of charities' financial affairs.

As the methods of collection are, generally speaking, fairly free and easy, the funds subscribed are at considerable risk and it is a common complaint that only a small portion of the funds collected actually reach the persons in need. This may be a quite unfair criticism – obviously a great deal of money subscribed in providing food for people struck by famine is going to have to be spent on transport, packaging and so on. This is essential and unavoidable. At the same time, where people are in paid positions working for a charity, a very large proportion of the funds collected are dissipated in their pay. To increase public confidence in charitable works, the 1993 Act now provides that the trustees of charities must keep accounting records that, in particular, contain:

- entries showing, from day to day, all the sums of money received and expended by the charity, and the matters in respect of which receipts and expenditure take place;
- a record of the assets and liabilities of the charity;
- the accounts should disclose at any time, with reasonable accuracy, the financial position of the charity at that time.

Before looking at the new regulations that have been made since the passing of the 1993 Act, one or two basic points.

In this book, the subject is dealing with the grass-roots work of keeping accounts. So, what does the phrase 'must keep proper books of account' mean in the case of any local charity? The answer includes the following points.

- Whenever money is collected, it should be done in as foolproof a manner as possible, and in as public a way as possible. Here are some examples.
  - If money is collected in a meeting place or at a social function of some sort, it should be counted by the treasurer in the presence of other members and the amount collected should be announced to the meeting. It is highly desirable that a receipt should be made out for the amount collected. The top copy – which would normally be given to the individual making a contribution to the charity – should be pinned on any noticeboard available and left up for at least one month.
  - If money is collected in collecting boxes, these should be efficiently sealed before use and should only be opened by the treasurer or an assistant treasurer in the presence of other people, including, if possible, the collector responsible for the box. A receipt for the amount collected should be made out and the top copy given to the collector. If several people took over the box

during the day, a note should be kept of the name of the person to whom the receipt is given. Preferably, this note should be made on the receipt itself so it is carbon copied onto the counterfoil.

- If collecting boxes are displayed in shops, public houses and so on, the box should be opened and counted in the shopkeeper's presence and a receipt given in the shopkeeper's name.
- All donations by private individuals should be acknowledged by receipts. All receipt books should be numbered consecutively with the year – that is 1/98; 2/98; 3/98 and so on, and kept for six years.

■ All money paid out should, so far as is possible, be paid against invoices or other documents, even if only a till receipt is available. These documents should be preserved in a lever-arch file or some other storage device. Small receipts should be stapled onto larger sheets of paper for safety, and a petty cash voucher number should be written on them so that they can be easily traced. The aim should be to have a piece of paper sanctioning every payment and a receipt to cover every piece of income.

■ All moneys received and paid should be recorded in an analysed cash book (such as the Simplex Club Accounts Book referred to earlier) and the columns should be totalled and carried to summaries for use in preparing the receipts and payments account for the year. This account is the essential record for drawing up the Income and expenditure account and balance sheet in the manner already described above.

THE NEW REGULATIONS FOR CHARITIES

Since the passing of the 1993 Act, new regulations have been made by the charity commissioners, and the accountancy bodies have produced a statement of recommended practice regarding charities that recommends to professional accountants the best way to comply with the new regulations. These documents are so clearly expressed and so readily available that there is little point in setting out any of the details here, but the following points are some of the most important. The actual documents may be obtained either free or at a small cost from the Charity Commission, St Albans House, 57–60 Haymarket, London SW1 4QX (telephone 0171–210 300).

If your charity income is less than £10 000 per year, and your charity expenditure is less than £10 000 per year (the £10 000 threshold), ask for the booklet *Charity Accounts Under the £10,000 Threshold*. If your charity income exceeds this figure, ask for the statement of recommended practice referred to above, which costs £5 (though the first copy is given free for an initial period). Referring chiefly to the small charity below the £10 000 threshold, the following points can be made.

- Accounts should be kept on a receipt and payments basis, like the Simplex Club Accounts Book described earlier, and the trustees should ensure that proper procedures are followed in collecting funds (receipts) and in preserving invoices and petty cash vouchers about payments made.
- End-of-year accounts may be in receipts and payments form, but if the treasurer prefers to keep accounts on an accruals basis (adjusting figures to refer to the particular year in question only, this is permissible.
- An external scrutiny of the accounts by a professional accountant is not generally required, but may be called for by the commissioners in doubtful cases (perhaps where an allegation has been made by some interested party). Where the receipts or payments exceed the £10 000 limit, an independent scrutiny, or even a full audit, may be required.
- Charities that have receipts and payments of less than £1000 a year are not required to register, but should still keep accounts in the style of club accounts described earlier in this chapter.
- Registered charities below the £10 000 threshold are required to produce both a set of accounts and an annual report, but will not need to send these in the charity commissioners unless they are asked to do so.
- The form of the accounts is set out in the form ACC–1371, which calls for a list of receipts and payments and a list of assets and liabilities. The form is very simply set out and may be obtained from the commission free of charge.

To conclude, it is clear that keeping proper accounts for both clubs and charities is very important. Even though you give your own time voluntarily to serve on club and charity committees, you need to be as professional as an amateur can be when handling money. Your good names are being held out in public as those of responsible and caring members of society. It is important to have all your records in impeccable order, so that your good name is preserved and reputation enhanced.

Index

Safety Crimes

Steve Tombs and
Dave Whyte

WILLAN
PUBLISHING

Published by

Willan Publishing
Culmcott House
Mill Street, Uffculme
Cullompton, Devon
EX15 3AT, UK
Tel: +44(0)1884 840337
Fax: +44(0)1884 840251
e-mail: info@willanpublishing.co.uk
website: www.willanpublishing.co.uk

Published simultaneously in the USA and Canada by

Willan Publishing
c/o ISBS, 920 NE 58th Ave, Suite 300,
Portland, Oregon 97213-3786, USA
Tel: +001(0)503 287 3093
Fax: +001(0)503 208 8832
e-mail: info@isbs.com
website: www.isbs.com

First published 2007

Hardback
ISBN 978-1-84392-086-1

Paperback
ISBN 978-1-84392-085-4

British Library Cataloguing-in-Publication Data
A catalogue record for this book is available from the British Library

Project managed by Deer Park Productions, Tavistock, Devon
Typeset by Pantek Arts Ltd, Maidstone, Kent
Printed and bound by T.J. International Ltd, Padstow, Cornwall

Contents

Acknowledgements

We wish to record publicly our thanks to those who have offered unswerving support for the rather unfashionable criminological concern which forms the subject matter of this book, as well as for their constructive criticism. Joe Sim, Frank Pearce, Laureen Snider, Paddy Hillyard. Anne Alvesalo, Simon Pemberton, Roy Coleman, Jonny Burnett, Pete Gill, Courtney Davis, Gary Fooks, Erja Virta, Kas Wachala and Andrew Watterson are owed debts of gratitude for their advice and insights on material contained herein. We are privileged to think of all of these people as friends as well as colleagues. Our thanks also go to the many people who have attended the various meetings of the European Group for the Study of Deviance and Social Control, which has consistently given us space to air arguments expressed here; particular mention amongst these should go to Andrea Beckmann, for her friendship, and for her work in sustaining the 'British' section of the aforementioned organisation.

For his ready acceptance of the litany of promised, then missed, deadlines over the past years we are grateful for the support of Brian Willan for this project – in even taking on the text, he has done something which most publishers of criminology texts would not have. And much more than a nod of appreciation is also due to Hazel Croall who, as series editor, has read every word of this book, providing supporting yet detailed feedback, without which any of its current failings would have been far greater.

This book could not, quite literally, have been written without those people who devote their lives to struggling around those issues which we have only dared to attempt to describe and account for here. Notable amongst these in terms of both the extent of their contribution and their comradeship have been John Bamford, Hilda Palmer, Rory O'Neill, and Anne and Tim Jones. Special thanks go to David Bergman and to the (past and present) staff, board members, volunteers and supporters of the Centre for Corporate Accountability; the CCA's particular role within the struggle for safer workplaces – to provide the bereaved with a path through the tortuous bias and lack of acknowledgement of the criminal justice system – is a vital and humbling one.

As with any venture that spans a period of years, we could not have written this without the support, love and sacrifices on the part of those who share our lives. Lyn and Patrick, that's you. Kathrin, that's you. Thanks.

Finally, we'd like to put on record that what is here is the result of a working relationship and a friendship that has been, and will remain, invaluable to both of us. This text, for all its omissions and weaknesses, is much more than the sum of its parts.

List of tables and figures

Tables

Figures

List of abbreviations

ATP	Automatic Train Protection
BCS	British Crime Survey
CCA	Centre for Corporate Accountability
CPS	Crown Prosecution Service
DPP	Director of Public Prosecutions
DWP	Department of Work and Pensions
HASAW Act	Health and Safety at Work Act (1974)
HSC	Health and Safety Commission
HSE	Health and Safety Executive
ILO	International Labour Organisation
IMO	International Marine Organisation
LFS	Labour Force Survey
LOSC	Labour Only Sub-Contracting
MIC	Methyl Iso-Cyanate
ODPM	Office of the Deputy Prime Minister
OECD	Organisation for Economic Co-operation and Development
OSD	Offshore Safety Division
RoSPA	Royal Society for the Prevention of Accidents
SOLAS	Safety of Life at Sea
SME	Small- and Medium-sized Enterprise
TSR	Temporary Safe Refuge
UCC	Union Carbide Corporation
UCIL	Union Carbide of India Limited

Foreword

Rory O'Neill

The date 23 March 2005 was a business-as-usual day for BP, Britain's largest private firm. The board was feted as a model of corporate probity, and was delivering soaring profits and share prices. The global chief executive Lord Browne – the poster boy for caring, successful business – had even done the seemingly miraculous and given the petroleum giant a green tinge.

But a 'corporate blindspot' on safety left this safe bet for shareholders less safe for the workforce. It was 23 March 2005 when the Texas City refinery explosion exposed the deadly flaws in BP's boardroom strategy. Fifteen died and 170 were injured in a blast which razed large sections of the plant.

There was nothing unique about events at BP, except the company's size and profile guaranteed the disaster would perhaps command closer scrutiny from the media and authorities. One investigation report noted it had failed to learn the lessons of previous incidents, particularly a series of serious safety offences in 2000 at its Grangemouth plant in Scotland. Another reported it had slashed costs, all part of its 'cheque book mentality' towards safety. But at all times it had done what companies are first and foremost required to do – to be as profitable as possible.

This book is concerned with the nature of production and how this impacts on the decisions made in boardrooms. It also deals with how infrequently these decisions, however deadly, lead from the boardroom to the courtroom. It is not filled with stories of comic book villains with no concern for the consequences of their actions, portraying safety crimes as bad deeds by bad people. Lord Browne no more set out that morning to kill 15 workers than he set out to stop it. But boardroom decisions made with a key objective of maximising profit have consequences, and safety can be a casualty. Nice guys can kill you.

In fact, this book sets out to deal with only a fraction of this killing. Work-related health problems, not 'safety', have for decades been the bigger workplace killer. We should remember that jobs in service-sector Britain may for the current working generation become safer, but remain just as deadly through causing illness. More of us are in work than at any time in history.

Exposing the links between boardroom behaviour and deaths and injuries at work requires information spanning an unusually broad range of disciplines, from business to criminal law, industrial relations to industrial safety and economics to sociology. It may be this complexity that has meant that being hurt at work is not recognised as a crime of violence in Home Office statistics, despite the location of the crime being the only major feature distinguishing it from other acts of violence.

We don't know how many people are killed or injured as a result of work. We do know official figures are substantial underestimates. As the authors here establish, the majority of work-related deaths are excluded from the official statistics. The systematic exclusions include road traffic accidents in work time, deaths reportable to agencies other than the workplace safety watchdog the Health and Safety Executive (HSE) and local authorities, or deaths while working abroad or arising from exposures while working abroad. Tot these up and you reach a total in excess of 1,600 deaths a year – at least seven times the officially recorded level.

Examples of recent deaths at work that don't count in official occupational fatality statistics include the seven workers killed on 23 December 2006 when a helicopter carrying rig workers, all UK residents, crashed over the Morecambe Bay gas field. The deaths were investigated by the Civil Aviation Authority. The death of bus driver Michael Hallinan in December 2005, trapped between two buses, again escaped the work death records. It's the same story for Lloyd's Bank worker Lucy Wilson, 23, who contracted a liver infection while training call centre workers in India on a short work trip for the company, succumbing to the disease within three weeks of her return.

Even deaths that should be included by HSE's criteria frequently miss out, because the doctors charged with making the reports sometimes fail to see beyond the fatal injury to the deadly workplace.

Thus, even in terms of 'safety', the price is greater than it might at first seem. There are also health care and welfare costs, heartache and poverty for bereaved families, trauma for injured workers. Thomas Corr had almost all his right ear severed at the Luton IBC van factory while fixing a machine. Six years later, in May 2002, he took his own life aged 37 after suffering headaches, tinnitus and severe depression. His job killed him and devastated his family, but you won't see that reflected in any workplace fatality statistics.

This all has implications for prevention. If you don't count the bodies, the bodies don't count. When allocating resources and deciding public health priorities, over 1,600 workplace injury deaths each year will command a more serious response from government than HSE's artificially deflated headline figure of fewer than 250 worker deaths a year.

Social class defines those who will die or be injured. By HSE's own estimates, 'process, plant and machinery operators' are about ten times more likely to die or suffer a serious injury at work as 'managers and senior officials'.

Workers, though, are blamed. Not dissimilar to Union Carbide's response following the Bhopal gas leak, a report released by BP within two months of the March 2005 Texas City blast alleged it was 'surprising and deeply disturbing' mistakes by workers that led to the explosion. In response, the firm was accused of 'corporate scapegoating', a charge completely vindicated in subsequent reports which instead highlighted the culpability of the global BP board.

The idea of the accident-prone worker, a myth which has been examined and discredited so thoroughly the language should sound quaint and archaic, is, in the words of Canadian academic Bob Sass, 'a dead horse that won't lie down'. Blame-the-worker behavioural safety systems are growing in popularity, putting the focus on the individual worker rather than on the management-designed, operated, supervised and profit-oriented system that placed them at risk. Through threats and incentives workers are coerced into not reporting injuries. In the US, they call it 'blood-in-pocket syndrome' – don't report it, hide the injury until you get home.

Safety crimes are sanitised with the use of blame-free language – disasters, abuses, scandals. They are 'accidents', despite there being nothing accidental in the decisions and circumstances that caused them to occur. They are called anything but 'crimes'.

By contrast, there's plenty of language to suggest the problem is overstated or the creation of vested interests. We talk of 'ambulance chasers', but when factories explode there's no equivalent criticism of 'ambulance fillers'. When deaths occur, they are the product of 'freak' accidents, not the wholly predictable outcome of the way the job was designed and executed. Deaths in trenches or in falls aren't the everyday and obvious outcome of a management neglect of basic, simple safety procedures, but are 'one in a million' tragedies, apparently unforeseen and unstoppable. The police conclude, with unseemly haste and usually long before any form of credible investigation has taken place, 'there are no suspicious circumstances'.

As this rigorous examination of the evidence demonstrates, there is a long distance from the boardroom to the courtroom. Managers, directors and those appointing them accept without question there is a direct correlation between boardroom decisions and the company's performance. Large pay packets, bonuses and pensions can all be justified because there is a straight line from the guiding hand of the board to the productivity and profitability of the firm. But when things go wrong and workers die or are injured, then that guiding hand is not raised in an admission of guilt. It is hard to reconcile the two positions.

Of course, when it comes to dealing with legal liability, the boardroom does have certain advantages. For starters, company directors do not on the whole look like the popular perception of a criminal. Stereotypes point to yobs and yoofs and spivs, but the corporate criminals, however yobbish and anti-social their boardroom behaviour, just don't look the part.

It's not that these bosses are without fault. Investigations cited in this book suggest in at least two out of three workplace fatalities there is a clear criminal case to answer. But the higher you get up the corporate ladder, the more likely you are to have the cash and connections – actual, class and cultural – to play and win the legal game, as blame is 'mystified and obscured'. The criminal justice system denies almost all occupational injury victims and bereaved relatives an admission of culpability by the guilty parties or a day in court. Redress is normally only available through common law compensation claims, which, if they go to court, can provide an admission of negligence on a balance of probabilities (rather than a criminal offence). Common law compensation cases require companies to answer for their unsafe and unhealthy behaviour 40 times more frequently than HSE prosecutions.

HSE – the default workplace safety police – is far more likely to seek informal solutions and measures in response to clear evidence of a safety crime. HSE's strategy puts a new emphasis on voluntary measures, education and support, backed up by an argument that the real benchmark is improving health and safety performance. This is patently an important goal – although the evidence suggests there are few grounds for complacency on this count, and it cannot, in any case, be the only goal. Quiet encouragement ignores the role of deterrence. It also dismisses notions of justice and fairness.

Criminal breaches of safety law have to be viewed in the context of the drive by successive governments to lift regulatory burdens from business. HSE has adopted a business-friendly persona, which could reflect both directives from central government and the 'capture' of the organisation by business interests, who over time have skewed its outlook and work to be closer to that of the business world. And so all the major indicators of workplace safety enforcement action plummet: prosecutions, convictions, notices, inspector contact time and inspections.

Companies, meanwhile, opt into voluntary 'compliance' programmes, evading regulatory attention because their *reported* incident rates are low. These programmes are widespread in the US; government-encouraged variations on the theme are now appearing in the UK. Voluntary approaches have the clear potential to undermine regulation. And regulation is more than a benchmark against which errant companies can be judged and punished. It also includes the package of rights available to workers to raise concerns, to call for information and to demand action.

If safety regulation is weakened, either by deregulation or by an incremental shift taking more and more companies into the world of self-regulation, then these workers' rights could be weakened by stealth. This has created the space for companies, particularly large companies, to create their own wholly voluntary and self-enforced 'ethical' alternative to traditional enforcement. Corporate social responsibility and ethical trading are buzzwords in the boardroom. They are also great PR without the discomfort of external policing.

HSE has obediently embraced this model of voluntary compliance. BP, the firm with the 'corporate blindspot' on safety, whose global board was savaged in 2006 and 2007 in reports after the Texas City explosion and which was the recipient of Britain's biggest safety fine in 2002, was still featured in 2007 on HSE's corporate social responsibility webpages as an example of good 'director leadership'.

Yet companies themselves can be victims of under-enforcement. Good firms that invest in prevention and who give a greater priority to safety suffer a competitive disadvantage compared to those who only expend time and effort in the unlikely instance they are caught. It is a system that encourages the good to be not so good and the bad to stay bad.

When companies commit safety crimes they are not in their own terms necessarily dysfunctional; in fact, they are acquitting most of their duties exactly as their legal constitution requires. Companies are constituted to maximise profits from commercial activities, and failure to do this is an offence for which shareholders can and do demand redress. The system of corporate law and governance rewards profit and gives primary oversight to shareholders, a group whose principal concern is the size of those profits. Like muggers, corporations don't set out to hurt you, they just want the money and accept someone might, when things go wrong, get hurt in the process.

Their guilt, though, can be shockingly apparent. The fire and explosions at Piper Alpha, the sinking of the *Herald of Free Enterprise* and the death of student Simon Jones at Shoreham dock were, in the words of the authors of this book, 'all crimes that could be traced back to the carefully planned decisions of accountants and managers'. These crimes, they add, are 'committed in cold blood' and are often 'committed in order to advance financial goals or maintain profitable systems of production'. As US work organisation expert Charley Richardson of the University of Massachusetts Lowell puts it: 'They are killing us by diligence, not negligence.'

It is the legal 'controlling mind' doctrine that affords corporate muggers a near impermeable defence. The 'corporate personality' which faces safety charges enjoys all the rights of a real flesh-and-blood person, without similar responsibilities. This is useful to companies, as the corporate person has one clear defining trait – greed. Corporations are first and foremost about making money. Safety responsibilities, in legal and business if not moral terms, are a lesser concern. The duties are not absolute. The law says an employer must do what is 'reasonably practicable' to ensure work is safe and healthy. The law as it stands is not good at laying liability at the door of companies – it leaves too much 'reasonable' wriggle room and the volume and sometimes vigour of enforcement action is low. It is singularly ill-suited to making directors and top managers liable for safety crimes.

While there's little chance of being caught, there's little incentive to be law abiding. Inspection backed by enforcement is the most successful way to secure compliance. This effect would be amplified if fines were more closely related to the gravity of the offence or ability to pay.

Punishment, of course, is not a solution to crime, but it should be a possible consequence of it. It could deliver both a deterrent effect and, just as crucial, a recognition that lives at work are important, and harming working people is, like other acts of violence, a serious crime.

Recent experiences suggest it will take bigger, better targeted penalties to spur change at major companies. For BP, it took nearly two years, three critical reports, intense media scrutiny, a $21m fine, serious pressure from corporate responsibility lobbying groups and a general conclusion from critics that the reputation of the company and its golden chief executive Lord Browne was 'down the toilet' before it conceded in February 2007 that production and safety priorities had been in conflict in the run-up to the Texas City explosion, and that this was a problem that must now be addressed by better investment in safety and by less emphasis on production. Lord Browne said the Texas City blast 'was a watershed' that would 'forever change BP'. But two workers had died at the same plant just six months before. Prior to Texas City, BP already had more fatalities than its major US competitors. Deaths alone were not enough to change BP's mind.

Back in the world of 'real' crimes, bosses can and do spend time behind bars. In October 2006, Jeffrey Skilling, Enron's chief executive, was sentenced to 24 years in a US jail for corporate fraud. The collapse cost workers their jobs and pensions, and investors their fortunes. The same company had been responsible for deaths in the UK, but faced the usual fines. It was Jeff Skilling who flew into the UK after three workers died and one was seriously injured in an August 2001 explosion at the company's Teesside power plant. His comment then: 'We pledge to work with the authorities to ensure it never happens again anywhere.'

This wasn't the plant's first death or its first explosion. The company – not its executives – had been prosecuted successfully on two previous occasions, once after a worker was killed in the plant's construction in 1992, and once in 1998 after a worker received horrific burns in an explosion. There were all the signs of a dysfunctional company, but the book work looked OK and Enron claimed its finances were good, so no one looked too closely. Worker deaths don't hurt shareholders.

Directors remain effectively immune from safety law. An average of 11 a year faced court action for workplace safety crimes in the decade up to December 2005; just 11 were jailed. In 2005 alone, inspectors from the animal welfare body the RSPCA secured 31 prison or suspended sentences for animal cruelty. This was down from 44 in 2004. It investigated 110,841 complaints and secured 2,071 convictions of 1,031 defendants. On every count, the RSPCA massively outperformed the HSE, the human cruelty at work watchdog.

If there is a slow recognition that workplace injuries and fatalities are often the result of corporate safety crimes, this has not come about because of the emergence of new evidence. The evidence has always been there and the case has always been watertight. The reason this is on the agenda at all is because there has been a campaign to put it there. Bereaved families, trade unions, campaign and advocacy organisations like the Hazards Campaign, the Centre for Corporate Accountability, Disaster Action, Inquest, Families Against Corporate Killers (Fack), the Construction Safety Campaign and the Simon Jones Memorial Campaign have all called for legislation, for action and for accountability. They have an unanswerable case.

Despite technological advances and the decline in more obviously hazardous industries like manufacturing and mining, some new trends in modern production are placing a large slice of the workforce at greater risk. More of us are now contingent workers – temporary and insecure, with few rights and little scope to object to safety abuses. The benefits system is getting meaner and sickness systems more punitive, so the pressure to stay in work, however hazardous, could be increasing. Working longer, harder and faster are not hazards dealt with under the current enforcement model, but they are the emerging problems of the twenty-first century workplace.

Workplace health and safety isn't a battle won; it is barely a battle started.

Rory O'Neill
Hazards magazine (*http://www.hazards.org*)
May 2007

Chapter 1

Introducing safety crimes

Introduction

If you were to stop one hundred people in the street and ask them to list, in their opinion, the five most serious crimes in Britain today, it's a very safe bet that in the vast majority of responses no form of corporate crime would feature. This is not to be disparaging of popular understandings of crime, for these ways of seeing are socially constructed. So, check today's newspapers for reports of political discussions or Home Office statements on law and order: again, corporate crime will be absent. Now scour those newspapers more thoroughly, and try to find corporate crime stories – corporate crime may be covered, but is unlikely to be given prominence, nor discussed in the language reserved for 'real' crime, and is more likely to be financial 'scandals', in specialist sections far from the headline-grabbing news pages. Check your TV guide for today's viewing, and search for corporate crime coverage amongst what will no doubt be a great deal of fictional, real-life and documentary programmes on crime – and it would be a surprise to find much, if any.

Now if corporate crime – in essence, crimes by corporations in pursuit of their legitimate goals[1] – is relatively invisible, then this invisibility is even more marked for some of the subcategories covered by this general term. One such sub-category – safety crimes[2] – is the subject of this text. Safety crimes – which we define as violations of law by employers that either do, or have the potential to, cause sudden death or injury as a result of work-related activities – are, we shall argue throughout this book, ubiquitous, have devastating physical (and psychological) effects, and carry with them enormous financial and social consequences. Despite this, such crimes remain relatively invisible at the level of political and

1

popular consciousness. Indeed, where events that *may* be represented as safety crimes do emerge in such contexts, they tend not to be represented as such: instead, they are likely to be viewed as accidents, disasters, tragedies, and so on. Even less forgivably, safety crimes as an area of focus is also obscured by the overwhelming focus of criminological teaching, research and writing.

It is this relative invisibility that is the central rationale for this text. We are concerned here with how this is achieved, why this is the case, and with the consequences of such crimes being obscured. Further, we wish to examine the role played by institutions and processes in maintaining definitions of crime from which safety crimes are marginalised. And, finally, we seek to set out some of the conditions for overcoming this relative invisibility. That is, we ask in what ways might governments, the media, the law and criminal justice system, and, indeed, criminologists, take safety crimes more seriously – and what might the effects be of any emergent focus upon this widespread area of offending.

If the invisibility of safety crimes is a central, recurrent theme of this book, then perhaps our first task is to put some safety crimes before our readers' eyes: what are safety crimes, what do they look like, what forms do they take, where do they occur, what consequences do they have, who are their victims, and how does law and its agencies respond to them? For this reason, the bulk of this chapter is devoted to a series of brief case studies of such crimes, to establish contours of the all-too-unfamiliar phenomenon with which the book is dealing. Prior to turning to these cases, we seek briefly to mark out the terrain of the book through a definition of safety crimes.

What are safety crimes?

As we have indicated above, safety crimes, as used throughout this text, are a subset of corporate crimes. And our understanding of the latter follows what has by now become a fairly standard definition, based upon the work of Kramer (1984), Clinard and Yeager (1980: 16), Schrager and Short (1978), and Box (1983). Thus, by 'corporate crime', we mean

> Illegal acts or omissions, punishable by the state under administrative, civil or criminal law which are the result of deliberate decision making or culpable negligence within a legitimate formal organisation. These acts or omisions are based in legitimate, formal, business organisations, made in accordance with the normative goals, standard operating procedures, and/or cultural norms of the organization, and are intended to benefit the corporation itself. (Pearce and Tombs 1998, 107–110)

We can, for the purposes of this text, simply replace corporate crime with safety crime in this definition. And this definition has a series of useful characteristics, to which it is worth drawing immediate attention.

Safety crimes may constitute violations of the Health and Safety at Work Act 1974, the primary piece of safety legislation in the UK, which is a criminal statute. Equally, however, there is legislation governing occupational safety that falls beyond the criminal law. Within the above definition, then, through reference to illegal rather than criminal acts, it avoids the restriction that follows from the fact that many laws, enforced by administrative bodies through the civil courts, also regulate actions which cause injuries to specific individuals or which undermine social institutions. Indeed, following Sutherland, the content of laws and the nature of legal distinctions such as those between crimes, torts and administrative sanctions, between acts *mala in se* and *mala prohibita*, are conventional, time-bound social products without an intrinsic substantive meaning that transcends their social or historical contexts; what acts or omissions constitute crime must be understood in terms of contingency (Lacey 1995). Thus, we extend our definition of crime beyond that proscribed by criminal law or indeed that which has been processed through the legal system.

Second, through references to negligence and the use of the phrase 'omission or commission', the definition avoids the trap of arguing that for corporate crime in general – and safety crime in particular – to exist there must be *actus rea* and *mens rea* ('knowing mind'). Given the organisational locus or origins of safety crime, to emphasise either an illegal *act* or an *intention* is often inappropriate, for two reasons. First, each term is anthropomorphic and individualising, and by definition is problematic in its application to a corporate entity which is more than, or different to, the sum of individual human actors. Second, intention implies a relatively unproblematic link between an act or omission and its consequence – yet this simplistic causal sequencing leads to an obscuring of the construction and maintenance of a situation or context which, as a consequence, is fertile ground for violations. Any focus upon safety crimes requires us to examine these in terms of their *organisational production*.

On the former point, it has been argued that 'most corporate crimes cannot be explained by the perverse personalities of their perpetrators' (Braithwaite 1984: 2), and this claim calls into question the proclivity within individualistic liberal or bourgeois cultures to locate the source of evil deeds in evil people (*ibid.*; see also Shrager and Short 1977: 410, Snider 1993: 61). Corporate and safety crimes can be produced by an organisation's structure, its culture, its unquestioned assumptions, its very modus operandi, and so on. Thus to understand such phenomena must not obscure human agency, but does require a shift from abstracted, atomised individuals to account for agency in the context of structures.

The definition of safety crime used in this text is, then, an explicitly inclusive one. That is, throughout this text we discuss *as crimes* many acts and omissions which have not been subject to any formal judicial process; thus these are phenomena which have not been interrogated as, let alone proven to be, violations of the criminal, or indeed any other form of law. To fail to do otherwise would lead us into the study of what Braithwaite called class-based administration of criminal justice, thereby obscuring precisely the most useful insights of Sutherland regarding the class-biased development of law and its differential implementation (see Chapter 4).

Other issues regarding our definition of safety crimes, and thus the scope of this text, require brief clarification.

First, we should emphasise that we focus here upon safety rather than health. While the commonly-used phrase 'health and safety', and the very object of legislation in this area, often reinforces the intimately linked nature of these two concepts, consideration of each raises some common, but many distinct, phenomena. Violations against worker or public safety are – usually – immediately apparent through near-miss, injury or even death; violations of occupational health law often involve a much more complex and contestable causal chain, the key factor often being a state of affairs rather than an event, such as long-term exposure to a noxious substance or endurance of a unhealthy mode of working which can produce cancer, stress or arthritis much later in one's life. This causal complexity makes the burden of proof a difficult one for victims of such crimes – involving, not least, often confounding resort to complex and often contradictory scientific claims. Similarly, the immediate visibility of safety offences as opposed to health offences means that it is the former that are much more likely to result in formal enforcement action on the part of regulators – rare though any form of such action is. Partly related to this is the fact that if occupational injury data is incomplete and problematic, to say the least, as we shall see in Chapter 2, that relating to occupational ill-health is almost non-utilisable – problems of measurement beset the area of occupational health to a far greater extent than that of occupational safety. And, again perhaps relatedly, there is also a sense in which meeting legal duties to provide a safe working environment imposes less costs in terms of changes to work organisation, practices and so on than dealing with less tangible ill-health effects.

None of this is to relegate occupational health crimes below that of safety crimes in social importance. But it is to say that there are important differences, so that an adequate treatment of each would require a much longer text than can be presented here. Further, none of this should imply that there are not common causes of occupational safety and health crimes – each can be understood, for example, through many of the causal factors or characteristics of acute deaths as set out in the table at the end of this chapter.

Second, we should clarify that while our focus is upon safety crimes, neither the legal duties that are being violated by these, nor the effects of such violations, are restricted to workers. Thus, for example, the Health and Safety at Work Act 1974 extends the duty of care owed by employers not simply to employees and the self-employed, but also to the general public as well as others, such as sub-contractors, not in direct employment but likely to be affected by the conduct of the employer's undertaking (sections 3–5). This is a recognition that whilst the victims of safety crimes are often employees, no actual nor metaphorical factory fence can exist that protects members of the public from decisions and omissions within companies that produce offences with actual or potentially dangerous effects. And the force of this legal requirement is under-scored in some of the cases selected for consideration below. Thus, for example, while the gas leak at Bhopal killed employees at the Union Carbide plant, arguably far greater devastation was wrought upon the local community, where tens of thousands were exposed to the gas, and to the surrounding natural environment, much of which remains despoiled to this day; the victims of the failure to ensure a safe system of work aboard the *Herald of Free Enterprise* were mostly consumers, that is, passengers; and the four deaths which arose as a result of the faults of Transco to work safely were of a family to whom the company supplied gas. Business organisations supply goods or services; those to whom those goods or services are supplied, or who live in the proximity of areas where some of that production or supply is undertaken, are just as likely to be victims of safety crimes as workers.

Finally, it remains here to be stated that throughout this text we view safety crimes as crimes of *violence*. Though this is not an original approach, it is, as we shall see, one which, in the context of academic criminology and general representations of occupational injuries, a rarity. For us, this lack of criminological attention to safety crimes as crimes of violence is less a quality of the latter phenomena, more a failure of the discipline to reflect upon long-standing, but ontologically weak, assumptions. Thus once occupational injuries are viewed not as accidents but as incidents which are not only largely preventable, but which the law requires to be prevented, then they fall within the ambit of criminology. Then, if we consider these illegalities in terms of their potential or actual consequences – injury and death – we realise that these look remarkably similar to the results of those events that most men and women, as well as policy-makers, politicians, and academics, deem to be 'proper' violence. Most crucially, these latter conceptions of violence are, as we shall see, based upon an implicit association of violence with the inter-personal and with intention, both qualities that are often absent from safety crimes.

That safety crimes are crimes of (actual or potential) violence is, for us, unequivocal; yet to reach this conclusion one must generally move beyond criminology, to understandings of violence developed in other disciplines.

One such holistic understanding of violence has been developed by Jamil Salmi who, following Galtung amongst others, has set out a systematic analytical framework which aims to explore a variety of dimensions of this phenomenon; he then identifies the patterns and relationships linking the various manifestations of violence to the prevailing economic, social and political power structures in an effort to establish accountability. Salmi sets out four broad categories of violence, and indicates a series of type within each category.

First, he identifies 'Direct Violence', that is, deliberate injury to the integrity of human life, which includes homicide, brutal acts and restrictions or physical constraints. It is within, though not encompassing all of, this category of violence that the overwhelming majority of criminological research proceeds. Highlighting intent through reference to *deliberate injury* (Salmi 2004: 56), this would exclude most forms of deaths and injuries associated with working.

Second, Salmi notes 'Indirect Violence', namely indirect violations of rights to survival; this includes the sub-categories of violence by omission, which 'draws on the legal notion of non-assistance to persons in danger' (ibid. 57), and mediated violence, 'which is the result of a deliberate human intervention in the natural or social environment whose harmful effects are indirect and often delayed' (ibid. 58). In the context of a discussion of the latter, Salmi considers the mediated violence generated through the capitalist production process, noting the tendency towards health and safety effects which is an effect of the inherent desire of employers to minimise 'unproductive' expenditures (Salmi 1993: 56).

Third, he refers to 'Repressive Violence', that is the 'Deprivation of Fundamental Rights' which includes violations of social, civil and political rights. This would incorporate as studies of violence much of the burgeoning literature around human rights and their violations – a literature dedicated to considering issues which if 'not completely ignored by criminology as a discipline' remains 'a minority pursuit', and for the most part a very recent one at that (Carrabine *et al.*, 2004: 352).

Fourth, and finally, Salmi identifies 'Alienating Violence' – 'Deprivation of "Higher" Rights' – based on 'the assumption that a person's well-being does not come exclusively from fulfilling material needs, the notion of alienating violence refers to denying a person the right to psychological, emotional, cultural, or intellectual integrity' (2004). This includes alienating living and working conditions, social ostracism and ethnocide (Salmi 1993, following Galtung 1981).

Categories of 'indirect violence' and 'alienating violence' are particularly important in thinking about safety crimes, as they direct our attention to the 'relations of domination, and the violences that are condoned as part of the "normal" and "healthy" functioning of a society such as ours' (Catley 2003: 5). Safety crimes, as we will argue at various points in this text, result from the organisation of production and working regimes that carry deadly consequences for some workers and members of the public. It is this that clearly puts safety crimes on the terrain of 'indirect violence', since safety crimes are the human consequences of mediated violence, inflicted indirectly through working. The concept of 'alienating violence' is relevant for safety crimes since it allows us to move from the level of the individual to *structural* violence, that is, violence that is produced systemically or structurally as a consequence of a variety of key organisational or social institutional arrangements. Key institutions that produce violence structurally and systemically in the context of work include labour markets, the occupational structure and the labour process, the uneven distribution of power within and around work organisations, the corporate form *per se*, and constituent parts of the state, such as criminal justice and legal systems, regulatory bodies and Government ministries. At various points throughout this text, we will therefore consider how those organisations and institutions play a role in mediating the conditions of indirect violence, and in the structural production of violence. This is how we approach the case studies that follow.

Case studies in safety crime

Introduction: using case studies

The case study approach has been, and remains, particularly important in all forms of corporate crime research. There are several reasons for this general tendency to produce case studies. First, in almost all jurisdictions there is a lack of consolidated corporate crime statistics that form basic raw material with which corporate crime researchers might work. Further, projects designed to generate large scale quantitative data with which then to work are extremely expensive and thus require funding – but such funding is unlikely to come from either governments or employers, each of which are likely to find corporate crime research unattractive; such funding has thus been extremely rare, is now virtually non-existent (Snider 2003), and there have been very few such large scale surveys (see Slapper and Tombs 1999: 37–41).

Thus there is a tendency in corporate crime research towards studies of discrete crimes or groups of crimes. Typically, these crimes have been large-scale in nature, that is, involving significant amounts of financial loss, or large numbers of victims (most commonly, consumers, employees, or local residents), or with particularly symbolic political or popular effects. These studies go beyond stating the 'facts' of particular cases, but generally involve detailed *post hoc* social scientific reconstruction of events and processes surrounding a particular crime or group of crimes; somewhat differently, some of these studies are based upon intimate, after-the-event accounts by whistle-blowers or investigative journalists. The result is generally a detailed case history which facilitates understanding of the processes by which corporate crimes emerge, occur, and are responded to. Albeit presented in truncated and outline form, this is precisely one of the tasks of the cases here.

Case study research within corporate crime does have advantages. First, a series of discrete case studies can provide an overall insight into the enormous *range* of offences in which corporations and organisations can and do become implicated, from the well-known to the obscure, from the 'trivial' to the more obviously serious. Second, taken together, this work reinforces the fact that business offending results from almost every business activity, in almost every area of economic activity, amongst corporations and organisations of all sizes. Third, a series of case studies, each of which is ostensibly quite different in terms of industrial and geographical location, the key actors involved, the scale and nature of consequences, and so on, may generate recurrent themes from which at least tentative generalisations can be generated. As Braithwaite has argued, case studies – producing a 'qualitative understanding of the contours of corporate crimes and how they unfold' – are 'most likely to advance our understanding of corporate crime as a social phenomenon' (Braithwaite 1984: 8, 7; see also Coleman 1987: 429).

The construction of case studies of offences (and of types of offence or offending industries), often involves trawling for evidence and source material beyond the confines of the discipline of criminology. Research on, and evidence concerning, corporate crime, needs to be collated from a range of disciplines which have no explicit concern with either of what Garland has called the Lombrosian or governmental projects, and out of which contemporary criminology has emerged (Garland 1994). Thus the sources upon which we draw in constructing our cases, and indeed which we use more generally throughout this text, are not primarily criminological, indeed criminological sources are often in little evidence here. Studying safety crime means moving well beyond criminology, drawing upon literature in business, management and organisational studies, economics, history, political economy, politics, and sociology, and which makes reference to substantive areas of study such as industrial relations, business ethics and/or studies in the social responsibility of business, studies of regulation, science–technology policy, studies of corporate failures, disasters and crises, and studies of social movements and activist politics.

Of course, care must be taken in interpreting cases, since, as we have already noted here, using and working with case studies, particularly in the context of safety crimes, raises issues of reliability. Thus it is important to note that in contrast with other methods used in the social sciences, case studies rely upon sources of evidence commonly derived from investigative journalists and whistleblowers rather than sources that can more easily be represented as 'hard' academic research (although, see George and Bennett 2005). Dependency upon investigative sources and whistleblowing therefore invites charges of politicisation, polemics, and moralising (for a somewhat scathing attack around precisely such points, see Shapiro 1983). Moreover, each of the events described of course raise specific issues that relate to very specific, contingent, circumstances. Having said this, in several of the cases highlighted, the failure to heed the warnings of whistleblowers and concerned members of the public were key features of the circumstances leading to the crime. Often investigators' and whistleblowers' voices are ignored until after the event. Thus, although we have to recognise that those voices may not be completely impartial, this is no reason to continue to ignore them. Indeed, the great tragedy is that it often takes a fatal incident to sit up and take whistleblowers and other marginalised sources of warning seriously.

Conclusions drawn from any particular case study may not necessarily apply beyond the specifics of the case; 'the use of a case study can be diminished by a belief that the findings may be idiosyncratic' (Bryman 1988: 88). The cases (at least those of *incidents*) presented here are *atypical*: most safety crimes are mundane rather than exceptional, do not result in deaths, let alone multiple fatalities; most are not subject to any investigation, let alone legal proceedings; most do not register at all in terms of publicity. These very characteristics combine to make such incidents, which occur every day up and down the UK and, in fact, across the globe, simply invisible and thus not amenable to study. The fact that most of the cases presented here are not typical therefore does not undermine their usefulness as case studies, for, as we have argued above, to present a case study is not to claim representativeness. Further, to echo Braithwaite, above, there is still much to learn from surveying these cases. It is important, therefore, not to draw general rules cast in stone from cases, but rather to identify common themes and features of cases to enable us to open up questions about the circumstances of causation which might shed some light upon how we might achieve more effective prevention. This at the very least makes them social facts that are worthy of critical attention.

Why these as opposed to other cases? Several criteria informed our choice of cases, but two are worth highlighting. First, to construct a case requires that one knows about it and that one can find out more about it – in other words, it requires a level of visibility that most safety crimes, mundane and routine as these are, simply never achieve. Notwithstanding this obvious but important limitation for presenting a range of case studies, we have sought here to include the most infamous and internationally-recognised cases, alongside some which caused barely a ripple beyond the immediate vicinity within which they occurred, or the group of people most immediately affected. Second, taken collectively, we have sought to illustrate safety crimes in all their variety. Thus, in the following, there are cases where one or several workers are the victims, and others where the victims are or include consumers, local communities and/or the natural environment. Third, the cases illustrate a range of organisations as offenders – from the large multinational conglomerate through to smaller companies to those operating at the borders of the legal/illegal economy. Fourth, we have sought to include cases where legality arises intentionally alongside those where the key issue appears to be that of negligence. Fifth, and finally, an industry focus was taken, in the case of the construction industry, to highlight how the structure and culture of a sector can be, at the very least, crime-facilitative.

Our first case study, then, focuses upon an industry which appears potentially criminogenic, at least if occupational deaths and injuries are an index of safety offences, namely the construction industry. Six further cases focus upon discrete 'events', setting out briefly the circumstances surrounding: the gas leak at the Union Carbide Chemical plant in Bhopal, India; the capsizing of the cross-Channel passenger ferry the *Herald of Free Enterprise*; the fire and explosion on the Piper Alpha oil installation; the death of Simon Jones; the gas explosion in Larkhall, Scotland that killed a family of four; and the deaths of 23 Chinese cockle pickers at Morecambe Bay. And a final case study focuses on an ongoing series of safety violations at the Sonae Chipboard factory in Kirkby, Merseyside. In sum, these cases represent a range of incidents and contexts, the scale of deaths and injuries produced, their visibility, their industry, and even their geographical location. All have been subject to some kind of legal process which places them firmly within the principal concern of this book: safety crimes.

UK construction

Key causal issues highlighted in this case include: casualised, sub-contracted and increasingly migrant workforce; long and complex supply chains; legal/illegal business relationships; aggressive management; market pressures; industry norms; problems in regulatory processes (see Table 1).

As the Health and Safety Executive's[3] most recent annual report notes, the construction industry is probably the last remaining heavy industry of any size in Britain. It employs 2.2 million people, and contributes up to 10 per cent of GDP, making it the single biggest industry. And it is a growing industry with significant labour turnover which, according to the Construction Industry Training Board, 'needs at least 87,000 recruits a year' (Construction Skills Network, 2006). But it is also rather a peculiar sector – and these peculiarities tend to combine to make its workforce particularly vulnerable.

The industry is characterised by a large number of companies, most of them small, which are linked through complex systems of sub-contracting and long supply chains. Eighty-five per cent of the work in the industry is done by supply chain organisations, the majority of which are regional small- and medium-sized enterprises (SMEs). This makes locating responsibility and accountability, training, and unionisation all very problematic issues. Self-employment is significant in the sector, and it is growing, given the spread of 'Labour Only Sub-Contracting' (Anderson and Rogaly 2005: 33, and passim). High levels of sub-contracting, agency workers, LOSC (Labour Only Sub-Contracting) and self-employment come together to give the construction industry the highest proportion of full-time self-employed workers of any industry in the UK (London Assembly Health and Public Services Committee 2005: 10).

There are substantial numbers of migrant workers from the EU accession countries working in the construction industry in London, especially workers from Poland and the Czech Republic. New arrivals might well have difficulty understanding health and safety briefings reporting processes or their rights at work.[4] Employers may also employ them illegally, both as a means of reducing costs and as a way of driving down labour conditions in general on a site or a job. More generally, the industry has a highly mobile workforce. Construction workers tend to move from project to project and this may mean that injuries often go unreported, while it also means workers receive little or no safety training (ibid.).

There is a large informal construction sector, with some £4.5 billion to £10 billion construction work nationally undertaken 'cash in hand'. Companies who do not pay their taxes are also likely to have a 'less safe working environment' for their workers; further, the informal economy creates market conditions that put 'pressure on legitimate builders to cut corners in order to compete for work' (ibid.: 10). It is, therefore, a highly casualised industry, and casualisation is a major source of danger for workers: according to the Health and Safety Commission,[5] the annual injury rate to workers with short job tenure (less than six months) is 5.7 times that for workers whose job tenure is at least five years (Health and Safety

Commission, 2003a: 3), while over one in five of all reportable injuries are sustained by workers who have been with an employer for less than a year (ibid.). Further, we know that the risk of death and injury is far greater for self-employed workers (see Chapter 2). Little wonder, given the above, that the HSE has characterised the national construction industry in the following way: 'no entry threshold, highly fragmented, itinerant and casualised' (London Assembly Health and Public Services Committee 2005: 10).

Little wonder, too, that construction is also one of the UK's most dangerous sectors. The sector has a fatal injury rate of over five times the all-industry average, and is the sector with the highest number of deaths (Health and Safety Commission 2005a: 13).[6] The number of workers killed in the construction sector each year in Britain has remained in the region of around 70–80 since 1996/97. In London the construction sector employs 5 per cent of London's workers, but accounts for 50 per cent of fatal injuries and nearly 20 per cent of major injuries in the city's workplaces' (London Assembly Health and Public Services Committee 2005: 1). Moreover, the high level of self-employment drastically undermines reporting rates – by up to 95 per cent. Yet even the reported figures, if a vast under-estimate, obscure even greater levels of risk for some workers within the sector. As the Southern and Eastern Regional Trades Union Congress (2005) has recently noted, 'What must also be taken into account is that up to a third of workers within the sector are employed in office and desk-based work and, as such, are not subject to construction-specific hazards. As such, accident rates as a percentage of the total construction workforce should be considered with this in mind'. Thus the rate of fatal and serious injury varies significantly between occupations within the industry. The most dangerous trades include steel erectors (41.2), crane drivers (32.8), roofers and cladders (24.6) and scaffolders/steeple-jacks (21.2).[7]

The main causes of fatal injuires are: falling through fragile roofs and rooflights; falling from ladders, scaffolds and other work places; being struck by excavators, lift trucks or dumpers; being struck by falling loads and equipment; and being crushed by collapsing structures (www.hse.gov.uk/construction). In other words, these are incidents with mundane, and highly preventable, causes. As the employers' body, the Federation of Master Builders, put it, 'there is nothing intrinsic about construction that suggests that somebody has to die ... [yet the] culture has become so engrained in that construction is dangerous, therefore someone is always going to get hurt' (cited in London Assembly Health and Public Services Committee 2005: 10–11).

While we would resist arguments which reduced the levels of injury and death in any industry to 'culture' (see Beck and Woolfson 1999), what the above does point to is that construction is not intrinsically dangerous, rather the source of risk for workers being found in the organisation of the sector and in work therein. These are socially constructed, and can and do vary between time and place. A similar point has been made about the very different 'safety' records of the Norwegian and UK offshore oil industries, a very useful comparison since it spans effectively the same work in the same context, that is, the North Sea which, whilst clearly inhospitable, is not inherently dangerous in the sense that it necessarily produces high numbers of worker deaths and injuries. Thus Ryggvik (2000) suggests that improved offshore safety in Norway is particularly the result of rights for union representatives to stop work when they feel safety is jeopardised, as well as the maintenance of strong offshore unions with a comprehensive network of trade union-appointed safety representatives; this is in marked contrast to the strident anti-trades unionism of the UK sector (Whyte 1999a).

The very scale of the industry (both in terms of numbers employed and worksites), the high level of sub-contracting and self-employment, the relatively short-term nature of many construction projects, and the scale of the informal economy make the work of the HSE particularly difficult in this sector (London Assembly Health and Public Services Committee 2005). Research using HSE internal data for the years 1996–2001 found a 52 per cent decline in the numbers of inspection contacts across the sector (Unison/Centre for Corporate Accountability 2002). Notices and prosecutions are in decline across the sector. Thus data for the most recent year, 2003/04–2004/2005, shows a decline in all formal enforcement activity in the construction industry: from 3,487 notices in 2003/04 to 2,481 in 2004/05 (from 798 to 548 improvement notices, from 33 to 20 deferred prohibition notices, and from 2,656 to 1913 immediate prohibition notices), an overall fall of almost 40 per cent (adapted from www.hse.gov.uk/statistics /enforce/index-ld.htm). Data for the same years also shows a fall in offences prosecuted in the industry (from 617 to 550 in 2004/05) and in convictions secured (from 418 in 2003/04 to 396 in 2004/05).[8]

Yet these trends fly in the face of evidence of the scale of offending across the construction industry: the subject of frequent enforcement 'blitzes' by the HSE, one such blitz in March 2005, for example, saw 214 enforcement notices issued and work stopped on 244 sites in the course of 1,170 visits which had been heavily publicised in advance (Trades Union Congress 2005a). In October 2005, targeted inspections of 1,379 contractors, focusing on falls from low height in the industry, led to 134 prohibition notices and 36 improvement notices being issued related to working at height (www.hse.gov.uk/construction/fitout). A 2003 blitz, involving 1,429 site visits, resulted in 332 prohibition and 82 improvement notices being served. Thirteen potential prosecutions were also

a blitz earlier in the same year (June 2003), HSE concluded
ʒain, over a third of construction sites were well below stan-
h and Safety Executive 2003a).

dicating a high level of safety crime across the sector, a recent
ı the industry, drawn up having taken evidence from a range
of interested parties, has noted the existence of a 'combative culture'
within construction:

> Several organisations identified a 'competitive combative culture'
> within the industry, in which the cause of safety problems is obscured
> as companies seek to avoid financial or legal penalties. This culture
> tends to reduce reporting of injuries both on sites and to HSE. Others
> noted a persistent complacency about worker injury. (cited in London
> Assembly Health and Public Services Committee 2005: 10)

There are good reasons, then, for thinking that the construction industry
is criminogenic.

Bhopal, December 1984

Key causal issues highlighted in this case include: power and reach of multi-national corporations; 'developed' versus 'developing' economy safety standards; poor design, maintenance, and management; global market pressures; victim blaming; power to circumvent/prevent legal processes; safety and environmental offences; long-term victimisation – lack of compensation (see Table 1).

In Bhopal, India, a chemical plant, operated by Union Carbide of India
Limited (UCIL), a subsidiary of Union Carbide Corporation (UCC), used
highly toxic chemicals, including methyl iso-cyanate (MIC), to produce
pesticides. On the night of Sunday December 2, 1984, water entered an
MIC storage tank setting in process an exothermic reaction. Soon, a cocktail of poisonous gases, vapours and liquids, including up to forty tons of
MIC, was spewing into the atmosphere.[9]

The Indian Government initially put the number of acute deaths at
1,700, a figure subsequently revised to 3,329. Twenty years after the leak,
in 2004, Amnesty International estimated that there had been over 7,000
such deaths, with 15,000 people having since died from longer-term
effects. About 100,000 'survivors' will never work again. These 'human'
effects do not begin to account for the environmental damage caused by
the leak – and still being caused, since Dow Chemical, the world's largest
chemical company which effectively took over UCC in 2001, refuses to
accept any responsibility for 'cleaning up' the affected surroundings.

14

Union Carbide Corporation worked hard at influencing both public opinion and the legal process through a series of largely spurious arguments about the incident, the nature of the Indian company, and the Bhopal plant and its employees. These included claims that: Bhopal's safety standards were identical to the standards at UCC's plant in Institute, West Virginia; it had an excellent safety record, and the design of the plant's Standard Operating Procedures – UCC's responsibility – was basically sound; the production of MIC in India, the siting of the plant and the quality of the materials used, were all the responsibility of UCIL and the Indian State; UCIL was an independent company responsible for its own affairs; India's 'cultural backwardness' was responsible for the poor maintenance and management, poor planning procedures and the inadequate enforcement of safety regulations; and, later, that the accident was due to sabotage, on the part of 'Sikh extremists' and then an errant tea-boy. These are classic strategies in the naming of an event as an 'industrial accident'.

When the leak occurred, key safety features were either inoperable or inadequate to their task: the vent gas scrubber was turned off, the flare tower was inoperative, and hoses that might have doused the gas had insufficient water pressure to reach the stack from which it was escaping. Further, while the storage tanks should have been refrigerated, the refrigeration unit had been turned off to save $50 per week. There are also serious questions that need to be addressed regarding the plant design itself. Plant instrumentation was inadequate to monitor normal plant processes. The refrigeration plant at Bhopal, even when working, was not powerful enough to cool all the MIC stored there, and the vent gas scrubber and flare tower were only designed to deal with a limited type of emissions.

In these respects, Bhopal was demonstrably inadequate and inferior to Institute. Nevertheless, even with this inferior technology, far fewer people would have died if: the plant had not been sited near shanty towns; there had been adequate risk assessment, modelling and monitoring of discharges, and emergency planning and management; plant personnel, local medical services and the state and national government had known more about the nature and effects of the deadly gaseous emissions – in the immediate aftermath of the leak, UCC refused to divulge any information about the chemical content of the leaked substances, making it very difficult to properly treat victims.

Further, UCC clearly owned and controlled UCIL; UCC owned 50.9 per cent of UCIL and exercised significant control over it. UCIL's production and marketing strategies were dictated by the corporate strategies of UCC; UCC had dictated how and which chemicals were produced and stored; UCC monitored safety procedures and UCIL was forced to rely upon UCC for technological assistance and updates. Indeed, UCIL's production of the pesticides Temik and Sevin took place under commodified conditions: they were to be produced and sold in such a way that sub-divisions of the company showed a normal profitable return on investment. It is questionable whether it was possible for UCIL to do so safely. And market conditions were changing: following two decades of huge growth, the pesticides market in India had become extremely competitive by the end of the 1970s, and by the beginning of the 1980s pesticide demand in India had all but collapsed. Thus the industry became characterised by harsher and increasing levels of competition.

What is clear is that UCC seems to have been responsible for both the acts of commission and omission that created the Bhopal disaster. The contentions made by UCC concerning the Bhopal disaster in its publicity and its legal arguments do not stand up to scrutiny.

On visiting Bhopal in the aftermath of the leak, Warren Anderson, UCC's CEO, was arrested – but released days later, never to return to India. Although, in December 1991, the Chief Magistrate in Bhopal ordered Anderson and the company to appear in court on charges of culpable homicide, neither appeared and are listed as 'proclaimed absconders'. Overwhelmingly, legal activity centred on civil suits for compensation – and, following a flurry of such suits, the Indian Government assumed legal powers to secure damages in March 1985 on behalf of victims who were not consulted. The initial sum demanded by the Indian government was $3.3 billion; in 1989, UCC and the Indian government reached an out-of-court settlement of $470 million. This rendered UCC immune from all litigation, including criminal charges. The money was to compensate the families of the 3,329 deaths and 20,000 seriously injured officially recognised by the Indian government.

But the money has still has not been fully distributed. Union Carbide, now owned by Dow Chemical, paid out £250m in compensation to residents in 1989, but only a part of that sum has been distributed. In July 2004, India's Supreme Court ordered the government to distribute money held in the bank, currently worth £174m, to the 566,876 Bhopal survivors and relatives whose claims have been successfully lodged. As late as September 2004, around US$330 million remained held by the Reserve Bank of India.

The Herald of Free Enterprise, March 1987

Key causal issues highlighted in this case include: market pressures; industry norms; systematic failure to heed warnings; poor design, maintenance, and management; victim blaming; and failings in legal and regulatory processes (see Table 1).

The *Herald of Free Enterprise* was one of the largest roll-on, roll-off (ro-ro) sea ferries – so-called because vehicles drive in through the bow and out through the stern at the destination. But when using the Belgian port of Zeebrugge, where turnaround time was longer than on other routes due to the design of loading facilities, it was commonplace to leave the port with the bow doors open – even though it was the formal responsibility of the assistant bosun to see them closed (Boyd 1992). Thus when the ferry left port, with its bow doors open on March 6, 1987, water began to flood through the open bow doors across the main car deck, which, as with other ro-ro ferries, lacked dividing bulkheads. The Herald quickly became unstable, and capsized in about 90 seconds. The sea was calm and there was only a light breeze, 193 passengers and crew members died.[10]

The Channel between England and continental Europe is one of the world's busiest waterways. During the 1980s, passenger ferries were facing the threat of new competition. Sealink UK Ltd had been privatised by the neo-liberal Thatcher Government in 1984, opening the market up to greater competition between operators. Reductions in crew numbers, modernisation of port facilities to speed ferry turnaround time, building of new, larger ro-ro ferries, and a range of cut-price fares began to characterise the market. And, after 1986, such trends were exacerbated when British and French Governments agreed to construct the Channel Tunnel, to be operative by 1994.

The findings of the Court of Formal Investigation into the *Herald* capsizing, held in 1987, were remarkable for their content and tone. It is worth quoting one key, and infamous, passage at length:

> ... a full investigation into the circumstances of the disaster leads inexorably to the conclusion that the underlying or cardinal faults lay higher up in the company. The Board of Directors did not appreciate their responsibility for the safe management of their ships. They did not apply their minds to the question: What orders should be given for the safety of our ships?

> The directors did not have any proper comprehension of what their duties were. There appears to have been a lack of thought about the way in which the Herald ought to have been organized for the Dover–Zeebrugge run. All concerned in management, from the members of the Board of Directors down to the junior superintendents, were guilty of fault in that all must be regarded as sharing responsibility for the failure of management. From top to bottom the body corporate was infected with the disease of sloppiness .... It

17

is only necessary to quote one example of how the standard of management fell short .... It reveals a staggering complacency. (Department of Transport 1987: Para 14.1)

The disaster had significant legal consequences. The inquest held later in 1987 into the capsizing returned verdicts of 'unlawful killing' – despite the coroner instructing such a verdict inadmissible – and created the possibility of a criminal prosecution. A manslaughter case – against P&O European Ferries, owners of the *Herald*, and seven individuals – did follow, but the judge closed proceedings before the prosecution had finished presenting its case on the basis that the legal test under current manslaughter law would not be met in this case. Indeed, whilst avoiding criminal sanction, the chairman of P&O European Ferries, Sir Jeffrey Stirling, became Lord Stirling in Prime Minister Thatcher's 1990 resignation honours.

This case was significant for several reasons. It had a symbolic significance, in several respects: due to the sheer scale of the tragedy, due to the images of it that pervaded the media of this enormous, everyday piece of technology capsized, and also due to the irony of its name – *Herald of Free Enterprise* – so that its sinking could be viewed as emblematic of the problems created for public and worker safety by a Government-led enterprise culture which seemed to valorise profit *and* risk taking. Further, in the failure of the prosecution, the problems of successfully holding large, complex organisations to account for the production of death was raised up political and popular agendas. The ensuing outcry was one factor leading, in 1996, to new proposals for a new law on 'corporate killing' – though at the time of writing, this has still to pass through the UK parliament.

Design changes to ro-ro ferries had been called for in 1985, following the capsizing of the vessel *European Gateway* off Harwich in 1982. Six people were killed in that incident. Following Zeebrugge, the United Nations body, the International Maritime Organisation (IMO) convened a special conference and eventually passed the Safety of Life at Sea Regulations (SOLAS 90). Regulation 8 of SOLAS 90 states that all ro-ro ferries must be able to stand upright long enough for passengers to evacuate. Although this applied automatically to vessels built after April 1990, it did not apply to those built before that date – it was argued that the cost of installing bulkheads on existing craft would, if passed on to passengers, increase fares by up to 35 cents per ticket. The standards agreed as suitable in SOLAS 90 were repeatedly postponed. They came into force in October 2005.

Yet ro-ro ferries seem inherently unsafe. Between 1989 and 1994, Lloyds register recorded 4,583 lives lost at sea – a third of which, 1,544, were lost in incidents involving ro-ro ferries, despite these being but a small fraction of the world's fleet. Then, infamously, on 28 September,

1994, the ro-ro ferry *Estonia* capsized in the Baltic sea killing – officially – 852 people (small children were not registered as passengers so the toll could have been significantly more). Water entered the vessel through defective bow doors. Most of these people died in the vessel because they did not have sufficient time to get on to the upper deck. Six weeks after this sinking, a report from the Department of Transport's Marine Safety Agency discovered that of the 107 ro-ro ferries it had inspected, bow door faults were found in one in three vessels.

In 2002, P&O announced a widespread reorganisation, cutting its fleet of ships from 24 to 17 and ending several 'uneconomic routes' – including services from Dover to Zeebrugge. P&O's ferry services director, Graeme Dunlop, stated at that time, eight years after the opening of the channel tunnel that, 'We knew the tunnel was going to open and we knew it was going to grab a share of the market. Our strategy was to increase the size of the market, so we each got a slice of a bigger pie'.

Piper Alpha, July 1988

Key causal issues highlighted in this case include: casualised/sub-contracted labour; aggressive management; industry norms; systematic failure to heed warnings; political economy of speed; global market pressures; failings in legal and regulatory processes (see Table 1).

Around 10 p.m. on 6 July, 1988, a series of explosions tore through the Occidental-owned Piper Alpha oil production platform in the Northern Sector of the British North Sea. One hundred and sixty seven were killed on Piper Alpha; 61 workers survived. Thirty bodies were never recovered from the North Sea after Occidental declined to pay for the excavation of the platform from the sea bed.

Subsequent accounts of events following the explosions indicate a high degree of management contribution to the events. Negligent emergency provision and under-maintained critical safety systems made a catastrophic situation worse: emergency lighting failed; there were hardly any torches available to the crew; each of the lifeboats was located in the same section of the platform, which also happened to be inaccessible; and no provision had been made for an alternative escape route to the sea. Most people on the platform gathered at the emergency muster point, the accommodation module, which due to its location above the gas compression module also happened to be one of the areas on the platform most exposed to fire and explosion. The accommodation module, constructed from wood and fibre-glass, quickly began to burn. The water deluge system – the platform's main defence against fire – failed. When two life rafts were launched, they failed to inflate. The standby safety vessel, a converted fishing boat, had no medical supplies to treat survivors as they were pulled from the sea, and the Tharos, Occidental's state-of-the-art floating fire engine, could not muster sufficient water pressure to reach the flames.

Occidental's senior management had been warned by their own consultants that the platform would not withstand prolonged exposure to high intensity fire. It was a warning that they chose to ignore since the company's assessment of the risk of such an incident occurring did not justify the expense of refitting the platform with high-grade fireproofing. The sequence of events that followed the initial explosions illustrate the strictly observed 'production first' dictum of offshore management. Managements on platforms connected by the same pipeline chain, the Tartan and the Claymore, declined to shutdown production, and instead continued to feed the blaze with oil as they obediently awaited permission for a costly closure of the pipeline from senior management onshore. There was no prosecution of Occidental, a firm that already had a criminal record for killing one of its workers in September 1987.

Piper Alpha, rather that being understood as a one-off, unpredictable event, should be understood as the culmination of a generalised safety crisis in the industry. The origins of this crisis are in the failure of both the regulatory system and the operating oil companies' management regimes. Also of key significance was the political economy that ensured the oil was to function as the motor of the neo-liberal restructuring of the UK economy in the 1970s and 1980s. This had three principle effects. First, as Carson (1982) argued, the conditions within which British oil policy developed are best described as 'the political economy of speed' whereby the speedy development of an industry – central to offsetting Britain's economic decline in the 1970s – came at great cost to the workers, measured in abnormally high rates of injury and death in the sector (11 times the fatality rate in the construction industry and nearly nine times the rate in mining). A related effect was regulatory acceptance, the 'institutionalisation of tolerance' of this appalling toll, indicated by the legal anomalies, jurisdictional gaps, and low level of resources available to the regulatory regime.

Second, the particular features of the labour process in the offshore oil sector were a major contributory factor. The use of casualised and sub-contracted labour was quickly established by the offshore drilling and operating companies in the early years of the industry. The legacy of this structure was that, over the years, the percentage of offshore workers employed as sub-contractors has remained at between 80 per cent and 90 per cent. In the pre-Piper Alpha period, workers were usually employed on short-term contracts that often lasted no longer than a few weeks or months, and contained few contractual rights. Trade union organisation was virtually unheard of. Brutal management styles ensured that those who were found to have trade union sympathies, or those who vocally expressed concerns about safety were routinely 'NRBd' (told they were not required back). Eighty three per cent of workers on board Piper Alpha on the night of the disaster were sub-contracted. The marginalisation of workers' expertise and knowledge of safety in the offshore management regime was to have catastrophic consequences. In the months preceding the disaster, management ignored a series of reports of gas leaks by workers on the Piper Alpha. On the day of the disaster, two workers had complained about a gas smell. Although one received permission by the platform safety officer to down tools, management had apparently declined to interfere with work routines and conduct an investigation.

Third, the contractual subordination of workers as a result of the offshore labour market structure had been exacerbated by a chain of events in the market which shook the industry in the mid-1980s. The collapse of the OPEC cartel quota system in 1985 (the average oil price per barrel plummeted from more than $30 in November 1985 to around $10 in April 1986) had a dramatic effect on the industry. In order to defend profit levels, oil companies slashed their operational budgets by between 30 and 40 per cent across the board. The impact on the workforce was devastating. Wage levels fell dramatically and 1906 saw up to 22,000 jobs lost in the industry. The operators' response to the oil price crash had far reaching implications for workplace safety in the industry. Funding allocated to ensuring the regular maintenance of plant equipment suffered the same fate.

Fatality and injury rates remain abnormally high in the industry, and, despite the introduction of some limited improvements to hardware and, a new regulatory regime following the official inquiry into the disaster, the workforce remains largely casualised and lacks trade union safety rights. In the years since Piper Alpha, the workforce has remained under pressure as a result of successive cost-cutting exercises aimed at recuperating the costs resulting from Piper Alpha.

Simon Jones, April 1998

Key causal issues highlighted in this case include: inter-firm relationships; casualised/sub-contracted labour; government sub-contracting out of employment responsibilities; changes in welfare state; failings in legal and regulatory processes (see Table 1).

In April 1998, Simon Jones signed on for casual work in Brighton with a local employment agency, Personnel Selection. According to Emma Ainsley, a friend, Simon had taken the job 'to get the dole of his back'.[11]

Simon was required to register with an employment agency, Personnel Selection, whose job it was to find him work. Under the Job Seekers Allowance scheme – part of New Labour's broader Welfare to Work strategy – claimants must continually demonstrate availability for and willingness to work; these conditions make refusing offers of work liable to lead to a withdrawal of state 'benefits'. Simon's first job with Personnel Selection was at Shoreham Docks, working for Euromin Limited, a Dutch cargo company. He went to work in a ship's hold, unloading its cargo. Within an hour of arriving for his first day of work, he was dead. His head had been crushed and partially severed when a three tonne 'crane' grab closed around it.[12] The grab should not have been there; it certainly should not have been open. The work required chains which should have been fastened to a hook instead. Changing back between a grab and a hook costs time and therefore money. Ten weeks prior to the incident, under Mr Martell's instruction, the chain had been welded to the inside of the grab so that the crane could be used for either purpose without delay (Kelso 2001). After Simon's death, co-workers were immediately required to clear up blood and debris from the bags of aggregates that were being shifted in the hold, and then to continue working. Emma Aynsley has since said that

> Immediately that me and Simon's family found out that he was working inside of a ship we all felt, as his mother put it, this wasn't an accident, because accidents are things that are avoidable and Simon should never, ever have been put in that situation.

As one of the campaigners in the Simon Jones Memorial Campaign said subsequently, in a strikingly clear analogy, it was like asking someone without a driving licence to drive an articulated lorry.

No prosecution was ever taken against Personnel Selection, though they are covered by the legal requirement to ensure the suitability of work which they assign or offer. Initially, the CPS also declined to prosecute Euromin, the firm for which the student was working (at just over £4 per hour). This is despite the fact that on visiting the scene of the death, the HSE issued two Prohibition notices – regarding the use of the crane – and an Improvement notice requiring the training and supervision of new workers.

A protracted and high-profile campaign by the Simon Jones Memorial Campaign developed. This involved a range of methods: lobbying via letters and phone calls; when the CPS and DPP initially declined to proceed with any case against Euromin or James Martell, legal pressure from lawyer Louise Christian – and an eventual judicial review of the decision not to prosecute; and various forms of direct action, such as occupying the Department of Trade and Industry and the offices of Personnel Selection, picketing the CPS offices and closing Southwark Bridge and the road outside the headquarters of the HSE in London.[13] In March 2000, at judicial review, two high court judges overturned the decisions of the DPP and

CPS not to prosecute. They stated that these had both behaved 'irrationally' by concluding that there was no realistic chance of conviction, and that their decision was based upon a misinterpretation of the law; they were directed to reconsider 'with dispatch' (Brooks 2001). In December 2000, the DPP reversed its decision and announced that James Martell and Euromin Limited. were to be tried for manslaughter and corporate manslaughter. On 29 November, 2001, Martell and Euromin were cleared of manslaughter; Euromin was fined £50,000 for two H&S offences. During the trial the judge described Euromin's and Mr Martell's attitude to safety as 'absolutely deplorable' and as giving 'wholly insufficient thought and attention' to safety. He also stated that the method of attaching bags to a hook welded to the grab should never have been used (ibid.).

Despite this, in his summing up the judge emphasised Martell's good character and, typically in cases of business offending where prosecutions are rare so that there is a high chance that companies and individuals will have no previous convictions, his 'clean record'. Speaking outside the Old Bailey after the verdict, Tim Jones, Simon's brother, criticised the judge for accepting Martell's claims of good character:

> Martell who, from the witness stand, said he would willingly send one of his own sons or his own daughter to work in the same conditions that killed my brother – is that his idea of a good character? He said that because Martell had no previous convictions, that he was unlikely to offend again, and that because he had no previous convictions, that made him a good character. (see also Brooks 2001)

In many ways, Simon's death was a routine killing. Hundreds of workers and members of the public die each year in Britain in work-related incidents. Rarely do these deaths make the headlines – unless they come in the form of 'disaster', that is, a multiple-fatality incident. But if it was routine, then Simon's death was also exceptional in several ways, certainly in its aftermath in terms of the campaign that was fought by the Memorial Campaign (friends, family, safety campaigners); and in successfully forcing the DPP and CPS to about-turn on their refusal to prosecute, it was far from routine. And, even though the case 'failed', a prosecution for manslaughter following a death at work is rare indeed – at the time of writing there have been only about 40 cases taken against individuals and/or companies in English and Welsh legal history;[14] most have been unsuccessful (see www.corporateaccountability.org/manslaughter/cases/main.htm).

The Simon Jones Memorial Campaign based their fight around the issue of casualisation – a growing feature of working life in neo-liberal Britain. For the campaign, casualisation translates into people being 'forced into low paid jobs with little or no training, no job security, no sick pay and no holiday pay means bigger profits for companies'. As one of the campaigners stated, 'Ten years ago, if you were going to work in a dock, you would had to have some training and knowledge. Nowadays, with the growth of casualisation, the search for cheap and throwaway labour, you have people who are doing work on docks that they have no training to do'. Casualisation, short-term employment, and agency work are all common features of the deregulated labour market. They are also furthered by a benefits system which forces claimants to take work – even work for which they are patently 'unfit' – on threat of withdrawal of financial support from the state. Finally, the role of Personnel Selection – acting as the 'middle-man' between the state and Euromin – is also symptomatic of a state contracting out its functions to the private sector. In short, Simon's death is only explicable in the context of neo-liberalism. It was quite literally neo-liberalism that, to refer back to Emma Aynsley's words, above, 'put [Simon] in that situation'; prior to neo-liberalism Simon Jones simply could not have been where he was to lose his life: in the heyday of the welfare state, there would have been no compulsion to work in exchange for benefit entitlement, no role for private companies in finding that work, and no chance of him working on the docks without having been certified as competent to do so under the national Dock Labour Scheme (Lavalette and Kennedy 1996). In other words, although a routine killing, Simon's death is only comprehensible in the context of wider social, political and economic trends. The vulnerability which exposed Simon Jones to circumstances that led to his death was created through structural factors.

Transco, December 1999

Key causal issues highlighted in this case include: poor design, maintenance, and management; market pressures; systematic failure to heed warnings; victim blaming; failings in legal and regulatory processes (see Table 1).

On the 22 December, 1999, Andrew and Janette Findlay and their children Stacey and Daryll were killed when a gas explosion completely destroyed their home at 42 Carlisle Road in Larkhall, Scotland. When investigators turned up at the wreckage of the house, they closed the 'slam shut' system to close off the supply of gas into the site of the explosion, but gas fires continued to burn as a result of 'gas coming up from the ground' (*BBC News*, 18 February, 2005). Readings taken at the front of the house registered 100 per cent gas. The explosion was conclusively found to have been caused by a leaking iron gas main which was subsequently found by investigators to have been severely corroded and had a total of 19 leaks (ibid.). Gas leaking from the mains had found its way under the kitchen of the house and ignited.

The prosecution in a subsequent court case alleged that Transco had failed to properly monitor its own records which showed that the mains had leaked 27 times. It was also recorded that escapes of gas at Carlisle Road had been reported on 13 occasions between July 1988 and December 1999. In a subsequent case on the 22 October, 2000, a couple in Dundee were killed in a gas explosion caused by a fractured iron gas main, the operation and maintenance for which Transco was responsible. Despite the close similarity with the Larkhall explosion, no criminal charges were laid against the company. Instead, the company came to an agreement with the HSE the following year on a new timescale for replacing cast iron mains piping (Health and Safety Executive 2004a).

Faulty gas mains are likely to continue to cause similar incidents in the UK. Most iron gas mains date from the Victorian and pre-war eras. The previously nationalised British Gas began to replace the corroding iron mains in the 1970s and since privatisation, this has primarily been the responsibility of Transco, the single largest gas supply company. In the 1980s, Transco began replacing the pipeline system with iron ductile mains which were subsequently also found to be at high risk of corrosion.

Britain's corroding system of gas mains have not been helped by Transco's failure to both replace and maintain its pipeline network. In the year following the Larkhall explosion, Transco were criticised by the industry regulator Ofgem, for failing to reach its target to replace corroding pipelines by 29 per cent (Hodge 2002). In 1997, Transco laid off 1,000 maintenance workers. Four years later, it admitted that it needed approximately 1,000 more workers to maintain the safety of the gas supply network (Lawrence 2001). In early 2002, Transco announced a 17 per cent reduction in its staff, cuts that amounted to the loss of 2,400 jobs.

In February 2002, Transco became the first company in Scotland to be charged with culpable homicide, the Scottish equivalent of the offence of corporate manslaughter in England and Wales. The prosecution had proceeded on the basis of a High Court ruling that it was not a requirement in Scots law for an individual to first be identified before the company could be found guilty of culpable homicide (see the *Herald of Free Enterprise* case). However, a Court of Appeal ruling dismissed the Crown's case that corporate liability could be imputed by aggregating several decisions that took place in the company in several different meetings by different company officers. The Court of Appeal effectively ruled that a corporate homicide case in Scotland also rests on the principle of identification and dismissed the charge of culpable homicide against Transco (see www.corporateaccountability.org/manslaughter-scot.htm). The failure of the corporate homicide case, the first of its kind in Scotland, appears to have severely dented the prospect of subsequent cases of corporate homicide being prosecuted, even in cases of small or medium-sized firms where identification would be less of an obstacle. There have been no attempts to prosecute such a case since. In December 2004, the Scottish Executive announced their intention to introduce a new offence of corporate killing.

Although the homicide case failed, the thoroughness of the corporate homicide investigation between the HSE and the police revealed serious failings in the company's management of risk to the public. This was important in a the subsequent prosecution of Transco for breaching the Health and Safety at Work Act at Larkhall. In this case, the company attempted to attribute blame for the explosion not to their own failings, but to a leak inside the house. It was an attempt to deflect responsibility that was not looked upon favourably by the court. Sentencing Transco in the High Court, Lord Calloway noted:

> the company have chosen to attempt to blame the explosion on an internal pipe leak (that is, something for which they are not responsible) despite overwhelming evidence to the contrary including the views of their own employees on the site after the explosion. There was no evidence at all in this case that such an internal leak had occurred. That aspect of the defence by the company serves only to demonstrate that the corporate mind of Transco has little or no remorse for this tragedy which, they ought at least now to accept, was exclusively of their own creation (*BBC News*, 25 August, 2005).

The company's records falsely showed that the mains outside the Findlay's house in Larkhall had been replaced by plastic pipes (*BBC Frontline Scotland*, 29 November, 2000).

The company was fined £15 million, a record fine for a health and safety offence, which Calloway described as '... an appropriate penalty for a serious failure over many years of one of our privatised utilities, a company in whom the public put their faith and to whom they pay substantial sums of money to ensure the safe transportation of their fuel'. The fine, despite its size, equated to less than 2 per cent of the company's post-tax profits for the previous year. In any case, because the company is able to choose how to spread the cost of the fine, the burden could be passed on to its consumers or workers in the form of higher charges or job cuts. Following the imposition of the fine, a company spokesperson declined to apologise for its crime (The *Observer*, 28 August, 2005).

Morecambe Bay Cockle Pickers, February 2004

Key causal issues highlighted in this case include: power and reach of multinational corporations; casualised/sub-contracted labour; legal/illegal business relationships; systematic failure to heed warnings; victim blaming; global market pressures; changes in welfare state; failings in legal and regulatory processes (see Table 1).

On 5 February 2004, 23 cockle pickers were drowned at Morecambe Bay on the Lancashire coast. This was the worst single industrial disaster in Britain since Piper Alpha. The dead were all immigrant workers from China who had been put to work on the highly profitable cockle beds of the Fylde coast. Two of the bodies were never found.

The tides in Morecambe bay are notoriously quick and the area was known for difficult currents and quicksands. On the day of the disaster, the tide times allowed only three hours of work before dusk. Because of high tides and weather forecasts, most of the British groups of cocklers had left the Bay at 5 p.m., the time that the Chinese workers arrived. The Chinese cocklers were organised by a 'gangmaster', Lin Liang Ren, who was responsible for feeding and housing the cocklers and supplying them with waterproof clothes and tools. On the night of the disaster, Lin Liang Ren drove the cocklers across the mud flats, several miles from the shore. The cocklers were caught in the dark in the midst of rapidly rising tides and although they managed to use mobile phones to call the shore, only one worker was rescued from the water. In March 2006, Lin Liang Ren was convicted for the manslaughter of 21 cockle pickers. The Liverpool Bay Fishing company that bought the cockles from Lin to sell on to larger producers was cleared of facilitating the crime.

There had been several clear warnings that had gone unheeded. In June 2003, the local MP Geraldine Smith had written to the Home Office with concerns that inexperienced Chinese cocklers were being employed on a fifth of the wages of British workers and that they were being exposed to dangers that experienced cocklers would not allow. A near miss, when 40 workers had to be rescued just six weeks before the disaster was reported and widely known about. Although the dangers to which Chinese cocklers were being exposed had been brought to the attention of the industry association responsible for issuing permits (the North Wales and North West Sea Fisheries Committee), no action was taken by the industry to limit those risks (*Liverpool Daily Post*, 7 December, 2005).

An ongoing dispute between British and Chinese gangs of cocklers intensified during the months and weeks leading up to the disaster. The dispute was partly about the territorial rights to work the bay, but was also fuelled by the assumption that Chinese labourers were more likely to take risks than locally-established cocklers. In the week before the disaster, buyers were being asked by British cocklers not to purchase cockles harvested by Chinese gangs (Herbert and Nash 2004).

The key legislative response to the Morecambe Bay disaster was the Gangmasters (Licencing) Act which passed into law in July 2004. The Act was supported by the government, the trade unions, all of the major supermarkets and the National Farmers Union. The new law stipulated that 'gangmasters' (employers that organise gangs of casual labourers, normally paid on a piece-work basis, in the agricultural industry) must now formally register with the Gangmasters Licensing Authority before they can operate. The Act created a skeleton regulatory structure for gang labour, but it did not specify a legal minimum for safety conditions, training or housing for immigrant workers. In the UK regulatory system, the HSE is responsible for monitoring safety standards in both illegal and legal enterprises. In practice, however, HSE has neither the resources nor the political will to inspect and investigate unregistered enterprises and seek compliance or take enforcement action in this sector. In the immediate aftermath of Morecambe Bay, the HSE carried out inspections and drew up safety guidance for the cockling industry. Yet the regulatory agency lacks the capacity to provide a sustained regulatory presence in the agricultural industries in which immigrant workers are concentrated.

The Trades Union Congress (TUC) estimates that around 2.6 million immigrant workers currently work in the UK and that only 1 per cent of newly immigrant workers are members of trade unions (Trades Union Congress 2003a). Lack of trade union membership is compounded by a lack of rights to minimal financial support. Immigrant workers are therefore easily recruited into the most casualised, low paid and dangerous work. The Transport and General Workers' Union estimates that after accommodation and travel, some migrant workers earn as little as 78p per hour and it is normal for wages to be paid below the legal minimum (*BBC News*, 25 February, 2004). It is likely that most of those that died had to been forced to work in the industry in order to repay the expenses of their passage to the UK. According to evidence revealed in court all of those who died had been smuggled into Britain and some owed up to £20,000 to people-smugglers (The *Guardian*, 25 March, 2005). In this sense, their position as workers can be described as 'indentured labour'. The immediate response of the UK government was to blame the workers for coming here to work in the first place. Home Secretary Charles Clarke and other government ministers argued that an ID card system would have protected migrant workers like those who were killed at Morecambe Bay because it would have prevented them entering the country and remaining here undetected (*The Times*, 20 December, 2004). Clarke's response echoed that of the tabloid newspapers in Britain which explained the cause of the disaster as the rise in illegal immigration as opposed to the absence of any safety controls. Morecambe Bay was therefore read as an 'immigration' or 'asylum' problem, rather than a failure of the health and safety regime.

A dramatic change in market conditions in the global market for cockles also helps us understand the broader economic pressures which speeded up the harvest. In 2002, an oil tanker, the *Prestige*, sunk off the west coast of Spain resulting in a massive oil slick. There was a subsequent banning of all fishing and shellfish harvest along the western and northern coasts of Spain which created a rise in the demand for cockles in the Spanish market. The Spanish company Conservas Dani bought a family-run firm based in Wales, Jones, in 2002 which had previously preferred to deal with established cocklers. Conservas Dani's arrival in Britain intensified demand and created new opportunities for gangmasters employing Chinese workers (Herbert and Nash 2004). The Morecambe Bay disaster can therefore be understood as resulting partly from pressures linked to changes in global markets and the role of transnational corporations in intensifying those markets.

The risks to workers in Morecambe Bay remain acute. In March 2006, more than two years after the disaster, the Royal National Lifeboat Institute reported that half of its 100 emergency call-outs in the Morecambe Bay area since the 2004 disaster were cockling related (*BBC News*, 24th March, 2006).

Sonae

Key causal issues highlighted in this case include: state support for investment of company; frequent offending ('recidivism'); safety and environmental offences; failings in legal and regulatory process; aggressive management; perceived conflict between safety and jobs (See Table 1).

In 1999, the Duke of Edinburgh opened a chipboard factory, run by Sonae UK, in Kirkby, Merseyside. As well as being the world's largest manufacturer of wood panels, Sonae – a Portuguese-based conglomerate – has major commercial interests in retail, telecommunications and a range of services. The new factory was located in Northwood, a poor ward in a poor town (Kirkby) in a poor borough (Knowsley). For example, in the Office of Deputy Prime Minister's list of the worst wards in the UK for employment in 2000, three wards in Knowsley – Longview, Princess and Northwood – were listed in the worst six, while on the Index of Multiple Deprivation, which includes indices for crime, health, housing, education and access to local services, Longview was fourth, Princess eighth and Northwood twentieth. Little wonder that the plant – employing 200-plus workers – was established with the financial and political backing of several public authorities, including Knowsley Borough Council, nor perhaps that it was awarded a grant of £1.95 million, by Peter Mandelson, as Secretary of State for Trade and Industry. The new factory had enormous economic, social and political significance for a regenerating town and region.

However, since its opening, the plant has been beset by health concerns among workers and by environmental fears among residents, and indeed a series of legal actions against it. For example, in 2003, the company received a fine of £37,000 after pleading guilty to five pollution offences.[15] Alongside these problems, the plant also has an extremely poor safety record – upon which this case study shall focus. A listing of key incidents and enforcement action illustrates this clearly, while also making it hard to resist the conclusion that, if the *Oxford English Dictionary* defines a recidivist as 'one who habitually relapses into crime', then that label applies to Sonae – even if it is almost entirely reserved, in popular and academic usage, to individual, lower-class offenders.

As early as April 2000, the HSE had instituted a prosecution after a Sonae employee, Ian Fairclough, had become trapped in the clamping mechanism of a Dieffenbacher hydraulic press. He suffered serious crush injuries to his arm and chest when he entered the line to release a trapped board and became trapped himself when the line activating the board was released. Sonae was fined £15,000 and ordered to pay £16,703 costs (*Liverpool Echo*, 25 February, 2003). Mr Fairclough was off work for more than three months, was left with a disability down his right side and – three years later, at the time of the prosecution – still needed treatment for post traumatic stress disorder. The judge said: 'It is important that firms such as Sonae do not sacrifice safety for profits. In this case, more care should have been taken and more precautions put in place to ensure such accidents do not happen' (ibid.).

Between October 2000 and April 2001, six over-three-day injuries and seven major injuries[16] at the site were reported to the HSE. In April 2001, Michael McNamara broke a leg after he caught it in a piece of machinery he was trying to unblock. On 20 May 2003, Sonae was fined £35,000 and ordered to pay £6,417.90 in costs, following successful prosecution by the HSE for two offences under the Health and Safety at Work Act 1974 related to this incident. Ian Connor from the HSE said:

> It is a lesson not just for Sonae, but for all employers to assess the risks and make sure proper safeguards are in place, as well as making sure employees are adequately trained and supervised ... The combination of a lack of safeguards with the lack of training and supervision left this an accident waiting to happen.[17]

In September 2001, there was a large fire at the factory, to which seventy firefighters attended. In the early hours (around 5.15 a.m.) of 17 December 2001, there was an explosion followed by a fire at the plant. No one was injured (*Liverpool Echo*, 17 December, 2001). Then, in June 2002, there was another dust explosion at the Sonae plant. Worker John Thomas's life was 'saved' when firefighters took him from the fire, though he was taken to hospital 'seriously ill' (*Liverpool Echo*, 3 June, 2002) with 'head, chest and back injuries' (*Liverpool Daily Post*, 27 July, 2002). He subsequently recovered. On 10 July 2006, Sonae was fined £70,000 and ordered to pay £77,046 costs at Liverpool Crown Court after pleading guilty to a charge arising from this incident. At the conclusion of the case, the HSE noted that as well as Mr Thomas being injured, 'many others were placed at risk and very substantial damage was caused to the premises'. HSE Inspector Tim Beaumont, who headed up the investigation, added, 'The basic problem uncovered by our investigation was that during the design and construction of the factory in 2000, Sonae did not take an overall view of safety in connection with the manufacturing process.'[18]

Safety 'problems' continued after the two fires and explosions in 2001. On 14 June 2002, a worker was run over at the plant by a reversing fork-lift truck. This led to a HSE prosecution in December 2004, which resulted in a fine of £12,000 and costs of £13,099.[19] In addition to the incidents noted above and the four HSE prosecutions, the HSE has also taken formal enforcement action at a quite staggering rate given what is known about the preferred modus operandi of the HSE and its inspectorates (see Chapters 4 and 7):[20]

- in May 2001, an improvement notice was issued on work in confined spaces;
- in September 2001, a prohibition notice was issued on the wood chip fuel feed area following an explosion;
- in November 2001, an improvement notice concerning automatic self-propelled transfer carriages was issued;
- a prohibition notice was issued on 25 June 2002, prohibiting the restarting of the plant involved in a recent explosion until a suitable and sufficient assessment of the risks associated with this plant was carried out;
- also in June 2002, an improvement notice on the safe use of industrial lift trucks was issued.[21]

A further five prohibition notices were served on the plant between 11 July 2002 and 15 October 2002.[22]

Then, in October 2003, a worker became trapped for around an hour, 50 feet in the air after being caught in a conveyor belt (*Liverpool Echo*, 28 October, 2003). He suffered serious leg injuries (*Liverpool Echo*, 29 October, 2003). By October 2003, Knowsley Council were reported as giving Sonae

'42 days to improve or face a £50,000 fine' – and the following summer local MP George Howarth demanded the closure of the factory (*Liverpool Echo*, 30 July, 2004). The factory continues to operate.

Safety crimes in outline

The above cases have been presented schematically only. But in presenting them, not only have we been able to mark out the broad territory with which this text is concerned, but we have also begun to highlight some key, recurrent themes which seem to arise in any *post hoc* analysis of a specific safety crime. These are presented in outline form in Table 1.

Table 1 Key causal issues highlighted in case studies

Case	Key Issues Highlighted
UK Construction	casualised, sub-contracted and increasingly migrant workforce long and complex supply chains legal/illegal business relationships aggressive management market pressures industry norms problems in regulatory process
Bhopal	power and reach of multinational corporations 'developed' versus 'developing' economy safety standards poor design, maintenance, management global market pressures victim blaming power to circumvent/prevent legal process safety *and* environmental offences long-term victimisation – lack of compensation
Herald of Free Enterprise	market pressures industry norms systematic failure to heed warnings poor design and maintenance, management victim blaming failings in legal and regulatory processes

Table 1 continued

Case	Key Issues Highlighted
Piper Alpha	casualised/sub-contracted labour aggressive management industry norms systematic failure to heed warnings political economy of speed global market pressures failings in legal and regulatory processes
Simon Jones	inter-firm relationships casualised/sub-contracted labour government sub-contracting out of employment responsibilities changes in welfare state failings in legal and regulatory processes
Transco	poor design and maintenance, management market pressures systematic failure to heed warnings victim blaming failings in legal and regulatory processes
Morecambe Bay	power and reach of multinational corporations casualised/sub-contracted labour legal/illegal business relationships systematic failure to heed warnings victim blaming global market pressures changes in welfare state failings in legal and regulatory processes
Sonae	state support for investment of company frequent offending recidivism safety *and* environmental offences failings in legal and regulatory processes aggressive management perceived conflict between safety and jobs

We wish finally to emphasise that despite these cases spanning more than 20 years, none of them remain a matter of history. The construction industry, at least in the UK, is booming, and continues to kill and injure disproportionate numbers. Many of the victims of Bhopal continue to suffer in terms of a polluted environment, inability to work, lack of compensation, and inadequate access to medicines. The post-Piper Alpha regulatory regime remains lax, a cost-cutting, bullying environment remains the norm offshore, and injuries and deaths continue. As we write,[23] the story of the sinking of another ro-ro ferry unfolds, this time in the Red Sea, off Egypt, with some 1,000 people dead – and many 'ro-ro' ferries continue to sail the seas. The Simon Jones Memorial campaign continues to fight against casualisation and for effective corporate manslaughter legislation, the latter being a fight that had really begun following the sinking of the *Herald of Free Enterprise,* and an issue on which successive Conservative then Labour Governments have 'committed' themselves, but have yet to introduce.[24] Migrant workers in the UK continue to be exposed to risks on a daily basis. Transco has been implicated in similar fatalities following the Larkhall explosion. The Sonae plant continues to operate, and to attract criticism for standards of safety *and* environmental management. None of these incidents is history in the sense that they have left thousands of grieving relatives.

The themes set out in figure 1 will recur throughout the following chapters – and we shall return to them in detail in Chapter 9, our concluding chapter. Of course, these common themes are refracted differently in specific case studies, have more or less significance and combine with other context-specific factors. But taken together, these cases indicate causes that reside in systems of management, in features of wider industry and market contexts which provide the conditions from which those crimes are produced, and in systems of law and regulation, which create opportunity structures for such offences. This is not to deny the role of contingent factors. But overwhelmingly the cases demonstrate – as will be explored empirically and theoretically through the chapters that follow – that to represent these, or safety crimes in general, largely in terms of 'accidents', or by attributing a key causal role to individualised 'human error', simply obscures rather than facilitates understanding, even if this mystification has particular benefits for certain social groups. If, then, this text is about rendering visible that which is obscured, as we noted above, then it is also about engaging directly and critically with the mystifications that separate off the phenomena with which we are concerned from crime, law and order agendas.

To these ends, then, the structure of the book is as follows. Having indicated what safety crimes look like in the above cases, we turn, in Chapter 2, to map occupational deaths and injuries, using various data to indicate the scale and distribution of these phenomena, of which safety crimes are a subset. Chapter 3 then assesses the ubiquitousness, power and significance of a series of related arguments which cast these deaths and injuries so mapped as *accidents* – that is, as quite distinct from crimes. In this chapter we also raise key questions about the failure of criminology as an academic discipline to incorporate safety crimes into mainstream understandings of violence. Chapter 4 then considers the extent to which we can estimate the scale of offending from this pool of death and injury data. While definitive answers are impossible to reach, we conclude that safety crimes represent at least as great a crime problem as those crimes of violence upon which the Home Office typically focuses, namely crimes of inter-personal violence recorded through official crime data.

Chapters 5–8 turn to focus upon the legal, regulatory and criminal justice approaches and responses to safety crimes. Specifically, Chapter 5 sets out, largely through an historical focus, the development of criminal law in ways that re-positioned safety crimes as distinct from 'real' crimes; Chapter 6 then examines the possibilities for re-assimilating safety crimes into existing structures of criminal law. How existing safety law is enforced empirically, and how we can understand such modes of enforcement theoretically, is the subject of Chapter 7, and in considering regulatory enforcement theoretically we are also attempting to grasp the prospects for, and limits of, changes in such practices. Similarly, Chapter 8 considers the empirical and theoretical dimensions of punishing and sanctioning corporations and employers following successful prosecution for safety crimes.

Finally, our concluding chapter sets out to theorise the nature of safety crimes, both through using the fragments of criminological theorising that can be turned to such a task, and by then developing a framework beyond criminology through which safety crimes can be better understood. This schematic political economy of safety crimes seeks also to set out the parameters of any more effective control. For that, unashamedly, is the aim of this book: to render safety crimes more visible not simply to know them better, but to prevent them and respond to them in ways that minimise and mitigate the exacerbation of social injustice that this book demonstrates is their central effect.

Notes

1   See Tombs and Whyte, 2006.
2   Note that although safety is often used in the couplet 'health and safety', the focus of this book is upon crimes of occupational safety *not* health. Crimes against occupational health do, of course, share some characteristics with safety crimes – yet are sufficiently distinctive to warrent separate treatment.
3   Throughout the rest of this book, the acronym HSE will be used instead of 'Health and Safety Executive' except in references to publications, where the full name will be used.
4   Southern and Easter Regional Traders Union Congress (2005).
5   Throughout the rest of this book, the acronym HSC will be used instead of 'Health and Safety Commission' except in references to publications, where the full name will be used.

6 It also has an 'especially poor' (Health and Safety Commission, 2005a: 13) record on ill-health.

7 The figures in brackets indicate accident rates per 100,000 for the GB as a whole 2003/04 (Southern and Easter Regional Trades Union Congress, 2005).

8 These compare to all industry averages which saw a 25% fall in all enforcement notices issued by HSE in the same years, a 26% decline in prosecutions instituted and a 24% decline in convictions secured www.hse.gov.uk/statistics/enforce/index.htm.

9 Case complied from the following sources: Amnesty International 2004; Cassells 1993; Everest 1985; Pearce and Tombs 1998, Shrivastava 1992.

10 Bergman 2000; Boyd 1992; Crainer 1993; Department of Transport 1987; Wells 1993.

11 All unattributed quotes, and much of the material upon which this case is based, is taken from the campaign's website; see www.simonjones.org.uk. Thanks to the campaign for permission to use this material extensively, and to Simon's brother, Tim, and mother, Anne for their help in checking this material.

12 The 'crane' was in fact an excavator which had been modified for use as a crane by welding hooks onto the grab.

13 Many of these actions, and the work of the campaign in general, is documented in the film. *Not This Time – The Story of the Simon Jones Memorial Campaign*; see www.simonjones.org.uk/newvideo.htm for details.

14 There has just been one analogous case under Scottish law, a charge of culpable homicide against Transco following the deaths of four people on December 22, 1999 when an explosion destroyed a family house in Larkhall. The case was dismissed by the trial judge in 2003.

15 'Sonae UK fined £37,500 for polluting brook' (6 October 2003), at http://www.letsrecycle.com/materials/wood/news.jsp?story=2667.

16 Definitions of these categories of injury are given in Chapter 2.

17 http://www.abertaytraining.co.uk/HomePage/healthnews.asp.

18 'Fourth HSE fine for Liverpool company after explosion', *Government News Network*, Press Release, GNN ref 135406P – see http://www.gnn.gov.uk/Content/Detail.asp?ReleaseID=213291&NewsAreaID=2.

19 Source: HSE prosecutions database – see http://www.hse-databases.co.uk/prosecutions/case/case_details.asp?SF=CN&SV=F170000429.

20 See http://ww.hse-databases.co.uk/notices/notices/notice_list.asp?rdoNType=&NT=&SN=F&EO=LIKE&SF=RN&SV=Sonae&ST=N&x=15&y=14, and also see Chapter 4 on the differences between the three types of notice issued by HSE inspectorates.

21 *Hansard*. House of Commons Written Answers – see http://www.publications.parliament.uk/cgi-bin/newhtml_hl?DB=semukparl&STEMMER=en&WORDS=sona%20notic&ALL=sonae&ANY=notice&PHRASE=&CATEGORIES=&SIMPLE=&SPEAKER=&COLOUR=red&STYLE=s&ANCHOR=20710w19.html_wqn6&URL=/pa/cm200102/cmhansrd/vo020710/text/20710w19.htm#20710w19.html_wqn6.

22 Source: http://www.hse.gov.uk/notices/notices/notice_list.asp?rdoNType=&NT=&SN=F&EO=LIKE&SF=RN&SV=Sonae&ST=N&x=19&y=11.

23 The Ferry sank on 3 February, 2006.

24 The Corporate Manslaughter and Homicide Bill 2006 was passing through the parliamentary process as this book was in its production stage (March 2007), but was subject to intense controversy, and threats to pull it by the Home Secretary. See http://www.corporateaccountability.org/manslaughter/reformprops/main.htm

Chapter 2

Mapping occupational death and injury

Introduction

In contemporary societies, work routinely kills workers and members of the public through acute injury and chronic illness. The scale of this routine killing – deaths occur across all industries, all types of companies – is almost incomprehensible. Although the focus of this text is upon safety, so that we are concerned here with deaths from acute incidents, a useful context for our considerations in this chapter is the International Labour Organisation (ILO) estimate that, at a bare minimum, 2.2 million workers die each year through work-related 'accidents' and diseases (International Labour Organisation 2005: 1). This means that annually there are more than 5,000 work-related deaths every day, while for every fatality there are another 500–2,000 injuries, depending on the type of job.

Of the 345,000 workers estimated by the ILO to have died in incidents (as opposed to occupational diseases and exposures) at the workplace in 2002, by far the greatest number, almost 220,000, were in Asia, with China having by far the highest number of deaths of any one Asian country – 73,595 – with the second highest number being India (48,176).[1] In Europe, Russia is the state with the highest absolute number of occupational fatalities – almost 7,000 – followed by Turkey, Ukraine, Poland and Romania. For Woolfson, flexibilisation – or, as he puts it, the creation of 'a deregulated low-cost, low-wage economy, where labour (preferably "union-free") is comprehensively subordinated to the needs of capital' – is the key to understanding why the states of the former Soviet Union mostly have safety records poorer than the rest of Europe: 'figures show that, as a whole, Central and East Europeans are three times as likely to die at work than those in the EU-15 (9.6 per 100,000 persons in employment compared to 3.4)' (Woolfson 2005).

Britain is not, then, one of the most dangerous places to work in Europe. Nor, however, is it one of the very safest, a claim that could be sustained precisely because of our lack of knowledge of the actual level of injuries *within* nations and the lack of utilisable data for comparison *between* nations (see Eurostat 2001; European Commission 2002). More recently, HSE has undertaken international comparisons of fatality and injury data across EU member states and the US for the year 2000, and was able to conclude that while Britain was one of the safest places, it was being caught up by other nation states (Health and Safety Executive 2000a). The fact of Britain's safety record deteriorating in relative terms is borne out by a recent EU survey which concluded that 'Accidents at work are generally decreasing, but not in all Member States'. Thus, while 'Between 1998 and 2001, serious accidents decreased by 6 per cent in the EU and fatal accidents by 21 per cent', this decrease being replicated across some of the newly acceded states such as Poland, Slovakia and Denmark, it was noted that, 'Despite this general downwards trend in most of the Member States, the incidence rate of serious accidents increased in Sweden (+13 per cent, between 1998 and 2001), the United Kingdom (+10 per cent), Spain (+6 per cent) and Ireland (+5 per cent)'.[2] Such comparisons are fraught with difficulty, and comparative analysis of injury data requires a whole series of factors to be taken into account, but such data do rather undermine the HSC and Government's long-term complacency regarding its safety record compared to other European nations.

In this chapter – which seeks to map the scale and distribution of occupational death and injury in Britain – we begin by setting out these officially recorded deaths and injuries, and note at the same time some of the data's limitations. From there, we seek to reconstruct fatality data, to arrive at a more utilisable figure for occupationally-related deaths than that recorded by HSE. The remaining sections of the chapter then consider the distribution of these deaths and injuries, noting their variation in terms of differential vulnerability, and paying particular attention to gender and ethnicity.

Using official injury data

The most common measurement of occupational 'safety' is recorded injury data; data for the United Kingdom are kept by the HSE and are currently collated under the Reporting of Injuries, Disease and Dangerous Occurrences Regulations 1995 (RIDDOR 1995), which place a legal duty upon employers to notify the HSE of injuries (and some 'dangerous occurrences') which are then categorised as 'fatal', 'major',[3] and 'over three-day' injuries, where 'incapacity for normal work [lasts] for more than three days'.

Unfortunately for those who would seek to make use of injury data (and of interest in the context of an employer's legal duty to report injuries) each category of *non-fatal* injury data maintained under RIDDOR is subject to significant under-reporting, a phenomenon highlighted over 30 years ago by the Report of the Robens Committee on Safety and Health at Work (Robens 1972: 135, and Chapter 15, *passim*). Although major injury data are more reliable than data for over three-day injuries, each data set is subject to processes of under-reporting which render them somewhat unreliable as measures of occupational injury (see Nichols 1997). In the late 1980s it was estimated that official data record on average just over 40 per cent of injuries which are notifiable to HSE, and just 10 per cent of injuries to the self-employed (Stevens 1992).

More recently, HSE has begun to make use of the regular Labour Force Survey. The Labour Force Survey (LFS) is a survey of some 60,000 private households in Britain, based upon a systematic random survey design, and carried out by the Office for National Statistics. Since 1992 it has been conducted on a quarterly basis, and HSE has asked four questions on (non-fatal) workplace injuries at each winter-quarter survey since 1993/94; HSE data are available for 1989/90, and then for each year from 1993/94 onwards. LFS data are of interest in their own right, since they indicate a widespread failure on the part of employers to meet the legal duty to report incidents, an offence under safety law. LFS data indicate that 'only one quarter of reportable non-fatal injuries to employees' and 'less than 5 per cent' in the case of self-employed workers, are reported by employers (Health and Safety Commission 1998: 1). These rates vary between 11 per cent in 'Finance and Business' and 17 per cent in 'Hotels and Restaurants' to 62 per cent in 'Public Administration and Defence' to 86 per cent in 'Extraction and Utility Supply'.[4] Whichever estimates are accepted, it is clear that reporting rates are extremely low. It has also been concluded recently that 'small firms are more likely to under-report or not report at all' (Daniels and Marlow 2005: iv). Yet while the LFS is a potentially useful adjunct to, and improvement upon, data collected under RIDDOR in terms of a measure of injuries, it is somewhat unreliable, given that there are just four questions asked at the end of a very long survey on a range of employment issues (Pickvance 2006).[5]

Generally, rates of mandatory reporting which appeared to improve briefly at the end of the 1990s are now in decline again (Daniels and Marlow 2005: 2–3). Moreover, given shifts in levels of non-reporting, these levels of under-estimate render any longitudinal analyses virtually impossible – a task already made difficult by the fact that there have been several changes in reporting requirements since 1974 (see Nichols 1997). Given the recognised 'poverty' of minor and major injury data, the variable social processes out of which they are produced, and the shifting legal categories into which they are organised, these need to be read with a whole series of caveats in mind and thus treated with extreme caution. For our purposes they are useful in telling us *something* about the sheer scale of the problem that we are indicating, the distribution of deaths and injuries by sector and so on, and for making some informed judgements about any trends in their incidence.

We can make several brief observations on the data presented in Tables 2–10. First, and not at all apparent from the data presented in the tables, the majority of the injuries recorded by the HSE are sustained by men rather than women – men are three times more likely to sustain a major injury, and about two-and-a-half times more likely to sustain an over three-day injury (Health and Safety Commission 2001: 56)[6]. To some extent, one might expect this on the basis of persistent gendered occupational segregation, at least horizontally. HSE research has concluded that:

> The higher injury rate in men is partly explained by the occupations, hours of work, and other job characteristics. However, after allowing for these characteristics of jobs, men continue to face a higher risk of reportable injury than women. Men face a 35 per cent higher risk of reportable injuries than women (not explained by the jobs held by men and women). (Health and Safety Commission 2001: 56)

This raises the issue of possible peculiarities in the risks faced by women, and subsequent 'official' attention accorded to these. We return to these issues in a later section.

Second, taking the data in Tables 1–3 together, it is clear that there are large *absolute* numbers of major injuries – around 30,000 such injuries to all workers in any given year – and over three-day injuries, up to and in some years above 130,000 recorded injuries across British workplaces. Workplace injury is far from an uncommon experience. Table 4 indicates that there is also an absolutely high number of injuries sustained by members of the public in any one year, even though movement between years is an erratic one.

Table 2 Reported major injuries[+]

	96/97	97/98	98/99	99/00	00/01	01/02	02/03	03/04	04/05
Employees (number)	27964	29187	28368	28652	27524	28011	28113	30689	30541
Rate per 100,000 employees	127.5	127.6	121.7	116.6	110.2	110.9	111.1	120.4	117.9
Self-employed	1356	815	685	663	630	929	1079	1283	1251
Rate per 100,000 self-employed	38.4	23.3	20.3	19.7	19.2	27.8	32.3	33.9	33.0
All workers	29320	30002	29053	29315	28154	28940	29162	31972	31702
Rate per 100,000 workers	115.1	113.8	108.8	104.9	99.6	101.2	101.9	109.3	107.1

Table 3 Reported over three-day injuries

	96/97	97/98	98/99	99/00	00/01	01/02	02/03	03/04	04/05
Employees (number)	127286	134789	132295	135381	134105	129655	128184	131017	121779
Rate per 100,000 employees	580.1	589.2	567.3	550.9	536.9	513.5	506.5	514.2	471.7
Self-employed	2282	984	849	732	715	917	951	1114	1143
Rate per 100,000 self-employed	64.6	28.1	25.2	21.8	21.8	27.5	28.4	29.5	30.2
All workers	129568	135773	133144	136113	134820	130572	129135	132131	122922
Rate per 100,000 workers	508.7	514.8	498.8	487.5	477.1	456.7	450.7	451.5	415.2

Table 4 Injuries to members of the public

	96/97	97/98	98/99	99/00	00/01	01/02	02/03	03/04	04/05(p)
Non-fatal *	35694	28613	23800	25059	20839	14834	12793	13679	14316

P is Provisional

* Injuries which result in the injured person being taken directly to hospital (Health and Safety Commission 2005a: 21).

[+] Injury data presented in the tables in this chapter is based upon HSE and HSE data, in addition to personal communication with HSE Statistics Unit, 26/10/2006, 20/04/2006. See www.hse.gov.uk/statistics/causacc/tables.htm, Health and Safety Commission 2000, 2003, 2005a, 2006b; Health and Safety Executive 2003b.

41

Third, Tables 2 and 3 both indicate that the recorded differences in fatality rates between workers and the self-employed (above, and Table 6) clearly do not hold with respect to injuries: Table 2 indicates that the rate of recorded major injuries to employees is some three to six times higher than that for the self-employed. This is clearly a reporting effect – if a self-employed worker *dies* then this is likely to be recorded, whilst an injury, even a major injury, is not, since there is no financial or other incentive to do so. Similar observations are relevant for the disparities in Table 3, and here we would expect the disparities in rates to be even greater given the far lesser seriousness of injuries. The data in Tables 2 and 3, then, need to be read in terms of non-reporting, bearing in mind the observation above, that only between 5 and 10 per cent of injures to the self-employed are actually reported.

Fourth, it again seems that over the time period covered there are no unequivocally clear, discernible trends, certainly given the problems of variable levels of reporting. In terms of those trends, we can see from Table 2 that there has been a small decline across the period in the rate of reported injury to both employees and the self-employed; there are slight decreases in rates across the period for both employees and the self-employed – though again, we would stress that the data for the self-employed are almost non-utilisable given that they are subject to up to 95 per cent under-reporting.

Now, notwithstanding the enormous problems in determining accurate figures for the numbers of occupational injuries, one consistent claim has been that the recording of fatal injuries is at least reliable (Health and Safety Commission 1996: 1, 1997: 1; Nichols 1989: 543, 1994: 104, 1997: 126). Indeed, the data on *fatal* injuries represents *the* most reliable available data on occupational injury, perhaps even having been improved recently with the introduction of new reporting requirements in 1995. However, as we shall see below, these data are far from complete.

Data for the reporting year 1996/97 is the first to be collected under new reporting requirements, RIDDOR 1995. Of interest in the context of the discussion regarding definitions of 'violence' that is to follow in Chapter 3 is that the new regulations had introduced an expanded definition of occupational fatalities, including inter-personal violence against employees and new categories of reportable occupational fatalities among members of the public by introducing the 'vital' test of 'arising out of or in connection with work' (Health and Safety Executive 1996: 14) in determining what injuries should be recorded as occupational. This phrase is intended to cover 'the manner or conduct of an undertaking', 'the plant or substances used for the purposes of the undertaking', and 'the condition of the premises used by the undertaking or of any part of them' (ibid.: 14). This new, more inclusive, definition simply renders reporting requirements consistent with the substance of the HASAW Act 1974, which requires an employer to 'conduct his undertaking, in such a way as to ensure, so far as is reasonably practicable, that persons not in his employment, but who may be affected, are not exposed to risks to their health and safety'. Under this expanded definition, a total of 593 fatal occupational injuries were recorded for 2004/05.[7]

Table 5 provides a broad overview of occupational deaths that have been recorded since these new reporting requirements were introduced. Several observations can be made about the data presented therein.

Table 5 Reported fatal injuries

	96/97	97/98	98/99	99/00	00/01	01/02	02/03	03/04	04/05
Employees (number)	207	212	188	162	213	206	183	168	172
Rate per 100,000 employees	0.9	0.9	0.8	0.7	0.9	0.8	0.7	0.7	0.7
Self-employed	80	62	65	58	79	45	44	68	51
Rate per 100,000 self-employed	2.3	1.8	1.9	1.7	2.4	1.3	1.3	1.8	1.3
All workers	287	274	253	220	292	251	227	236	223
Rate per 100,000 workers	1.1	1.0	0.9	0.0	1.0	0.9	0.8	0.8	0.8
Members of the public†	367	393	369	436	444	393	396	374	370
Total (workers + public)	654	667	622	656	736	644	623	610	593

† HSE typically notes that about two-thirds of fatalities to members of the public are the result of suicide or trespass on the railways. Of course, these, as all HSE data, exclude fatalities from work-related road traffic incidents.

First, when these data are presented, HSE refer not to deaths including those to members of the public, but rather utilises what has been labelled a 'head line figure' (Health and Safety Executive 1997; Tombs 1999a), referring only to totals of workers (employees and the self-employed). Now, it should be noted that deaths to members of the public are consistently high. But HSE's justification for omitting these from the headline figure is presumably based on some claim that these are not 'real' workplace deaths – in fact, a significant number of these deaths are suicides, and HSE typically notes that about two-thirds of fatalities to members of the public are the result of suicide or trespass on the railways. Nevertheless, this is a rather curious sleight of hand by HSE, since these deaths are reported to and recorded by them as occupational fatalities, and they may well constitute failures of employers to meet legal duties.[8] In any case, such *ad hoc* alterations to what constitutes legitimate injury data are not made in the opposite direction – that is, by counting *in* deaths which are clearly occupational, but which are not covered by HSE's remit. The most notable example in this context are the 1,000 or so fatal injuries sustained whilst driving each year – there is now almost universal agreement that these are occupational fatalities, but they are not reportable under RIDDOR, and are never referred to as possible 'additions' by HSE when their headline figures are released (see below).

Second, these totals are historically low figures. Clearly work is far safer in Britain than it was in the era of early industrialisation when the factory inspectorate was established and described, for example, in Marx's *Capital Volume 1*, or Engels's *The Condition of The Working Class*. Further, it is possible to argue that the HASAW Act (1974) gave a particular impetus to this long-term improvement, not least since the Committee of Inquiry that ultimately led to the Act and the changes it introduced had itself been established in the context of some rises in industrial injury rates (Dawson *et al.* 1988: 9). However, it would be wrong to attribute too much to the Act *per se*. As Nichols has argued, a crucial factor to be taken into account in this long-term improvement was the relative strength of labour vis-à-vis capital (Nichols 1997: 122, and *passim*). Further, the long term downward trend seemed to be an instance of a 'secular tendency' for fatality rates to fall across industrialised countries due to advances in medical care, improvements in communication and transport, knowledge regarding safer working practices, and levels of investment in technology (ibid.: 128). More latterly, and more specifically, injury rates have declined partly as a result of changes in the occupational structure in British workplaces; HSE has noted, for example, that construction is probably the last remaining heavy industry of any size in Britain (Health and Safety Commission 2005a: 13). Since the introduction of the HASAW Act in 1974, for example, employment has shifted significantly from manufacturing to services: three million jobs in manufacturing have gone, while the service sector now employs more than three-quarters of the British workforce compared with two-thirds of workers in 1974.

Third, within the data presented in Table 5, the absolute figures indicate small declines in the numbers of fatalities to employees, the self-employed and members of the public over the nine-year period. In none of these categories, however, is there a clear year-on-year decline in the absolute number of fatalities. As also indicated in Table 2, the rate of non-fatal injuries has also seen a small decline in this period.

Fourth, it should be noted that the rate of fatalities for the self-employed is higher, and typically about double, the rate for employees – an issue that is discussed below in terms of the relative vulnerability of the self-employed vis-à-vis employees.[9]

Finally and most important of all, whilst those figures might allow us to make some very general year-on-year comparisons in the period since RIDDOR was introduced, the problem is that their usefulness is limited because they cannot be regarded as representing anything close to the full picture of deaths and injuries at work in Britain. Whilst fatal injury data are clearly more utilisable than other injury data, because of the relatively lower chances that fatalities will not be reported, and while the requirements of RIDDOR 1995 are an improvement, there are considerable anomalies within the construction of those figures that render them grossly incomplete.

Now, if there are problems regarding fatality data, this can at least be reconstructed and, as we shall argue in Chapter 4, it can also be used to say something about the level of safety *crimes*. But any such reformulations would still exclude the vast majority of potential safety crimes, since incidents that result in fatalities represent only a small minority of workplace injuries, recorded or otherwise. We have also noted that there are enormous problems of under-reporting of non-fatal injuries, whilst variability in reporting rates over time makes any longitudinal analysis difficult, if not impossible. Injury data does, however, remain of *some* use for us. First because it again indicates the sheer scale of the phenomenon with which this text is concerned. And, second, because we can say *some thing* about the relative distribution of injuries. The latter point will be picked up again later in the chapter. For the time being we discuss how the available data can be more usefully constructed.

Reconstructing official data

The gap in accounting is best illustrated by the stark contrasts between the consistently higher injury rates amongst the self-employed in the context of fatal injury which are not repeated when we look at non-fatal injury data, where the contrast with data on fatalities is clear. Official data shows that being self-employed makes a worker about twice as likely to be fatally injured, whilst at the same time, being self-employed makes it four to five times *less* likely that a worker will sustain a major injury (Tables 2 and 5). This is, of course, a reporting effect and can only be explained by understanding the relative difficulty with which fatalities as opposed to injuries can be hidden. In crude terms, it is more difficult to hide a body than it is to hide a broken wrist.

Having noted this distinction, we should be careful not to simply assume that fatality data are infallible. Indeed, we can identify at least three separate problems with HSE-published data of fatalities which render their use problematic, and any claims regarding their 'virtual' completeness simply wrong.

First, the coverage of RIDDOR 1995 continues to exclude significant numbers of occupationally-caused deaths, for which there do exist officially collected data. Some of these omissions are at the very least curious – notably fatalities relating to the supply and use of flammable gas[10] – but the least excusable, and numerically most significant, is the exclusion of road traffic fatalities which involve 'at work' vehicles. RoSPA (1998) estimated that there are 800–1,000 such fatalities per annum (see also Bibbings 1996), HSE and the Department of Transport have estimated up to 20 such fatalities a week, indicating just in excess of 1,000 per annum (Health and Safety Executive/Department for Transport 2003), while a recent study confirmed the number of deaths at the highest figure in that range, 1,000, concluding that 'Britain's roads are the country's most dangerous workplace' (Trades Union Congress 2005b; see also Campbell 2005). Incorporating existent, omitted data[11] increases the total of occupational deaths from the HSE's recorded figure of 593 for 2004/05 to somewhere close to 1,700 deaths.[12]

Second, the data maintained under RIDDOR with respect to occupational fatalities remain internally incoherent. Anomalies arise, in particular, from inconsistent reporting requirements depending upon: where a fatality occurs; the length of time between sustaining the injury and death (and here there is a disjunction between the regulatory requirement and its actual operation); and whether the fatal injury is sustained by an employee, a self-employed worker, or a member of the public. To provide an illustration of a situation bordering on absurdity: in 2005 a farmworker, having completed his shift, was being given a lift on the back of a tractor when he fell, and died – but since his death occurred outside working hours, it did not get recorded as an occupational fatality ('Work Deaths are Off the Record', *Hazards*, 93, 2006: 31). The net effect of such anomalies is to omit significant, but unquantifiable, numbers of relevant fatal injuries (see Tombs 1999a: 356–9).

Third, and finally, RIDDOR reflects an under-recording of fatal injuries due to social processes of under-reporting.[13] Before a death can be registered, a valid certificate giving the cause of death must be completed and signed by a registered medical practitioner who attended the deceased during her/his last illness; if a death is shown to be 'violent or unnatural', the Coroner is required by law to conduct an inquest. Two studies (Start *et al.*, 1993 and 1995) have highlighted the inability of both hospital clinicians and general practitioners to recognise some categories of reportable deaths. The first (Start *et al.* 1993) indicated that individual clinicians at all grades showed a variable appreciation of the different categories of cases which should be reported, being mistaken in up to 60 per cent of individual cases. Indeed, 'Deaths resulting from accidents were often unrecognised' (ibid.: 1039). In a second study involving general practitioners (Start *et al.* 1995), only 3 per cent recognised all those deaths which should be reported for further investigation; deaths from industrial or domestic 'accidents' were recognised as cases requiring referral by fewer than half of all general practitioners. Both studies indicate that certifying doctors tend to consider only the eventual cause of death rather than the sequence of events leading to death (ibid.: 193).

There can be no doubt that the published fatality data are inadequate: they project only a minimal number of occupationally-caused deaths in Britain on an annual basis. However, from the points of critique that we raise above, it is clear that these data are liable to some reconstruction, through resort to other, official measures of occupationally-caused fatalities. It remains clear that inconsistencies within the reporting requirements themselves, along with various social processes of under-reporting, mean that the HSE's 'headline' figure – that which is trumpeted in press releases but is merely a combination of fatal injuries to workers and the self-employed required by law to be reported to and recorded by HSE – is a dramatic under-estimate of the numbers killed in work-related incidents in the UK each year. For 2004/05, the headline figure would be 223 – the figure for 'All Workers' (see Table 5). The actual figure is somewhere between 1,600 and 1,700. This more accurate figure would include: deaths to members of the public (recorded under RIDDOR), totalling 370 in 2004/05 (see Table 5); deaths incurred whilst driving and 'at work', about 1,000 per annum; and a small number of miscellaneous categories, such as fatalities relating to the supply and use of flammable gas (23 in 2005), and those arising in the course of sea fishing (10 fatalities in 2004) and merchant vesseling (20 fatalities in 2004) in British waters or on British vessels at sea (Marine Accident Investigation Branch 2005: 27, 19). In other words, to obtain a more accurate figure of officially recorded occupational fatalities, we need to apply a multiplier of between seven or eight to the headline figure.

Having attempted to reconstruct the data more usefully, we would argue that a figure between 1,600–1,700 deaths is workable as a *minimum* estimate of annual deaths from sudden injuries. There are, however, two more major caveats to be made. The first is that this figure, as we remind readers throughout the book, does not include the deaths caused by industrial illnesses and exposures. As we indicated in the introduction, the total figure for deaths caused by work in the UK is likely to be in the tens of thousands. Our 1,600–1,700 therefore represents a minimal figure of a small subset of the total death toll. The second is one that all social scientists will be familiar with, namely that quantitative data, let alone 'official' statistics, alone can allow us to make only very rudimentary observations about any social phenomenon (see Levitas 1996). Statistics may allow us to make some comparisons across time and may allow us to make some estimates about scale and incidence, but they can tell us very little about more complex social features of deaths and injuries at work. They can tell us little about the processes by which deaths and injuries are socially distributed or about the processes that produce deaths and injuries in the first place. Nor can they tell us anything about the differential social *impacts* of deaths and injuries amongst different sectors of the population. What the preceding data fail to convey is the fact that risks faced at work are neither evenly nor randomly distributed: not only are such deaths, injuries and illnesses unequally distributed, but this unequal distribution mirrors well-known structural inequalities within nations – between regions, social classes and communities – as well as between nations.

Dimensions of vulnerability

There are good theoretical reasons and some empirical evidence to indicate that these deaths, injuries and illnesses disproportionately fall upon members of the lowest socio-economic groups. If we ask *who* gets killed and injured, the answer is to be found in certain manual occupations – and is comprehensible in traditional class terms (see Table 10). Thus, for example, HSE data indicate that 'process, plant and machine operatives' are 15 times more likely to incur a reportable injury than 'managers and senior officials', and more than ten times more likely than those in 'professional occupations'.

Historically, then, it is perhaps unsurprising that the key source of opposition to workplace risks has been organised labour, and a key political tactic has been to seek more effective regulation, at best regulation involving workers' representatives themselves – in other words, struggles to secure safer and healthier workplaces have historically been classic struggles on the part of labour and its allies to attenuate management's right to manage and expropriate surplus value. This is a key explanatory factor in the long-term historical trend towards safer workplaces within industrialised economies. It also helps to explain why there is no ineluctable trend towards safer working, somehow associated with industrialisation, benign employers or the enlightened state – elements of a so-called Whig version of history whereby capitalism became progressively more humane. Rather, pointing to the struggles of organised labour, historically and contemporaneously, indicates that fluctuations in levels of workplace safety can partially, but crucially, be related to the strength of organised labour or, more accurately, the strength of balances of forces between states, capital and labour.[14]

These points being made, then, there can be no doubt that the relative decline in trade union membership and the erosion of a range of rights held by workers in the post-war liberal democracies has more recently re-shaped the balance of power between capital and labour. The internationalisation of neo-liberalism has profoundly repositioned labour markets and labour processes in favour of capital, particularly in the developing world, and this has had profound implications for the way that nation states imagine and act out their relationship to national and transnational capital. These relationships are increasingly creating and intensifying job insecurity – and all that accompanies it, including the increased likelihood of exposure to workplace risk and harm. For example, as Doogan's analysis of labour turnover in the UK in the 1990s indicates, while long-term employment actually *increased* for skilled, managerial and professional groups, job turnover increased 'absolutely and relatively in elementary occupations in lower skilled occupations and absolutely in low skilled agricultural jobs' (Doogan 2001: 432).

Such specifics are crucial in terms of the production and distribution of workplace harm. HSE research, based upon UK Labour Force Survey returns, has found significant correlations between injury rates and job tenure. Thus: the rate of injury to workers in their first six months is over double that for workers who have been with an employer for at least a year (Health and Safety Executive 2000b: 3), a correlation that holds after allowing for occupations and hours of work (Health and Safety Commission 2001: 62). Even more strikingly, higher rates of injury are associated with shorter working weeks, so that 'those working less than 16 hours per week have double the rate of injury compared with those who work 30–50 hours per week' (ibid.: 4). Thus, '[w]orkers on a low number of weekly hours have substantially higher rates of all workplace injury than those working longer hours, and the rate gets lower as the number of weekly hours increases' (ibid.: 61). Again, this holds even after allowing for other job characteristics (ibid.).

Now, there is an obvious issue here about the extent to which people learn on the job, but such facts should also raise concerns about the exacerbation of vulnerability through casualisation of work: temporary and part-time workers – workers who are likely to enjoy far fewer forms of employment protection than those in full-time, permanent employment – are, once all other factors have been controlled for, more likely to be injured at work. To these conclusions we can safely add that child workers, home-workers and those working 'illegally' are at the same time likely to face extreme risks whilst also being invisible to almost any 'official' considerations of the distribution of injury and disease. And the converse of these arguments is that the safest workplaces in the UK are those with strong trade unions and effectively functioning, union-backed safety representation. This has been confirmed in numerous research studies. What the most recent studies have found is that strong worker representation in the workplace has a markedly beneficial impact upon health and safety performance (Walters *et al.* 2005) and that trade unions are the key organisations in providing this support. Strong trade union representation reduces injury rates dramatically, by perhaps as much as 50 per cent (Reilly *et al.* 1995). Moreover, a review of the research confirmed the consistency of those findings on an international basis (James and Walters 2002). This review of evidence underlines two points. First, at the level of the workplace, the crucial risk controls are those that are exerted by well-organised workers themselves. This suggests that rather than having been made redundant in the current phase of capitalism, 'traditional' forms of labour organisation remain just as important as they have ever been. Second, it suggests that were a de-institutionalisation process to occur, it would, quite literally, have catastrophic affects. Despite the efforts of employers in particular sectors to remove negotiations around safety from the sphere of industrial relations, this strategy has only had limited success (see for example, Woolfson *et al.* 1996). Regardless of the relative decline in trade union membership, trade unions and other 'traditional' forms of worker organisation remain crucially important to the mitigation of risks in the workplace. Safety conditions remain institutionalised in collective bargaining agreements in the UK. Thus if there are clear roles for a range of campaigning groups and NGOs in seeking to intervene in safety politics,[15] these complement, rather than substitute for, 'old' forms of collectivism.

This point also helps us to explain differences in risk of death and injury in terms of sector as opposed to occupation. About half of the fatalities incurred by employees in Britain occur in two of the most casualised sectors – construction and 'agriculture, forestry and fishing' – which, along with 'recycling of scrap and waste', also have the highest injury rates to employees (Health and Safety Executive 2004b). Tables 6–9 provide some data on the distribution of various types of injury across different sectors of the economy. It is clear from these tables that the most dangerous sectors in terms of fatal and non-fatal injuries to employees are agriculture, construction and the extractive industries. In particular, the relative dangerousness of agriculture and construction is borne out strikingly in the data for fatal injuries to the self-employed, presented in Table 7. Comparing the data here with that in Table 6, we find that, on average, across all industries, being self-employed makes you twice as likely to incur a fatal injury. It should also be noted that there are no clear downward trends in any of the sectoral fatal injury rates here.

Table 6 Fatal injuries reported to all enforcing authorities by industry 1996/97–2004/05, incidence rates per 100,000: employees

	1996/97	1997/98	1998/99	1999/2000	2000/01	2001/02	2002/03	2003/04	2004/05
Agriculture, hunting, forestry and fishing	7.6	6.7	5.4	4.53	4.7	7.9	7.3	2.8	7.0
Extractive and utility supply	4.2	7.9	4.7	3.1	4.6	6.9	1.6	5.1	1.3
Manufacturing	1.3	1.3	1.6	1.0	1.2	1.3	1.2	0.8	1.3
Construction	8.2	5.7	4.4	5.5	6.5	5.3	4.9	4.3	4.8
Services	0.4	0.4	0.3	0.2	0.4	0.3	0.3	0.4	0.3
All industries	0.9	0.9	0.8	0.7	0.9	0.8	0.7	0.7	0.7

Table 7 Fatal injuries reported to all enforcing authorities by industry 1996/97–2004/05, incidence rates per 100,000: self-employed

	1996/97	1997/98	1998/99	1999/2000	2000/01	2001/02	2002/03	2003/04	2004/05
Agriculture, hunting, forestry and fishing	14.3	8.7	15.0	13.0	19	11	12.9	21.3	14.7
Extractive and utility supply	-	10.3	13.0	13.7	-	-	-	0.4	-
Manufacturing	2.3	2.7	2.2	1.2	1.8	0.4	0.5	1.2	0.4
Construction	3.0	3.1	2.8	3.2	5	2.9	2	2.5	1.7
Services	0.7	0.5	0.4	0.5	0.4	0.2	0.4	0.3	0.4
All industries	2.3	1.8	1.9	1.7	2.4	1.3	1.3	1.8	1.3

Table 8 Non-fatal major injuries reported to all enforcing authorities, incidence rates per 100,000, by industry 1996/97–2004/05: employees

	1996/97	1997/98	1998/99	1999/2000	2000/01	2001/02	2002/03	2003/04	2004/05(p)
Agriculture, hunting, forestry and fishing	256.9	222.3	205.6	224.4	213.9	238.5	262.5	235.2	228
Extractive and utility supply	315.1	282.7	246.8	244.1	267	222.9	222.7	228	232.5
Manufacturing	206.4	216.1	201.5	204.1	194.2	194.9	194.3	194.1	192.3
Construction	403.0	382.3	402.7	395.9	380.9	356.1	354.9	327.7	299.4
Services	90.8	88.4	83.7	79.3	75.3	79	80.7	94.5	93.4
All industries	127.5	127.6	121.7	116.6	110.2	110.9	111.1	120.4	117.7

p is provisional

Table 9 Non-fatal major injuries reported to all enforcing authorities, incidence rates per 100,000, by industry 1996/97–2004/05: self-employed

	1996/97	1997/98	1998/1999	1999/2000	2000/01	2001/02	2002/03	2003/04	2004/05(p)
Agriculture, hunting, forestry and fishing	40.9	32.3	36.9	41.0	34.5	54.4	43.2	42.7	41.8
Extractive and utility supply	211.7	780.8	441.5	532.7	67.2	41.4	140.7	84.8	106.4
Manufacturing	41.7	35.7	35.2	25.9	22.9	44.4	45.5	46.8	39.9
Construction	104.9	65.4	56.5	57.7	62.7	79.5	99.1	97.8	89.4
Services	13.7	4.6	5.1	5.3	4.9	8.5	9.3	12.8	13.2
All industries	38.4	23.3	20.3	19.7	19.2	27.8	32.3	33.9	32.9

P is Provisional

Table 10 Injuries to employees by occupation 2004/05(p), incidence rate per 100, 000 employees *

Occupation	Fatal	Major	Over three-day	All reported injuries
Managers and senior officials	0.3	43.0	89.2	132.5
Professional occupations	0.1	52.3	138.4	190.9
Associate professionals and technical occupations	0.3	66.9	335.3	402.5
Administrative and secretarial occupations	-	29.1	80.6	109.8
Skilled trade occupations	1.6	226.3	746.1	973.9
Personal service occupations	0.1	112.7	516.0	628.8
Sales and customer service occupations	-	83.9	316.8	400.7
Process, plant and machine operatives	3.0	408.8	1733.7	2145.4
Elementary occupations†	1.2	200.6	943.8	1145.6
All occupations	0.7	117.7	469.0	587.4

P is Provision

* Source: www.hse.gov.uk/statistics/employment/index.htm

† The elementary occupations category includes occupations non specified above in agriculture, construction, plant processing and services.

Now, in terms of relative danger across different sectors, one point needs to be made here regarding levels of 'inherent' danger, the kind of arguments that support glib assertions such as the phrase 'occupational hazard'. Whilst it is accepted that there may be greater risks to be faced on a building site than in an office, for example, the idea that certain occupations are so inherently dangerous that they necessarily produce certain levels of injury cannot be sustained. Thus within construction it is clear that there are more or less dangerous ways in which working can be organised – a crude but clear illustration of this can be witnessed in the oft-made observation that the construction work in preparation for the Sydney Olympics in 2000 produced no fatal injuries amongst construction workers, while those in Athens in 2004 produced some 40 plus (McCartney 2005). The contrast between these two contexts is generally, and plausibly, explained by, on the one hand, the strength of Australian construction unions and the legal rights they have secured in terms of workplace safety, and, on the other, the overwhelming reliance in the Athens project upon casualised, non-union, migrant labour (Australian Broadcasting Company 2004; BBC Radio 4 2004). For considerations of the organisation of danger within a different industry, the studies by both Carson (1982) and Woolfson and colleagues (1996) of work organisation in the UK offshore oil industry are instructive. Indeed, these latter studies also demonstrate that, in a sector that has drawn labour from the high unemployment areas of Scotland and Northern England, the idea that workers exchange exposure to risk for higher wages is also more myth than reality (see also Moore 1991). Thus structural vulnerability in the workplace and economic marginalisation have mutually reinforcing effects that manifest themselves in terms of exposure to workplace risks.

Gender, ethnicity and patterns of risk

While 'danger' has traditionally been associated with male occupations (Harrison 1993), and despite the fact that research has mostly ignored womens' occupational health and safety issues (Szockyi and Frank 1996: 17), trends in the data indicate that those areas in which women are over-represented, notably services, are those which exhibit both persistently high, and rising, rates of injuries and ill-health (see Craig 1981; Labour Research Department 1996). Indeed, both popular and academic understandings or considerations of the relationships between 'risk' and work views these through the prism of (declining) hazardous and male dominated occupations (mining, shipbuilding, heavier forms of manufacturing, and so on), so that much work within this area (see below) has highly, if implicit, masculinist connotations.[16] That there are both gender and ethnic both gender and ethnic dimensions to this unequal victimisation is evidenced in the work of John Wrench (Wrench 1996; Lee and Wrench 1980; Wrench and Lee 1982; see also Boris and Pruegl 1996).

An OECD report recently noted that 'Historically, work environment research has largely concerned industry work, thus the male worker' (Trades Union Congress 2002). So if there is very little social science which focuses upon occupational safety (Nichols 1997), work which does exist tends to focus predominantly upon men's work. As TGWU national organiser Diana Holland said:

> Health and safety problems are often associated with heavy industry, and jobs mainly done by men, yet accidents occur in all types of workplace and many women face hazards at work. Often it is the least obvious environments that can be most dangerous as risks go undetected and can develop into health and safety problems (Trades Union Congress 2003b).

Yet as we indicate throughout this book, occupational death and injury are routine and ubiquitous phenomena. So, if, as we noted above, 95 per cent of reported fatalities are sustained by men, and if in 2004/05 men were 2.5 times more likely to suffer a reported non-fatal injury than women (www.hse.gov.uk/statistics/tables/table11e.htm), these observations obscure a mass of relatively hidden victimisation suffered by female workers.

Thus, as Harrison has noted, if we confine ourselves to letting these overall figures 'speak for themselves', we 'miss other important issues' (1993: 258). This confirms our need to move from beyond a purely quantitative overview of occupational injuries. In the specific case of the relatively low number of injuries sustained by women, Harrison observes that this should not detract from an analysis of those industries where injuries are incurred by women since 'we would fail to appreciate the significance of injuries and disability and possible consequences for women's lives' (ibid.: 258), including particularly acute financial disadvantage (ibid.: 260).

Yet there is a prior issue here, one which reappears contemporaneously in relation to, for example, stress and musculoskeletal disorders, both of which are noted below. Each of these categories of 'ill-health' is currently a site of contestation,[17] with campaigners arguing that they are in fact matters of occupational injury/safety. This both under-scores and develops the point made in Chapter 1 that safety is not health. There is a close relationship between these different categories of detrimental effects in causation as we noted, but there is also a close relationship in their manifestations. Thus a consideration of women's safety is one way to address the problematic distinction between ill-health on the one hand, and an injury on the other – since women experience less of the latter but may experience much more of the former, even if these effects are unrecorded. For example, women constitute of 80 per cent of 'cleaners and domestics' (the *Guardian*, 28 February, 2006: 4), and are thus exposed to a whole series of chemical hazards, biological hazards and physical agents (noise, vibration) and noxious substances, yet the translation of exposures into notified cases is negligible. Indeed, the very couplet, with an implied distinction between, 'health and safety' may itself incorporate a gendered division (Harrison 1993). It has now become commonplace within trade union circles to refer to the 'gender gap' in occupational safety.

Such considerations are all the more salient given that, in Great Britain for example, women now constitute 46 per cent of the workforce (Equal Opportunities Commission 2005: 8), but many tend to work part-time – this is the case for 44 per cent of all women workers (compared with 11 per cent of men; ibid.). Further, women are three times more likely than men to be homeworkers, they tend to stay with the same employer for shorter periods, and over a third stay with an employer for less than two years. These are all characteristics of particular vulnerability. Female vulnerability at work and in the labour market is further under-scored by the fact that women remain under-paid compared to male counterparts: female full-time average hourly earnings are 19.5 per cent lower than equivalent male earnings; female part-time average hourly earnings 40 per cent lower than equivalent male full-time earnings (Trades Union Congress 2005c: 1). Moreover, vertical segregation, the under-representation of women at higher levels in occupational life, remains entrenched. According to the Government's Women and Equality Unit, women comprise 30 per cent of managers in England, while just 4 per cent of directorships are held by women; women make up 73 per cent of managers in health and social services, yet constitute over 80 per cent of the workforce; they account for just 6 per cent of managers in production.[18] Horizontal segregation also has implications for victimisation to safety crimes – if less obviously so. Women's employment remains grossly over-represented in various service occupations – 84 per cent of women employees work in the service sector (Equal Opportunities Commission 2005: 9). If women do not work in traditionally dangerous occupations, those areas of work in which they predominate are characterised by gender-specific, and less visible, risks. For us, there are clear safety correlates of this skewed distribution of poorly protected work. Moreover, women workers still experience the classic double burden, a function of their continuing to bear predominant responsibilities for child-rearing and domestic labour (Doyal with Pennell 1979: 216).

The TUC regularly surveys its safety representatives to identify what problems, caused or made worse by work, are being raised by women workers (Trades Union Congress 2002). Successive surveys have found stress to be the most frequently identified issue (ibid.). Stress affects working women more than men, and is a function of vulnerability. As the ILO has noted, 'The relation between gender, work and stress is complex and varied' (ibid.). Factors which exacerbate women's exposure to stress include low pay, repetitive, monotonous work, low autonomy and a lack of control, over-demanding jobs and greater total workload, and employers' failures to accommodate family responsibilities.

After stress, the most recent TUC survey revealed 63 per cent of women citing manual handling as the most problematic safety issue, reinforcing previous surveys 'showing that women at work are exposed to heavy lifting. Many women work in jobs where frequent manual handling is expected' (ibid.).

Third in the list are repetitive strain injuries (RSI), which are also known as work-related upper limb disorders. Fifty three per cent of the safety reps identified this category as a problem caused or made worse by work. This figure is higher than the 37 per cent who identified RSI as a problem for men and women workers in the 1998 TUC Safety Reps Survey, and reinforces the view that women are at particular risk of repetitive strain injuries: telephone operators, typists and Display Screen Equipment workers, packers, supermarket checkout operators and light assembly workers are all overwhelmingly associated with RSI. A large TUC affiliate that organises in the public sector has previously stated that

> Women are at particular risk of developing work related upper limb disorders (WRULDs) ... . Women often have to work at repetitive tasks, working long shifts or on piece rates. Women are also more likely to be put upon. Bad employers (and low wages) force women workers into not taking breaks; working longer hours in poorly designed workplaces; and not complaining. Women workers are also less likely to be able to rest once they get home: instead of recovering they often have to do the housework. (ibid.)

Women also suffer more back pain at work than men – yet they are less likely than men to take time off. A HSE poll also found women were less likely to tell their bosses they were in pain. Forty-nine per cent of female workers said they suffered from recurrent back pain, compared to 40 per cent of men. But women who suffer from back problems take an average of 10.4 days off per year, compared to their male colleagues who take 33 days sick leave per year for back pain. HSE's Elizabeth Gyngell said: 'In 2004, 205,000 women took time off work to recover from back injuries, and no doubt many more suffered in silence' (Trades Union Congress 2005d).

Musculoskeletal disorders are the most prevalent recorded form of occupational injury in Britain – over 1 million cases are reported by workers per year (www.hse.gov.uk/msd/index.htm). Incidence rates for these conditions – low back pain, joint injuries and repetitive strain injuries of various sorts – are slightly higher for women than for men (www.hse.gov.uk/statistics/causdis/musc.htm). It is of interest that these are classified as ill-health, and do not figure in injury data. Though long contested by medicine and the law, and often dismissed as the complaint of the malingerer, these injuries – to the hands, the back, the arm and the shoulder – vary from acute pain, to chronic, long-term, progressively intensifying pain, to disfigurement and crippling. A list of the popular names associated with some of these injuries says something of their association with women: 'typist's cramp, washer-woman's wrist, mother's shoulder' (Huws 1987: 50–1). If we add to that list a term that emerged in Australia in the 1970s – 'ethnic wrist' – then it is clear that these are injuries associated with poorly protected, marginalised workers.

Women also experience significant levels of inter-personal violence in the workplace. British Crime Survey estimates of violence at work – threats and assaults – indicate that men and women face similar levels of risk of being assaulted at work, but that women had a higher risk of being threatened (www.hse.gov.uk/statistics/causdis/violence.htm). And HSE's survey of self-reported working conditions reveal 'a greater proportion of females than males reported being physically attacked (8 per cent compared with 6 per cent) or threatened (18 per cent compared with 15 per cent) in their current job' (ibid.). While BCS data indicate that 'protective service occupations' have the greatest estimated rates of assaults and threats, these are followed by 'health and social welfare associate professionals' – which tend to be female jobs. Employers have a legal duty to risk assess to prevent violence, and this assessment must account for the specific risks faced by female workers. Compliance with and enforcement of this duty is poor (Trades Union Congress 2002).

Given the peculiar nature of women's vulnerability to certain kinds of injuries, the legal requirements for employers to assess risks should often include a gendered element. However, recent survey evidence indicates the failure of employers to meet their legal duties in this respect. Thus, of employers' responses to problems raised by women workers, this evidence concludes that: 26 per cent of employers always take the problems seriously; 56 per cent of employers sometimes take them seriously; 12 per cent of employers rarely take them seriously; and 3 per cent of employers never take them seriously (ibid.). Thus, only in one out of four cases does management always take the problems raised by women workers seriously. The particular health and safety concerns of working women need to be effectively addressed and taken seriously on all occasions by all employers. Twenty seven per cent of risk assessments have not addressed women's concerns, and 41 per cent have only partly addressed them. So in less than three out of ten cases are employers fully addressing the risks faced by women workers despite the legal requirement to do so (ibid.). This is as likely to be borne of an implicit assumption of 'the worker' as being male rather than out of any conscious discrimination; but whatever the reason, the effects are the same. Thus, for example where women and men are performing the same tasks, women could be placed at greater risk of injury than men because the job equipment and personal safety equipment are designed to fit the average man (Smith and Mustard 2004). In its respect, one could conclude that the relative invisibility of women's safety issues is exacerbated by employers' safety compliance efforts, in turn reproducing women's invisible victimisation.

The association between vulnerability and victimisation is further highlighted in recent HSE-sponsored research examining the experiences of different ethnic groups of work-related stress (Smith *et al.* 2005). Nationally, HSE estimates that about half a million people in the UK experience work-related stress at a level they believe is making them ill, with a total of 12.8 million working days lost to stress, depression and anxiety in 2003/4. Stress, of course, has multiple causes, but is generally experienced more greatly by those who are least able to exert any control or influence over workplace demands placed upon them. It is, then, a classic disease of workplace marginalisation and vulnerability. Smith *et al.* found a 'significant correlation' between work stress and ethnicity. In summary, they concluded that '[r]acial discrimination, particularly in combination with gender and ethnicity, was identified as having a strong influence on work stress . . . certain work characteristics were also associated with work stress: higher effort reward imbalance, greater job demand, and lower control over work were all associated with work stress' (ibid.: viii). Put simply, despite popular myths about stress being associated with high flying corporate executives, if you are a minority-ethnic female, low down the occupational hierarchy with little or no control over your work, and both over-worked and under-paid, then you are likely to be subject to this form of occupational disease. Understanding exposure to and victimisation from risk, and differential responses to and public knowledges of this victimisation, thus requires an understanding of various forms of class–race–gender articulations. Such an understanding requires deconstructing traditional representations of workplace risk and hazards.

Globally, a particularly heavy toll of death and injury occurs in developing countries where large numbers of workers are concentrated in primary and extraction activities such as agriculture, logging, fishing and mining (Takala 2002: 2–3). This unequal international distribution of risk is further exacerbated by the struggle to secure safer and healthier workplaces in developed countries having as one effect the relocation of risk and hazard to developing economies – creating a key advantage for Transnational Companies in their ability to 'export' hazardous work from more to less regulated contexts economies (Castleman 1979; Ives 1985). The classic and most infamous manifestation of this was the Bhopal 'disaster'. While the gas leak was the result of a combination of production and cost-cutting decisions (Pearce and Tombs 1998), the very fact that MIC was on-site at all in Bhopal was the consequence of successful resistance by French chemical workers to a prior Union Carbide intention to store and use MIC at its plant in Beziers, France (ibid.).

The long and still largely unsuccessful struggle of the victims of the Bhopal gas leak to gain compensation for human and environmental suffering also indicates a further structural inequality associated with global risk distribution: for the economic consequences of death, injury and disease associated with working are also differentially distributed. Thus, for example, occupational health and safety compensation schemes differ enormously – while workers in Nordic countries enjoy nearly universal coverage, 'only 10 per cent or less of the workforce in many developing countries is likely to benefit from any sort of coverage. Even in many developed countries, coverage against occupational injury and illness may extend to only half the workforce' (Takala, cited in Demaret and Khalef 2004).

Finally, to talk of deaths and injuries is not merely to refer to *physical* harms. Occupational injuries – however 'minor' – have widespread, if largely unrecognised, financial, psychological, as well as social effects. However, it is the financial costs of injuries and ill health which have been the focus of recent attention by official organisations and interest groups. Thus the HSE and governments have, for over a decade now, sought (erroneously – see Cutler and James 1996) to argue the 'business case' for improved health and safety (Health and Safety Executive 1993; Davies and Teasdale 1994; Health and Safety Commission/Department of Environment, Transport and the Regions 2000), seeing the costs to companies of injuring and causing illness as a lever to raise standards of compliance! In this context, it has been estimated that the costs of injury and ill health is £18 billion a year (see, for example, Health and Safety Commission/Department of Environment, Transport and the Regions 2000, *passim*). Yet one of the contradictions within such an argument is that employers *do not* actually meet the costs of workplace injuries and illness: most of the £18 billion cost of workplace injury and illness is paid for by the government and the victims. Indeed, notwithstanding the contemporary prevalence of claims about a 'compensation culture', currently fewer than one in ten workers entitled to compensation for a work-related injury or disease actually receive this (Pickvance 2005). Even the HSE itself estimates that employers, who cause the health and safety risks, pay between £3.3 billion and £6.5 billion (Trades Union Congress 2003c). In other words, costs associated with injuries and ill health represent a socialisation of the costs of private production, in effect a massive redistribution of wealth from the poor to the rich. That is, through supporting the cost of industrial injury benefit, health and other social services, paying higher insurance premiums, paying higher prices for goods and services so that employers can recoup the costs of downtime, retraining, the replacement of plants and so on, private industry is subsidised on a massive scale by employees, taxpayers and the general public. This in turn has knock-on effects on governments' ability to use revenue from general taxation for more socially productive purposes.

Such bald statistics of deaths or losses to corporate profits or GDP mask a wide array of searing, but less quantifiable, social and psychological harms. Families and communities are subjected to trauma in the event of death and injury. Children lose mothers and fathers, spouses lose partners, sports teams lose coaches and players, church and social clubs lose their members, and workers lose their colleagues – to the extent that such psychological and social costs are immeasurable. Moreover, such losses and harms have effects across generations, so that, for example, children who experience poverty following the death of the main wage earner are themselves more likely to grow up in conditions of relative insecurity, a condition then more likely to be experienced by their own offspring.[19] It remains to be noted that the psychological trauma heaped upon the bereaved is often magnified greatly by the consistent inability of the state, through the criminal justice system, to provide 'answers' as to why someone who leaves for work either does not return, or returns in a considerably less fit condition – despite central elements to law's own stated 'promise' being, first, to provide mechanisms for bringing the perpetrators of illegal harms to account, and, second, indeed increasingly, to provide redress for victims of such harms (Tombs 2004).

Conclusion

The data that has been reviewed in this chapter indicate that no matter how incomplete the officially recorded deaths and injuries caused by work, the toll is undoubtedly huge. The reconstruction of UK fatality data presented here produces a minimal estimate of 1,700 people killed annually. However, this exercise still tells us relatively little about how victimisation is distributed. In a global or even European context, as we have pointed out, the UK may not represent an exemplar case, but it is by no means the most dangerous country in which to work. The annual death toll of people caused by work globally rivals the death toll caused by wars and dwarfs the death toll caused by acts of terrorism, no matter how broadly 'terrorism' is defined (International Labour Organisation 2005).

To the inadequacies of the headline figures on deaths and injuries, we can add major inadequacies in our knowledge of how deaths and injuries at work are distributed. Yet our review of the limited conclusions that we can draw from existing data and the few empirical studies that exist on the distribution of victimisation provides a powerful illustration of the extent to which position in the workplace, socio-economic group, gender and ethnicity structure the risk of being injured or killed. Moreover, when it comes to absorbing the social and economic costs of deaths and injuries at work, it is the most vulnerable that bear the greatest burden. None of this is revealed in any of the officially published data sets; precious little is revealed in government-funded research into the subject.

More meaningfully, this discussion has urged us to explore how exposure to risks through work produces a highly concrete manifestation of what has been called the structuring of vulnerability (Nichols 1986) – it is one of the means by which the poorest, most disadvantaged people in our society are further, systematically discriminated against in terms of the quality, longevity, even preservation of their lives. At the same time, as is often the case with structured inequalities, these exposures remain relatively invisible, further exacerbating social, economic and political marginalisation of those who face them.

Notes

1 Further details can be found at International Labour Organisation (2005) and at www.corporateaccountability.org/internationsl/deaths/tables/summary/main.htm

2 Source: www.europa.eu.int/rapid/pressReleasesAction.do?reference=STAT/04/55& format=HTML&aged=0&language=EN&guiLanguage=en. See Eurostat, Population and Social Conditions, 'Work and health in the EU – A statistical portrait'. Eurostat is the Statistical Office of the European Communities.

3 HSE note that examples of major injuries include 'fractures (except to fingers, thumbs or toes), amputations, dislocations (of shoulder, hip, knee, spine) and other injuries leading to resuscitation or 24-hour admittance to hospital' (source www.hse.gov.uk/ statistics/sources.htm).

4 Moreover, even this recognised level of under-reporting still in principle excludes three potentially significant – if somewhat overlapping – areas of occupational injuries, namely those incurred by workers in the illegal economy, as well as by home- and child-workers (see, for example, O'Donnell and White 1998, 1999).

5 In the supplementing of officially-recorded data with self-report data via the Labour Force Survey, there is some similarity with the Home Office's development of the British Crime Survey as a self-report, victimisation survey aimed to overcome some of the problems associated with recorded crime statistics and the so-called hidden figure of crime; it is clear, however, that the two exercises are very differently resourced, and attract very different levels of political commitment. It should also be noted that in 2005, the HSE conducted its first Workplace Health and Safety Survey, completed by 996 employer respondents, aiming to 'record health and safety conditions across British workplaces'. One aim of this is to supplement recorded injury data. A worker survey is planned for 2006 (www.hse.gov.uk/statistics/ pdf/whassnotes.pdf).

6 This calculation is made upon the basis of a combination of reported injuries under RIDDOR and self-reported injury through the Labour Force Survey.

7 Though not apparent from the data in the table, over 95 per cent of fatal injuries to workers in any one year are overwhelmingly sustained by men (Health and Safety Commission 2001. 56–7).

8 As is just as likely to be the case with the one hundred plus annual fatalities to members of the public that are not suicides on railways.

9 Moreover, self-employment has grown dramatically in recent years, rising from just over 2 million workers in 1974 to a current total of around 3.8 million (www.hse.gov.uk/statistics/empolyment/index.htm).

10 The numbers of fatalities relating to the supply and use of flammable gas are hardly irrelevant in the context of the overall total of fatalities. In the five reporting years between 2000 and 2005, 33, 26, 25, 18 and 23 such deaths respectively were reported to HSE (www.hse.gov.uk/statistics/tables/tablegs1.htm).

11 Also excluded are injuries reportable under separate merchant shipping, civil aviation and air navigation legislation; injuries to members of the armed forces; and fatal injuries to the self-employed arising out of accidents at premises which the injured person either owns or occupies (source: www.hse.gov.uk/statistics/sources.htm).

12 For a more detailed treatment of the reconstruction of fatality data, see Tombs 1999a.

13 Thanks to Gary Slapper for first bringing these points to our attention.

14 We shall return to these arguments regarding what Snider (1991) has called the dynamics of regulatory reform in Chapter 7.

15 For example, the Simon Jones memorial campaign (www.simonjones.org.uk) or the Centre for Corporate Accountability (www.corporateaccountability.org).

16 We acknowledge both that there are exceptions to this criticism, and that the criticism applies to our own work.

17 For example, the first campaigning aim of the UK National Stress Network, part of the Hazards Campaign, is for 'the recognition of stress-related illness as an industrial injury' (UK National Work Stress Network 2006: 3).

18 Source: www.womenandequalityunit.gov.uk/women–work/women_top.htm

19 Thanks to Paddy Hillyard for first pointing out to us this particular dimension of the harms associated with occupational injury and ill health.

Chapter 3

Obscuring safety crimes

Introduction

In previous chapters – through a brief consideration of a series of case studies within the rubric of safety crimes, and then through presenting a range of data regarding the scale and distribution of occupational deaths and injuries – we have indicated that in objective, if sheer physical, terms, deaths and injuries at work represent a significant social problem. Of course, as we have emphasised, this does not necessarily mean that this social problem is recognised popularly nor politically: that is, such injuries and deaths may remain relatively invisible, or if visible, be perceived as neither a significant social nor indeed a crime problem; and each of these is in fact the case. The anomaly apparent here – a significant toll of death and injury which seems to barely register as a social or crime problem – needs further consideration. In short, how is it that safety crimes are obscured from view?

The very fact that these deaths and injuries tend *not* to be counted as crimes within official data is one in a series of intimately linked social processes through which their existence and nature is obscured and distorted. Law and legal processes play a key role in rendering such events as separate from real crime, and we consider these in subsequent chapters. Here, however, we note some of the general processes related to their more general invisibility from crime, law and order discourses, before focusing in particular upon a key element of this invisibility, namely the ways in which safety crimes are represented both as accidents, and then as phenomena that imply various degrees of culpability on the part of victims.

The invisibility of safety crimes

At the broadest level, safety crimes remain socially, politically, and academically invisible in ways which mirror the invisibility of corporate crimes in general. Thus there is an array of social processes that contribute to removing such offences from dominant definitions of 'crime, law and order' (Slapper and Tombs 1999).

Here, what has been increasingly recognised as 'the politics of law and order' is clearly important (Hale 2004; Downes and Morgan 2002; Brake and Hale 1992). Generally, as law and order has become a politicised area, then law and order discourses have drawn various events and processes *onto* the terrain of crime, expanding the reach of the criminal justice system. But this 'net-widening' (Cohen 1985) has not extended to safety crimes. Here, the effect has been quite different: in simply not considering occupational deaths and injuries within crime, law and order discourses, the difference between the former and real crime has been further cemented. More generally, beyond this rhetorical level, there are a whole series of ways in which political processes exclude safety crimes from considerations of crime, law and order.

Firstly, it is clearly Governments that formally define crime, that pass or block legislation, that fund enforcement bodies, that send formal and informal signals to the ways in which laws are to be enforced, and so on. These considerations, to the extent that they deal with the passage and implementation of the law, will be dealt with in a later chapter, where we consider the myriad ways in which law *separates out* safety offences from 'real' crimes (Chapter 5). But here we might also add some further – perhaps disparate – observations which point to the de-criminalisation of safety offences through political processes. Institutionally, the Government department that deals with crime is the Home Office; the office of state that covers safety regulation is (currently) the Department of Work and Pensions – not exactly synonymous with crime-fighting. Running the Home Office – that is, being Home Secretary – is now one of the highest profile Government offices, ranking close to Chancellor and Foreign Secretary in seniority. Responsibility for health and safety, by contrast, is located at junior minister level, within the DWP. A further contrast is found in the level of political stability afforded to these different areas. From the election of the first Blair Government in 1997, to 2007, three Labour Governments have seen just four ministers running the Home Office (Straw, Blunkett, Clarke and Reid)[1]; in 2007, Lord McKenzie became the seventh minister responsible for safety and health at work in seven years, and the ninth since Labour came to power in 1997. Long before Lord McKenzie's appointment, unions, safety campaigners, RoSPA and even the Institute of Directors bemoaned the lack of ministerial continuity, prompting the hardly radical Institution of Occupational Safety and Health to note how this game of 'pass the safety parcel' . . . 'begs the question of how seriously the government takes safety, when it still hasn't delivered on its manifesto commitments' (Jolliffe 2004: 2).[2]

Of course, a key product of the lack of political priority attached to safety offending is the very poverty and paucity of data in this area which was the focus of the previous chapter. If, as Maguire notes, 'a salient feature of almost all modern forms of discourse about crime is the emphasis placed upon terms associated with its quantification and measurement' (Maguire 1994: 236), then it is hardly surprising that neither safety crime in particular nor corporate crimes in general 'feature in . . . debates about the "crime problem"' (Nelken 1994: 355; Green 1990: 27).

This separation of safety crimes from the proper sphere of crime, law and order politics is reflected in, and in turn reinforced by, the sheer torrent of criminal justice legislation aimed at the usual 'suspects'. Thus it has been estimated that the period of Labour Governments since 1997 has seen over 50 pieces of crime and immigration legislation pass through Parliament (Hillyard 2006), while it has been generally claimed that over 1,000 new criminal offences had been created up to May 2005.[3] None of these of course has impinged upon safety crimes with the one major piece of legislation in this area, new legislation to make it easier to prosecute companies for corporate manslaughter, taking ten years from the point at which it first appeared in Labour's manifesto to the point at which it appeared in Parliament for debate (see also Chapter 6).

If we leave the sphere of formal politics, it is also clear that in any case long-standing constructions of crime and the criminal create obstacles to businesses and business people being viewed in similar ways to conventional offenders: thus there is also a significant lack of fit between offenders in the sphere of safety crimes, and those in the context of conventional crimes. In terms of business organisations, corporations may have been granted the status of legal persons, but they do not equate with popular images of real persons, let alone 'criminal' ones; similarly, directors of and managers within them simply do not fit our popular images of offenders (see Lacey 1995: 21). Individual business offenders simply do not 'look the criminal type'. Although any first year student of criminology can articulate a series of critiques of Lombrosian categories, the idea that criminals look a certain way – or at least do *not* look certain ways – is, in our view, enormously powerful. When the photographs of six men (four from the former line operator Railtrack and two from the construction firm Balfour Beatty) appeared on the front of national and regional newspapers on the day that their trial for manslaughter charges following the Hatfield train crash commenced (Tuesday February 1, 2005), it was immediately apparent that *they simply did not look like killers.*

Moreover, if it has *historically* jarred to think of businesses and business people as offenders, this has become even more the case under the emergence to dominance of neo-liberalism, where the legitimacy afforded to businesses and business people has been significantly augmented (Snider 2000; Tombs 2001). Indeed, more recently, far from being potential criminals, business people are those whom we are supposed increasingly to aspire to be, role models of synoptic societies, and even – as in the case of some like Branson, Sugar and Trump – celebrities. Corporations and those who work within them, then, are viewed quite differently to the objects of 'traditional' crime concerns; 'conventional criminals' tend to be represented as a burden upon society in a way that corporations will not be. Further, where business organisations engage in criminal activity, this tends to be cast as involving technical infringements of law, rather than real crimes. Finally, and crucially, as we have argued elsewhere with respect to corporate crimes in general, offences are represented as an aberration from their routine, legitimate activities – a point we shall take up below with respect to the power of the language of accidents.

These assumptions, and the general contrast with 'real' crime and 'real' criminals, are reflected in and reinforced by the media. Whether we survey fictional or documentary-style treatments of crime on TV, or newspaper and other print media coverage of the issues, we find that while there may be some attention to safety crime – specialist documentary programmes, for example – representations of crime converge to produce 'blanket' conceptualisations regarding 'law-and-order' that reinforce dominant stereotypes of crime and the criminal (Chibnall 1977). Thus, as with corporate crimes in general, where safety crime is covered, its presence is vastly outweighed by treatments of conventional crime, it is treated in lower profile outlets or formats, and is often represented in the rather sanitising language of scandals, disasters, abuses and accidents rather than as criminal activity (Tombs and Whyte 2001).

The point here is not, of course, to claim that the media creates our images, ways of seeing and understanding: the situation is much more complex than that. But one of the reasons why the media is particularly powerful in the context of corporate crimes in general and safety crimes in particular, is because these already seem for many of us to be far removed from our immediate experience. And this is partly an effect of the relationship between the offender and the victim in many corporate offences. In most forms of traditional crime there is, or must at some point be, a degree of proximity between offender and victim. By contrast, with safety crimes, there are frequently enormous distances between offender and victim, in terms of both space and time – many of the operating conditions on Piper Alpha or at Bhopal or the ship on which Simon Jones was working were determined many miles away in the United States or Holland, by 'faceless' managements in Union Carbide or Occidental Petroleum or Euromin Limited., who had no contact, *let alone any relationship*, with the workers or passengers who were to die as a result of decisions taken – or not taken – some time in the past (see Chapter 1).

Indeed, many victims of both corporate and safety crimes may never be aware of their status as victims (Croall 2001; Meier and Short 1995). A response to sustaining an injury at work may be to chide ourselves to be more careful in the future – we are at least as likely to blame ourselves (below) rather than think that we may be the victim of an offence. And even if people are, or become, aware of their status as victims, acting upon this awareness is often extremely difficult. While it is an issue of health rather than of safety, if we return to asbestos-caused diseases, this much is clear. Thus, the asbestos-industry tried to suppress information about ill-health effects for over 100 years by co-opting the medical community, attacking critical science and funding industry-friendly research, by forming apparently 'independent' lobbying groups, and through quite simple and routine cover-ups, manipulation of data, and lying to workers and regulators; and then Governments failed to support victims in their efforts to secure compensation.

Finally, even if aware of their victimisation, it may be perfectly rational for injured workers or their bereaved families *not* to act on this – for example, to attempt to pursue the issue of any criminal offence having been committed. For one thing, HSE and its inspectorates, while formally charged with responding to complaints, are notoriously reluctant to be seen to take the side of workers since they have been adamant since their formation that they do not become involved in 'industrial relations issues' – and, as we shall see, operate on the basis of there being a natural 'identity of interests' between employers and employees on the issue of safety at work. Thus the chances of 'success' of working through formal channels are slim indeed. And against this need to be balanced the reactions of employers to those raising safety complaints – which can range from intimidation through to barring an employee from a whole industry (see Tombs and Whyte 1998). Finally, the widespread focus upon behaviour-based safety schemes (see below) and their links to 'no-accident' bonus schemes within workplaces and companies acts as another powerful disincentive against acting upon one's recognition of possible victimisation.

Now, none of the various mechanisms whereby safety crimes are rendered relatively invisible are particularly remarkable in isolation. What is crucial, however, *is their mutually reinforcing nature* – that is, they all work in the same direction and to the same effect, removing these crimes from 'crime, law and order' agendas. Moreover, they operate alongside a powerful set of discourses which create injuries within the context of the workplace as something always/already distinct from crimes – that is, as *accidents*.

Occupational *accidents*

It remains common, indeed ubiquitous, to refer to incidents that lead to death or injury at work as 'accidents'. This term is a neutral, 'anaesthetising' one; by contrast, alternative terms, such as industrial killing, wounding, or violence, would carry with them quite different connotations and logically be related to quite different legal, political and social responses. The language of accidents infects almost all statements and documents on the issue of workplace deaths and injuries, on the part of Governments, regulators, NGOs, academics and even trade unions and campaigning groups. Thus, for example, in his Foreword to the Government's flagship strategy document, *Revitalising Health and Safety*, Deputy Prime Minister Prescott refers to the 'tragic rail accident' at Ladbroke Grove – an incident still subject to a criminal legal investigation at that time[4] (Health and Safety Commission/DETR 2000: Foreword, and *passim*). A major HSE report on 30 years of health and safety legislation and enforcement presented a self-congratulatory table headed 'The Decline in Fatal Accidents', despite the fact that HSE does not record *accidents*, only fatal injuries (Health and Safety Executive 2004c: 5) – a nomenclature repeated by academics when they speak of this area, even when they claim awareness of some of its problematic implications (see Hutter 2001: 50, *passim*). As we noted at the outset to Chapter 2, the ILO has recorded how the number of 'fatal occupational accidents' is increasing internationally (International Labour Organisation 2005: 1).

Now, these observations are not raised in any point-scoring fashion. The point is that all of those who comment upon safety incidents in the workplace tend to fall easily at times into using the language of accidents – including ourselves, we are sure – and this indicates its ubiquitousness, its pervasiveness, its all-too-easy commonsensical appeal. The language of accidents is both socially available and socially prioritised. And it is for these reasons, and as a preface to our discussion here, we also need to make clear that this language is not generally used consciously. At the same time, though, we must recognise that at times use of this language *is* the result of conscious corporate manipulation, both generally and in relation to specific events (Wells 1993: 40). As Wells notes, and as is particularly of relevance given the nature of victimisation in the case of many forms of safety crimes, the further removed the harms they cause are from the public experience, then the easier is such manipulation (ibid.: 40).

But of more interest to us are the ways in which the use of particular forms of language need not be understood simply, or perhaps even largely, as the result of conscious manipulation, since 'The social construction of behaviour and events results from a complex interaction between a number of factors, including cultural predispositions, media representations, and legal rules, decisions, and pronouncements' (Wells 2001: 11). That is, we need to know something of how this language is sustained and, further, what its power and effects are.

One observation that needs to be made is that the applicability of the term accident can be sustained partly due to the low level of investigation of industrial injuries, near-misses, and so on, as we shall see in Chapter 4. This systematic lack of analysis of the causes of workplace incidents is one of the key mechanisms by which the ideology of the accident can persist, both for the very lack of scrutiny of actual causes and also because the fact of an investigation immediately raises a particular incident as unusual, and thus anomalous, or, in Mathiesen's (2004: 37–48) terms, 'isolated'. In mutually reinforcing fashion, of course, the lack of investigation itself is partly based upon the idea of the 'accident': in their study on the police investigation of safety crimes, Alvesalo and Jauhiainen (2006) found how incidents were often described and defined as accidents, with the contributory negligence of the victim emphasised; such constructions influenced police work, and were used as reasons *not* to proceed with a crime investigation.

In our view, then, the predominance of the language of accidents (and associated terms like tragedy) – along with derivatives reserved for multiple fatality incidents such as disaster – to refer to workplace deaths and injuries carries with it several, reinforcing, sets of implications, each of which even in isolation renders it less rather than more likely that the events and processes thus obscured can be viewed as crimes:

First, the term 'accident' carries with it implications regarding intentionality, or the lack of it, which are crucial in the context of safety and health crimes. Thus Goldman notes that what she calls 'accidentality terms',

> provide us with an account of the mental element – intention, will, desire, deliberation, purpose, etc. – in some event. When describing some incident or process as an 'accident', or having 'occurred/been done accidentally' rather than 'deliberately' or 'intentionally', we conflate information not just about causation, and perhaps (if pertinent) degrees of culpability and fault to be imputed, but also about the element of consciousness that intruded into the event (Goldman 1994: 51–2).

As we shall demonstrate in Chapters 5 and 6, the concept of intent enjoys significant legal status – and, relatedly, for some it is a key distinguishing criterion between conventional ('real') crime and corporate crime (merely technical offences). Below, in this chapter, we shall also set out how it is in fact problematic when set against common-sense standards of moral seriousness. For now, it is enough to say that, given that intent is deemed intrinsic to crime, or at least to serious crime, then to ascribe to deaths and injuries a status implying a lack of intent, that is, 'accidental', is immediately to obscure an inter-related set of issues around seriousness, criminality, fault, causation, and so on.

Second, the language of 'accidents' is one which focuses upon specific events, abstracting them from a more comprehensible context (Scheppele 1991). It evokes discrete, isolated and random events, processes, systems and carries with it connotations of the unforeseeable, unknowable and unpreventable, despite the fact that any examination of a range of incidents reveals common, systematic, foreseeable and eminently preventable causes and consistent locations of responsibility. Such language is one way of performing the techniques of isolation referred to above, following Mathiesen, whilst it also already helps to pre-empt further, and certainly critical, scrutiny – or, scrutiny of certain kinds. Thus 'If accidents are discrete, unforeseen and chance events . . . then it becomes difficult to see them as social events, as socially contexted' (Harrison 1993: 255).

In these uses of apparently innocent, or neutral, linguistic terms which in fact carry enormous social and political meaning, there are striking parallels here with Mathiesen's recent, and brilliant, analysis of political repression in advanced capitalist economies. Whilst accepting that in such efforts physical coercion still has key roles to play, Mathiesen emphasises 'silent silencing'. Silencing is the creation of acquiescence to dominant ways of understanding the world:

> Silence in this sense is a continuum, from silence despite disagreement (grudgingly you go along) to silence as an accepting attitude (you accept the standpoint, not even noticing that silencing has taken place, or at least not taking the fact of silencing seriously). (Mathiesen 2004: 9)

The silent element of the silencing process refers to the creation of acquiescence 'through a process which is quiet rather than noisy, hidden rather than seen, non-physical rather than physical' (ibid.).

And these are precisely the ways in which the processes pointed to above operate. Indeed, a key illustration of silent silencing for Mathiesen is afforded by the capsizing of the Alexander Kielland, an oil installation in the Norwegian North Sea, in 1980, which resulted in 123 deaths. For Mathiesen, the scale of this event was one which posed fundamental questions regarding the extraction of oil from the North Sea, that is, as an event it became a challenge to authority and to a key economic activity. To some extent, then, the incident is similar to the fire and explosion on Piper Alpha in July 1988 (a threat to oil production and thus to the British economy), the capsizing of the *Herald of Free Enterprise* (a threat to passenger ferry services within an increasingly competitive market, and to a large conglomerate, P&O), the gas leak at Bhopal (which put into focus the activities of chemicals companies across the developed and developing worlds), or the series of train crashes that beset the UK in the 1980s and 1990s (which, by the late 1990s, finally threw the network into chaos, this leading eventually to the demise of Railtrack). In the case of the Alexander Kielland, such was the threat posed, claims Mathiesen, that a concerted response was required:

> because people's perception of totality or context is dangerous to an activity like oil extraction it becomes important for the representatives of the activity to pulverise the relationships which people begin to see (ibid.: 37).

Silencing through pulverisation – which becomes 'more important the more extensive and sensational the event is' (ibid.) – requires a series of techniques to be deployed, and for us these are useful when thinking about the ways in which power deals with the mundane, routine industrial deaths and injuries and the acute events that erupt into public consciousness from time to time.

Most crucially, the event in question needs to be isolated. Pulverisation through isolation encompasses a series of techniques in the form of messages through mass media and political discourse. Of particular interest in the context of this discussion is that for Mathiesen this firstly entails the event being 'individualised', that is, the event is 'made into something unique, something incomparable, and something quite special, individual and atypical', far too exceptional for any generalised lessons to be drawn or arguments made (ibid.: 38). The event may also be 'normalised'. Although this may seem contrary to individualisation, it is perfectly comprehensible as a complementary technique: for normalisation can only proceed effectively if the event is pulled out of a regular, familiar context and placed into another; and within this other context – the high risk industry or the inherently dangerous activity or, we would add here, the at–risk worker (below) – then this apparently unique event becomes entirely usual, relatively typical and ordinary. The event may also be 'split up', by which it is meant that the event is reduced to a series of loosely connected, relatively minor details of an incident – often technical in nature – which are thereby torn from their systemic context and their systematic relationship with this context; thus post-Piper discussions could come to revolve endlessly around by the availability of Temporary Safe Refuges, post-Zeebrugge by technical questions of ro-ro ferry design, or train safety by the cost and merits of Automatic Train Protection systems.

Now these arguments are important in themselves. But what is also crucial about them, for us, is how Mathiesen's claims regarding isolation are crystallised through the language which sits at the heart of discussion – official, political, academic or popular – of occupational safety, namely the language of accidents. And it is to a further, more specific consideration of the nature and power of such language that we now turn.

Victim blaming and the accident-prone worker

If the language of accidents carries with it a whole series of connotations, there is one further set of consequences to be discussed here, in some detail, which revolve around the issue of victim blaming. The basis of victim-blaming discourses is to be found in the idea of 'accident-prone-ness' which, in the context of occupational safety, has a very specific history. Sass and Crook (1981) note that the term 'accident prone' was first coined in 1926,[5] when studies conducted in the UK concluded that 'varying individual susceptibility to "accidents" is an extremely important factor in determining the [accident frequency] distribution' (ibid.: 183). Latterly, Grayson and Goddard set out its meaning:

> Accident proneness is generally used to mean that accidents are caused by a few individuals who tend to have a large number of accidents – and that they have repeated accidents *no matter what precautions the employer takes* (Grayson and Goddard 1976: 17, emphasis added).

According to these definitions, then, accident proneness is a 'quality' of individuals, something associated with personality types, personal characteristics and/or lifestyles, and a 'quality' that they bring with them into the workplace. And it is with the emergence of this notion of accident proneness that we can perceive some kind of foundation or basis for the prevalence of the plethora of arguments (and tactics) that can be subsumed under the practice of worker/victim blaming. We also see the basis for a whole series of professional/'expert' interventions into the workplace which address not dangerous work organisation or plant, but which attempt to modify the behaviour of workers. In this, there is perhaps an analogy to be drawn with the 'birth' of criminology, as documented by Foucault, this taking on a particular form on the basis of a specific definition of the problem to be treated:

[An individual] steals because he is poor, certainly, but we all know that all the poor don't steal. So, for that individual to steal, then there must be something wrong with him. This something is his character, his psyche, his education, his unconscious, his desires. And with that the delinquent is handed over to a penal technology, that of the prison, and a medical technology, if not of the asylum, at any rate that of specialised supervision (Foucault 1977 : 12).

Thus, as not all workers are involved in accidents, despite working in the same environment as colleagues, then some of them are defined as accident-prone (or a variation upon this – lazy, stupid, careless, and so on) just as the poor who steal are defined as 'criminal' or 'criminogenic', since not all the poor steal. The fault is not in the system which maintains the poor in poverty, just as it is not in the working environment which presents hazards to a workforce.

Fifty years after the 'discovery' of accident-proneness in studies by Greenwood and others, the Robens Committee – whose report largely determined the nature and substance of the 1974 Health and Safety at Work Act – itself explicitly recommended that government address this problem in its approach to health and safety regulation. According to the particular version of this concept contained in the Committee's Report, the single most important reason for accidents at work was worker apathy (Robens 1972: 1). Asserting that 'Safety is mainly a matter of the day-to-day attitudes and reactions of the individual', it concluded that accident prevention should focus upon the fostering of safety awareness (ibid.: 1-2). Thus the Robens Committee pinpointed those workers involved in, or close to the scene of, industrial accidents, rather than unhealthy and unsafe working conditions, as the locus of potential improvements in industrial health and safety.

There is no intention here to enter into a critical commentary upon the original studies conducted by Greenwood and others on the distribution of accidents among a particular cohort of workers – this has been done more than adequately elsewhere (Sass and Crook 1981). What is important for our purposes is to note the shift in the use of, or reference to, accident-proneness. This 'concept' is no longer used in any specific sense, as originally developed – that is, referring to workers who have been 'shown' statistically to be more likely than others to have accidents. Rather, it has come to be used in a much more generalised, vague but highly functional fashion – workers as a whole are viewed as a group of people predisposed towards accidents, through incompetence, carelessness, apathy, recklessness, and so on. Accidents are linked with workers. Those on the scene of accidents are held, almost automatically, as responsible. In a generalised sense, then, 'workers' become the problem at the heart of occupational safety – and this in turn is the basis for worker, and often victim, blaming in discourse and practice around occupational safety (and, moreover, this set of tactics is one amongst a variety of strategies by which the victims of social problems in general are held responsible for their plight – see Ryan 1971; Goodey 2005: 96–9).

Where a worker is blamed (either explicitly or implicitly) in practice, this tactic will at times involve resort to one or several characteristics – that they are incompetent, lazy, apathetic, inattentive, careless, reckless, and so on. Crucially, although the notion of risk is directly invoked, it is seen not as something that exists apart from, and thereby imposing itself upon, the worker; rather, risk is viewed as something which originates in / is brought on by the behaviour of workers. Thus the most obvious consequence of accident-proneness and worker/victim blaming is the diversion of attention from the fact that risks are built into the very system of capitalist production, and subsequent lack of emphasis upon the nature of the workplace, the processes involved therein, and their particular rationales. If the focus on the aftermath of an incident were not to be upon workers but shifted to employers – to their employment practices (levels of training, or pressures in terms of the speed or intensity of work, for example), or to the design of the workplace and/or the job – such attention may logically lead to either cost implications, to redress the lack of investment in plant or people, or have legal ramifications, or both. As Robertson notes, 'The use of the word "accident" to describe when a worker is injured or killed hides the fact that often this is a result of a criminal act by the employer . . . . Words are being used to change the way we deal with health and safety' (2004: 6).

This strategy has a long history. Doran has argued that the very concept of an industrial accident was 'reorganised' by official discourse through the early Factory Acts, so that these events labelled accidents became separated from workers' own experiences of the broader problem of their health (understood within the organisation of production), and became subject to routine interpretation (observation, recoding, codifying) by factory inspectors (Doran 1996; see also Watterson 1991). This reorganisation itself created the possibility for the emergence of the statistically recorded unavoidable accident, subsequently situated within discourses of risk and insurance rather than negligence, culpability or criminality (Doran 1996; Defert 1991; Ewald 1991).

More generally in the context of occupational safety the idea of accident proneness has been deployed quite explicitly also to invoke events or phenomena in which victims are implicated, via their carelessness, apathy, or lifestyles (alcohol or drug abuse, poor sleeping habits, and so on; Tombs 1991). That is, victims become complicit in their victimisation –

so that they are either to be blamed or at least not to be viewed as inno-cent.[6] Thus Robertson reports how, in 2000, the *British Medical Journal* reported that it would no longer use the word 'accident' in its pages, since this was 'inappropriate': 'it argued that "most injuries and their precipitating events are predictable and preventable". It added that by using the word "accident" we were encouraging victim-blaming and reduced support for those who survived' (Robertson 2004: 6). Such assumptions of responsibility are made all too easy by the prevalence of victim-blaming strategies that have emerged around, and continue to cloud, considerations of occupational deaths and injuries.

Thus the term 'accident' both invokes and reinforces resort to an individualising lens for viewing and 'understanding' safety incidents, and this lens extends to quasi-legal approaches to such events. Law's complex reasonings in relation to defining crime, while not exclusively focused on the individual, have an individualising effect which extends beyond the notion of intent *per se*. Thus, even where intent is not the issue in determining legal liability – such as in the case of corporate manslaughter – then the individualising ethos of criminal law has militated against such successful prosecutions, whilst in contexts where this charge has been raised, such as following the Zeebrugge or Southall 'disasters', then charges of manslaughter have been raised against relatively low-level individuals on the scene of the incident – namely, the assistant bosun or the train driver (see Tombs 1995, Slapper and Tombs 1999: 30–4, 101–107, and Chapter 10, *passim*).

These legal responses are reinforced by, and themselves reinforce, the immediate 'commonsense' appeal of accident-proneness. This is clearly illustrated in media coverage of the recent disasters in the UK. In the immediate aftermath of many of these incidents, there emerged initial popular attributions of blame directed against individuals on the scene of these 'accidents'. In such cases, the power and appeal of accident proneness is only diminished through the long detail of a public inquiry, at which there is (often) a complex tracing of events surrounding an incident in order to arrive at its 'fundamental' cause(s), located within managerial and organisational systems.

Such inquiries may be contrasted with the general lack of a search for 'fundamental' causes following minor, 'day-to-day' incidents, causes thereby remaining obscured. Hughes has noted how 'social attitudes to safety tend to blame an individual for his own death through carelessness or bad luck', whereas following disasters there is at least more likelihood that there will be a public focus upon 'management' or 'systems' (Hughes 1984 : 15).

These types of argument, then, are espoused (and believed) not only by those individuals and groups that may have a vested interest in seeing their acceptance – in particular, here, we think of employers who, were workers not thus blamed, might find themselves being held responsible for a much larger proportion of industrial accidents with the possible consequence of coming to be considered as blameworthy – but indeed also by other groups who have, or have had, a direct interest in industrial health and safety – in particular, here, we refer to governments and their appointees, but also to health and safety 'experts' or professionals and, most surprisingly, to some workers themselves (Leopold 1985: 265; Watterson 1988: 293).

The practical nature and effects of the ideology of accident-proneness and worker-blaming are perhaps most clearly exemplified in the reactions of Union Carbide Corporation (UCC) to the gas release at Bhopal (see Chapter 1) – in this particular case, the 'incompetent' worker is invoked although, through the use of racist and imperialist stereotypes, this more specifically becomes the incompetent *Indian* worker (Everest 1986: 107). Thus in attempts to 'explain' the circumstances surrounding the accident, UCC refused to countenance any suggestion that the methylisocyanate leak may have resulted from fundamental inadequacies in the Bhopal plant's basic design, state of maintenance, staffing levels, and so on. In fact, UCC claimed, variously, that the leak had been caused by: a failure on the part of operators to comply with basic safety procedures; a purely mistaken introduction of water into an MIC storage tank by an unwitting employee; an act of terrorism by Sikh extremists; and, most recently, and it appears 'definitively', an act of sabotage by a disgruntled employee. More generally, UCC cast the Indian workers (and, indeed, government regulators) as technologically unsophisticated, and incapable either of understanding or adhering to basic safety procedures (ibid.).

It is not the intention here to enter into a discussion of the causes of the Bhopal disaster, nor to engage in a detailed critique of UCC's final version of the 'sabotage theory'.[7] It is sufficient to state here that, although it took UCC nearly three-and-a-half years to develop this 'theory', the idea of sabotage as the main cause of the accident had been mooted by UCC in the immediate aftermath of the tragedy; thus there is a real sense in which UCC *assumed* sabotage to be the cause of the disaster and then set out to prove in detail how this could have been the case (see, for example, Kalelkar 1988: 557, emphases added).

UCC is not exceptional. But the Bhopal disaster is particularly interest- ing for us, because the almost automatic responses of UCC to the 'accident', plus the difficulties encountered subsequently by those attempting to oppose such 'common-sensical' accounts of its causes, attest to the significance – that is, the deep-rootedness and pervasiveness – of the concept of 'accident-proneness'; and this is so even where the incident has been subject to as much publicity, investigation, and even court hearings, as has this one.

In general, then, the most important consequences of the ideological thrust of 'accident-proneness' is to assign responsibility for, and identify the objects of improvement in relation to, industrial injuries. Accepting the nature of the workplace and work processes as given means that the management of safety becomes a task of controlling the potentially hazardous actions or omissions of workers. Further, the predominance of the notion of accident-proneness meant that only *certain types* of experts entered the field of safety and health (those concerned with health sciences and the law, rather than, for example, engineers or designers of work organisation); moreover, this ideology remained virtually unquestioned by these experts, so that the very expertise which they possessed, which might in fact have proved to be a resource upon which workers could draw in the course of struggles over health and safety, was very often exercised upon workers, in the sense of being used to justify an ever-increasing regulation of the details of their behaviour, both inside and outside the workplace (Lessin and O'Neill 2002).[8] The issue becomes behaviour modification through control of workers rather than modification of dangerous workplaces – and, coupled with reward programmes for 'accident-free' working, through creating a culture of non-reporting of industrial injuries, such programmes have in-built tendencies to appear 'successful' (ibid.).

At a 'macro' level, then, the acceptance that most 'accidents' are caused by workers has key implications in terms of the necessary level and nature of regulation: that companies do not necessarily need to be subjected to more stringent state regulation in the sphere of health and safety, but rather should be left, to a large degree, to self-regulation. As Harrison has put it in her historical analysis of the role of the idea of an accident in factory regulation, it is 'a means of dealing with the difficulty for factory administration of directly interfering with employers' interests' (Harrison 1993: 269). Such approaches within both the US and the UK, then, need to be linked to the increasingly strident logic of self-regulation being espoused in many parts of the advanced capitalist world. In short, victim blaming and the 'concept' of accident-proneness are analogous to other key elements of capitalist ideology – they individualise structural issues. At a 'micro' level, then, companies, being left to self-regulation, and defining the problems of health and safety in terms of their workforce, can engage in a stricter disciplining of, and control over, the behaviour of that workforce, so that individual workers find themselves subjected to increasing levels of regulation over the minutiae of everyday behaviour in the workplace (and, indeed, outside of the workplace, too). The recent re-emergence of behaviour-based safety programmes (Lessin and O'Neill 2002) – essentially forms of behaviour modification which cover a range of techniques from disciplining to training – also involve a form of *responsibilisation* of individual workers. As recent criminology has demonstrated in the context of crime control, responsibilisation of individuals is integral to a realignment of the state's responsibilities.

The possible pincer-like combination of these macro- and micro-effects is stunningly exemplified in new regulatory practices which impose tickets (akin to parking tickets) for health and safety violations. Discussing this new practice in Ontario, Gray has argued that under 'neo-liberal self-regulation, workers are essentially forced to police their own hazards through individual responsibility', and that such an approach

> is a key example of the diffusion of employer responsibility and blameworthiness for unsafe working conditions. The ticketing practice not only directly polices workers in health and safety, but it also forces workers to practice individual responsibility. Workers must not only enforce regulation themselves to avoid unsafe work (a physical harm), but they must also be cautious of health and safety tickets (a financial harm) (Gray 2006: 879).

Indeed, a study of the rationales for the types of violations to which tickets might be attached found that these were all of a 'clear and visible' nature, and that they excluded both 'organisational factors' and 'organisational/managerial decision-making' (Gray, 2006). This, then, represents a clear blurring of responsibility for unsafe conditions, as well as 'the notion of who is a health and safety offender' (Gray 2006: 888). And its very existence is, if not wholly explained by, logically related to, ideas of accident-proneness and associated tactics of victim blaming.

Safety crimes as violence?

Now, if safety crimes tend to be obscured, rendered (relatively) invisible, while the phenomena to which this label points are in fact misrepresented as 'accidents', then one issue raised is the extent to which academic social science has sought either to address this misrepresentation, or to bring to light a relatively hidden social problem – each, surely, key rationales for academic investigation. Since our particular concern here is with the excavation of crimes, then the obvious discipline to which we might turn is criminology, in order to assess how safety crimes are considered therein. Now, on one level, this query can be answered very curtly – for if criminology has historically marginalised the crimes of the powerful, then it has paid particularly scant attention to safety crimes. For us, while this is hardly surprising, it is in one respect very curious – for within criminology there is a significant level of attention devoted to the phenomenon of violence in general. Yet if it is within this rubric of 'violent crimes' that we would argue safety crimes should be considered, any survey of criminological work on violence would conclude that such considerations are notable for their absence.

In short,[9] while there are obviously enormous epistemological, theoretical and political differences between the various approaches to violence taken within what stands for academic criminology, these approaches share, virtually without exception, certain characteristics or, more accurately, assumptions – assumptions which essentially rule out any consideration of safety crimes. Thus crucial within the definitions of violence deployed or included within these approaches are two central assumptions: first, a primacy granted to intention; and, second, a focus upon individual as opposed to collective sources of violence, and thus the centrality of violence as inter-personal as opposed to structural.

Now, intent enjoys significant legal status – while, relatedly, for some it is a key distinguishing criterion between conventional ('real') crime and corporate crime (merely technical offences) (see Pearce and Tombs 1998: 231). However, it is worth noting here that the notion of intent presupposes, and then concretises, a moral hierarchy which, once examined, is counter common-sensical. This point was first made – to the best of our knowledge – by Reiman in a simple but striking fashion. Reiman contrasts the motives (and moral culpability) of most acts recognised as intentional murder with what he calls the indirect harms on the part of absentee killers, by which he means, for example, deaths which result where employers refuse to invest in safe plant or working methods, where manufacturers falsify safety data for new products, where illegal discharges are made of toxic substances into our environment, and so on. Reiman notes that intentional murderers commit acts which are focused upon one (or, rarely, more than one) specific individual, a point which we know holds for contemporary Britain, despite moral panics about 'stranger danger'[10]; thus in such cases the perpetrator – whom in many respects fits our archetypal portrait of a criminal – 'does not show general disdain for the lives of her fellows' (Reiman 1998: 67). Reiman contrasts such forms of intentional killing with the deaths that result from 'indirect' harms. For Reiman, the relative moral culpability of the intentional killer and the mine executive who cuts safety corners is quite distinct and, he argues, contrary to (indeed diametrically opposite to) that around which criminal law operates. Thus the mine executive

wanted to harm no-one in particular, but he *knew his acts were likely to harm someone* – and once someone is harmed, the victim is someone in particular. . . . there is no moral basis for treating *one-on-one harm* as criminal and *indirect harm* as merely regulatory. (Reiman 1998: 67–70, original emphases)

Thus, Reiman concludes, offenders of intentional, one-on-one harm are less likely to represent some generalised threat to others than the mine executive. The reasoning is convincing, and points to indifference or 'indirect' harm as at least, if not more, culpable than intention and 'direct' harms – with implications for how these are treated by any criminal justice system (see Pemberton 2004). Yet the greater moral culpability that is attached both legally and popularly to acts of intention can also allow those implicated in corporate crimes to rationalise away the consequences of their actions – techniques of neutralisation made possible through, and supported by, key institutions such as the media, formal political debate, and so on (see above, also Slapper and Tombs 1999: 105–7, 118–22; and Chapter 5 *passim*).

If intent is central to dominant legal and academic understandings of violence, also significant is the primacy attached to explanations at the level of the individual. As Salmi has written, the 'usual treatment of violence' is infected with '[e]xcessive individualisation', 'attributing solely to individual factors actions that cannot in reality be accounted for in individual terms. By so doing, the possibility of a causal link between the violence observed and the surrounding social structure is systematically dismissed' (Salmi 1993: 8). Rather, focus remains upon 'the individual and the eradication of such deplorable behaviour' (Catley 2003: 4). This is unsurprising in advanced capitalist societies, since analysis at this level coheres entirely with the ethos of individualism upon which such societies are maintained.

Certainly once one abandons an epistemological commitment to individualism, then more encompassing definitions and considerations of violence become possible. For example, among the work on the issue of workplace violence, that of Bowie stands out, since he has sought to develop the category of 'organisational violence', and although this is partially limited by some commitment to intention, it is far more useful than other definitions of violence. Thus, for Bowie, organisational violence 'involves organisations knowingly placing their workers or clients in dangerous or violent situations or allowing a climate of abuse, bullying or harassment to thrive in the workplace' (Bowie 2002: 6). If this still retains some commitment to intention, it at least moves beyond simple understandings of individual action, not least because it acknowledges how a general organisational demeanour of generating or turning a blind eye towards violence can be fostered 'in a growing economic rationalist climate of decreasing job security, massive retrenchments and expanding unemployment that pitted workers and unions against employers' (ibid.: 9). Of particular interest for us is that Bowie also notes that such violence is much harder to recognise due to the tendency to 'blame' (ibid.: 6) individuals, and to develop strategies for responding to violence which are 'based on a pathology model of "mad, bad or sad" employees or clients and patients who are seen as individually responsible for the violence occurring at work' (ibid.: 8).

Similarly, Hills, in introducing a collection of case histories of 'corporate violence', defines this phenomenon as

> Actual harm and risk of harm inflicted on consumers, workers, and the general public as a result of decisions by corporate executives or managers, from corporate negligence, the quest for profits at any cost, and wilful violations of health, safety and environmental laws (Hills 1987: vii).

Through the cases presented in this collection, and in his final considerations regarding these, Hills concludes that such violence is understood 'not in the pathology of evil individuals but in the culture and structure of large-scale bureaucratic organisations within a particular political economy' (Hills 1987a: 190). Hills's understanding of violence seems to shift beyond both intention and individuals. These shifts beyond intention can also be discerned in some other, recent criminological work which, if not explicitly couched in the language of violence could be re-framed as such – we are thinking in particular here of a variety of work within the rubric of 'green' criminology (Lynch and Stretesky 2003; White 2003), within which we would include the systematic (state-corporate) exploitation of whole classes of people (Walters 2006). Indeed, across such work, the use of 'violence' starts to resemble some of the characterisations of the Holocaust, of genocide, and of other forms of state violence, and even in this very fact, the marginality of such modes of arguments to, and substantive focus within, criminology becomes apparent. So if the (partial) transgressing of the boundaries of dominant understandings of violence by Bowie and Hills are not unique, they are, within criminology, extremely rare. All too often, one must move beyond criminology – as we did in Chapter 1, where we utilised briefly the work of Salmi – to arrive at more accurate ways of describing, analysing, then theorising about violence.

Conclusion

We have sought to demonstrate in this chapter how safety crimes are systematically obscured through a series of mutually reinforcing processes. At the broadest level, safety crimes remain socially and politically invisible in ways which mirror the invisibility of corporate crimes in general. Thus there is an array of social processes that contribute to removing such offences from dominant definitions of 'crime, law and order' (Slapper and Tombs 1999).

The obscuring of the criminal aspect of safety crimes has been crucially generated and strengthened historically and contemporaneously by the idea of the accident-prone worker, which in turn legitimates strategies of victim blaming, that is, assigning responsibility for, and identifying the objects of improvement in relation to, industrial injuries onto individuals rather than the nature of the workplace, work processes, managements, cultures of an industry or sector, and so on – that is, the very causal factors we highlighted as crucial in producing safety crimes in our presentation of case studies in Chapter 1. The ideology and practices of accident-proneness thus need dismantling if we are to treat 'accidents' as (potential) safety crimes.

Indeed, once occupational injuries are viewed not as accidents but as incidents which are not only largely preventable, but which the law requires to be prevented, then they fall within the ambit of criminology. Then, as we have argued in this text, if we consider these illegalities in terms of their consequences – injury and death – we realise that these look remarkably similar to the results of those events that are deemed as 'proper' violence. However, as we have seen in the latter section of this chapter, dominant criminological conceptions of violence are based upon an implicit but tenaciously-held association of violence with both the inter-personal and with intention, both qualities that are often absent from safety crimes. That safety crimes are crimes of (actual or potential) violence is, for us, unequivocal; yet to reach this conclusion one must generally move beyond criminology, to some well-accepted understandings of violence which allow us to move beyond the interpersonal and intention, and within which safety crimes clearly fall.

It is the very organisational locus or origins of safety crime which makes the emphasis upon either an illegal *act* or an *intention* usually inappropriate, for two reasons. First, each term is anthropomorphic and individualising, and by definition is problematic in its application to a corporate entity which is more than, or different to, the sum of individual human actors. Second, intention in particular implies a relatively unproblematic link between an act or omission and its consequence, yet this simplistic causal sequencing leads to an obscuring of the construction and maintenance of a situation or context which, as a consequence, is fertile ground for violations. We reiterate a point we have made several times in this text: any focus upon safety crimes requires us to examine these in terms of their *organisational production*.

In Chapter 2, we sought to set out the extent of occupational deaths and injuries across British workplaces; we made clear at that point, however, that we were speaking of incidents rather than crimes *per se* – that is, not all deaths and injuries are the result of safety crimes. In this chapter, we have further considered the nature of these phenomena, and paved the way for considering some of these deaths and injuries as safety crimes, indeed crimes of violence. In the following chapter, Chapter 4, we turn directly, through a combination of theoretical and empirical arguments, to an attempt to reveal the extent of corporate violence in the form of safety crimes.

Notes

1   And had not Blunkett resigned following the nanny/passport/Kimberley Clarke row, he may have continued in the office, thus lending even greater continuity to this Office.

2   Safety is not of course unique in some of these respects; prisons, for example, have been presided over by a long line of junior ministers since 1997. However, the prisons minister *is* located within the Home Office. Moreover, as we argue throughout this section, the key issue is not about any specific element of the processes we describe, but the fact that they are all mutually reinforcing.

3   Such figures are difficult to establish beyond doubt, of course. This claim began to circulate on the basis of a calculation made by the Liberal Democrats Press Release at www.libdems.org.uk/story.html?id=8180 and also BBC NEWS/POLITICS, May 12, 2005, at http://newsimg.bbc.co.uk/1/low/uk_politics/4541377.stm. Given the source of this claim it needs to be treated with particular caution – but it remains that there is no doubt that a great deal of new criminal offences have been created, whether or not these can actually be counted in four figures.

4   In fact, it was only in 2005 that it was finally decided by the CPS that no individuals would face charges over the 1999 Ladbroke Grove rail crash which claimed 31 lives, the CPS citing 'insufficient evidence': Network Rail, formerly Railtrack, did face criminal charges under the Health and Safety at Work Act 1974 (BBC News, December 6, 2005, http://news.bbc.co.uk/1/hi/uk/4504696.stm).

5   Although without being named formally, claims which amount to accident proneness were in circulation well before then; see, for example, Harrison 1993, on factory inspection at the turn of the nineteenth century.

6   And thus not deserving of the state's support. Contrast with New Labour's (claimed) championing of the victim as being at the centre of the criminal justice system.

7   The former has been dealt with exhaustively, most adequately in Everest 1986; Jones 1988; Morehouse and Subramaniam 1986; and Shrivastava 1992, while the latter has been attempted in Bergman 1988 and Bhopal Action Group 1988. See, more generally, Pearce and Tombs 1998: 194–219.

8   In the previous chapter, we referred to recent research findings that about 1,000 deaths on the roads are actually work-related fatalities, concluding that 'Britains roads are the country's most dangerous workplace as under-pressure workers, struggling to meet deadlines and suffering fatigue from long hours, become a danger to themselves and others' (Trade Union Congress 2005b). In response to this, a Cranfield School of Management expert on driver behaviour said: 'Companies need to conduct psychological profiling of employees to see who has a tendency towards aggression or thrill seeking' (Campbell 2005).

9   A detailed examination of the taken-for-granted assumptions within criminology regarding what constitutes violent crimes – and the implications these assumptions have for any potential criminological focus upon safety crimes – can be found in Tombs, 2006.

10 BCS figures for 2002/03 show that 'In over half of violent incidents the offender/s were known to the victim in some way; in one-third of incidents they were known well' (Smith and Allen 2004: 11).

Chapter 4

Discovering safety 'crimes'

Introduction

In Chapter 2, we explored the extent to which we can treat official statistics on deaths and injuries at work as accurate, and argued that, whatever the limitations of the data, it is clear that occupational injuries constitute a major social problem. We have also argued that injuries and deaths at work are generally misrepresented when cast as 'accidents' – a label that has a series of problematic specific connotations and social effects. But our considerations thus far have not established the extent to which, occupational deaths and injuries can be regarded as crimes.

Now, it is important to be clear that in the context of a treatment of safety crimes, we cannot assume that all injuries are the result of some violations of the law. This assumption is made even in two of the best pieces of work within criminology that raise the issue of safety crimes: Box's (1983) classic chapter on 'Corporate Crime' in *Power, Crime and Mystification*, and Reiman's (1979) similar, US-based discussion in *The Rich Get Richer and the Poor Get Prison*. These classic texts of critical criminology each contain important, and at the time of publication largely novel, insights into the problem of safety crimes – yet they can also be criticised for treating in their data all workplace injuries and death as crimes. That is, in their attempts to criticise dominant understandings of the crime problem, they seek to include within the category of crime phenomena such as occupational injuries and ill health. Yet, while we certainly agree with the need to reformulate dominant constructions of 'crime', there is a danger in using the term 'crime' *too* loosely, without grounding it in the real processes of law enforcement and criminalisation. The danger, which these authors run into, of allowing subjective opinions to lead our analysis (and thus exposing our work to the charges of 'moral entrepreneurship': Shapiro 1983). A generally applicable definition of crime cannot be anything that we merely feel is wrong or distasteful. 'Crime', if it is to retain any meaning at all, must always be related to the material processes and institutions of criminal justice. To put it bluntly, just because someone is killed or injured at work does not necessarily mean death or injury is the result of a crime – this needs to explored then demonstrated, rather than assumed or asserted.

Our previous comments notwithstanding, a key message from the work of Box and Reiman is that the very notion of crime is contested. An important way of approaching crime as a contested concept has been developed by European writers who come from the 'abolitionist' perspective (Bianchi and van Swaaningen 1990; de Haan 1990). Abolitionists such as Hulsman (1986) point out that 'crime' has no intrinsic, objective property: it has no ontological reality outside the social institutions and processes that define it. What we know as crime should be understood as merely the types of behaviour and conduct that the state defines as worthy of control and punishment: some forms of harmful conduct are deemed worthy of control and others are not. This is a point that we will return to in the conclusion where we will argue that – counter to the received wisdom in criminology – the criminalisation of safety offences is entirely consistent with this perspective. The point to bear in mind at the moment is that crime is a relative concept which is defined in relation to the process of making and enforcing the criminal law. It is this point of critique that provides a starting point for understanding both why most injuries and deaths at work are not criminalised *and* how criminal law and criminal justice institutions perpetuate our understanding of them as 'accidents' or 'technical offences', and therefore not really crime at all.

Understanding the process of criminalisation requires us to broaden our horizon of inquiry beyond a narrow consideration of state-defined crime. The forms of conduct that are criminalised in society can be considered as part of a wider spectrum of social harms (Hillyard *et al.* 2004). It is particularly important when we are dealing with corporate harm to consider that conduct which is defined as crime will only ever represent the tip of the iceberg (Whyte 2004).

The intention of this chapter, however, is to show that the marginalisation of safety crimes within mainstream criminal justice discourse and practice cannot be justified with reference to the definition of crime set by the criminal justice system itself. At the same time, we would argue that to engage on the terrain of crime and criminal justice, we need to retain some workable definition of 'crime'. Describing all injuries and deaths at work as crimes may have some justification, but it reduces our approach to crime to a labelling or a moralising exercise.

We do not seek to resolve the contradictions that underpin the notion of crime here (although we will say something more about those contradictions in Chapter 6). The important thing for the purposes of this book is to recognise that 'crime' is a term that has no settled meaning, but that it always carries an ascribed, or socially constructed meaning. We recognise that the harms that result in criminalisation are not fixed in time, but are subject to prolonged struggles over their definition and enforcement. We also recognise that the process of criminalisation is not fixed either. Thus, as we shall see in Chapters 6 and 7, we can find at different moments in history movements both to criminalise and to decriminalise safety crimes.

Using official crime figures?

Despite their well-documented limitations, 'official crime statistics' remain predominant as a 'descriptive medium' (Maguire 1997: 139) in crime debates, constituting at least a starting point for almost all efforts to quantify the extent of various forms of offences. The particular concern of this chapter is with the availability – or otherwise – of official data on safety crimes, that is, infractions of a legal duty placed upon an employer or a corporate entity, this legal duty defined within the framework of the criminal law, most notably the Health and Safety at Work Act (HASAW Act) 1974.

Even a cursory examination of 'notifiable offences' for England and Wales reveals the extent to which their focus is almost exclusively upon 'conventional' crimes. Home Office data collated under the category 'Violence against the person' includes the following categories and sub-categories of violent offences:[1]

- *Homicide*, including: murder, premeditated and unlawful killing of another person; manslaughter, unintentional killing of another person; infanticide, intentional killing of an infant under 1-year-old by a mother suffering from post-natal depression or other post-natal disturbance.
- *Causing death by dangerous driving*: killing another person by driving a motor vehicle dangerously on a road or in a public place.
- *Causing death by careless driving when under the influence of drink or drugs*: killing another person by inattentive driving, the driver having recently consumed alcohol or drugs.
- *Causing death by aggravated vehicle taking*: killing another person by dangerous or careless driving of a stolen motor vehicle on a road or in a public place.
- *More serious wounding or other act endangering life*: viciously intending to cause grievous bodily harm to another person.

- *Other more serious violence offences,* including: attempted murder, attempting to kill another person in a premeditated and unlawful manner; threat or conspiracy to murder; stating an intent to kill or solicit, encourage, endeavour, or persuade someone to do so; child destruction, intentional killing of an unborn child capable of being born alive by its mother; endangering railway passengers, placing railway passengers in danger by interfering in any way with the railway system.
- *Less serious wounding,* including: maliciously inflicting grievous bodily harm, with or without a weapon' and 'assaulting someone and causing him or her actual bodily harm'; racially or religiously aggravated other wounding, 'maliciously inflicting grievous bodily harm, with or without a weapon' and 'assaulting someone and causing him or her actual bodily harm, where there is a racial or religious motive to the offence'; common assault (includes some minor injury); common assault (no injury), 'assaulting another person where the victim receives a minor injury or … no injury'; racially or religiously aggravated common assault, 'assaulting another person where the victim receives no injury and there is a racial or religious motive to the offence'; harassment, 'putting people in fear of violence; also continual, persistent attacks causing alarm or distress'; racially or religiously aggravated harassment, 'putting people in fear of violence; also continual, persistent attacks causing alarm or distress where there is a racial or religious motive to the offence'; possession of weapons, 'being found in possession of an object or instrument', and assault on a constable, 'when a police officer is assaulted in the course of his or her duty'.

Now, *none* of the above categories – as diverse and all-encompassing as they appear to be on first reading – include occupational injuries. One obvious category for including records of safety crimes is that covering homicide, manslaughter and violent crime. However, the crime of manslaughter in England and Wales has been legally and socially constructed in a way that renders it inapplicable to corporate offences/offenders, not least because of the centrality of *mens rea* ('knowing mind') to this offence (see Chapter 7). Perhaps a more fruitful source of data on safety crimes is the offence category of manslaughter (culpable homicide in Scotland). The problems in attempting to apply this charge successfully to both the corporate entity and/or individual employers are well-known (see Slapper and Tombs 1999; Tombs and Whyte 2003a), and given that, at the time of this book going to press, at the end of January 2007, just fourteen successful manslaughter prosecutions for safety offences have been recorded,[7] such data are unlikely to make much of an impact in the relevant Home Office data column. And the sub-categories of wounding and assault might also legitimately include reference to infractions of the criminal law which resulted in injury (fatal or otherwise) to an employee or member of the public. Again, this is not actually the case. One of the most striking aspects of legal – not to mention political and academic – treatments of violence is the general absence of the production of violence by corporate activities (Wells 1995; Pearce and Tombs 1992; Tombs 2006), an issue upon which we focus in Chapter 3.

Despite the problems with working with the available death and injury data (see Chapter 2), the complete absence of safety crimes from mainstream crime figures urges us to draw comparisons, no matter how crude, between homicides recorded in the Home Office notifiable offences and deaths and injuries at work. First, in terms of deaths, it is possible to compare the numbers of people killed at work with those recorded by the Home Office as homicides (that is, murder, manslaughter and infanticide).

Now, from these data we can make several observations. Initially it appears that one is more than twice as likely to be a victim of homicide in England and Wales than to die as a result of an acute workplace-related incident. However, against this we need to bear in mind that the fatality data above is for workers only – that is, it excludes members of the public. Further, as we indicated in Chapter 2, the headline figure that Table 11 uses only captures somewhere between one-seventh to one-eighth of the occupational fatalities which we know about for the most recent year, 2004/05. On the basis of these qualifications, being a victim of a work-related fatality looks much more likely than being a victim of homicide.

Table 11   Reported fatal injuries to all workers and rates per million workers, 1996–2005[3]

1996/ 1997	1997/ 1998	1998/ 1999	1999/ 2000	2000/ 2001	2001/ 2002	2002/ 2003	2003/ 2004	2004/ 2005
287	274	253	220	292	251	227	236	223
11	10	9	8	10	9	8	8	8

Table 12   Homicides in England and Wales, 1995–2005 and rates of homicides per million population, England and Wales, 1995–2003[4]

1996	1997	1997/ 1998	1998/ 1999	1999/ 2000	2000/ 2001	2001/ 2002	2002/ 2003[5]
678	735	731	744	763	849	863	1043
11.4	11.0	11.9	12.6	13.2	15.1	15.7	19.3

A similarly crude, but instructive, comparison can be made in terms of injuries. According to the 2003/04 British Crime Survey, there were a total of 2,780,000 violent offences in England and Wales, and 4.1 per cent of people experienced a violent incident, half of which resulted in no injury.[6] Smith and Allen (2004: 1) noted that 'The majority of violent crimes involve no significant injury to the victim and about half (51 per cent) involve no injury at all. In the 2002/03 BCS, 11 per cent resulted in medical attention from a doctor and 2 per cent in a hospital stay'. In terms of risk of violence, respondents to the 2002/03 BCS were calculated to be at a 4.1 per cent – or 41 in a thousand – risk of being a victim of violent crime (ibid.: 6).

If we turn back to Tables 2 and 3 in Chapter 2, we can indicate some illuminating comparisons with violent crime recorded by the BCS. In terms of the injury data, we need to recall the high levels of under-reporting, particularly amongst self-employed workers and particularly for minor injuries, but even if we take the over three-day injury rate for all workers (that is, employees and the self-employed), we find a rate of 415.25 per 100,000 for the most recent year (2004/05). Putting this in percentage terms, this means that 4.15 per cent of workers have reported an injury that caused them to be absent from work for three days or more – this compared to 4.1 per cent of BCS respondents citing their victimisation to violent crime. What is important here is to recall that over half of the latter incidences of violence resulted in no injury at all, and only 11 per cent resulted in any form of medical attention.[7] Then, if we turn to the data in Table 2, in Chapter 2, we find the percentage of workers experiencing a major injury – defined by HSE as 'fractures (except to fingers, thumbs or toes), amputations, dislocations (of shoulder, hip, knee, spine) and other injuries leading to resuscitation or 24-hour admittance to hospital' – standing at 1 per cent (100.3 in 100,000). This can be compared with the *less than 0.4 per cent* of BCS respondents (11 per cent of the 4.1 per cent who experienced violence) needing medical attention. The comparisons are crude, unsatisfactory, beset by methodological and statistical problems, so that the exact figures are almost meaningless – but they are broadly indicative of a rather undeniable conclusion, namely that work is more likely to be a source of violence in Britain than those 'real' crimes recorded by the Home Office.

The absence of safety crime data from Home Office statistics outlined above is significant in terms of the separate ontological status accorded to safety crime. The fact that the safety crime count is not published by police forces or by the government department responsible for crime, but by a separate agency, reinforces the exclusion of safety crime from mainstream debates on crime. Constructing safety crime as something that has to be acted on and counted not by police forces, nor by the Home Office or Scottish Executive, but by regulatory agencies, reinforces the idea that safety crime is not 'real crime'. The institutional segregation of safety crimes by the state therefore has profound implications for how we think about safety crimes. Further, this means that we must look to what those agencies do if we are to discover more about how safety crime is actually defined: it is in investigative, administrative, enforcement and juridical processes that crime is recognised and defined (Alvesalo 2003a).

Normally in criminal justice systems we can find a distinction made between *regulatory offences* and *crimes of violence*. While it is important to recognise that regulatory offences are a sub-category of criminal offences, it is also important to recognise the features that distinguish them from other (mainstream) criminal offences. There are three features of the regulatory process that act upon the definition of safety crimes. First, the investigation and prosecution of safety crimes is in the remit of *regulatory* authorities rather than police forces. This procedural feature of safety crimes differentiates those offences immediately from the mainstream criminal justice system. This has an important bearing upon how safety crimes are regarded by their perpetrators, victims, and the wider public. If the police are not involved in the investigation of safety crimes, then those crimes are less likely to be socially constructed as 'real' crimes. It is their enforcement by a specialist organisation, the HSE, that is the most important factor in distinguishing regulatory offences from other criminal offences. In England and Wales, the relatively rare investigation and prosecution of safety crimes as manslaughter (as opposed to Health and Safety at Work Act) cases involve the police in collaboration with the regulatory authorities. Second, this process of administrative differentiation also places responsibility for a huge number of offences in the hands of a relatively small agency. The average workplace can expect a visit approximately every 20 years (Centre for Corporate Accountability 2004: para 3.30). This limits the extent to which safety crimes can be identified and processed, since offences will generally only come to the attention of HSE inspectors during investigations, routine inspections and 'blitzes' (discussed below). The third feature that allows us to distinguish between regulatory crimes and crimes of violence is the way that the criminal law has developed specific procedures for dealing with safety crimes. Regulatory offences often involve the use of low level pre-court penalties or administrative notices which can be issued by inspectors on the spot (normally improvement notices and prohibition notices). This automatically creates a question about whether we can described such offences, dealt with outside the normal rules of criminal procedure, as 'crimes'. Closely related to the previous point is that regulators very often seek to deal with many of the offences they come across informally. We pick this point up later in the chapter in a discussion of compliance approaches to regulation.

The gap between 'enforceable' and 'enforced' crime

We set out our definition of safety crimes earlier as 'infractions of a legal duty placed upon an employer or a corporate entity, this legal duty defined within the framework of the criminal law.

Yet, the points made in the preceding section highlight the fact that, very often, the differential treatment of safety crimes – the informal way that safety crimes are often dealt with by regulatory agencies – produces a gap between the breaches of criminal law that are uncovered by the authorities on the one hand, and the breaches that are processed and recorded as such on the other. Indeed, it was this point that prompted Edwin Sutherland to argue for a broad definition of white-collar crime. It is worth exploring this argument in a little detail here.

In a series of papers, articles and a book published between 1940 and 1949[8] Sutherland developed the concept of 'white-collar crime' – 'a crime committed by a person of respectability and high social status in the course of his occupation' (Sutherland 1983: 7). He thus challenged the stereotypical view of the criminal as typically lower class since 'powerful business and professional men' also routinely commit crimes. Criminal acts are not restricted to those dealt with in criminal courts. Other agencies such as juvenile courts may deal with 'violations of the criminal law' and some offences can be dealt with by either criminal courts or civil courts. Some individual white collar offenders avoid criminal prosecution because of the class bias of the courts – although businessmen could often be charged as accessories to such crimes as bribery unlike politicians they usually escape prosecution – but more generally they are aided by 'the power of their class to influence the implementation and administration of the law'. Thus the crimes of the upper and lower classes 'differ principally in the implementation of the criminal laws that apply to them' (Sutherland 1940: 35–37). Given that 'upper class' criminals often operate undetected, that if detected they may not be prosecuted, and that if prosecuted they may not be convicted, Sutherland argued that the criminally convicted are far from the closest approximation to the population of violators.

In his 1945 article 'Is "White-Collar Crime" Crime?' Sutherland set out to produce a more encompassing and abstract definition of crime. Crime requires the 'legal description of an act as socially injurious and legal provision of a penalty for the act' (Sutherland 1945: 132). Notice that while Sutherland holds on to the law in his definition of crime, he extends relevant bodies of law beyond the criminal law. He recognised that many laws which are enforced by administrative bodies through the civil courts also regulate actions which cause injuries to specific individuals or which undermine social institutions, and they also routinely impose punitive sanctions. Moreover, *contra* the view that such acts are merely 'technical violations and involve no moral culpability' in fact they are 'distributed along a continuum in which the *mala in se* are at one extreme and the *mala prohibita* at the other' (ibid.: 139). The content of laws and such legal distinctions are themselves social products (Sutherland 1945).

In other words, Sutherland argues that crimes are illegalities which are contingently differentiated from other illegalities by virtue of the specific administrative procedures to which they are subject. The corollary of this is that 'successful' criminalisation of the illegalities of the powerful would pre-empt them from arguing that their illegalities are merely 'regulatory offences', merely *male prohibita*. And there are persuasive arguments that it *matters* both practically and ideologically whether something is defined as a crime or a civil offence: that is, to be subject to one rather than another set of procedures has important differential effects.[9]

Sutherland's argument regarding the most appropriate definition of crime – itself essentially an argument for incorporating corporate and white collar offences into the study of crime – is a detailed one, much of which must be read alongside the responses of his critics, not least the legalistic, and well-known, response from Paul Tappan (1947)[10]. There is not the space to fully rehearse this debate here. Most fundamentally, though, Sutherland raises the crucial issue of how the relative power of different social groups affects what became criminalised and when:

> Embezzlement is usually theft from an employer by an employee, and the employee is less capable of manipulating social and legal forces in his own interest than is the employer. As might have been expected, the laws regarding embezzlement were formulated long before laws for the protection of investors and consumers. (Sutherland 1940: 36)

Nor is the 'meaning' of law closed nor simply to be read off from the avowed intentions of legislators. Thus he notes how the Sherman anti-trust legislation, while 'enacted primarily because of fear of the corporations', was mostly used as the basis for criminal prosecutions against trades unions in its first thirty or so years (Sutherland 1983: 57).

Further, he demonstrated the contingent nature of the distinction between criminal and other offences by tracing the genealogy of the laws regulating competition (antitrust), false advertising, labour relations, and infringements of patents, copyrights, and trademarks. Each:

> … has a logical basis in the common law and is an adaptation of common law to modern social organisation. False advertising is related to common-law fraud, and infringement to larceny. The National Labour Relations Board Law, as an attempt to prevent coercion, is related to the common-law prohibition of restrictions on

freedom in the form of assault, false imprisonment and extortion. For at least two centuries prior to the enactment of the modern anti-trust laws, the common law was moving against restraint of trade, monopoly and unfair competition. (Sutherland 1945: 133)

Thus there are good reasons for suspecting that the differential application of law, the development of different legal categories, and distinct enforcement *modus operandi* for 'street' and corporate offenders are not rooted in any intrinsic differences in the offences *per se*.

Finally, Sutherland is quite clear that the differential interpretation and enforcement of law against white-collar crime is partially based upon the fact that legislators, judges and administrators within the criminal justice system are either subject to the material and ideological influence of business-people, or share common ideological and/or cultural worldviews (Sutherland 1945: 137–8). Concomitantly, when what Sutherland calls the 'status' of business people declines, so they become more prone to the development of rigorous enforcement of laws designed to regulate their anti-social conduct (ibid.).

Sutherland therefore approached the problems of accounting for the under-enforcement of white-collar crime by emphasising what is 'enforceable' rather than what is actually enforced. By doing so he managed to retain a robust notion of 'crime' – and the location of the deaths and injuries that can be logically described as crime within this definition – which allowed him to legitimately ask questions about the absence of white-collar crime from mainstream crime control agendas. He is therefore deriving his definition of white-collar crime from the 'gap' been what could be enforced and what actually is enforced.

Enforcing the law

An alternative approach to Sutherland's emphasis upon the 'enforceable' would be to link definitions of crime much more closely to the criminal, or at least to a formal legal process. For example, a definition of safety crimes could read as follows: acts or omissions which are dealt with by a criminal justice agency (including regulatory agencies with enforcement powers) using an enforcement procedure specified in criminal law.

The use of the words 'enforcement procedure' is significant here because, as Figure 1 indicates, enforcement notices issued by the UK HSE are a much more frequent response to safety crimes than prosecution. This definition excludes breaches of the law that are discovered but are not processed by criminal justice agencies. The weakness of this approach to safety crimes, therefore, is that it depends upon the agency's or, at a micro-level, the individual front line inspector's, decision to take action or not against safety crimes. In a given year, if enforcement notices or prosecutions for safety crimes are lower than the previous year, this is not necessarily because fewer crimes have been committed, but is more likely to be due to changes in enforcement practices, priorities, resources, and so on. This certainly creates a definitional weakness, but the strength of this approach is that it allows us to remain more clearly within the definitional boundaries of the criminal justice system.

Enforcement data, then, merely represent an index of offences against health and safety legislation that have – in differing ways – been subject to processing by regulatory agencies; that is, unlike injury data, enforcement data needs no reconstruction before we can speak unproblematically of safety crimes (at least on the definition of safety crimes used here). We must, however, keep in mind the key caveat that such data may tell us less about the volume of crime uncovered and more about the enforcement practices and priorities of inspectorates. (On this as a more general problem within criminological research see Coleman and Moynihan 1996: 32–9).

As we note above, breaches of safety law are more likely to be met by the issuing of various notices rather than prosecution. This works out at a ratio of around nine administrative notices issued by all enforcing agencies (HSE and local authorities) to every prosecution, a pretty consistent measure over the past five years or so. The figure below represents recent trends in HSE enforcement activity.

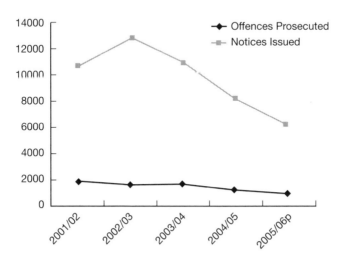

Figure 1   Cases prosecuted and notices issued by the UK Health and Safety Executive[11]

The first thing to note from Figure 1 is the consistently large gap between enforcement notices and prosecutions. Notices tend to be issued for lesser, but hardly non-serious offences, as the following quotation, from the most recent HSE Offences and Penalties report makes clear:

> A proportionate approach is taken to any breaches, so in less serious cases, the inspector will explain how the dutyholder is not complying with the law and advise them how to put the problem right ... *Where the breach of the law is more serious*, the inspector may serve a notice to the duty holder. (Health and Safety Executive 2005: 4–5, emphasis added)

Three types of notice may be issued. An *improvement* notice requires breaches (offences) to be remedied within a specified period of time; a *deferred prohibition* notice is an order that a certain piece of plant or type of work activity will be shut down unless a breach is rectified within a specified period; an *immediate prohibition* notice – the most serious enforcement order – effects an immediate closure of a worksite, part of that worksite, or particular work process until a company complies with legislation of which it is in breach.

On the basis of the above, then, let alone in terms of what we know qualitatively about how inspectors actually enforce the law (see Chapter 7) – that is, on the basis of a general reluctance to use any kind of formal enforcement action – it is clear, then, that the total number of notices issued in any one year does provide a minimal indication of the numbers of safety crimes for that period.

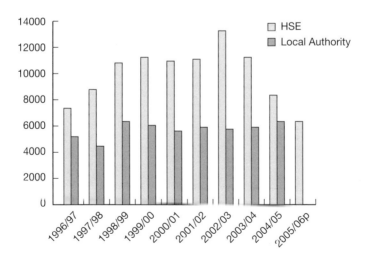

Figure 2 Total enforcement notices issued by UK authorities[12]

Now, again to be clear, these data tell us something about enforcement but, certainly on a year by year basis, are not indicative of the scale of safety offending. That is, they tell us less about the numbers of offences *encountered* by inspectors, much more about changes in enforcement policy, resources, year-on-year priorities, and so on.

Returning to Figure 1, the second thing to note from this graph is the recent steep decline in both enforcement notices issued, and prosecutions laid by, the HSE. We can thus observe a reduction of 42 per cent in enforcement notices issued over the most recent five years and an even steeper reduction of 49 per cent in prosecutions.

Prosecuting safety crime

What makes this decline even more striking is that it should be read within the context of historically low absolute numbers of prosecutions taken. This much is indicated by the data presented in Table 13 below, which compares prosecution data for nine years from 1975, roughly the period since the establishment of HSC/E[13] – with the nine years' data between 1996/97 and 2004/05.

Table 13 Prosecutions by inspectorates, 1975–1983 and 1996/97–2004/05[14]

Year	HSC/E	LA	Total	Year	HSE	LA	Total
1975	1588	78	1666	1996/97	1490	n/a	n/a
1976	1327	106	1433	1997/98	1627	506	2133
1977	1623	97	1720	1998/99	1759	424	2183
1978	1671	335	2006	1999/2000	2115	412	2527
1979	1373	211	1584	2000/01	1973	401	2374
1980	1443	307	1750	2001/02	1986	350	2336
1981	1260	291	1551	2002/03	1659	330	1989
1982	1427	296	1723	2003/04	1720	410	2130
1983	1366	261	1627	2004/05	1320	332	1652

It is clear that there is a slightly higher level of prosecutorial activity in the second than in the first period, notwithstanding the sharp drop in the most recent year for which confirmed data is available (2004/05). What is important for us here, however, is that we find across the years 1975–2005 both relatively consistent and absolutely low numbers of total prosecutions.

This rough consistency that Table 13 points to in the two periods is even more remarkable when one considers changes in a whole range of relevant variables across that 30-year period. These include, in no order of priority:

- dramatic changes in the macro-political climate, from the establishment of HSC/E during the high-point of corporatism, through the laissez-faire economics of Thatcherism, to the contemporary antipathy to any regulation of business on the part of New Labour;
- waves of both resource retrenchment and periods of increased resources;
- various shifts in enforcement priorities;
- significant changes in the economic structure, notably a shift from manufacturing to services, as well as a mushrooming of, and high turnover among, small businesses;
- a massive growth of self-employment;
- changes in economic performance, meaning that this 30-year period has witnessed several business cycles;
- changes in the organisation of production, summed up by many in terms of 'Post-Fordism';
- an increase in the absolute volume of law to be enforced, much of which has been EU-inspired.

If nothing else, the above data points to the enduring status of prosecution as the 'last resort' for regulators (Hawkins 2002). If there is a more recent decline, this is likely to be a result of the re-assertion of a concerted policy of de-regulation on the part of the Labour government that is beginning to undermine HSE enforcement strategy under intensifying budgetary pressures (and we will discuss this in more detail in Chapter 7).

The way that safety crimes are processed before they are considered for prosecution is crucial to understanding rates of prosecution. Regulators generally do not investigate or respond formally to all breaches of the law. Just as when a crime is reported to the police, at some point there will be a decision taken by the regulator about whether a reported incident is worth taking action over or not. As we have already seen in this chapter, most safety crimes in the UK, if they are acted upon in the first place, are dealt with using administrative notices. In other words, where inspectors opt for formal enforcement measures, these tend overwhelmingly to be procedures that fall short of prosecution. Indeed, in all categories, including the most serious injuries and deaths, only a minority of cases end up being prosecuted in the courts.

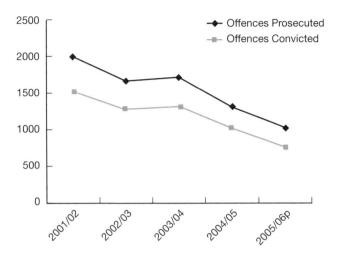

Figure 3 HSE prosecutions and convctions[15]

Figure 3 demonstrates a parallel decline in prosecutions taken by HSE and convictions for health and safety offences in the courts.

According to HSC enforcement policy, prosecutions are used where there is 'sufficient evidence to provide a realistic case of prosecution.' (ibid.: 12). Official policy statements such as this, however, mask the complexities of the prosecution process. Indeed, it is clear that the proportion of prosecutions to recorded injuries is very low indeed. To get an idea of this, we can set the total number of prosecutions, 652, against the level of recorded injuries for the same year, as set out in Tables 2–5, in Chapter 2. There we noted that for 2004/05, there were 593 fatalities to workers and members of the public, 31,702 major injuries to employees, 122,922 over three-day injuries to employees, and 14,316 non-fatal injuries to members of the public reported, even allowing for the various elements of under-reporting that were discussed. Thus, the ratio of total prosecutions to recorded injuries of varying severity (169,533 in total) is just in excess of 1:100.[16] If, as we argue in Chapter 2, that some two-thirds of injuries sustained in relation to work can be defined as 'crimes' then the ratio of prosecutions to recorded criminal injury appears very low indeed.[17]

Formal enforcement data therefore record only a tiny proportion of an as yet unquantifiable level of safety offences. The best that can be said regarding the extent of safety crimes on the basis of offence data is that the latter provides an absolutely minimal indication of the volume of the former. These data can therefore really only get us closer to understanding what the HSE do, as opposed to estimating the scale of safety crimes.

Low prosecution rates are to some extent driven by low detection. Thus, for example, some reported deaths are still not investigated, despite a HSE commitment to investigate all work-related fatalities. According to one analysis by the Centre for Corporate Accountability (CCA), in the five-year period 1996/97–2000/01, 75 worker deaths and 212 deaths to members of the public were not investigated (Unison/Centre for Corporate Accountability 2002). In cases of the most serious of non-fatal injuries, defined as 'major injuries', between 1996/7 and 2000/01, the percentage investigated almost doubled from 11 per cent to 19 per cent, with an increase in the actual number of major injuries investigated from 2,532 to 4,335; however, this increase still meant that, in 2000/01, *81 per cent of major injuries were not investigated*. Indeed, looking at the whole five-year period, some of the injuries to the most vulnerable workers remained un-investigated: there was no investigation into 905 of the 1,144 reported major injuries to trainees, or into 126 of the 164 injuries to those involved in work experience. Moreover, still by 2000/01, some of the most serious among the major injuries were not investigated, including: 72 'asphyxiations' (44 per cent of the total), 31 'electrical shocks' (35 per cent of the total), 333 'burns' (57 per cent of the total) and 418 'amputations' (41 per cent of the total; ibid.). In short, most safety crimes – including many of the most serious crimes – remain undetected and outside the radar of the criminal justice system.

This evidence also points clearly to a considerable variation in the chances of an incident being prosecuted across industry, region and type of incident. The research cited above found that 67 per cent of deaths of workers were prosecuted in 1998/99 compared with 11 per cent of major injuries. The large variation of prosecution across sectors is indicated by the finding that in the manufacturing and construction industry, 12 per cent of major injuries that were investigated were prosecuted. In agriculture, the comparable rate was 7 per cent and in the extraction industries (including the oil and gas industry), it was 3 per cent. The report found major discrepancies across regions. In Wales, for example, 20 per cent of major injuries were prosecuted, and in the West Midlands, the rate was 6 per cent. Although our concern here is with safety crimes rather than the much larger figure of occupational illness and ill health (see Chapter 1), it is worth noting that only 1 per cent of industrial diseases investigated by HSE were prosecuted.[18]

Those variations immediately alert us to the central role that the discretion of the inspector and the prosecutor has in those cases. In England and Wales the decision to prosecute (with the exception of corporate manslaughter cases where the decision rests with the Crown Prosecution

Service) is normally made by the HSE. In Scotland, the decision is made by the Procurator Fiscal after considering the evidence from an HSE investigation. HSE data set out in Table 14 below highlights starkly how this discretion can result in a variation of prosecution rates over time.

It is rarely the case that the failure to prosecute is merely down to insufficient evidence. It is the under-investigation of safety crimes and the lack of resources dedicated to inspection that are the key factors in keeping detection rates low. It is likely, then, that the very recent fall in rates of prosecution that we can see in Table 14 is directly related to a recent fall in inspection. As O'Neill (2006) has noted, the rate of inspection in the Field Operations Division of the HSE (the largest division in the inspectorate and one with comparatively high average rates of inspection) has reduced dramatically so that premises that could have expected on average one inspection every 6.99 years in 2001/02 could only expect one inspection per 10.84 years in 2004/05.

The data here indicates how a shift in prosecutorial decisions can produce dramatic changes – here, a decline – in absolute numbers and in the proportion of fatalities that result in a prosecution.

Table 14   Fatalities resulting in prosecution in the UK[19]

Year of fatality	Fatalities reported to HSE	Number of offenders prosecuted	% Fatalities resulting in prosecution
2000/01	350	149	43
2001/02	278	85	31
2002/03	256	68	27

At this point, it is important to recall our discussion in Chapter 2, where it was shown that the actual number of fatalities caused by working is seven to eight times the number of fatalities reported to HSE. Given that very few of the fatalities that are in this revised figure are likely to be subject to prosecution, the 'real', underlying rate of fatalities resulting in prosecution is likely to be much lower than the figures in Table 14 indicate.

Estimating safety crime

If this discussion indicates that, due to under-recording, under-investigation and under-enforcement, it is almost impossible to estimate the scale of offending in any complete sense, then an approach is to attempt to *estimate* the proportion of injuries and deaths (discussed in Chapter 2) that might be defined as 'crimes'. Given the acute problems with recording injuries also discussed also in Chapter 2, our most robust, albeit still hopelessly incomplete, measure of safety crimes is fatality data. At least we know pretty accurately which fatalities are included in the figures and which are excluded. Using this data as a baseline allows us to say *something* about the proportion of HSE recorded fatal injuries which might be the result of safety *crimes.*

First, there are three types of quasi-'official' evidence now available which allow some – albeit tentative – conclusions on the volume of this most egregious form of safety crime, namely: a series of special investigations into groups of fatalities undertaken by HSE in the 1980s; a now considerable stock of Commissions of Inquiry into a whole series of disasters that occurred in the UK; and a series of (HSE) Accident Investigation Reports, comprising one-off but highly detailed examinations of particular incidents. These have been discussed elsewhere (Tombs 1999b: 80–2), suffice to say here that each attempts to locate *responsibility* for injuries and incidents, and the focus of each is mainly on fatalities. The data presented in those various sources tends to the conclusion that in the clear majority of cases of workplace fatalities – in some two out of three fatal injuries – there is at least prima facie evidence of violations of duties placed upon employers by the HASAW Act, and thus at the very least a criminal case to answer. This general conclusion – based upon evidence indicating attribution of responsibility for the fatalities in question – also holds in the case of deaths at work whilst driving, with employers failing to meet their legal duties to provide safe systems of work, and to reduce risks 'so far as is reasonably practicable', where they are requiring employees to drive as part of their employment. Key causal factors in fatalities include: the failure to consider safer, alternative means of transport or indeed routes; the setting of unsafe schedules, journey times and distances; failures to maintain vehicles adequately; failures to invest in vehicles with additional safety features; and the lack of specialised training on offer for regular drivers (RoSPA 1998; see also Campbell 2005, Trades Union Congress 2005b).

To the above quasi-official evidence we might add a growing weight of academic research which attests to the fact that workplace deaths might usefully be explored as crimes, even in the absence of any legal process. While there has been relatively little attention to corporate crime in general within British criminology, the work that has been developed has often taken health and safety offences against employees as its focus.[20] Within this it is possible to discern work which provides an indication of the scale of such offending, though not in any complete quantifiable sense. Much of this work takes the form of case studies which re-create sociologically specific cases which were not dealt with adequately via the criminal justice system.

Thus work by Bergman (1991, 1993, 1994), Carson (1982), Pearce and Tombs (1993, 1997), Tombs (1995, 1996), Tombs and Whyte (1998), Slapper (1993), Woolfson *et al.* (1996), Woolfson and Beck (1997), and Whyte (1999a), for example, has all taken some aspect of safety crime as one focus, and all attest to the fact that the actual level of corporate offending not only far outweighs that recognised by official data, but is in some generalised sense comparable to conventional offending.

Exceptional within this tradition are the few attempts to re-analyse a series of deaths that have been processed (or not) through the criminal justice system. Notable here is the work of David Bergman and the work of Gary Slapper. Bergman (1991, 1994) re-analysed a subset of workplace deaths, both in terms of their causes and also by exploring the actual legal processes that did or did not follow each of them – with particular reference to the tendency of the 'near opaque filter' of the HSE 'preventing these cases from ever reaching the CPS's over-cautious scrutiny' (Bergman 1994: 2). Thus, his re-analysis of 28 deaths in the West Midlands between 1988 and 1992 concluded that:

> Four should have resulted in a manslaughter prosecution. Seven should have been referred to the police for a criminal investigation and subsequently to the Crown Prosecution Service. Eight were inadequately investigated by the enforcement authorities and require further investigation. Five should have resulted in a prosecution under health and safety law. (Bergman 1994: 90)

In only four of the 28 cases was the legal process found adequate.

The only comparable work to that of Bergman is Slapper's *Blood in the Bank*, which is based around a detailed analysis of 40 cases of death at work, following these through the inquest process.[21] For the record, juries returned verdicts of 'accidental death' in 33 of these cases and death by 'misadventure' in another five. Thus there was an essentially common finding in 38 of the 40 cases, or in 95 per cent of them – a figure considerably higher than that for verdicts in *all* inquests (that is, for all suspicious deaths, deaths in custody, and so on), where the equivalent figure is about 48 per cent (Slapper 2000: 98) – that deaths were caused by 'accidents' or 'misadventure'. Of the remaining two cases, one saw an open verdict returned, while in the other, death was found to be the result of 'the breakdown of safety procedures and lack of supervision'. The responsible company – British Gas – was fined £2,000 in this case, following a HSE prosecution under health and safety law (ibid.: 242–3). Such prosecutions – that is, for breaches of health and safety law – followed in 13 of the 40 cases examined in Slapper's book. All were successful and resulted in fines, ranging from £500 to £50,000. Ten of the 13 fines imposed were for £10,000 or under. Through his re-analysis of these deaths, Slapper argues that in 24 of the 40 cases, deaths were attributable to:

> the pressures of the profit driven economy. Thus, the work practice being used, the disregard for safety equipment or training, were the result not of ignorance but of unwillingness or inability to pay the necessary extra in order to ensure that the work would be safe. (ibid.: 164)

Such a conclusion indicates that there might be a far higher level of criminal culpability than is indicated by the fact that, to date, there have only ever been 14 successful prosecutions for corporate manslaughter following a workplace death in England and Wales, and no equivalent corporate homicide cases in Scotland.

The evidence documented in this section reinforces the importance of retaining Sutherland's distinction between what is enforceable and what is enforced. At the same time, the Slapper and Bergman studies discussed here attempt to understand the scale of safety crime whilst being guided carefully by a precise legal reasoning: the un-enforced crimes highlighted by those authors are only defined as crimes with close reference to the criminal law. So, even staying within the strict parameters of criminal legal reasoning, the conclusion is that most of the deaths analysed can be regarded as safety crimes.

Conclusion

In previous chapters we have demonstrated, first, that there are significant numbers of deaths and injuries caused by working and, second, that these are misunderstood if cast as 'accidents'. In this chapter, we have arrived at some sense of the scale of offending related to these deaths and injuries, that is, to discover the extent of safety crimes.

From this exercise, we can draw several conclusions. First, that the scale of such offending is not captured in 'official' crime statistics – if safety offences are crimes then these are separated out from the 'real' crimes recorded by the Home Office. Second, this separation of safety (and, more generally, most corporate) crimes from real crimes is subject to historical dispute, and having important contemporary resonances, remains central to debates around, and obstacles to furthering, safety crimes as a legitimate area of criminological study. Third, we found that in this area (as in many others), studies of the activities of enforcement bodies did not produce reliable estimates of crime *per se*.

That said, we have also insisted that there is enough available evidence – quantitative and qualitative – to justify several further conclusions. Most fundamentally, we have argued that being a victim of workplace violence is more likely than being a victim of 'conventional' violence. But if there is a significant crime problem here, one at least comparable with the crimes of violence upon which the criminal justice system, its political masters, and indeed criminologists focus their overwhelming attention, it remains relatively invisible. Thus, political and popular discussions of crime in general, and crimes of violence in particular, do not include safety crimes. And at the same time, as the previous chapter indicated, when we talk about workplace injuries, it is not to invoke crime or violence, but to imply almost the opposite: namely that these injuries are somehow 'accidents', to the extent that the latter terms remain predominant in academic, policy and popular discourse for referring to those phenomena with which this chapter in particular, and this book in general, is concerned.

If we have established thus far that occupational death and injury represent a significant, yet mystified or obscured, crime problem, then a key, remaining aim of the text is to consider how this crime problem might be reconstructed through law and the criminal justice system. And it is to these tasks that the book now turns as a basis for considering the reform in the treatment and perception of such crimes.

Notes

1   For the sake of completeness, also listed are a series of offences under the heading 'Other', including endangering life at sea, cruelty to or neglect of children, abandoning a child under two years, child abduction, procuring illegal abortion and concealment of birth. See www.crimestatistics.org.uk/output/Page78.asp.

2   Those figures are not made public in official data sources. The figures we use are derived from the monitoring work of CCA (see http://www.corporate accountability.org/manslaughter/cases/convictions.htm).

3   This table is adapted from Table 5, Chapter 2. The absolute numbers are not wholly compatible in the sense that HSE data covers Scotland also. However, the key point of the comparison is with regard to *rates*.

4   In any one year, some of the cases initially recorded as homicide by the police will be reomoved from these records as the police or courts subsequently determine that no homicide has taken place (see Cotton 2004: 4). For the purposes of these tables, the higher – i.e. original – figure has been retained.

5   This figure includes the 172 recorded victims of Dr Harold Shipman.

6   http://www.crimestatistics.org.uk/output/Page63.asp.

7   As Smith and Allen note, 'this is not to suggest that worry about violent crime is unjustified' (Smith and Allen 2004: 1). The point is made here for sake of a crude but, in our view, highly instructive comparison.

8 The original year of publication of Sutherland's classic text *White-Collar Crime*, not to be published in its full, 'uncut' version, until 1983; see Geis and Goff 1983: x–xi.

9 It is in such a context that David Nelken has reminded us that 'the topic of white-collar crime illustrates the possibility of divergence between legal, social and political definitions of criminality – but in so doing it reminds us of the artificiality of all definitions of crime' (Nelken 1994: 366).

10 For a detailed discussion of the debate between Sutherland and Tappan, and the significant implications of their contrasting positions for treating 'corporate crime' as crime, see Pearce and Tombs 1998: 83–124.

11 The source for this data is Health and Safety Commission (2006a) 2005/2006 data are provisional.

12 Based upon data derived from Health and Safety Executive (2005) and Health and Safety Commission (2006a). 2005/2006 data are provisional (p).

13 HSC was established by the HASAW Act 1974, while the HSE, as an amalgamation of existing inspectorates, formally came into being on January 1, 1975.

14 Source of data for 1975–1983 is Dawson *et al.* 1988: 228.

15 Source of data is Health and Safety Commission (2006a) 2005/2006 data are provisional.

16 This is indicative only. For the most part, it is not possible to refer to the percentage of injuries which result in a prosecution, since any prosecution arising from an injury is likely to take place in a subsequent year to that in which the injury itself is recorded, while HSE does not generally make available raw data with which to trace through these linkages. However, see the CCA's analysis of prosecutions following deaths, major injuries, and other categories of incidents (Unison Centre for Corporate Accountability 2002). HSE has since begun to present rates of prosecutions following investigated workplace deaths.

17 We should add a provisos here: while these data cover safety *and health* offences, the data are still utilisable for us since we know that health offences are far less likely to result in prosecution. For example, a CCA analysis of all HSE prosecutions for the three years 1996/97–1998/99 found that there were only 11 prosecutions in total for breaches involving occupational health (cited in Tombs 2004: 172). On this basis, it is likely that the overwhelming majority of the cases that reach court relate to safety rather than health offences. Similarly, the above points do not include reference to dangerous occurences, responding to which appears to be crucial to prevention in HSE's own terms, and those of the Robens system of self-regulation (see Chapter 7). The same CCA analysis referred to above found that in the three-year period under examination, less than 4 per cent (39 recorded dangerous occurences of a total of 927) resulted in a prosecution (ibid.).

18 All figures cited here are from 1998/99. The full analysis can be found in Unison/Centre for Corporate Accountability (2002).

19 Source of data is Health and Safety Executive (2005).

20 There is no simple explanation for this, but some plausible elements of one; see Slapper and Tombs 1999: 45–6.

21 A summary of the cases is included in an appendix (Slapper 2000: 240–68).

Chapter 5

Differentiating safety crime from 'real' crime in law

Introduction

How have safety crimes developed in relation to the mainstream criminal legal process? This is the first of two chapters that focuses upon various dimensions of this question. This chapter discusses the way in which the law has sought to deal with safety crimes, on one hand as 'regulatory' offences, and on the other, as 'crimes of violence'. The question of how the criminal legal process deals with safety crimes immediately raises questions of power. In nineteenth-century Britain, the very first criminal laws that were introduced to protect workers from unsafe working practices, the Factories Acts, proved difficult to implement because of the state's institutional failure to impose criminal status on members of the wealthy class of factory owners. This story provides a key focus of this chapter. The fate of the Factory Acts is also a starting point for this chapter because it illustrates a perennial problem for those who argue for the criminalisation of safety offences: how can a criminal justice system that is designed to deal with lower class offenders be mobilised to punish the relatively powerful individuals and organisations (directors, senior managers and companies) who commit safety crimes?

We approach this chapter from a perspective that views the law not as a naked instrument of power that is always used to control subordinate groups, but as a complex and often contradictory system of rules and practices that ultimately aims to maintain and stabilise the existing social order (Lacey 1994). We therefore take a perspective that is rooted in critical legal studies and neo-Marxist approaches to the law (Grigg-Spall and Ireland 1992) as opposed to instrumentalist approaches (which view law simply as a direct expression of the will of the ruling class) or liberal legal scholarship (which views law as an expression of consensual social values). In order to understand the particular contradictions that lie at the heart of the criminal law, Norrie (2001) argues that we have to explore how the law developed at very particular moments in history and how its shape is derived from the development of social relations at those moments. The development of law as it might apply to corporate offenders in safety crimes is characterised by Norrie as a process of *differentiation* – whereby corporate deviance is strictly segregated – and *assimilation* – whereby corporate deviance is dealt with by adapting the existing criminal law rules that apply to individuals. Differentiation implies the creation and development of a separate sphere of regulatory law and assimilation the re-shaping of corporate liability to integrate corporate offenders into the mainstream criminal process. The criminal law has created a different process for dealing with safety crimes as regulatory offences on one hand and as crimes of violence on the other. This, and the following, chapter is concerned with the legal reasoning behind what we might call a 'bifurcated' model of criminal process. In this chapter, we focus on the ways in which safety crimes are differentiated from 'real' crime, while our next chapter considers some of the details of, and obstacles to, an assimilation of safety crimes into law, a process which grants them the status of 'real' crimes. We begin this chapter by summarising the history of the criminalisation of safety offences, before turning to explore the contradictions and dilemmas that processes of criminalisation create in present day criminal justice systems.

The Factory Acts: the first safety crime laws

The first legislation to intervene in the organisation of factory production came in Britain, in 1802, in the form of the Health and Morals of Apprentices Act, designed specifically to regulate the working conditions of 'Poor Law' apprentices in the textile industry. Then, from 1831 onwards, a series of Factory Acts were passed – regulating the hours and conditions of young workers and women, extending across industries and workplaces of different sizes, until the consolidation of existing legislation in the Factory Act of 1878. Although largely concerned with limiting the working day, the debates that framed the emergence of this legislation were dominated by concerns about the horrific rate of injuries and deaths by 'overwork' of factory workers, and particularly children. Accounts of those conditions published at the time reveal that children were forced to work shifts, sometimes in excess of 24 hours, in overcrowded, filthy and dangerously confined spaces. In Karl Marx's (1887/1954) account of the emergence of the laws aimed ostensibly at curbing the industrial carnage experienced in nineteenth-century Britain, masters of the cotton, silk, and mining industries are revealed as merciless and murderous. Children as young as two were forced into labour in the lace industries and the average labourer in some industrial towns might not be expected to live past their teens.

During this period there existed what Carson has termed a 'logic of enforcement' (Carson 1979: 44–7). If the period between 1802 and 1831 has been characterised by a law that was 'almost entirely ineffectual' (ibid.: 40), with the new law 'contravened on a substantial scale' so as to make it 'a dead letter' (Carson 1981: 136), several somewhat disparate sources of pressure for more effective law and enforcement emerged. Certainly in the debates around the passage and implementation of the Acts in the run up to and then following the 1833 Factory Act (the latter creating the factory inspectorate in the form of four paid inspectors), there was a brief moment during which there was a real impetus to use the criminal law to control the human carnage produced as a result of Britain's industrial revolution – in particular 'to foster a public identity of unambiguous criminality for the delinquent' factory owner (Carson 1974: 129).

A viable class society

Karl Marx's analysis of the emergence of the Factory Acts proposes that the carnage in the factories had created an urgent need for the state to use the law to control factory owners who demonstrated little respect for the rule of law. First, Marx argued that there was an intensification of class conflict between the ruling class and those who worked in the factories. This level of conflict was played out at a level that was threatening the efficient organisation of production. Second, it became clear the industrial system of production could not be trusted to regulate its own rampant physical abuse of labour, and thus threatened the long-term viability of the factory system. The following passage summarises concisely Marx's analysis of regulation as necessary both to dissipate conflict and to check the greed of the factory owners from exhausting its most valuable commodity.

> These Acts curb the passion of capital for a limitless draining of labour power, by forcibly limiting the working day by state regulations, made by a state that is ruled by capitalist and landlord. Apart from the working class movement which daily grew more threatening, the limiting of factory labour was dictated by the same necessity which spread guano over the English fields. The same blind eagerness for plunder that had in one case exhausted the soil, had, in the other, torn up by the roots the living force of the nation. (1887/1954: 229)

The legal protections for workers enshrined in Factory Acts therefore originated in the need to resolve a contradiction inherent in capitalism: the relentless demand for profit in the short term threatened to exhaust the capacity for sustaining profits in the long term. Marx therefore argues that the general impulse to regulate is not simply the result of a consensual or philanthropic decision to make work more humane, but that it is in the very conditions of the factory, the 'dens of misery in which capitalistic exploitation obtains free play for the wildest excesses', that the need for regulation is created (ibid.: 460). Carson later summed this process up by arguing that the Factory Acts helped ensure a 'viable class society' (Carson 1980a).

The introduction of the Factories Acts was central to the process of industrialisation itself. Crucially, through limiting the length of the working day, factory owners were forced to consider ways of extracting greater value from employees in shorter working hours and under ostensibly 'safer' working conditions. The class of factory owners as a whole was impelled to develop technology that would enable the offsetting of costs incurred by regulation. Regulation thus gave capital the impetus to revolutionise production in order to guarantee its own expansion. Paradoxically, then, the Factories Acts hastened the development of the factory system and encouraged the monopolisation of capital (the latter because the increased necessity for a greater outlay of capital forced the smaller factory owners out of business (Marx 1887/1954: 447–8)).

Thus, for Marx, through the imposition of a minimal level of protection for workers, the state played a crucial role in forcing the qualitative leaps in the nature of capital investment and concentration of production that were crucial to the development of the factory system – so effecting the real rather than the formal subsumption of labour. In imposing upon capital conditions of production that were required for what in retrospect was a crucial shift in the development of capitalism, the state helped to establish the conditions of existence and further development of capitalism while apparently acting against the interests of individual employers. It is no casual turn of phrase, then, when Marx refers to this period of early factory regulation (1846–1867) as both 'epoch-making' and constituting the arrival of 'the millennium' (Marx 1954/1887: 268).

Struggles for criminalisation

Throughout his account, Marx takes a great deal of care to underline the contradictory politics at work within the 'bourgeoisie' (ruling class) in the reform process. The compassionate tone of the concerns expressed by wealthy reformers pepper Marx's prelude to the emergence of the Factory Acts. Here we find discontent swelling amongst members of the ruling class, including magistrates who compare children working in the lace trade to slaves in Virginia, alongside establishment newspapers such as

The Times condemning the cruel treatment of factory operatives. The government's own reports to the Childrens' Employment Commissioners on the occupational health of workers in the potteries, match making and paper industries are cited throughout. Those reports document in gruesome detail the physically and morally degenerating conditions of work: vulnerability to disease; low life expectancy; and the mutilation of children, many suffering stunted growth and premature aging.

A succession of Inspectors' reports are quoted for their sustained condemnation of the Factory masters and this condemnation appears to intensify over the years following the Inspectorate's establishment. In particular, *Capital* draws out the different positions adopted within and between different branches of the state. When the Home Secretary eventually appealed to the Inspectorate to treat factory owners who were in breach of the 1844 Act leniently, via a Home Office circular, the Inspectorate refused. The internal divisions within the Factory Inspectorate are also prominent in Marx's account. The least punitive of the four factory inspectors, J. Stuart is singled out for allowing the relay system to flourish in Scotland, whilst in England, the Inspectorate continued 'their legal proceedings against the pro-slavery rebellion' (Marx 1887/1954: 273).

The analysis of the Factory Acts developed by Marx, and latterly Carson, both emphasised the importance of struggles around the *enforcement* of those laws. It is notable that in both of those author's accounts, it was often the case that bitter struggles between employer and factory hand intensified *after* the passage of legislation. For example, the factory owners mobilised against the 1844 Act coming into full force in 1848 with an unremitting lobby of Parliament and appeals to the workforce that their jobs were at risk. Their assault was also directed at the Factories Inspectorate who were denounced as 'a kind of revolutionary commissioners . . . ruthlessly sacrificing the unhappy factory workers to their humanitarian crochet' (ibid,; 270) Marx discussed at length conflicts over the implementation of a 'relay system' by the Factory masters. The relay system, introduced to exploit loopholes in the Factory Acts, enabled masters to circumnavigate the legal limits on the working day by employing workers concurrently across different shifts. The introduction of the relay system represented the manufacturers' 'revolt' against government (ibid.: 397). In response to this revolt the factory workers held protest meetings across Yorkshire and Lancashire, creating a counter revolt so ferocious that the Factories Inspectorate 'urgently warned the government that the antagonism of classes had arrived at an incredible tension' (ibid.: 276). The relay system was finally abolished by the Factory Act of 1850.

Marx is rarely given credit for producing a subtle analysis of state power, but as this discussion shows, his description of the state during this period rejects a crude instrumental notion of the state's relationship with the factory owning class or indeed a crude characterisation of class struggle.

The emergence of strict liability offences

Any zeal for criminialisation in those debates at the birth of the Factories Acts was to fade fast. The courts from an early point had used their prerogative to avoid conviction where it could be shown that the offence was not wilfully or grossly negligent. They also tended to impose the minimum penalties. Just over two thirds of convictions between 1836 and 1842 resulted in a minimum £1 fine (Carson 1979: 50). The discretion being exercised in the courts indicated a major problem of political will to enforce the law.

Proposals for imprisonment as punishment for the most serious offences were rejected in the framing of the 1833 Act. The newly formed inspectorate actually lobbied on occasion for a repeal of the most onerous parts of the law having being advised to co-operate closely with employers so as to make the new law acceptable to them (ibid.: 11–13). The problem the Inspectorate faced was that factory inspectors were being formally

> required to criminalise what was normal within the factory system … to criminalize a body of men not on the periphery of moral life, such as displaced or poverty-stricken workers, but men who were at the centre of the emerging political and social order (Norrie 2001: 85).

Given the routine nature of breaches of the Acts, a response that prosecuted each and every offence would have resulted in a 'collective criminalization which extended far beyond some opprobrious minority' (Carson 1979: 48). With the courts in the main unwilling to embark upon a collective criminalisation of the 'respectable' class of factory owners, the Factories Inspectorate very quickly learned to apply the law selectively. They did this by adopting a system of bargaining and low-level sanctions. Inspectors were given powers to exercise their own discretion, and the Inspectorate powers to devise regulations, which normally imposed an administrative responsibility upon employers (such as keeping time-books, certificates of employees age and so on). Criminal prosecution only came after initial attempts to persuade had failed. Inspectors actually drafted a bill (that was in the event never implemented) to introduce a system of on-the-spot fines to pre-empt criminal proceedings to ease the tricky task of dealing with individuals of high social standing. Despite Hawkins's (2002) failure to consider this history, this is in fact the very origin of 'a strategy of last resort prosecution' (Norrie 2001: 85) with which his work is centrally concerned (see Chapter 7). It is significant that the decision to prosecute came after inspectors had decided that there was some clear intention on the part of the factory owner to commit an offence. This Carson describes as the incorporation of the criminal law concept of *mens rea* into inspectors' decisions to prosecute (Carson 1979: 52–3).[1]

At the same time as the notion of intentionality (and therefore moral blameworthiness) was informally introduced into the investigation process, the legislative reforms of the 1844 Factory Act diluted the normal *mens rea* requirement in criminal process. Specifically, the 1844 Act deemed an employer 'guilty in the first instance' and required the employer to 'prove his due diligence' in defence of any case (Carson 1980b: 164), thus reversing the traditional requirement in criminal law to identify *mens rea* before guilt can be established. This change enabled a second class type of offence to be effectively created within which breaches of the Factory Act would inevitably fall. And *this* offence – since it did not require a state of mind to be demonstrated and carried low-level administrative penalties in the first instance – was more easily constructed as an 'administrative breach' or a 'technical offence', rather than an unambiguously criminal offence. This is essentially why strict liability offences came to be regarded as something other than 'real crimes'. The 1844 Act therefore took a major step towards the concept of 'strict liability' offences which removed the label of criminal from Factory Act prosecutions and thus enabled such prosecutions to be more acceptable to the magistrates who were asked to impose sanctions against members of their own social class. The courts – by ensuring that a separate, lower level of offence was created – assisted in decriminalising breaches of health and safety law in the eyes of the law and thereby legitimated the conventionalisation of those crimes in the workplace.

'Community settlement' and regulation

The analysis developed by Marx, Carson, and Norrie identifies class conflict as the motor of those historical developments. This can be contrasted with liberal perspectives on the development of law which propose that this period was less one of struggle and more simply one of a humanitarian response to exploitation. Changes in the law, from a liberal perspective, arose not from the contradictions created by the system of production and the struggles that arose from those contradictions, but from an almost natural process of finding an optimal level of labour efficiency. For example, in Clarke's overview of the emergence of 'the regulatory society', there is no sense of what this conflict or struggle meant in relation to the regulatory outcome:

> technology, the means to success of industrialisation, brought with it new dangers. In deep mines and factories contracted workers were subject to appalling degradation and exploitation and suffered increasingly from the hazards of new industrial processes. After some opposition, the first Factory Acts were introduced. Their requirements for safer working conditions were respected, on the whole, by the larger manufacturers, but ignored by many of the smaller ones, who could not afford to implement their provisions. (Clarke 2000: 13)

Such a characterisation contains many of the assumptions that infect current debates regarding regulation: that it emerged as part of some unfolding, humanising response to dangers created by 'technology'; that the legitimacy of the law is generally respected by the regulated; and that where regulations are flouted, this tends to be on the part of marginal, less responsible, usually 'small', companies.

Bartrip and Fenn have similarly argued that the Factory Acts emerged from a general consensus that efficient legislation, and its enforcement, rely upon achieving a balance between the benefits of doing business and its 'harmful concomitants' (Bartrip and Fenn 1980a: 178). Safety crimes – because they result from the general momentum of progress – 'differ from other crimes' (ibid.), and thus require a different regulatory response; occasional 'failures' to enforce the criminal law were in fact a function of the constraints within which inspectors were working, so that 'there is no need to look beyond' such constraints 'to explain the evolution of their policy' of enforcement (ibid.: 183); the constraints were 'a reflection of the resources that the community was prepared to devote to enforcement taking into account not only efficiency considerations, but reluctance to erode laissez-faire principles and advance the bureaucratic state' (ibid.: 182); and, as the Inspectorate's practices evolved, it gained 'a more realistic appreciation of what could be carried out in an imperfect world'. (ibid.: 184)

Carson's rejoinder to Bartrip and Fenn identified in the Factory Acts not a 'balance' based upon a community settlement, but an ongoing conflict between pro-regulatory forces and the economic exigencies of the emerging order:

> who exactly is meant to have been making all these rational community choices between lost production levels of 'acceptable' criminality, gains to the community and the like? ... Of course the early factory inspectors were operating under constraints; of course they were compelled to balance factors like rigorous enforcement against others such as lost production; but the constraints, I suggest, emanated from something rather more tangible than some ephemeral 'community' sitting down to do its cost-benefit analysis on factory conditions. Rather ... they stemmed from a collision between the impetus towards regulation, on the one hand, and basic structural and ideological features of the new order on the other. (Carson 1980a: 190)

The outcome of the implementation and enforcement of the Factory Acts (whether read in the differing historical accounts as 'community settlement' or 'conflict') can hardly be in dispute.

This period of the implementation of the Factory Acts represented a seminal moment in the development of safety law, one in which there were moments of a real possibility of an assimilation of safety crimes into a wider system of criminal law. Through a combination of novel law, emergent forms of enforcement, and the development of a rationale in the courts for treating these crimes in particular ways, that moment was lost, and safety crimes were segregated into a differentiated category of ('strict liability') offences. And this creation of a distinct category of 'regulatory' law in nineteenth-century Britain was to set an enduring pattern which has been followed in many jurisdictions since.

Differentiating liability for safety crimes

The category of strict liability offences that emerged at the end of the nineteenth century facilitated the differentiation of regulatory offences and mainstream crimes of violence. In the UK, this distinction endures, and is made between those offences that are prosecuted as breaches of health and safety law, under health and safety legislation (regulatory offences) and offences that are prosecuted as common law crimes of violence. The most significant category of the latter group of offences are 'corporate manslaughter' offences which are prosecuted in England and Wales using the rules of manslaughter, rules that have been developed to apply to cases involving deaths that result from the involuntary or negligent actions of individuals.

This is not to imply that each of those types of offences can be regarded wholly separately in law. Both are criminal offences. Regulatory offences are defined as criminal offences because, like other crimes, they involve prosecution by the state, they require a pre-determined standard of proof to be demonstrated to the court, and the state imposes a penalty that is linked to the potential social consequences of the offence. Those are the most important characteristics that determine whether a given legal procedure is 'criminal' or not.[2] Offences against regulatory law are governed by criminal rather than civil law. It is this feature of those offences that means that in strict law-book terms we can describe safety crimes unequivocally as crimes. This is important since: 'discussions of corporate crime often ignore altogether the possibility that corporate activity might breach not just the regulatory codes but the criminal law "code" itself' (Wells 2001: 11).

Now, while it is important to recognise that regulatory offences are a sub-category of criminal offences, it is also important to recognise the features that distinguish them from other (mainstream) criminal offences. It is to this task that the chapter now turns.

Inchoate offences

Normally regulatory offences are defined in relation to a breach of law rather than the specific outcome of that breach. Crimes of violence, on the other hand, are defined by the result or outcome of any criminal act or omission, that is, strictly in relation to the harm that has been caused. Thus a corporate manslaughter or homicide charge is only relevant in cases where someone has died, while a company or an individual can generally be prosecuted for a breach of regulatory law regardless of whether some identifiable harm has resulted. Thus, regulatory law 'fails to distinguish those companies which have caused death and injury from those companies which may be unsafe but which have not yet caused harm' (Bergman 2000: 39). Liability that is attributed without any reference to the harm caused is known in legal terminology as inchoate liability.

The removal of the presence of a harm in inchoate offences has been justified by the idea that the primary purpose of the law when it comes to safety crimes is to prevent the harm occurring in the first place, rather than to punish wrongdoing. (Wells 2001: 5–6). This process of disconnecting harm from offence is crucial in reframing the 'criminal' nature of the offence. Some notion of 'harm' has always been a central notion in modern criminal justice systems.[3] If we examine all of the established criminal law textbooks, we find that the notion of preventing harm to individuals and to the public features in any discussion of the founding principles of the criminal law (see, for example, Smith and Hogan 2002: 16–17). The harm principle, as set out by John Stuart Mill ('the only purpose for which power can be rightfully exercised over any member of a civilized community, against his will, is to prevent harm to others'; 1859/1962: 135) was, for early liberal theorists, a precondition for justifying the use of the state's coercive powers over the individual. Harm as a basis for criminal justice intervention remains significant in so far as most criminal acts are in some way connected to the harms that they produce. In cases where the 'harm' is separated from the 'crime', we begin to lose sight both of the gravity that is attached to the offence and, at the same time, of the legitimate basis for state intervention.

Social condemnation of offences under the HASAW Act 1974 may be weakened simply because the offence is not determined by the seriousness of the injury or the harm that results. Because there is no charge of corporate injury or corporate killing under the HASAW Act, it means that the Act generally is not regarded as one designed for punishing serious harms. Rather, it is seen as a statute which aims to prevent a range of unspecified harms before they occur. But those unspecified harms, because they have no label attached to them which draws attention to their status as a 'crime' or to the serious consequences of the crime, are therefore more difficult to comprehend as crimes. Safety offences that use the inchoate mode are described not as 'grevious bodily harm', or 'assault', but instead as 'breaches' of the relevant statute. The effect of all of this is a deepening of the differentiated character of regulatory offences and a reinforcement of the general assumption that they are 'not real crimes'.

Having made this point, it is important to note that the inchoate form does not shape the entire response of the criminal justice system to safety violations. Thus, in the UK, the HSE sets a minimum threshold in the criteria that determine which injuries will be investigated. Some serious injuries are investigated and some are not. According to this policy, all deaths at work are investigated – though this in fact means deaths to employees (see Chapter 2) – as are all amputations, serious multiple fractures, crush injuries leading to internal organ damage, head injuries involving loss of consciousness, burns of more than 10 per cent, blinding, scalping and asphyxiation. The assessment of harm also undoubtedly features in the sentencing process. We will note in Chapter 8, how, through case law, it has been established that the courts should consider higher penalties if the outcome has been a serious injury, ill heath, or a death. Typically the highest fines imposed under the Health and Safety at Work Act are those that involve fatalities. In effect, both regulator (in decisions to prosecute) and the courts here are working within a framework of inchoate offences but are applying harm-based or result-based decisions when it comes to investigation and sentencing respectively.

Corporate liability

Regulatory crimes and crimes of violence are also distinguished by the way in which the criminal law has developed specific procedures for dealing with safety crimes. When safety crimes are processed as crimes of violence (for example corporate manslaughter and corporate homicide cases), the rules of liability closely approximate the normal rules of attributing liability for inter-personal or 'mainstream' crimes of violence. On the other hand, regulatory offences generally imply a method of attributing liability that has been designed for the purpose.

We have already noted the criminal justice system's pre-occupation with *individual* culpability for safety crimes. The central problem with the criminal law's methodological individualism for our discussion here is that responsibility for safety crimes can rarely be meaningfully attributed to one or several specific individuals, as is the case with inter-personal crimes. Safety crimes often result from a series of decisions made at different levels of the organisation. In the case of Piper Alpha (see Chapter 1), the decision to reduce the maintenance programme on the platform and at the same time push the production system beyond its capacity was crucial to the genesis of this safety crime. The decisions that led to this state of affairs were made at various levels in Occidental's corporate hierarchy. They were also directly the result of poor management–workforce relations and the lack of any formal worker representation which could force management to respond to workers' complaints about safety on the plant (Woolfson *et al.* 1996; Whyte 1999a; Tombs 1990). Thus the killing of 167 workers on the Piper Alpha platform cannot be understood in terms of the result of a decision of any one individual. The cause of the Piper Alpha disaster, as is often the case with other safety crimes, can only meaningfully be understood in terms of its organisational causation or production.

There are a variety of types of employing organisation that can be implicated in safety crimes: corporations, government and public sector organisations, charities and associations and various other forms of unincorporated organisations. The constitution of public sector organisations is generally governed by public law and the constitution of private sector organisations by corporate law. However, most organisations have similar safety responsibilities in regulatory law. In general, regulatory law applies to both public and private sector organisations.

For Glasbeek (2005), however, there is an important distinction to be made between corporations and other types of organisation. What makes corporations different is that they are constituted, socially and legally, for one primary purpose: to maximise profits from commercial activities. This means that law reformers must recognise corporations as a special case. Corporations will make profits in whichever way they can and this includes cutting corners and exposing workers to risk (unless there are restrictions in place which can limit such exposures). Law reformers, however, tend to work within a consensus perspective (see Chapter 7) and work on the assumption that good safety is in the best interests of all organisations. For Glasbeek, lumping all organisations together in one category supports a very specific approach to criminalisation. The primary aim is to find reforms that will deal with the complexity of organisations rather than those that seek to change the institutional basis of the corporation and limit the murderous effects of the pursuit of profit. This is a point that has resonance with Norrie's (2001) argument on the removal of *motive* from the criminal process. Motive – in this case, profit motive – is irrelevant to the process of establishing liability for a crime. By obscuring the profit motive, the law 'serves another unmentioned purpose: it supports the status quo in respect of occupational health and safety regulation' by preserving the consensus view that safety crimes are generally 'accidents' rather than the avoidable consequences of an industrial profit-maximising process. Thus, the consensus view of safety crime and how to regulate it (see Chapter 7) is preserved: 'when it comes to the risks of any for-profit activity, the employer is in the best position to know what they are likely to be and how they could be minimised' (Glasbeek, 2005: 25).

Having made the point that there is good reason for corporations to be treated as a special case, it remains the case that safety crimes – albeit in different forms and for different motivating factors – are committed by a range of different types of organisations. In the UK, part of the debate on the form that a new offence of corporate manslaughter might take has revolved around the extent to which crown bodies (institutions which represent the state such as government ministries) should be held responsible for criminal offences. It is the desire to ensure that crown bodies and non-incorporated bodies do not remain exempt from prosecution which has led to calls for the law to be reformed to allow all types of organisation to be held accountable. The implication of Glasbeek's argument, however, is that the law must be sensitive to the constitution of different organisational forms and therefore be sensitive to the underlying reasons behind the organisational production of safety crimes.

The argument that profit-making corporations should be treated as special cases is supported by the fact that, as we shall see in the following chapter, corporations are able to fall back upon a legal principle which protects them from liability known as 'corporate personality'. Indeed, it might be said that the problems that have been historically created by the process of assimilating corporations into the mainstream criminal law stem from the special status that corporations are given; a status which enables the corporation to own property formally and to make profits for the individuals that in reality own and control them, *without* those individuals incurring full liability for any harms that they may cause vicariously through the corporation. In other words, corporations present specific problems for the criminalisation of safety crime.

Principles of corporate liability

A key period in the development of strict liability offences – outlined above – was undoubtedly the struggle to implement the Factory Acts. However, this is not to imply that the concept of strict liability was only developed for the purpose of dealing with safety crimes. As Wells (2001: 68) noted, the concept in the nineteenth-century was 'more commonly found in the area of morals, minors and drink'. Yet the concept does have a property that makes it particularly amendable to corporate offending. In strict liability offences, it does not matter if the accused is an individual or an organisation: the absence of *mens rea* ensures that either the organisation or the individual (or both) could be held liable where relevant causation is shown. Normally, however, it is the corporation that is prosecuted for safety crimes. In this sense, the legal category of strict liability has allowed law enforcers to avoid a central dilemma in debates around the criminalisation of safety crimes: should the law focus on the organisation or on an individual within the organisation? Historically, the development of differentiated forms of liability for safety crimes has focused predominantly upon how to attribute liability to the organisation rather than the individuals who contribute to organisational decision making; we shall see in the following chapter the extent to which regulatory offences in the UK that apply to directors and senior managers are ill-designed for this purpose.

Methods for imputing liability to corporations generally use mechanisms that impose criminal responsibility for the conduct of employees of the corporation upon the corporation itself. Although the meaning of the term changes according to the context in which it is applied, 'vicarious liability' is normally used to imply that the corporation's liability can be imputed using the conduct of one or more of its employers. A pure form of vicarious liability would enable the actions of any employee at any level of the organisation to be imputed to the corporation. Some selective forms of vicarious liability restrict this mechanism only to a specified group within the organisation. It is often said that US law uses a system of vicarious liability. Normally what is being referred to here is a very particular form of vicarious liability known as *respondeat superior* which applies in the US Federal Courts. Under the doctrine of *respondeat superior*, corporate liability can be triggered by the criminal conduct of any employee of the corporation, as long as the conduct occurred within the scope of their employment (that is, the employee was conducting a work-related activity) and the conduct was intended to benefit the corporation (see Gobert and Punch 2003: 55–9; Wells 2001: 132–6). There are two main problems with this doctrine. The first is that the relative ease with which *respondeat superior* can be used to attribute liability means that the courts have developed a relatively low level of punishment, in other words, a similar effect to the differentiation of strict liability cases. Vicarious liability cases in the US courts are regarded as part of a system of rules that do not fall squarely within the parameters of the criminal law. The second is a more conceptual problem that raises questions about whether vicarious liability can fully capture the *corporate* nature of the offences it is used to prosecute. Although *respondeat superior* represents a relatively broad method of attributing liability, it still relies upon identifying the conduct of an individual who can be said to have triggered corporate liability. This may, particularly in complex organisational structures, be difficult, in spite of the fact that this individual can be at any level of the organisation. Vicarious liability-based systems therefore do not take us closer to a meaningful attribution of the offence to corporations because they constitute a form of liability in which the individual remains central to the establishment of fault.

This latter problem reminds us that when thinking about corporate crime it is always necessary to understand the relationship between the offence, the corporation, and the individuals who make up the corporation. Understanding these relationships accurately is necessary if we are to reverse a situation in which corporations continue to escape criminal responsibility (Kaye 1992). At the beginning of this chapter, we asked: how can a criminal justice system that is designed to deal with lower class offenders be mobilised to punish the relatively powerful individuals and organisations (directors, senior managers and companies) who commit safety crimes? At the end of the chapter, the question has become rather more complex: how do we use a body of law designed for individual offenders when we are dealing with a form of crime that very often can only meaningfully be attributed to collective action and collective decision making, perhaps at multiple levels in the corporate organisation?

Conclusion

The origins of a differentiated system of law for safety crimes can be traced to the moment at which the criminal courts saw the punishment of the wealthy or the ruling class as somehow beyond their remit. The process of law reform and the process of law implementation remains guided by a logic of social ordering – of mediating over conflict in a way that will not disturb the status quo. We cannot escape the fact that a necessary, key logic of capitalist social orders is to maintain the predominance of capital – and its institutional form, the corporation – in social relations. It is this fact above all else that shapes the criminal law's relationship to safety crimes (Slapper 1993; Glasbeek 1989).

The process of differentiating law identifies an enduring paradox in the criminalisation of safety crimes. In the case of the Factory Acts, a new principle of liability that emerged after protracted struggles around the implementation and enforcement of the criminal law enabled a second class of crimes to be created which would never be able to attract the same level of moral opprobrium or condemnation attached to other crimes of violence. The effect of 'strict liability' in the case of the Factory Acts was not to make the criminalisation process any easier, but to differentiate safety offences as a distinct category of crimes. This process of *differentiation* is deepened by the creation of separate systems of policing and punishment that apply to safety crimes. Because strict liability offences are not regarded as 'real' crimes, the public relations consequences of regulatory offences and the relatively low-level sanctions imposed by the courts (if those cases actually reach the courts) are absorbed rather more easily by convicted corporations and individuals.

There is a very crude principle of law reform in operation here: if you make the route to establishing liability easier, then it is the instinct of the court to interpret a lower degree of seriousness and therefore attach a less severe punishment to the offence. Lower thresholds of liability imply a relative ease with which prosecutions for safety crimes can be secured. However, this possibility of easier criminalisation is offset by the lack of resources that investigating and prosecuting authorities can draw upon, the resort to less punitive pre-court sanctions, and consequent low rates of prosecution for safety crimes. This effect highlights an inherent contradiction in the legal rules that have been developed to hold corporations accountable. Put simply, a process of decriminalisation has occurred at the same time as the rules of prosecution being developed in a way that makes it easier to convict. If we are effectively to criminalise corporate crimes, then the most obvious conclusion to draw from this contradiction is that we should seek to assimilate safety crimes into the system of criminal law. Yet, developing the law in this direction has also been beset by a similarly perplexing contradiction: if we are to fully criminalise safety crimes, does this mean that we have to assimilate safety crimes into a system that has not been designed for the purpose? It is to the key legal issues raised by this question that we now turn.

Notes

1   In criminal cases, the latin phrases *actus reus* and *mens rea* are used to describe the basic elements of a crime. For a crime to have been committed, there needs to be presence of criminal conduct or the physical cause of a criminal event (the *actus reus*) and an identifiable individual with a criminal state of mind (*mens rea*). Actus reus is often referred to as the 'physical' element of the crime and *mens rea* as the 'mental' element of the crime. The literal translations of *mens rea* is 'knowing mind'. The term is used in a legal sense to mean that intent or knowledge on the part of the offender is required before a crime can be said to have occured.

2   By contrast, civil law cases involve no prosecution, but are in essence applications to the court by private citizens for adjudications to be made on a balance of probabilities. There is no 'accused' in a civil court case; court decisions are normally made to establish liability on one side or the other, between the plaintiff (the person applying to the court for a settlement) and the appellant (the person who defends him/herself against the case made by the plaintiff).

3   Even if, far from dealing with the most pressing public harms, the crime that is generally dealt with by the apparatuses and technologies of crime control involves a few, highly individualised harms (Hillyard *et al.* 2004).

Chapter 6

Assimilating safety crimes

Introduction

In the previous chapter, having introduced Norrie's (2001) distinction between the processes of *differentiation* and *assimilation*, we considered the historical basis for the fact that safety crimes are not regarded as real crimes in law. Thus we argued that organisations and their directors are rarely exposed to the same criminal controls or level of punishment as relatively lower status individuals (Sanders 1985). Offenders who are responsible for committing safety crimes are generally regarded as socially useful and respectable, and often – because of their status, wealth and other resources – enjoy some measure of influence over public policy decisions. Moreover, employing organisations, and their individual directors and senior managers, are insulated by a separate set of rules that guide criminal prosecution for safety crimes. In this chapter, we turn to examine a process of assimilation, whereby corporate deviance is dealt with by adapting the existing criminal law rules that apply to individuals. On the face of things, a process of assimilation allows corporate crime – including safety crime – to be treated as 'real' crime. Having said this, the process of assimilating crimes of the powerful more generally is one that is rare in any criminal justice system. Nonetheless, it is a process that deserves particular explanation in this text in order to consider the potential for safety crime to be dealt with effectively by a legal system that is designed to deal with the crimes of the relatively powerless.

The first, and perhaps most fundamental, problem with the assimilation of safety crimes into the mainstream criminal legal process is that the criminal law in the western legal jurisdictions has been designed with lower-class individual offenders in mind. The rules of *mens rea* that have been developed in Western jurisdictions tend to involve several levels of culpability. This is necessary because it is not always the case that individuals can be said to have clearly intended the consequences of their actions. In safety crimes, it is not often the case that an act or omission is intended to injure or kill. Often in those cases, risks to workers or the public might be created without any clear intention to kill or maim. Cases of safety crimes therefore normally imply a lower level of culpability than intent. Safety crimes are more likely to result from the *reckless* or *careless* disregard for the consequences of taking risks.

In most Western legal systems, this distinction can be characterised as the essential difference between 'murder' and 'manslaughter'. The offence of murder normally implies intent to kill, whereas manslaughter normally implies that a death has arisen from reckless, unintentional conduct. In such cases, the test for criminal liability is normally that the risk was foreseen or was foreseeable. In other words, the risk should have been foreseen by any reasonable person. In English law, the test is that risk must have been serious and obvious enough for it to have been appreciated by the accused and that the accused was capable of appreciating the risk.

However, if manslaughter has been a frequent analogy drawn upon by academics and safety campaigners alike – and indeed has been one route that the criminalisation of safety crimes has followed – there are other properties of safety crimes that make them appear rather more like murder than manslaughter. It is possible to argue that, although their consequences tend to be unintended, safety crimes are often committed under conditions that of greater pre-meditation and planning than many murders. As we have seen in Chapter 1 (and we develop this discussion in the conclusion), the typical causes of safety crimes can often be linked directly to the demands of cost-driven managerial regimes. Thus aggressive managements, pressures upon employees through time or resource constraints, inherently dangerous ways of working established as standard operating procedures, inadequate training, poorly designed or maintained equipment, the absence or lack of robustness of basic safety equipment, and the use of casualised, overworked or under-qualified staff can all be understood as consequences of profit-motivated decisions made, or cultures set, by managements. In Chapter 1, we saw how decisions to cut the maintenance budget on Piper Alpha, to decrease the harbour turnaround time in P&O channel sailing or to put untrained staff into high risk work, as in the case of Simon Jones, were all causal factors in those crimes. In those terms, they were all crimes that can be traced back to the carefully planned decisions of accountants and managers. Notwithstanding the stereotypes of crime fiction, most murders do not tend to arise from premeditated, calculating plans, but are often the result of a pattern of violent interactions, commonly between individuals who know each other. Safety crimes on the other hand are, by definition, committed in cold blood and often are committed in order to advance financial goals or maintain profitable systems of production. We therefore need to think through carefully the distinctions between safety crimes and other types of crimes of violence – distinctions that we began to draw out in Chapter 3. At the very least, however, it is perfectly plausible to suggest that the differentiated treatment of safety crimes is not a consequence of properties inherent to such offences which render them less blameworthy. As we noted in Chapter 3, following Reiman, it may be reasonable to attach a higher degree of moral blameworthiness to such crimes. In other words, it is the concepts and categories that are used in mainstream law, and the distinctive approaches that have been adapted to safety crime, rather than the characteristics of the offence *per se*, that stand in the way of criminalisation of safety offences.

Acts and omissions

In cases of safety crimes, the concept of 'knowledge' is likely to be defined as an individual's awareness of the consequences of taking a particular risk in the workplace. So if a manager knowingly allows employees to work from a height without a safety harness, then it might be argued that sufficient *mens rea* is present to allow the incident to be defined as a crime. But a safety crime rarely arises directly as a result of a positive decision. Safety crimes are more likely to result from indifference, and the failure or refusal to provide adequate protection from harm. In the case of workplace safety, offences tend to be caused by failures to comply with the minimum legal requirements, where the deadly effects of those are entirely predictable. Safety crimes may often be the result of management failure to do something they should have done to protect workers and the public. In other words, safety crimes tend to be produced by acts of *omission*, rather than acts of *commission*.

A criminal omission is generally more difficult to pin down than a criminal act. It may often be much harder to identify the lack of action on the part of a particular manager or boardroom, than it is to identify an act that creates a serious risk to workers or the public. Of course there are some cases where omissions are clear. In the Lyme Bay case, it was relatively easy for the prosecution to show that the accused, Peter Kite, was aware of the consequences of his inactions. In December 1994 the company concerned, OLL Ltd, became the first company in English legal history to be convicted of homicide. Peter Kite, its managing director, also became the first director to be given an immediate custodial sentence for a manslaughter conviction arising from the operation of a business. Both Kite and the company were found guilty on four counts of manslaughter arising from the death of four teenagers who drowned in Lyme Bay while on a canoing trip organised by OLL. Kite was sentenced to three years imprisonment, and the company was fined £60,000. But the case was arguably atypical of corporate homicide scenarios. In this case, there was evidence that the risks had been made clear to him by employees and that he had chosen to ignore those risks. The key evidence presented to the court was a letter from a previous employee warning Kite of the serious risks of loss of life created by company procedures. Without this evidence, the court may not have found it easy to convict.

By contrast, in the case of the Transco Larkhall explosion in 1998 (see Chapter 1), the neglect of the gas pipeline system took place over a number of years and the failure to take action to upgrade the system was identified as the responsibility of a number of individuals in a number of committees and working groups. Ultimately, then, the case against the company did not proceed because the Crown did not identify one individual with sufficient authority and responsibility for the offence to trigger corporate *mens rea*.

These points being made, we must emphasise that there is no necessary antagonism between the criminal law as it is currently organised, and the criminalisation of omission. As Jefferson (2001: 132) has noted, if 'English law traditionally does not always hold a person guilty for failing to act', there 'are exceptional cases', and these 'exceptions have grown in recent years'. Thus, discussing a series of 'established exceptions', Jefferson notes the following, of particular interest to, and relevance for, us: failure to perform a duty imposed by contract; failure to perform a duty imposed by law; and the unwitting – that is, where there is no *mens rea* – creation of a dangerous situation, since this creates a duty to put that situation right (ibid.: 132–41). Moreover, he notes that, 'Since death may be caused by omission, so also may the lesser statutory offence of causing grievous bodily harm with intent' (ibid.: 135).

Now, there is no doubt that some of the specific claims made by Jefferson may be contested, the relevant case law being open to differing interpretations. But what his discussion absolutely clarifies is that there is no necessary technical impediment in criminal law to dealing with crimes of omission. In turn this indicates that there is space for judicial development and/or legal reform, so that the lack of such development or failure to reform is less a technical or legal issue, and more a political or ideological one.

Corporate criminal personality

In regulatory law, as we have seen in the discussion of the history of the Factory Acts in the previous chapter, the test of *mens rea* was removed to produce a new principle of liability, thereby differentiating corporate from individual offending. The effect of this legal invention of strict liability was to sidestep the thorny issue of assimilating safety crime into the system of criminal rules that apply to individuals. The convenience of strict liability was that it removed the 'mental element', or the need to retain a concept of intent, and therefore it could eventually be applied relatively unproblematically both to corporations and to individuals. But strict liability was not to remain as the only basis for attributing liability in safety crimes. As case law developed throughout the twentieth century, the courts developed a method of using the rules of individual liability in relation to corporations. In essence, what happened was that the criminal law principle of *mens rea* was reshaped to enable liability to be imputed to organisations and collective entities. As part of this process of reform, the law contrived a way of manufacturing a 'corporate criminal personality'.

The corporate criminal personality is analogous to, but significantly more complex than, the legal personhood ascribed to the corporation in corporate law. In the latter, the concept of limited liability allows for corporations to be granted a separate 'personality' which is distinct from the individuals and organisational processes that comprise the corporation. Corporate personhood allows the financial liability of shareholders and managers to be limited because those liabilities are deemed to be held by separate legal entity in the 'person' of the corporation. Limited liability thus disconnects the corporate person from the persons that make up the corporation. The principle of limited liability is therefore the defining feature of the modern corporation. Limited liability effectively reduces exposure for investors in the event of financial losses being incurred by the corporation. The principle of limited liability which protects corporations in Western systems of law ensures that owners (normally shareholders) are not responsible for the financial liabilities of the corporation (Glasbeek 2002; Spencer 2002). If senior managers take a series of decisions that plunge the company into debt, managers or owners of the company usually will not be held liable for that debt. Investors can only lose the shares they invested in the first place, nothing more. In legal terminology, this protection for owners is known as the 'corporate veil'. In human rights law, corporations can claim the same 'rights' (to life, privacy, freedom of expression, and so on) as can individuals. The principal effect of the fictional legal form of the corporate person is to protect the property rights of capital and to encourage the reproduction and accumulation of capital by corporations.

At the same time as corporate personhood is held in company law to be a fixed legal state in which the limited liability corporation is protected by the same rights as any individual, the criminal law constructs a parallel but very different conceptualisation of corporations. The corporate *criminal* personality is brought to life only after an individual within the organisation is first implicated in the offence. This legal principle is captured in the relatively new doctrine of corporate *mens rea*.

The identification doctrine

Whilst *mens rea* can be said to be a relatively new doctrine, the notion of collective or group liability is an old one. In twelfth-century England, communities were held collectively liable for murder. As Wells notes, in medieval thinking, the individual was regarded as being inseparable from group and community membership. Now, the individual has been abstracted 'from the complex of relationships, such as nationality, class, or occupation, by which she was previously defined' (2001: 72). The enlightenment notion of the autonomous, rational self-interested individual therefore precipitated a shift in the way we think about both individual and collective liability. This methodological individualism – which became embedded in eighteenth- and ninteenth-century English law – has had profound consequences for how the courts developed a concept of corporate liability.

The concept of corporate *mens rea*, which evolved in the English courts and was followed by other common law jurisdictions throughout the twentieth century, assumes that a corporation can not be held liable for a crime unless an individual within the organisation with sufficient knowledge of the offence and with the necessary responsibility and authority in the organisation can first be identified. In other words, corporate *mens rea* depends upon identifying a particular 'controlling mind' within the organization that can be said to be responsible for the offence. There is a long and complex case history of the evolution of corporate *mens rea* and we are therefore wary of over-simplifying the issues (see Wells 2001; Slapper and Tombs 1999: 26–35; and Gobert and Punch 2003: 59–69). Having noted this as a word of caution, a good illustration of the origins of principle applied for determining who are the people representing the 'controlling minds' of the corporation is summed up in a dictum of Lord Denning's in the 1957 case of *H.L. Bolton (Engineering) Co. Ltd.* v. *T.J. Graham & Sons*:

A company may in many ways be likened to a human body. It has a brain and a nerve centre which controls what it does. It also has hands which hold the tools and act in accordance with directions from the centre. Some of the people in the company are mere servants and agents who are nothing more than hands to do the work and cannot be said to represent the mind or will. Others are directors and managers who represent the directing mind and will of the company and control what it does. The state of mind of these managers is the state of mind of the company and it is treated by the law as such.[1]

Latterly in a key case, Viscount Dilhorne in the case of *Tesco Supermarkets Ltd.* v. *Nattrass* defined the controlling mind:

> … who is in actual control of the operations of a company or of part of them and who is not responsible to another person in the company for the manner in which he discharges his duties in the sense of being under his orders.[2]

The 'identification doctrine' can be understood as an extension of the notion of 'corporate personality' since it establishes the corporation as a separate entity from the directors and managers that make decisions on behalf of the corporation. Yet it departs from 'corporate personality' in so far as it establishes a complex and often difficult-to-establish route to establishing the organisation's criminal state which, unlike the concept of corporate personality, rests on the identification of an individual's acts or omissions. The key problem that has been experienced in a succession of cases is the difficulty of actually identifying one individual who can be said to constitute the controlling mind of the organisation. This individual must also be shown to have been grossly negligent and to have been aware that the risk of causing death is both serious and obvious. Although in a series of cases in the 1980s the courts failed to make the basis for prosecution clear, it seems that this test remains a tough one (for a discussion of the complexities of this debate, see Hartley 2001; and Bergman 2000).

Referring back to the Lyme Bay case outlined above, the relatively small size of the company OLL Ltd made it reasonably easy to identify an individual who can be said to have been the 'controlling mind'. The case for the prosecution was bolstered by the evidence of a letter from the former employees that indisputably made the managing director aware of the risks in question; serious risks that, as the prosecution was able to show, were not subsequently addressed with any urgency. Between the OLL Ltd prosecution and April 2006, six more companies have been convicted for corporate manslaughter. Most of those convictions have been against very small companies.[3] As Sullivan (2001: 33) has noted, the law as it stands 'ensures that, *de facto*, liability is confined to small companies' (see also Dunford and Ridley 1996). Here we find an increasingly glaring irony: while the very size and complexity of large organisations have been key features in *producing* disaster, those same features have rendered the identification of a controlling mind, and thus corporate prosecution, virtually impossible (Tombs and Whyte 2003a).

The most notable challenges to the identification doctrine came in the P&O case (see Chapter 1) and then in the prosecution of Great Western Trains over the Southall train crash, where, in 1997, six people died and some 150 were injured after an InterCity passenger train ploughed into a freight train. In the latter case, the Crown tried to argue that the doctrine of identification no longer applied and that it was possible to consider the conduct of the 'company' as a whole rather than the conduct of an individual 'controlling mind'. The trial judge however ruled that:

> There is, I accept, some attraction in the fact that gross negligence manslaughter, involving as it does an objective test rather than *mens rea* in the strict sense of the expression, is in some ways closer to statutory offences of the kind in the cases relied on by Mr Lissack than it is to the ordinary run of criminal offences. But I do not think this is a good reason for no longer having to look for a directing mind in the company to identify where the fault occurred. In my judgment it is still necessary to look for such a directing mind and identify whose gross negligence it is that fixes the company with criminal responsibility.

> Accordingly, I conclude that the doctrine of identification which is both clear, certain and established is the relevant doctrine by which a corporation may be fixed with liability for manslaughter by gross negligence.

As a result of this ruling, the Attorney General asked the Court of Appeal for a clarification of the law on this point. In Attorney General's Reference No 2/1999, the court held that the Trial judge was correct and that 'the identification principle remains the only basis in common law for corporate liability for gross negligence manslaughter'. In other words, at least as we write,[4] *mens rea* remains a pre-requisite for corporate manslaughter cases to proceed.

The corporate *mens rea* approach was developed in order to allow organisations to fit within a body of law that, as we have seen earlier in this chapter, is underpinned by methodological individualism. This attempt to resolve a contradiction thrown up by the criminal law has also created a new internal contradiction: that organisational prosecutions are ultimately dependant upon the case against an individual. As Tim Kaye has remarked, ' … it is a very strange form of legal personality which says that a person is legally responsible only when someone else is guilty as well' (1992: 354; see also Neocleous 2003: 84).

The principle of aggregation

Safety crimes, like many corporate crimes in general, are rarely imputable to the actions of one individual or a group of individuals acting alone. The principle of aggregation presumes that corporate *mens rea* can be imputed to an organisation by combining the acts or omissions of several different agents of the corporation across managerial levels of the organisation and across time. Claims that a principle of aggregation might apply in law have been raised in arguments heard at two landmark trials, the P&O case in England and the Transco case in Scotland.

Consistent with the doctrine of identification, in order to establish that P&O itself was guilty of manslaughter, the prosecution had to first prove that one of its controlling directors or senior managers was guilty of manslaughter. When the prosecution against five senior employees collapsed, the case against the company inevitably went too. Further restrictions on the criminal responsibility of corporations were set out in a High Court ruling which in effect precluded the aggregation of fault from several directors as being sufficient to incriminate the company. On this matter, Bingham L.J. ruled that:

> Whether the defendant is a corporation or a personal defendant, the ingredients of manslaughter must be established by proving the necessary *mens rea* and *actus reus* against it or him by evidence properly to be relied on against it or him. A case against a personal defendant cannot be fortified by evidence against another defendant. The case against a corporation can only be made by evidence properly addressed to showing guilt on the part of the corporation as such.[5]

If this sounds complex, that's because it is. But we can cut through the circularity of the argument to some extent if we retain some notion of a simultaneous process of *assimilation* and *differentiation*. What Lord Justice Bingham is arguing here is that if we apply the normal rules of criminal process, the courts would not usually allow the actions of one individual to contribute to another's guilt. By doing so, the precedent that has followed this case has effectively fixed the notion of corporate personhood firmly in the arena of criminal law. In other words, he is therefore assimilating very narrowly the corporation into the criminal process. Because often corporate killing involves aggregation, for reasons indicated above, the precedent set here has ensured that a great many cases will not be heard in front of a criminal court. This ruling shows therefore that attempts to assimilate corporations into a system of law designed for individuals can actually have the effect of differentiating safety crimes. This is the paradox that the law has created with the doctrine of identification, one which others have pointed out, stems from Bingham having 'knotted himself' in a circular argument (Slapper, personal interview cited in Hartley 2001). It is this paradox that, as Kaye (1992: 349) observes, makes the criminal law look decidedly 'schizophrenic' when it is applied to the corporation.

The key advantage in the principle of aggregation is that individual states of mind can be added together in order to produce a corporate guilty mind. The P&O ruling following the sinking of the *Herald of Free Enterprise* denied the legal integrity of this principle and a very similar endpoint was reached by the court in the Transco case (see Chapter 1). In the latter case, the failure to review and replace dangerous piping by the firm took place in several meetings at different levels of the organisation which spanned a number of years. The prosecution's novel argument that such decisions and non-decisions could be aggregated across time to impute corporate liability was also denied by the court. The case was widely known as 'Scotland's Herald of Free Enterprise', a title which has an unintended, but pointed, double meaning.

The P&O and Transco cases highlight important contradictions in the law as it applies to corporations. First, they highlight a general paradox. Organisational crimes are very often more easily committed because of the diffusion of responsibility and blame that occurs in large organisations. Complicity in crimes of a bureaucracy or an organisation is much more amenable to techniques of neutralisation on the part of individuals involved, quite simply because they may be able to point to multiple causes at several levels of the organisation. The very same features of an organisation that make safety crimes more likely, then, are the features that prevent the perpetrator being held culpable for manslaughter/homicide in a criminal court. Second, these cases also denied the possibility that the actions of different individuals at different stages of the decision-making process could be aggregated to produce organisational fault. Yet, as we have seen already in this chapter, there is a contradiction in company law, whereby corporations are constructed in a very specific way that enables the various components of the organisation and its decision making processes to be considered as a singular whole. The P&O and Transco rulings reveal an inherent bias in the law's concept of corporate personhood. In those cases, the idea that the corporation could be regarded as a integrated decision-maker for the purposes of criminal conduct was effectively rejected. The courts dispensed with the principle of aggregation at the point when its application would implicate the company in a serious crime. The law, in other words, grants the corporation a singular, human-like identity that protects it from the legal liabilities that human beings cannot escape – yet this singular identity apparently does not apply when the corporation is being held to account for its crimes.

Generalising corporate liability

To this point, we have been examining how the criminal law in England and Wales[6] has developed a form of corporate liability for manslaughter. Yet we might extend our deliberations beyond deaths, to consider how the law might proceed against corporations for crimes of violence resulting in injuries short of death.

Now there is no reason, theoretically at least, why corporate *mens rea* could not be applied to a whole range of crimes of violence caused by corporations (such as corporate endangerment or corporate assault offences; Bergman 2000). In practice, of course, prosecuting authorities have not been minded to bring such cases. If there is no doctrinal legal reason for this, then the explanation of such a limited approach to assimilation must lie somewhere beyond the legal process. In England and Wales, there has been no sustained public debate about corporate violence beyond the high profile 'disaster' cases.

The idea that corporations can be held liable for all criminal offences is by no means a new one. In the 1699 edition of George MacKenzie's *Law and Customes of Scotland in Matters Criminal*, a text that is recognised as the first attempt to codify the criminal law in Scotland, the author, who was Scotland's most senior jurist of the time, discusses whether a collective body of people or an 'incorporation' can commit a crime or not. His conclusion was that, under certain circumstances, incorporations could indeed commit crime and could be punished for those crimes, and that 'rulers' of the incorporation – the individuals responsible for the incorporation's crime – should be likewise punished. Some have speculated that had it not been for the 1707 Act of Union, Scots law under MacKenzie's influence would have been codified. Had this transpired, it is possible that a general principle of corporate liability might have featured in Scotland's criminal code since the early eighteenth century. Of course this did not transpire. A more recent Draft Criminal Code published by the Scottish Law Commission (Clive *et al.* 2003) notes that 'the existing law on corporate liability is not satisfactory' and argues that corporations as 'legal persons' should be liable for a range of offences in the criminal code.

Some jurisdictions, such as France, have sought to introduce corporate criminal liability based upon rigid principles of corporate *mens rea* (Wells 2001). In Canada, the C-45 Bill, introduced by a reform process triggered by the Westray disaster in which 26 miners died, created a new way of attributing criminal liability for organisations. The reformed Criminal Code in Canada allowed 'organizations' to be prosecuted for any of the criminal offences set out in the Criminal Code – not just involving deaths.

It covers, for example, the offence of 'causing bodily harm by criminal negligence' as well as financial and other offences which go beyond the realm of safety crimes. At the time of writing, the reforms in Canada are relatively new and have yet to be fully tested by the courts.

A particularly interesting attempt to create a novel form of corporate liability known as the 'corporate culture model' has been developed recently in Australia. Under the Australian Federal Criminal Code Act (1995), liability can be attributed to a corporation if its board of directors or a senior manager intentionally, knowingly or recklessly carried out the relevant conduct. Intention, knowledge or recklessness can be also attributed to a corporation where it is established either that a 'corporate culture existed within the body corporate that directed, encouraged, tolerated or led to non-compliance with the relevant provision' or where the corporation failed to create and maintain a corporate culture that ensured legal compliance. Corporate culture is defined in the Act as 'an attitude, policy, rule, course of conduct or practice existing within the body corporate generally or in the part of the body corporate in which the relevant activities takes place'.[7] In the corporate culture model, liability can be imputed where the individual who committed the unlawful act reasonably believed that an authoritative member of the corporation would have authorised or permitted the commission of the offence. An authorisation or permission can be established by proving that, on the one hand, the board of directors, or a high managerial agent of the body corporate, directly authorised, or implied authorisation, or permitted the commission of the offence. On the other hand, the authorisation or permission can also be established by proving that a corporate culture existed within the body corporate or that the body corporate failed to create and maintain a corporate culture that required compliance with the relevant provision. Effectively, then, in the corporate culture model, there is no need to show that any one person acting within the corporation was negligent. Negligence can be found in the conduct of the corporation viewed as a whole. This is reflected in Section 2 of Section 12.4 of the Act which states that 'fault element may exist on the part of the body corporate if the body corporate's conduct is negligent when viewed as a whole (that is, by aggregating the conduct of any number of its employees, agents or officers)'.[8]

It is also worth drawing attention to recent, novel attempts in Italy to develop a model of corporate criminal liability – albeit one generated in the context of efforts to pursue financial rather than safety offences. In March 2002, legislation was passed to create two types of corporate liability. One invokes crimes committed by the head of a corporation, and thus is not far removed from the principle of identification. Much more significant, however, is a second, 'innovative element', which has established the concept of 'structural negligence' (Gobert and Punch 2003: 111). This refers to the negligence of a corporation as an organisation or entity, thus rooting liability in 'organisational fault' (ibid.: 110). In defending itself against any prosecution, and to demonstrate due diligence, a corporate body must show that it had considered the possibility of an offence *and* had put into place measures to avoid this outcome. A clear implication is that 'the company needs to have established guidelines and control systems that take into account the risk of the offence being committed. If it has not, then it will be found to be "structurally negligent". 'It is not enough that the company has set up a generic control system' (ibid.: 111). This again is an innovation which attempts to reflect the actual nature and functioning of the modern corporation – and, though not developed for the purpose, there is no reason why it could not apply to safety offences.

In the Netherlands, where there has been a specified principle of corporate liability in the Dutch Penal Code since 1976, the courts have very slowly and tentatively moved towards establishing organisational criteria for attributing liability and fault. The Dutch approach is based upon the two principles of 'power and acceptance' developed in case law. Corporate liability in the Netherlands rests upon showing whether the defendant (the corporation) had the necessary power to determine whether an employee acted in a particular way; and whether the corporation normally accepted such conduct (Field and Jorg 1991: 163–64). The concepts of power and acceptance

> point not to the judgment of isolated positive acts by individuals, but to continuing collective processes. Both suggest more than just a generalised value judgement: ought this to have been allowed to happen? They require concrete examination of the relationship between individuals and corporate groups and a focussing on corporate decision making processes. (ibid.: 166)

This produces, in principle at least, the recognition that corporate crimes are produced by ongoing managerial processes that are routinely tolerated, thus accounting for the fact that, as we note above, corporate crimes often stem from omissions rather than commissions. Yet Field and Jorg's discussion of the development of corporate liability in the Netherlands also raises similar tensions as those discussed above in relation to identification. Although the 'power and acceptance' model allows us to aggregate a series of decisions made (and not made) in the body corporate across time and in a range of different situations, there remains a need to identify where liability rests for the general practices of the corporation. The division of where the power lies in the corporation (or in Anglo-doctrinal terms, the distinction between the 'hands' and the 'brain' of the corporation) is not formally made.

A *de facto* corporate veil

So far, this chapter has argued that the 'identification doctrine' conjures up a rather odd conceptualisation of the relationship between the corporation and the individual. For the purposes of identifying the defendant, the identification doctrine separates the organisation from its constituent parts (its workers and its senior managers and directors). The corporate entity, as in corporate law, is envisaged as a separate person. This corporate person enjoys the same protections and rights as an individual (it has recourse to appeal, to the provisions of the Human Rights Act and so on) but it does not have the same liabilities as individuals. The law insists upon the identification of a rational, free-acting and thinking individual who can be said to possess the necessary *mens rea* before a company can be regarded as guilty.

This has resulted in two key effects. First, reluctance on the part of the CPS to prosecute for corporate manslaughter indicated by the low number of prosecutions taken, and second, the failure of some high profile, and apparently clear-cut, cases. Each of these likely consequences was illustrated starkly in October 2005[9] when Network Rail and Balfour Beatty were fined an unprecedented total of £13.5m for breaches of health and safety regulations related to the Hatfield train crash in 2000[10] (Balfour Beatty's fine was later reduced from £10 million to £7.5 million on appeal). Earlier, Balfour Beatty and five rail executives had faced charges of corporate manslaughter, only for the case to be halted by the judge due to a lack of evidence. Two weeks later, the CPS decided not to proceed with manslaughter charges following the Potters Bar train crash,[11] on the grounds that there was no realistic prospect of conviction; yet in 2004, Network Rail and Jarvis had accepted legal responsibility for claims arising from the crash, to provide 'comfort and assistance' to the victims.

There is no little irony here when we consider the point made in the previous chapter that the criminal law and its guiding principles are designed to deal with individual offending. The criminal justice process takes some odd twists and turns in order to guarantee that individual directors and senior managers are unlikely to be held liable for safety crimes. This is underlined by a clear preference for *corporate* as opposed to individual prosecutions in regulatory cases. Normally, it is the organisation, rather than its senior officials, that is prosecuted for safety crimes. And in most cases, the company faces a fine which, as we will see in Chapter 0, is neither particularly punitive nor likely to secure a deterrent effect. We will also argue in this chapter that the debate on criminalising safety crimes quickly loses its meaning if we only concentrate on the legal process of law itself without considering the form of punishment and what it aims to achieve (Dunford and Ridley 1996; Wells 2001). We will also set out why the use of fines against corporations is not a particularly effective means of punishment. The key point is that corporation can act as a convenient shield for the key decision makers in the corporation. The corporation can effectively absorb the punishment, normally in the form of a fine, while its directors and senior managers are relatively rarely exposed to sanction. Between 1980 and 2004, only 11 directors were convicted for manslaughter. Of those, five were imprisoned, one received a community sentence and five were given suspended sentences. The average custodial sentence was two and a half years.[12] We can say, therefore, that just as the notion of corporate personhood erects a veil which protects both the owners and the senior officers of the company, a corporate veil also exists in a *de facto* sense when it comes to safety crimes.

The UK government's Corporate Manslaughter and Corporate Homicide Bill (see note 4) explicitly denies the possibility of individual liability. Section 16 of the Bill specifically excludes offences that will apply to individuals and notes that: 'an individual cannot be found guilty of aiding, abetting, counseling or procuring an offence of corporate manslaughter'. This clause is particularly interesting since most criminal offences can be prosecuted if someone has been complicit in the crime by aiding and abetting. It is significant in the context of this debate that the Institute of Directors moved from opposition to the Government's reform proposals to vociferous support for a change in corporate manslaughter law (see, for example, *The Safety and Health Practitioner*, December 2002: 4) in 2002, just as the Government's position changed. By contrast, those groups with an interest in the protection of workers and members of the public (such as trade unions and victims organisations) argued equally vociferously for individual liability.

The Bill's rejection of an individual offence contrasts with the position taken by the Canadian government which noted that under their new legislation a corporate executive or board member can also be liable under the Criminal Code for aiding or abetting an offence, counselling a person to be a party to an offence, or being an accessory after the fact to an offence.[13] The Australian Capital Territory (ACT) enacted a separate individual offence in the Crimes (Industrial Manslaughter) Amendment Bill 2003 to allow for the prosecution of 'senior officers' if they negligently or recklessly caused the death of a worker. Senior officers face a maximum penalty of 25 years' imprisonment if they are convicted.[14]

Prosecutions of directors under regulatory law in the UK are also relatively rare. In the ten years up to December 2005, HSC have calculated that, under the HASAW Act, 'proceedings have been brought against a total of 111 directors, of which 86 were convicted and 11 were jailed' (Health and Safety Commission 2005c: 2); moreover, these prosecutions had 'disproportionately impacted on small firms' (Health and Safety Commission 2005d, para 5.2). Similarly low levels of prosecution are revealed in research by the CCA which shows that, in the three years between 2002/03 and 2004/05, there were only 28 convictions of company directors for breaching the HASAW Act.[15] In the context of the total figure of convictions for health and safety offences (around 1,000 a year on average), convictions of directors represent less than 3 per cent of all health and safety prosecutions. We can therefore identify another feature of the *de facto* corporate veil which protects both the owners and the senior officers of the company; a veil that is created in the application of regulatory law.

There are a whole set of separate issues relating to the failure to prosecute directors for HASAW Act offences. The most important reason appears to be that the law does not specify duties for individual directors. This arises from the emphasis in health and safety law upon the duties of 'employers', a term that the courts have consistently interpreted as meaning the company rather than the individual directors of the company. In other words, the duties placed upon companies generally do not impose duties on directors. Section 37 of the HASAW Act does allow for company directors to be prosecuted if an offence has arisen from the 'consent', 'connivance' or 'neglect' of the director. However, the absence of positive safety duties placed upon directors makes the avoidance of prosecution relatively easy because there is no onus on the individual director to take any action to ensure the law is not broken. This relates directly to the points we have already made about acts and omissions in this chapter. It might be relatively easy to prosecute a director for committing a criminal act. But an omission that leads to a crime – which is a much more likely form of culpability for safety crimes – does not necessarily imply a breach of Section 37.[16] The significance of this loophole in failing to provide adequate incentives for directors to maintain a safe workplace is confirmed by a comprehensive review of evidence on the effectiveness of health and safety regulation. This review, *Making Companies Safe: What Works?* (Davis 2004), identifies the need to close the current legal loopholes that enable directors to 'abrogate *all* responsibilities for ensuring that their companies comply with the law and operate safe systems of work' (ibid.: 28; emphasis in the original).

A set of proposals on directors' duties proposed by Glazebrook argues that a tighter form of directors' liability could be secured by the adaption of directors' liability clauses, not only in the HASAW Act, but in a range of regulatory statutes. This would involve the creation of new offences of causing death or serious injury by breaching safety regulations (including the Environmental Protection Act and Nuclear Installations Act, as well as the HASAW Act). The offences would be pinned to directors by asserting that '[e]very person who is (or has the duties of) a director of a corporation is under a duty to prevent the commission or continuance of scheduled offences by the corporation' (Glazebrook 2002: 420). In these proposals, breaches of those offences would carry sentences of up to ten years.

What is rather odd about the current debate about accountability for directors and senior managers is that proposals to improve directors' accountability are generally split between those who advocate the creation of a new crime of violence, and those who would amend existing regulatory law. In the UK, individual accountability is always posed as a choice between the creation of a new crime of violence that can more easily attribute liability for safety crimes to individual directors or senior managers, or amendments to the HASAW Act. In other words, the debate is always framed in terms of a choice between differentiation and assimilation. There is no logical reason not to seek reform by both routes (see, for example, Hall and Johnstone 2005). In most jurisdictions, directors are granted the opportunity in law to hide behind the *de facto* corporate veil that is erected by criminal law. Dealing effectively with safety crimes means that we must adapt the law to deal with the full range of obstacles that lie in the road to accountability for directors and senior managers.

Conclusion

For Glasbeek (2005), the choice facing law reformers seeking to assimilate safety crimes into the mainstream of crimes of violence can be expressed as a choice between corporate personality-based methods of attributing liability (such as corporate *mens rea*) and the creation of a new basis for liability which stretches the boundaries of the identification doctrine. As we have demonstrated, technical legal problems appear to beset both approaches. In sum, the courts have tended to construct an extremely rigid route to the former, and the latter route has tended to lead to a watering down of the criminal status of the offence and the offender. This does not mean, however, that it is beyond our imagination to *develop* laws which seek a new approach to corporate liability which do not decriminalise safety crimes. The route to law reform in Canada, although it also contains some potential flaws, is important because it explicitly attempted to find this balance.

In this and the previous chapter we have discussed the historical and technical processes of 'assimilation' and 'differentiation' in the criminalisation of safety offences. This historical perspective instructs us that there is nothing 'natural' or 'handed down' about the criminal law. Rather, the criminal law evolved in response to a need to maintain a particular social order and to mediate in conflicts that threaten to disrupt that order. The arguments of Carson, Marx, and others[17] are not simply that the criminal law rigidly and reflexively defends the interests of the ruling class to the exclusion of other groups. To maintain order effectively, institutions of the law also need to retain plausible claims to equity and fairness – and on this basis alone, powerful members of society can never be completely exempted from systems of crime control. Thus it is more accurate to see the impulse of Western legal systems not simply as one which protects the powerful, but one which establishes and maintains a particular social order, or, in the words of Carson, a 'viable class society'.

This and the previous chapter have merely provided an overview of the intricate debates and finer points of law and policy that contribute to the predominance of capital in modern liberal democracies. And if this chapter has sought to demonstrate ways in which, and the extent to which, reform in law in this area might be secured, it is to a consideration of regulation that we must now turn in order to further explore these possibilities.

Notes

1   *H.L. Bolton (Engineering) Co. Ltd v. T.J. Graham & Sons* [1957] IQB 159, at 172.
2   *Tesco Supermarkets Ltd. v. Nattrass* ([1972] AC 153), at 171.
3   Those figures are not made public in official data sources. The figures we use are derived from the monitoring work of CCA (see http://www.corporate accountability.org/manslaughter/cases/convictions.htm).
4   The long awaited Corporate Manslaughter Bill was finally introduced in Parliament on the last day of the 2005/06 session. A stated aim of the Bill is to remove the principle of identification, even if this may not be its actual effect, at least in practice; see www.corporateaccountability.org/manslaughter/reformprops/main.htm for a detailed, critical appraisal of the Government's proposals.
5   *Rv. HM Coroner for East Kent ex parte Spooner* (1989) 88 Cr. App. R 10 at 17.
6   In Scotland, where there has never been a successful equivalent corporate homicide offence, the Transco case has effectively put Scottish law on par with the law of England and Wales.
7   Section 12.3 of the Australian Federal Criminal Code (1995). Full text of this section of the code is available at the Australian Attorney General's website: http://scaletext. law.gov.au/html/pasteact/1/686/0/PA000730.htm.
8   Full text of this section of the code is available at the Australian Attorney General's website: http://scaletext.law.gov.au/html/pasteact/1/686/0/PA000740.htm.
9   Source of the following discussion and all quotations is BBC News, *Safety on the Ralways*, at www.news.bbc.co.uk/1/hi/in_depth/uk/2004/safety_on_the_railways/.
10 In October 2000, four people were killed and a further 102 were hurt when a GNER train derailed at Hatfield, Hertfordshire; a broken rail was found to be the 'substantial' cause of the accident.

11 In May 2002, seven people died and 76 were injured when a WAGN service crashed at Potters Bar in Hertfordshire, the triggering cause being a faulty set of points.

12 Figures derived from www.corporateaccountability.org/directors/convictions/manslaughter/main.htm.

13 Full text of the Act can be obtained at: http://www2.parl.gc.ca/HousePublications/Publication.aspx?pub=bill&doc=C-45&parl=37&ses=2&language=E.

14 Full text of the Act can be obtained at: www.corporateaccountability.org/d1/International/australia/ACTManslaughter03.pdf.

15 Available online at www.corporateaccountability.org/directors/convictions/safety/main.htm.

16 For a more detailed analysis, see the CCA briefing at www.corporateaccountability.org/directors/duties/law.htm.

17 For example, Thompson's classic *Whigs and Hunters* (1975).

Chapter 7

Regulating safety crimes

Introduction

A succession of British Ministers have declared that the aim of the Labour Government is to make the UK the most business-friendly environment in the world.[1] Such claims are normally accompanied by the phraseology of 'burdens on business' and 'red tape' to refer to law regulating economic activity, with the unquestioned implication being that such 'burdens' and 'tape' should be reduced as far as possible. In the UK, such terms have entered the political lexicon to such an extent that they are used ubiquitously when the regulation of safety crime, and other aspects of corporate activity, is debated in political circles. As Blair argued in a 2005 speech, this has clear implications for safety regulation and enforcement, 'We cannot guarantee a risk-free life', adding: 'We cannot respond to every accident by trying to guarantee ever more tiny margins of safety. We cannot eliminate risk. We have to live with it, manage it. Sometimes we have to accept: no-one is to blame' (cited *Hazards*, 91, August 2005). To regulate to eliminate risks, he continued, means that 'we lose out in business to India and China, who are prepared to accept the risks'. Notwithstanding that it is no collective 'we' who face risks, but very particular groups of workers (see Chapter 2), this claim also rather obscures the fact that China and India each have occupational fatality rates more than ten times that of Britain (ibid.).

Within this sentiment resides an assumption that to be successful in the modern, globalised world, states have to compete against each other to attract capital. The British government, like most liberal democracies across the world, has accepted the 'realities' of a globalised world order. No matter how contested the idea of globalisation is, there are two major assumptions that are made when the idea of globalisation is accepted as a hegemonic 'truth' or a 'new orthodoxy' (Goldblatt 1997: 140). The first is the assumption that Governments now exert less political control over economies – economic management is relegated to the task of over-seeing the operation of 'free' markets – and over the key actors in these economies, namely corporations and, most significantly, multi- or trans-national corporations. The second is that this is an inevitable process, or to recall Margaret Thatcher's words, 'there is no alternative'.

Neither are convincing, since governments still do a great deal of regulating. If we consider that regulation is much more than something state agencies 'do' to business, then the totality of government regulatory activity must be viewed through a much wider lens (Baldwin *et al.* 1998). Governments are continually introducing, refining and enforcing a complex web of regulations that do much more than control harmful corporate activities. Governments set the rules of entry to markets, the rules that allow markets to function efficiently, and establish the infrastructure and the legal framework that allows corporations to employ workers, to produce and exchange goods and services, to invest, speculate and so on. Of course, since this chapter is about safety crime, it specifically addresses the regulation of corporate harm. But at the same time, it is important to bear in mind that safety crime regulation is part of a much larger system of rule making and enforcement.

The reconstruction of government controls on the harms caused by business as 'burdens' on business or as 'unnecessary red tape' is a common theme in contemporary debates on the regulation of safety crimes. It is a theme that is sustained by particular theoretical claims vis-à-vis the nature of corporate offending, the relationship between employing organisations and their employees, and ultimately about how we understand the role of business activity in society. This chapter begins by providing an introduction to the way in which such theoretical claims underpin the approach to regulation adopted in the UK, and examines how they shape the regulation of safety at a workplace level, before turning to explore the range of theoretical explanations that inform our understanding of safety regulation. In essence, this chapter shall explore the origins of consistent under-enforcement that we documented in Chapter 4.

Regulation-in-action: dimensions of under-enforcement

The key, overarching piece of relevant legislation in the UK is the Health and Safety at Work Act 1974 which is underpinned by the philosophy of self-regulation. The Robens Committee, which sat between 1970–1972 to review the existing state of occupational safety (and health) legislation in the UK, concluded that the most fundamental defect of the statutory system was that there was too much law. This resulted in 'apathy' amongst those at work, since 'people are heavily conditioned to think of safety . . .

as . . . a matter of detailed rules imposed by external agencies' (Robens 1972: 7). Moreover, Robens argued that safety is an area in which there is a far greater 'identity of interests' between the 'two sides' of industry than most other aspects of workplace relations. Concluding that the 'primary responsibility' for improving occupational safety lay 'with those who create the risks and those who work with them' (ibid.: 152), the Robens Committee urged the establishment of a 'more effectively self-regulating system' (ibid.). Robens' recommendations concerning the nature of this self-regulating system were formalised in the subsequent HASAW Act 1974, and later provided a model for occupational safety legislation in Canada and a number of Australian states. According to Robens' version of self-regulation, then, criminal law and its enforcement has a fundamental, but minor, role to play in ensuring occupational health and safety protection – the principal responsibility for achieving protection is to be left to those who create and work with the risks, namely employers and employees (see Tombs 1996).

Without entering into detailed discussion of the Act here (see Dawson *et al.* 1988), it is important to highlight key elements of the self-regulatory philosophy, developed by Robens, subsequently institutionalised by the HASAW Act. Regulatory inspectorates, brought together under the umbrella organisation of the HSE, were not conceived of as any kind of 'police force' for industry. Rather, employers and employees should co-operatively self-regulate (Robens 1972: 18–19), through formal and informal structures, while the HSE and its inspectorates disseminate advice, encouraging and overseeing compliance (ibid.: 80). Key elements of this regulatory approach are the use of negotiation and bargaining on the part of regulators to raise, incrementally, general standards of safety management rather than to ensure compliance with detailed, prescriptive regulations. Emphasis is upon prevention, which is represented as distinct from punitive modes of regulation (Pearce and Tombs 1990). Nevertheless, Robens was clear that 'flagrant offences call for the quick and effective application of the law' and that enforcement should be 'rigorous where necessary' (Robens 1972 : 80).

The HASAW Act certainly ushered in some significant improvements to existing safety legislation (Pearce and Tombs 1991: 422), yet in fundamental respects it remained wedded to long-standing assumptions regarding appropriate modes of regulation (Nichols 1990: 330). Critics unsurprisingly rejected its assumption of a fundamental unity of interests within the workplace, and urged the establishment of something akin to a safety policing agency (Nichols and Armstrong 1973; Woolf 1973).

But despite its assumptions of a basic mutuality of interests between employers and employees, even the self-regulatory philosophy of the

HASAW Act 1974 recognised the likelihood of some non-compliance with safety regulations, and the need to *force* compliance upon employers. This pressurising role was assigned mainly to trades unions within workplaces, and to regulators as a source of external pressure. However, this also meant that if either of these should become unable adequately to fulfil their role, then self-regulation could give way to deregulation.

First, then, this philosophy places an enormous onus upon the balances of power – within and beyond workplaces – between capital and labour. At the policy level, self-regulation is linked to a system of tripartism, whereby employees and employers determine policy within the HSC – though this is clearly an organisation in which employers' interests predominate (Dalton 2000). At the level of workplaces, the balance of power is intimately related to the level and strength of the workers' organisation, not least because subsidiary legislation grants formal roles to trade union representatives in the organisation of health and safety. This is a crucial point, since the most well-cited, and widely accepted, finding regarding safety protection at work is that it is best delivered by strong, active trades unions working through safety committees and safety representatives (James and Walters 2005: 98–102) – with HSC finding that workplaces where these conditions are in place experience over 50 per cent fewer injuries than those where such conditions are absent (ibid.: 99).

Second, in terms of the functions of law, it must be clear that any system of self-regulation is predicated upon a range of credible enforcement techniques to which regulators have access and which allow an escalation of sanctions if the regulated body fails to co-operate. Such an enforcement philosophy, however, can only effectively function where three conditions are met: (i) that inspectors actually have a credible presence (to inspect routinely, to investigate incidents) within workplaces; (ii) that escalation towards greater punitiveness on the part of inspectors is possible and, where the circumstances demand it, likely; and (iii) that sanctions formally at the disposal of both regulators and, then, the courts are credible ones. Yet both historically and currently, it is difficult to see any of these conditions of existence of a Robens-style enforcement philosophy actually in place.

Examining the work of HSE inspectors[3]

It is notoriously difficult to gain a detailed insight into what HSE inspectors actually do. Frequency of inspection has always been a thorny issue in relation to the enforcement of safety law. Under-inspection is, as we note in Chapter 4, a primary factor in keeping detection rates low. In its evidence to the Robens Committee, the TUC had 'reminded Robens that the ILO in 1961 had recommended that workplaces should be inspected at least annually' (cited in Dawson *et al.* 1988: 224), a level of inspection that is very far from the original target, with employers being inspected anywhere between once every ten and once every 20 years. As we saw in Chapter 4, low rates of investigations after incidents have been reported to HSE remains another recurrent issue of contention.

Thus the HSE has *never* been granted the resources to act as any kind of police force for industry. At April 1, 1976, after the formal establishment of HSE, there was a total of 3,282 HSC/E staff in post (including temporary staff). This rose to a peak of 4,226 total staff in post in 1979, before beginning an almost year-on-year decline up to 1990, when resources were increased, leading to a new peak of 4,545 staff being reached in 1994. Since that time, numbers have fluctuated, but total staff has never surpassed that 1994 total. At 1 April 2005, there were 3,903 staff in post. Of course, it should be emphasised that, in any one year, a minority of these staff are actually inspectors, the remainder being engaged in a range of support functions. Budget pressures have begun to force resources even lower. A further 250–350 posts are to be lost by 2008, and this, combined with real terms decline in HSE's grant since 2002, means that 'HSE will by 2008 have lost around 17 per cent of the staff it had in 2002 when comparing like with like' (Trades Union Congress 2006).

Just as the only way to relieve the pressure on front-line HSE staff is to reduce their responsibilities and reduce the amount of work they do, the ability of HSE and its inspectorates to do what they are legally charged with is dependent upon the volume and range of regulation to be enforced, the loss or addition of new areas of enforcement responsibilities, and the numbers and types of workplaces[4] across which law is to be enforced. There is therefore a close relationship between the structure and style of the regulatory regime and the resources available to do the job of regulating.

Low rates of investigations *may* indicate a low level of actual offending – so that, for example, the vast majority of occupational injuries do not occur as a result of safety offences. This does, as we argued in Chapter 4, fly in the face of almost all existing available evidence on the scale of safety crimes. Moreover, given the level of discretion of enforcement officers, here as in other areas of criminal justice, the evidence outlined in Chapter 4 is more plausibly a reflection of the general enforcement strategy of HSE (Whyte 2006) and the constraints placed upon it by increasingly scarce resources.

When HSE *do* conduct investigations in the course of routine, proactive inspections, or following incidents that have been reported to them, their primary, often sole, concern is with locating source problems and recommending remedial measures, if they deem any are required, in order to prevent future occurrence of such an event. The HSC's enforcement statement notes that '[g]iving information and advice, issuing improvement or prohibition notices and withdrawal or variation of licences or other authorisations are the main means which inspectors use to achieve the broad aim of dealing with serious risks, securing compliance with health and safety law and preventing harm' (Health and Safety Commission 2004a: 4). Rarely do inspectors seek to gather evidence or information upon which any future prosecution might be based. In other words, the HSE inspection mindset is not one that is geared towards the detection of 'crime' or 'criminals'. Bergman noted that inspectors consistently fail to examine the role of senior company officers in relation to deaths at work, since they 'are not viewed as potential criminals whose conduct requires investigation'(Bergman 1994: 97). More generally, it is widely accepted that inspectors neither enter premises in order to seek out violations, nor respond to the vast majority of observed or known offences by resort to formal enforcement action. Except in the case of the most egregious safety offences, enforcement action is only invoked where processes of persuasion, negotiating and bargaining, often over a very protracted period, have proven 'unsuccessful'. Law is, indeed, the 'last resort' (Hawkins 2002) – a point noted in Chapter 5 and one to which we shall return below.

HSC's recently (2004) launched *Strategy for Workplace Health and Safety in Great Britain to 2010 and Beyond* – a rather bland document of very little substance – further downplays the role of formal enforcement in the work of the HSE inspector, dedicating two paragraphs of its 17 pages to this issue. This is one index of what appears to be a shift in HSE enforcement practice further towards greater voluntarism. Evidence of such a shift is also to be found in a discussion paper by HSE's then Deputy Director-General, Justin McCracken, urging a shift of emphasis to 'educate and influence', so 'using a smaller proportion of [the HSE's] total front line resource for the inspection and enforcement aspects of [HSE's] work'.

Opposed to the general direction in HSE enforcement policy, a July 2004 Parliamentary Select Committee added the recommendation that 'the HSE should not proceed with the proposal to shift resources from inspection and enforcement to fund an increase in education, information and advice', the central component of HSE's new enforcement strategy. 'The evidence supports', it continued, 'that it is inspection, backed by enforcement, that is most effective in motivating duty holders to comply with their responsibilities under health and safety law' (ibid., para 142). Now, despite the Select Committee's findings, and a major meta-review of existing research that concluded that law enforcement is a necessary if not sufficient condition of effective safety protection (Davis 2004), the Government has remained committed to a path away from already meagre levels of enforcement, and towards even greater focus on 'advice' and 'education'.[5] As an internal HSC paper, entitled *Becoming a modern regulator* (dated March 23, 2004) noted, 'there has been deregulatory pressure from within government to reduce burdens on business, be clearer about the benefits of regulation, and more sympathetic to business needs', adding that 'HSE has responded positively to the debate' (cited in *Hazards* 88, October–December 2004). Here there truly are echoes of the response of the first Factory Inspectors to the advice from Government that, in the context of enforcing the 1833 Factory Act, they should co-operate closely with employers so as to make the new law acceptable to them (see Chapter 5).

Subsequently, the Government and HSC launched a complementary set of initiatives around regulation and enforcement. The Hampton Review – established by the Treasury in 2004 to 'consider the scope for reducing administrative burdens on business by promoting a more efficient approach to regulatory inspection and enforcement without reducing regulatory outcomes'[6] – published its report in March 2005, tellingly entitled *Reducing Administrative Burdens: Effective Inspection and Enforcement.*[7] The Hampton Report called for more focused inspections, greater emphasis on advice and education, and in general a removal of the 'burden' of inspection from most premises, and, with full acceptance by the Government, 'were aimed at promoting effective, risk-based enforcement'. Also in March 2005, the Cabinet Office's Better Regulation Task Force published its review of regulation, *Less is More: Reducing Burdens, Improving Outcomes.*[8] The recommendations of these reports came together in the Legislative and Regulatory Reform Bill,[9] which was published in January 2006. The new Bill aims to 'enable delivery of swift and efficient regulatory reform to cut red tape' (Cabinet Office News Release January 11, 2006).

In this fiercely anti-regulation political context, HSC had launched, in July 2005, its own review of regulation, under the rubric of 'a debate on the causes of risk aversion in health and safety', and, in the words of safety minister Lord Hunt, called for 'a common sense approach to risk management'. Thus 'excessive risk aversion does damage too. It hits organisational efficiency, competitiveness, restricts personal freedoms and damages the cause of protecting people from real harm'. Similarly, HSE Deputy Director General Jonathan Rees added that 'HSE's approach to regulation is very much based on sensible risk management. Risk is ubiquitous. Some degree of risk whether financial, environmental or in terms of safety is necessary for progress'.[10]

Unsurprisingly, then, this recent period has seen a renewed interest in experiments aimed at replacing 'traditional' modes of regulation – that is, inspection. Among the experiments in shifts from enforcement that have been rolled out by HSC/E in the past year are the following:[11]

- HSC's intervention strategy, a September 2005 Report, committed HSE to piloting 'ways to identify and recognise good performance', meaning that in exchange for commitments to institute certain safety measures, companies can gain exemption from inspectors' visits;
- HSE's draft 'simplification' plans, published in November 2005, set out HSC/E's 'determination to develop legislation that is easy to understand and comply with to help secure stronger commitment from business', supporting a 'risk-based, targeted approach to enforcement';
- in October 2005, the HSE, in co-ordination with local authorities, launched a Large Organisations Project Pilot (LOPP), which may prove a key, fully-blown self-regulating alternative to enforcement, and which at the pilot stage covered about 1 million workers;
- a Department of Trade and Industry's (DTI) enforcement pilot, begun in June 2005, which uses a 'traffic light' system in which businesses which have demonstrated excellence in health and safety and food standards are no longer subject to inspection.

There is evidence that this shift away from enforcement is beginning to bite. A sharp down-turn in enforcement activity (outlined in Chapter 4) has been accompanied by a reduction in inspections. In the Field Operations Division of HSE, the inspection rate has fallen from an average workplace inspection every 6.99 years to every 10.84 years between 2001/02 and 2004/05. With a reduction in scheduled inspections, and other visible shifts away from enforcement activity, it is inevitable that fewer safety crimes will be brought to the attention of regulatory authorities, never mind the courts. Low rates of prosecution for safety crimes outlined in Chapter 4 can be largely explained by both the acceptance of the importance of industry's commercial 'imperatives' by the HSE (Tombs and Whyte 1998), and its view of itself as a body which must co operate with and advise industry (Pearce and Tombs 1998). The Hampton Agenda and the associated policy shift further towards a model of self-regulation is driving down levels of prosecution and other enforcement activity. The problem of regulatory under-enforcement is therefore likely to get much worse. The effect is that self-regulation gives way to deregulation, and, as we have seen in Chapter 4, more and more safety offences effectively become decriminalised.

Government resourcing commitments which ensure that there are fewer HSE inspectors than traffic wardens in central London (Trades Union Congress 2006) and concomitant low levels of investigation and inspection, will reduce yet further the pool of incidents upon which inspectors can intervene. Beyond the issue of 'visibility' of safety crimes, the discussion set out here raises major questions about how this shift away from enforcement towards self-regulation, persuasion and bargaining can be legitimised. It is to a consideration for the various theoretical understandings of, and justifications for, regulatory 'under-enforcement' set out in this chapter and in Chapter 4 that we now turn.

How and why is law enforced? Theorising regulation

The picture above – of consistent under-enforcement of safety law and the push for more, rather than less, enforcement activity – is typical. There now exists a mass of studies – mostly nationally based, though with some useful cross-national comparative studies also, some on safety in particular, but many on other forms of regulation of business activity – regarding the practices of a whole range of regulatory bodies. Of the few, broad generalisations that can be drawn from these studies about the practices and effects of regulatory enforcement agencies, non-enforcement of law is the most frequently found characteristic (Snider 1993: 120–4).[12]

Now, within this literature, where the concern is regulatory enforcement *per se*,[13] it is generally recognised, and here this is particularly the case with regard to 'social regulation', that across both business sectors and discrete areas of legislation, one mode of enforcement predominates, namely a compliance-oriented approach. Indeed, some have argued that there is a generalised convergence across enforcement bodies, jurisdictions, bodies of law, and so on, towards such an enforcement approach (Hutter 1997: 243). Within this enforcement mode, as we shall see in the following section, regulators overwhelmingly enforce through persuasion – they advise, educate, bargain, negotiate and reach compromises with the regulated.

If we have demonstrated, to this point, the fact of regulatory under-enforcement, we still have to *explain why*, rather than simply report that, for instance, regulators are so reluctant to prosecute even when detected offences are deemed serious and sufficient evidence of those offences has been gathered (Hawkins 2002). Regulation needs to be theorised rather than simply described; and, as we have indicated in Chapters 5 and 6, part of this theorisation is understanding its emergence in an historical perspective (for example, it was in our discussion of the early Factory Acts that we were able to comprehend the historical basis for a strategy of prosecution as last resort on the part of the factory inspectorate). Indeed, a wide range of explanations for, and ways of thinking about, the phenomenon of 'regulatory under-enforcement' have been developed over the past 150 years or so. We will now consider the most influential perspectives that have been developed in this body of work.

Consensus theories of regulation

First, we wish to consider a variety of perspectives grouped together under the umbrella term 'consensus'. While there are clearly differences between these, they all share a series of fundamental, pluralist assumptions, including the idea that power in modern social orders is dispersed rather than concentrated, that a variety of interests can be mobilised to influence the formal political agenda (which is where effective power lies), and that while the basic contours of these social orders are supported by a general social consensus, social change, through mobilisation of interests, is possible (see Pearce 1976: 38–41). In effect, these are liberal theories of regulation.

One perspective that has been loosely described as the 'public interest' approach (for discussions see French and Phillips 2000; Baldwin and Cave 1999; Ogus 1994) looks at regulation as a process that occurs as a protective state response to the public 'good' being threatened. In this perspective, systems of regulation are the outcome of dialogue between a range of diffuse competing interests. Regulation is conceived of as the outcome of an open and ultimately benevolent decision-making process that reaches a conclusion after weighing up the pros and cons involved in imposing new restrictions upon business. The assumption in public interest models is that a cross-industry consensus involving relevant stakeholders (generally understood as workers, employers and government) is required for a system of regulation to work.

A body of work produced from a consensus perspective has been developed by a group of researchers mainly based in the Oxford School of Socio-legal Studies (Baldwin 1995, 1997; Black 1997; Hawkins 1984, 1997 and 2002; Hawkins and Thomas 1984; Hutter 1988, 1997, 2001). According to this 'compliance school' of regulation, the most successful regulatory strategies are likely to be those involving persuasion, bargaining, and compromise between regulator and regulated. 'Self-regulation'[11] is therefore to be encouraged, since corporations do not respond particularly well to – indeed they are more likely to be alienated by – the full force of the criminal law. From this perspective, corporations have the capacity to act as good corporate citizens, capable of responsible and moral decision-making. Therefore, regulators must appeal to the better nature of corporations by nurturing co-operative relationships with managements. Compliance writers argue that building a consensus around appropriate forms of corporate crime control is a pre-condition of effective regulation. For compliance styles of regulation to work, they must secure the broad agreement and political support of the 'regulatory community'.

When a consensus is achieved and maintained through a close relationship between regulators and regulated, businesses can be expected to self-regulate effectively (Hutter 1988; 1997). To those ends, strict application of the law is inappropriate for corporations (Bardach and Kagan 1982), and it is therefore important from this perspective that regulators are flexible and use discretion in determining which rules to apply (Black 1996; Hawkins 1996a; Lange 1999). Thus, according to Hawkins (1990: 461): '[g]iven the vast numbers of regulatory violations, many of which would be widely regarded as minor, others of which would be seen as serious or even potentially disastrous, and given the scarcity of regulatory resources, a more discriminating approach to regulatory enforcement is needed'. Consensus theories thus support the view that regulatory officials must act as consultants rather than police (Pearce and Tombs 1990).

Now, on one level, the characterisation of the approach to enforcement on the part of inspectors entailed in this perspective is an accurate one in descriptive terms – witness the detailing of such attitudes in Hawkins's recent study of prosecutorial decision-making in HSE (Hawkins 2002). Thus, from this viewpoint, the under-enforcement of safety law that we described in the earlier sections of this chapter is inevitable, since it is a reflection of organisational mission and values, refracted through organisational cultures. However, the compliance school goes further than this, arguing not only is such an approach to enforcement inevitable, but that it is both necessary and desirable. In other words, they move from describing, usually through inspectors' own rationalisations, a situation *as is* to arguing that this is how things *must* be and indeed how they *should* be, slipping between the empirical and the normative. Thus the majority of texts in this area both *document* the predominance of this approach, and *endorse* (some version of) this as the most appropriate enforcement approach.

A variant upon these arguments, but one which shares many of their basic assumptions, is to be found in the voluminous work of John Braithwaite and a series of colleagues over the past 20 years.[15] This influential work, whilst recognising that there are a range of options along the regulatory continuum, argues that 'monitored' or 'enforced' self-regulation is the most pragmatic regulatory outcome (Braithwaite 1982; Braithwaite and Fisse 1987). Braithwaite is in favour of compliance strategies, but only when the threat of tough sanctions remains an option to regulators (Braithwaite 2000). In one of the most sophisticated arguments for self-regulation, Braithwaite and Fisse argue from the starting point that state regulators will never have the resources to enforce regulatory law effectively, whilst adding that internal regulators enjoy certain technical and social advantages over those on the outside (Braithwaite and Fisse 1987). Self-regulation is described and prescribed as being based upon a 'carrot and stick' approach: where self-regulation proves ineffective, the next preferred regulatory tactic is to move to 'enforced self-regulation', this requiring a company to develop a tailored set of rules by which it intends to comply with law which, once approved by external regulators, would then be 'enforced' internally. Where evidence of non-compliance emerges, the potential of punitive external intervention remains (Ayres and Braithwaite 1992: 102–16).[16]

Strategies of enforcement are thus conceived of in terms of a pyramid, where non-compliance leads to the invoking of ever more interventionist or punitive modes of enforcement on the part of regulators. In essence, this is an incrementalist and compliance-oriented strategy based on the principle of deterrence. The issue of deterrence is also considered at length by Braithwaite herein, and elsewhere. In general, Braithwaite argues that there are some contexts in which deterrent-based strategies work, whilst in others these are simply counter-productive. Thus, deterrence must be 'integrated into a strategy that tries persuasion first . . . then incapacitation where deterrence fails' (Braithwaite 2000: 114). Regulatory agencies are best able to do their job when they are 'benign Big Guns' – that is, when they view corporate actors as both rational and moral actors, but assume the latter until proven wrong, thus emphasising persuasion and self-regulation until the point at which greater punitiveness becomes necessary.

Increasingly allied to arguments around self- and enforced self-regulation are descriptions of, or prescriptions regarding, the utility of 'goal-oriented' over prescriptive ('command and control') legislation. While the latter is said to specify the means of securing compliance, the former entails an agency negotiating 'the substantive regulatory goal with industry, leaving the industry discretion and responsibility of how to achieve this goal' (Ayres and Braithwaite 1992: 38). This process of negotiation, based upon a dialogue or conversation both depends upon, but is also one way of achieving, shared, informed interpretations (and the norms, values, and conventions that give rise to them). Thus, 'interpretive' or 'regulatory' communities allow mutual understanding to be secured without further resort to rules.

'Consensus' has been a dominant guiding principle for regulatory policy in the UK, but also in virtually all capitalist economies. Thus, for example the Robens philosophy that, as we have noted earlier in the chapter, provides the foundations for UK Health and Safety regulation (and, indeed, in other jurisdictions), is based upon the idea that there is a natural affinity between senior managers and workers on workplace safety (Nichols and Armstrong 1973; see also Nichols 1990). There is therefore an important link between theory and policy to be observed here. Consensus theories of regulation tend to reflect the dominant themes in 'official' doctrine and policy on controlling safety crime. As a result, we might say that consensus theories analyse the regulatory process from a perspective that incorporates many of the assumptions that governments, regulatory officials and businesses use to inform policy. This conflation between what 'is' and what 'ought' to be renders consensus and compliance theories relatively difficult to criticise (consensus theorists can always deflect criticism by saying they are merely describing rather than prescribing; see Hawkins 1990 for an example of this defence). Despite this tautological insulation from critique, consensus and compliance theories have been exposed to sustained criticism. Five of those main criticisms can be summarised as follows.

First, some commentators argue that there is little empirical evidence for the claims of consensus theories about the desirability of self-regulation (Dawson *et al.* 1988; Smith and Tombs 1995). Indeed, while its desirability is often based upon the undesirable nature and effects of the enforcement approach with which it is contrasted – so called 'punitive' enforcement – the case against strict enforcement regulation is always made hypothetically, since it has never been tried in practice over a sustained period (although see Alvesalo and Tombs 2001; Alvesalo 2003b). At the same time, there is a significant body of *official* evidence that contradicts the feasibility of self-regulation, not least in post-disaster inquiry reports. Thus, for example, Lord Cullen's enquiry into the Ladbroke Grove train crash identified shortcomings in the enforcement of health and safety legislation. Criticisms by then Director General of HSE Jenny Bacon went beyond the issues of HSE resources, and she identified a lack of vigour in the HSE Railway Inspectorate's regulatory duties and the 'placing of too much trust in the duty holders [employers]' (Cullen 2001: para.10.18).

Second, critics argue that consensus models fail to recognise how the concentration of power in business organisations impacts upon strategies of control of safety crime. Although some consensus models take some account of the wider social and economic frame within which regulatory strategies are shaped (for example, Grabosky 1997; Hawkins 2002), this is too easily relegated to one among a number of factors, and certainly the immense resources of financial and political power that (particularly larger) corporations draw upon to bargain with governments and with regulators are glossed over in such models of regulation (see Hawkins 1984: 192).

Third, consensus models see conflicts over regulation as a peripheral rather than central feature of regulation. Corporate or organisational resistance to regulation is precipitated by small numbers of malicious deviants or 'bolshie types' (Hawkins 1996b: 312). Workers and popular movements against corporate crime are also characterised as peripheral, and rarely warrant more than a passing mention in many of those texts. Accounts of regulation from this perspective too easily forget two lessons from history. On one hand (as we saw in the case of the emergence of the Factory Acts) historically, businesses and their representatives have fought bitterly in opposition to regulation when it is not in their clear interest. To this we can add a large contemporary body of evidence that demonstrates how companies obfuscate, lie, cheat and make threats to disinvest, often engaging in fierce public relations campaigns and behind-the-scenes political maneouvres to avoid regulatory reform (Monbiot 2000; Tombs and Whyte 1998; Woolfson *et al.* 1996; Tweedale 2000). On the other hand, consensus models fail to recognise that regulatory controls have often been established only after long and bitter struggles by organised groups of workers and other social movements. A recent example of this tendency is exhibited by Hawkins in his book *Law as Last Resort* (2002). In this text, the only nod to the significance of social movements that support progressive social regulation is found in one reference to Ralph Nader (Hawkins 2002: 14), and even then, this is to set up a crude (and misleading) link between his own criticisms of command and control regulation and Nader's attack on corrupt regulation. The book fails even to make mention of organisations such as Hazards or Disaster Action, or other high profile public/trade union organisations, that have consistently, often very effectively, campaigned for more effective regulatory enforcement. The cases of Simon Jones, Sonae, Bhopal, and the *Herald of Free Enterprise* (as we saw in Chapter 1) are all further testimony to the importance of local, national and indeed international protest movements in pursuing enforcement and/or prosecution in particular cases of safety crimes.

Fourth, because it is myopic when it comes to this aspect of the regulatory dynamic, consensus theorists are highly selective about the 'consensus' they describe. As Davis has argued in the context of the UK, the criminal law has failed to reflect the growing consensus in public support for greater corporate and managerial accountability for deaths at work (Davis 2000: 18).

Fifth, the assumption that corporations are essentially responsible, moral, decision makers underplays both the routine and pervasive nature of corporate offending and the fact that social regulation is often adopted after corporations have committed the least responsible, reckless and most socially damaging acts. Moreover, this assumption obscures the techniques of 'creative compliance' that corporations use systematically to avoid the law (McBarnet and Whelan 1991; McBarnet 1988). Finally, it rather side-steps the *sina qua non* of the corporation – that it is legally bound to maximise profitability for its shareholders.

Neo-liberal theories of regulation

Neo-liberal theorists, most closely associated with the Milton Friedman's Chicago School of Economics, argue that, in general, states have an interventionist tendency that obstructs the efficient regulation of economic activity. Neo-liberals argue that we are over-regulated. Thus, within this general perspective, better safety protection should be secured not through legal regulation and its more adequate enforcement, but through the natural, invisible, disciplining hand of the market.

Market mechanisms are constructed as more appropriate and efficient means of allocating resources and exerting control on participants in markets than governments. Neo-liberal market logic holds that workers enter employment after freely agreeing contractual terms with employers. The risks that workers are exposed to will have a nominal value in those negotiations, and employers will find an optimum level of safety provision that is necessary to attract workers on competitive wages (Moore 1991). Where this optimal level is not reached, then an excess of injuries and the subsequent reaction within the labour market will naturally adjust to eschew employment in a particular firm, or encourage premiums to be paid for 'danger'. This market adjustment results in higher prices than competitors for similar good or services, and thus a loss of business. Thus, the working of the market, left freely to operate, will correct the original 'error'. No state intervention can achieve optimal efficiency so perfectly. However, if neo-liberals are opposed to legal interventions by the state but are broadly supportive of the individual's right to seek legal redress, so, if the market mechanisms fail workers or consumers, then compensation can be provided by the civil law resort to litigation.

The neo-liberal economic perspective is of course associated with the policies of the Thatcher and Reagan governments of the 1980s, but latterly has been embedded in subsequent governments in the US and the UK albeit in a range of slightly modified forms (Jessop 2002). A key element of the neo-liberal ideology that took hold of political systems in the late 1970s and 1980s was the institutionalisation of 'deregulation' as a centrepiece of economic policy. In fact, this was a highly selective deregulation. Whilst states actually expanded their capacity for intervention in social life (for example criminal justice and penal systems in most western states grew rapidly in the same period), some forms of social regulation were deemed unsustainable and damaging to the economy. It was the Reagan and Thatcher governments that first used the language of 'red tape' or 'burdens on business'. In the UK, a Deregulation Unit was established at cabinet level,[17] with the remit to spark a 'bonfire of controls', to take place in concert with a mass privatisation of publicly owned industries. What followed in the US, UK and in other prominent OECD countries was a twin pronged attack upon the legislative safeguards governing some forms of anti-social business activity, perhaps most notably worker safety. This took different forms in different states, depending upon the level of resistance met from pro-regulatory forces (see below). Whether ultimately material or ideological in character, deregulation became the order of the day. And neo-liberal, deregulatory tendencies have been given further impetus as neo-liberalism has, over the past quarter of a century, achieved an international predominance as the 'one best' way of organising economies – a process that is signified by the term globalisation, to which we shall return, below.

Thus an increasingly important arena where we find the influence of neo-liberal ideas is in the global trade regime. Latterly, this ideology has supported the coerced expansion of privatisation and attacks on safety standards and other regulatory protections in the developing world (Michalowski and Kramer 1987; Tombs and Whyte 2003b). Thus, for example, the World Trade Organisation has forced the repeal of food, environmental and workplace safety regulations where they have been deemed to impede 'free trade' (Peet 2003; Wallach and Sforza 1999). Yet it is important to note that despite its seemingly unassailable position in world politics, neo-liberal free market ideology has never been implemented in its purest form. Rather, it has provided a set of guiding principles of minimal interference and enterprise promotion.

The following three criticisms can be made about the neo-liberal perspective. First, neo-liberal explanations of regulation have been criticised roundly for refusing to recognise that capitalist markets – especially those structured along the lines of neo-liberal prescriptions – fail to protect us because they create and support a concentration of power and information in the hands of a small elite (Chomsky 1999; Pearce and Tombs 1998: 17–25; Snider 2003). The need to earn a living, combined with lack of choice and intense competition in job markets, forces many people to work in unsafe workplaces. Second, even the 'freest' of markets do not and cannot operate without the active intervention of states (Jessop 2002; Moran and Wright 1991, Soros 1998: 36–42). As the economic sociologist Karl Polanyi once argued, even nineteenth-century *laissez faire* economic principles had to be enforced by the state (1944/1957: 139). States establish the market conditions, rules and infrastructures within which businesses operate. If we recall the argument in the introduction to this chapter, states do a great deal to 'regulate' industry and commerce – to maintain its steady progress – even where safety crime controls are weak. A third point follows this critique of 'market freedom'. Markets are never likely to be truly 'free' since even the most profit-oriented businesses themselves often recognise that regulation is in their long-term interests. Large firms in particular are generally unwilling to subordinate themselves to the vagaries of the market (Pearce 1976: 82–4).

Even under the most extreme versions of neo-liberal capitalism, then, regulation (even social regulation) cannot disappear altogether – not least for some of the very same reasons that the Factory Acts needed to be ushered in at the birth of fully-fledged industrial capitalism (see Chapter 5). Yet, neo-liberalism has been highly effective in its assault upon workers' safety and pollution standards and in attacks upon the funding of regulatory agencies. On this point, some neo-liberal theorists argue that government regulation, especially in monopoly industries, has a tendency to produce a corrupting influence between large companies and state regulators (Peltzman 1976; Stigler 1971). State regulation will only ever produce unequal and unfair competition in the market place, because it encourages a mutually re-inforcing relationship between governments and big business. In this sense, this body of theorists, sometimes known as the 'law and economics' movement, has similarities to another perspective on regulation: 'capture theory'.

Capture theories of regulation

Capture theories characterise governments and state regulatory agencies as vulnerable to 'capture' by big business. Regulatory capture theory's most well known exponent is Marver Bernstein (1955) who conceptualised the regulatory process as a 'life cycle' where regulatory agencies tended to go through various stages of maturity. In essence, his argument was that regulatory agencies are born out of a general concern about some social problem which appears amenable to a regulatory solution – and, in the early stages, although they tend to be outmanoeuvred by business, regulatory agencies retain a certain zeal (or a strong political will in favour of regulatory control). This zeal ebbs away as the agency reaches maturity, and in 'old age' is debilitated to the point of emasculation in its final 'capture' by industry. Capture is achieved by a mixture of intense corporate lobbying, the consolidation of elite interests in public and private sectors, and a 'revolving door' of personnel between regulator and regulated. The implication of capture theory is therefore that regulation is counterproductive, since it has an inherent tendency to institutionalise corporate influence. Once the capture process has been set in motion, regulatory agencies are doomed to intervene on behalf of the corporations they regulate, and ultimately to advance the interests of big business.

Other advocates of 'capture' depart from life cycle theory and simply argue that in advanced stages of capitalism the state and its administrative apparatuses will become colonised and ultimately controlled by large corporations. This perspective has been used widely to explain the corporate manipulation of government in a so called 'globalised' world order (see, for example, Sklair 2001). Thus, Noreena Hertz's widely acclaimed book, *Silent Takeover,* argued that corporate power is now unassailable, since 'Governments are now like flies caught in the intricate web of the market' (2001: 140). The influence of unelected, pro-business 'experts' upon UK government (through their role in policy circles around the Prime Minister and the Treasury, or via appointment to the House of Lords), the colonisation of government think tanks by business and the proliferation of government–industry decision-making partnerships all provide us with strong evidence of a 'capture' tendency in contemporary Britain (Monbiot 2000). And this increasingly incestuous relationship between business and government elites has spilled over into the regulatory field.

If one thinks back to the evidence of under-enforcement set out at the beginning of this chapter, we are presented with a powerful case for capture. But the degree to which the government–industry relationship in any capitalist social order is best described in terms of capture remains questionable. For one thing, at the empirical level, many, if not most, of the agencies to which this approach might be applied have hardly had any (early) period of zealous enforcement – the factory inspectorate, for example, almost immediately reached accommodation with the interests of (large) manufacturers and the sympathies of a class-conscious magistracy, as we described in Chapter 5.[18] Further, theoretically, this approach over-simplifies the role of governments as the instruments or pawns of business. The regulatory process is constructed as uni-directional, with decision-making power moving from business down through states and societies. Three points flow from this critique of capture theory. First, it denies or underplays the possibility for resistance, and – like consensus theories – marginalises the centrality of social movements against corporate crime (Kramer 1989). Capture theories view the potential impact of social movements on the regulatory system as minimal since, if, as capture theory argues, regulatory agencies are doomed to lurch from one captured state of existence to the other, there is little point in pro-regulatory movements focussing their efforts on regulatory policy. Second, it cannot explain why at particular moments, 'stricter' regulation that is clearly antithetical to the immediate interests of corporations but is in the long-term interests of capital as a whole – can be introduced (Marx 1887/1954; Carson 1979; Stolberg and Harris 2003). Third, capture theory can't explain why over time, regulatory agencies can revert to more punitive strategies, even after the point at which they appear to have been captured, or that there may be variations in enforcement policy within agencies (Hutter 2001).

All of this is not to say that the capture thesis does not have any conceptual value, or that 'capture' does not happen to government agencies at particular moments (for example, Carson 1980c; 1982). The value of capture theories is that they are able to highlight systematic bias in regulatory agencies. An alternative approach is to point to the 'balance of social forces' in any regulatory regime. That is, to look at the balance of power between dominant and sub-dominant groups. Few would disagree that in capitalist societies states tend to act in ways that promote dominant business interests above other interests. A second value of capture theories is that they can explain how regulatory regimes can facilitate corporate crimes by establishing the framework for collusion between industry and government officials. In capitalist social orders, the relationship between business and state agencies is bound have a mutual, even symbiotic, political tendency. Indeed, this point is recognised to some extent by each of the perspectives that we have reviewed so far. Consensus theorists accept that regulatory settlements often favour big business. For neo-liberals, over-concentration of power in the hands of business elites is highlighted as a serious threat to market democracy. For capture theorists, the colonisation of the state by business is inevitable in regulated market societies. So, one point that these perspectives all recognise (albeit to varying degrees) is that *state regulation has a tendency to favour organised business interests.*

What is missing from each of those perspectives, however, is a detailed understanding of how regulation is also used by relatively powerless groups to *resist* corporate power and *oppose* business interests. To the extent that it does occur, regulatory 'capture' is a process that is never complete. Regulatory agencies remain vulnerable to external pressures from labour and from public pressure and popular campaigns. This latter point, on the significance of conflict and resistance, is one of the distinguishing characteristics of Marxist, neo-Marxist and radical approaches (grouped together here as 'critical approaches') on regulation and safety crime.

Critical approaches to regulation

Before we examine this latter point, it is worth noting that the capture thesis is often attributed to Marx and to Marxist analyses that over-simplify the capitalist state as an instrument of ruling class domination. Such critiques often trot out the well worn quote: 'The executive of the modern state is but a committee for managing the affairs of the whole bourgeoisie'[19] (Marx and Engels 1968/1890: 37). This quote is usually deployed not to examine why or on what basis Marx might have developed such a view of the state, but – reproduced devoid of context[20] – to demonstrate the extent to which Marx held to a rudimentary or primitive understanding of the state. Our earlier discussion in Chapter 5 of Marx's analysis of the Factory Acts passages noted a subtle understanding of the fragmented and often contradictory way in which regulation develops. In stark contrast to his intellectual reputation as an 'instrumentalist' or 'economic determinist', Marx portrays the British state as contradictory and institutionally divided over the struggle for regulation. Regulation is passed in the midst of bitter struggles against legal intervention by the factory owners themselves, and capital at some points is itself divided over its opposition to regulation. Although the significance of Marx's analysis for thinking about the complexity of the capitalist state – and in particular the importance of his observations for understanding the regulatory process –

has rarely been acknowledged, it is his insistence on viewing regulation and its enforcement as an outcome of the struggle between antagonistic class interests that has endured in critical and neo-Marxist analyses of regulation. A number of writers have drawn upon this tradition of viewing struggles and conflict between economic groups or social classes as central to understanding the regulatory process (Carson 1979; Davis 2000: 14–18). Mahon (1979) draws upon the work of the Greek Marxist Nicos Poulantzas, arguing that the state is an 'unequal structure of representation' which absorbs and dissipates conflicts between opposing interests. This has the effect of maintaining the long-term stability of the social order. Regulatory agencies are created following particularly contentious conflicts of interests precisely because conflict needs to be absorbed and dissipated. In turn, regulatory agencies ensure that particular business interests are subordinated to the long-term interests of capital as a whole. This is why we might expect tough regulatory responses after a prolonged campaign against, or public debate over, an issue of corporate crime. It is also why we might expect to see regulation implemented against the wishes of business at particular times (Wilson 1980; Woolfson *et al.* 1996). At times some bids from pro-regulatory forces are irresistible. For example, the Offshore Safety Division (OSD) of HSE was established as a new regulator for the offshore oil industry under the rabidly pro-business Conservative governments of the 1990s. The OSD was formed after the moment of political exposure precipitated by the Piper Alpha disaster and the subsequent campaigns of industrial action for safety rights for workers on North Sea oil platforms (Woolfson *et al.* 1996). This reinforces the central point of the critical and neo-Marxist thinkers, then, that regulatory controls can be most effectively fought for at times when the state – indeed the social order – is vulnerable to pressure from subordinate groups.

Consistent with this analysis, some academic writers have highlighted the centrality of 'pro-regulatory forces' in securing demands for tighter regulation, and in ensuring the effective enforcement of the law. Thus, for Snider for example, regulation is best understood as a dialectical process, determined by the outcome of struggle within two sets of relationships, namely the relationship between states and capitals, and the relationship between states and their broad electorates. Thus key factors in identifying regulatory outcomes are: the interests and strength of various forces within capital, the nature and strength of various pro-regulatory groups, and the interests within and strength of local and national states (Snider 1991). This indicates that understanding the level of regulation at any one time is both an empirical and theoretical task.

Such an approach coheres with a wider body of neo-Marxist and critical literature that views the law as a site of struggles over the definition of 'crime' and over who constitutes the legitimate objects of crime control.[21]

Thus, the emergence of the UK Corporate Manslaughter and Corporate Homicide Bill was only possible due to the combined efforts of workers groups, victims and relatives campaigns, supported by the work of critical academics and lawyers. Although, as we indicated in Chapter 6, the campaign for an effective corporate killing law has been by no means 'successful', what this story does indicate is that struggles for stricter regulation can make progress – and gain widespread popular support – even in the face of hostile economic and political conditions. Indeed, the watered down form that the Bill has taken suggests a process of government mediation between pro-regulatory forces and corporations and their representatives, albeit one which has taken unequal account of the competing demands of these groups.

This view of the state as an unequal structure of representation therefore allows us to see how spaces for challenging power are not necessarily closed down or captured, no matter the intensity of a prevailing pro-business ideology. To return to the point raised at the start of this chapter, despite the current rhetoric of neo-liberal discourse, a diminution of safety standards is not a necessary or inevitable consequence of global competition. States as regulators remain dominant players in, indeed essential to, the functioning of the global economy (Jessop 2002).

Conclusion

Of the four perspectives on regulation that we have explored here, it is the consensus perspective – underpinned by the idea that effective regulation is best secured by building a consensus around the regulatory community – that remains dominant in Western regulatory systems. But we should not necessarily think that the perspectives that underpin regulation are diametrically opposed, or operate in a mutually exclusive way. It appears that in the case of health and safety, the rise of neo-liberalism as an organising political ideology in Western democracies remains unchallenged by the consensus approach. As Hawkins has noted, via the idea of the 'surround' within which regulation proceeds (Hawkins 2002: 48–9, and *passim*); macro economic and political factors play an important role in shaping inspectors' world-views. This throws light on the supine response of HSE to the Government's deregulatory messages, and also indicates that inspectors increasingly enter their bargaining and negotiation with employers with some sense of the greater power of capital, the increased urgency of threats to relocate investment abroad, or the realities of diminished state capacities under conditions of deregulation and privatisation, and so on. Under neo-liberal conditions, in other words, punitive enforcement becomes less feasible, and co-operative or compliance-oriented approaches become much more likely. And it is here that we can see – again – a coherence with policy, since the current and recent British Governments are, for all their deregulatory rhetoric, probably less interested in the removal of law *per se* (which, as Thatcher found in the 1980s, invites political confrontation), but much more interested in changing the terms of that enforcement, towards greater compliance-type techniques which imply less actual impact upon business.[22] The prospects for worker protection are not good if this analysis is accurate. If consensus theories have accommodated and provided intellectual legitimacy to the 'deregulation' strategies promoted by neo-liberals, then capture theories cohere with a different set of neo-liberal claims. Capture theorists, on the left and the right of the spectrum, share the idea that in the current social order, there is no alternative to the triumph of the market over state regulation. TINA (there is no alternative) is essentially the normative equivalent of capture theory's resignation to the corruption of state regulation by the market. Capture theory is therefore unable to produce an alternative to the domination of the regulatory system by corporate interests.

Our discussion in this chapter, however, raises the possibility that an analysis of struggles for regulation is of a complexity that moves us beyond a bilinear struggle between state and capital. The complex struggle for regulation is not resolved only in the formal political arenas of government. Neither is it resolved at the level of the regulatory agency or even the individual workplace. As we argued in Chapter 5, the rule of law in capitalist societies is as much about social order maintenance as it is about control efforts *per se*. Crucially, states continue to set the rules of the market nationally and trans-nationally (Underhill 1994) and reconstruct regulatory and infrastructure systems when markets break down (Alvesalo and Tombs 2001). In other words there is clearly room for manoeuvre on the part of states as to how to regulate and enforce – requiring us again to confront the specificities of balances of power within concrete social orders. If both capture and consensus theories are compatible, in different ways, with the current political mantra of 'there is no alternative', then critical approaches open up considerations of precisely what alternatives do exist – and how they might be pursued and secured.

Notes

1 See, for example, Osler 2002, *passim*.
2 The Safety Representatives and Safety Committee (SRSC) Regulations 1978, and tellingly the one part of health and safety legislation of this period that caused real political controversy (Walters 1987: 48).

3   This chapter does not focus upon the work of Local Authority inspectors, known as Environmental Health Officers (EHOS). But it should be noted that these have significant worker safety enforcement functions in almost 1.2 million establishments.

4   For example, since 1974, the numbers, and rapid turnover, of small businesses in the UK has increased exponentially.

5   See, for example, the Government's Response to the Select Committee Report, in the form of a letter from the Secretary of State for Work and Pensions, published as an Appendix to the House of Commons Work and Pensions Committee. *Government Response to the Committee's Fourth Report into the Work of the Health and Safety Commission and Executive. HC 1137.* London: the Stationery Office; and Health and Safety Commission 2004b.

6   Hampton (2005) *Reducing Administrative Burdens: Effectice Inspection and Enforcement.* London: HM Treasury/HMSO, available at www.hm-treasury.gov. uk/hampton, 1.

7   Available at www.hm-treasury.gov.uk/budget/budget_05/press_notices/bud_bud05_presshampton.cfm.

8   Available at www.cabinetoffice.gov.uk/regulation/documents/pdf/br_act_review.pdf.

9   www.publications.parliament.uk/pa/cm200506/cmbills/111/en/06111x--.htm.

10 Health and Safety Executive Press Release E094:05 July 13, 2005, at www.hse.gov.uk/press/2005/e05094.htm. Quotations from this source.

11 Source: *Risks*, no 235, December 1, 2005, p5..

12 While this holds as a generalisation, it remains a generalisation; there are important national differences in enforcement strategies across differences spheres of regulatory activity (Snider 1991).

13 As opposed, for example, to studies of regulatory policy formation.

14 A model of regulation where corporations are trusted to monitor and control their own compliance with the law under a minimalist regulatory framework.

15 See Braithwaite 2000 for an excellent overview of this work.

16 Gunningham and Johnstone (1999) have recently developed this model in order to argue for a 'twin track' approach to regulation.

17 The fore-runner of what is now known as the Better Regulation Executive, referred to earlier in the chapter as leading the review of regulation which resulted in the Legislative and Regulatory Reform Bill (2006).

18 By contrast, some have argued that in the US, the Occupational Safety and Health Administration did begin life with a zealous approach to enforcement, even if this was more expressive than symbolic (Calavita 1983), so that here a capture theory based upon a life-cycle approach might have somewhat more force.

19 Marx's term for the ruling class of property owners.

20 The statement was made in his polemical political programme, *Manifesto of the Communist Party.*

21 The same issues are at stake in campaigns to hold war criminals to account at the International Criminal Court, for the criminalisation of violence against women and in campaigns for the decriminalisation of drug use.

22 In the UK now, any proposal for law reform which may affect business must be accompanied by a 'Regulatory Impact Assessment' which sets out in detail – and costs – the potential impacts that the new law and its enforcement may have upon business.

Chapter 8

Punishing safety crimes

Introduction

This chapter is concerned with how the perpetrators of safety crimes are dealt with after they have been found guilty in a criminal court. Before starting our discussion of how court sanctions and punishment are applied in the context of safety crimes, we begin with a couple of important background issues that need to be borne in mind when reading this chapter. First, it is likely that in most jurisdictions, safety crimes do not attract the most punitive response from the state when compared with other forms of white-collar and corporate crime. Bernie Ebbers, the World Com Chief, was sentenced to 25 years in jail in July 2005 for his part in the corruption that brought down his business empire; and, in October 2006, Jeffrey Skilling, the Enron Chief Executive, was sentenced to 24 years in jail for his part in those frauds. No employer to our knowledge has ever faced such a lengthy sentence for killing – let alone injuring – in the workplace. This can be partly explained as a function of the differentiated way in which states respond to different forms of crime. Large scale crimes of corruption subvert and threaten the smooth operation of legitimate markets in the way that safety crimes generally don't. Therefore it is the former types of crime that may produce more punitive state responses than other forms of white collar and corporate crime (Slapper and Tombs 1999), although as we indicated in the previous chapter, safety crimes and the popular opposition that they often generate can present a crisis of stability for the social order. It is at those moments that law reformers, legislatures and courts are more receptive to arguments for more punitive responses.

The second thing to bear in mind is that this book is concerned with safety *crimes,* and therefore we include no commentary or analysis in relation to the role of civil proceedings in the punishment of corporations. A broad distinction between civil and criminal procedure can be made as follows. The former normally involves an individual initiating a case against another individual or a private corporation to seek compensation. The latter involves an infraction of the criminal law normally (although not always) initiated by a representative of the state. The difference in the gravity or seriousness with which each legal procedure is generally regarded can be illustrated by examining the technical characteristics of each procedure. Criminal courts make a decision on the guilt or otherwise of the defendant; if guilt is proven, the court will normally impose criminal penalties. Civil cases deal with the allocation of costs and damages to one part or the other and normally involve a decision about whether or not the respondent must pay damages. In most civil cases, the plaintiff or applicant seeks damages for a personal injury against them (which may include disease, impairment of physical or mental condition, or death, where the action is initiated by the bereaved). Very few damages cases actually ever reach the courts since the vast majority are subject to out-of-court settlements (Harpwood 1993: 18.1). Personal injury actions against corporations are notoriously difficult to win since corporations have the resources to delay proceedings; there are considerable risks for the plaintiff, since potentially huge court costs have to be paid for by the losing party, costs which are usually much more easily absorbed by the defendant, certainly if the defendant is a large corporation. These factors combine to encourage plaintiffs to settle out of court for a reduced compensation sum rather than seeking full compensation in the courts (Harris 1984). In criminal cases, the relationship between the two parties is entirely different. The state punishes crime on behalf of us all, whereas individuals pursue civil action on behalf of themselves. The fact that punishments can be imposed in the criminal courts once an accused is found guilty further distinguishes criminal procedure from civil procedure. No matter how punitive the latter may often appear, it is criminal cases that imply the state's right to punish, and by extension, the seriousness with which the state regards criminal behaviour.

This point immediately alerts us to how the criminal law acts as a mechanism of social censure (Sumner 1990), or as Mathiesen (1990) put it, a 'message from the state'. The criminalisation of conduct by the State carries a gravitas and social opprobrium that is not comparable with the cases that are pursued in the civil courts simply because the State, rather than the individual, acts as the accuser and the prosecutor on behalf of its citizens.

The argument running through this book is that not all crimes are treated by the state equally; as a result, the social opprobrium carried by legal censure varies across different criminal offences and changes over time and place. Discussions in previous chapters have detailed how safety crimes came to represent a different class of offence. On one hand, safety crimes are very often segregated in law as 'regulatory' or 'administrative' offences, and on the other hand, they tend to be exposed to 'compliance' rather than 'strict enforcement' styles of policing. Moreover, as Chapters 5, 6 and 7 have indicated, the seriousness with which safety crimes are treated is not fixed. This chapter explores how safety crimes are currently treated, and how they might be treated differently, by the courts. It starts by examining how safety crimes fit with the key theoretical perspectives that have been developed to justify contemporary forms of punishment, before going on to describe how safety offences are dealt with in the UK. The final section of this chapter will then propose a range of alternative penalties and sanctions for safety crimes.

Theories of punishment and safety crimes

The observation that deterrence theory is much more applicable to safety crimes when compared with 'mainstream' crimes has become commonplace in the study of white-collar and corporate crime (Sutherland 1983; Chambliss 1967; Geis 1996; Pearce and Tombs 1998). Deterrence theory is based upon the idea that individual conduct – deciding, for example, whether or not to commit a criminal act – is shaped by the costs and benefits that might arise from the conduct. Individuals therefore make a rational calculation that weighs the chances of being caught and the severity of the punishment against the 'benefits' of committing a crime. It is a perspective that is neatly summed up in Jeremy Bentham's idea of *homo economicus*, the self-interested, rational thinking 'economic man'. In theoretical terms, deterrence theory has been most commonly challenged on two counts. First, rational choice depends upon the subject having perfect knowledge of the risks of being caught. Second, rational choice depends upon individuals' being capable of exercising rational judgement. Generally, the model is applied to those who are *least* capable of acting rationally. Pierre Bourdieu (1998: 83), referring to the capacity of lower-status populations to mobilise and improve their conditions of existence, has made this point:

> The unemployed and the casualised workers, having suffered a blow to their capacity to project themselves into the future, which is the precondition for all so-called rational conducts, starting with economic calculation . . . are scarcely capable of being mobilised ... in other words, a reasoned ambition to transform the present by reference to the projected future, one needs some grasp on the present.

The ability to act rationally, in other words, is severely compromised where people do not have any control over the social conditions that shape their present and their future.

Conversely, companies and their senior officers do have some motivation to consider the long term consequences of their decisions, and the costs of punishment to their business and their social position. They are much more likely to commit crime only after making a reasoned assessment and choice to act rationally. Corporations are 'future oriented' (Braithwaite 1989). Moreover, although most individuals do not possess the information necessary to calculate rationally the probability of detection and punishment, large bureaucratic organisations do have the resources to deploy sophisticated information gathering systems and to call upon lawyers and accountants. Both companies and their directors do make calculated decisions, not based upon perfect knowledge, but based upon a range of knowledge resources available to them which allow them to make calculated decisions. Chambliss (1967) argued that deterrence can appropriately be used against white collar offenders because they satisfy two conditions. First, they do not have a commitment to crime as a way of life; and second, their offences are instrumental rather than expressive. In other words, the crimes they commit are less likely to be spontaneous or emotional as we might find in many 'street' crimes, but are often the result of calculated risks taken in boardrooms. Organisations and their senior officers use cost-benefit analysis to assess the implications of strategic decisions as a routine procedure.

There are some key examples here. Perhaps the most infamous case is the decision to proceed with the production of the Ford Pinto, despite corporate knowledge of a lethal design flaw, based on the calculation that the explosions that would follow impact upon the fuel tank would cause a projected total of 180 deaths and 180 serious injuries. On the company's reckoning, each death would cost them $200,000, each injury $67,000 and each car $700. Thus while the total cost of allowing the dangerous car to leave the production line was $49.5m, the costs of design change were estimated at $137m; the company therefore decided to produce and market the car with the fault. Dowie's investigation into the Ford Pinto revealed that in fact 500 people had died as a result of Pinto explosions (Dowie 1977). This type of calculation is also used when firms consider major safety investments. The British Railways Board and Railtrack, used a cost-benefit calculation to decide against installing the Automatic Train Protection (ATP) system. The company's estimation was that the system would cost approximately £14m per human life saved. The cost of instalment greatly exceeded the projected economic value of the lives that would be saved (£3m per life). The calculation was brought into sharp relief by the Ladbroke Grove train crash in 1999. Had ATP been installed, it would most likely have saved the lives of 31 people killed at Ladbroke Grove (Whyte 1999b).

Those are perhaps the most dramatic and extreme examples of the application of rational decision-making in business contexts and it is important to note that we would not expect to see this level of analysis in the everyday decisions that businesses make. However, it remains the case that businesses do routinely make decisions based upon the projected cost implications of a particular activity or strategy. In other words, perpetrators of safety crimes are better equipped and more likely to be rationally focused upon the future consequences of their policies, strategies and the way that they organise their activities.

Deterrence theory is the bedrock of contemporary western systems of criminal punishment. However, saying that deterrence theory underpins our approach to punishment is not to say that it is the only philosophical basis that we find influential in systems of punishment. Deterrence theory is typically contrasted with retribution or 'just deserts' theory, the latter conceiving of punishment as a means of repaying society for transgressing rules. The basis for this philosophy is not that citizens do act rationally, but that they *should* act rationally. It is also underpinned by the liberal assumption that the State's rules are there to benefit all. If some choose to break the rules, it is normal to achieve some kind of pecuniary advantage over others. Therefore, punishment should be conceived of as repaying a debt to society. Penal theorists like Andrew von Hirsch (1976/1996) also argue that the just deserts perspective clarifies the appropriate penalty for the crime and therefore improves transparency and accountablility in the penal system. Murphy (1973/1995) has criticised just deserts from a similar position to that outlined above, namely that the retributive conception of justice masks an inherent contradiction: because repaying a debt to society means the least to those who are the least well positioned within the social structure, punishment which seeks retribution is likely to be least effective when applied to the social groups which are, overwhelmingly, the principal target of contemporary criminal justice systems.

Rehabilitative theories of punishment are based upon the idea that punishment should make interventions that are likely to transform the criminal into a law-abiding citizen. Rehabilitation aims to reform the criminal and re-integrate them into the community. John Braithwaite has developed perhaps the most influential perspective on rehabilitation over the past 20 years or so. He argues that rehabilitation fails to work because often punishments are disconnected from the social environment that they seek to change. In order to reconnect the offender to the community that he or she has offended against, Braithwaite's (1989) 'reintegrative shaming' thesis proposes that punishment is less likely to work by exclusionary or stigmatising practices, than if the offender has a chance of being re-integrated into society. Influenced by forms of punishment found in Japanese and in Maori culture, Braithwaite argues that a process of public shaming can facilitate the re-integration of the offender into the community. The criticism that has been levelled against reintegrative shaming is that it is difficult to re-integrate individuals of low social status, since they are likely to be in a social position that is disconnected from the 'community' dealing out the punishment in any case and will therefore not necessarily respond to a process of shaming. However, what is interesting for the purposes of the argument here is that for Fisse and Braithwaite (1983) this principle of re-integration can be most effective when dealing with organisations and individuals of high status in the community, since they have a great deal to lose in terms of reputation.[1]

A final justification for punishment that is commonly applied to western criminal justice systems is incapacitation (Greenwood 1983). In the case of the most dangerous or persistent offenders, prison or intensive monitoring can be used to remove an individual from the social environment he or she is deemed to be a danger to. Incapacitation is therefore normally achieved by long prison sentences. Aside from the brutalising effect that long prison sentences have on those that are subjected to them, the key problem with this approach is that it disconnects the criminal conduct from the motivations or conditions that give rise to the crime in the first place and instead superimposes upon the offender another set of harsh and brutalising conditions. Incapacitation in the context of safety crimes might take a different form. Incapacitation of organisations can be achieved by isolating a particular activity or part of the organisation where offending is identified, or by targeting the whole organisation and intervening to physically prevent it from committing criminal activities. A fuller discussion of the ways in which this can be done is provided below. Incapacitation of senior managers or directors who are found guilty of safety crimes can be achieved by prison of course, but this is problematic because it does not deal with motivation or causation, and, in capitalist social orders, only a tiny minority of criminal directors and senior managers are ever likely to be given prison sentences. We might propose a more viable form of incapacitation that does not aim to remove the offender from society altogether, but only from the community he or she is a danger to. By disqualifying criminal directors and senior managers from holding high office in an organisation, we can ensure that they will be incapacitated and at the same time retain a clear connection between the punishment and the specific conditions that give rise to the crime. It is important not to lose sight of the fact that effective incapacitation might be achieved by withdrawing the privilege to make profits in the case of the corporation, or the privilege to hold high office in the case of an individual who is the target of the sanction. Incapacitation in this context is therefore better understood as incapacitation of privilege (since it is from a position of privilege that safety crimes are committed), rather than isolation from the social body.

In short, then, there is reason to expect that each of the key philosophies of punishment discussed above can be appropriately applied in the use of sanctions against companies and high status individuals. The theoretical bases of each of those philosophies of punishment are challenged when we take into account the social status and relative position of privilege/deprivation held by those that are punished. Deterrence is compromised because lower status individuals are least well placed to exercise rational choice. Retribution is compromised because the concept of the social contract means little to those that have little to gain from fulfilling their part of the social contract in the first place. Rehabilitation is compromised by the false hope of self-improvement when re-integration into society may mean little more than re-integration into the conditions that led one to commit criminal acts in the first place. Incapacitation is compromised because it seeks merely to disconnect offenders temporarily from the social body. When it comes to dealing with safety crimes committed by relatively powerful offenders, however, the key problems in each of those cases might be negated by the relative privilege or relatively higher social status of the offender, particularly if the form of punishment can be shaped in a way that takes account of this position of power and privilege.

In theory, all of this appears relatively unproblematic. But we should be very careful about oversimplifying systems of punishment. It is not enough to say in some general way 'criminal sanctions work', because the effectiveness of the punishment is likely to vary so much depending upon the receptiveness of those punished, the circumstances that led to the offence, the likelihood of future prevention and so on. We therefore need greater theoretical clarity that allows us to see which types of punishments might be most effective when applied to specific criminal offences and when applied against specific perpetrators. In the case of sanctions that seek deterrence, the aim is to create either a general or individual effect of discouraging crime by making the costs too high. In the case of retributive punishment, the aim is to ensure that the individual repays a debt to society that is commensurate with the offence. In the case of rehabilitation, the aim is to reform the individual. In the case of incapacitation, the aim is physically to prevent the perpetrator from committing crime again. It is the degree to which those aims of penal theory might be met that the rest of this chapter seeks to unravel by considering, first of all, how safety crimes are currently punished, and second, how this system of punishment might be reformed.

Fines and safety crimes

Most offences that are prosecuted, including the most serious crimes, will, if the prosecution is successful, incur a fine. Fines following health and safety convictions are notoriously low. This is partly because, although the higher courts are permitted to impose an unlimited fine, the maximum that can be imposed by the Magistrates Courts is £20,000. Since most safety crimes in England and Wales are prosecuted in the Magistrates Courts, the average fine remains low. Although, as Figure 4 below shows, there has been a sharp trend upwards in the size of fines imposed for safety crimes over the past eight years, the average remains under £14,000. The UK Treasury's review of enforcement (Hampton 2005) concluded that fines in the Magistrates Courts were often too low to eliminate the economic benefits derived from law breaking.

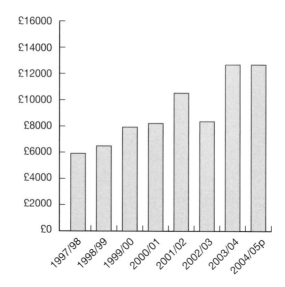

Figure 4   Average fine following conviction of a safety offence in the UK[2]

Figure 4 shows the average fine in convictions of cases taken by the Field Operations Division (FOD) of HSE (which comprises around 60 per cent of total convictions). It shows a steady rise in level of fines imposed by the courts. Another way that this data can be represented is by taking away some of the larger fines that tend to skew the figures. Thus, HSE has published a figure that excludes all fines over £100,000 (which added up to only 13 convictions in 2005/06). The average for all HSE health and safety convictions for 2005/06 when removed of those 13 convictions was £6,219.

As we might expect, the fines for offences that result in a fatality are higher. This partly reflects the gravity of the offence, but it also reflects that fact that those offences are more than twice as likely to be heard in a higher court (Unison/Centre for Corporate Accountability 2002: 15). Figure 5 below sets out the level of average fine for a prosecution following a fatality.

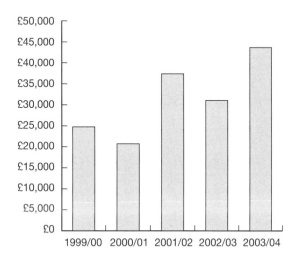

Figure 5   Average fines following work related fatalities in the UK

As this figure demonstrates, the average fine for a fatality has risen steadily in recent years. The first issue that we should note in relation to this data is that it tells us very little about the real impact of fines upon the offender. We know from the preceding discussion that most of the convicted parties are companies, but this is about all that we do know. We have no way of knowing, for example, what those fines are in relation to the turnover or the profits of the firm that has been fined. Of course, a fine of £45,000 is unlikely to make an impact on a large trans-national firm, when compared with, say, a small family partnership. Having said this, we can identify at least five high profile cases involving large firms since 1999 that have attracted fines of over £1m. In 1999, Balfour Beatty was fined £1.2m for the collapse of a tunnel during the construction of a new rail link to Heathrow airport (a record fine for an incident that didn't involve a death). Also in 1999, Great Western Trains were fined £1.5m for causing the Southall train crash that killed seven and injured 150. In 2002, BP were fined £1m for causing an explosion at its Grangemouth plant. In

2005, the gas company Transco was fined £15m for killing a family of four in a gas explosion (see Chapter 1). In 2006, Balfour Beatty was again fined a record-breaking amount. The company was ordered to pay £10m for the causation of four deaths and 102 injuries in the Hatfield crash (later cut to £7.5m on appeal).

Fines of this magnitude, when considered alongside the upward trend indicated in Figures 4 and 5 above, appear on the face of things to indicate a gradual acceptance by the courts that higher penalties should be imposed for safety offences. A system that is almost exclusively reliant upon a system of fines, however, is likely to remain problematic for five main reasons.

First, if we take the large fines noted above, they are very often not particularly large when taken in comparison with the profits of the companies they seek to penalise. They are even less significant when set against the annual turnover of a company – turnover being the appropriate figure if one wants, for example, to measure the impact of any particular fine when compared to a fine against an individual based on his/her annual income. As we have noted already in Chapter 1, the £15m record fine for a health and safety offence in the UK levied on Transco Plc in August 2005 amounted to less than 2 per cent of the previous year's after-tax profit. Another way of expressing the value of the fine is as 0.16 per cent of turnover for 2004, equating to a fine of £40 for someone earning £25,000 a year. This record fine for such a grave offence hardly dented the company's revenue. In relative terms, it is typically lower than that imposed by local authorities upon local citizens who allow their dogs to foul public spaces. And, of course, the problem of the low level of even 'record' fines is exacerbated when the chances of prosecution, as we have already seen in previous chapters, are rather low. Thus, it might be said that a fine even at this record level, might have very little impact upon the management of an organisation unless it knows that either the chances of being caught, or the size of the fine, amount to too great a risk to take. Even the highest levels at which fines are imposed at the moment are hardly likely to provide a deterrent to offending, or to put it another way, can hardly provide an incentive to be law abiding.

Second, because of the tendency for the average fine to be relatively low, fines certainly have most acute effect on the smallest firms. It is small firms that, as we have seen in Chapter 6, are most readily prosecuted for the offence of corporate manslaughter. Therefore the current system of punishment for safety crimes can be said to be inequitably applied to organisations depending upon their size.

Third, because safety crimes are constructed using the 'inchoate mode' (see Chapter 5), fines are primarily related to the gravity of the breach of health and safety/corporate manslaughter law, as opposed to the outcome of that breach. In case law, it has been established that the courts should also consider higher penalties following a health and safety breach if the outcome has been a serious injury, ill heath, or a death, but this is very often a secondary consideration of the courts.[4] This means that fines do not necessarily correspond to the harm caused and may appear derisory when they are imposed to punish debilitating injuries or deaths. In the Transco case, the size of the fine was ostensibly not related to the fact that the firm had killed a family of four in their own home, rather the presiding Judge Lord Calloway noted that fine was imposed on the company because of the seriousness of the offence, and because of the lack of remorse shown by the firm's representatives (a justification that is consistent with *R v Howe* – see footnote 4 – since prompt admission of responsibility can be considered a mitigating factor in sentencing such cases in the UK).

Fourth, because fines are levied on the organisation generally, rather than targeted at a particular group within the company, those costs can be absorbed by the organisation as it sees fit. The costs of even the largest fine might be offset against a particular budget heading (they might result in cuts to running or maintenance costs that may even worsen the management of safety in an organisation), or they may be passed on to customers and clients in the form of price rises, or to suppliers by reducing the market value of a product. The costs of fines may even be passed on to workers – those most endangered by safety offences – in the form of wage cuts or adverse changes in working conditions.

Fifth, fines are wholly counter-productive when they are applied to public sector or government organisations. The effect on such organisations is similar to that set out in the previous point, since, as Fisse (1990) argues, fines in this context simply result in 'some budgetary shuffling with money deducted from one arm of government passing back into general revenue' (cited in Clarkson and Keeting 1994: 243). Since those organisations are funded by public revenues, the effect of fining public sector organisations is ultimately that the costs of organisational offending are transferred to taxpayers.

If the system of fines used to punish corporate offenders for safety crime can hardly be seen to impose a binding penalty on individual firms and public sector organisations, a measure of their more general punitiveness is illustrated neatly by Figure 6, below, which sets out the total value of fines for safety crimes to British industry.

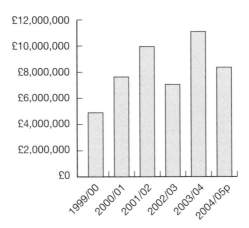

Figure 6   Annual total of all UK health and safety fines[5]

We should read this figure with caution, since the data is from the Field Operations Division of the HSE and although it is the largest division, it represents only around two thirds of the annual convictions in cases laid by HSE and excludes data from chemicals, mining, railways and offshore industries, sectors that have historically attracted higher than average fines. Even with this proviso in mind, though, the HSE FOD data reproduced here is worth commenting upon since the total figure reproduced here does not approach anything close to a sum that might be described as a 'burden' imposed upon business. In fact, the total penalty imposed for safety crimes in the UK in 2004/05, outside of the four sectors noted above (£8,442,340) more or less equates to the combined value of pensions that the top dozen FTSE 100 directors will receive every year when they retire (approximately £8,810,000; Labour Research Department 2006).

Think back to the discussion at the start of this chapter on the key theories of punishment: deterrence, retribution, incapacitation and rehabilitation. Most clearly, the system of fines that we have at present fails as a form of deterrence largely because the penalty is very often, in both absolute and relative terms, set at a derisory level. Relatively low levels of fine mean that this form of penalty fails as an adequate repayment to society for the harm that those crimes incurr. Neither can it be said that fines have the ability to incapacitate offenders, since few are pitched at a level that threaten the continuation of the business. Lastly, the fine as a one-off penalty, unless it has lasting effects (for example if it produces some adverse publicity for the organisation) or is sufficiently harsh, provides no ongoing incentive to organisations to adjust their policies or practices. In other words, fines in this form do not necessarily encourage rehabilitation.

Rethinking punishment for safety crimes

A starting point for thinking about how we might make fines more effective is to return to our five criticisms of the current system of fines outlined above:

1 Unless the organisation faces a high chance of being caught and receives a potentially debilitating fine, there exists no incentive to be law abiding.
2 Fines are not related to the gravity of the offence.
3 Fines do not correspond to ability to pay and therefore tend to penalise the smallest firms.
4 The cost of fines can be absorbed and redistributed by convicted organisations.
5 The effect of fining public sector organisations is counter-productive.

The chapter now turns to an exploration of how reforms to the system of punishment might address each of those criticisms in turn.

Accounting for the chances of being caught

It is important at this point in the discussion to recognise that there is a distinction to be made between theories of *individual* and *general* deterrence. Sentencing can have the aim of either deterring the future conduct of the individual or company being sentenced, or sentences can be aimed at sending a message to companies and directors more generally that criminal conduct will not be tolerated by the state. Given the low rates of detection for safety crimes, the general deterrent effect is crucial for optimising the return on the resources dedicated to the prosecution process and the more general aim of promoting compliance (Bergman and Fooks, forthcoming). In both cases, we might expect the organisation to make a similar calculation that aims to answer the question: is it likely that an offence will be detected at all? In the case of individual deterrence, the question is: will the punishment prevent the organisation from committing the same, or similar, offences again? Either way, the calculation will be made not only on the basis of the severity of the punishment, but also on the chances of being caught. One proposal to deal with problem 1, noted above, then, is to ensure that fines are moderated so as to reflect the chances of being caught. As Etzioni (1993) points out, the detection rate for the crime in question is crucial. As not all crimes are detected and punished, fines should be raised as detection ratios decrease. An organisation might calculate that it has, say, only a one in ten chance of being caught. The organisation may also calculate that the likely fine has a value to the company of the average fine for a safety offence in the courts. But the value of that fine to the organisation, since it only has a one in ten change of being caught, would effectively be a tenth of the value that the courts are likely to impose.[6] Such calculations are of course bound to be based upon rather contrived assumptions and projections. But as we have seen earlier in this chapter, this is very often how organisations, particularly profit-making corporations, do make, or strive to make, decisions about organisational or business strategy. At their heart lies an effort to reach an accurate assessment of the chances of detection, prosecution and conviction. Etzioni presents evidence (ibid.: 153–4) to show that only about one in 50 corporate crimes is detected. Assuming the rational calculation of corporations, fines would thus have to be multiplied by 50.

Fines reflecting the gravity of the offence

Dealing with problem 2 would mean refocusing the way that safety crime offences are generally punished. Specifically, it would mean a shift away from the inchoate mode within which those offences are currently located. As we saw in Chapter 5, an assessment of the gravity of the harm caused does feature in the investigation and in the sentencing process. To argue for a shift towards a consideration of the harm done would therefore merely be to argue that we should move the system a little further in the direction it is already going in. Thus we might recommend a minimum penalty to be linked to an offence in which endangerment was particularly acute or where a minor injury, a major injury or a death had been caused. Those minimum sentences would be applied alongside the existing minimum sentences referred to above. A combination of the gravity of the offence and the chances of being caught might bring the system of fines closer to the kind of rational decision making that might incentivise organisations not to break the law. Rather than moving towards a deterrence model, this approach would be in line with a retributive model, with the penalty fixed to sum that would indicate the appropriate penalty for the offence.

An accurate assessment of the costs of safety crimes to society is, just like any other type of crime, very difficult to achieve. For example, in the case of a street robbery, we may be able to put a price on the loss incurred by the item stolen, but there is also a range of hidden costs: perhaps the victim has been physically or psychologically damaged, for example, and may need medical or welfare support. Safety crimes raise similar problems. The scale and the impact of safety crimes (as we saw in Chapters 2 and 3) suggest that the external costs, those costs never borne by offending companies or their officers, are huge. These include medical costs, funeral expenses, the loss of income to an individual or a family caused by long-term illness or disease, before even thinking about the huge long-term emotional and physical costs that are borne by victims and the bereaved. Once we begin to add those costs on, any fines that could come close to accounting for the true costs of serious safety crimes would most probably be far too high to expect any but the largest of companies to pay.

Unit fines

If fines were reformed along the lines of a retributive or just deserts penalty, then, this would still raise key problems of inequitable sentencing and the likelihood of bankruptcy. It is likely that the smallest companies would be more acutely penalised and the largest firms would be much better placed to absorb and redistribute the costs. An alternative proposal to deal with the problem of uneven impact across large and small companies is to establish a system of unit fines that is linked to ability to pay. This is consistent with current sentencing guidelines. For example, the guidelines issued to magistrates in England and Wales stipulate that: 'In all cases with corporate offenders, the company's financial circumstances must be carefully considered … Turnover, profitability and liquidity should all be considered … If the company does not produce its accounts, the court can assume that the company can afford to pay whatever fine it imposes' (Magistrates Association 2001: 3) The problem is that fines are applied highly inconsistently across the country (see Unison/Centre for Corporate Accountability 2002; Hampton 2005). Sentencing guidelines have not in their present form produced consistency.

The CCA has set out a formula for a unit fine that would take account of the gravity of the offence and ability to pay. In this formula, the courts would set a percentage at a level somewhere in the range of 5 per cent to 15 per cent that would reflect the seriousness of the offence. The level would be set according to the degree to which the company was culpable of an offence and the degree of harm caused. Thus, a high degree of culpability and a high degree of harm would place the company towards the higher end of that scale. This percentage could then be applied to an average of either the firm's turnover or profit to determine the level of fine (Centre for Corporate Accountability 1999).

One problem with imposing unit fines is that sentencers currently have very little knowledge about the financial status, or indeed other important aspects of the offender that might affect the sentence. Currently, David Bergman has noted that, when sentencing convicted companies, the courts do not have access to the same level of detail of background information about the offender in comparison to other crimes. Social inquiry reports for the latter are likely to include educational details, income and expenditure. Often inquiry reports will also be furnished with an assessment of the offender's likely response to probation. Yet, in safety crime cases:

> No police officer or similar person gives evidence and there is no document available to the court similar to the social inquiry report. The court remains unaware of the most basic information on the company – its turnover, annual profits, history of relationship with the regulatory agency or its general health and safety record. (Bergman 1992: 1312)

Bergman, in arguing for higher fines, advocates the use of 'corporate inquiry' reports detailing essential financial and safety information. He cites as a model the system in the United States under which a federal probation officer is required to undertake a pre-sentencing investigation into each convicted company to help the court decide an appropriate level of fine.

Equity fines

Problem 4 set out above – the ease with which the cost of fines can be absorbed and redistributed by convicted organisations – raises the question that setting an appropriate level of fine for a company may be futile in any case, since managers and directors can simply pass on the burden to consumers, shareholders or workers, especially in the largest firms. One solution developed by Coffee (1981) is to impose fines upon the value of the firm, rather than upon its running costs. This proposal for 'equity fines' proposes that offending companies would be ordered to issue a set number of new shares in the firm, to be controlled by a state-controlled compensation fund. The argument is that this process, which effectively dilutes the value of shares held by the owners of the company, would not penalise the most vulnerable groups, since the funds for investment would not be depleted, merely re-allocated to the compensation fund from existing shareholders.

The major criticism of equity fines is that those who are penalised, the shareholders, are likely to have little knowledge of the offending and are not in a position to influence the day-to-day decisions made by a company; equity fines therefore target innocent shareholders (see, for example, Croall and Ross 2002: 541). This criticism is countered by the argument that it is ultimately shareholders who benefit from the proceeds of crimes committed by the company in their name. Further, a system of equity fines should encourage shareholders to take an active interest in the degree to which their firm complies with the law and pressurise the company to ensure it is law abiding. To this end, Glasbeek (1989) has suggested that equity fines might be strengthened to apply to major shareholders: those shareholders with sufficient equity to exert substantial influence or control over the affairs of the company. A formula to define who might be considered a major shareholder, Glasbeek notes, is already applicable in existing corporate statutes in Canada. Such a formula, he suggests, could also be applied to parent companies and holding companies where it is a subsidiary that has committed the crime.

To this, we might add, there is no reason why equity fines could not be based upon the type of graduated formula that we describe above; thus they could be set at levels that reflect the seriousness of the offence and the ability of the company to pay.

Beyond financial penalties and 'pure' deterrence

The fifth problem, that of sentencing organisations that are in the public sector, immediately demands that we need to look beyond the realm of financial penalties, simply because of the contradictions that are raised by state judiciaries punishing public authorities when the costs will be paid for out of public funds. In any case, if our aim is the reform of organisation – and the provision of incentives to organisations to be law abiding – then perhaps we need to be thinking more imaginatively beyond the realm of deterrence.

Deterrence has always been attractive to white collar and corporate crime scholars, simply because the positivist assumption that lies behind deterrence theory (that individual action is shaped by a rational calculus and therefore produces a relatively easy solution to the crime problem for which crime experts can take credit) proposes similar remedies for crimes in the suites as mainstream criminology has proposed for crimes in the streets: all we have to do is remove the gain to be made from crime and we will eradicate the crime. Unfortunately there are several reasons to expect that things might not quite be as easy as this.

First, decision makers work within what has been called 'bounded' rationality. This means that other factors beyond economic calculus tend to shape their decisions. They may be influenced, for example, by what their peers expect of them or by what they perceive as normal practice in an industry, or they may make decisions for very specific reasons that are related to the structure or practices of the organisational bureaucracy (Bergman and Fooks forthcoming). This suggests that financial considerations might never fully capture the decision-making process.

Second, even if we could assume that decision makers even in the most profit-orientated organisations do structure their actions and inactions according to a carefully worked through calculus, then because of the problem of identifying the true costs of crime captured by externalities, this calculus could never be expected to produce a 'pure' form of deterrence.

Third, and following the previous point, we should be wary of relying upon financial costs, particularly since the actuarial science of cost-benefit analysis can never be an exact one. The rational calculations made by corporate accountants do not always produce rational results (as we saw in the examples of Ford and Railtrack cited above). The risk is that an organisation's or its senior management's commitment to the law is reduced to a figure on a balance sheet by financial penalties, regardless of whether this figure is accurate or not (on this point, see Becker 1968).

Fourth, a problem arises that Coffee (1981) has described as 'the deterrence trap'. Introducing fines that would be large enough to truly act as a deterrent would mean that most corporate offenders, if they were caught, would simply end up bankrupt. For Coffee, this is pointless since those that are penalised by bankruptcy are generally not those that are responsible for safety crimes. It is workers through job losses and clients and contractors through unpaid bills that are generally penalised by bankruptcy. This effect, termed 'spillover' by Coffee, is one of the reasons that led him to develop his proposals for equity fines, but it also gives us reason to think that non-financial penalties might be necessary when punishment is aimed at reforming rather than destroying corporate offenders. Having said this, there may well be firms or organisations that society deems so beyond reform and so criminogenic that we would not wish them to continue in existence. In such cases, several solutions have been proposed.

Incapacitation

The corporate death penalty is the ultimate sanction against an organisation. In cases where the organisation is put to death, companies would effectively be nationalised or put into the hands of a receiver (as is the case in bankruptcy procedures in many jurisdictions). Braithwaite and Geis (1982) argue for sentences which might fall short of the corporate death penalty, such as limiting the charter of a company to prevent it from continuing the criminal aspects of its operations, or withdrawing its licence to operate in a particular sphere of activity. The option to nationalise is attractive because it can limit the spillover effect of job losses or economic harm to a particular section of the community. In other words, it avoids victimising the most vulnerable populations. The transferral of a company to a new parent company with an established law abiding record might provide an option here. A corporation may also be barred from engaging in a particular form of economic activity or prohibited from operating in particular geographical regions (Moore 1987: 395–6). A similar and less permanent option that has been suggested has been the freezing or confiscation of the assets of a company.

Similarly, it is common in other types of white collar crimes that senior managers and directors are disqualified from holding high office, either permanently or for a set period of time. This would seem to provide a means of incapacitating individuals from committing similar crimes in the future. The weakness of using this resort exclusively is that the organisation can easily find someone to take the place of the disqualified director; the removal of one or more individuals will not necessarily reform organisational behaviour. As Levi (2000) has pointed out, it is also the case that this can be relatively easily circumnavigated by individuals who have a controlling position in their own firm, since they may simply establish a partnership (rather than an incorporated firm) and continue to conduct business.

One final means of incapacitation is to exclude companies – and directors – from bidding for central or local Government contracts. The role of government as a customer of private business firms is significant and, following the recent waves of privatisation in the UK and beyond, a growing one; thus governments have considerable leverage that could be wielded in order to exclude those with convictions, or poor safety records, from bidding for, or receiving, Government work; or, somewhat less bluntly, such information could at least be used as one factor to discriminate between bids. This would both operate as a form of disqualification and potentially force companies to take a future-oriented, bottom line view in the day-to-day management of safety and compliance with legal requirements.

Rehabilitation

Lofquist (1993) draws an important distinction between 'market-based sanctions' and 'politics-based sanctions'. The former are founded upon the assumption that corporations are unitary, rational profit-maximising entities, and that crime results from these characteristics. So, *corporate* crime control might be more appropriately achieved by increasing the costs of safety crimes above their potential benefits. The latter are founded upon the assumption that organisations are complex, differentiated entities, simultaneously in pursuit of different and often conflicting goals. Safety crimes can therefore be understood as emanating from the structural characteristics of the organisation. Punishments that are aimed at altering organisational structures and procedures in order to improve internal accountability and law observance might therefore be more appropriate (ibid.: 165; see also Piquero *et al.* 2005). Some have argued that punishments are more feasible and more likely to be effective if their aim is the reform of the criminogenic structures, policies and practices of profit-making organisations. As we have seen in Chapter 6, the focus upon the criminal features of the organisation is an approach that has been adopted in Canada and advocated in Australia, where in the case of the latter, the national penal code allows for prosecutions on the basis of a criminogenic 'corporate culture'. We might in some cases expect responses that seek to change the corporate culture, or organisational rehabilitation, to be more valuable than a simple deterrent effect.

The concept of organisational rehabilitation, however, raises a series of other issues. As the case studies in Chapter 1 demonstrate, safety crimes very often arise from defective control systems, insufficient checks and balances within the organisation, and poor communication systems or authoritarian managerial regimes. These failings are sometimes deliberate, and made to facilitate the commission of offences or the avoidance of detection, and sometimes the failings are inadvertent. Either way, it may be possible for court orders to force corporations to correct criminogenic polices and practices. Rehabilitation, according to Braithwaite and Geis, is a more workable strategy with corporate crime than with mainstream crime because organisational structures are more easily reformed – they are more malleable – than human personalities. As they argue, 'a new internal compliance group can be put in place much more readily than a new superego' (1982: 310). Moreover, Croall (2005) points out that since corporate penalties are a response to corporate 'fault', it is appropriate that penalties are directed at the underlying circumstances of this fault in the organisation. Corporate probation, she suggests, is likely to be effective in this respect.

Corporate probation, an established punishment used in the US courts, involves imposing a specified set of conditions on the convicted company. Corporate probation might involve, for example, the introduction of specified safety procedures and/or the employment of specialist safety staff. The first time probation was used against a corporation in the US was in 1971 where the oil company ARCO was ordered to develop an oil-spill response programme during its probation period (Lofquist 1993). Under US sentencing guidelines, certain mandatory conditions of the probation are now specified. If a company commits a further crime during probation, it must pay a fine or restitution or it must engage in a programme of community service. In the US system, regulatory officials act as probation officers and report to the court on whether or not conditions of probation have been satisfied. Court orders, known as 'punitive injunctions', have been proposed as a more stringent form of corporate probation. The point of punitive injunctions is that the form of remedial action required by the courts is linked very closely to the process of triggering a criminal penalty if the injunction is breached. Punitive injunctions tend also to specify the personnel responsible for ensuring their compliance (Croall 2005).

In the US, offenders' rehabilitation programmes for senior officials in the organisation who are convicted of safety crimes normally involve a range of professionals who encourage the offender to face up to the impact and thus understand the consequences of his/her behaviour. However, the use of such programmes can be questioned since, if we accept that often the senior officers who commit safety crimes are likely to be in a much better position to appreciate the consequences of their actions for themselves and for others (they would for example normally be sufficiently expert to appreciate, prior to the offence, exactly what damage, loss or injury could follow from their wrongful conduct and why it is wrong), then such programmes may be of limited value.

Restitution for safety crimes

Some commentators have noted the possibility of community service as a means of corporate recompense for the damage caused to the individual, the family and the community. Punch (1996) has pointed out the advantages of corporate community service (for example making a company lend an executive to a charity for a year), and direct compensatory orders which enable the punishment to be designed to offset the costs of the crime to the victim. Corporate community service is a remedy that is widely used in the US courts, as is the imposition of community service upon individuals associated with organisational crimes. Often the courts design community service in a way that allows the organisation or individuals within the organisation to contribute to the community using their specialist skills. It is this latter feature of community service for safety crimes that has often exposed such penalties to criticism for their inappropriateness. Thus, for example, in August 2006, a former President of a sewer company was sentenced to seven years probation and 840 hours community service by an Arizona court after he had been found guilty of homicide and reckless endangerment for causing the death of an employee, James Gamble, who was poisoned by sewer gas whilst unblocking a sewer tank. The court found that the main cause of the death was that the air had not been adequately tested, and crucially that workers were not properly trained in the correct procedures for entering sewer tanks or in the proper rescue procedures. The community service, the court ordered, should be spent teaching safety classes. This caused controversy since the victim had died precisely because the company had failed to provide the necessary safety training. Critics argued that the company was clearly not capable of providing this training to the necessary standard.[7]

Shaming provisions

Public shaming provisions, such as publishing an advertisement in a newspaper that publicly announces a conviction for safety crimes, or being ordered to show a sign detailing the conviction outside a firm's premises, have been used in several jurisdictions.

For Braithwaite and Geis (1982: 301), those punishments can act as a deterrent simply because '[c]orporations and their officers are genuinely afraid of bad publicity arising from their illegitimate activities'. Publicity orders by their nature are dependant upon how their message is communicated and the medium through which this message is communicated. This might be particularly important when they are applied to safety crimes, since publicity orders depend upon public reaction. Public reaction against some safety crimes – those that involve no injury or death particularly – may be more difficult to secure precisely because of processes of decriminalisation that safety crimes are vulnerable to (Dunford and Ridley 1996: 15). Communicating a strong message of the seriousness of the offence may be all the more important in the context of safety crimes. As Levi (2002) has noted, this type of penalty is likely to be more effective when it is applied to large household name companies, since they are the companies that have the most to lose in terms of reputation. However, it is significant in this respect that Fisse (1971) argues that publicity orders and similar techniques of shaming rely less on public reaction than on the reactions of business executives, official persons and 'opinion leaders'.

Publicity orders can impose punitive burdens on management which are more difficult to quantify and therefore less calculable than fines. Ultimately, publicity orders are more likely to affect the organisation's reputation than have a lasting impact on a chief executive or a director. Therefore, those are punishments for which the costs will always be disproportionately borne by the organisation rather than by individual senior managers. A related requirement that has been used in the US in particular is the requirement that a senior manager/director appears in court during the trial and sentencing process where it is an organisation that is being prosecuted so that the company or organisation's senior officers are not allowed to use the shell of the organisational form to remain anonymous.

The requirement for a human face to be given to the corporation in court is significant since it takes a major leap of the imagination to conceptualise how the corporation can exhibit an emotional response such as shame. The internalisation of shame by the corporation rather than the individual is more likely to be realised in a completely different way and it more likely to be internalised as a measure of the extent to which bad publicity costs companies in the long term. Shaming itself may therefore be regarded as a financial deterrent to companies as opposed to an emotional response capable of allowing individuals to contemplate the consequences of their offending. It may also be the case that precisely because they are less quantifiable than fines and the fact that their long-term effects are less amenable to quantification, reputational penalties can impose greater punishment and deterrence than mere economic sanctions.

Friedrichs (1998: 13) however, has argued that 'sophisticated public relations operations have the means to transform attempts to shame corporations to their advantage, or at least to neutralise those efforts'. In other words, this is a form of punishment that may be easily countered by the larger corporations with large public relations departments, or those that can afford to hire PR firms. At least two further problems are associated with this sanctioning strategy. One is that it requires firms to have some visibility – or indeed engage in direct business with – the general public. Yet often the public fails to identify which firms are the source of goods or services they might purchase – how many of us would be aware, for example, that Dixons is actually part of a European multinational company that includes Currys, PC World and the Link, companies to whom we might as consumers direct our business were there to be any reaction to the public 'shaming' of Dixons. Second, even in the event of effective shaming, if the impact of reputational damage is to lose custom, then this requires choice – however, for those who buy petrol, and might want to respond to the public shaming of a leading retailer, they would find not only little choice (petrol all emanating from one of the big five oil giants), but they would also find there is little to choose between any of these in their long-term safety management/compliance record, for example.

Towards a sentencing mix?

Differentiating between those different aims of punishment (deterrence, retribution, rehabilitation and incapacitation) does not imply that those philosophies of punishment produce mutually exclusive solutions to the punishment of safety crimes. As the preceding discussion indicates, there are likely to be cases where deterrence is not likely to be achieved (not least if punishment comes be regarded simply as the 'add-on' cost of conducting business); equally, there are likely to be cases where the most appropriate 'just deserts' is impossible to establish, or where rehabilitative aims are simply not appropriate. If we imagine that the penalties imposed for safety crimes might not be merely restricted to a financial deterrent, then there is reason to think that we can combine deterrence and just deserts to good effect. But because the real value of the external costs generated by safety crimes is unlikely to be quantifiable, we will always need to have the option to either seek rehabilitation or, in the worst cases, incapacitation. This suggests that the most effective way of dealing with safety offences is by deploying a 'mix' of sentencing options that could be made available to the courts (Croall and Ross 2002). In other words, because of the complexities of the way that safety crimes are produced and the complexities that we face in seeking to prevent future crimes taking place, we have to think about the most appropriate 'sentencing mix'. This is not to say that each punitive aim should be given equal weight. Indeed,

Braithwaite (2002) has suggested an adaption of his pyramid of enforcement along the lines of a sentencing mix. Here, he recommends restorative justice as the first resort at the bottom of the pyramid, then if this fails, regulators should appeal to the rational capacities of offenders and impose deterrent penalties. Where those fail and the offender is deemed an 'incompetent or irrational actor', then incapacitative penalties should be imposed.

All of the evidence that we have points to the relatively high chance of securing deterrence where financial penalties are appropriately apportioned and where those penalties are most clearly targeted (for detailed overviews of this evidence, see Davis 2004 and Bergman and Fooks forthcoming). For this reason, we would argue that a system of fines that reflects both the gravity of the offence and the ability of the offender to pay seems to be the most justifiable and the most likely to achieve deterrence. In cases where the organisation has the necessary capital to sustain equity fines, we see no good reason why this penalty should not be levied on investors. The fact that the punishment of investors is hardly likely to find favour in capitalist social orders, where a range of legal protections are already afforded to the owners of businesses (and here we refer the reader back to our discussion of corporate personality in Chapter 6) does not mean that we should not continue to argue for equity fines as a likely means of achieving results. After all, we do not consider the interests of those that profit most from law breaking when framing punishments for any other crime.

It is also important not to underestimate the importance of attaching moral condemnation to punishment and the way that this might supplement purely instrumental punishments such as effective fines or reforming the structures and policies of the organisation. As Bergman and Fooks have noted, the key weaknesses of those instrumental approaches is that they fail to communicate and transmit the requisite moral opprobrium that is central to the process of criminalisation. Publicity orders thus are important as supplementary penalties, since they provide a different function: 'as a sanction that can work to reaffirm the moral importance of meeting the terms of legal duties under health and safety legislation, publicity orders represent a potentially powerful means of reinforcing the normative basis of compliance with health and safety regulation' (Bergman and Fooks, forthcoming: npn).

Sentencing individuals

Thinking about the most appropriate 'sentencing mix' also returns us to the question of whether we punish the individual or the organisation. If this chapter has concerned itself almost exclusively with corporate and organisational penalties, this is merely because of the infrequency with which individuals are punished for safety crimes. Yet, again we might raise issues about the extent to which this is driven by the discretionary decision of investigators and prosecutors. HSE prosecution policy currently notes that the regulator will seek to prosecute individuals using the same evidence test noted above, and instructs inspectors that '... prosecuting individuals will be warranted where there are substantial failings by them, such as where they have shown wilful or reckless disregard for health and safety requirements, or where there has been a deliberate act or omission that seriously imperilled their health and safety or the health and safety of others' (Health and Safety Executive 2003c: 2). The policy also emphasises that decision to prosecute also rests upon a 'public interest test', so that investigators must ask themselves: would prosecution be in the public interest? Either due to the evidential test, or the public interest test, or a combination of the two, however, individual prosecutions are relatively rare. For the individual the maximum penalty for a summary health and safety offence in the UK is six months imprisonment or a £5,000 fine or both. Yet, as we noted in Chapter 6, it remains overwhelmingly the company that is punished for safety crimes. To recap, we reported that in the ten years up to December 2005 only 86 directors were convicted and 11 jailed for breaches of health and safety law. We also reported that between 1980 and 2004, 11 directors were convicted for the common law offence of manslaughter. Of those, five were imprisoned, one received a community sentence and five were given suspended sentences.

Fisse and Braithwaite (1993) argue in favour of corporate criminal liability but are also conscious of the need in many cases to punish or discipline individuals within the corporation. Geis and Dimento (1995: 84) conclude that punishing the individual *and* the corporation offers the best chances of securing deterrence, but speculate that results 'might more readily be achieved by concentrating all criminal resources on individual malefactors'.

It is at the punishment stage of the criminal process that the *de facto* corporate veil discussed in Chapter 5 comes to life. For if it is companies rather than their senior officers that pay the penalty for committing crime, the only penalty to senior officers is that their reputation as managers may be damaged. But if the individual responsible is not prosecuted for, or directly implicated in, the crime, then this is hardly likely to affect their managerial reputation. It is equally arguable that imprisoning directors will not really make an impact upon levels of safety crime because companies will always be able to find someone willing, in exchange for the right sort of remuneration, to take very high-risk decisions. The US phenomenon of appointing a 'vice president in charge of going to jail' (Braithwaite 1984) thus threatens to undermine the effectiveness of punishment. If we accept the principle of *corporate* or *organisational* punishment, a principle that allows organisational offences to be regarded as conceptually independent from the offences committed by the individuals within the corporation, this does not mean that we are left with an either/or choice. Segregating organisational from individual punishments merely gives us the opportunity to use either or to use both. As we have seen, there is reason to think that neither on their own can be effective and, following a long-standing tradition of research in white collar and corporate crime we would argue in most cases an appropriate sentencing mix directed against both corporations and individuals will be the only way to make the punishment stick.

Conclusion

As the previous section in this chapter has argued, the complexities of the motivations and factors that encourage safety crimes demand an appropriate punitive 'mix'. This is not to undervalue the centrality of punishments that aim to provide a necessary deterrent. Safety crimes arise very often from reasoned and cost-balanced decisions. The principle of deterrence therefore must be placed at the heart of any punitive strategy if it is likely to have any effect in preventing future offending at all. Punishment in other words, where rational decision-making has resulted in a crime, has to be constituted in a way that makes crime unattractive to offenders.

It is the principle of 'less eligibility', or the idea that the material conditions of an offender's punishment are regulated to a level far below the conditions experienced by the average non-criminalised citizen, that has historically underpinned the application of deterrence theory (Rusche 1933/1980). Since the imprisoned population tends to be overwhelmingly comprised of those from the lower social stratum, the conditions of imprisonment must be seen to impose more hardship than the social conditions normally experienced by the lowest strata of society. This principle of less eligibility, as we have seen, does not apply to offenders associated with safety crimes (also Munro 2006). Ruche and Kirchheimer noted in their classic work *Punishment and Social Structure* that the general principle of ensuring that punishment negates the proceeds of crime was never applied in relation to the regulation of factory safety (1939/2003: 174), and they reproduce data from French labour law violations to demonstrate this point. Their argument is that the system of punishment encourages rather than discourages offending in the case of safety crimes. As we have seen in relation to our discussion of the form that punishment takes in the case of the UK, their basic argument remains prescient. As Rusche (1933/1980) has argued, the existence of a principle of less eligibility is necessary because the form that punishment takes is always related to structural inequality.

Punishment is less related to crime, as we have already seen in our discussion of the historic origins of the criminal law, than to the defence of a particular social order, one that is based upon unequal relations of property (see also Rusche and Kirchheimer 1939/2003: 5). Safety crimes, just like many forms of mainstream crime, ultimately arise from unequal social relations of power. As we have seen in Chapter 2, those are offences that tend to victimise disproportionately the most vulnerable groups in society precisely because of their subordinate position in the labour market, and more generally, the social hierarchy. In Chapter 6, we argued that the processes of law reform and implementation of the law are intimately connected to a process of social ordering; a process that is geared towards maintaining the status quo. In capitalist social orders, maintaining the status quo means ensuring the predominance of capital and therefore the right of its institutional form, the corporation, to remain profitable. To this we can also add that maintaining the status quo ultimately means ensuring that other key institutions such as branches of the state and public sector enterprises are not fundamentally undermined by the criminal law. It is those rules of thumb that have historically ensured that safety crimes – and the forms of sanction that are used to punish them – are differentiated from 'real' crimes. Just as the magistrates of the nineteenth century found ways of reconstructing offences against the Factory Acts as less blameworthy, a range of judicial techniques continue to undermine the seriousness with which the courts deal with safety crimes (Bergman and Fooks forthcoming).

So what does the preceding discussion tell us about the form that punishments for safety crimes should take? First that the punishment of safety crimes, if it is to be effective, must overcome the major contradiction that we point to above: it must challenge, rather than reinforce, the conditions that give rise to safety crimes in the first place. Some of the suggestions outlined above seek to do so, but ultimately criminal law and a system of punishment cannot achieve the broader aim of social (as opposed to criminal) justice. The key problem with relying merely on punishment as a panacea for crime is that the conditions that give rise to crime in the first place cannot be changed by the way that we punish the small minority of offenders that end up in court. Punishment can never, therefore, be seen as the solution to crime.

Some forms of punishment can provide a general deterrence against particular forms of offending if organisations and their senior officers calculate that it will not be worth their while to continue to commit safety crimes. Punishment in the courts can also send an important expressive message from the state to assert social disapproval of such offending.

Punishment can also be targeted so as to produce less tangible, but nonetheless effective results, such as reinforcement of the moral importance that should be attached to safety crimes. There are also, as we have seen, punishments that can go some way to repairing the social damage that a particular crime has inflicted. Finally, as we have argued here, the particular forms that punishment take are likely to be a great deal more effective if they are designed to take into account the specificities of the crime and the offender in safety crimes (not least a recognition that they are very often highly profitable crimes conducted from behind the corporate veil). It should also be added that the discussions that we have had in this chapter are not merely theoretical, since versions of each of the punishments discussed in this chapter (with the exception of equity fines) have been, or are currently, in use in the US, Canada, Australia or Europe (ibid.).

Indeed, any review of both literature and international practices in relation to the sentencing of corporations and/or individuals involved in corporate crime more generally attests clearly to the fact that this is an area in which there now exists a range of imaginative proposals, some of which have been introduced in limited fashion, others of which remain at the proposal stage (Croall 2005). These sanctions each have their drawbacks, none is a panacea, and each is more or less appropriate for particular types of corporation and following specific forms of offence (Slapper and Tombs 1999). Ultimately, while there are clearly enormous difficulties in developing effective sanctions in the case of corporate crime these tend to be political rather than technical (Lofquist 1993, Etzioni 1993). Again, the key issue is the political refusal to treat corporate crime in general, and safety crime in particular, as real crime.

This reference to the politics of safety crime reminds us that, while the importance of the forms of punishment adopted by any given society should not be underestimated, the key features of societies that produce safety crimes remain, as this book has indicated, located in the organisation of production (Chapters 1, 2 and 3) and the political construction of the form of regulation designed to control safety crimes (Chapter 7), rather than the outcome of the criminal justice process. It is those central features of the production and control of safety crimes that urge us to reconsider the centrality of political economy, rather than the peripheral amelioration of particular crimes that might be provided by reforming systems of punishment. It is to a development of this political economy approach to understanding the production of safety crimes that our concluding chapter turns.

Notes

1 A practice for which there are clearly limits; see, for example, Tombs 2002.
2 Source of data is Health and Safety Executive (2005).
3 Source of data is Health and Safety Executive (2005).
4 *R v Howe and Son* (Engineers) Ltd [199] All ER 249.
5 Source of data is Health and Safety Executive (2005).
6 It is worth noting in the context of our discussion above that if the chance of being prosecuted for a detected death is 29 per cent, and the number of detections is between $\frac{1}{7}$ and $\frac{1}{8}$ of the true figure of people who are killed by working, then in fact the chances of being prosecuted for killing a worker, never mind for less serious offences, is likely to be a great deal less than one in ten.
7 See www.occupationalhazards.com/articles/15516.

Chapter 9

Conclusion: making sense of safety crimes

Introduction

Safety crimes are a significant crime problem, as we have sought to demonstrate throughout this text. Yet, despite this, we have also indicated various ways in which political, social, legal and regulatory processes combine to obscure their nature, extent, scale and consequences. This social construction of safety crimes as something other than a crime problem extends to the discipline of criminology which, through its definitions of 'crime', 'violence' and 'policing' further marginalise such phenomena – yet a central theme of this book is that safety crimes are a proper and legitimate focus of analysis for criminology. Indeed, it is a remarkable feature of criminology that this is the first text in the discipline devoted to this subject. It remains for us to consider the extent to which, theoretically and empirically, safety crimes might be placed upon the criminological agenda.

We saw in the previous chapter how there are good theoretical and empirical reasons for at least considering the application of classicist or 'rational choice' forms of reasoning to the area of corporate crime control. Whilst the rational choice perspective pre-dates modern criminology, as we have noted, it has made an indelible mark upon the development of deterrence perspectives. To argue, as we have, that rational choice theory is more applicable to safety crimes than to the types of crimes to which it is normally applied, assumes broadly two things about safety crimes. First, that safety crimes result from profit-seeking (see, for example, Grayson and Goddard 1976; Nichols and Armstrong 1973; Woolfson *et al.* 1996; Work Hazards Group 1988). And, second, that safety crimes are produced through the functioning of rational, profit-maximising entities.

In for-profit organisations, the claim that accumulation (to sustain or expand profitability) ultimately takes priority over safety – indeed, any other goal – within a corporation seems incontrovertible. Thus it would be ludicrous to ignore the dynamic tendency to accumulate within a capitalist system, since this provides the *raison d'être* of the private corporation. However, the primacy of accumulation does not mean that there cannot be some congruence between occupational safety and efficiency/profitability within a given organisation. There is no need to accept uncritically a business case for improved safety[1] or to accept the tenets of consensus theory (see Chapter 7) to recognise that, under certain conditions, there is some coincidence of interests between accumulation and safety, and between capital and labour. To pose a mutual exclusivity between safety and profitability leads to a misunderstanding of the causes of industrial injuries in general, and safety crimes in particular, and – crucially – an under-estimation of any prospects for their prevention. Such a view for example fails to account for the fact that some companies manage safety much more effectively than others, and are also in some cases among the world's most profitable corporations, and that safety measures over and above those required by the law are taken by some companies at certain times, and so on. Moreover, the safety–profits dichotomy downplays important points about the way in which profitability is calculated. For example, a corporation that engages in long-term calculations of profitability is more likely to provide safer workplaces than one driven by short-term rationalities. Equally, large organisations engaged in a range of more and less hazardous activities are able to subsidise improved safety in some aspects of their operations, and even to sustain loss-making units, for some (albeit not indefinite) period of time (Pearce and Tombs 1997). Finally, some versions of the safety–profits dichotomy tend to pose an overly rationalistic concept of corporate managements, safety efforts, and the production of industrial injury. In other words, there is an implication, at least, that deaths and injuries can simply be attributed to acts or omissions based upon (financial) calculation. While this may be so in some cases, it is clearly not applicable to all safety crimes. Moreover, to attribute rationality to the corporation is to recognise that this is its *raison d'être*, rather than a description of how real companies actually operate at all times; as we have seen in our case studies, managements often manage poorly, so that calculations are either not made or, if they are made, are in fact erroneous. It should also be added, of course, that safety crimes may also be produced in the context of not-for-profit organisations (see Chapter 6).

For these reasons, then, while there is an ultimate and inevitable 'truth' to the argument that profit maximisation within capitalist economies is the most fundamental cause of safety crimes, we need to move beyond this level of analysis if we are to explore fully how safety crimes are produced. It is to the use – the potential and limitations – of criminological theory (beyond the rational choice perspective) in furthering this understanding, that we now turn.

Criminology, theory and safety crimes

Various forms of individual positivism that emerged after the heyday of the eighteenth- and nineteenth-century classicist theorists sought to identify the 'abnormalities' that either propelled individuals into crime, or ensured that they were more predisposed to committing crime than the general population. Now, there have been some attempts to apply an individual positivist type analysis to corporate crime, though these have been marginal to criminology, conducted mostly within business or management studies. These have tended to seek to identify those 'personality' factors associated with people who succeed in private companies, and tend to highlight features such as being innovative, ambitious, shrewd, aggressive, impatient, and possessing a 'moral flexibility' (see Snider 1993). More recently, however, and squarely within a 'criminal justice' framework, Babiak and Hare (2006) have examined the role of the 'psychopath' in corporations. As Hare has claimed,

> The world of unfeeling psychopaths is not limited to the popular images of monsters who steal people's children or kill without remorse. After all, if you are bright, you have been brought up with good social skills, and you don't want to end up in prison, so you probably won't turn to a life of violence. Rather, you'll recognise that you can use your psychopathic tendencies more legitimately by getting into positions of power and control. What better place than a corporation? (Hare, cited in Hilpern 2004)

Now, we do not need to accept pseudo-scientific categories such as 'psychopath' (see also Bakan 2004), nor the theoretical framework of individual positivism, to see how certain qualities are likely to be both valued within the corporate world, while at the same time individuals possessing such characteristics may also be more likely to be involved in corporate illegalities, either as leading figures or as individuals prepared to turn a blind eye to organisational illegality.' If corporations seek to recruit particular types of people, and if it is the case that the higher one goes up the corporate hierarchy the more likely are certain characteristics to be present, valued and accentuated, then we need to know something about the culture and functioning of the corporation itself, as well as the environments within which it operates, to understand how its employees, from the most senior downwards, act, think, rationalise, and so on. For example, to understand how Bhopal was produced requires more than understanding the actions and omissions of Warren Anderson; on the other hand, Anderson clearly typified many of the qualities valorised by corporate America, and thus requires some place in an overall story of the production of thousands of deaths. In this context, it is important to bear in mind that very often there is an almost total lack of meaningful differences between corporate offenders and corporate non-offenders (Snider 1993: 61; see also Virta 1999; Weisburd and Waring 2001).

If a myopia towards corporate offenders has been a hallmark of individual positivisms, so too has this been the case with the vast range of sociological positivisms that have come to dominate criminological theorising since the 1930s. Here, however, we come to some notable exceptions. As a criminological theorist working within the Chicago School, Sutherland himself attempted to develop a general, sociological, theory of crime causation, claiming that 'differential association' could explain both upper-class and lower-class crimes: crime arises from an excess of definitions favourable to law violation over definitions unfavourable to law violation. Criminal activity – motivations, *post-hoc* rationalisations and actual techniques of commission – is, like all behaviour, learnt. This learning, and exposure to different definitions regarding the appropriateness or otherwise of certain behaviours, emerges out of our various associations – and these associations vary by frequency, duration, priority and intensity.

Moreover, we know, on the basis of documented evidence, insider accounts, and, indeed, reasonable inference, that within certain corporations or even industries, certain forms of activity are prevalent, both in terms of knowing how to engage in them and knowing why one must engage in them. So presumably if this holds for legal activity, it holds for illegal activity too. For example, in the cockling industry off the northwestern coast of England, one must assume that 'everyone knows' that there is available a pool of illegal labour, and how to draw upon this, just as in the construction industries of many of our regenerating urban centres, it is common knowledge that there are armies of migrant labour, where the pick up points and times to collect these each day are, and how these should be treated to conceal them from any external authority, and so on. Further, and crucially, there may also be generalised knowledge within a particular sector that 'everyone is doing it' – which not only provides a motivation, since not to do it is to place one's own workplace or company at a competitive disadvantage, but also that to do it is so generalised that it is acceptable, not really criminal.[3]

Differential association is a problematic concept, and has been subjected to stringent criticism (Taylor *et al.* 1973: 125–30). It is of interest, however, precisely because it attempted to incorporate corporate crime within a general theory of crime. Other variants of sociological positivism have not sought to do so in such an explicit manner, yet there still remain elements or forms of these modes of explanation that can be or have been utilised by subsequent theorists to explain incidences of corporate crime. Notable here is Mertonian strain theory and its central concept, anomie. For example, Passas (1990) has linked deviant behaviour to the disjunction between institutionalised aspirations and the accessibility to legitimate opportunity structures. Although Merton saw these phenomena as confined to the lower classes, Passas argues that there is no compelling reason why anomie theory cannot be applied to high-class and corporate deviance:

> As the meaning and content of success goals vary from one part of the social structure to another, similar difficulties in attaining diversely defined goals may be faced by people in the upper social reaches too; they are, therefore, far from immune to pressures towards deviance (ibid.: 158).

Of course, the pressures to succeed exist for businesses and organisations in terms of maximisation of profit, growth and efficiency. These goals may have to be obtained *by all* or *any means*, particularly when the continuation of the corporation is at stake and key actors have come to equate the furthering of their own ends as largely dependant on the prosperity of the firm, an attitude underpinned by the system of financial rewards which apply to senior management, not least bonus and share schemes linked to stock market performance. Structural pressures and strains may be applied both to those at the top as well as to employees, and the employment of deviant methods may be the only possible way of dealing with problematic situations, or may be perceived as such (see Box 1983).

Finally, in this whistle-stop tour of criminological perspectives, various forms of critical and radical criminologies – including Marxisms and feminisms – have made important contributions to our body of knowledge regarding corporate crime causation. Notable here are: Stuart Hills's edited collection *Corporate Violence* (Hills 1987b), precisely because it consists of a series of empirical and theoretical case studies of the ways in which injury and death are produced systematically by the drive for profit; *Crimes of the Powerful* (Pearce 1976), where it is argued that corporations act systematically to control the markets within which they operate, often criminally, and often doing so with the connivance of the (here, American) state; and Szockyi and Fox's (1996) anthology of analyses of the myriad ways in which corporations exploit constructions of gender to victimise female consumers, workers and recipients of health care.

The processes which result in deviance and anomie thrive in an environment dominated by concerns of costs and benefits and are reinforced by the structural pressures generated within a capitalist mode of production. Sometimes the connections between market pressures and corporate crime are easily seen. Companies often end up committing crimes or making terrible reckless errors because they are desperately endeavouring to acquire, retain or re-gain a significant slice of the market, as was clearly the case with the *Herald of Free Enterprise*. Thus, as we have seen throughout this text, but especially in relation to the case studies in Chapter 1, there are clear structural pressures upon and within organisations which seem to provide a crucial motivation for safety crime – as a desirable, or even 'necessary', response to the demands of profitability. This opportunity-motivation is clearly heightened when these structural pressures are faced in contexts where workers are relatively weak or vulnerable.

Beyond criminology

One obviousness that emerges from this brief appraisal of criminological theory, and indeed throughout the text, is that understanding safety crimes requires us to look far beyond the individual on the scene – the ship's assistant bosun who did not check whether the ferry's bow doors were closed before leaving port, the chemical plant worker who attached the hose to the tank, the shipping manager who sends a young man to unload cargo. This is to deny neither human agency, nor that individuals at times act (or fail to act) in ways that are decisive triggers for safety crimes. Individual, low-level employees at times may act in violation of safety law, behave stupidly, carelessly, recklessly, and so on. Having said this, as we have argued throughout this text, and in particular in Chapter 3, the extent to which safety incidents and safety crimes are represented as being the effects of one or several low-level individuals acting in such ways is both enormously exaggerated, and indeed ideologically and strategically so.

To examine incidents and offences in terms of individuals is to fail to ask the question, what kind of organisation or process is it that allows the actions or inactions of one or several low level employees unintentionally to cause significant physical harm, as is often the case? Here, we can usefully turn to Charles Perrow's (1984) *Normal Accidents*. Perrow begins his text by outlining, and not entirely dismissing, 'conventional' explanations for accidents – not least 'operator error', lack of attention to safety features, lack of operating experience, and so on – but goes on to argue that there are more basic and important contributory factors to the failures of systems (ibid.: 63). This more fundamental phenomenon is the very nature of the processes and organisation that characterise some forms of production.

Thus Perrow claims that, for example, chemical plants are based on complex rather than linear reactions, the former being interactions 'in which one component can interact with one or more other components outside of the normal production sequence' (ibid.: 77–8). Indeed, complex systems are increasingly the norm in certain industries given their 'advantages' over linear systems:

> Complex systems are more efficient (in the narrow terms of production efficiency, which neglects accident hazards) than linear systems. There is less slack, less underutilised space, less tolerance of low quality performance, and more multifunction components. From this point of view, for design and hardware efficiency, complexity is desirable. (ibid.: 88)

Moreover, according to Perrow, some industries which are based on complex rather than linear reactions are also characterised by 'tight' rather than 'loose' coupling. Tight coupling suggests that: delays in processing are not possible; little slack is possible in supplies, equipment and personnel; there are limited possibilities of substitution of these resources; and there is an absence of designed-in buffers and redundancies (ibid.: 96). In other words, the nature of disasters and 'accidents' (for Perrow), and the nature of safety crimes (for us), is misunderstood by remaining at the level of the individual; one must focus upon the nature of the system of which the individual is a part.

The actions, inactions, decisions, and so on of individuals must therefore be placed in the structures within which they operate – and this means taking cognisance of their immediate workgroup, their workplace, their organisation/company as well as, beyond these, a far wider complex of factors. This highlights the need to move beyond individualised or environmental explanations, to engage in the theoretical and empirical work required to develop an understanding of safety crimes. And the urgency of developing such a wide-ranging explanatory framework has been raised by some commentators on corporate crime, who have emphasised the need to incorporate explanatory variables which range from the micro (individual) through to the macro (socio-structural) levels (Coleman 1987; Punch 2000; Vaughan 1992, 1996). As with theory-building in corporate crime research in general (Cressey 1989), theoretical development here remains at an early stage, although there are now a number of book-length studies which attempt to use some of this range of factors. These include studies of safety crimes in the offshore oil industry (Whyte 1999a, Woolfson *et al.* 1996), corporate crime in the asbestos (Tweedale 2000), chemicals (Pearce and Tombs 1998) and pharmaceutical (Braithwaite 1984) industries, corporate manslaughter (Slapper 2000), corporate and state illegalities associated with the fateful launch of the Challenger space shuttle (Vaughan 1996), and a national case study in the micro/macro control of 'economic' crime (Alvesalo 2003b). All of those latter studies integrate analyses of systematic features in the production of corporate crimes. The same features can be identified in the case studies that we set out in Chapter 1. Here we organise those features into three levels.

First, at the micro-level of the individual and of inter-personal relations, we need to take account of individual personality and characteristics, not least in terms of the kinds of personalities that are recruited or encouraged within the organisation, as well as 'individual' factors that are socially constructed as relevant such as rank/position within hierarchy, age, gender, and ethnicity. Shifting to the level of the immediate work-group or sub-unit within the organisation, we must take account of inter-personal dynamics (and particularly the possibility of 'groupthink'), the culture of the work-group (and the extent to which this coheres or clashes with the culture of the wider organisation), and its location within the overall organisation, both structurally and geographically – that is, is it relatively autonomous or highly supervised? Is it part of one large organisational complex, or is it geographically isolated?

Second, at what might be called the meso-level, there are also key sets of issues to be raised in relation to the organisation itself. At this level, we need to understand something of its organisational structure, its internal lines of decision-making and accountability, its geographical scope of operations, and the nature, volume and complexity of internal transactions. Issues of organisational culture must also be addressed: is the organisation risk taking or risk averse; it is gendered; is it authoritarian; and is it one where a blame culture predominates? Crucially, we must also enquire into what kind of management is either valorised or deemed acceptable by the organisation; and related to this point are issues concerning workforce organisation, notably the existence, and strength, both of trade unions, as well as of safety reps and safety committees. Of further relevance are the very products or services that are the focus of the organisation: are these opaque or transparent, are they sold to consumers or other organisations, is their production labour intensive or capital intensive? Perhaps most obviously, we need to know something of the economic 'health' of the company, and of specific organisational units, as well as the ways in which, and the time-scales across which, profitability is calculated.

Finally, there are key sets of questions to be broached regarding the macro-economic, political and social environments within which the organisation operates. Amongst these extra-organisational features are: the nature of the market structure; the size and scope of the market; the predominant form of inter-organisational relationships within any given market; the material and ideological state of regulation; the more general nature of state–business relationships; the dominant form of political economy, and concomitant societal values, including the nature and degree of pro- or anti-business sentiment. Thus an understanding of changing levels of occupational 'safety' requires attention to factors which include the following: the abilities of capital to relocate within and beyond national boundaries, and thereby to export hazard and risk; trends in labour markets and employment patterns, not least attempts to imitate models of flexibility claimed to exist in the US and Japan; the nature of, and changes in, contractual arrangements and methods of payment; and the introduction of new technologies and new forms of work organisation, particularly in terms of the impact of these upon workers' skills and functions. Crucially, as the case studies on Piper Alpha, Bhopal, Morecambe Bay and the *Herald of Free Enterprise* illustrate most clearly, we need to gain an understanding of the national and international economic conditions that shape organisational strategies.

Whether examined in isolation, or in their combination through attempts to conceptualise the range and relative importance of such factors in terms of an overarching framework, the production of safety crimes therefore needs to be conceptualised at a range of micro, meso and macro levels. And this requirement, for an integrated understanding of these complex levels of analysis, takes us beyond criminology. Indeed, even in our brief discussion of classicisms, and individual and sociological positivisms, it is clear that we needed to move towards disciplinary areas such as organisation theory and organisation studies, economics, and political science in order to fully understand how corporate crimes are produced in any given society. This task in fact requires a political economy (Gill and Law, 1988: xviii) of safety crimes, one which understands their production through prevailing systems of economic, social and political organisation, dominant value systems and beliefs, and the differential distribution of power. Further, the integrated historical and international focus of political economy forces us to recognise that we cannot understand safety crimes in the UK without some understanding of how these, first, have emerged, and, second, fit within broader market processes that are increasingly played out globally. If we return to the case of Simon Jones, we see just how vital a broader political economy is to glean a full understanding of the production of safety crimes. Thus, we find that just as changes in the labour market summarised under the label casualisation explain why he was able to work in a high risk industry with neither training nor supervision, we need to turn to an analysis of a welfare state under reconstruction to understand what led him to be working at all. Remember that Simon Jones was a student, taking a year out before completing his degree programme. He had signed up with Personnel

Selection, in the words of his friend, to 'get the dole off his back'. His being in the place where he could be killed was partly the result of a benefit system which, under the guise of encouraging people to work, penalises them for failing to do so, particularly in the case of young people. For some, these may be taken-for-granted facts of life. But it was not always so, and indeed the state of affairs is both recent and can only be understood in the context of macro-level social processes, on both national and international levels.

A thematic political economy of safety crimes

Understanding the complexities of safety crimes therefore means that we need to move beyond criminological theory and take account of the micro, meso and macro processes that we noted in the previous section. One way to develop a systematic analysis of safety crimes is to formulate a more thematic analysis of the material that we have discussed in this book. This is the point at which we can begin to make more sense of the themes that were sketched out in Table 1, in Chapter 1, and to ask, in particular, how do they help us to understand the incidence of (and various reactions to) safety crimes? To this end, we can identify six key features in the production of safety crimes that emerge from our analysis of safety crimes throughout this text and elaborate upon our initial analysis in Chapter 1.

1. Worker's vulnerability to victimisation

The cases raised various factors related to the nature of workforces, which may also be viewed as the *objects* of managerial practices and cultures. When grouped together, we find a key theme is that workers at plants or in sectors where safety crimes occur are disproportionately likely to be casualised, sub-contracted and/or increasingly migrant workforces. This is not to claim that these are the *only* workers who are victims of safety crimes – victimisation by such crimes is ubiquitous – but as we saw in Chapter 2, for example, *vulnerability* is often a characteristic of those who are victimised by such crimes. More generally, vulnerability in relation to death and injury, let alone safety crimes *per se*, is a function of the strength of workers in relation to managements. As we also noted in Chapter 2, research evidence overwhelmingly points to the finding that the safest workplaces are those workplaces that have strong trade union representation (James and Walters 2002; Reilly *et al.* 1995; Walters *et al.* 2005) suggesting that the relative strength of workers in the workplace is the key factor in the amelioration of the risk of safety crimes.

2. The nature of management

First, there are features about the companies themselves, in terms of how they are managed, how workers are treated, and the standards of management that can be regarded as 'acceptable'. Here we find numerous references to aggressive managements, and to managements who ensured that warnings, usually from below, were being systematically ignored. Moreover, we identify a generalised lack of management accountability for safety crimes. Management decisions and failures to heed warnings are subject to very little external counter-balancing in terms of regulation. Indeed, through processes of victim blaming, those providing warnings – and who were ultimately to pay a high price for these being ignored – are often cast as the problem itself. As we saw in Chapter 3, these claims both produce and are in turn supported by generalised discourses of victim blaming via the notion of the 'accident-prone' worker. Moreover, as we noted, this victim blaming can have long-term consequences, leading, for example, to a lack of compensation for victims. Further, we find managements who design or maintain plant badly – that is, managers who do not manage very well. And this is further reflected by the fact that among the cases in Chapter 1 we find several instances not just of safety crimes but of environmental offences, and of companies that frequently offend or sectors where recidivist employers appear to be commonplace. Thus managerial practices – and the cultures within which these are embedded – are crucial in understanding the production of safety crimes.

3. Inter-organisational factors

If the relationship between workers and managers is the key factor in determining the risk of safety crimes being produced, then this is also related to features in the labour market that enable work to be sub-contracted or sub-divided between organisations. There is strong evidence that points to a weakening of workers' position in relation to the labour market through casualisation and sub-contracting and their vulnerability to workplace risks (Mayhew and Quinlan 1998; Mayhew *et al.* 1997). That is, workplace balances of power are related to, though not simply determined by, wider social relations of power. Clearly, this needs to be understood in an extra-organisational context. Beyond the organisational structures and cultures of companies, there are key *inter*-organisational features which seem to emerge consistently. These include the ways in which different parts of the same firm relate to each other (parent–subsidiary relationships, for example, in the case of Bhopal, and agency–contractor relationships, in the case of Simon Jones and Piper Alpha), how different firms were linked to each other within or across particular sectors, perhaps in terms of long and complex supply chains, or indeed in terms of systematic relationships between legal and illegal businesses (in the case of Morcambe Bay).

4. Market factors

A further group of factors, both cultural and organisational, is located at the level of the market or industry in question. These include the norms that predominate in an industry for what is acceptable or even 'required' in terms of how production of goods and services is organised – characterised, for example, in the 'political economy of speed', alongside a series of (more or less real, but perceived in any case) market pressures, operating locally, nationally, and internationally, or even globally. Thus in *each* of the cases examined in Chapter 1, particular features of a market create quite specific demands for profitability, speed or cost-cutting. This location of the problem of workplace safety in the market has been developed by Moore (1991). He examined the creeping casualisation of the organisation of work in a number of industries and, in the context of a deregulated economy and the reassertion of the supremacy of the market, describes the result as 'cash-nexus carnage'. As others did before him did (for example, Nichols and Armstrong 1973; Carson 1980c), Moore sees the intensification of increasingly unfettered markets as the greatest threat to the health and safety of workers, thus offering the combination of opportunity plus motivation for safety crimes.

5. Law and regulation

A key group of factors to be considered in any explanation of safety crimes is located in law and regulation. Occupational safety is regulated in a way that, as we found systematically through our discussion in this text (particularly in Chapters 6, 7 and 8), there are consistent failings in or problems with legal categories and reasoning, ongoing regulatory oversight, and in post-event legal and regulatory processes. But even before we can understand contemporary law and enforcement with regard to occupational safety, we need to recognise that the bases of these are to be found in the ways in which legal systems have been constructed either to separate out safety crimes from real crimes, or even to deny the notion of safety crimes. Thus, low levels of inspection, detection, formal enforcement and sanctions ensure that safety offences are regarded as less serious than other crimes of violence, an enduring phenomenon that acts to reduce the social opprobrium that is attached to those crimes. Crucially, the way the state responds to safety crimes shapes the way that those crimes are tolerated from the boardroom to the workplace.

6. Unequal distribution of power

This takes us, finally, to a common theme of this text, namely power, one which clearly links our discussions on the production of safety crimes, their representation, and their regulation, but which also can be seen as a particular quality that accrues to businesses in relation to states, other organisations and populations. Thus we found in the cases in Chapter 1 and the discussion of 'structured vulnerability' in Chapter 2, how changes in social policy through the structure of the welfare state, as well as changes in state forms and public policy more generally, have augmented the leverage enjoyed over populations and states by private capital. This may be seen locally, as in local and/or national state support for investment by an offending company in a particular locale, or in the conflict this appears to raise between safe jobs or no jobs at all, or more generally in the power of business to circumvent, or prevent resort to, legal processes. And, finally, and to reassert the international dimension of the phenomena with which we are dealing in this text, the significance of the power and reach of multinational corporations, and their ability to trade off 'developed' versus 'developing' economy safety standards, illustrates the insidious ways in which unequal power relations can act to encourage safety crimes.

Conclusion

The constituent themes of a political economy of safety crimes, sketched above, do not fit well with the way that criminology and law constructs these phenomena. If we have already discussed previously, and in this chapter, various aspects of the ways in which criminology acts to obscure safety crimes, we have also pointed in Chapters 5–8 to the ways in which safety crimes are constructed through law and its application to them. One feature that unites both criminology and law in this respect is that they both reject political economy explanations in favour of a highly individualised explanation of 'accidents' at work, which separates out the phenomena with which we are concerned from 'real' crimes. To illustrate, as we saw in Chapter 7, health and safety law is underpinned by a philosophy that asserts a natural identity of interests between workers and management in the organisation of workplace safety. This idea is enshrined in the Robens Report which formed the basis of the Health and Safety at Work Act (1974). Particularly important points are made in this respect about Robens's conviction that 'safety is mainly a matter of the day to day attitudes and reactions of the individual' (Robens Report: para 13). Robens had argued that the key problem in effective safety organisation was 'worker apathy': the reluctance of workers to play an active role in preventing 'accidents'. Indeed, he argued that if safety law was structured in a rigid and prescriptive way, and if state regulators adopted strict enforcement policies, then this might discourage workers from being involved in taking appropriate action to prevent 'accidents'. In other words, for Robens, stricter enforcement might actually encourage rather than prevent safety crimes. Anthony Woolf, however, pointed out in his critique of the Robens Report that the weakness of the 'natural identity of interests' philosophy is principally located in its inability to grasp that 'nearly all accidents are the inevitable result of unsafe working systems which could themselves be made safe by the employers, by a combination of hazard analysis, planning, training and supervision' (1973, ibid.: 90). Woolf questioned Robens's assumptions on apathy, arguing that: 'if they are false, as I believe them to be, the role envisaged by Robens for law and order enforcement will itself have to be examined' (ibid. 89). If this text has demonstrated one thing, then it is that, more than 30 years after Woolf's assessment of Robens, enforcement around safety crimes remains wholly inadequate.

A fundamental question that has not been stated, but is at least implicit throughout much of this book, is whether, given the manifest failure of the criminal justice system to prevent crime (Hillyard and Tombs 2004), we should or could expect things to be any different when it comes to safety crime. But for us this is perhaps the wrong way of posing a potentially significant question. For, although the State has indeed failed, particularly in relation to under-enforcement, to talk only of State failure in the face of rising crime rates encourages us to think of the State in a particular way: that the State has lost control *over* society. This may be true, but a more useful way of thinking about State power is how it operates *through* society. The State is not simply an open system, vulnerable only to the demands of the most powerful or effective lobbying by interests groups. States in capitalist social orders are precisely that: capitalist states. States pursue policies that privilege the interests of capital over labour, reinforce unequal gender relations, and reproduce racist and other forms of social divisions. But, although social divisions are manifestly reinforced and exacerbated by the State, State institutions, as we noted in Chapter 7, also remain (unequal) structures of representation. The stability of the social order is only guaranteed after struggles between different groups are absorbed by the State. This involves not simply a process of ruling over sub-dominant groups, but also a compromise that secures the legitimacy of the rulers and consent of the ruled. One consequence of this process is that State institutions remain vulnerable to counter-hegemonic demands. If the recent history of capitalist societies has taught us anything, it is that the struggle against State–corporate power is most effectively resisted by collective opposition from workers and from other popular movements in workplaces, at sites of consumption and on the streets. So whilst there is a case for bringing the *State* back into our understanding of how best to oppose power, we must at the same time recognise the pivotal position that workers and the public have in struggles against safety crimes (Tucker 1990).

Both the under-enforcement of regulation and the absence of controls for serious corporate harm provides us with a perfect illustration of Lacey's (1994) point that we cannot take 'crime' for granted. Neither can we take its enforcement for granted. The criminal justice system remains pre-occupied with a relatively limited number of interpersonal crimes. With the key exception of the so-called 'war on terror', Home Office priorities have been, and remain, a limited number of 'headline' crimes of interpersonal violence, property and public 'nuisance'. And criminology by and large obediently falls into line behind this 'official' version of what constitutes the crime problem (Hillyard *et al.* 2004; Walters 2003). The law's embedded bias, which – as we saw in Chapter 5 – is historically inscribed, forces us to think about a much more profound question in relation to regulation: whether under capitalist social orders, State regulation can ever adequately guarantee our protection? Can workplace deaths and injuries ever be sufficiently harnessed in states that see as their primary aim the encouragement of private profit maximisation and capital growth? Given that under-regulation and an absence of safety crime controls appears to be as much an embedded feature of capitalist social orders as safety *crime* itself is, our greatest challenge is perhaps not simply to reform or tinker with the means we have to control individual corporations. A much greater and more pressing challenge is to seek an alternative means of organising production regimes that will neither encourage nor sustain the routine killings and injuries committed by employers.

Notes

1 For the HSE Better Business strategy, see www.hse.gov.uk/betterbusiness/large/index.htm.
2 One has only to watch *Wall Street* to see that the personality traits that helped to make Gecko a success were the same characteristics that allowed him, through a combination of intention and negligence, to break the law.
3 This is also one example of 'techniques of neutralisation', which are crucial to understanding motivation in the context of corporate crime: see Box 1983; Slapper and Tombs 1999.

Sources of further information

Almost all of the key texts – books, chapters, journal articles, reports – which deal with safety either from a criminological or social science perspective have been cited in this book. We will not rehearse these in detail here, save to point again to a few key items. Our discussion of these follows the structure of the book.

Numerous case studies of safety crimes exist – though these are overwhelmingly written from the US and thus the selection of such cases is also biased either towards their occurrence in the US or to US-based companies. This small caveat aside, most collections of case studies of corporate crimes contain some examples of safety crimes, but see in particular a useful selection of cases across various chapters of Hills (1987b), Pearce and Snider (1995) and Tucker (2006).

The relative invisibility of safety offences has been considered, in terms of the various elements of this legal, political and social process, in Bergman (1991), Glasbeck and Rowland (1979), Glasbeek (1989), McMullan and McClung (2006), Tombs (1999b, 2000) and Tombs and Whyte (2001). Two classic texts in which safety crimes are considered – however briefly – in the context of an excellent general critique of the biases of criminal justice systems and representations of the crime problem towards the crimes of the relatively powerless are Box (1983) and Reiman (1998). Efforts to document the *actual* scale of death, injury and safety crimes are very rare – not least because of the problems of access to data. For this reason, despite it now being a *little* dated, the work undertaken by David Bergman and the CCA remains seminal here (see, in particular, Bergman 1993, 1994 and 2000; and Unison/CCA 2002). A more forensic approach to a much smaller selection of cases (all involving legal responses to work-related death) can be found in Slapper (2000), a key text for understanding the failures of the criminal justice system to treat safety crimes *as crimes*.

The classic texts on the emergence of law with respect to health and safety are undoubtedly those by Carson (1970a, 1970b, 1974, 1979, 1980a and 1980b); see also the critique offered by Bartrip and Fenn (1980a, 1980b, and 1983). For an historical discussion that bears similarity in approach to that of Carson, albeit in a Canadian context, see Tucker (1990). An excellent general context for understanding the nature and historical emergence of contemporary law and legal systems can also be found in Norrie (2001).

On regulation, a debate often referred to is that around the relative strengths and merits of a 'compliance-oriented' versus a more punitive regulatory approach – see Hawkins (1990 and 1991), and Pearce and Tombs (1990 and 1991). For critical, and more recent, commentary on the debate, see Davis (2004), Hopkins (1994), Johnstone (1999) and Gray (2006). On the regulatory mix, the work of Braithwaite and colleagues is currently dominant: see Ayres and Braithwaite (1992), Gunningham and Johnstone (1999), Haines (2005) and Johnstone (2003). For a typology of approaches to regulation, see Whyte (2004). Hawkins (2002) is a fascinating study, based upon rare insider access, of the decision-making processes employed by safety inspectors in the UK as to whether or not to prosecute for safety offences. The classic piece on regulatory reform – including a specific discussion of safety regulation – remains Snider (1991). On the sanctioning of safety offenders, the most useful – and still very recent – overviews are set out by Croall (2005) and the CCA.[1]

A general political economy of occupational safety is set out in Nichols (1997), though this is not organised around safety crimes *per se*. Attempts to account for the production of safety crimes in an integrated fashion – encompassing the various levels and elements of analysis that we have argued must be part of any adequate account – can be found in Carson (1982), Davis (2000), Whyte (1999a), Woolfson et al. (1996), Pearce and Tombs (1998), Slapper (2000), Vaughan (1996), and, though couched somewhat differently, an excellent and concise discussion of the wide range of factors to be taken into account in any causal explanation of safety crimes is set out in Punch (2000).

Beyond these texts, journals and book chapters, for us the key source of critical information on the state of British safety – and one which frequently discusses safety crimes in particular – has long been, and remains, *Hazards* magazine. *Hazards* aims to look behind the company safety hype, and provide practical tools for workplace safety representatives to prevent safety crimes. Using a global network of union safety correspondents, *Hazards* provides the best first port of call for information on safety and safety crimes. It can be accessed at www.hazards.org/.

More generally, there is, of course, a great deal of information available electronically. There are few, if any, websites devoted to safety crimes *per se*, but there are, first, many devoted to issues of safety and, second, to corporate crime in general (among the latter, those with the best coverage of safety crimes are listed).

On 'safety' and safety crimes, see the following:

www.hazardscampaign.org.uk

The Hazards Campaign, a network of resource centres and campaigners on health and safety at work, and the best source of safety contacts and campaigning groups information in the UK.

www.corporateaccountability.org

The Centre for Corporate Accountability, a charity concerned with the promotion of worker and public safety, provides free advice to victims of safety crimes, campaigns around law and enforcement, and undertakes related research, much of which is available at the site.

www.tuc.org.uk/h_and_s/index.cfm

The health and safety section of the Trades Union Congress website. Note, in particular, the newsletter *Risks*, which can be accessed from this site.

www.worksmart.org.uk/rights/viewsection.php?sen=9

Advice on health and safety law provided to workers by the Trades Union Congress.

www.labournet.net/default.asp

LabourNet aims to be in the forefront of using the resources of the internet to provide communications, news and information for the labour movement, seeking to strengthen organised labour. There are excellent sections on safety.

www.iosh.co.uk

Website of the Institution of Occupational Safety and Health which is the UK professional body for health and safety practitioners. The Institution of Occupational Safety and Health's stated aims are to regulate and steer the profession and provide members and groups outside the organisation with guidance on health and safety issues.

For sites devoted either specifically, or with useful material on, corporate crime in general, and with some useful coverage of safety crimes, see the following:

www.corpwatch.org

Corporate Watch (US) tracks illegal and unethical corporate activity, and business–industry relations. Its parent organisation is the Transnational Resource and Action Center (TRAC), based in San Francisco.

www.corporatewatch.org

Corporate Watch (UK) tracks similar forms of corporate activity to the US journal of the same name (above), but is independent of and unrelated to the US publication.

www.essential.org

Multinational Monitor, published by Essential Information, Inc., tracks corporate activity, especially in the 'Third World', focusing on the export of hazardous substances, worker health and safety, labour union issues and the environment.

www.corporatepredators.org

Here you will find 'Focus on the Corporation', a weekly column on illegal and unethical corporate activity, posted by two North American journalists/activists.

http://paulsjusticepage.com/elite-deviance.htm

An excellent source of corporate crime material, and many links, maintained by Paul Leighton, co-author of Reiman's *The Rich get Richer and the Poor Get Prison.*

www.nader.org

The Nader Page. The site of Ralph Nader, long time US anti-corporate campaigner, this site seeks to further the ability of consumers to be heard and to have a real voice and a significant role in the legislative and regulatory decision-making processes.

www.motherjones.com

Mother Jones is an independent not-for-profit US-based campaigning site and magazine whose roots lie in a commitment to social justice implemented through first rate investigative reporting.

www.citizen.org

Public Citizen, an organisation that campaigns for openness and democratic accountability in government; for the right of consumers to seek redress in the courts; for clean, safe and sustainable energy sources; for social and economic justice in trade policies; for strong health, safety and environmental protections; and for safe, effective and affordable prescription drugs and health care.

'Official' information on health and safety can be found at the following sites, each of which also has plenty of useful links:

www.hse.gov.uk

The Health and Safety Executive, contains an increasingly useful body of information; see especially sections on Enforcement, the (searchable) Notices and Prosecutions database, Statistics, Annual Reports, Local Authorities, and Press Releases.

http://uk.osha.eu.int

European Agency for Safety and Health at Work, established by the EU to collect, analyse and promote OSH-related information, with the stated aim of making Europe's workplaces safer, healthier and more productive, and in particular to promote an effective prevention culture.

www.osha.gov

Occupational Safety and Health Administration, US equivalent to HSE, its stated aim is to prevent work-related injuries, illnesses and deaths for every American worker.

www.cdc.gov/niosh/homepage.html

The National Institute for Occupational Safety and Health, a US federal agency responsible for conducting research and making recommendations to the US government on work-related injury and illness.

www.ilo.org

The International Labour Organization, a UN agency, sets, promotes and supervises international labour standards, and is the UN's main source of expertise about workers' rights and conditions, social protection and labour law.

Note

1   See, in particular, 'Sentencing Issues' briefing at: www.corporateaccountability.org/rb/sentencing/sentencing.htm, downloaded, December 3, 2006.

References

Alvesalo, A. (2003a) 'Economic Crime Investigators at Work', *Policing and Society*, 13(2): 115–38.

Alvesalo, A. (2003b) *The Dynamics of Economic Crime Control*, Espoo: Poliisiammattikorkeakoulun tutkimuksia.

Alvesalo, A. and Tombs, S. (2001) 'The Emergence of a "War" on Economic Crime: The Case of Finland', *Business and Politics*, 3(3): 239–67.

Amnesty International (2004) *Clouds of Injustice. Bhopal disaster twenty years on*, Oxford: Amnesty International, at web.amnesty.org/wire/December2004/Bhopal, downloaded, December 2, 2006.

Anderson, B. and Rogaly, B. (2005) *Forced Labour and Migration to the UK*, London: COMAS/TUC.

Australian Broadcasting Company (2004) Protests held over death of Olympic construction workers – Wednesday, August 11. www.abc.net.au/sport/content/200408/s1173882.htm, downloaded, December 2, 2006.

Ayres, I. and Braithwaite, J. (1992) *Responsive Regulation: Transcending the Deregulation Debate*, Oxford: Oxford University Press.

Babiak, P. and Hare, R.D. (2006) *Snakes in Suits. When Psychopaths Go To Work*, New York: HarperCollins.

Bakan, J. (2004) *The Corporation. The Pathological Pursuit of Profit and Power*, New York: Free Press.

Baldwin, R. (1995) *Rules and Government*, Oxford: Clarendon Press.

Baldwin, R. (1997) 'Regulation: After "command and control"', in K. Hawkins (ed.) *The Human Face of Law*, Oxford: Clarendon Press: 65–84.

Baldwin, R. and Cave, M. (1999) *Understanding Regulation: Theory, Strategy and Practice*, Oxford: Oxford University Press.

Baldwin, R., Scott, C. and Hood, C. (eds) (1998) *A Reader on Regulation*, Oxford: Oxford University Press.

Bardach, E. and Kagan, R. (1982) *Going by the Book: The Problem of Regulatory Unreasonableness*, Philadelphia: Temple University Press.

Bartrip, P. and Fenn, P.T. (1980a) 'The Conventionalization of Factory Crime – A Reassessment', *The International Journal of the Sociology of Law*, 8: 175–86.

Bartrip, P. and Fenn, P.T. (1980b) 'The Administration of Safety: The Enforcement Policy of the Early Factory Inspectorate 1844–1864', *Public Administration*, 58: 87–102.

Bartrip, P. and Fenn, P.T. (1983) 'The Evolution of Regulatory Style in the Nineteenth Century British Factory Inspectorate', *Journal of Law and Society*, 10(2): 201–22.

BBC Radio 4 (2004) *You and Yours – Transcript*, Friday, July 23, www.bbc.co.uk/radio4/youandyours/yy_ftf_athens_230704.shtml, downloaded, December 2, 2006.

Beck, M. and Woolfson, C. (1999) 'Safety Culture – A Concept Too Many?', *The Health and Safety Practitioner*, 16(1): 14–16.

Becker, G. (1968) 'Crime and Punishment: An Economic Approach', *Journal of Pol.itical Ecomony*, 76(2): 169–217

Bergman, D. (1988) 'The Sabotage Theory and the Legal Strategy of Union Carbide', *New Law Journal*, 138, June.

Bergman, D. (1991) *Deaths at Work. Accidents or Corporate Crime*, London: Workers' Educational Association.

Bergman, D. (1992) 'Corporate Sanctions and Corporate Probation', *New Law Journal*, 142, September.

Bergman, D. (1993) *Disasters. Where the Law Fails. A New Agenda for Dealing with Corporate Violence*, London: Herald Families Association.

Bergman, D. (1994) *The Perfect Crime? How Companies Can Get Away with Manslaughter in the Workplace*, Birmingham: West Midlands Health and Safety Advice Centre.

Bergman, D. (2000) *The Case for Corporate Responsibility: Corporate Violence and the Criminal Justice System*, London: Disaster Action.

Bergman, D. and Fooks, G. (forthcoming) *Sentencing Health and Safety Offences: A Report for the Health and Safety Executive*, London: HSE.

Bernstein, M. (1955) *Regulating Business by Independent Commission*, Princeton, New Jersey: Princeton University Press.

Bhopal Action Group (1988) *Sabotaging the Sabotage Theory: A Critique of the Paper by Ashok Kalelkar*, London: Transnational Information Centre.

Bianchi, H. and van Swaaningen, R., (eds) (1986) *Abolitionism. Towards a Non-Repressive Approach to Crime*, Amsterdam: Free University Press.

Bibbings, R. (1996) *Managing Occupational Road Risk. Discussion Paper*, Birmingham: RoSPA.

Black, J. (1996) '"Which Arrow?": Rule Type and Regulatory Policy', in D. Galligan (ed.) *A Reader on Administrative Law*, Oxford: Oxford University Press: 165–93.

Black, J. (1997) *Rules and Regulators*, Oxford: Clarendon Press.

Boris, E. and Pruegl, E., (eds) (1996) *Homeworkers in Global Perspective. Invisible No More*, London: Routledge.

Bourdieu, P. (1998) *Acts of Resistance: Against the Tyranny of the Market*, New York: The New Review Press.

Bowie, V. (2002) *Workplace Violence*, New South Wales: Workcover.

Box, S. (1983) *Power, Crime and Mystification*, London: Tavistock.

Boyd, C. (1992) 'The Zeebrugge Car Ferry Disaster', in W. Frederick, J. Post and K. Davis, *Business and Society. Seventh Edition*, Hightstown, NJ: McGraw Hill: 498–511.

Braithwaite, J. (1982) 'Enforced Self Regulation: A New Strategy for Corporate Crime Control', *Michigan Law Review*, 80: 1466–1507.

Braithwaite, J. (1984) *Corporate Crime in the Pharmaceutical Industry*, London: Routledge and Kegan Paul.

Braithwaite, J. (1989) *Crime, Shame and Reintegration*, Cambridge: Cambridge University Press.

Braithwaite, J. (1993) 'Responsive Regulation for Australia', in P. Grabosky, and J. Braithwaite (eds) *Business Regulation and Australia's Future*, Canberra: Australian Institute of Criminology: 81–96

Braithwaite, J. (2000) *Regulation, Crime, Freedom*, Aldershot: Ashgate.

Braithwaite, J. (2002) 'Rewards and Regulation', *Journal of Law and Society*, 29(1): 12–26.

Braithwaite, J. and Fisse, B. (1987) 'Self Regulation and the Control of Corporate Crime', in C. Shearing, and P. Stenning (eds), *Private Policing*, Beverly Hills: Sage: 221–246.

Braithwaite, J. and Geis, G. (1982) 'On Theory and Action for Corporate Crime Control', *Crime and Delinquency*, 28(2): 292–314.

Brake, M. and Hale, C. (1992) *Public Order and Private Lives: The Politics of Law and Order*, London: Routledge.

Brooks, L. (2001) 'Alarm as employer cleared in death case', the *Guardian*, November 30.

Bryman, A. (ed) (1988) *Doing Research in Organisations*, London: Routledge.

Calavita, K. (1983) 'The Demise of the Occupational Safety and Health Administration: A Case Study in Symbolic Action', *Social Problems*, 30(4): 437–8.

Campbell, D. (2005) 'Working drivers responsible for 1,000 road deaths a year', *Observer*, November 13.

Carrabine, E., Iganski, P., Lee, M., Plummer, K. and South, N. (2004) *Criminology. A Sociological Introduction*, London: Routledge.

Carson, W.G., (1970a) 'White-Collar Crime and the Enforcement of Factory Legislation', *British Journal of Criminology*, 10: 383–98.

Carson, W.G. (1970b) 'Some Sociological Aspects of Strict Liability and the Enforcement of Factory Legislation', *Modern Law Review*, 33 (July): 396–412.

Carson, W.G. (1974) 'Symbolic and Instrumental Dimensions of Early Factory Legislation: A Case Study in the Social Origins of Criminal Law', in R. Hood (ed.) *Crime, Criminology and Public Policy*, London: Heinemann: 107–138.

Carson, W.G. (1979) 'The Conventionalisation of Early Factory Crime', *International Journal of the Sociology of Law*, 7(1): 37–60.

Carson, W.G. (1980a) 'Early Factory Inspectors and the Viable Class Society – A Rejoinder', *International Journal of the Sociology of Law*, 8(2): 187–91.

Carson, W.G. (1980b) 'The Institutionalisation of Ambiguity: Early British Factory Acts', in G. Geis and E. Stotland (eds.) *White-Collar Crime. Theory and Research*, London: Sage: 142–173.

Carson, W.G. (1980c) 'The Other Price of Britain's Oil: Regulating Safety on Offshore Oil Installations in the British Sector of the North Sea', *Contemporary Crises*, 4: 239–66.

Carson, W.G. (1981) 'White-Collar Crime and the Institutionalisation of Ambiguity: The Case of the Factory Acts', in M. Fitzgerald, G. McLennan, and J. Pawson, (eds) *Crime & Society. Readings in history and theory*, London: RKP/OUP.

Carson, W.G. (1982) *The Other Price of Britain's Oil: Safety and Control in the North Sea*, Oxford: Martin Robertson.

Cassells, J. (1993) *The Uncertain Promise of Law. Lessons from Bhopal*, Toronto: University of Toronto Press.

Castleman, B. (1979) 'The Export of Hazard to Developing Countries', *International Journal of Health Services*, 9(4): 569–606.

Catley, B. (2003) *Philosophy – the Luxurious Supplement of Violence*, paper presented at Critical Management Studies 2003, Lancaster, July, available at www.mngt.waikato.ac.nz/ejrot/cmsconference/2003/proceedings/philosophy/catley.pdf, downloaded December 2, 2006.

Centre for Corporate Accountability (1999) *Response to the Consultation of the Sentencing Advisory Panel, November 1999*, London: CCA.

Centre for Corporate Accountability (2004) *Evidence to the House of Commons Work and Pensions Committee, The Work of the HSC/E*, London: CCA.

Chambliss, W. (1967) 'Types of Deviance and Effectiveness of Legal Sanction', *Wisconsin Law Review*, 3, Summer, 703–19.

Chibnall, S. (1977) *Law-and-Order News. An Analysis of Crime Reporting in the British Press*, London: Tavistock.

Chomsky, N. (1999) *Profit Over People: Neo-Liberalism and Global Order*, New York: Seven Stories Press.

Clarke, M. (2000) *Regulation. The Social Control of Business Between Law and Politics*, London: Macmillan.

Clarkson, C. and Keating, H. (1994) *Criminal Law: Text and Materials*, 3rd edn, London: Sweet and Maxwell.

Clinard, M. and Yeagar, P. (1980) *Corporate Crime*, New York: The Free Press.

Clive, E., Ferguson, P., Gane, C. and McCall Smith, A. (2003) *A Draft Criminal Code for Scotland with Commentary*, Edinburgh: Scottish Law Commission.

Coffee, J. (1981) 'No Soul to Damn, No Body to Kick: An Unscandalised Inquiry Into the Problem of Corporate Punishment', *Michigan Law Review*, 79(3): 386–459.

Cohen, S. (1985) *Visions of Social Control*, Cambridge: Polity.

Coleman, C. and Moynihan, J. (1996) *Understanding Crime Data*, Buckingham: Open University Press.

Coleman, J.S. (1987) 'Toward an Integrated Theory of White-Collar Crime', *American Journal of Sociology*, 93(2): 406–39.

Construction Skills Network (2006) *Blueprint for UK construction skills 2006–2010*, www.constructionskills.net/research/constructionskillsnetwork/forecastmodel/constructionskillsnetworkoutputs/uk/, downloaded December 2, 2006.

Conscious Cinema (2000) *Not This Time – The Story of the Simon Jones Memorial Campaign*, film available at www.simonjones.org.uk.

Cotton, J. (2004) 'Homicide', in D. Povey, (ed), *Crime in England and Wales, 2002/2003. Supplementary Volume 1. Homocide and gun crime*, 01/04, London: Home Office.

Craig, M. (1981) *Office Workers' Survival Handbook. A Guide to Fighting Health Hazards in the Office*, London: The Women's Press.

Crainer, S. (1993) *Zeebrugge. Learning From Disaster*, London: Herald families' Association.

Cressey, D. (1989) 'The Poverty of Theory in Corporate Crime Research', in F. Adler and W.S Laufer (eds), *Advances in Criminological Theory*, New Brunswick, NJ: Translation, 31–55.

Croall, H. (2001) 'The Victims of White-Collar Crime', in S-Å. Lindgren (ed.), *White-Collar Crime Research. Old Views and Future Potentials. Lectures and Papers from a Scandinavian Seminar* (BRÅ-Rapport 2001:1), Stockholm: Brottsförebyggande råde/Fritzes.

Croall, H. (2005) 'Penalties for Corporate Homicide', annex to *Scottish Executive Expert Group Report, Corporate Homicide,* Edinburgh: Scottish Executive.

Croall, H. and Ross, J. (2002) 'Sentencing the Corporate Offender: Legal and Social Issues', in N. Hutton and C. Tata (eds) *Sentencing and Society: International Perspectives,* Aldershot: Ashgate: 529–47.

Cullen, Lord (1990) *The Public Inquiry into the Piper Alpha Disaster (2 volumes), Cmnd 1310,* London: HMSO.

Cullen, Lord (2001) *The Ladbroke Grove Inquiry: Part 1 Report,* Norwich: HMSO.

Cutler, T. and James, P. (1996) 'Does Safety Pay? A Critical Account of the Health and Safety Executive Document: "The Costs of Accidents"', *Work, Employment & Society,* 10(4): 755–65.

Dalton, A. (2000) *Consensus Kills. Health and Safety Tripartism: Hazard to Workers' Health,* London: AJP Dalton.

Daniels, C. and Marlow, P. (2005) *Literature Review on the Reporting of Workplace Injury Trends. HSL/2005/36,* Buxton: Health and Safety Laboratory, www.hse.gov.uk/research/hsl_pdf/2005/hsl0536.pdf, downloaded December 2, 2006.

Davies, N.V. and Teasdale, P. (1994) *The Costs to the British Economy of Work Accidents and Work-Related Ill-Health,* London: HSE Books.

Davis, C. (2000) *Corporate Violence, Regulatory Agencies and the Management and Deflection of Censure,* unpublished doctoral thesis, University of Southampton.

Davis, C. (2004) *Making Companies Safe: What Works?* London: Centre for Corporate Accountability.

Dawson, S., Willman, P., Bamford, M. and Clinton, A. (1988) *Safety at Work: The Limits of Self-Regulation,* Cambridge: Cambridge University Press.

de Haan, W. (1990) *The Politics of Redress: Crime, Punishment and Penal Abolition,* London: Unwin Hyman.

Defert, D. (1991) '"Popular Life" and Insurance Technology', in G. Burchall, C. Gordon, P, Miller (eds), *Foucault Effect: Studies in Governmentality with Two Lectures by and an Interview with Michel Foucault,* Brighton: Harvester Wheatsheaf: 211–234.

Demaret, L. and Khalef, A. (2004) *Two million work deaths a year: carnage is preventable, ILO says,* www.hazards.org/wmd/ilobriefing2004.htm, downloaded December 6, 2006.

Department of Transport (1987) *The Merchant Shipping Act 1894, mv Herald of Free Enterprise, Report of Court No 8074 (Sheen Report),* London: HMSO.

Doogan, K. (2001) 'Insecurity and Long-Term Employment', *Work, Employment & Society*, 15(3): 419–41.

Doran, N. (1996) 'From Embodied "Health" to Official "Accidents": Class, Codification, and British Factory Legislation, 1831–1844', *Social & Legal Studies*, 5(4): 333–57.

Dowie, M. (1977) 'How Ford Put Two Million Firetraps on Wheels', *Business and Society Review*, 23(Fall): 46–55.

Downes, D. and Morgan, R. (2002) 'The Skeletons in the Cupboard: The Politics of Law and Order at the Turn of the Millennium', in M. Maguire, R. Morgan, and R. Reiner (eds) *The Oxford Handbook of Criminology, Third Edition*, Oxford: Clarendon.

Doyal, L., with Pennell, I. (1979) *The Political Economy of Health*, London: Pluto.

Dunford, L. and Ridley, A. (1996) 'No Soul to Be Damned, No Body to Be Kicked: Responsibility, Blame and Corporate Punishment', *International Journal of the Sociology of Law*, 24(1): 1–19.

Equal Opportunities Commission (2005) *Facts About Men and Women in Britain*, at www.eoc.org.uk/pdf/facts_about_GB_2005.pdf, downloaded, December 2, 2006.

Etzioni, A. (1993) 'The US Sentencing Commission on Corporate Crime: A Critique', in G. Geis and P. Jesilow (eds) *White-Collar Crime*, Philadelphia: The Annals of the American Academy of Political and Social Science.

European Commission (2002) *European Social Statistics. Accidents at Work and Work-Related Health Problems. Data 1994–2000*, Luxemburg: European Commission.

Eurostat (2001) *European Statistics on Accidents at Work. Methodology*, Luxemburg: European Commission.

Everest, L. (1986) *Behind the Poison Cloud: Union Carbide's Bhopal Massacre*, New York: Banner Press.

Ewald, F. (1991) 'Insurance and Risk', in G. Burchall, C. Gordon and P. Miller (eds), *The Foucault Effect: Studies in Governmentality with Two Lectures by and an Interview with Michel Foucault*, Brighton: Harvester Wheatsheaf: 197–210.

Field, S. and Jorg, N. (1991) 'Corporate Liability and Manslaughter: Should we be Going Dutch?', *Criminal Law Review*, 156–71.

Fisse, B. (1971) 'The Use of Publicity as a Criminal Sanction Against Business', *Melbourne University Law Review*, 8: 107–50.

Fisse, B. (1990) 'Recent Developments in Corporate Criminal Law and Corporate Liability to Monetary Penalties', *University of New South Wales Law Journal*, 13: 1–19.

Fisse, B. and Braithwaite, J. (1983) *The Impact of Publicity on Corporate Offenders*, Albany, NY: State University of New York Press.

Fisse, B. and Braithwaite, J. (1993) *Corporations, Crime and Accountability*, Cambridge: Cambridge University Press.

Foucault, M. (1977) 'Prison Talk: An Interview with Michel Foucault', *Radical Philosophy*, 16: 10–15.

French, M. and Phillips, J. (2000) *Cheated Not Poisoned? Food Regulation in the United Kingdom, 1875–1938*, Manchester: Manchester University Press.

Friedrichs, D. (1998) 'Interview', in *Corporate Crime Reporter*, November 30th.

Galtung, J. (1981) *Violence and its Causes*, Paris: UNESCO.

Garland, D. (1994) 'Of Crimes and Criminals: The Development of Criminology in Britain', in M. Maguire, R. Morgan and R. Reiner (eds), *The Oxford Handbook of Criminology*, Oxford: Clarendon.

Geis, G. (1996) 'A Base on Balls for White Collar Criminals', in D. Shichor and D. Sechrest (eds) *Three Strikes and You're Out: Vengeance as Public Policy*, Thousand Oaks: Sage: 244–264.

Geis, G. and Dimento, J. (1995) 'Should We Prosecute Corporations and/or Individuals?', in F. Pearce and L. Snider (eds) *Corporate Crime: Contemporary Debates*, Toronto: University of Toronto Press: 72–86.

Geis, G. and Goff, C. (1983) 'Introduction', in E. Sutherland, *White Collar Crime: The Uncut Version*, London: Yale University Press: ix–xxxiii.

George, A. and Bennett, A. (2005) *Case Studies and Theory Development in the Social Sciences*, Cambridge, MA: The MIT Press.

Gill, S. and Law, D. (1988) *The Global Political Economy*, Hemel Hempstead: Harvester Wheatsheaf.

Glasbeek, H. (1989) 'Why Corporate Deviance is Not Treated as a Crime', in T. Caputo, M. Kennedy, C. Reasons and A. Brannigan (eds) *Law and Society: A Critical Perspective*, Toronto Harcourt Brace Jovanovich: 126–145.

Glasbeek, H. (2002) *Wealth by Stealth: Corporate Crime, Corporate Law and the Perversion of Democracy*, Toronto: Between the Lines.

Glasbeek, H. (2005) *Canada's Take on Corporate Killing: the Westray Bill*, London: Institute for Employment Rights.

Glasbeek, H. and Rowland, S. (1979) 'Are Injuring and Killing at Work Crimes?', *Osgoode Hall Law Journal*, 17: 506–94.

Glazebrook, P. (2002) 'A Better Way of Convicting Businesses of Avoidable Deaths and Injuries?', *Cambridge Law Journal*, 61(2): 405–22.

Gobert, J. and Punch, M. (2003) *Rethinking Corporate Crime*, London: Butterworths.

Goldblatt, D. (1997) 'At the Limits of Political Possibilities: The Cosmopolitan Democratic Project', *New Left Review*, 225: 140–50.

Goldman, L. (1994) 'Accident and Absolute Liability in Anthropology', in J. Gibbons (ed.), *Language and the Law*, London: Longman: 51–99.

Goodey, J. (2005) *Victims and Victimology. Research, Policy and Practice*, London: Longman.

Grabosky, P. (1997) 'Discussion Paper. Inside the Pyramid: Towards a Conceptual Framework for the Analysis of Regulatory Systems', *International Journal of the Sociology of Law*, 25(3): 195–201.

Gray, G. (2006) 'The Regulation of Corporate Violations. Punishment, Compliance, and the Blurring of Responsibility', *British Journal of Criminology*, 46(5): 875–92.

Gray, G. (2006a) 'Ticketing Health and Safety Offenders. A Socio-Legal Examination of Ticketing in High-Risk Firms', *Policy and Practice in Health and Safety*, 4(2): 77–97.

Grayson, J. and Goddard, C. (1976) '*Industrial Safety and the Trade Union Movement, Studies for Trades Unionists*, 1(4).

Green, G.S. (1990) *Occupational Crime*, Chicago: Nelson Hall.

Greenwood, P. (1983) 'Controlling the Crime Rate Through Imprisonment', in J.Q Wilson (ed.), *Crime and Public Policy*, San Francisco: Institute for Contemporary Studies: 251–69.

Grigg-Spall, I. and Ireland, P. (1992) *The Critical Lawyers' Handbook*, London: Pluto.

Gunningham, N. and Johnstone, R. (1999) *Regulating Workplace Safety: Systems and Sanctions*, Oxford: Oxford University Press.

Haines, F. (2005) 'Tracking the Regulation Debate', *The Australian and New Zealand Journal of Criminology*, 38(1): 141–7.

Hale, C. (2004) 'The Politics of Law and Order', in C. Hale, K. Hayward, A. Wahidin and E. Wincup (eds), *Criminology*, Oxford: Oxford University Press: 427–446.

Hall, A. and Johnstone, R. (2005) 'Exploring the Re-criminalisation of OHS Breaches in the Context of Industrial Death', *Flinders Journal of Law Reform*, 57(8): 57–92.

Hampton, P. (2005) *Reducing Administrative Burdens: Effective Inspection and Enforcement*, London: HM Treasury/HMSO.

Harpwood, V. (1993) *The Law of Tort*, London: Cavendish.

Harris, D. (1984) 'Claims for Damages', in D. Harris (ed.) *Compensation and Support for Illness and Injury*, Oxford: Clarendon Press.

Harrison, B. (1993) 'Are Accidents Gender-Neutral? The Case of Women's Work in Britain, 1880–1914', *Women's History Review*, 2(2): 253–75.

Hartley, H. (2001) *Explaining Sport and Leisure Disasters*, London: Cavendish.

Hawkins, K. (1984) *Environment and Enforcement: Regulation and the Social Definition of Pollution*, Clarendon Press: Oxford.

Hawkins, K. (1990) 'Compliance Strategy, Prosecution Policy and Aunt Sally: A Comment on Pearce and Tombs', *British Journal of Criminology*, 30(4): 444–66.

Hawkins, K. (1991) 'Enforcing Regulation: More of the Same from Pearce and Tombs', *British Journal of Criminology*, 31(4): 427–30.

Hawkins, K. (1996a) 'Compliance Strategy', in D. Galligan (ed.) *A Reader on Administrative Law*, Oxford: Oxford University Press: 299–325.

Hawkins, K. (1996b) 'Using Legal Discretion', in D. Galligan (ed.) *A Reader on Administrative Law*, Oxford: Oxford University Press: 247–273.

Hawkins, K. (ed) (1997) *The Human Face of Law*, Oxford: Clarendon Press.

Hawkins, K. (2002) *Law as a Last Resort: Prosecution Decision Making in a Regulatory Authority*, Oxford: Oxford University Press.

Hawkins, K. and Thomas, J. (eds) (1984) *Enforcing Regulation*, Boston: Kluwer.

Health and Safety Commission (1996) *Health and Safety Statistics, 1995/96*, Sudbury: HSE Books.

Health and Safety Commission (1997) *Health and Safety Statistics, 1996/97*, Sudbury: HSE Books.

Health and Safety Commission (1998) *National Picture of Health and Safety in Local Authority Enforced Industries 1998*, London: HSC/Government Statistical Service.

Health and Safety Commission (2000) *Health and Safety Statistics 1999/2000*, London: HSE Books.

Health and Safety Commission (2001) *Health and Safety Statistics 2000/01*, London: HSE Books.

Health and Safety Commission (2003) *Health and Safety Statistics Highlights 2002/03*, London: Health and Safety Commission/National Statistics, www.hse.gov.uk/statistics/overall/hssh0203.pdf, downloaded December 4, 2006.

Health and Safety Commission (2003a) *HSC Changing Patterns of Employment Programme*. Annual Report on Progress. HSC 03/91, http://www.hse.gov.uk/aboutus/hsc/meetings/2003/110203c91.pdf, downloaded December 2, 2006.

Health and Safety Commission (2004a) *Enforcement Policy Statement*, Sudbury: HSE Books.

Health and Safety Commission (2004b) *Strategy for Workplace Health and Safety in Great Britain to 2010 and Beyond*, Sudbury: HSE Books.

Health and Safety Commission (2005a) *Health and Safety Commission Annual Report and the Health and Safety Commission/Executive Accounts 2004/2005*, London: The Stationery Office.

Health and Safety Commission (2005b) *Directors Responsibilities for Improving Health and Safety Performance – Proposed Report to the Government, Health and Safety Commission paper HSC/05/90. Annex 1,* www.hse.gov.uk/aboutus/HSC/meetings/2005/061205/c90.pdf, downloaded, December 2, 2006.

Health and Safety Commission (2005c) *Directors Responsibilities for Improving Health and Safety Performance – Proposed Report to the Government, Health and Safety Commission paper HSC/05/90,* www.hse.gov.uk/aboutus/HSC/meetings/2005/061205/c90.pdf, downloaded, December 2, 2006.

Health and Safety Commission (2005d) *Minutes of the Health and Safety Commission,* HSC/06/M09.

Health and Safety Commission (2006a) *Health and Safety Statistics 2005/06,* London: National Statistics.

Health and Safety Commission (2006b) *Statistics of Fatal Injuries,* www.hse.gov.uk/statistics/overall/fatl0506.pdf, downloaded December 2, 2006.

Health and Safety Commission/Department of Environment, Transport and the Regions (2000) *Revitalising Health and Safety. Strategy Statement,* London: Department of Environment, Transport and the Regions.

Health and Safety Executive (1993) *The Costs of Accidents at Work,* London: HSE Books.

Health and Safety Executive (1996) *A Guide to the Reporting of Injuries, Diseases and Dangerous Occurrences Regulations 1995,* Sudbury: HSE Books.

Health and Safety Executive (1997) *Press Release E133:97 – July 28, 1997. Headline Workplace Health and Safety Statistics 1996/97.*

Health and Safety Executive (2000a) *Statistics of Workplace Fatalities and Injuries in Great Britain. International Comparisons 2000,* London: HSE.

Health and Safety Executive (2000b) *Key Messages from the LFS for Injury Risks: Gender and Age, Job Tenure and Part-Time Working.* Available at: www.hse.gov.uk/statistics/keyart.pdf, downloaded December 4, 2006.

Health and Safety Executive (2003a) *HSE Press Release: E193:03, October 3 2003,* www.hse.gov.uk/press/2003/e03193.htm.

Health and Safety Executive (2003b) *Statistics of Fatal Injures 2002/03,* London: Health and Safety Executive/National Statistics, available at: http://213.212.77.20/statistics/overall/fatl0203.pdf, downloaded December 4, 2006.

Health and Safety Executive (2003c) *Prosecuting Individuals,* Operational Circular OC 130/8, HSE internal policy document.

Health and Safety Executive (2004a) *HSE Publishes Investigation into Fatal Gas Explosion in Dundee,* Press Release, April 5.

Health and Safety Executive (2004b) *Health and Safety Statistics Highlights 2003/04*, Bootle: HSE Statistics Co-ordination Unit.

Health and Safety Executive (2004c) *Thirty Years On and Looking Forward: The Development and the Future of the Health and Safety System in Great Britain*, London: HSE Books, at www.hse.gov.uk/aboutus/reports/30years.pdf, downloaded December 2, 2006.

Health and Safety Executive (2005) *Health and Safety Offences and Penalties 2004–05. A Report by the Health and Safety Executive*, Sudbury: HSE Books.

Health and Safety Executive (2006) *Health and Safety Offences and Penalties 2003/04 – Key Statistics,* available online at http://www.hse.gov.uk/enforce/off03-04/statistics.htm, downloaded December 2, 2006.

Health and Safety Executive /Department for Transport (2003) *Driving at Work. Managing Work-Related Road Safety, INDG382*, Sudbury: HSE Books.

Herbert, I. and Nash, E. (2004) 'How Spain's insatiable appetite fuels a desperate pursuit of cockles in Morecambe', *The Independent on Sunday*, February 15, 2004.

Hertz, N. (2001) *The Silent Takeover: Global Capitalism and the Death of Democracy*, London: Arrow.

Hills, S. (1987) 'Preface', in S. Hills (ed.), *Corporate Violence. Injury and Death for Profit*, Totowa, NJ: Rowman and Littlefield: vii–viii.

Hills, S. (1987a) 'Epilogue: Corporate Violence and the Banality of Evil', in S. Hills (ed.), *Corporate Violence. Injury and Death for Profit*, Totowa, NJ: Rowman and Littlefield.187–206.

Hills, S. (ed) (1987b) *Corporate Violence. Injury and Death for Profit*, Totowa, NJ: Rowman and Littlefield:

Hillyard, P. (2006) 'Criminal Obsessions: Crime Isn't the Only Harm', *Criminal Justice Matters*, 62(Winter): 26–27, 46.

Hillyard, P. and Tombs, S. (2004) 'Beyond Criminology?', in P. Hillyard, C. Pantazis, S. Tombs and D. Gordon (eds), *Beyond Criminology? Taking Harm Seriously*, London: Pluto Press, 10–29.

Hillyard, P., Sim, J., Tombs, S. and Whyte, D. (2003) 'Leaving a "Stain Upon the Silence": Critical Criminology and the Politics of Dissent', *British Journal of Criminology*, 44(3): 369–90.

Hillyard, P., Pantazis, C., Tombs, S. and Gordon, D. (eds) (2004) *Beyond Criminology? Taking Harm Seriously*, London: Pluto Press.

Hilpern, K. (2004) 'Beware: danger at work', The *Guardian,* September 27, 2004.

von Hirsch, A. (1976/1996) 'Giving Criminals Their Just Deserts, Civil Liberties Review, no 3', in J. Muncie, E. McLaughlin and M. Langan (eds) *Criminological Perspectives: A Reader*, London: Sage: 315–324.

Hodge, N. (2002) *Scotland: Gas Monopoly Faces Killing Charge over Death of Family*, World Socialist Website, March 15, available at www.wsws.org/articles/2002/mar2002/tran-m15_prn.shtml, downloaded December 2, 2006.

Hopkins, A. (1994) 'Compliance with What? The Fundamental Regulatory Question', *British Journal of Criminology*, 34(4): 431–43.

Hughes, P.W. (1984) 'Cost Effective Health and Safety', *The Safety Practitioner*, May.

Hulsman, L. (1986) 'Critical Criminology and the Concept of Crime', in H. Bianchi and R. van Swaaningen (eds), *Abolitionism. Towards a Non-Repressive Approach to Crime*, Amsterdam: Free University Press: 25–41.

Hutter, B. (1988) *The Reasonable Arm of the Law? The Law Enforcement Procedures of Environmental Health Officers*, Oxford: Clarendon Press.

Hutter, B. (1997) *Compliance, Regulation and Environment*, Oxford: Clarendon Press.

Hutter, B. (2001) *Regulation and Risk: Occupational Health and Safety on the Railways*, Oxford: Oxford University Press.

Huws, U. (1987) *VDU Hazards Handbook*, London Hazards Centre.

International Labour Organisation (2005) *World Day for Safety and Health at Work 2005: A Background Paper*, Geneva: International Labour Office.

Ives, J. (ed) (1985) *The Export of Hazard. Transnational Corporations and Environmental Control Issues*, Boston: Routledge and KeganPaul.

James, P. and Walters, D. (2002) 'Worker Representation in Health and Safety: Options for Regulatory Reform', *Industrial Relations Journal*, 33(2): 141–156.

James, P. and Walters, D. (2005) *Regulating Health and Safety at Work: An Agenda for Change*, London: Institute of Employment Rights.

Jefferson, M. (2001) *Criminal Law*, London: Longman.

Jessop, B. (2002) *The Future of the Capitalist State*, Cambridge: Polity.

Johnstone, R. (1999) 'Putting the Regulated Back into Regulation', *Journal of Law and Society*, 26(3): 378–90.

Johnstone, R. (2003) *From Fiction to Fact - Rethinking OHS Enforcement, National Research Centre for OHS Regulation Working Paper 11*, at www.ohs.anu.edu.au/publications/pdf/wp%2011%20%20Johnstone.pdf, downloaded December 3, 2006.

Jolliffe, E. (2004) 'Comment. Pass the Safety Parcel', *The Safety and Health Practitioner*, May.

Jones, T. (1988) *Corporate Killings. Bhopals Will Happen*, London: Free Association Books.

Kalelkar, A. (1988) 'Investigation of Large Magnitude Incidents – Bhopal as a Case Study', in *Institute of Chemical Engineers Symposium Series No.110. Preventing Major Chemical and Related Process Accidents*, Rugby: IChemE: 553–575.

Kaye, T. (1992) 'Corporate Manslaughter: Who Pays the Ferryman?', in D. Feldman and F. Meisel (eds) *Corporate and Commercial Law: Modern Developments*, London: Lloyds of London.

Kelso, P. (2001) 'Student killed on first day at docks. Employer and manager deny charges of manslaughter', The *Guardian*, November 8.

Kramer, R. C. (1984) 'Corporate Criminality: The Development of an Idea', in E. Hochstedler (ed.), *Corporations as Criminals*, Beverly Hills: Sage Publications, 13–37.

Kramer, R. (1989) 'Criminologists and the Social Movement Against Corporate Crime', *Social Justice*, 16(2): 146–64.

Labour Research Department (1996) *Women's Health and Safety*, London: Labour Research Department.

Labour Research Department (2006) 'Survey Exposes FTSE Directors', Luxury Pension Packages, Press Release, 3 September.

Lacey, N. (ed) (1994) 'Introduction', *A Reader on Criminal Justice*: Oxford: Oxford University Press: 1–35.

Lacey, N. (1995) 'Contingency and Criminalisation', in I. Loveland (ed.), *Frontiers of Criminality*, London: Sweet and Maxwell: 1–28.

Lange, B. (1999) 'Compliance Construction in the Context of Environmental Regulation', *Social and Legal Studies*, 8(4): 549–67.

Lavalette, M. and Kennedy, J. (1996) *Solidarity on the Waterfront. The Liverpool Lock-Out of 1995/96*, Birkenhead: the Liver Press.

Lawrence, F. (2001) 'Running Up a Profit', The *Guardian*, May 17.

Lee, J. and Wrench, J. (1980) 'Accident-Prone Immigrants: An Assumption Challenged', *Sociology*, 14(4): 551–66.

Leopold, J.W. (1985) 'Workers Participation and Joint Union-Management Health and Safety Committees in the United Kingdom', in S. Bangara, R. Misiti and H. Wintersberger (eds), *Work and Health in the 1980s. Experiences of Direct Workers' Participation in Occupational Health*, Berlin: Wissenscahaftszentrum.

Lessin, N. and O'Neill, R. (2002) 'Bad Behaviour', *Health and Safety Bulletin*, 312, (October): 24–27.

Levi, M. (1997) 'Violent Crime', in M. Maguire, R. Morgan and R. Reiner (eds), *The Oxford Handbook of Criminology: Second Edition*, Oxford: Clarendon Press. 841–889.

Levi, M. (2000) 'Shaming and the Regulation of Fraud and Business "Misconduct": Some Preliminary Explorations', in S. Karstedt and K. Bussman (eds) *Social Dynamics of Crime and Control: New Theories for a World in Transition*, Oxford: Hart: 117–132.

Levi, M. (2002) 'Suite Justice or Suite Charity: Some Explorations of Shaming and Incapacitating Business Fraudsters', *Punishment and Society*, 4(2): 147–63.

Levitas, R. (1996) 'The Legacy of Rayner', in R. Levitas and W. Guy (eds), *Interpreting Official Statistics*, London: Routledge.

Lofquist, W. (1993) 'Organisational Probation and the US Sentencing Commission', in G. Geis and P. Jesilow (eds) *White Collar Crime*, Newbury Park, California: Sage: 157–69.

London Assembly Health and Public Services Committee (2005) *Building London, Saving Lives. Improving Health and Safety in Construction*, London: Greater London Authority.

Lynch, M. and Stretesky, P. (2003) 'The Meaning of Green: Contrasting Criminological Perspectives', *Theoretical Criminology*, 7(2): 217–38.

MacKenzie, G. (1699) *Law and Customes of Scotland in Matters Criminal*, Edinburgh: Andrew Anderson.

McMullan, J. and McClung, M. (2006) 'The Media, the Politics of Truth, and the Coverage of Corporate Violence: The Westray Disaster and the Public Inquiry', *Critical Criminology*, 14(1): 67–86.

Magistrates Association (2001) *Fining of Companies for Environmental and Health and Safety Offences: Magistrates Court Sentencing Guidelines, issued May 2001*, London: Magistrates Association.

Maguire, M. (1994) 'Crime Statistics, Patterns, and Trends: Changing Perceptions and their Implications', in M. Maguire, R. Morgan and R. Reiner (eds), *The Oxford Handbook of Criminology*, Oxford: Clarendon Press.

Maguire, M. (1997) 'Crime Statistics, Patterns and Trends: Changing Perceptions and Their Implications', in M. Maguire, R. Morgan and R. Reiner (eds), *The Oxford Handbook of Criminology: Second Edition*, Oxford: Clarendon Press.

Mahon, R. (1979) 'Regulatory Agencies: Captive Agents or Hegemonic Apparatuses?' *Studies in Political Economy*, 1(1): 162–200.

Marine Accident Investigation Branch (2005) *Marine Accident Investigation Branch Annual Report 2004*, Southampton: Marine Accident Investigation Branch.

Marx, K. (1954/1887) *Capital: Volume 1*, London: Lawrence and Wishart.

Marx, K. and Engels, F. (1890/1968) 'The Manifesto of the Communist Party', in *Karl Marx and Frederick Engels, Selected Works*, London: Lawrence and Wishart: 35–68.

Mayhew, C. and Quinlan, M. (1998) *The Effects of Outsourcing on Occupational Health and Safety: A Comparative Study of Factory-Based and Outworkers in the Australian TCF Industry*, Occupational Health and Safety Commission, Australian Government Publishing Service, Canberra.

Mayhew, C. Quinlan, M. and Ferris, R. (1997), 'The Effects of Subcontracting/Outsourcing on Occupational Health and Safety: Survey Evidence from Four Australian Industries', *Safety Science*, 25: 163–78.

Mathiesen, T. (1990) *Prison on Trial: Second Edition*, Winchester: Waterside Press.

Mathiesen, T. (2004) *Silently Silenced. Essays on the Creation of Acquiescence in Modern Society*, Winchester: Waterside Press.

McBarnet, D. (1988) 'Law, Policy and Legal Avoidance: Can Law Effectively Implement Egalitarian Policies?', *Journal of Law and Society*, 15(1): 113–21.

McBarnet, D. and Whelan, C. (1991) 'The Elusive Spirit of the Law: Formalism and the Struggle for Legal Control', *Modern Law Review*, 54(6): 848–73.

McCartney, J. (2005) 'Foreword' to *London Assembly Health and Public Services Committee, Building London, Saving Lives. Improving Health and Safety in Construction*, London: Greater London Authority.

Meier, R.F. and Short, J.F. Jnr. (1995) 'The Consequences of White-Collar Crime', in G. Geis, R.F. Meier and L. Salinger (eds), *White-Collar Crime. Classic and Contemporary Views. Third Edition*, New York: The Free Press: 80–104.

Michalowski, R. and Kramer, R. (1987) 'The Space Between Laws: The Problem of Corporate Crime in a Transnational Context', *Social Problems*, 34(1): 34–53.

Mill, J.S. (1859/1962) 'On Liberty', in M. Warnock (ed.) *Utilitarianism*, London: Fontana.

Monbiot, G. (2000) *Captive State: The Corporate Takeover of Britain*, London: MacMillan.

Moore, C. (1987) 'Taming the Giant Corporation? Some Cautionary Remarks on the Deterrability of Corporate Crime', *Crime and Delinquency*, 33(3): 379–402.

Moore, R. (1991) *The Price of Safety: The Market, Workers' Rights and the Law*, London: Institute of Employment Rights.

Moran, M. and Wright, M. (eds) (1991) *The Market and the State: Studies in Interdependence*, London: MacMillan.

Morehouse, W. and Subramaniam, M.A. (1986) *The Bhopal Tragedy*, New York: Council on International and Public Affairs.

Munro, W. (2006) 'Market Discipline', paper to the *Neo-liberal Scotland Conference*, University of Strathclyde, May 19–21.

Murphy, J.G. (1973/1995) 'Marxism and Retribution', in A. Duff, and D. Garland, (eds) *A Reader on Punishment*, Oxford University Press: Oxford.

Nelken, D. (1994) 'White Collar Crime', in M. Maguire, R. Morgan and R. Reiner (eds) *The Oxford Handbook of Criminology*, Oxford: Clarendon Press: 355–392.

Neocleous, M. (2003) *Imagining the State*, Maidenhead: Open University Press.

Nichols, T. (1986) *The British Worker Question*, London: RKP.

Nichols, T. (1989) 'The Business Cycle and Industrial Injuries in British Manufacturing over a Quarter of a Century: Continuities in Industrial Injury Research', *Sociological Review*, 37(3): 538–50.

Nichols, T. (1990) 'Industrial Safety in Britain and the 1974 Health and Safety at Work Act: The Case of Manufacturing', *International Journal of the Sociology of Law*, 18: 317–342.

Nichols, T. (1994) 'Problems in Monitoring the Safety Performance of British Manufacturing at the End of the Twentieth Century', *Sociological Review*, 37(3): 538–50.

Nichols, T. (1997) *The Sociology of Industrial Injury*, London: Mansell.

Nichols, T. and Armstrong, P. (1973) *Safety or Profit: Industrial Accidents and the Conventional Wisdom*, Bristol: Falling Wall Press.

Norrie, A. (2001) *Crime, Reason and History: A Critical Introduction to Criminal Law*, 2nd edn, London: Butterworths.

O'Donnell, C. and White, L. (1998) *Invisible Hands. Child Employment in North Tyneside*. London: Low Pay Unit.

O'Donnell, C. and White, L. (1999) *Hidden Danger: Injuries to Children at Work in Britain*. London: Low Pay Unit.

O'Neill, R. (2006) 'Come Clean', *Hazards Magazine*, 95, July/Sept: 6–7.

Ogus, A. (1994) *Regulation: Legal Form and Economic Theory*, Oxford: Oxford University Press.

Osler, D. (2002) *Labour Party Plc. New Labour as a Party of Business*, Edinburgh: Mainstream.

Passas, N. (1990) 'Anomie and Corporate Deviance', *Contemporary Crises*, 14: 157–78.

Pate-Cornell, E. (1993) 'Learning From the Piper Alpha Incident: A Post-Mortem Analysis of Technical and Organisational Factors, *Risk Analysis*, 13(2): 60–78.

Pearce, F. (1976) *Crimes of the Powerful: Marxism, Crime and Deviance*, London: Pluto.

Pearce, F. and Snider, L. (eds) (1995) *Corporate Crime: Contemporary debates*, Toronto: University of Toronto Press.

Pearce, F. and Tombs, S. (1990) 'Ideology, Hegemony and Empiricism: Compliance Theories of Regulation', *British Journal of Criminology*, 30(4): 423–43.

Pearce, F. and Tombs, S. (1991) 'Policing Corporate "Skid Rows": A Reply to Keith Hawkins', *British Journal of Criminology*, 31(4): 415–26.

Pearce, F. and Tombs, S. (1992) 'Realism and Corporate Crime', in R. Matthews and J. Young (eds) *Issues in Realist Criminology*, London: Sage: 70–101.

Pearce, F. and Tombs, S. (1993) 'US Capital Versus the Third World: Union Carbide and Bhopal', in F. Pearce and M. Woodiwiss (eds) *Global Connections: National and International Aspects of Crime and Crime Control*, London: MacMillan: 187–211.

Pearce, F. and Tombs, S. (1997) 'Hazards, Law and Class: Contextualising the Regulation of Corporate Crime', *Social & Legal Studies*, 6(1): 79–107.

Pearce, F. and Tombs, S. (1998) *Toxic Capitalism: Corporate Crime in the Chemical Industry*, Aldershot: Ashgate.

Peet, R. (2003) *Unholy Trinity: The IMF, The World Bank and WTO*, London: Zed.

Peltzman, S. (1976) 'Towards a More General Theory of Regulation', *The Journal of Law and Economics*, 19(2): 211–40.

Pemberton, S. (2004) 'A Theory of Moral Indifference: Understanding the Production of Harm by Capitalist Society', in P. Hillyard, C. Pantazis, S. Tombs and D. Gordon (eds), *Beyond Criminology? Taking Harm Seriously*, London: Pluto Press: 67–83.

Perrow, C. (1984) *Normal Accidents. Living with High-Risk technologies*, New York: Basic Books.

Pickvance, S. (2005) 'A Little Compensation', *Hazards*, 90, April/June: 18–19.

Pickvance, S. (2006) *Preventing Ill-Health Caused by Work: What Progress?* Paper presented at Health and Safety – revitalised or reversed?, London: Institute of Employment Rights, January 18.

Piquero, N., Exum, M. and Simpson, S. (2005) 'Integrating the Desire-for-Control and Rational Choice in a Corporate Crime Context', *Justice Quarterly*, 22(2): 252–80.

Polanyi, K. (1944/1957) *The Great Transformation: The Political and Economic Origins of Our Time*, Boston: Beacon.

Punch, M. (1996) *Dirty Business: Explaining Corporate Misconduct*, London: Sage.

Punch, M. (2000) 'Suite Violence: Why Managers Murder and Corporations Kill', *Crime, Law and Social Change*, 33: 243–80.

Reilly, B., Pace, P. and Hall, P. (1995) 'Unions, Safety Committees and Workplace Injuries', *British Journal of Industrial Relations*, 33(2): 273–88.

Reiman, J. (1998) *The Rich Get Richer and the Poor Get Prison*. Fifth Edition, Boston: Allyn & Bacon.

Reiman, J.H. (1979) *The Rich Get Richer and the Poor Get Prison. Ideology, Class, and Criminal Justice*, New York: John Wiley & Sons.

Ridley, A. and Dunford, L. (1997) 'Corporate Killing – Legislating for Unlawful Death?' *Industrial Law Journal*, 26(2): 99–113.

Robens, Lord (1972) *Safety and Health at Work, Report of the Committee 1970–72. Cmnd. 5034*, London: HMSO.

Robertson, H. (2004) 'Bad Language', *Hazards*, 86, April/June: 6–7.

Royal Society for the Prevention of Accidents (RoSPA) (1998) *Managing Occupational Road Risk*, Birmingham: RoSPA.

Rusche, G. (1933/1980) 'Labour Market and Penal Sanction: Thoughts on the Sociology of Criminal Justice', in T. Platt and P. Takagi (eds) *Punishment and Penal Discipline*, Berkley California: Crime and Justice Associates: 10–17.

Rusche, G. and Kirchheimer, O. (1939/2003) *Punishment and Social Structure*, Transaction: New Jersey.

Ryan, W. (1971) *Blaming the Victim*, New York: Pantheon.

Ryggvik, H. (2000) 'Offshore Safety Regulations in Norway: From Model to Systems in Erosion', *New Solutions*, 10(1–2): 67–116.

Salmi, J. (1993) *Violence and Democratic Society. New Approaches to Human Rights*, London: Zed Books.

Salmi, J. (2004) 'Violence in Democratic Societies. Towards an Analytic Framework', in P. Hillyard, C. Pantazis, S. Tombs and D. Gordon (eds), *Beyond Criminology? Taking Harm Seriously*, London: Pluto Press: 55–66.

Sanders, A. (1985) 'Class Bias in Prosecutions', *Howard Journal*, 24(3): 176–99.

Sass, R. and Crook, G. (1981) 'Accident-Proneness: Science or Non-Science?', *International Journal of Health Services*, 11(2): 175–90.

Scheppele, K.L. (1991) 'Law Without Accidents', in P. Bordieu and J.S. Coleman (eds), *Social Theory for a Changing Society*, Boulder: Westview: 267–93.

Select Committee on Environment, Transport and Regional Affairs, Fourth Report, *The Work of the Health and Safety Executive* (2000) HC31, London: The Stationery Office.

Shapiro, S.P. (1983) 'The New Moral Entrepreneurs: Corporate Crime Crusaders', *Contemporary Sociology*, 12: 304–7.

Schrager, L.S. and Short, J.F. (1977) 'Towards a Sociolgy of Organisational Crime', *Social Problems*, 25: 407–19.

Shrivastava, P. (1992) *Bhopal: Anatomy of a Crisis*, London: Paul Chapman Publishing.

Sklair, L. (2001) *The Transnational Capitalist Class*, Oxford: Blackwell.

Slapper, G. (1993) 'Corporate Manslaughter: An Examination of the Determinants of Prosecutorial Policy', *Social and Legal Studies*, 2(4): 423–443.

Slapper, G. (2000) *Blood in the Bank. Social and Legal Aspects of Death at Work*, Aldershot: Ashgate.

Slapper, G. and Tombs, S. (1999) *Corporate Crime*, London: Longman.

Smith, A., Wadsworth, E., Shaw, C., Stansfeld, S., Bhui, K. and Dhillon, K. (2005) *Ethnicity, Work Characteristics, Stress and Health. Health and Safety Executive Research Report 308*. London: HSE Books.

Smith, C. and Allen, J. (2004) *Violent Crime in England and Wales. Home Office Online Report 18/04*, www.homeoffice.gov.uk/rds/pdfs04/rdsolr1804.pdf, downloaded December 2, 2006.

Smith, D. and Tombs, S. (1995) 'Beyond Self-Regulation: Towards a Critique of Self-Regulation as a Control Strategy for Hazardous Activities', *Journal of Management Studies*, 35(5): 619–36.

Smith, J. and Hogan, B. (2002) *Criminal Law*, 10th edn, London: Lexis Nexis Butterworths Tolley.

Smith, P.M. and Mustard, C.A. (2004) 'Examining the Associations Between Physical Work Demands and Work Injury Rates Between Men and Women in Ontario, 1990–2000', *Occupational and Environmental Medicine*, 61: 750–56.

Snider, L. (1991) 'The Regulatory Dance: Understanding Reform Processes in Corporate Crime', *International Journal of Sociology of Law*, 19(2): 209–37.

Snider, L. (1993) *Bad Business: Corporate Crime in Canada*, Toronto: Nelson.

Snider, L. (2000) 'The Sociology of Corporate Crime: An Obituary (or: Whose Knowledge Claims Have Legs?)', *Theoretical Criminology*, 4(2): 169–206.

Snider, L. (2003) 'Captured by Neo-liberalism: Regulation and Risk in Walkerton, Ontario', in *Risk Management*, 5(2): 17–27.

Soros, G. (1998) *The Crisis of Global Capitalism: Open Society Endangered*, London: Little Brown and Company.

Southern and Eastern Regional Trades Union Congress (2005) *Evidence from Southern and Eastern Regional Trades Union Congress to the Greater London Assembly Scrutiny Inquiry. Health and Safety of Construction Workers in London*, http://www.tuc.org.uk/h_and_s/tuc-9752-f0.cfm?regional=7, downloaded December 2, 2006.

Spencer, R. (2002) *Corporate Law and Structures: Exposing the Roots of the Problem*, Oxford: Corporate Watch.

Start, R.D., Delargy-Aziz, Y., Dorries, C.P., Silcocks, P.B. and Cotton, D.W.K. (1993) 'Clinicians and the Coronial System: Ability of Clinicians to Recognise Reportable Deaths', *British Medical Journal*, 306(April 17th): 1038–41.

Start, R.D., Usherwood, T.P., Carter, N., Dorries, C.P. and Cotton, D.W.K. (1995) 'General Practitioners' Knowledge of When to Refer Deaths to a Coroner', *British Journal of General Practice*, 45: 191–3.

Stevens, G. (1992) 'Workplace Injury: a View from HSE's Trailer to the 1990 Labour Force Survey', *Employment Gazette*, December, 621–38.

Stigler, G. (1971) 'The Theory of Economic Regulation', *Bell Journal of Economics and Managerial Science*, 2(3): 3–21.

Stolberg, S. and Harris, G. (2003) 'Industry fights to put imprint on drug bill', *New York Times*, September 5.

Sullivan, B. (2001) 'Corporate Killing – Some Government Proposals', *Criminal Law Review*, January, 31–39.

Sumner, C. (ed) (1990) *Censure, Politics and Criminal Justice*, Milton Keynes: Open University Press.

Sutherland, E. (1983) *White Collar Crime, The Uncut Version*, New Haven: Yale University Press.

Sutherland, E. (1940) 'White-Collar Criminality', reprinted in G. Geis, R.F. Meier and L.M. Salinger (eds) (1995) *White-Collar Crime. Classic and Contemporary Views*, New York: The Free Press, 29–38.

Sutherland, E. (1945) 'Is "White-Collar Crime" Crime?', *American Sociological Review*, 10(2): 132–39.

Sutherland, E. (1949) *White-Collar Crime*, New York: Holt Reinhart and Winston.

Sutherland, E. (1983) *White Collar Crime. The Uncut Version*, New Haven: Yale University Press.

Szockyi, E. and Fox, J.G. (eds) (1996) *Corporate Victimisation of Women*, Boston, MA: Northeastern University Press.

Szockyi, E. and Frank, N. (1996) 'Introduction', in E. Szockyi and J.G. Fox (eds), *Corporate Victimisation of Women*, Boston, MA: Northeastern University Press, 3–32.

Takala, J. (2002) Introductory Report: Decent Work – Safe Work, paper presented at *XVIth World Congress on Safety and Health at Work*, Vienna, May 26–31.

Tappan, P. (1947) 'Who Is the Criminal?', *American Sociological Review*, 12(1): 96–102.

Taylor, I., Walton, P. and Young, J. (1973) *The New Criminology*, London: RKP.

Thompson, E.P. (1975) *Whigs and Hunters: The Origin of the Black Act*, Harmondsworth: Penguin.

Tombs, S. (1990) 'Industrial Injuries in British Manufacturing', *Sociological Review*, 38(2): 324–343.

Tombs, S. (1991) 'Injury and Ill-Health in the Chemical Industry: De-centring the Accident-Prone Victim', *Industrial Crisis Quarterly*, 5 (January): 59–75.

Tombs, S. (1995) 'Law, Resistance and Reform: "Regulating" Safety Crimes in the UK', *Social & Legal Studies*, 4(3): 343–65.

Tombs, S. (1996) 'Injury, Death and the Deregulation Fetish: The Politics of Occupational Safety Regulation in UK Manufacturing Industries', *International Journal of Health Services*, 26(2): 309–26.

Tombs, S. (1999a) 'Death and Work in Britain', *Sociological Review*, 47(2): 345–67.

Tombs, S. (1999b) 'Health and Safety Crimes: (In)visibility and the Problems of "knowing"', in P. Davies, P. Francis. and V. Jupp (eds), *Invisible Crimes: Their Victims and their Regulation*, London: Macmillan: 77–104.

Tombs, S. (2000) 'Official Statistics and Hidden Crimes: Researching Health and Safety Crimes', in V. Jupp, P. Davies and P. Francis (eds) *The Practice of Criminological Research*, London: Sage: 64–81.

Tombs, S. (2001) 'Thinking About "White-Collar" Crime', in S-Å. Lindgren (ed.), *White-Collar Crime Research. Old Views and Future Potentials. Lectures and Papers from a Scandinavian Seminar* (BRÅ-Rapport 2001:1). Stockholm: Brottsförebyggande råde/Fritzes: 13–34.

Tombs, S. (2002) 'Understanding Regulation?', *Social and Legal Studies*, 11(1): 113–33.

Tombs, S. (2004) 'Workplace Injury and Death: Social Harm and the Illusion of Law', in P. Hillyard *et al.* (eds), *Beyond Criminology? Taking Harm Seriously*, London: Pluto Press: 156–77.

Tombs, S. (2005) 'Commentary. The Conventionalisation of Early Factory Crime', *Policy and Practice in Health and Safety*, 3(2): 103–5.

Tombs, S. (2006) 'Violence, Safety Crimes and Criminology', *British Journal of Criminology*, Advance Access published on December, doi: 10,1093/bjc/az1095.

Tombs, S. and Whyte, D. (1998) 'Capital Fights Back: Risk, Regulation and Profit in the UK Offshore Oil Industry', *Studies in Political Economy*, 57(September): 73–101.

Tombs, S. and Whyte, D. (2001) 'Media Reporting of Crime: Defining Corporate Crime Out of Existence?', *Criminal Justice Matters*, 43(Spring): 22–3.

Tombs, S. and Whyte, D. (2003a) 'Two Steps Forward, One Step Back: Towards Accountability for Workplace Deaths?', *Policy and Practice in Health and Safety*, 1(1): 9–30.

Tombs, S. and Whyte, D. (2003b) 'Corporations Beyond the Law? Regulation, Risk and Corporate Crime in a Globalised Era', *Risk Management*, 5(2): 9–16.

Tombs, S. and Whyte, D. (2006) 'Corporate Crime', in E. McLaughlin and J. Muncie (eds), *The Sage Dictionary of Criminology. Second Edition*, London: Sage: 74–76.

Trades Union Congress (2002) *No More 'Men Only' Health and Safety*, available online at: www.tuc.org.uk/h_and_s/tuc-4838-f0.cfm, downloaded December 2, 2006.

Trades Union Congress (2003a) *Migrant Workers – Overworked, Underpaid and Over Here*, Press Release, 10th July.

Trades Union Congress (2003b) *Risks*, 96, March 8, www.tuc.org.uk/h_and_s/tuc-6365-f0.cfm#f1, downloaded December 2, 2006.

Trades Union Congress (2003c) 'Employers are not meeting the costs of workplace injuries and illness', *TUC Press Release*, March 18.

Trades Union Congress (2005a) *Risks*, 201, April 9, www.tuc.org.uk/h_and_s/tuc-9652-f0.cfm#o1, downloaded December 2, 2006.

Trades Union Congress (2005b) *Risks*, 233, November 19, www.tuc.org.uk/h_and_s/tuc-11021-f0.cfm#tuc-11021-15, downloaded December 2, 2006.

Trades Union Congress (2005c) *TUC Submission, Women and Work Commission*, www.tuc.org.uk/equality/tuc-9391-f0.pdf, downloaded December 2, 2006.

Trades Union Congress (2005d) *Risks*, 212, June 25, www.tuc.org.uk/h_and_s/tuc-10093-f0.cfm#o3, downloaded December 2, 2006.

Trades Union Congress (2006) *HSE Funding, a case for more resources*, briefing available online at: http://www.tuc.org.uk/h_and_s/tuc-12542-f0.cfm, downloaded November 25, 2006.

Tucker, E. (1990) *Administering Danger in the Workplace. The Law and Politics of Occupational Health and Safety Regulation in Ontario 1950–1914*, Toronto: University of Toronto Press.

Tucker, E. (ed) (2006) *Working Disasters: The Politics of Recognition and Response*, New York: Baywood Press.

Tweedale, G. (2000) *Magic Mineral to Killer Dust: Turner and Newall and the Asbestos Hazard*, Oxford: Oxford University Press.

UK National Work Stress Network (2006) *Information Pack 2006*, Norwich: UK National Work Stress Network.

Underhill, G. (1994) 'Introduction: Conceptualising the Changing Global Order' in R. Stubbs and G. Underhill (eds) *Political Economy and the Changing Global Order*, New York: Palgrave MacMillan, 17–44.

Unison/Centre for Corporate Accountability (CCA) (2002) *Safety Last? The Under-Enforcement of Health and Safety Law. Full Report*, London: Unison/Centre for Corporate Accountability.

Vaughan, D. (1992) 'The Macro-Micro Connection in White-Collar Crime Theory', in K. Schlegel and D. Weisburd (eds) *White-Collar Crime Reconsidered*, Boston, Mass: Northeastern Universtiy Press: 124–45.

Vaughan, D. (1996) *The Challenger Launch Decision. Risky Technology, Culture, and Deviance at NASA*, Chicago: Chicago University Press.

Virta, E. (1999) 'A Thief is a Criminal Who has Not Had Enough Time to Start a Company', in A. Laitinen and V. Olgiati (eds), *Crime-Risk-Security*, Turku: University of Turku, 91–128.

Wallach, L. and Sforza, M. (1999) *The WTO: Five Years of Reasons to Resist Corporate Globalisation*, New York: Seven Stories Press.

Walters, D., Nichols, T., Conner, J., Tasiran, A. and Cam, S. (2005) *The Role and Effectiveness of Safety Representatives in Influencing Workplace Health and Safety, HSE Research Report 363*, London: HSE Books.

Walters, D.R. (1987) 'Health and Safety and Trade Union Workplace Organization: A Case Study in the Printing Industry', *Industrial Relations Journal*, 18(1): 40–9.

Walters, R. (2003) *Deviant Knowledge. Criminology, Politics and Policy*, Cullompton: Willan.

Walters, R. (2006) 'Crime, Bio-Agriculture and the Exploitation of Hunger', *British Journal of Criminology*, 46(1): 26–45.

Watterson, A. (1988) *Industrial Relations and Health and Safety at Work in Post-War Britain: A Study of Conflict and Control in the Workplace*, unpublished PhD thesis, University of Bristol.

Watterson, A. (1991) 'Occupational Health in the UK Gas Industry: A Study of Employer, Worker and Medical Knowledge and Action on Health Hazards in the Late 19th and Early 20th Centuries', paper presented to the *Annual Conference of the British Sociological Association*, Manchester, March.

Weisburd, D. and Waring, E. (2001) *White-Collar Crime and Criminal Career*, Cambridge: Cambridge University Press.

Wells, C. (1993) *Corporations and Criminal Responsibility*, Oxford: Clarendon.

Wells, C. (1995) 'Cry in the Dark: Corporate Manslaughter and Cultural Meaning', in I. Loveland (ed.), *Frontiers of Criminality*, London: Sweet & Maxwell: 109–125.

Wells, C. (2001) *Corporations and Criminal Responsibility, Second Edition*, Oxford: Clarendon.

White, R. (2003) 'Environmental Issues and the Criminological Imagination', *Theoretical Criminology*, 7(4): 483–506.

Whyte, D. (1999a) *Power, Ideology and the Regulation of Safety in the Post-Piper Alpha Offshore Oil Industry*, unpublished PhD thesis, Liverpool John Moores University.

Whyte, D. (1999b) 'Rail Crash Inquiry: A Public Stitch Up?', *Socio-Legal Newsletter*, no. 29, November.

Whyte, D. (2004) 'Regulation and Corporate Crime', in J. Muncie and D. Wilson (eds), *Student Handbook of Criminal Justice and Criminology*, London: Cavendish: 133–152.

Whyte, D. (2006) 'Regulating Safety, Regulating Profit: Cost Cutting, Injury and Death in the North Sea after Piper Alpha', in E. Tucker (ed.) *Working Disasters: The Politics of Recognition and Response*, New York: Baywood Press: 181–206.

Wilson, J. (1980) 'The Politics of Regulation', in J. Wilson (ed.) *The Politics of Regulation*, New York: Basic Books: 357–94.

Woolf, A. (1973) 'Robens – The Wrong Approach', *Industrial Law Journal*, 2(1): 88–95.

Woolfson, C. (2005) 'Un-Social Europe', *Transitions Online*, June 10, 2005, www.tol.cz/look/TOL/article.tpl?IdLanguage=1&IdPublication=4&NrIssue=119&NrSection=4&NrArticle=14149&tpid=6, downloaded December 2, 2006.

Woolfson, C. and Beck, M. (1997) *From Self-Regulation to Deregulation: The Politics of Health and Safety in Britain*, Mimeo, Universities of Glasgow and St Andrews.

Woolfson, C., Foster, J. and Beck, M. (1996) *Paying for the Piper: Capital and Labour in Britain's Offshore Oil Industry*, London: Mansell.

Work Hazards Group (1988) *Death at Work*, London: Workers' Educational Association.

Wrench, J. (1996) 'Hazardous Work: Ethnicity, Gender and Resistance', paper presented at the British Sociological Association Annual Conference, University of Reading, April 1–4.

Wrench, J. and Lee, J. (1982) 'Piecework and Industrial Accidents: Two Contemporary Case Studies', *Sociology*, 16(4): 512–25.

Index

Added to a page number 'f' denotes a
  figure, 't' denotes a table and 'n'
  denotes notes.